Composers of Classical Music of Jew

Composers of
Classical Music
of
Jewish Descent

LEWIS STEVENS

Foreword by
Rabbi Julia Neuberger

VALLENTINE MITCHELL
LONDON • PORTLAND, OR

First published in 2003 in Great Britain by
VALLENTINE MITCHELL
Suite 314, Premier House
Edgware, Middlesex HA8 7BJ

and in the United States of America by
VALLENTINE MITCHELL
c/o ISBS, 920 NE 58th Avenue, Suite 300
Portland, Oregon 97213-3786

First published in paperback in 2005

Website: **www.vmbooks.com**

British Library Cataloguing in Publication Data

Stevens, Lewis
    Composers of classical music of Jewish descent
    1. Composers, Jewish – Biography 2. Composers, Jewish –
    History 3. Music –19th century – Jewish influences 4. Music
    – 20th century — Jewish influences
    I. Title
    780.9'23924

ISBN 0-85303-613-6

Library of Congress Cataloging-in-Publication Data

A catalog record for this book is available from
the Library of Congress

Typeset in 11/12.5pt Palatino by Vitaset, Paddock Wood,
Kent Printed in Great Britain by
MPG Books Ltd, Bodmin, Cornwall

To my mother, Sarah, *née* Isaacs,
and my grandchildren, Alwin, Edwin and Lewis

By the waters of Babylon,
There we sat,
Sat and wept,
As we thought of Zion.
There on the poplars
We hung up our lyres,
For our captors asked us there for songs,
Our tormentors, for amusement,
'Sing us one of the songs of Zion.'
'How can we sing a song of the Lord
    on alien soil?'
If I forget you, O Jerusalem,
Let my right hand wither;
Let my tongue stick to my palate
If I cease to think of you,
If I do not keep Jerusalem in memory
Even at my happiest hour.

Psalm 137:1–5

Contents

Illustrations

FIGURES

MAPS

PLATES

(Between pp. 136–137 and pp. 264–265)

Foreword

Lewis Stevens has provided the reader with a wonderful collection of over 250 biographies of composers of classical music of Jewish descent, a valuable and entertaining work of reference. He uses the most inclusive of definitions of 'Jewish descent', and makes his selection on the grounds of at least one Jewish grandparent – plus some sense of knowing of the Jewish 'part' of their identity. That definition is difficult, of course. The Nazis used one Jewish grandparent as well, but with very different aims.

What Stevens sets out to demonstrate is that Jews have made an extra-ordinary contribution to classical music in the West since the Enlightenment, disproportionate to their prevalence in the population. Of course, it is difficult to know exact numbers if one includes those who converted themselves, or whose parents or grandparents did. Equally, the sense of 'Jewishness' was very varied, and the pride in name and origins varied hugely, from Felix Mendelssohn who refused to use the visiting cards printed for him in the name of Bartholdy, despite his own commitment to Protestantism, to Gerald Finzi's dissociation from Jews and Judaism and embracing of the all-English view of the world.

Stevens suggests that a sense of being 'on the edge', new insiders, or insiders/outsiders simultaneously, may have had some part to play in the outpouring of creative talent after 1800. Equally, the general outpouring of talent amongst Jews post-Enlightenment suggests a pent-up well of creativity, a longing to perform on a broader stage, a yearning – as we know existed amongst many – for secular learning. What emerged was a series of Jewish communities with distinction in music, law, medicine and science, to name but a few areas. Yet Jews had been musicians within their own communities since Temple times, as well as court musicians in Europe in the Tudor period, lawyers par excellence as Talmudists, medical men from the rabbinic period on, with great distinction at many European courts from Moorish Spain on, and scientists since inheriting the Greek mantle and translating their know-ledge into Latin and French for the non-Jewish world. These were not new interests or skills. But, as well as being well entrenched, they were also largely portable. If Stevens is correct in suggesting that the proliferation is, in part at least, due to being 'on the edge', then one must add to that the sense that many

Jews had that they might need to move around. Within the Habsburg Empire and beyond, many people felt that Europe was a small place, where one could function in one city as much as in another, hence portability of skills had an important role to play, and especially for Jews.

Stevens also attempts to examine the genetic make-up of Jews, and the possibility that this may be a contributory factor. It is probably far too early to be certain. Suffice it to say that Liszt, no Jew lover, was deeply moved by hearing Sulzer in Vienna: 'For moments we could penetrate into the real soul and recognise the secret doctrines of the fathers. Seldom were we so deeply stirred by emotion as on that evening, so shaken that our soul was entirely given to meditation and to participation in the service.' Jews did – in many cases – hear fine music and fine renditions as a matter of course in the synagogues. That must have been an influence, as must the learning of an instrument one could take wherever one went.

Some non-Jews despised Jews and their music, most notably Wagner. But for that loathing to be so deep rooted, there must have been something that they heard or saw – a creative impulse that was different, a critical faculty that was sharp, a style of playing that had a different timbre – as strange and different. For they regarded Jews, however much they were composing or playing within the great European traditions, as imitative and outsiders. Stevens begins to list those so-called outsiders, and shows how far their influence has reached. The reader will learn a great deal from these biographies – even if not always agreeing with Stevens' interpretation of Jewish history – and come to see that modern classical music is suffused with Jewish composers, some Jewish themes, and a sense of experimentation that is very healthy.

The one exception Stevens cites is Israel, where he regards the rather self-conscious striving to create a national style as having resulted in music that so far appears to have had a limited appeal outside Israel. He quotes Schoenberg and Hans Keller in support of his argument, but in fact he made his case earlier; if being an outsider is part of the prompt, and evokes the talent, then a new sense of being an insider may not be the best of settings. Equally, he suggests most of the composers he lists either did not practise, or had never practised, Judaism – outsiders again, not part of the community, or new, and sometimes uncomfortable, members of the Christian world. If he is right – and it is highly debatable – then Israel, where people are either very religious or deeply secular but strongly nationalistic, is not the setting to produce the creative talent. That debate will run and run, whilst we enjoy klezmer, folk music, and even Jewish rock and roll, as well as the works of a few very distinguished Israeli classical composers.

Rabbi Julia Neuberger

Acknowledgements

I am very grateful to David Betteridge, a friend for nearly 60 years, to Marilyn Scott, a friend and former colleague at Stirling University, and to my wife Evelyn, all three of whom have spent much time reading through and making helpful and perceptive comments on the text. I am also grateful to Heather Valencia, a former colleague at Stirling University, for translating the foreword of *Lexikon der Juden in der Music*, and I would like to thank Eric Gordon for his comments on the entry for Marc Blitzstein.

I am grateful for permission to reproduce the following material in this book: cover illustration: Rheinisches Bildarchiv, Cologne; plates 1, 2, 8 and 17: Gallica-Bibliotheque Nationale de France; plate 3: John Calder Publications; plates 4 and 20: *Wieniawski: His Life and Times*, Neptune City, NJ: Paganiniana Publications; plate 5: Kurt Weill Foundation for Music, New York; plate 6: Eric A. Gordon, *Mark the Music: The Life and Work of Marc Blitzstein*, New York: St Martin's Press; plates 7, 12, 16, 18 and 19: *David Popper*, Neptune City, NJ: Paganiniana Publications; plate 9: Hans Eisler Archive, Berlin; plate 10: Boosey & Hawkes, London; plate 11: S. Frederick Starr, Johns Hopkins University, Washington, DC; plate 13: Milan Slavický, Charles University, Prague.

Notes on the Text

For cross-referencing purposes, small capitals are used for the names of composers at first citation in the chapters of Part I and in Part II to indicate that the composer is included as an entry in Part II.

In Part II composers are listed in alphabetic order, followed by their date of birth and death, as appropriate. Where a composer has changed his or her name, the most recent name is given and the former name is placed in square brackets. For a small number of entries, where two dates of birth are given the former refers to the Julian (Old Style) calendar and the latter to the Gregorian (New Style) calendar. Until February 1918 Russia adhered to the Julian calendar. On 31 January 1918 (Julian) the next day was declared 14 February (Gregorian). Where the name of a town or country has changed, the names given are those used at the time of birth or death followed by the current name, where necessary, in square brackets. The name Palestine is used when describing events occurring in that country before 1948 and the name Israel used from 1948 onwards. Readers should note that details of websites were correct at the time of writing, but may subsequently have been updated or replaced.

A brief bibliography accompanies each composer entry in Part II. Here a number of standard reference works are frequently cited, the abbreviations of which are as follows.

AG *New Grove Dictionary of American Music*, ed. H. W. Hitchcock and S. Sadie (London: Macmillan, 1986).

CC *Contemporary Composers*, ed. B. Morton and P. Collins (Chicago and London: St James Press, 1992).

G *The New Grove Dictionary of Music and Musicians*, 2nd edn, ed. S. Sadie and J. Tyrrell (London: Macmillan, 2001).

Grad Gradenwitz, P. *The Music of Israel: from the Biblical Era to Modern Times*, 2nd edn (Portland, OR: Amadeus Press, 1996).

GW *The New Grove Dictionary of Women Composers*, ed. J. A. Sadie and R. Samuel (London: Macmillan, 1994).

HBD *The Harvard Biographical Dictionary of Music*, ed. D. Randel (Cambridge, MA: Harvard University Press, 1996).

Ho   Holde, Arthur, *Jews in Music* (New York: Bloch Publishing, 1974).
Ken   Kennedy, M., *The Oxford Dictionary of Music*, 2nd edn (Oxford: Oxford University Press, 1994).
Leb   Lebrecht, N., *The Companion to Twentieth-Century Music* (London: Simon & Schuster, 1992).
Ly   Lyman, D., *Great Jews in Music* (New York: Jonathan David, 1994).
Pan   Fuller, S., *The Pandora Guide to Women Composers: Britain and United States 1629–Present* (London: Pandora, 1994).
WW   Warrack, J. and West, E., *The Oxford Dictionary of Opera* (Oxford: Oxford University Press, 1992).

Web sites are also listed for some composers, and in some cases references are made to sleeve notes. Where an asterisk is given against a reference, it indicates that the reference contains information about the composer's Jewish descent.

Glossary of Hebrew, Musical, Scientific and Related Terms

The following abbreviations are used in the glossary: H, Hebrew or Yiddish; S, scientific; and M, musical terms.

Hebrew words are transliterated. This sometimes leads to alternative spellings, and some alternatives are given under specific entries. The only spelling that might cause confusion, since it is the first consonant in a number of words, is the transliteration of the Hebrew letter ה (Hay), which may be transliterated as *h* or *ch* depending on whether the Sephardic or Ashkenazic pronunciation is used.

Where a definition is cross-referenced in a different part of the glossary, it is given in small capitals.

aleatory music (M) Music in which chance or indeterminacy are compositional elements. *Alea* is Latin for 'dice'.

aliyah la-aretz (H) literally 'Going up to the land'. Used to mean 'visiting or emigrating to the land of Israel'. Only the journey from Egypt or from the desert involves an increase in altitude, but going to Israel or the Holy Land is regarded as going up in a spiritual sense.

allele (S) One of a pair or series of alternative forms of a gene that occurs at a given position in a chromosome. All higher organisms, including humans, have paired sets of chromosomes, one of paternal and one of maternal origin. For each gene there are two copies, which may either be identical or alternative forms.

Anschluss German for 'connection, annexation'. Used specifically for the annexation of Austria by Nazi Germany in 1938.

Aryan In Nazi ideology, a Caucasian of non-Jewish descent, especially of the Nordic type.

Ashkenazim Jews whose ancestors lived in the Middle Ages in Germany and the surrounding countries, as distinct from those with Spanish or oriental ancestry, the SEPHARDIM. 'Ashenazic' is the adjectival form.

atonality (M) Music not in any key. All twelve notes of the CHROMATIC scale are used impartially in contrast to the normal major and minor scales of tonal music. The twelve notes of the octave function independently, unrelated to a key centre. The finale of Schoenberg's second string quartet (1908) is often regarded as the first atonal composition, although it is foreshadowed in the music of Debussy and Skriabin. Schoenberg continued to develop his ideas and compositional practice, and in 1921 announced a further development in the form of SERIALISM.

Bar mitzvah (H) literally 'son of commandment'. Sometimes written as a single word. At the age of 13 and one day a boy is considered a responsible adult for most religious purposes. The associated ceremony dates from the Middle Ages.

BCE Before the Common Era, equivalent to BC.

cantillation (M) The mode of chanting the TORAH and other scriptures in the synagogue and the system of musical notation for this.

cantor The synagogue official who leads the prayers, particularly on the Sabbath and at festivals.

carrier (genetic) (S) An individual who carries a recessive ALLELE that is not expressed. For example, the allele for Tay Sachs disease is a recessive allele. An individual having two copies of the allele will have Tay Sachs disease, but an individual having one Tay Sachs allele and one normal allele will not have the disease but will be able to transmit the allele to offspring and is thus a carrier.

CE The Common Era, equivalent to AD.

Chanukah (H) [alternative spelling *Hanukkah*] Hebrew for 'dedication'. The minor festival, usually in mid-December, to celebrate the victory of the Maccabees over the forces of Antiochus in 165 BCE. The Maccabees rededicated the Temple altar to Jewish worship.

Chassidism (H) [alternative spelling *Hassidism*] A revivalist movement that began in the eighteenth century in south-east Poland and was led by Israel Baal Shem against the 'dry-as-dust' bookishness of TALMUDIC Judaism. Baal Shem shifted the emphasis from scholarship to piety, from the Talmud to the Prayer Book. He preached that one must serve God with joy. This new message had a particular appeal for the masses of ordinary Jews unlearned in the Talmud. There are adherents of Chassidism today living in Israel, USA, England, France and many other countries.

chazzan (H) [plural *chazzanim*; alternative spelling *hazzan*] Hebrew for 'CANTOR'.

chazzanuth (H) The art of the CANTOR, i.e. the style in which the cantor intones or sings the liturgy.

cherem (H) [alternative spelling '*Herem*'] Hebrew for 'excommunication'. A ban imposed on an individual to separate him from the other members of the community. There are 24 offences for which it can be invoked, including insulting rabbinic authority, testifying against a fellow Jew in a non-Jewish court and flouting Jewish customs. In modern times the institution of *cherem* has largely fallen into disuse. Moses Mendelssohn (1729–86), on the grounds of religious tolerance, expressed opposition to the right of the rabbis to impose the cherem.

chromaticism (M) The use of a musical scale that divides the octave into 12 equal intervals of a semitone.

counterpoint (M) The simultaneous combination of two or more melodies to make musical sense. The term derives from the expression *punctus contra punctus*, i.e. 'point against point', or 'note against note'.

Degenerate Music see ENTARTETE MUSIK.

Diaspora Used generally to describe the dispersion or spreading of a people originally belonging to one nation or having a common culture, but specifically, when capitalized, to describe the dispersion of the Jews after the Babylonian and Roman conquests of Palestine.

diatonic (M) From the Greek meaning 'at intervals of a tone'. Pertaining to a given major or minor key in contrast to CHROMATICISM.

dibbuck (H) [alternative spelling *dybbuk*] The soul of a person pursued by demons that has found temporary security in the body of a living person. First reference to a dibbuck is found in the seventeenth century in the writings of the KABBALA.

Dorian mode (M) See MODE.

Entartete Musik (M) 'Degenerate or decadent music'. Originally the name given to a propagandist, racist exhibition in Düsseldorf in 1938 featuring works of composers and musicologists proscribed and banned by the Nazi Party. It was modelled on a widely publicized exhibition of 'degenerate visual art' held in Munich in 1937. The cover of the guide to the exhibition featured a caricature of a black man playing a saxophone and wearing a Star of David. The composers and writers featured were deemed to have detrimentally affected German culture during the years of the Weimar Republic (1918–33); they included Adorno, Berg, Bloch, Eisler, Hindemith, Korngold, Krenek, Schoenberg, Schreker, Stravinsky, Toch, and Weill.

gene (S) The heredity unit that determines a specific biological function or character. Located on chromosomes.

gene frequency (S) Genes may exist in alternative forms known as ALLELES. The gene frequency is the percentage of different alleles at one given position or locus in a population.

genizah (H) Hebrew for 'hiding place'. A room or container in which worn-out holy texts and pages containing the name of God are stored.

genotype (S) The genetic constitution of an organism, or the actual ALLELES present in an individual, as distinct from its physical appearance, or PHENOTYPE.

ghetto An area in a European city in which Jews were formerly required to live. The term is derived from the Italian for an iron foundry and was to refer to the Venetian quarter, near a foundry, to which Jews were restricted in 1516. It is also used nowadays more generally to describe a densely populated slum area of a city, inhabited by a socially and economically deprived minority.

Halakhah (H) Hebrew for 'way' or 'path'. The legal tradition of Judaism, which is usually contrasted with the theology, ethics and folklore known as 'Aggadah'. It has come to denote Jewish law as a whole; the rules and regulations by which the Jew 'walks' through life.

halil (H) [alternative spelling *hallel*] Hebrew for 'praise'. A joyous recital of Psalms 113–18 during the morning sevice on festival days.

Hashkivienu (H) Hebrew for 'Let us lie down'. The first lines of the central part of the prayer said at night before retiring, asking for protection against enemies, famine and sorrow. 'Let us lie down, O Lord our God, in peace, and let us rise up, O our King, to life.'.

Haskalah (H) Hebrew for 'knowledge', 'education' or 'enlightenment'. It is used to describe the movement that originated in eighteenth-century Germany with the aim of broadening the intellectual and social life of Jews, to enable them to take their place in western society.

Hatikvah (H) Hebrew for 'The Hope'. National Anthem of the State of Israel, sung to a folk tune of Moldavian origin.

Hebrew See Chapter 3, section 3.1 for definition. Note: 'Hebrew' is used as a noun or adjective; an alternative adjectival form is 'Hebraic'.

heritability (S) The degree to which a trait or character is controlled by inheritance. For example, if a trait such as height had a heritability value of 0.4, this would mean that height was controlled 40 per cent by inheritance, and 60 per cent by nurture or environmental factors.

heterozygote (S) An organism with unlike members of any given pair or series of ALLELES.

histocompatibility antigens (S) A complex set of antigens present on the surface of cells which allow the body's immune system to distinguish foreign, or 'non-self' cells from 'self'. There are a large number of different histocompatibility antigens, which differ from one individual to another. Only in identical twins are they the same. This is why tissue matching is so important in tissue or organ transplants, if rejection is not to occur.

Holocaust The word derived from the Greek meaning 'whole burnt offering'. Since World War Two used to describe the mass murder by the Nazis of Jews of continental Europe between 1940 and 1945.

Israelite see Chapter 3, section 3.1.

Jew See Chapter 3, section 3.1. Note: 'Jewish' or 'Judaic' are alternative adjectives for 'relating to Jews'.

kabbalah (H) Hebrew for 'received tradition'. A general term for Jewish mystical tradition, but, more exactly, the teachings which first began to emerge in southern France and Spain in the thirteenth century. Kabbalists claimed that their tradition had originally been given to Moses at Sinai, together with the TORAH. Kabbalistic theosophy explored the inner workings of the divine in its relationship to man and the magical influence of man's actions on God. It has played an important part in the literature of both Jews and Christians since the Middle Ages.

Kaddish (H) Aramaic for 'sanctification'. The prayer glorifying God's name, recited at the close of synagogue prayers; it is the most solemn and one of the most ancient of all Jewish prayers. Mourners also recite it during the period of mourning and on the anniversary of a death.

klezmer (H) A Yiddish term meaning 'musician'. Generally, an informal group of musicians, often itinerant, playing traditional music, folk songs or solemn hymns. Used also to denote a musical tradition cultivated by ASHKENAZIM in the east European DIASPORA.

Kol Nidre (H) Aramaic for 'all vows'. The opening words of a solemn declaration at the beginning of the evening service on YOM KIPPUR. It is a formal abrogation of all vows made during the past year. This affects only the obligations of man towards God but not those towards his fellow men. Many Jews were forcibly converted during the Inquisition and this abrogation would absolve them from such vows.

Kristallnacht 9 November 1938. The night on which the Nazis decided to carry out a general POGROM against all Jews under their rule. This was in retaliation for the assassination of a German diplomat in Paris by the young Polish Jew Herschel Grynspan on 7 November. Grynspan declared that he was taking revenge for the injustice done to his parents, who were expelled, along with many other Jews, by the Nazis from Germany. On 9 November stormtroopers together with a Nazi mob attacked Jewish homes, injuring and murdering Jewish victims. Hundreds of synagogues were destroyed, 7,500 Jewish shops were burnt to the ground and 90 were left dead.

Marrano The Spanish name given to Jews who converted to Christianity under threat of death or persecution at the time of the Inquisition, but who retained a secret adherence to Judaism.

Maskilim (H) [singular, *Maskil*] Hebrew for 'enlightened ones'. Those who followed and furthered the HASKALAH movement called themselves 'enlightened ones'.

microtone (M) Any interval smaller than a semitone.

minimalism (M) The name given to a style of musical composition that originated in the USA in the 1960s. Minimalism is based on slow transformations of small musical elements. The elements undergo substitution and changes of phasing. Stasis and repetition replaced the melodic line of conventional tonal music. The music appears to move slowly without apparent direction or climaxes.

mitzvah (H) Hebrew for 'commandment'. A term originally used of divine commands in the Bible, but which eventually came to refer to any good deed. See also BAR MITZVAH.

mode (M) A way of ordering a musical scale. From about 400 CE to 1500 CE the dominant modes used by European composers were known as the Church modes. These arose out of the modes devised by Pythagoras and the Greek thinkers. Church modes (and the Greek modes before them) differed from one another in their placing of the semitones within a scale (for details, see Chapter 1, sections 1.1 and 1.2 and Figure 1). Church modes were given the following names: Ionian, Mixolydian, Dorian, Aeolian, Phrygian, Locrian and Lydian. Since the sixteenth century most European composers have used the major and minor scales of the diatonic systems rather than modes, with the exception of composers writing in a pastoral, folk or church tradition.

neume (M) A system of musical notation used from the seventh to fourteenth centuries.

Pentateuch (H) The five books of Moses – Genesis, Exodus, Leviticus, Numbers and Deuteronomy.

Pesach (H) Hebrew for 'passover'. The spring festival celebrating Israel's dramatic deliverance from enslavement in Egypt, as recounted in the Book of Exodus. It is called 'Passover' because God passed over the houses of the captive children of Israel when he slew the Egyptian first-born.

phenotype (S) The observable characteristics of an organism, produced by the GENOTYPE in conjunction with the environment. Not all ALLELES present in a genotype are expressed. For example, an individual who is a CARRIER for Tay Sachs disease has one Tay Sachs allele and one normal allele. Because the normal allele is dominant over the Tay Sachs allele, such an individual will not suffer from Tay Sachs disease, because it will not be expressed in his phenotype.

Phrygian mode (M) See MODE.

Pogrom (H) From Russian, via Yiddish meaning 'like thunder'. An organized persecution or extermination of an ethnic group, especially of Jews.

Polymorphism (S) The occurrence of more than one form of a gene.

polyphony (M) The word applied to 'many-sound' or 'many-voice' music. Music made up of several strands moving with apparent independence and freedom, though fitting together harmonically. This is in contrast to 'monophony', i.e. a single sound or voice, and 'homophony', i.e. all sounds or voices moving in the same rhythm, like a melody with each note harmonized. The polyphonic period – the age of unaccompanied choral music associated with Palestrina, Byrd, Lassus and their contemporaries – was pre-eminent in the sixteenth and early seventeenth centuries.

recombination (S) The occurrence of progeny with combinations of genes other than those that occurred in the parents. This occurs as the result of a process known as 'crossing over' and assortment of genes, which occurs during the formation of both male and female gametes (sperm and ova), and/or the fusion between sperm and ovum.

Reform movement (H) A movement that arose in nineteenth-century Germany with the aim of reforming Judaism in the light of western thought, values and culture, where such a reinterpretation would not conflict with Judaism's basic principles.

répétiteur (M) One who coaches the singers or instrumentalists, or both, in an opera house.

Rosh Ha-Shannah (H) Hebrew for 'head of the year'. The festival celebrating the Jewish New Year.

Sabra a native-born Israeli. The word is derived from the Arabic name for a plant of the aloe species with spiky outer leaves and sweet, juicy flesh.

Second Viennese School (M) The group of composers who worked in Vienna (and Berlin) between 1910 and 1930 under the leadership of Arnold Schoenberg, e.g. Berg and Webern. Commonly linked to the SERIAL method of composition.

Sephardim (H) Jews of Spanish and Portuguese origin who spread throughout North Africa, the Ottoman Empire, parts of South America, Italy and Holland after the expulsion of the Jews from the Iberian peninsula at the end of the fifteenth century. 'Sephardic' is the adjectival form.

serialism, serial music, serial technique or twelve-note music (M) A progression of ATONAL music. It uses all twelve notes of the CHROMATIC scale, but in an ordered way. The system is based on a series of intervals referred to as a note row (hence serialism), which involves all twelve notes of the chromatic scale in the order selected by the composer. In its strictest application no note should be repeated until all the other eleven have appeared, and the order of the series remains unchanged throughout the work, unless with certain permitted modifications. It can be used harmonically as well as melodically; the whole note row can be transposed, inverted, reversed or inverted and reversed. Schoenberg first began using serialism in 1923. Further developed in the 1940s as TOTAL SERIALISM.

shamash (H) [alternative spellings *shammes, shamus, shammus*] Hebrew for 'beadle'. The sexton or caretaker of a synagogue; the 'servant' of a congregation of worshippers.

Shema (H) Hebrew for 'hear' also referred to as *Shema Yisroal*, 'Hear O Israel'. The most common of Hebrew prayers, recited three or four times a day by Orthodox Jews. The declaration of faith in one God. It is also the last prayer a Jew utters on his deathbed.

Shoah (H) Hebrew meaning 'catastrophe'. The Hebrew word for the HOLOCAUST.

solfeggio or **solfège** (M) Italian and French terms for a method of ear training and sight-reading in which the names of the notes used are a fixed-doh system, i.e., doh is always C, ray is D, soh is G, etc. A type of vocal exercise serving the purpose of voice training and also practice in sight-reading, by recognizing the intervals and notes. It is believed to have originated with Guido of Arezzo at around the eleventh century CE, using the first syllables (Ut, Re, Mi, Fa, So, La) of each phrase of the hymn *Ut queant laxis*. Ut was replaced by Do in the seventeenth century. Solfeggio is sometimes also used to mean the whole system of rudimentary musical instruction, e.g., sight-singing, ear training and study of notation. Extensive courses in *solfège* were first introduced into conservatories in Brussels and Paris.

Sprechgesang, Sprechstimme (M) A type of vocal performance between speech and song. Towards the end of the nineteenth century several composers sought to control the interaction of a speaking voice with a musical accompaniment, not only rhythmically but also in terms of pitch. Schoenberg used it in *Gurrelieder, Die glückliche Hand, Pierrot Lunaire* and *Moses und Aron*. In *Pierrot Lunaire* he wrote a melodic line for vocal declamation, in which the speaking voice must momentarily touch the indicated pitch, then rise and fall away from it in a *glissando*. In general usage, *Sprechgesang* is the term for the vocal technique, *Sprechstimme* for the vocal part employing it.

Synagogue (H) Greek word meaning 'place of gathering'. The building in which Jews worship and offer their prayers. The synagogue is assumed to have begun as an institution during the Babylonian Captivity, after the destruction of the First Temple in 586 BCE.

tallit (H) Hebrew for 'cloak'. The prayer shawl used by males at prayer at religious services.

Talmud (H) Hebrew for 'study'. The Talmud is a massive compendium of 63 books that includes the learned debates, dialogues and commentaries of scholars who for over 1,000 years have interpreted the TORAH.

Tetrachord (M) A succession of four notes contained within the compass of a perfect fourth, e.g., A-G-F-E, where the intervals between the notes are tone, tone, and semitone, respectively.

tonality (M) The way elements are arranged in a musical work to make it coherent. All systems of tonality share the idea that music progresses away from and towards fundamental pitches, which control the relative importance of all sounds used within a work. Music is drawn to a particular tone as if by gravitational pull.

Torah (H) Hebrew for 'teaching'. In its narrowest meaning Torah refers only to the first five books of Moses – the Pentateuch. The term is also used to refer to the whole of the Old Testament, i.e., the Pentateuch, the Prophets and the Writings. This is sometimes referred to as the 'Written Torah'. In its broadest sense Torah represents the whole of Jewish teaching from the commencement of the Bible through to the present day.

total serialism or **generalized serialism** (M) Composition that treats all musical parameters SERIALLY, not only pitch but also time values, volume (amplitude) and timbre.

twelve-note music (M) See SERIALISM.

yahrzeit (Y) [alternative spelling *yohrzeit*] Yiddish from the German *Jahrzeit*. The anniversary of the death of a parent or relative for whom the rites of mourning are carried out. A memorial candle or lamp is lighted in the home, and another in the synagogue, where it burns from sunset to sunset.

yarmulkah (H) [alternative spellings *yarmulke, yarmulka*]. The skullcap worn so as not to pray or study the TORAH with bare head. Sometimes called a *cappel* or *kippa*.

Yigdal (H) Hebrew for 'May He be magnified'. A popular hymn from the thirteenth century sung on the Sabbath and at religious festivals.

yishuv (H) Hebrew for 'settlement'. The Jewish community in pre-state Palestine, i.e., Jews settling in Palestine before the existence of the State of Israel.

Yom Kippur (H) Hebrew for 'Day of Atonement'. The last of the annual Ten Days of Penitence, which begins with ROSH HA-SHANNAH; one of the two high holy days of the Jewish calendar. Yom Kippur is, perhaps, the day that has the strongest hold on the Jewish conscience.

Introduction

Jews have made an enormous contribution to western music over the last 200 years, as composers, performers, impresarios, writers and critics. Their contribution to western civilization far outweighs that of non-Jews when viewed in terms of numbers of individuals in relation to the total population of the western world. The period coincides roughly with the time of emancipation of the Jews in Europe, that is, their entitlement to equal rights with other citizens of the state, following the French Revolution, and continued to progress throughout Europe up to the twentieth century. It can be seen as a natural development from the European Enlightenment, which elevated the individual, the 'human being', and aspired to liberate him or her from historically evolved social and religious frameworks.

The Jewish Enlightenment movement (*Haskalah*) was an offshoot of the European Enlightenment. Its spiritual father was the philosopher Moses Mendelssohn (1729–86), the grandfather of Felix and Fanny Mendelssohn. Mendelssohn endeavoured to link the faithful observance of religious injunctions with tolerance and the widest possible freedom of opinion. The movement aimed to keep religious observance, and at the same time to be compatible with obligations to the state. It encouraged the reform of Jewish education to include both secular and religious education. All this had the effect of enabling Jews to play a much fuller role in many spheres in the wider community, including science, politics and the arts, including music.

The title of this book, *Composers of Classical Music of Jewish Descent*, requires definitions of both 'classical music' and 'Jewish descent'. Classification is a useful tool for attempting to understand a wide range of subjects including science, philosophy, politics and the arts, although it has limitations. Whilst many people have an understanding of what they mean by 'classical music', many would have difficulty in defining its precise limits. This is in part because there is a complete spectrum of types of music, each of which has features in common and which influences one another, and in a sense compartmentalization creates artificial boundaries. The *New Grove Dictionary of Music and Musicians* (2nd edn, 2001) has widened its scope, when compared to that of the first edition, to include pop and rock music, and to give wider coverage of world music: this decision has been questioned by a number of

1

critics.[1] Although some music lovers have strong interests in many different musical genres, most have a preference for just one genre.

The classification of music appears to pose no problems for record shops. When I was a student in the late 1950s the local record shop segregated customers on two floors: the upper, carpeted floor was for the sale of classical records and had ample-sized listening booths with comfortable chairs; the lower floor, covered with linoleum, was for popular music and had much smaller booths without seating. Now, over 40 years later, the typical record shop has usually only a small section of classical music, which is tucked away in a tiny corner of the shop, swamped both aurally and visually by the other genre. Nevertheless, in spite of these major changes, classification does occur, and the vast majority of composers appear only under one category. This is also obvious from the many books and periodicals devoted to classical music.[2]

The scope of this book is limited to composers of western classical music. This includes music that has sprung broadly from the European musical tradition, and is generally included in standard works on classical music.[3] Not included is music from India and eastern Asia, jazz, musicals or folk music, including, for example, *klezmer*. However, during the twentieth century, as travelling has become much easier, many composers who are included in this book, for example, Milhaud, Gershwin, Reich and Glass, who have been brought up in the European musical tradition, have absorbed influences from other cultures. Composers, such as Gershwin, Wilhelm Grosz, Friedrich Hollaender, and André Previn, who have composed some 'classical music', are included, but Irving Berlin, Jerome Kern, Richard Rodgers, and Stephen Sondheim, who have not, are omitted. There are a number of musicians who are best known as conductors, performers, or musicologists, but who nevertheless have composed, for example, Klemperer, Maazel, Kreisler, Schnabel and Adorno; these have been included.

The second definition is that of 'Jewish descent'. A number of books have been written about Jews in music, and about Jewish music.[4] Both of these are subject to different interpretations. The definitions of what it means to be a Jew are discussed in Chapter 3, section 3.1. Jewish music can either mean music written by Jews, or music that is recognizable by its structure or its function as distinctly arising from Jewish culture.

The purpose of this book is to identify the contribution that Jewish culture has made to 'classical music'. For this we need to include any composer who has been imbued with Jewish culture or tradition. This will not be restricted to those who are considered Jews by Jewish law (*Halakah*), but will include those who have a heredity or cultural connection with Judaism. As discussed in Chapter 3, both inheritance and upbringing are undoubtedly important in determining aptitude and success in composing, although they are not the only factors. It is more logical, in this context, to consider composers of Jewish descent, rather than composers who are Jewish according to Jewish law. If there is a genetic contribution to this aptitude (the ability to successfully compose music), then it is more important to consider Jewish descent. For example, an individual with a Jewish mother and non-Jewish father will have 50 per cent of his or her genetic make-up from a Jew, but equally so will a person with a Jewish father and non-Jewish mother. However, according to Jewish law, with its adherence to matriarchal descent, the former is Jewish while the latter is not. If there is any genetic basis for this attribute, that is, ability to compose, then it is as likely to come from the mother as it is from the father.

Adopting this approach raises the question of how many generations back to trace the Jewish descent. For each generation back one goes, the likelihood of having a Jewish ancestor doubles, for example, the probability of having a single Jewish great-grandparent is four times greater that of having a single Jewish parent. For the purposes of my study I have restricted the scope to individuals who have at least one Jewish grandparent. The reason is that most individuals will know or have known their parents and in many cases their grandparents, but few will have known their great-grandparents. If upbringing is important, then if an individual knows, or has known his or her grandparents, then they are likely to be aware of their Jewishness, even if only to a small degree, and this could be regarded as an influence on their personality. An individual with one Jewish grandparent will have a 25 per cent Jewish contribution to their genetic make-up, regardless of whether they themselves are Jewish, that is, whether their maternal grandmother and mother are Jewish or non-Jewish.

There are, of course, non-Jewish composers who may have been influenced by Jewish culture through friends or colleagues. Shostakovich and Ravel are obvious examples. But it is necessary to have a cut-off point, and so I have excluded this category, together with those having less than a quarter Jewish genetic contribution.

This book is divided into two parts. The first part attempts to account for the emergence over the last 200 years of composers of Jewish descent and to assess their contribution to European classical music. The first two chapters form a brief historical sketch of composers of Jewish descent from earliest times up to the present day and are subdivided into the period before 1800 and the period after 1800. In the earlier period, following the destruction of the Second Temple in 70 CE many Jews began dispersing throughout Europe and North Africa. However, up until about 1800 they lived within their host countries largely in communities separated from their surrounding populations, and so made little contribution to the development of western classical music, or indeed any other aspect of culture. This is in marked contrast to their contribution after 1800.

Chapter 3 considers the nature of the contribution Jews made after 1800, and to what extent this can be accounted for by Jewish culture or by Jewish inheritance. Can their contribution be considered innovative, or was it simply a case of adapting to the developments that had already occurred in western classical music? The views of other musicians, both positive and negative, are considered.

In order to consider the 'inheritance' question it is necessary to address the question of whether the Jews constitute a distinct group or race. Is there any genetic evidence to indicate that any specific genes or combinations of genes are present to a higher degree in Jews than in their surrounding populations? With the completion of the genetic sequence of the human genome, one might anticipate that Jews could potentially be defined in terms of DNA sequences. However, this seems highly unlikely, given the intermarriage that has occurred over many generations. The present evidence suggests that the human genome has in the region of 30,000 to 60,000 genes, which is about twice the number that are present in 'simple' organisms such as worms or fruitflies.[5] However, over 90 per cent of the genes present in worms and fruitflies are also common to humans. Thus, when considering differences between very closely related organisms, such as different human races, very few if any genes are likely to be unique to a particular race or group, although combinations of genes may be more common in certain groups than in others.

The majority of composers of Jewish descent living from 1800 onwards either renounced their Jewish faith or at least were not practising Jews, although many had spiritual beliefs, for example, Copland, Joachim, Mahler, Mendelssohn, Moscheles, Offenbach, Schoenberg, Ullman, Weill and Zemlinsky. Some, like Bernstein, were proud to be Jews; others, like Finzi, wanted to completely dissociate themselves from Judaism. In chapter 4 I consider whether, or to what extent, composers of Jewish descent were conscious of their Jewish inheritance, and whether this was reflected in their composing.

The second, longer part of the book takes the form of biographies of composers of Jewish descent. Here over 250 composers are listed, together with biographical sketches. Each entry includes a brief bibliography where further information about the composers can be found. For the majority, their Jewish origin is well known, but for some this is not so. In most cases references to their Jewish origin are given. I have aimed to be inclusive rather than exclusive, and it is possible in a few cases, where the evidence for Jewish descent is from indirect sources or is flimsy, that future research may refute it. The biographical sketches focus on the life and works of the composers, but do not include any musical analysis except where a composer may have been responsible for a major development, for example, Schoenberg and serial music.

Appendix 1 contains a list of those composers who were included in the Nazi-authorized *Lexikon der Juden in der Musik* by Stengel and Gerigk, together with a translation of its foreword, in which the purpose of the lexicon is explained.

4

NOTES

1. See *Gramophone*, 78 (April 2001), pp. 4 and 108–9.
2. *Gramophone, International Record Review, BBC Music Magazine, Classic fM, Gramophone Classical Good Guide, Classical Music on CD*.
3. Gerald Abraham, *The Concise Oxford History of Music* (Oxford: Oxford University Press, 1979); Stanley Sadie and Alison Latham (eds), *The Cambridge Music Guide* (Cambridge, Cambridge University Press, 1985); Donald J. Grout and Claude V. Palisca, *A History of Western Music*, 6th edn (New York: W. W. Norton, 2000).
4. Abraham Z. Idelsohn, *Jewish Music in its Historical Development* (New York: Dover, 1992); Aron M. Rothmüller, *The Music of the Jews: an Historical Appreciation* (London: Vallentine Mitchell, 1953); Arthur Holde, *Jews in Music* (New York: Bloch Publishing, 1974); Irene Heskes, *Passport to Jewish Music* (Westport, CN: Greenwood Press, 1994); Darryl Lyman, *Great Jews in Music* (New York: Jonathan David, 1994).
5. A number of papers in the February 2001 issue of *Nature* magazine.

Part I
HISTORICAL SURVEY
AND ANALYSIS

Chapter 1

Musical Developments in Jewish Communities from Biblical Times until the End of the Eighteenth Century

Music has had a secular and a sacred role from earliest biblical times. Although there is no record of its actual sound, since an accurate written musical notation for western music did not evolve until about the tenth century CE,[1] less precise notations, for example, neumes, were in use earlier.[2] From descriptions of the instruments and their pictorial representation, and descriptions of the type of music, some deductions are possible. The first mention of music in the Bible is in Genesis 4:21, where Jubal is described as the 'ancestor of all who play the lyre and the pipe'. However, it is unlikely that any systematic development of music occurred before the time of the first kings of Israel, around 1000 BCE. From the time of Abraham (1800–1700 BCE) up until around 1000 BCE the Israelites had been either nomadic or in bondage in Egypt (for definition of Israelites, Hebrews and Jews, see Chapter 3, section 3.1). During this early period the Hebrews were one of many Semitic tribes and would have had contacts with the Sumerians and the Egyptians. Sumeria formed the southern region of Mesopotamia (the land between the Tigris and Euphrates) and extended to the tip of the Persian Gulf. The area is now part of southern Iraq and Kuwait.

From 1550 to 1080 BCE there was a cultural explosion in Egypt that included music. The development of new instruments can be discerned from the many wall paintings of the period. It seems most probable that the Israelites drew from the developments of both their Sumerian and Egyptian neighbours and adapted them to their own requirements. Any significant innovations appear to have come from outside, that is, from neighbouring nations. Throughout their history the Hebrews have been quick to accept from other cultures whatever features were compatible with their own religious institutions.

1.1 MUSIC UP UNTIL ROMAN TIMES

After the building of the First Temple (*c.* 970 BCE) music played an important part in religious ceremonies. King David chose the Levites to be responsible for providing musical accompaniment, both vocal and instrumental, to the sacrifices. When Solomon married Pharaoh's daughter, she is said to have brought with her a large variety of musical instruments, and so developments in Egyptian music were undoubtedly absorbed into the music of the Temple. Accounts of Solomon's Temple describe 24 choral groups consisting of 288 musicians performing in 21 weekly services.[3] The instruments described include the *nevel* (a large harp), the *kinnor* (a lyre), the *halil* (a double reed pipe) and the *shofar*. The shofar, made from a ram's horn, produces limited tones and served for signalling purposes only. By the time of Nebuchadnezzar (539 BCE), an even wider range of instruments are mentioned: 'horn, pipe, zither, lyre, psaltery, bagpipe and other types of instrument' (Daniel 3:4). True biblical chanting seems to have originated in the fifth century BCE.

By the second century BCE a Hellenistic influence on Hebrew music is evident, as the musical instruments referred to in the book of Daniel written in the second century BCE are given their Greek rather than Hebrew names. After the destruction of the Second Temple (70 CE) musical instruments were not used in religious services, with the exception of the least musical instrument, the shofar. Although it is often believed that the reason for this was a token of mourning for the destruction of the Temple, the use of musical instruments in the Temple had been discouraged before then in order to safeguard the purity of religious music 'against the musical and orgiastic mystery cults', in which Syrian and Mesopotamian Jews not infrequently participated. Secular music was believed to have a bad influence on people, and spiritual leaders discouraged it. The destruction of the Temple reinforced this view, and led to a ban.[4]

The earliest foundations of musical theory are generally attributed to the Greek philosopher and mathematician Pythagoras (572–497 BCE), although the Sumerians and Babylonians may have had rudiments of musical theory before that time, as did the Chinese.[5] Even earlier, Tubal-Cain, Jubal's half-brother, has been attributed as having an understanding of the relation between pitch and linked mathematical parameters, but this is highly speculative, on the basis of Genesis 4:21–2.[6] Pythagoras left no writings; his theory of music was recorded about 200 years later. He used a stretched string to establish the relationship between length and the pitch of the note. He found that if a stretched string is 'stopped' at one-half, two-thirds or three-quarters of its length and then plucked, the musical consonances known as the *octave, fifth* or *fourth*, respectively, are produced.[7] These intervals provided the theoretical basis for western music until the end of the Middle Ages. Pythagoras had, in effect, discovered the physical basis of harmony.[8] He established the octave and musical intervals within the octave. The tetra chord (four notes descending through a perfect fourth) became the basis of Greek music and, depending on the intervals between the four notes within the tetra chord, the different modes (e.g. Lydian, Phrygian and Aeolian) were assigned. By extending the range to a second tetra chord, with an interval between them, complete octave scales were possible.

Thus, up until the time of the destruction of the Second Temple (70 CE), Jews and their ancestors had largely adapted developments in musical practice and theory from their neighbours or captors, the Egyptians, Babylonians and Greeks, rather than initiating new developments. With Alexander the Great's conquest of the Middle East in 330 BCE, Jewish culture came under Greek influence. This affected Jews living in the southern Middle East (Egypt) much more than those living in Judea, who were able to better retain their own cultural heritage. The Greek influence was strongest between about 200 BCE and the beginning of the Common Era. Secular music was most affected, whereas music used in the Temple was highly conserved and little affected.

In 165 BCE Judas Maccabeus recaptured Jerusalem from the Seleucid Greeks and the Temple was rededicated. However, in 63 BCE Jerusalem was captured by the Romans, and Judea became a Roman province. The Greeks had undoubtedly influenced Jewish culture. In contrast, the Romans made little impact. At the time of the destruction of the Second Temple most of the Jewish nation lived within the domain of the Roman Empire, in the Land of Israel and in the large Hellenistic Diaspora extending west to present-day France and east into Asia Minor, but a large minority lived in Babylonia. During the next 500 years Jews dispersed further within what was initially still the Roman Empire and also beyond it. Jewish cultural centres such as Jerusalem and Alexandria fell into decline whereas Babylon once again became an important cultural centre. Here, the rabbinical edicts concerning the prohibition of musical activity were almost completely ignored.[9] The Roman Empire collapsed after 500 years, when the territories were overrun by the Arabian conquest.

Unlike Greek music, the music composed for the Temple was not written down but was passed on orally. The Levites, members of the tribe of Levi, were responsible for providing the music to accompany the offering of sacrifices in the Temple. After the destruction of the Temple the instrumental music of the Levites fell into oblivion and the associated technical skills were lost. A vocal musical tradition continued in the synagogues and in gatherings of Christians, originally a Jewish sect, until they were formally anathematized by Orthodox Judaism around 80 CE. The early Christian psalm adhered closely to the music of the Jewish psalm, whereas the development of the Christian hymn took a more independent course. *Zemirot* (hymns that formed part of the Jewish liturgy, and also Sabbath table hymns) were introduced into Jewish ritual around the sixth century CE. Secular Jewish music at this time was much the same as most secular music from other parts of the Near East. Greek songs spread to Palestine at the beginning of the Common Era.

11

1.2 MUSIC IN THE MIDDLES AGES

Church services were more or less standardized by the eleventh century. The earliest music of the medieval church was plainsong, often known as Gregorian chant. It was in the period that Pope Gregory was pontiff that much of the plainsong was collected and categorized. The chanting of the Pentateuch, which is still heard in Yemenite synagogues in modern Israel, shows striking similarities to the probable state of Gregorian chant before the advent of neume notation, and the origins of Gregorian chant can be traced back to Jewish religious music.[10] Secular music was also being developed at this time, in particular by minstrels. In France these travelling minstrels were known as *jongleurs*, and in Spain the equivalent was *juglar*. They earned their living writing poems, composing songs and acting, performing throughout the country, especially at the royal courts. Although historical records are sketchy, it is clear that there were a number who had obviously Jewish names. If a *jongleur* was a nobleman, he was known as a *troubadour* or *trouvère*. A *trouvère* composed his own poems, but he did not necessarily perform them himself; he may have employed a singer or *chanteor* to do this. The subject matter of these poems was almost exclusively courtly love. However, since there were no Jewish noblemen, Jews might be *jongleurs* but not *troubadours* or *trouvères*.[11]

Early polyphony began to develop in the late Middle Ages. Prior to this time monophony was the main vocal style. The initial progression was of two melodic lines moving in exactly the same rhythm and in parallel: this is known as organum and dates from about 900. The Cathedral of Notre Dame in Paris was the focus of its further development in the late twelfth century, by Léonin and Pérotin. The development of polyphony gave music a depth that was paralleled in developments in painting from the early Renaissance. It was developing in secular music too, particularly in Italy. One of its earliest exponents was Francesco Landini, who lived in Florence from *c.* 1325 to 1397. The first collection of German polyphonic secular songs appears in the *Locheimer Liederbuch* (Locheimer songbook) compiled *c.* 1450.[12] The author of the songbook was Wölflin von Lochheim; he may also have been the composer of the 48 vocal compositions set for two and three voices. The dedication in the songbook is in German, but it is written in Hebrew characters. This and other evidence suggests that Wölflin von Lochheim was a Jew.[13]

The Renaissance brought about further developments, among them the beginnings of western harmony, a system that was to dominate western music for at least 450 years, and although since the end of the nineteenth century the rules that this embodies have been progressively broken, western harmony still forms the core of much contemporary music. An important change that occurred from the time of the Middle Ages was that musical tradition was no longer an oral tradition. Whilst monophonic music (a single melodic line) can be learned and handed down orally, it is all but impossible to memorize polyphonic music, which not only requires remembering each line, but also how they fit together. For the development of complex polyphonic music, a system of notation was a prerequisite. As early as the Greek and Roman era, a system of lettering was used. From about the seventh century a system of signs, known as neumes, began to be used to indicate to a singer of a plainsong the general curves and rhythms of the melody, but they were not initially an accurate indication of pitch. As they became more widely used, they were also used more precisely. Guido of Arezzo (c. 991–post-1033), a Benedictine monk from the Abbey of Pomposa on the Adriatic coast, devised the elements of musical notation that form the basis of the system that is used today. By the eleventh century this notation was used in conjunction with lines to indicate pitch, although at this stage there was no indication of the notes' durations. The modes, originally devised by the Greeks much earlier (see section 1.1) became generally known as church modes, not because they had become exclusive to church music, but because the church helped to classify them and codify the system of their employment. Each of these modes differs in the arrangement of tones and semitones within the octave (see Figure 1). From about 1600 the seven modes gradually became replaced by the diatonic scales,

Figure 1
TONE INTERVALS IN MUSICAL MODES.

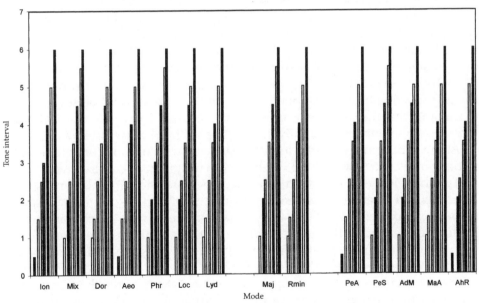

Church modes: Ionian (Ion), Mixolydian (Mix), Dorian (Dor), Aeolian (Aeo),
Phrygian (Phr), Locrian (Loc), Lydian (Lyd)
Diatonic: Major (Maj), Relative minor (Rmin)
Synagogue modes: Pentatonic Ashkenazic (PeS), Pentatonic Sephardic (PeA),
Adonay-Malach (AdM), Magen-Abot (MaA), Ahavah-Rabba (AhR)

with their major and minor modes forming the basis of western European classical music. Further developments led to proportional notation indicating the duration of a note, and bar lines were also used. These developments in musical notation were essential tools for the composition of polyphonic music.

Up to the time of *Haskalah* in the eighteenth century, Jews made an insignificant contribution to the overall development of western music. Organs came into use in churches by the twelfth century, but apart from a few exceptions – the Altneu, Pinkus and Meisel synagogues in Prague – they were not used in synagogues until the rise of the Reform Movement, when the first organ was installed in the Reform Temple in Seesen, Germany, in 1810. They are not used in present-day orthodox synagogues.

After the destruction of the Second Temple religious services took place in the synagogues. The date of the origin of synagogues is unclear. The earliest historical records date back to the period immediately preceding the Common Era, when the synagogue already formed the central form of Jewish worship.[14] The earliest reference to synagogue worship is to be found in the writings of the Jewish philosopher, Philo (20 BCE–50 CE). Services in the Temple had been performed by priests and Levites, but now the organization became democratic. A precentor was chosen from among the congregation by the elders of the synagogue to lead the service (see Glossary for definition of synagogue). This role developed so that by about the sixth century it became that of a professional precentor or *chazzan* (sometimes spelt *hazzan*; also known in different countries as the *cantor*, *chanter*, *Vorbeter* and *Vorsänger*; the English term *cantor* is used here). Texts from the Bible were chanted (cantillation) and this form of cantillation changed little throughout the generations. However, over a period of time a collection of prayers grew. Prayers became more intricate with the introduction of metrical poetry or *piyyut* and they could be sung. It was in this area that the cantor was most able to use and display his musical skills. This development arose initially among the Sephardic Jews of Spain.

At the southern end of the Jewish Diaspora Arabian influences took hold, initially in secular Jewish song but later also in synagogue music. Arab meter and Arab melodies were used in the synagogue services in Babylonia, Syria, Morocco and Spain by the tenth century. A difference of emphasis arose between Ashkenazic and Sephardic rituals: in the former the cantor was the leading force shaping the music, whereas in the latter more stress was put on the role of the congregants and the chanting was simpler. In the former the cantor was expected to enliven Sabbath services and religious festivals with vocal music. He also became in some ways like the French *troubadour* or the German *Minnesinger*, having to satisfy the popular demand for music, although this was not without opposition from those who felt that music should not get the upper hand over religious observance. This music was memorized until the beginning of the sixteenth century, when attempts were made to write it down. However, there is evidence that neumes were used sporadically well before this time.

Signs or *ta'amim* were added to liturgical texts used in the Temple and in synagogues at the beginning of the Christian Era. The *ta'amim* were used, not to indicate a single note or an accurate pitch, but rather to suggest the melodic manner of rendering a phrase or word.[15] Some examples of the 28 *ta'amim* used are given in Figure 2. These are unique to the chanting of the Torah and are still used in synagogues throughout the world today. A more complex and

Figure 2
EXAMPLES OF *TA'AMIM* AND THEIR USE:
Above, *ta'amim*; below, Genesis 21:14 in modern Hebrew print showing vowels and *ta'amim*.

⅄ *Etnacha* (to rest)	⊆ *Darga* (stepwise)
⌐ *Munach* (sustained)	∪ *Paser* (to scatter)
⚲ ⚲ *T'lisha g'dola* (to draw out)	⅀ *Shalsheles* (chain)
⁄ *Mercha* (to lengthen)	∩ *Pashta* (extending)
∣ *Silluk* (cessation)	< *Yethib* (Staying)

וַיַּשְׁכֵּ֨ם

אַבְרָהָ֣ם ׀ בַּבֹּ֜קֶר וַיִּֽקַּֽח־לֶ֣חֶם וְחֵ֣מַת

מַ֡יִם וַיִּתֵּ֣ן אֶל־הָ֠גָר שָׂ֥ם עַל־שִׁכְמָ֛הּ

וְאֶת־הַיֶּ֖לֶד וַֽיְשַׁלְּחֶ֑הָ וַתֵּ֣לֶךְ וַתֵּ֔תַע

בְּמִדְבַּ֖ר בְּאֵ֥ר שָֽׁבַע׃

15

precise notation using neumes was developed around the twelfth century for both liturgical and non-liturgical music. A notated manuscript by Obadiah, a Norman Proselyte from that date, was found in the Cairo *Genizah* in 1965.[16] The first written sources of Ashkenazi chants appeared in the sixteenth century.

By the sixteenth century synagogue song was well established. Because many Jewish communities were not stable, frequently being expelled from one place to another, they often did not engage a 'permanent' cantor. Cantors were often peripatetic musicians wandering from town to town as guest performers in both synagogues and at concerts in the towns.[17]

1.3 MUSIC FROM THE RENAISSANCE UNTIL THE END OF THE EIGHTEENTH CENTURY

The first Jewish musician with a reputation outside the Jewish community in western Europe was Salamone ROSSI (1570–1630). He was both a composer and a performer. For most of his working life he was employed at the court of Mantua. The time of the Renaissance in Italy marked the full development of polyphony and harmony. Rossi performed at court and also composed madrigals, canzonettes, instrumental music and polyphonic settings of Hebrew Psalms and prayers for use in the synagogue. Although the text of his liturgical music was in Hebrew, the music itself was pure contemporary Italian. Initially there was opposition to using the music in synagogues, although it was used in Italy for a short period before Mantua was swept by war in 1630. Later, in Paris in 1877, Samuel Naumburg edited Rossi's settings using modern musical notation. Rossi's most important contribution to western music was in providing a connecting link between music of the Renaissance and the early baroque by developing the *Sonate a Tre* (trio sonata).

In medieval times and up to about 1600 western music generally used church modes. This system was gradually replaced by the diatonic system (see section 1.2). Both systems are based on intervals of a semitone. Much synagogue music of oriental origin is based on microtone intervals and does not fit exactly with western modal systems. Synagogue music used five modes, two of which were biblical modes used for chanting the various portions of the Scriptures and the other three, prayer modes used for musical recitations of extra-biblical texts. The two biblical modes are the Pentateuch mode generally used in Sephardic Jewish melodies (*e-f-g-a-b-c-d-e*) and the Pentateuch mode of the Ashkenazim (*f-g-a-b♭-c-d-e-f*). The principal prayer modes are the *Adonay-Malach* mode (*c-d-e-f-g-a-b♭-c*), the *Magen-Abot* mode (*d-e-f-g-a-b♭-c-d*) and the *Ahavah-Rabba* mode (*e-f-g♯-a-b-c-d-e*).[18] The last of these, *Ahavah-Rabba*, named after the prayer used in the morning ritual, is important in Jewish secular music. It was used in Hungary, Poland and Russia. Its musical aesthetic quality, characterized by the interval of the augmented second (1½ tones), was considered not only appropriate for synagogue services but also for folk music as well.[19] These five modes can be compared with church and diatonic modes (Figure 1) in such a way as to show the interval between successive notes in the scales. In this way the equivalence between certain modes is evident. See for example: (i) Mixolydian (church mode), Major and Pentateuch Ashkenazic; (ii) Lydian (church), relative Minor and *Magen-Abot*; (iii) Aeolian (church) and Pentateuch Sephardic; and (iv) Locrian (church) and *Adonay-Malach*. Note also the unique 1½ tone interval in the *Ahavah-Rabba* mode.

Over a period of two centuries, from the time of Rossi to the time of Salamon SULZER (1804–90), the harmony of synagogue song was largely accommodated into the major and minor modes of the diatonic scale. Of the well-known composers of synagogue music during the nineteenth century Sulzer, Naumbourg (1815–80) and Louis LEWANDOWSKI (1821–94) used almost exclusively classical western harmony; only Hirsch Weintraub (1811–82) broke free of it. For example, Naumbourg's *Zemiroth Yisrael* consists of chants and recitatives in the south German style and choruses influenced by French Grand Opera, whereas Lewandowski introduced a Mendelssohnian, Romantic style into the synagogue.[20] Sulzer is generally considered as being responsible for the foundations of modern synagogue music. As a cantor himself, he restored the position of cantor from that of itinerant Jewish 'minstrel' to that of a trained, organized office, both musically and spiritually.

From the destruction of the First Temple up until the nineteenth century, music was undoubtedly very important to Jewish communities throughout the Diaspora. However, it is clear that music composed by Jews had very little impact on the development of classical western music. An important factor in this was that Jewish communities were prevented from interacting socially with the peoples amongst whom they dwelt, often being confined to ghettos and restricted in their employment. Exceptions were instances where Jews composed and occupied positions of standing within the courts of other nations, for example David Sacerdote, Abramo dall' Arpa Ebreo, Abramino dall' Arpa, Isacchino Massarano, Davit da Civita Hebreo and Salamone Rossi all at the court of Mantua; Allegro Porto Hebreo, whose music was dedicated to Emporer Ferdinando of Austria;[21] the Bassano family who settled in London in 1539 and played with the King's musicians; and Thomas and Joseph LUPO, whose families also played in the Tudor court.[22] But examples like these were few and far between. After the *Haskalah*, however, all this was to change.

NOTES

1. CE (Christian Era) and BCE (Before the Christian Era) are equivalent to AD and BC.
2. Gerald Abraham, *The Concise Oxford History of Music* (Oxford: Oxford University Press, 1979), pp. 62–3.
3. Abraham A. Schwadron, 'On Jewish Music', in E. May (ed.), *Musics of Many Cultures: an Introduction* (Berkeley, CA: University of California Press, 1983), p. 286.

4. See Abraham, *Concise Oxford History of Music*, pp. 39–40.
5. Howard Goodall, *Big Bangs: the Story of Five Discoveries that Changed Musical History* (London: Vintage, 2001), pp. 110–11.
6. Peter Gradenwitz, *The Music of Israel: from the Biblical Era to Modern Times*, 2nd edn (Portland, OR: Amadeus Press, 1996), pp. 29–30.
7. Alexander Wood, *The Physics of Music*, 6th edn (London: Methuen, 1961), pp. 181–8.
8. Alison Latham (ed.), *Oxford Companion to Music* (Oxford: Oxford University Press, 2002), 'harmonic series', pp. 558–9.
9. Alfred Sendrey, *The Music of the Jews in the Diaspora* (New York: Yoselof, 1970), p. 73.
10. Yehezkel Braun, 'Aspects of Melody: an Examination of the Structure of Jewish and Gregorian Chants', in J. Paynter, T. Howell, R. Orton and P. Seymour (eds), *Companion to Contemporary Musical Thought* (London: Routledge, 1992), vol. 2, pp. 858–84, and Goodall, *Big Bangs*, pp.168–9.
11. See Sendrey, *Music of the Jews*, pp. 84–111.
12. See Gradenwitz, *Music of Israel*, pp. 130–1.
13. See Sendrey, *Music of the Jews*, pp. 144–9.
14. Alfred Sendry, *Music in the Social and Religious Life of Antiquity* (Rutherford, NJ: Fairleigh Dickinson University Press, 1974), p. 145.
15. Schwadron, 'On Jewish Music', pp. 291–4.
16. See Gradenwitz, *Music of Israel*, pp. 85–9, and Sendrey, *Music of the Jews*, pp. 150–65.
17. A. Z. Idelsohn, *Jewish Music in its Historical Development* (New York: Dover, 1992), pp. 101–9.
18. See ibid., pp. 478–84, and Sendrey, *Music of the Jews*, pp. 174–7.
19. Schwadron, 'On Jewish Music',p. 294.
20. See Gradenwitz, *Music of Israel*, pp. 267–73.
21. Ibid., p. 145.
22. Ibid., p. 165.

Chapter 2

Composers of Jewish Descent from the Beginning of the Nineteenth Century to the Present Day

From the beginning of the Jewish Enlightenment (*Haskalah*), towards the end of the eighteenth century, musicians of Jewish descent have played a prominent role in the development of western classical music, as composers, performers, musicologists, writers and organizers. In order to understand how this occurred it is necessary first to consider the historical and sociological backgrounds. This includes the demography of Jews throughout the period (section 2.1), the changing political map of nineteenth-century Europe (section 2.2), the introduction of civil rights in different countries of Europe (section 2.3) and the origins and spread of the *Haskalah* throughout Europe (section 2.4). Composers of Jewish descent in the nineteenth century lived almost entirely in Europe, whereas in the second half of the twentieth century they were more widely distributed, in America and Israel. For this reason these composers are discussed in two different sections, the nineteenth century (section 2.5) and the twentieth century (section 2.6).

2.1 JEWISH DEMOGRAPHY: 1800 TO THE PRESENT DAY

At the beginning of the nineteenth century the world Jewish population was about 3.3 million, 2.73 million of whom lived in Europe. The largest Jewish community in the Diaspora was in Poland, prior to its partitioning in 1795 between Russia, Prussia and Austria (Map 1). By the end of the nineteenth century the Jewish population of Europe had increased to 8.5 million. Of these, 5.1 million lived in the Russian Empire, 1.95 million in the Austro-Hungarian Empire and 587,000 in Germany (see Map 5 for the geographical boundaries). There were smaller numbers in other countries, for example, 267,000 in Romania, 200,000 in England, 104,000 in France, 104,000 in Holland and 43,000 in Italy. Within the Austro-Hungarian Empire, half of the Jews lived in Galicia, a quarter in Bohemia, Moravia and Silesia and a quarter in

19

Hungarian land. Poland re-emerged as an independent state after the Treaty of Riga in 1921, by which time its Jewish population was about 2 million, increasing to 2.7 million in 1930 and 3.35 million in 1939. In the Soviet Union in 1921 there lived approximately 1 million Jews.[1]

In western and central Europe Jews were predominantly urban dwellers; this was particularly so in Austria and Hungary, where Vienna and Budapest were by far the largest centres in Europe. Warsaw also had a large Jewish community, comprising 42 per cent of its total population in 1918. By contrast, in Germany the Jewish population was more scattered throughout a number of towns. After the failed revolutions in Europe in 1848, and the general population increases throughout the nineteenth century resulting in severe economic problems, many Jews began to migrate, principally from eastern Europe to western Europe, but after 1880 an increasing number left for America, up to one million by 1900.

At the end of the twentieth century the world Jewish population was about 13 million, with the highest number (about 6 million) living in the USA and Canada, 3.5 million in Israel, 1.5 million in the USSR shortly before its demise in 1991, about 1 million in western Europe and less than 130,000 living in eastern Europe, excluding the former USSR. In 1800 the largest Jewish community in the Diaspora was in Poland, but by the year 2000 it was in North America.

The changing distribution of the main centres of Jewish population throughout this period is shown by continent in Figure 3. The changes were

Figure 3
DISTRIBUTION OF JEWISH POPULATIONS, 1800–1986.

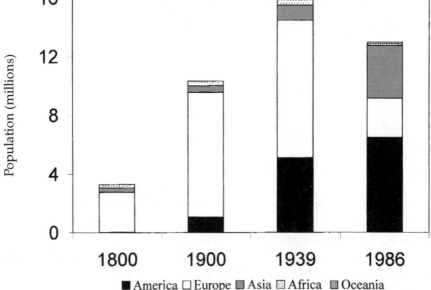

■ America □ Europe ■ Asia ▨ Africa ▥ Oceania

driven by a number of factors: changes in the political map; the growth of populations throughout Europe, coupled with the more rapid growth of the Jewish population; the granting of civil rights to Jews in different countries; restrictions in the employment of Jews; the Jewish tax burden; and anti-Semitism, which in its most extreme form led to the Holocaust.

2.2 THE CHANGING POLITICAL MAP OF EUROPE

The most important political events affecting the lives of Jews living in Europe during this period were: the French Revolution and the rise of Napoleon; the three partitions of Poland; the establishment of the Pale of Settlement by Catherine of Russia; the revolutions in central Europe of 1848; the fall of the Austro-Hungarian Empire and the founding of the German Empire; the Russian revolutions of 1905 and 1917; World War One; World War Two and the Holocaust; the creation of the State of Israel in 1948; and the changing conditions in the former USSR before its demise (see Table 1).

Table 1
MAJOR POLITICAL EVENTS AFFECTING JEWS LIVING IN EUROPE IN THE NINETEENTH AND TWENTIETH CENTURIES

Event	Date
1st, 2nd and 3rd partitions of Poland	1772, 1793, 1795
French Revolution	1789–94
Establishment of the Pale of Settlement by Catherine II	1791
Treaty of Vienna	1815
Founding of the German Empire	1871
Russian Revolutions	1905, 1917
World War One	1914–18
Removal of the Pale of Settlement	1917
World War Two	1939–45
Formation of the State of Israel	1948
End of the Stalinist era	1953
Demise of the USSR	1991

2.2.1 POLAND

Jews began settling in Poland in the eleventh century and by the late seventeenth century three-quarters of the world's Jewry lived in the Polish Lithuanian Commonwealth. In 1795 Poland became partitioned between Austria, Prussia and Russia and no longer existed as a distinct state (see Map 1), a condition that was to continue until 1918. At the time of partition, Jews made up about 10 per cent of the population of Poland – the largest minority in the country. Between then and the eve of World War Two that percentage increased to 13 per cent. By contrast, Jews formed a much smaller minority in other European countries, for example, less than 2 per cent of the population of Germany. A number of factors favoured Poland as a place for Jews to settle. This was particularly so during the reign of King Casimir the Great (1333–1370). Polish attitudes towards religious minorities were relatively liberal and Jews were protected by law. Casimir's reign is sometimes likened to that of a second 'King Solomon'. Poland was free from the ravages of the Hundred Years' War (1337–1453) affecting most of western Europe. It lay outside the Holy Roman Empire and the state was generally more liberal. Polish bishops consistently refused to take part in the Crusades and the Polish Church refused to keep Jews separate from the rest of the population, to the displeasure of the Vatican. During the Renaissance Jews saw Poland as a refuge.

Towards the end of the eighteenth century the political situation changed dramatically. King Stanislaus Augustus Poniatowski (1764–95), although intelligent and well educated, was a weak monarch. The Enlightenment was spreading throughout Europe, and Poniatowski tried to introduce reforms that would improve the position of burghers and peasants, grant rights to religious dissenters, and also curb the power of the conservative gentry. An armed rebellion in 1768 with support from Russia followed. King Frederick of Prussia, fearing that Russia might seize the whole of Poland, also became involved. This culminated in the First Treaty of Partition in 1772. Poland lost territory – Pomerania to Prussia, and Byelorussia and Southern Poland to Austria. Further attempts at reform led to conservative magnates inviting Catherine II of Russia to bring in troops to prevent reform, and this led to the second partition in 1793 in which Poland was further reduced. Further resistance and battles ended with the third and complete partitioning of Poland in 1795, in which Russia gained 62 per cent of the remaining territory, Prussia 20 per cent and Austria 18 per cent (Map 1). Although the third partition meant that Poland disappeared as an independent country until 1918, it failed to annihilate the Polish nation. During the nineteenth century there were a number of Polish uprisings, albeit largely unsuccessful. After the 1831 uprising many Poles emigrated, two-thirds of whom found asylum in France.

2.2.2 THE RUSSIAN EMPIRE AND THE PALE OF SETTLEMENT

Up to the time of the partitioning of Poland, Russia had a very small Jewish population, but as a result of successive partitions it acquired a large increase, so much so that by the second half of the nineteenth century there were 5 million Jews living within the Russian Empire (50 per cent of the world population of Jews). Whereas other autocracies, such as Austria and Prussia, maintained an ambivalent attitude towards Jews, both protecting and exploiting them, the tsarist regime had always regarded Jews as unacceptable aliens. Its policy had been one of keeping Jews out of the Russian Empire.

Map 1

THIRD PARTITION OF POLAND, 1795 (Territorial boundaries are shown with broken lines)

Acquiring the former Polish territory after the partitions forced Russia to 'deal' with the Jewish population. On 23 December 1791 Catherine II decreed the setting up of the so-called Pale of Settlement. This consisted of the western and south-western provinces of the Russian Empire, to which Jews were confined (Map 2). The geographical area of the Pale was expanded, reaching its final form in 1835, when it comprised 15 provinces in western Russia and 10 in the Kingdom of Poland. It remained in existence until 1917.

Various restrictions were placed on Jews living within the Pale, but these were not necessarily uniform throughout the area. In the Duchy of Warsaw, which included most of the territory of the Kingdom of Poland (Map 2), the decree of 1807 on personal liberty that ended serfdom was suspended in relation to the Jews, and was never fully implemented. From 1794 Jews in Byelorussia and the Ukraine had to pay a double poll tax, and their settlement in the eastern part of the empire was limited, but at the same time Catherine II decided that Jews should continue to maintain their internal autonomous administration, for example, be responsible for collection of the double tax. Beginning in 1804, two years after the accession of Alexander I to the throne, a statute was issued ordering Jews to leave their villages and defining the areas in which they could live. They were prohibited from leasing, inn-keeping and selling alcohol. These measures destroyed the livelihoods of one-third of the Jewish population. Further statutes were introduced, the most severe of which were the 'Cantonist Decrees' of Nicholas I in 1827. These conscripted all male Jews from 12 to 25 for military service, which, at that time, was for 25 years. The regime in the cantonist institutes was very harsh and Jews were often forcibly baptized. Jewish communities had to provide a quota of recruits, and this led to children of poor families being kidnapped to rescue sons of the more wealthy from service.

During the 125 years that the Pale existed, conditions sometimes became more restrictive, sometimes less. During Nicholas I's reign (1825–55) conditions were particularly harsh, but under Alexander II's reign (1855–81) some restrictions were eased and the recruitment of Jews for the armed forces was placed on the same basis as for other subjects within the empire. Selected categories of Jews were allowed to live outside the Pale. The situation deteriorated again during Alexander III's reign (1881–94), when Jews were blamed by anti-Semites for the assassination of Alexander II, although there was no real basis for this accusation. This and other factors led to pogroms in 1881 in Kiev, Odessa, Elizavetgrad and Warsaw. Warsaw and Odessa were the two largest centres of Jewish population in the Russian Empire at the time. In May 1882 the government introduced the Temporary Laws. These imposed further restrictions on Jews and were intended to keep Jews apart from the rest of the population and to encourage them to emigrate. They prohibited town Jews from entering villages, even those within the Pale, prohibited the purchasing of real estate outside the towns, and prohibited shops opening on Sundays and Christian holidays. The years 1881–2 marked the start of massive migrations of Jews out

Map 2
PALE OF SETTLEMENT, 1835.

BALTIC SEA

• St Petersburg

• Riga

Dvinsk •

Moscow •

Konigsberg •

Kovno •

• Vilna

Vitebsk •

Smolensk •

PRUSSIA

KINGDOM OF
POLAND

• Bialystok

Minsk •

RUSSIA

Warsaw •

Lodz •

• Pinsk

PALE OF SETTLEMENT

Lublin •

• Kiev

• Berdichev

• Yekaterinoslav

AUSTRIA-HUNGARY

• Kishinev

Odessa •

BLACK SEA

of the Russian Empire, and this was to continue for many years. Over 10,000 Jews were expelled from Moscow in 1891, and huge expulsions from the non-Pale area occurred between 1894 and 1896. Pogroms continued, particularly in the southern and western provinces of the Pale in 1905. The October Manifesto for the 1905 Revolution appeared to offer hope that conditions might improve, and that Jews would have a vote in the *Duma* (the elected lower house of the Russian parliament, 1906–17), but no action was taken to remedy the restrictions on Jews, which remained much the same until the 1917 Bolshevik Revolution.

The few Jews living outside the Pale, but within the Russian Empire, were greatly restricted. They were banned from state service in Moscow and St Petersburg. However, the discrimination was largely religious and could be circumvented by baptism, for example Anton and Nikolay RUBINSTEIN, whose parents had converted to Christianity, ran the Moscow and St Petersburg Conservatories. Anton, particularly, dominated the musical scene in Russian for many years.

2.2.3 CENTRAL AND WESTERN EUROPE

By the end of the first decade of the nineteenth century the western half of present-day Germany formed the Confederation of the Rhineland (Map 3) and was part of the Napoleonic Empire. Prussia was sandwiched between the Confederation of the Rhineland, to its west, and the Russian Empire, the Grand Duchy of Warsaw and the Austrian Empire to its east. After the fall of Napoleon the Congress of Vienna was convened in 1815 to establish a balance of power and a lasting peace in Europe. In place of the defunct Holy Roman Empire, a German Confederation was created (Map 4). This included Prussia, part of Austria, Bavaria, Saxony, Hanover, Hesse, Mecklenburg and Holstein. The weakened Austrian Empire continued to exist despite the failed internal revolutions of 1848 but became further weakened after defeat by Prussia in 1866. In 1867 the Hungarians demanded equal status within the empire, and it was divided into two states. Ruler Franz Joseph then assumed the titles of Emperor of Austria and King of Hungary. This status held until 1914. After 1866 Germany was reorganized under Prussian leadership into the North German Confederation, from which Austria was excluded. In 1871 Bismark was the driving force for the formation of the German Empire, which included the Prussian part of the North German Confederation together with Bavaria, Hesse, Würtemburg and Baden (Map 5).

2.3 CIVIL RIGHTS AND JEWS

The speed with which Jews were emancipated varied in different parts of Europe.[2] In France the relatively small Jewish population comprised four distinct ethnic and geographical groups: the Ashkenazim of Alsace and parts

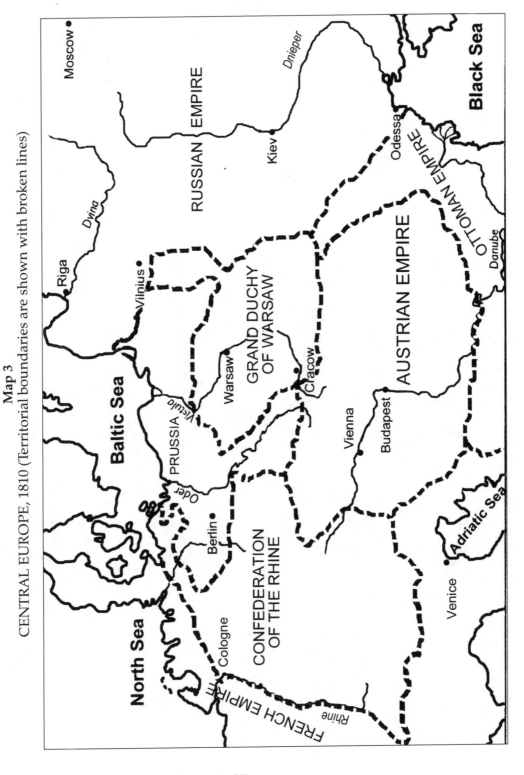

Map 3

CENTRAL EUROPE, 1810 (Territorial boundaries are shown with broken lines)

27

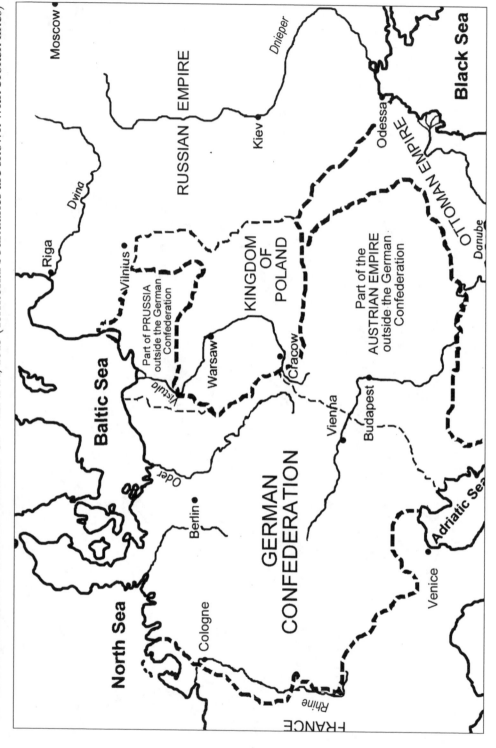

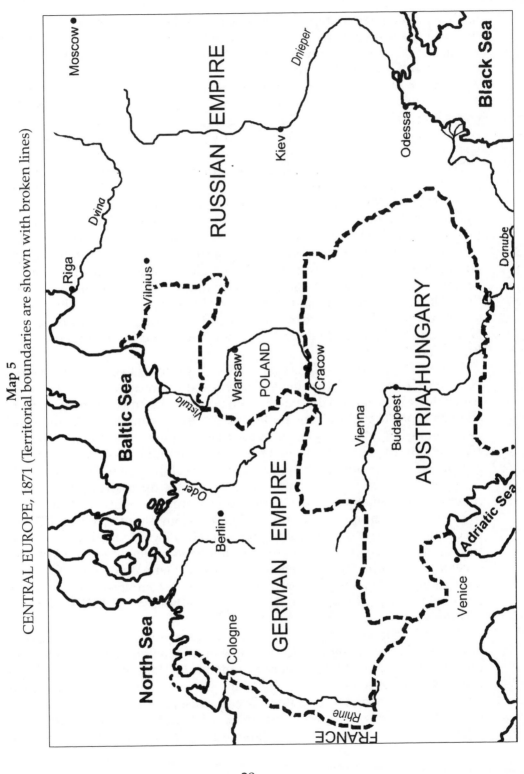

Map 5

CENTRAL EUROPE, 1871 (Territorial boundaries are shown with broken lines)

distinct ethnic and geographical groups: the Ashkenazim of Alsace and parts of Lorraine; a small Jewish population living in Paris; the Sephardim in Bordeaux, Bayonne and the south-west; and the Jews of the papal territory of Avignon, Carpentras, Cavaillon and L'Isle-sur-la-Sorgue (Map 6). The last group were under the control of the Pope from the thirteenth century until 1791. Darius MILHAUD's forebears for many generations were part of this community. His opera buffa *Esther de Carpentras* is set in this 'papal' Jewish community. The Sephardim in the south-west and those living in the papal territory had certain privileges not accorded to the Ashkenazim of Alsace. In 1791 the French National Assembly accorded full civil rights to all Jews in accordance with the Declaration of the Rights of Man and of the Citizen, which included the articles 'All men are born, and remain, free and equal in rights' and 'No person shall be molested for his opinions, even such as are religious.' This, in many ways, became the model for civil rights in many other countries. However, there were also implications for Jews, as is most clearly enunciated by the liberal Count Stanislas de Clermont-Tonnerre in his famous speech: 'To the Jews as a Nation, nothing; to the Jews as individual, everything.' In other words, it would be unacceptable for Jews to be a 'nation within a nation'. In 1798 the civil rights, initially accorded in 1791 under the Napoleonic code, were extended to Jews living in the Confederation of the Rhineland (Map 3).

Joseph II (Archduke of Austria, 1765–90) promulgated several decrees between 1781 and 1789 that generally reduced the restrictions on Jews. He sought to bring Jews into the mainstream of public life and culture. Jews were allowed to practice agriculture, trades and professions and attend schools and universities, but full civil rights throughout the empire were not granted until 1867. Joseph II's policies promoted the Enlightenment, and although he died in 1790, he set the trend for the dissolution of the Holy Roman Empire in 1806.

In 1900 Jews comprised less than 5 per cent of the Austrian population, but they were overwhelmingly concentrated in Vienna. Between 1848 and 1914 the Jewish community in Vienna increased from about 5,000 to 175,000, becoming 9 per cent of the total population. They included a complete spectrum, from cosmopolitan, German-educated Jews to newly arrived Yiddish-speaking Jews from the east. Their influence in Vienna greatly outweighed their numbers, but they never really acquired a completely secure social position. For example, MAHLER converted to Catholicism in 1897 in order to become *Kapellmeister* at the Vienna Court Opera.

Full civil rights were granted to Jews in the German Empire in 1871. Earlier, in 1812, the Prussian Reform Movement obtained civil rights for Jews but not full equality, for example Jews were excluded from state employment such as teaching posts in schools and universities. Between 1812 and 1871 progress towards full civil rights oscillated. The increasing prominence of German Jewish bankers caused resentment and in part led to the *Hep Hep* riots (so-called after the battle cry of the rioters) of 1819 and caused the government

Map 6
CENTRES OF JEWISH POPULATION IN FRANCE AT THE BEGINNING OF
THE NINETEENTH CENTURY.

to delay reform. After 1830 the tide turned in favour of emancipation. The revolutions of 1848 were aimed at freedom of speech, assembly and religion for the different nationalities within the Confederation. The failure of the revolutions led to monarchs delaying reforms and Jewish rights became restricted. With the formation of the North German Confederation in 1869, Parliament granted complete emancipation. When the German Empire was formed in 1871, full emancipation was extended to the additional states (Bavaria, Würtemburg, Hesse and Baden). In spite of having civil rights there were still subtle forms of discrimination. Restraints remained that blocked Jewish social advancement, for example, foreclosure of the higher ranks of the civil service and the near impossibility of a Jew winning a university professorship. The Weimar Constitution of 1919 confirmed both freedom of religion and absolute separation of political citizenship from religious belief and gave Jews a fuller degree of freedom than ever before. However, this also marked a rise in anti-Semitism and the emergence of Nazism. In 1935 the Nuremberg Laws (see Chapter 3, section 3.1) denied citizenship to German Jews and ethnic cleansing was to follow.

In Hungary after 1867, although the Magyars were a minority (48 per cent of the total population), they became the principal ruling nationality assisted principally by Germans and Jews. The Magyars wanted to see assimilation rather than elimination of other nationalities. The Jews were the foremost advocates of assimilation and contributed – in literature and the arts – a brilliance that the native gentry lacked.[3] They also became prominent in the press, in banking and in finance. Many Jews emigrated from the east and settled in the towns. Budapest had a 25 per cent Jewish population in 1900.

In 1848 Jewish equality was proclaimed in the Italian states, and when Italy was finally reunited by 1870 there was full emancipation throughout Italy. Switzerland, with a very small Jewish population, was the last European state to have full emancipation included in its Constitution in 1874.

In England, Jews were expelled from the country in 1290. By the mid-seventeenth century, during Cromwell's time, there were a small number of *Marrano* merchants living and trading in England. After 1656 they were allowed officially to resettle in England. Initially, the small Jewish population was mainly Sephardim from Holland, whose ancestors had fled Spain at the time of the Inquisition. Significant numbers of Ashkenazic Jews from central Europe did not arrive until the nineteenth century. In 1753 the government introduced the Jewish Naturalization Act, allowing foreign-born Jews to become naturalized. One of the reasons for this was to facilitate commerce and increase revenue. For example, with the Jacobite uprising of 1745, the City panicked and it was Sampson Gideon, a Jewish financier, who raised £1,700,000 to help restore government calm. However, there was considerable opposition to the Naturalization Act, and also increasing anti-Semitism, so much so that the act was withdrawn a year later because of the outcry from Christian merchants.

In England there were no special laws defining the status of Jews; this was in contrast to many countries in continental Europe; in theory every Jew born in England was a full citizen. However, the oaths required for public and government office in which a candidate was expected to swear by 'the true faith of a Christian' debarred practising Jews from a number of positions. The same oath was required to receive a university degree and to purchase certain types of real estate. The Jewish Civil Disabilities Act of 1833 gave a Jew civil rights as an individual citizen, distinguished only by his particular creed. There were no more restraints upon Jews than there were on any other British subject. At the time, Felix MENDELSSOHN, who was visiting England, commented in a letter to his family:[4] 'This morning they emancipated Jews, which makes me proud, especially since a few days ago, your miserable Posen Statutes were attacked here, just as they deserve.' (The Posen Statutes were a series of laws handed down by Prussia's Frederick William III on the rights and responsibilities of Jews in the recently acquired Polish Duchy of Posen. They required the ability to speak German well, the adoption of a special family name, residence in Posen since 1815, and a skill in a trade or art.) Full political rights were granted in 1858. With the founding of University College London in 1837, Jews were permitted to study for degrees, but a Christian religious test was still in force at Oxford and Cambridge until 1871.

In the Netherlands there was a *Marrano* community by the end of the sixteenth century and Jews were recognized as subjects in 1657. They were granted equal rights in 1796.

Looking at Europe as a whole at the end of the eighteenth century, conditions for Jews varied greatly from country to country. In Holland and in England Jews were least burdened with economic restrictions, this being an acknowledgement of their contribution to the expansion of trade, and there was no interference by the state in their religious affairs, but there were restrictions on the owning of real estate, becoming naturalized and holding public office. At the opposite end of the European continent, in Poland, before the nineteenth century, Jews formed a sizeable middle class with relatively few restrictions. By contrast, in central Europe, Jews were much more restricted. As part of the legacy of the Middle Ages the attitudes of the monarchs was often that Jews should not cause harm to Christians. To this end there were many restrictions on Jews, limiting where they could live and burdening them with additional taxes, for example, the *Leibzoll*, a body toll on Jewish travellers passing through a city or principality, akin to that collected on the movement of livestock. During the nineteenth century this all changed in parallel with the *Haskalah* or Jewish Emancipation.

The earliest Jews to settle in America were Sephardim. Columbus's first crossing to America in 1492 coincided with King Ferdinand's announcement expelling Jews from Spain. It is believed that several of the crew of this expedition were *Marranos*, perhaps even Columbus himself.[5] In the 1630s Jews settled in a Portuguese colony in Brazil, later in the West Indies and then in

New Amsterdam, which after 1664 became New York. The legal position of Jews in the English and Dutch colonies was favourable, since the respective governments wanted active colonization. Jews were given full rights to worship, to trade and to own property. The 1740 Plantation Act granted full civil rights to Jews and other religious groups who had been living in British colonies for seven years. The American Constitution of 1789 provided that 'no religious test shall ever be required as a qualification to any office or public trust under the United States'. The First Amendment of 1791 went further, renewing the commitment to religious freedom: 'Congress shall make no law respecting an establishment of religion, or prohibiting the free exercise thereof.' These declarations were all essentially federal, not state guarantees. Eight of the original thirteen states continued to deny Jews equal political rights. In 1868 North Carolina was the last of the original states to grant Jews political equality.

At the beginning of the nineteenth century the Jewish population of America was about 3,000, two-thirds of whom lived in North America. This number increased to 15,000 in North America by 1820. The Jewish population continued to grow steadily throughout the nineteenth century. Between 1881 and 1914, 2.5 million Jews (largely Ashkenazim) left eastern Europe and 2 million of these entered the USA. The reason for this mass migration was the pogroms in eastern Europe, together with the increase in both the Jewish population and the population as a whole, thus creating a need for more 'living space'. There was a further wave of migration before and during World War Two, of Jews fleeing Nazism. This time the immigrants were mainly well-educated German Jews.

2.4 THE JEWISH ENLIGHTENMENT (*HASKALAH*) AND ITS SPREAD THROUGHOUT EUROPE

There gradually evolved a transformation in European thought throughout many parts of Europe during the seventeenth century. The authority of the Church diminished as 'natural reasoning' became the driving force behind many advances in science and philosophy. A new confidence in the power of the human mind was evident and the importance of reasoning became paramount. For example, philosophers and scientists such as Descartes, Locke, Hume, Bacon, Newton and Galileo furthered knowledge and understanding by the appeal of reason rather than the authority of the Church. Nevertheless, Descartes, Locke, Newton and Galileo did not see this as contradicting their Christian faith. This changed way of thinking became known as the Enlightenment. It epitomized a new attitude and gave rise to an optimism and confidence that the lot of mankind could and would be improved. Since Jews, particularly in central Europe, lived as separate communities, often restricted as to where they were allowed to live, they were initially unaware of these developments and so the spread of the Jewish Enlightenment, or *Haskalah*, occurred later than that of the European Enlightenment.

Moses Mendelssohn (1729–86) is regarded as the early driving force of the *Haskalah* movement. The term *Haskalah* is derived from the Hebrew word *sekhel*, meaning 'intellect', and the followers of the *Haskalah* movement were known as *maskilim*, men of understanding. Moses Mendelssohn was the son of a poor Torah scribe from Dessau. He was given a traditional Jewish education, including the study of Talmud and medieval Jewish philosophy, by David Fränkel. When the latter moved to Berlin, where he was appointed rabbi, Moses Mendelssohn, then aged 14, moved with him. At the time the Jewish population of Berlin was restricted to 120 families. There Mendelssohn met other Jews who were exploring secular knowledge, and he was able to broaden his education to include learning French, Latin and standard German and also to study the philosophies of, for example, Leibniz and Locke. He developed a close friendship with the dramatist and literary critic Gotthold Lessing, who had written a play entitled *The Jews*, which sought to undermine common prejudices against Jews. Lessing encouraged Mendelssohn to publish his philosophical essays. Mendelssohn felt it was possible to actively participate in the Enlightenment and at the same time to remain true to his Jewish faith. He was also concerned that his fellow co-religionists should do likewise, rather than remain in a time warp. The maxim of the *Haskalah* was: 'Be a Jew in your home, and a man outside.' Mendelssohn wanted to discourage German Jews from using Yiddish, which he regarded as a debased form of German and the language of the ghetto, and instead to use German and Hebrew. With this in mind he translated the Pentateuch into German, with a Hebrew commentary.

In the history of Jewish thought Mendelssohn's philosophy serves as the link between mediaeval rationalist philosophy and the newer eighteenth-century ideas. His last major work was *Jerusalem; or On Religious Power and Judaism* (1783). In this he emphasized that while the state could coerce, religion should be based on persuasion. Like Descartes and Locke, he felt that his rational approach was not incompatible with his religious beliefs. Nowadays he is regarded as a key figure in the Jewish Enlightenment, rather than as a philosopher of world status. By contrast, Baruch Spinoza (1632–77), who was educated in Judaism and mediaeval Jewish philosophy, came to a pantheistic view of the universe and considered there was no need for Jews to remain a separate people who worship God in a special way. He is regarded as a philosopher of world stature, but his philosophy was incompatible with Judaism and during his lifetime he was placed under a ban (*cherem*) by the Amsterdam Jewish community.

The *Haskalah* movement met with resistance from conservative Jewry, but nevertheless soon spread from Berlin to Breslau and Konigsberg (Map 7). By the 1820s the Austrian Empire, rather than Prussia, was the main centre of the movement, particularly Bohemia, northern Italy and Galacia. By the 1840s it had spread to the Russian Empire. By then Vienna, Prague, Zamosc, Warsaw, Brody, Tarnopol, Lemburg (Lvov), Odessa, St Petersburg and Vilna were becoming important centres of *Haskalah*. As a result of its spread, Jews were better educated and the structure of Jewish society changed. *Maskilim* emphasized the importance of a broader education, not one that concentrated solely on Talmudic studies. It included scientific developments and knowledge of the main European languages. Jewish schools were set up and textbooks were written in Hebrew for Jewish students educated according to the programme.

Nevertheless, Talmudic studies may have been a good springboard for 'sharpening the mind'. An analogy can be drawn between Talmudic studies in the early nineteenth century and the widespread retention of Latin in British schools until well into the twentieth century. Much of the argument for the retention of Latin was that the study of Latin was a good mental exercise and gave insight into Roman civilization. This of course was true, but there were more persuasive arguments for proficiency in modern languages. A comparable case could be made for study of the Talmud, that is, that it stimulated an aptitude for polemics and also gave an insight into one's culture.

2.5 THE EMERGENCE OF COMPOSERS OF JEWISH DESCENT IN NINETEENTH-CENTURY EUROPE

Composers of Jewish descent began to contribute to western classical music at about the time the Jewish Enlightenment began to spread from its first centres such as Berlin. Some composers came from wealthy families, but for several this was not the case. Those coming from less wealthy families were, nevertheless, often sent to first-class teachers in some of the larger centres, such as Vienna, Berlin, Budapest, Warsaw and Prague. Felix MENDELSSOHN and many of his friends are good examples of the former. Although born in Hamburg, Felix and Fanny MENDELSSOHN lived in Berlin from an early age. Their father was assimilated and a wealthy banker, for whom a broad education for the family was of paramount importance. Giacomo MEYERBEER'S background was similar in many respects, except that he remained a practising Jew. He also lived near Berlin and his father was the wealthy owner of a sugar refinery. He, too, was given a broad education. Of Mendelssohn's associates, Ferdinand DAVID was born in Hamburg in the Mendelssohn family home and was a family friend. Ferdinand von HILLER was the son of a wealthy Jewish merchant and was ensured a good musical training, being one of the few pupils that Hummel took on. Adolph MARX was the son of a doctor and was sent for composition lessons to Zelter, who was also Mendelssohn's teacher. Moritz MOSZKOWSKI was born in one of the centres of the *Haskalah*, Breslau. He was the son of a businessman and was sent to Berlin for further study.

Map 7
CENTRES OF *HASKALAH* IN THE FIRST HALF OF THE NINETEENTH CENTURY.

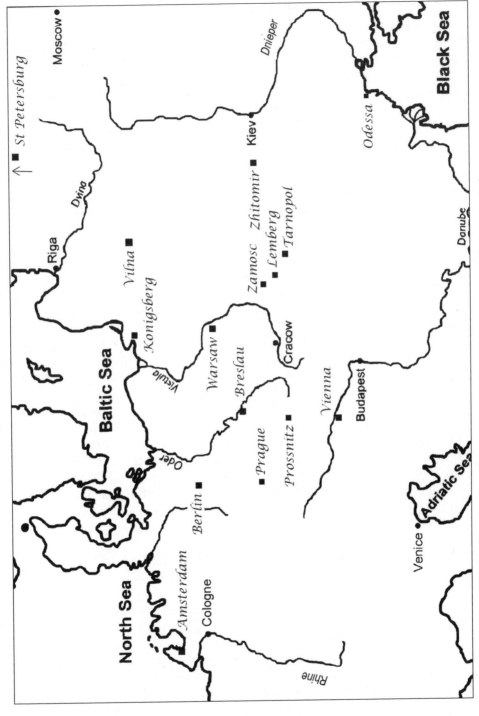

Note: Centres of *Haskalah* are indicated by squares and given in italics.

Not all were from wealthy backgrounds. One such was Ignaz MOSCHELES, who was born in Prague, where the family was not wealthy. However, his parents realized his talent and he was able to go to Vienna for further training, although his father died and the family finances were particularly precarious. David POPPER was also born in Prague, the son of a cantor, and he studied at the Prague Conservatory. Louis Lewandowski, who is known only through his liturgical music, came from a poor family living near Posen but was sent to Berlin where he met Mendelssohn's cousin. Friedrich GERNSHEIM's father was a doctor and he was sent to the Leipzig Conservatory, where Moscheles taught him.

The *Haskalah* spread south from Berlin through Austria and Hungary (see Map 7). Joseph JOACHIM was born in a ghetto in Hungary, but the family moved to Pest and Joachim continued his training in Vienna. Karl GOLDMARK came from a lower middle-class Jewish family of 20 children. He was sent to Vienna for further training at the age of 14. However, his parents could not continue to support him and he had to earn a living by teaching from an early age. Karl DAVIDOV was brought up in Kurland, a region of Latvia outside the Pale of Settlement. His father was a doctor and also an amateur violinist. Davidov was sent to St Petersburg and then to Leipzig for his musical training. Ignaz FRIEDMAN was from Krakow and he also went to Leipzig for musical training. The parents of Anton and Nikolay Rubinstein lived in the Ukraine, within the Pale of Settlement, but both sons went to Moscow for their education. Henryk and Józef WIENIAWSKI's father was a doctor living in Lublin. The family was musical and both sons studied at the Paris Conservatory.

The pattern that is evident from the examples cited above is that whether or not the composers came from poor or wealthy families, their parents generally recognized their talent, encouraged them in their musical education, and sent them to the well-established conservatories to ensure they had the best education. The composers whose families were living within the Pale of Settlement generally established themselves a little later than those living in Europe to the west of the Pale of Settlement.

2.6 COMPOSERS OF JEWISH DESCENT OF TWENTIETH-CENTURY MUSIC

The development of music is a continuous process, but within this process there are certain 'landmarks'. Although 1 January 1900 did not mark a particular musical development, nevertheless a fundamental change gained momentum between the music of the nineteenth and twentieth centuries. This was the loosening of the constraints of diatonic harmony that had been the framework for most music of the nineteenth century and earlier. In works such as the opening of Wagner's *Tristan and Isolde* (1865) and Debussy's *Prélude à l'après-midi d'un faune* (1894) diatonic relationships are no longer of binding significance. Many other musical constraints were lifted and new innovations occurred throughout the twentieth century. There are two ways in which composers of Jewish descent have contributed. The first is from a national perspective, by contributing to the music of the country in which they lived. The second is from a developmental perspective, contributing to particular musical developments that were not restricted to national boundaries.

2.6.1 MUSICAL DEVELOPMENTS IN DIFFERENT COUNTRIES

It is interesting to contrast the two largest countries of the northern hemisphere, namely Russia and the United States of America. In Russia there was an established musical tradition by the beginning of the twentieth century. A generation of gifted composers including Mussorgsky (1839–81), Balakirev (1837–1910), Rimsky-Korsakov (1844–1908) Borodin (1833–87) and Tchaikovsky (1840–93) had ensured a national tradition and a body of compositions that were known throughout the western world. By contrast, in the realm of classical music America was hardly on the 'musical map'. A distinctly American style had not yet emerged, and many of the composers of classical music were still following the 'European' tradition. The only notable nineteenth-century composer of Jewish descent, who was living in America, was Louis GOTTSCHALK. However, composers of Jewish descent made a major contribution to American music in the twentieth century and have done much to create 'American music', for example, Aaron COPLAND, Leonard BERNSTEIN, George GERSHWIN, Morton FELDMAN, Steve REICH, and Philip GLASS. In addition, there were many composers who took on American citizenship after fleeing from Europe, for example, Wolfgang KORNGOLD, Kurt WEILL and Arnold SCHOENBERG. Here I am considering only classical music, but it should be noted that composers of Jewish descent have also made major contributions to jazz, musical theatre and film music (see section 2.7).

By contrast, the only major composer of Jewish descent in Russia to make any real impact outside Russia has been Alfred SCHNITTKE. There are other, less well-known composers such as Maximilian STEINBERG, Reinhold GLIÈRE and Moisei WEINBERG. Musicians of Jewish descent from Russia have made a major impact as performers and educators. Anton Rubinstein is best known as a virtuoso pianist, while his compositions are only occasionally played today. However, he played a major role in musical education as founder of the St Petersburg Conservatory in 1862, where he was concerned to raise standards of musical education to a level comparable to those in western Europe. His brother Nikolay also played an important role in musical education, founding the Moscow Conservatory in 1866. Mikhail GNESIN (1883– 1957) and his family founded the Gnesin Institutes that were established throughout the Soviet Union as musical training institutes. Steinberg taught at the St Petersburg Conservatory for the whole of his working life, where his pupils included

Shostakovich, Shaporin and Popov.

2.6.2 CENTRAL EUROPE

The territories of twentieth-century Germany, Austria, Poland, Czechoslovakia and Hungary are best considered collectively here, since the boundaries of the states of central Europe have changed much throughout the course of this period. Of the composers of Jewish descent living in central Europe, Gustav Mahler was undoubtedly the greatest from the late Romantic period. Most of those who succeeded him, for example, Schoenberg, Korngold, Weill and GOLDSCHMIDT, were forced to flee the Nazis.

When Schoenberg first invented serialism (see Glossary) in 1921, he confided to a friend that it would guarantee the supremacy of German music for centuries to come.[6] However twelve years later his pupil, Alban Berg, wrote in a letter to Anton Webern: 'When "the new Germany" officially banned their revered master's music as symbolic of all that was un-German, indeed anti-German, in modern art and music, there is but one word to characterize his musical achievements adequately: German.'[7] Schoenberg's claim was arrogant; although his influence on much twentieth-century music is undeniable and in the twenty-first century it is still felt, serialism itself has not guaranteed German supremacy in music.

Whilst Schoenberg claimed to have created a system that would maintain the supremacy of German music for centuries to come, musicologists of the Nazi era saw this in a very different perspective. They were concerned about the relationship between race and music and attempted to prove that all 'great music' was Aryan or Nordic in conception, whereas 'degenerate' music was primarily Jewish in conception. Several claimed that the major triad and polyphony originated in tribes of Germanic origin, and that atonalism and the destruction of harmony was the work of the Jews.[8] This appears to ignore the chromaticism in works such as Wagner's *Tristan and Isolde*.

Large numbers of musicians fled Germany with the advance of Nazism, and large numbers perished under the regime. Nevertheless, Schoenberg has had a considerable influence, although not always a positive one, on Austro-German composers in the twentieth century. Consider the composers Berg, Webern, Eisler, Krenek, Hindemith, Orff, Henze, Pfitzner, Stockhausen, Hartmann, Zimmerman and Weill. The most important pupils of Schoenberg were Berg (1885–1935), Webern (1883–1945) and EISLER (1898–1962). Berg and Webern were strongly influenced by Schoenberg, whom they regarded as their mentor. Eisler, on the other hand, studied with Schoenberg from 1919 to 1923, composed some early works using serial technique, but then fell out with Schoenberg and did not pursue serial technique. Of the other composers of the period, Krenek (1900–91) adopted serialism independently in his opera *Karl* V (1930–3), Hindemith (1895–1963) unequivocally rejected Schoenberg's method, and Pfitzner (1869–1949) and Orff (1895–1982) did not use it. Hartmann (1905–63) studied briefly with Webern and learned much from his method without adopting serialism. Weill was recommended by Hermann Scherchen to study with Schoenberg in 1919, but the family's ailing financial situation kept him from studying in Vienna, where Schoenberg taught at the time.[9] Although Weill flirted briefly with atonality, the main thrust of his musical development was in music theatre. How his musical development would have fared had he studied with Schoenberg is a matter for speculation.

After World War Two, René LEIBOWITZ (1913–72), who had studied with Schoenberg and Webern in Berlin, settled in Paris. There he became an important teacher and advocate of Schoenberg's music. Among his pupils were Boulez (1925–), Henze (1926–) and Zimmermann (1918–70). Boulez and Stockhausen (1928–) saw in Webern's later works the precedent for a more generalized form of serialism,which was not only concerned with pitch but also with rhythm, amplitude and timbre. Henze's early music shows the influences of Stravinsky, Hindemith, Bartok and Schoenberg. Although Henze took an interest in serialism for a short period, he abandoned it as being insufficiently communicative. Music theatre and political issues have been an important element in his compositions. Zimmermann's compositional techniques range from serialism to electronic music. His best work is the opera *Die Soldatem*, which has a plot similar to that of Berg's Wozzeck. Thus while some composers have been influenced by Schoenberg, if only indirectly, others have been antipathetic towards his methods.

György LIGETI (1923–) was born and brought up in Hungary. Initially he was cut off from new developments in serialism and electronic music because of the communist prohibitions. In 1955 he heard music by Schoenberg and Berg for the first time and he began writing a twelve-note work, *Requiem*. In 1956 he managed to escape from Hungary. He made his way to Cologne, where he met Stockhausen and absorbed the more generalized forms of serialism that were being developed. He has become one of the most well-known composers of Hungarian origin in the twentieth century. He has, however, lived most of his life in Hamburg and Vienna and became an Austrian citizen in 1967.

2.6.3 FRANCE

In twentieth-century France the most significant composer of Jewish descent was Darius Milhaud (1892–1974). He was a member of a group that included Auric, Durey, Honegger, Poulenc and Tailleferre and was known as *Les Six*. The six colleagues followed Satie (1866–1925) in mocking accepted musical conventions by being strongly anti-Romantic and flippant. This was something of a mixed blessing; it brought publicity, but at the same time labelled the composers as not serious. After a few years the three leading members – Honegger, Poulenc and Milhaud – sought more positive and promising directions. Milhaud is best known as the composer of the ballet *Le Boeuf sur le toit* and *La Création du monde*, and as being one of the most prolific composers of the twentieth century. One of his teachers at the Paris Conservatory was Paul DUKAS (1865–1935), who is known principally today for his composition *The Sorcerer's Apprentice*. Other twentieth-century French composers of Jewish descent include ROLAND-MANUEL, WIENER and ROSENTHAL. In addition, Leibowitz and TANSMAN, who were both from Poland, spent large parts of their lives in Paris.

2.6.4 ENGLAND

One of the havens for Jews fleeing Nazi persecution was England. Egon WELLESZ (1885–1974), Berthold Goldschmidt (1903–96), Matyas SEIBER (1905–60), Franz REIZENSTEIN (1911–68), Walter Goehr (1903–60) and his son, Alexander GOEHR (1932–), all arrived in England during the 1930s. Many became established figures in British academia. Wellesz left Austria in 1938 for Oxford, where he was appointed lecturer in music history in 1943 and reader in Byzantine music in 1948. Although he wrote all nine of his symphonies in England, he is best known as a musicologist of Byzantine music. Goldschmidt had an established reputation as a composer by the time he fled the Nazis in 1935. Subsequent to this he composed very little, and few of his earlier compositions were heard until 1984. After 1984 he resumed composing, aged over 80 years, in what might be described as his Indian summer that lasted until his death in 1996. Seiber, who came to England in 1935 and taught music at Morley College for 15 years, is perhaps best remembered as a teacher. Reizenstein came to England in 1934 and was professor of piano at the Royal Academy of Music (1958–68) and at the Royal College of Music at Manchester (1962–68).

Walter and Alexander Goehr came to England in 1934. Walter was best known as a conductor. He conducted a number of orchestras, including the BBC Symphony Orchestra. Noted among his premiere performances were Tippett's *A Child of Our Time* (1944) and the British premieres of Mahler's Sixth Symphony (1950) and Messian's Turangalîla Symphony (1953). His son Alexander is a prolific composer, but is perhaps more widely known as a broadcaster and writer on music. He was professor of music at Leeds University (1971–6) and professor of music at Cambridge from 1975 until his retirement in 1999.

Of the British-born composers of Jewish descent that include Gerald FINZI (1901–56), Benjamin FRANKEL (1906–73), Minna KEAL (1909–99), Robert SENATOR (1926–), Wilfred JOSEPHS (1927–97), Malcolm LIPKIN (1932–), Melanie DAIKEN (1945–), Robert SAXTON (1953–), Malcolm SINGER (1953–) and Adam GORB (1958–), Finzi is undoubted the most widely known, particularly for his song settings and for the quintessentially English character of his compositions. He has followed in the footsteps of English songwriters that include Elgar, Parry and Vaughan Williams. Frankel composed eight symphonies and orchestral works and also five string quartets. These are only occasionally played in concert halls at the present time, but many of them have been recently recorded for the first time. He is perhaps still more widely known for the large number of film scores that he composed. Josephs was also a prolific composer, but is best known as a composer for films and television. Of the composers born after World War Two, Saxton has been the most successful to date. Senator, Lipkin, Daiken, Saxton, Singer and Gorb hold or have held teaching posts in British universities or music colleges.

2.6.5 AMERICA

It is in the USA that composers of Jewish descent have made the most significant contributions to the development of music of their country in the twentieth century. At the beginning of the twentieth century composers living in America were by and large composing in the European tradition. The first major composer to set what might be described as a distinctively American style was Charles Ives (1874–1954), most of whose compositions date from the two decades up to 1918. Ives was unfettered by European norms, ready to go his own way and unashamed of the incongruous. The atonal aspects of his *Unanswered Question*, dating from 1906, antedate Schoenberg's first properly atonal compositions. Other composers of the period include Cowell (1897–1965) and Varèse (1883–1965). The latter, although born in Burgundy, composed all his surviving music in America.

In spite of the emergence of Ives as a composer by 1920, attitudes in the American music establishment were still highly conservative. Aaron Copland relates how his teacher, Rubin GOLDMARK, when seeing that Copland was examining the score of Ives's Concord Sonata, warned him not to 'contaminate' himself with such things. Copland (1900–90) was determined to see American music sounding as distinctly American as Mussorgsky's and Stravinsky's sounded Russian. He was the first American composer of Jewish descent to have his music widely performed outside the USA. In 1921 he was one of the first Americans to enrol at the New School for Americans at Fontainbleau, as a pupil of Nadia Boulanger. Many Americans followed him in studying with Nadia Boulanger. Those of Jewish descent included Marc BLITZSTEIN in 1927, Elie SIEGMEISTER from 1927 to 1931, David DIAMOND in 1937, Arthur BERGER from 1937 to 1939, Irving FINE in 1939, Harold SHAPERO from 1942 to 1943, and Philip Glass from 1963 to 1965. By 1932 Copland was affectionately known by younger American composers as 'Dean of American music', and the epithet stuck. He had gone some way towards the establishment of a distinctive American music.

Another composer to bring a distinctive American style to his music was George Gershwin (1898–1937). He used distinctly American forms, such as ragtime, blues and jazz, both in concert works such as *Rhapsody in Blue* and in his folk opera *Porgy and Bess*

Leonard Bernstein (1918–90) was an important figure in American music in the middle of the twentieth century. His main compositions date from the mid-1940s to the mid-1960s. He composed in a number of different styles, including jazz, but excluding serial music. The genre in which he was probably at his best was music theatre, in works like *West Side Story* (1957). In his symphonies his style is likened to that of Mahler, Berg and Shostakovich. Besides composing, he was a concert pianist, conductor and educator. His television programmes, such as *Young People's Concerts* (1958–73), were very popular with a wide audience. He was the first American-born conductor of a major American orchestra.

Whilst the American musical tradition was forged by composers such as Ives, Gershwin, Copland, Sessions, Piston, Carter, Barber and Bernstein, after World War Two other factors and undercurrents came into play. Many European composers had fled Europe and were now living in America. These included Hindemith, Milhaud, Korngold, WOLPE, Weill, Schoenberg and Bartok. Bartok fled to America, but died in 1945. Stravinsky emigrated to the USA in 1939, although he left Russia in 1914 and was living in Paris and Switzerland until 1939.

After 1945 a number of aspiring young American composers felt there was a need to move away from a central European tradition. The idea that young American composers needed to study with Nadia Boulanger in order to establish their music compositional credentials became less important. Schoenberg, writing in 1949, was highly critical of her influence on American composers:

> One of the influences which is a great obstacle to richer development is the models which they imitate. It would not be so bad to imitate Stravinsky, or Bartok, or Hindemith, but worse is that they have been taught by a woman of Russian-French descent, who is reactionary and had much influence on many composers. One can only wish that this influence might be broken and the real talents of the Americans be allowed to develop freely.[10]

Centres of experimental and electronic music were founded at Darmstadt and Cologne, where Boulez and Stockhausen were the leading figures. In America this trend originated with Cowell and Varèse and continued with composers such as Partch (1901–74), Cage (1912–92), Feldman (1926–87), Nancarrow (1912–97) and others. Evolving from Schoenberg's serialism, Boulez developed the concept of a more generalized form of serialism that not only involved pitch but also rhythm, amplitude and timbre. In America, Milton Babbitt also developed his own form of serial control of rhythm. Explained simply, pitch has a simple repeating unit, namely the octave; Babbitt developed a system in which rhythm also has a repeating unit. Musical developments in general became more technical and more mathematical, and the music became more predetermined.

The developments of John Cage, in many ways, moved in the opposite direction, towards aleatoric or chance music. Cage studied musical theory with Schoenberg from 1935 to 1937 and was also interested in fine art and Asian philosophy. This set him thinking along opposite lines to that of 'total' control, as advocated by Boulez and Babbitt. In his early compositions Cage developed his own form of serialism. By the late 1930s he began experimenting with the piano, by inserting a variety of different objects between the strings to create a variety of sounds, developing the prepared piano. Increasingly, chance played an important role in his music and by 1952 it reached an extreme in a piece called 4' 33", in which there is no notated music and a pianist sits at a piano for the required time without performing, so that the audience listens to whatever sounds they become aware of. By this time Cage had attracted a number of like-minded colleagues, including Christian Wolff (1934–), Earl Brown (1926–) and Morton Feldman. By the 1970s Cage's music was out of fashion, even in many academic circles. The most influential member of his immediate circle was Feldman. Feldman did not commit himself fully to loss of composer control. He attempted to reach a workable compromise between the plasticity in musical structure and clarity in his instructions to performers. He experimented with graphic notation of his music. In some of his compositions he indicated only the register, the relative length of an event, and the number of notes to be included, leaving the performers considerable freedom. One aim was to use sound as painters use colours. His music is characterized by soft dynamics, understated gestures, consonance and repetition. The last two of these are also common to minimalism.

Minimalism sprang up in the 1960s, also partly as a reaction to serialism. It marked a departure from the extremes of the more generalized forms of serialism developed by Boulez and others (see section 2.6.2) and the indeterminacy developed by Cage and others. After World War Two there was an expansion of university education, and in America, where there was no government patronage of music, an increasing number of young composers were financially supported by their university teaching posts. In this climate there was less pressure for these composers to be worried by audience numbers and so serialism thrived. At its extreme, the development of music in universities could be seen in the same light as developments in science and mathematics. If it was difficult for the general public to appreciate, this appeared to be secondary to its academic importance. In this climate the highly structured, technical and mathematical aspects of generalized serialism seemed in tune with academia.[11] One of its exponents, Babbitt, even criticized uninformed listeners, who judged his music by whether or not they liked the sound!

In the wake of developments by Boulez and Stockhausen in Europe, and the legacy of Schoenberg's teaching in America, the syllabuses at music schools during the 1950s had a strong emphasis on serialism. A number of composers born in the 1930s began composing using serial techniques, but there was also a reaction against this, both on the part of emerging composers and the listening American public. This took a number of forms. George ROCHBERG was prominent among the composers who reassimilated the practices of earlier western music. Of his third string quartet, which signalled this reassimilation, he wrote:

> By embracing the earlier traditions of tonality and combining them with the more recently developed atonality, I found it possible to release my music from the over-intense, expressionistic manner inherent in purely serially organized, constant chromaticism, and from the inhibition of physical pulse and rhythm which has enervated so much recent music.[12]

Whereas in Europe the musical establishments were quite receptive to complex dissonant music, in America music was regarded more as entertainment. Against this backdrop the development of minimalist music was particularly strong in America. The label 'minimalist' has evoked some controversy, and some composers dislike being described as such. It can be regarded as the musical equivalent of minimalist art, in much the same way that expressionism is used, both to describe a form of art (e.g., Kandinsky, Munch, Klee) and music (e.g., Debussy, Ravel). One of the aims of minimalist artists was to reduce materials, structure and colour to their most basic or minimal elements. Minimalist art influenced pop art, but the converse was more generally the case in music, where pop music had an influence on minimalist music.

Minimalists set out to reject the complexities of serialism and to replace them by a return to tonality and modality in their most elementary forms, often using small diatonic units and repetition of rhythmic patterns. The music is often trance-inducing and has had an immediacy of appeal to audiences. Far from being miniscule in length, as well as minimal in content, minimalist compositions project audible change slowly, over extended periods of time. In its early days such music was often performed in galleries as part of visual art exhibitions, rather than in concert halls. LaMonte Young (1935–) is generally considered to be the founder of the movement, with Terry Riley (1935–), Steve Reich (1936–) and Philip Glass (1937–) collectively associated with its development (the last two are of Jewish descent). All four had conventional musical educations, after which they studied music of other cultures. Both Young and Riley became pupils of Pran Nath in India. Reich studied African and Balinese music, and Glass worked with Ravi Shankar in Paris transcribing Indian music into western notation.

Glass is the son of a record store owner, and is quoted as saying: 'The first thing I knew about music was that you sold it.' Nevertheless he opted for a conventional American music education, including studying with Nadia Boulanger in Paris. He was also much influenced by Cage's book, *Silence* (1961), which was also to influence the next generation of minimalists including John Adams. The book strongly advocated experimentation. Minimalism appears to be a significant force and lasting influence on music in the late twentieth century. The operas of Glass and the more recent *Nixon in China* (1987) and *The Death of Klinghoffer* (1991) by Adams have been particularly successful. Minimalism has continued to evolve under the influence of those described as the next generation of composers. John Adams explains that what sets him apart from Reich and Glass is that he is not a modernist. He embraces the whole musical past and does not have the kind of refined, systematic language that they have. He relies more on his intuitive sense of balance.[13]

Another feature of this generation of American composers, which in many ways is like a return to the eighteenth century, is that not only do they compose, but they are active in performing their music. Glass and Reich recruited their own groups of performers. No more is this true than of Meredith MONK (1943–) who, although not so widely known, came from the same lower Manhatten artistic community that nurtured Reich and Glass. Her emphasis has been on a form of vocal minimalism. Many of her compositions are for the unaccompanied voice and vocal groups. She has developed vocal techniques sometimes using simple intervals and motifs often repetitively, using gestures that she describes as transcultural, for example, Inuit throat singing, Balkan nasality and Tibetan chanting. She rejects the label minimalist, as do other composers, saying that she is from the folk music tradition and that repetition is a feature of much folk music, with the alternation of verse and chorus.

America was clearly the main base from which minimalism emerged. It also spread to Europe, with composers such as Nyman (1944–), Andriessen (1939–), Górecki (1933–), Pärt (1935–), Martland (1959–), Kancheli (1935–) and Tavener (1944–).

To summarize, at the beginning of the twentieth century America was a backwater of classical musical development. During the twentieth century American composers established an American identity not only in classical music, but also in jazz and in the development of the stage musical. American composers were active in the development of serial music in its broader sense and in the minimalism that followed. Important in the American musical arena of the twentieth century have been composers of Jewish descent, who have played leading parts both as composers known throughout the world, for example, Copland, Gershwin and Bernstein, and as leaders in the development of new styles, for example, Feldman, Reich and Glass. They have made even greater contributions to film music (see below), jazz and the musical, but only the first of these is within the scope of this book.

2.7 SEIZING OPPORTUNITIES: FILM COMPOSERS

Since the Middle Ages and earlier, Jews living throughout most countries of the Diaspora had been restricted in where they have been allowed to live and in what employment they may undertake. Over many years they have become both skilful and adaptable; these attributes being necessary for their survival throughout many parts of the Diaspora. Their role as money-lenders and their subsequent dominance in banking and finance illustrates this. During the twelfth and thirteenth centuries Ashkenazic Jews from north-western and central Europe found that the type of employment open to them was becoming increasingly restricted. Prior to this time many had been craftsmen and traders, but Christian merchants' guilds then organized themselves on the basis of social ties reinforced by Christian oaths of mutual loyalty. At the same time, with the rise in the money economy, loans were required for a wide range of purposes, for example, for construction costs in monasteries and church buildings, for the ransom of knights caught up in the Crusades, for monarchs equipping armies, and for craftsmen needing money for business purposes. Since Jews had been forced out of the trades, money-lending was one of the few openings left to them.

Here Jews had an advantage in being outside the jurisdiction of the Church. Both Christians and Jews found a convenient interpretation of Deuteronomy 23:20.

> You shall not deduct interest from loans to your countrymen, whether in money or food or anything else that can be deducted as interest; but you may deduct interest from loans to foreigners. Do not deduct interest from loans to your countrymen, so that the Lord your God may bless you in all your undertakings in the land that you are about to enter and possess.

An interpretation of this was that Christians could not charge interest for loans to Christians, nor Jews for loans to Jews, but Jews could charge interest on loans to Christians and vice versa. Jews increasingly took on the role of money-lender; this made them unpopular with Christian traders and often posed considerable risk to their safety. Rulers would often tax Jewish money-lenders highly for the profits from their loans. This often meant that Jews were in effect being used indirectly as tax collectors for the monarch, sometimes in exchange for a measure of protection. Although Jews were made particularly unpopular by taking on this role, it undoubtedly meant that they evolved skills that would stand them in good stead to become bankers and financiers in more recent times.

Another example of how Jews, because of their sometimes disadvantageous position in society, were quick to seize an opportunity, was in the film industry in general, and in the context of this book, in composing film music. The first known use of music to accompany a film was a showing by the Lumière family of film with a piano accompaniment in Paris in 1895. In the early days of the silent film, the purpose of music used as accompaniment was often to drown the sound of the projector; it was chosen from whatever happened to be at hand. As the silent film industry developed, the musical accompaniment became more refined, first by the use of musical extracts composed by classical composers that had been adapted to the timescale of the film, and then later by the composition of music specifically for a silent film. Examples of the latter include Meisel's music to accompany the Eisenstein films *Battleship Potemkin* and *October*, Honegger's scores for *La Roue* and *Napoléon*, Milhaud's for *L'Inhumaine* and *Petite Lili*, Arthur BENJAMIN's for *The Clairvoyant* and *The Turn of the Tide*, and Shostakovich's for *The New Babylon* (Milhaud and Benjamin were both Jewish). However, the most significant stage in the development of film music occurred after the development of sound films. The 'talkies', as they were referred to, became so popular that by 1938, 65 per cent of the American population attended 'movies' every week.

The development and production of film music reached its peak between 1935 and 1950, the golden age of Hollywood film music. After 1950 television became its big competitor, but during the 1930s and 1940s American studios were producing over 500 films per year. The composer of film music during this period was expected to be eclectic, composing for anything from classical or historical drama to a gangster film. It often required composing short stretches of music that had to fit a precisely timed film sequence. During this period composers set the styles of film composing for years to come. The late 1930s was also the time when Jews were fleeing Nazi persecution in Europe. The three composers most responsible for setting the style of film music were Korngold, Max Steiner and Alfred Newman, all of whom were of Jewish descent, although only Korngold had fled from the Nazis.

By the 1930s Korngold had a reputation as a composer of classical music. He had also collaborated with Max Reinhardt on a number of operettas. In 1934 Reinhardt invited him to Hollywood to collaborate on the film production of *Midsummer Night's Dream*. After this he returned home to a worsening situation in Austria. In January 1938 he received a telegram from Warner Brothers: 'Can you be in Hollywood in ten days' time to write the music for *Robin Hood*.' He phoned the director of the Staatsoper, Dr Eckmann, who at the time was involved in organizing the premiere of Korngold's opera *Die Kathrin*, telling him of the telegram message. Dr Eckmann's reply was 'Professor Korngold, take this as an omen and go.' Within a week Korngold and his wife were sailing for America. In effect *Robin Hood* had saved their lives.[14] Korngold adapted extremely well to the new genre and composed for a large number of successful films, receiving two Oscars. He composed 18 film scores between 1935 and 1944, returning to classical music after the death of his father in 1945. The trilogy of Korngold–Eroll Flynn spectaculars, *Robin Hood*, *The Sea Hawk* and *The Private Lives of Elizabeth and Essex* – were landmarks in the composition of film music. Korngold used musical themes in much the same way as Wagner used *leitmotifs* to emphasize in an unspoken language emotions and relationships.

Max Steiner was an Austrian Jew. He was born in Vienna in 1888 and began composing operettas at the age of 15. He moved to New York in 1914, working as a conductor and arranger in the American musical theatre on Broadway. With the Wall Street Crash of 1929 and the coming of sound films, there was an over-capacity in Broadway, and by 1931 45 per cent of Broadway had shut down. Steiner moved to Hollywood, composing for his first film in 1931. By 1965 he had written over 300 film scores and was largely responsible for setting the stylistic norm generally considered the characteristic 'Hollywood sound'.[15]

Alfred Newman was born in New Haven in 1901. His family was of Russian–Jewish origin and he was the oldest of ten children. In spite of the family's precarious financial situation, money was found for him to have piano lessons with teachers including George Wedge and Rubin Goldmark. When the family moved to New York, his father could find no work, so by the age of 13 he was obliged to start supporting his entire family. By the age of 15 he was a piano accompanist on Broadway, and at 17 became its youngest musical director. Like Steiner, Newman moved to Hollywood in 1930. In the late 1930s he studied composition with Schoenberg. He was head of the musical division of Twentieth-Century Fox from 1940 to 1960. By the time he resigned from this post, in 1960, he had written scores for 250 films and helped establish the romantic symphonic style in Hollywood.[16]

Dimitri Tiomkin was another composer who found his way to Hollywood in 1929. He was born in 1894 in the Ukraine of Jewish descent and studied under Glazunov and Blumenthal at the St Petersburg Conservatory. After the Russian Revolution he left for Berlin to study with Busoni and Egon Petri. As a concert pianist he gave the first European performance of Gershwin's piano concerto in F in 1928. For a period he continued both as a concert pianist and a film composer, but an injury to his right arm committed him fully to the latter. He brought a nineteenth-century Slavic style to his film music, but his most enduring claim to fame is through his scores for epic Westerns such as *High Noon* (1952), *The Alamo* (1960) and *Gunfight at the OK Corral*. Other important film scores were for *Lost Horizon* (1937), *Cyrano de Bergerac* (1950), *The High and Mighty* (1954), *Giant* (1956), *The Old Man of the Sea* (1958), *The Fall of the Roman Empire* (1964) and *Tchaikovsky* (1971).[17]

Some composers regarded film music as an inferior genre. Korngold's father, the music critic Julius Korngold, regarded his son's move to film music as a step down and always hoped he would return to operatic composition. Schoenberg had a number of offers to compose film music but none materialized. The most well known was a possible collaboration with Irving Thalberg to compose music to accompany the filming of Pearl S. Buck's novel *The Good Earth*. Schoenberg's demand for a fee of $50,000 has sometimes been interpreted that he derided the film industry. However, this seems to be a misinterpretation. What seems to have caused all negotiations for this and other films to come to nothing was Schoenberg's difficulty in accepting the division of labour required in film production; he needed to be in full control of the creation.[18] The norm was for the film's director to be in charge. Composers handed over their composition to the 'in-house' musical editor, who orchestrated the music as he saw fit for the film. Composers were rarely present when the adaptations took place.

This was not the case with Bernard HERRMANN, who is most widely known as a film composer but who regarded himself as a composer who also scored films. His first two films, *Citizen Kane,* in collaboration with Orson Wells, and *All That Money Can Buy*, which won an Oscar, were so successful that he was able to 'call the tune' with film directors. He insisted on his own orchestration, and also on being present during the shooting of the film. He was one of the most highly regarded film composers; his scores are characterized by an uncompromising darkness and sombre urgency.[19] He went on to compose 61 film scores in total.

Herrmann was born in America, and, like many other composers of Jewish descent, for example, Copland, ANTHIEL, Newman, GRUENBERG, and LEVANT, he was brought up in America. He took the opportunities that film music presented. However, Copland composed music for only eight films, a small proportion of his total output. Antheil wrote background scores for 11 films between 1936 and 1957. Gruenberg wrote scores for ten films and received three Academy Awards between 1940 and 1942.

Other composers of film scores had fled Nazi Germany to live in America for example, WAXMAN, TOCH, ZEISL, HOLLAENDER and Gold. Friedrich Holländer (anglicized to Frederick Hollaender or Hollander), the son of violinist and composer Victor Holländer, fled to California in the mid-1930s. He composed songs and wrote scores for over 150 films, beginning in 1929. He is perhaps most famous for his score for Josef von Sternberg's *Der Blaue Engel* starring Marlene Dietrich. Hollaender, who had been a refugee in Paris, knew Waxman since they had both stayed in the same cheap boarding-house, the Hotel Ansonia. Hollaender engaged Waxman, then aged 24 and relatively unknown, to orchestrate and conduct the score of *Der Blaue Engel*, but Waxman was to receive no screen credit. Nevertheless, this was the start of many more screen commissions for Waxman, who was to go on to become a very successful composer of music for over 140 films, winning two Oscars. Waxman's aspirations were to be more than just a film composer, and by the late 1940s he became more interested in composing concert music and conducting. Although he is still best known as a film composer, he wrote three major concert works: *Sinfonietta* for strings and timpani (1955), the oratorio *Joshua* (1959), and *The Song of Terezin* (1965). His most popular work is undoubtedly the *Carman Fantasy* (1947), which was commissioned by Heifetz.

Ernst Toch had already established a reputation as a composer before he fled to America in 1934. He turned to film composing, but with less distinction than some of his compatriots, although he did compose for 21 films between 1928 and 1945. Erich Zeisl escaped Vienna in 1938 and moved to Hollywood in 1941, composed for two films, but became disillusioned with the film industry and in 1949 went into music teaching.

Ernest Gold (originally Goldner) fled from Vienna to America in 1938. Prior to this he had composed some concert pieces, but he was more successful with popular songs. He began working in Hollywood in 1945 and became one of the world's greatest composers of background film music. His films include *On the Beach* (1959), *Exodus* (1960), *Judgement at Nuremberg* (1961), *Pressure Point* (1962), *Inherit the Wind* (1960), *The Secret of Santa Vittoria* (1969) and *Cross of Iron* (1977). Hans Eisler had also left Nazi Germany for America in 1933, but he was deported for 'un-American activities' in 1948. Whilst in America he composed for eight films.

Much of the film music composed up until the 1950s was in the lush romantic style of the late nineteenth century, which used large orchestras, but by the mid-1950s twentieth-century influences were creeping in. Copland was one of the first to make this advance by using a modern style while at the same time providing memorable melodies and powerful underscoring of the dramatic action, but of those who were primarily film composers Leonard Rosenman and Elmer Bernstein, both of Jewish descent, were at the forefront of this change. Rosenman was born in Brooklyn and studied composition with Schoenberg, Sessions and Dallapiccola. The film scores for which he is remembered are *East of Eden* (1954) and *Rebel Without a Cause* (1955). Both films are concerned with severely disturbed adolescents and Rosenman created a sound completely new to Hollywood, which gave James Dean, the principal star, a musical identity. Like Herrmann, Rosenman worked with the director at all stages of the production.

Elmer Bernstein, also born in New York, studied composition with Wolpe and Sessions and began his career as a concert pianist. In the 1950s he began composing for films. His two major achievements in the development of film music were the introduction of jazz and the use of a much smaller orchestra, giving the music a chamber-music-like concentration. His second and third film scores for *Sudden Fear* (1952) and *The Man with the Golden Arm* (1955) brought him to prominence and he continued scoring for many films until the mid-1980s.

Although film music is most frequently associated with America and Hollywood, the English composer Benjamin Frankel composed over 100 film scores and had an association with British cinema and television for some 37 years. His first film score was in 1934. His score for *Curse of the Werewolf* (1960) contains the first twelve-note serial work in a British feature film. Wilfred Josephs also wrote film scores. He was a music consultant at the London International Film School, but concentrated more on television than cinema.

In conclusion, composers of Jewish descent have made a substantial contribution to film scores, not only in terms of the total number of successful films but also by playing a major role in the development of the genre.

NOTES

1. Evyatar Friesel, *Atlas of Modern Jewish History* (Oxford: Oxford University Press, 1990).
2. H. H. Ben-Sasson (ed.), *A History of the Jewish People* (Cambridge, MA: Harvard University Press, 1969), pp. 750–63; and Robert M. Seltzer, *Jewish People, Jewish Thought* (New York: Macmillan, 1980), pp. 513–46.
3. Alan J. P. Taylor, *The Hapsburg Monarchy 1809–1918* (Harmondsworth: Penguin, 1964).
4. Jeffrey S. Sposato, 'Creative Writing: the [Self-]Identification of Mendelssohn as Jew', *Musical Quarterly*, 82 (1998), pp. 190–209.
5. Paul Johnson, *A History of the Jews* (London: Weidenfeld & Nicolson, 1987), p. 230.
6. Charles Rosen, *Arnold Schoenberg* (Chicago: University of Chicago Press, 1975), pp. 70–1.
7. Alexander L. Ringer, *Arnold Schoenberg: The Composer as Jew* (Oxford: Clarendon Press, 1990), pp. 18–19.
8. Pamela M. Potter, *Most German of the Arts* (New Haven: Yale University Press, 1998), pp. 134, 179–80 and 255.
9. Jürgen Schebera, *Kurt Weill: an Illustrated Life* (New Haven: Yale University Press, 1995), pp. 20–1.
10. Erwin Stein (ed.), *Arnold Schoenberg: Letters* (London: Faber, 1964), p. 267.
11. Richard Crawford, *America's Musical Life* (New York: W. W. Norton, 2001), pp. 689–713.
12. George Rochberg, 'On the Third String Quartet', in O. Strunk (ed.), *Source Readings in Music History* (New York: W. W. Norton, 1998), pp. 1504–8.
13. K. Robert Schwarz, *Minimalists* (London: Phaidon, 1996), pp. 170–87.
14. Brendan G. Carroll, *The Last Prodigy: a Biography of Erich Wolfgang Korngold* (Portland, OR: Amadeus, 1997), p. 268.
15. Christopher Palmer, *The Composer in Hollywood* (London: Marion Boyars, 1990), pp. 15–50.
16. Ibid., pp. 68–92.
17. Ibid., pp. 118–59.
18. S. M. Feisst, 'Arnold Schoenberg and Cinematic Art', *Musical Quarterly*, 83 (1999), pp. 93–113.
19. Howard Goodall, *Big Bangs: the Story of Five Discoveries that Changed Musical History* (London: Vintage, 2001), p. 172.

Chapter 3

Accounting for the Preponderance of Composers of Jewish Descent in the Nineteenth and Twentieth Centuries

In the previous chapter I have shown that since the beginning of the Jewish Enlightenment (*Haskalah*), composers of Jewish descent have made a significant impact on the development of western classical music. Although this book is restricted to composers, it is important to note also the major contribution of performers, librettists and impresarios of Jewish descent. The following examples illustrate this. Eminent conductors in the twentieth century of Jewish descent include Rudolf Barshai, Antal Dorati, Bernhard Haitink, Jascha Horenstein, Eliahu Inbal, Otto KLEMPERER, Serge Koussevitzky, Erich Leinsdorf, James Levine, Lorin MAAZEL, Pierre Monteux, André PREVIN, Eugene Ormandy, Landon Ronald, Fritz Reiner, Joshua Rifkin, Kurt Sanderling, Rudolf Schwarz, Georg Solti, George Szell, Michael Tilson Thomas and Bruno Walter. Great violinists of the twentieth century include Samuel Dushkin, Mischa Elman, Ivry Gitlis, Ida Haendel, Josef Hassid, Jascha Heifetz, Bronislaw Huberman, Leonid Kogan, Rudolf Kolisch, Yehudi Menuhin, Nathan Milstein, Shlomo Mintz, David Oistrakh, Itzhak Perlman, Arnold Rosé, Isaac Stern, Henryk Szeryng, Josef Szigeti, Maxim Vengerov and Pinchas Zuckerman; pianists include Daniel Barenboim, Annie Fisher, Emil Gilels, Myra Hess, Vladimir Horowitz, Louis Kentner, Wanda Landowska, Josef Lhevinne, Benno Moiseiwitch, Murray Perahia, Menahem Pressler, Arthur Rubinstein, Andras Schiff, Solomon (Solomon Cutner) and Rosalyn Tureck. In other areas of music librettists of Jewish descent include Lorenzo da Ponte, Ludovic Halévy, Hugo von Hofmannsthal, Stefan Zweig, Marie Pappenheim and Ira Gershwin; music critics include Eduard Hanslick, Julius Korngold, Alfred Einstein and Hans Keller; and impresarios include Johann Peter Salomon, Rudolf Bing, Rolf LIEBERMANN and Jeremy Isaacs.

In this chapter I shall consider the kind of explanations that have been put forward to explain the over-representation of composers of Jewish descent when compared to the small fraction that Jews comprise of the world's population. It is not only in music that this occurs; it can also be seen in other areas, for example, in medicine, science and law, to name a few. Although Jews formed less than 10 per cent of the population of Vienna in 1910, for example, they made up over 50 per cent of the medical faculty and by 1936 over 60 per cent of the city's lawyers.[1] To analyze this phenomenon with respect to music, I consider whether there are genetic or environmental factors at work accounting for this; in other words, whether it is a matter of nature or nurture, or a combination of both. First, though, in order to set the parameters, we need to define a Jew and thus someone of Jewish descent.

3.1 DEFINITION OF A JEW

The definition of a Jew is not something universally agreed upon, and has caused controversy from both within and without Jewish communities. Does it define an individual belonging to a particular religion or a particular race? Historically the origin of the word *Jew* is derived from the name Judah (*c.* 1600 BCE),[2] one of Jacob's 12 sons, and was originally used to describe members of the tribe of Judah. After the death of King Solomon, in *c.* 922 BCE, the tribes of Israel (the name used to describe the descendants of Jacob, who was also called Israel) split into two, the southern kingdom of Judah and the northern kingdom of Israel. After that time the term *Yehudi* (the Hebrew for Jew) could be used to describe anyone from the kingdom of Judah, which included the tribes of Judah, Benjamin and Levi. The northern kingdom was conquered by the Assyrians and 10 of the 12 tribes mixed with the local population and ceased to exist as a distinct group. A historian has calculated that the Jews alive today are descended from a mere 2 per cent of those alive at the time of the Second Temple.[3]

The term *Jew* is now commonly used more widely to refer to all the physical and spiritual descendants of Jacob, as well as of the patriarchs Abraham and Isaac and their wives. The term *Hebrew* was first used to describe the descendants of Abraham. Two years after the establishment of the State of Israel, the Law of Return (1950) was enacted. This defined a Jew as 'a person who was born of a Jewish mother or who has become converted to Judaism and who is not a member of another religion'. The interpretation of this definition has been actively debated by many sectors of the Jewish community. Orthodox Jews only accept matrilineal descent or conversions that they recognize, and this excludes some conversions performed by the Reform Movement (see Glossary). The Orthodox interpretation also includes in its definition a person descended from a Jewish mother who has converted to another religion. Within the Reform Movement, some consider a person Jewish if either parent is Jewish and the child is raised as Jewish, but if the mother is Jewish and the father is not, and the child is not raised as Jewish, then according to some in the movement, the child is not Jewish. The two extremes attach differing importance to hereditary and religious elements in the definition. The origin of matrilineal descent, although not explicitly spelt out in the Bible, is inferred from various statements (Deuteronomy 7:1–5; Leviticus 24:10; and Ezra 10:2–3) and appears to have been the tradition only since about 500 CE.[4]

The way in which Jews define themselves is not necessarily the way others define them, particularly anti-Semites. For example, Karl Lueger, the leader of an anti-Semitic movement and mayor of Vienna in 1895 said: 'A Jew is anyone I say is a Jew.' The Nazis were more specific when enacting the Nuremberg Laws in 1935. These laws were aimed at removing citizenship from Jews. Jews were divided into categories according to the number of Jewish grandparents. One Jewish grandparent was sufficient to be regarded as of mixed Jewish blood. To be a full Jew required either three Jewish grandparents, or two Jewish grandparents and belonging to the Jewish religious community. So although the definition was based primarily on heredity considerations, belonging to the Jewish religious community could also be a factor. In their book *Lexikon der Juden in der Musik* compiled on the orders of the leadership of the National Socialist Workers' Party, Stengel and Gerigk based their criteria for inclusion on the Nuremberg Laws (see Appendix I).

Some authors define as Jewish any person who considered or considers him- or herself as such, or who was or is so regarded by his or her contemporaries,[5] whereas others use the strict *Halakhic* (legal) definition.[6] With regard to the composers of Jewish descent included in Part II of this book, I have aired on the inclusive side, generally including those who have at least one Jewish grandparent, and who would thus be likely to be aware of some Jewish heritage, whether they liked it or chose to ignore it. This is discussed further in Chapter 4.

3.2 THE QUESTION OF A JEWISH RACE

In their comprehensive survey *The Myth of the Jewish Race*,[7] published in 1975, Raphael Patai and Jennifer Wing consider the evidence for distinctiveness of the Jewish Race. They discuss a wide range of evidence including historical, psychological and genetic evidence. A race can be described as a group having a common ancestry distinguished by physical characters, and in more biological terms, a geographically isolated group having gene frequencies (see Glossary) distinct from other races.[8] There are conceptual difficulties associated with this definition. The average divergence in gene frequencies between individuals *within* a race is often much greater than the average divergence in gene frequencies *between* races. It has been estimated that only 15 per cent of genetic diversity occurs between races or ethnic groups as compared to 85 per cent occurring within groups. Most of today's ethnic groups that are described as races are not the genetically coherent groups they are often thought to be, although the gene frequencies for a large number of alleles (see Glossary) differ between the five major racial groups (Caucasian, African, Asian, Hispanic and American Indian), and these differences have been used to compute the time at which the major racial groups diverged.[9] However, the idea that there are distinct racial groups is not scientifically sustainable. Owens and King assert that, 'The possibility that human history has been characterized by genetically relatively homogeneous groups (or races), distinguished by major biological differences, is not consistent with genetic evidence.'[10]

The Jewish religion can be traced back about four thousand years and the large-scale dispersal of the Jewish population began with the Babylonian exile in 586 BCE. The present-day Jewish population can be classified according to the location in which each community developed. These include: the Middle Eastern communities of former Babylonia and Palestine; the Jewish communities of North Africa and the Mediterranean basin; and the Ashkenazic communities of central and eastern Europe. The first and second of these include Sephardic communities.

3.2.1 HISTORIC EVIDENCE

It is clear that Jews throughout their history have rarely been a completely isolated population. From the earliest times there has been admixture from local surrounding populations and invaders. At many stages different genes will have been introduced into the population as the result of proselytism and intermarriage. It is difficult from historical records to quantify the extent of these processes. There are many relevant references in the Bible, but in general the 'high profile cases' of interbreeding are the ones that are described in detail, as the following examples illustrate. At about 1800 BCE Abraham had six children by Keturah, variously described as his wife (Genesis 25:1) or concubine (First Book of Chronicles 1:32), and he sent the children 'to the land of the East'. He also had a son, Ishmael, by his Egyptian handmaid, Hagar. Later, his great-grandson, Joseph, married Asenath, daughter of Poti-phera, priest of On (Heliopolis). Moses married a Midianite, Zipporah (Exodus 3:21), and also a Cushite (Ethiopian) (Numbers 12:1). David had at least two non-Israelite ancestors, his great-grandmother Ruth, a Moabite, and 10 generations back the Canaanite woman, Tamar (First book of Chronicles 2:4–15).

Proselytizing was carried out in Roman times and earlier. Some Romans and Greeks converted to Judaism because they were attracted to the concept of monotheism. After the dispersal of the Jews after 70 CE, the population moved into Arab-controlled lands, and wherever they settled they attracted converts to Judaism. The Yemenite Jews are thought to be largely proselytes, dating back to about the second century CE, and remained an isolated community until they were resettled in Israel after 1948. There are examples from biblical times of slaves who converted to Judaism, and this also occurred in

the Middle Ages. One view, of Talmudic origin, was that the act of proselytizing was itself a work of piety. Between the seventh and the eleventh
centuries it has been reckoned that the Jewish population of the Middle East
and North Africa may have even doubled as the result of proselytizing slaves.

Interbreeding is also an important factor in introducing new genes into the
Jewish gene pool. Although it is difficult to quantify, it is clear that interbreeding occurred from the earliest times. Jews have very often been surrounded by much larger populations of non-Jewish neighbours. At the time
of King David the army contained foreigners. King David himself had many
non-Jewish concubines. During the Babylonian exile interbreeding occurred
between Jews and Babylonians. Rabbinic legislation forbids sexual relations
with gentiles, but is tolerant of marriage to proselytes. Intermarriage increased
during the twentieth century. What is important in cases of interbreeding is
the religion of the offspring, since only those brought up as Jews will
contribute to the Jewish gene pool.

In addition to outbreeding by intermarriage, there is also the converse,
namely inbreeding. The marriage between cousins goes back as far as
Abraham's time, around 3,500 years ago, and although it is now very much
less frequent, it is still a factor to take into account. In Israel a number of
surveys have been carried out. In the period 1955–7 it was found that 1.4 per
cent of Ashkenazic Jews married their first cousins, whereas among non-
Ashkenazic Jews as many as 8.8 per cent did so. At least two composers listed
in Part II (i.e., 2 out of over 250 listed, or 1%) married their cousins (for example,
Meyerbeer and Milhaud).

3.2.2 GENETIC EVIDENCE

In contrast to historical evidence, the geneticist examines genetic differences
within present-day populations and uses these to infer how these changes
have arisen. (Readers who do not wish to read the detailed genetic evidence
will find a summary of the conclusions in the last paragraph of this section.)

A number of different factors have contributed to the unity and diversity
of the present-day Jewish population; these include common ancestry,
genetic drift, natural selection and admixture with the gene pool from surrounding non-Jewish populations. Assessing the contribution of each of these
is a complex task. Up until the 1960s observable morphological characters,
such as height, body weight, skin colour, shape of nose, shape of head or hair
colour were used to distinguish different ethnic groups. However, there is a
problem in that many of these morphological characters are affected both by
genetic make-up and by environmental factors. It is often difficult to separate
these components. Since the 1960s evidence from the study of biochemical
traits has been increasingly used. The polymorphs (see Glossary) that exist in
the well-known blood groups and also in a number of blood proteins have
been used to compare gene frequencies, both between and within different

groups. The distribution of particular blood groups and blood proteins has been compared within the whole Jewish population and also between specific Jewish populations and their non-Jewish neighbours.

The conclusion from most of the work carried out up until the 1980s was that the Jewish population showed considerable heterogeneity or variation. More heterogeneity has been found to exist between different groups of Jews (e.g., Ashkenazim compared to Iranian, Iraqi and Kurdish Jews) than between Jews and their non-Jewish neighbours (e.g., Ashkenazic Jews and their neighbours in eastern Europe). Results such as this have been found in many cases where different races throughout the world have been compared: that is, the genetic variation within a race is greater than that between races. Nevertheless, the results do suggest that European Jews retain elements of their Mediterranean Jewish ancestry. When a number of different traits or characters are compared, it is possible to compute a composite score of the differences, or genetic distance. This measures how genetically different groups are from one another. It has been found that the genetic distances within extremes of the Jewish population are greater than between specific Jewish groups and their non-Jewish neighbours.

Since the publication of Patai and Wing's book in 1975 there have been many advances in the understanding of molecular genetics and in the methods used for analysis. In particular, individual genes can now be examined in great detail. It is also possible to trace matrilineal and patrilineal descent. Human males have a single X and a single Y sex chromosome, whereas females have two X chromosomes. This means that the Y chromosome is present in males only and it is transferred from father to son in strict patrilineal descent (see Figure 4). In addition to the main set of chromosomes in each cell there is also a small chromosome present in the organelle known as the mitochondrion. This particular chromosome is present in the ovum but not in the sperm. Therefore, in contrast to the Y chromosome, the mitochondrial chromosome is transferred by matrilineal descent only. The constitution of chromosomes in general may change as a result of (i) mutation or (ii) a process known as recombination. The latter occurs during the formation of the male and female gametes. Recombination is a type of molecular cutting and pasting between the chromosomes of maternal and paternal origin (Figure 5). However, this process occurs in all chromosomes except the Y chromosome and the mitochondrial chromosome. An advantage arising from this difference is that changes in the Y chromosome or mitochondrial chromosome only occur as a result of mutation and not recombination, and thus can be used to obtain a gender-specific record of the past. Whereas other chromosomes have multiple origins, because of recombination that may have occurred in previous generations the Y chromosome and mitochondrial chromosome can be traced back to a single paternal or maternal origin, respectively. In addition, the genetic markers used on these chromosomes are described as 'selectively neutral', so that differences in the environments in which the different

Figure 4
TRANSMISSION OF X AND Y CHROMOSOMES FROM PARENTS TO OFFSPRING.

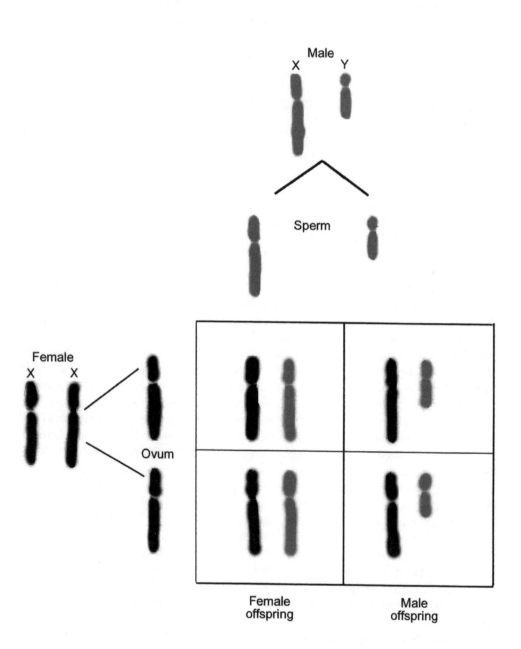

Figure 5
RECOMBINATION DURING GAMETE FORMATION.

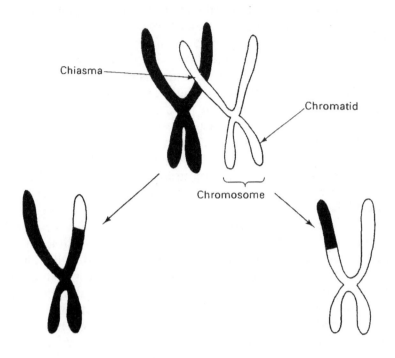

populations evolve will not have a selective effect, which might otherwise bias the evolutionary origins. These two chromosomes have been very useful in studying Jewish ancestry.

When a number of different biochemical traits, for example, blood groups and histocompatibility antigens (see Glossary), were studied and improved methods of analyses used to compute a composite measure of differences between groups (i.e., genetic distance), Livshits *et al.*[11] found that the genetic distances within Jewish populations were lower than those between particular Jewish populations and their non-Jewish neighbours. Similar results have been obtained from a number of studies with Y and mitochondrial chromosomes.[12] The results are consistent with (i) a common origin of Ashkenazic and Sephardic Jews in a Middle Eastern ancestral population, (ii) a clear distinction in ancestry of Ashkenazic Jews and their neighbouring non-Jewish populations of central and eastern Europe, and (iii) some admixture from the surrounding populations, amounting to less than 1 per cent per generation.

A further interesting observation arises from a study of the Y chromosome in the Jewish priesthood or *Cohanim*.[13] According to the Bible, the priesthood was established about 3,300 years ago and, unlike Judaism itself that is inherited by matrilineal descent, the priesthood is by strict patrilineal descent. The study showed a clear distinction between the priesthood and the lay Jewish population, and this difference was observed in both Ashkenazic and Sephardic populations. This suggests that the origin of the priesthood pre-dates the division into Ashkenazic and Sephardic communities.

Further light concerning the origins of Ashkenazic Jews comes from the study of genetically inherited diseases. Four diseases in particular, namely, idiopathic torsion dystonia, Tay Sachs, Gaucher and Niemann-Pick diseases, show a higher incidence in Ashkenazic Jews than in other populations. Two explanations have been offered to explain this. The first is known as the founder effect, in which a mutation arises in a small closed breeding popu-lation, which then expands rapidly. The mutation causing the disease idio-pathic torsion dystonia, in this case is thought to have arisen in the northern part of the Pale of Settlement (Lithuania and Byelorussia) about 300 to 500 years ago, and it is also thought that present-day Ashkenazim are descended from a relatively small number of ancestors, perhaps between 10,000 and 20,000. The data are consistent with historical investigations that suggest that the wealthier classes of this population expanded rapidly despite many losses in subsequent pogroms. A number of genealogical studies of business leaders, prominent rabbis and community leaders have found that on average they had between four and nine children who reached adulthood, that is, con-sistent with a rapid expansion. The ancestors of a large number of the composers of Jewish descent are likely to have been amongst them.

On the basis of the evidence from Tay Sachs, Gaucher and Niemann-Pick diseases, in which there at least eight different mutations known, Diamond[14] argues that the occurrence of eight deleterious mutations striking the Ashkenazic populations is too great to be simply coincidence. The second explanation offered is that there may be some compensating advantage to maintaining these mutations in the population. The selective advantages that have been proposed are, firstly, that carriers (see Glossary) of these diseases have greater resistance to tuberculosis, which was prevalent in the cramped conditions of the ghettos of eastern Europe. There is evidence for lower fre-quency of death from tuberculosis in Tay Sachs heterozygotes (see Glossary), although the evidence is inconclusive. A parallel situation is well documented to account for the prevalence of sickle cell anaemia in Africa, in that the heterozygote confers resistance to malaria. A third suggestion is that greater intelligence was required to survive persecution and to make a living through commerce, since Jews were barred from agricultural jobs available to the non-Jewish population, and that this was a selective factor. These and other possi-bilities are highly speculative, and conclusive evidence is difficult to obtain.

A particular mutation known as G197delLDLR, causing a form of familial hypercholesterolaemia, has also been studied in a group of Ashkenazic Jews from Israel, South Africa, Russia, the Netherlands and the United States, all of whom can trace their ancestry to Lithuania.[15] Genetic analysis suggests that this mutation arose between 15 and 26 generations ago. This corresponds approximately to the founding of the Jewish community in Lithuania (1338 CE). In this case no evidence for any selective advantage of this mutation has been deduced. It has been attributed to a founder effect in what was then a rapidly expanding population, from a limited number of families.

Two different conclusions can be reached from the large number of scientific studies aimed at assessing whether or not Jews represent a distinct biological race or group. From studies using morphological features and from earlier biochemical studies it appears that there is greater genetic variation within present-day Jewish populations than there is between particular Jewish populations and their surrounding non-Jewish populations. This highlights one of the conceptual difficulties in defining race mentioned at the beginning of this section. However, more recent molecular genetic evidence, particularly that from studying the chromosomes present only in a single sex suggests a common ancestry for both Ashkenazic and Sephardic Jews, albeit with admixture from external gene pools. Nevertheless, it suggests more common features within present-day Jews than between certain groups of Jews and their surrounding neighbours. Recent evidence from certain genetically inherited diseases is consistent with present-day Ashkenazic Jews having arisen from a much smaller founder population in the northern part of the Pale of Settlement between 300 and 500 years ago, and that within that population the wealthier and better-educated Jews had large families that also had a good rate of survival.

In conclusion, it is clear that a Jew cannot be defined as a particular genotype (see Glossary), and that there are no known genes exclusive to Jews. However when comparing Jewish and non-Jewish populations, there are certain alleles (see Glossary) that occur with a higher frequency *on average* in Jewish populations than in non-Jewish populations; there will nevertheless be some Jews lacking these alleles and some non-Jews who possess them.

Recent research on the human genome has set important limits to possible genetic differences between races. When the human genome sequence was published in February 2001, one surprise was the small number of genes it contained – around 30,000. Earlier biologists were predicting between 60,000 and 100,000 genes. This number is less than twice that found in a worm.[16] Furthermore, about 45 per cent of the worm's genes are almost identical to those of humans. Just as striking is the 98 per cent overlap between the human genome and that of our nearest evolutionary neighbour, the chimpanzee.[17] This leaves a very small genetic difference to account for such vast differences, especially in brain development and cognitive function, between humans and chimpanzees. Any genetic differences between human races are undoubtedly even smaller.

One factor that compensates to some extent for this small number of genes is a process known as alternative splicing. Alternative splicing enables DNA to be read from a number of different starting points, and this means that considerably more than 30,000 gene products can be encoded by 30,000 genes. This process of alternative splicing appears to be more common in humans than in other species. At least 40 to 60 per cent of human genes have alternative splice forms and this greatly increases the functional capacity of the human genome. Nevertheless, when the diversity of genes or gene products occurring within one human race or group is compared with the diversity between two races, for example, Jews and their surrounding non-Jewish neighbours, the results are very interesting. For example, if you were to sample a gene at random from two humans at random, there is an 86 per cent chance they will be identical and a 14 per cent chance that they will not. If you sample a gene at random from two individuals belonging to the same race, there is an 86.5 per cent chance they will be identical and 13.5 per cent chance that they differ. Thus practically all human genetic variation occurs within rather than between races or groups.[18]

3.3 MUSICAL APTITUDE: NATURE OR NURTURE?

One topic that has been highly controversial and emotive for many years is whether certain races or social groups are more intelligent than others. This controversy came to prominence in 1969, when a psychologist, Arthur Jensen, claimed there were inherent differences in the average intelligence of different racial groups, with blacks scoring significantly lower intelligence quotients (IQs) than whites. His ideas and conclusions have been strongly criticized on a number of grounds, not least because some of the data Jensen cited have since been shown to be fraudulent.[19]

Patai and Wing discuss a number of studies, mainly with children, carried out between 1936 and 1960 showing that on average Jews scored significantly higher than non-Jewish groups in intelligence tests.[20] It should be noted that only Ashkenazic Jews were involved in most of these tests. They go on to consider the possible reasons for the higher score, and suggest this may have come about largely by environmental selection. Jews have a long history of oppression and persecution and it has been suggested that this has been a selective factor favouring those most capable of surviving. Intelligence would undoubtedly be one of many factors that would be important. Patai and Wing also point out that Jews have a long tradition of Talmudic scholarship and scholarship in general. It is not possible to prove whether these factors have resulted in higher IQs, since such tests only originated at the beginning of the twentieth century.

The concept of IQ has been used to assess both individuals and populations. Some studies have also claimed that when the heritability of the IQ in populations is apportioned between hereditary and environmental factors, as much as 80 per cent may be attributed to hereditary, that is, IQ is determined far more by inheritance than by upbringing. Inevitably this type of study has political implications, but it is also questionable whether such measurements as the average IQ are meaningful when applied to a population. Rose, Kamin and Lewenton[21] question the notion of race and the whole validity of IQ tests, particularly their wider interpretation, pointing out flaws and biases in early studies. Proponents[22] claim that more recent studies support the older claims that genetic factors set the potential limits of behaviour of the human animal, while environmental circumstances and events influence the individual organism within the limits of its potential as determined by heredity. Gould[23] makes a substantial case that intelligence cannot be measured as a single heritable quantity, attacking the very idea of intelligence as a unitary rankable genetically based entity. Intelligence is a multifactorial trait. It is difficult to define precisely, unlike other human attributes such as height, weight or skin colour, although its meaning is generally understood. At least seven types of related mental activities make up this multifactorial trait, which are used to generate a single number, the IQ. Although performance in an intelligence test may be a useful predictive indicator of performance in a specified area, it cannot be a composite measure of all aspects of intelligence.

There is general agreement among scientists that most human attributes are the product of interaction between genes and the environment, but the relative contributions of heredity and environment for many of these are difficult to quantify.[24] We cannot, for example, partition attributes such as aggression, altruism, charisma or intelligence between genetic make-up and nurture, although partitioning may be possible for attributes such as height, fertility or susceptibility to certain diseases. Thus, the results purporting to show differences in average intelligence between samples of Jewish and non-Jewish populations cited above must be taken with a high degree of scepticism.

With regard to IQ measurements, the areas that are still being actively debated are (i) whether IQ is a meaningful measure of intelligence, (ii) whether IQ can be accurately apportioned between hereditary and environmental factors, and (iii) whether this apportionment is meaningful between two different populations. Also related to these issues are those of methodology and evidence. For example, it may in principle be possible to link intelligence to genes, but as yet no methods, for example, molecular biological methods, are able to do so. These issues have been fully reviewed by Segerstråle (2000).[25]

Intelligence and IQ has been extensively researched for many years; in contrast, the assessment and quantifying of musical aptitude has been much less studied. The questions that one might like to ask are: (i) is it possible to assess musical aptitude, (ii) is there a link between musical aptitude and intelligence, and (iii) can an understanding of (i) and (ii) help to understand the disproportionate contribution that Jews have made to western music since the beginning of the nineteenth century. I have shown that intelligence testing is fraught with difficulties; musical aptitude is just as difficult to define and also includes within it a number of different factors. As in the

65

field of intelligence testing, numerous tests have been devised for testing musical aptitude.[26] Although many observers would claim to be able to pick out individuals having great musical ability or talent, there is a great difficulty in defining musical ability in such a way that a generally acceptable method of measurement would be possible. Musical ability can manifest itself in a number of different situations, for example performing, composing and listening. Many scientists have rightly questioned quantification of intelligence as a single parameter, namely IQ; with musical ability this is an even more complex issue. The 'ideal' intelligence test would be one in which innate intelligence is measured independently of upbringing, but this is impossible. The same applies to tests designed to test musical aptitude as opposed to musical attainment. All aptitude tests designed to measure potential will inevitably require a certain level of attainment. Many different tests have been devised to test different aspects of musicality. However, these have been used to test an individual's ability and it is very doubtful that they could form a sound basis for comparing different populations, or indeed could add anything to the question of why Jews are 'over-represented' in many spheres of music.

Two questions of potential relevance need to be considered. Firstly, is musical talent inherited, or, at least, does it have a genetic component? There are of course well-known examples of music running in families, for example, the Bach and Couperin families. Menuhin was reportedly a believer of the view that musicians are 'born and not made'. He started his music schools to nourish exceptional musical talent. Karl Popper, the philosopher of science, who was also a member of Schoenberg's Verein für musikalische Privataufführungen (Society for Private Music Performances), although convinced that music ran in families, was puzzled because he felt that European music was too recent an invention to be genetically based, as genetic changes would be expected to take longer.[27] There is one reported study[28] purporting to show that musicality is transmitted as a dominant Mendelian trait. However, this or related studies have not been followed up and so cannot be given much credence. The second question is whether there is a relationship between musical ability and intelligence, as measured by IQ. A number of studies have been made, most of which show a low positive correlation between intellectual and musical ability. Some correlation is hardly surprising, but Shuter-Dyson concludes, 'however valuable intelligence may be in the development of musical ability, mere intellectual efficiency, however highly oriented towards music, will not make a musician'.[29]

In a recent study one particular aspect of musical aptitude has been examined to determine the extent to which it is inherited. This concerns the perception of pitch, which is clearly an important aspect of 'musicality'. In a series of tests carried out on monozygotic (identical) and dizygotic (non-identical) twins, Drayna et al.[30] found that the ability to recognize pitch has a high heritability of between 0.71 and 0.80. This means that genetic factors can contribute as much as 80 per cent of the ability to discriminate pitch whereas environmental differences, for example upbringing, contribute only up to 20 per cent. When compared to many other complex human traits this is a very high heritability, however it is only one small aspect of musicality, albeit an important one. So far no studies have been carried out to see whether this trait shows differences between groups of people.

In conclusion, there is little scientific evidence, so far, to indicate the relative importance of nature versus nurture on musical aptitude. In the next section the composers listed in Part II of this book are examined to see if there are any common factors that may help explain the preponderance of composers of Jewish descent in the past 200 years. Section 3.5 examines the importance of cultural evolution.

3.4 AN EXAMINATION OF THE COMPOSERS LISTED IN PART II

Part II of this book lists over 250 composers of Jewish descent. Although this is not a large number, and the information available for each composer varies in the amount of detail, it is nevertheless large enough to analyze some of the factors that may be common to a number of these composers. Figure 6 shows the distribution by country of birth for composers of Jewish descent. Usually

Figure 6
DISTRIBUTION OF COMPOSERS OF JEWISH DESCENT BY COUNTRY OF BIRTH.

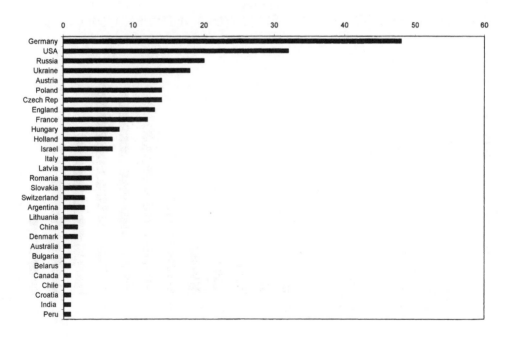

the country of birth is the same as the country of origin, but not in every case: for example, SCHREKER's father was a German-speaking Bohemian who was working as a court photographer in Monaco at the time of Schreker's birth, and Meredith Monk was born in Lima, Peru while her mother, a popular singer, was on tour, although the family lived in New York. The largest number of composers listed were born in Germany, but subsequently, during the twentieth century, many migrated from Germany to America.

The dramatic increase in the number of composers of Jewish descent from the beginning of the nineteenth century is evident from Figure 7.This is based on the number of such composers alive during 20-year blocks from the beginning of the eighteenth century onwards. Unless a composer is quite exceptional, he or she will not become widely known until at least 30 years of age, and so 'potential' composers born after about 1970 will not contribute to the numbers, which accounts for what is an apparent decrease after the 1970s. If we look at the migrations of composers, the results are quite revealing, as Table 2 shows. A number of different categories of migration is considered. The first is simply that of comparing the country of birth and country of death. From these I have excluded any that are only apparent changes, that is, where the boundaries of the countries have changed. The second category I have described as East to West movement, and this is intended to include migration to avoid persecution and for economic reasons. In this category I have counted as East to West migration movement from any of the following countries – Germany, Russia, Lithuania, Latvia, Poland, Ukraine, Belarus, Hungary,

Figure 7
COMPOSERS OF JEWISH DESCENT LIVING BETWEEN 1550 AND 2000

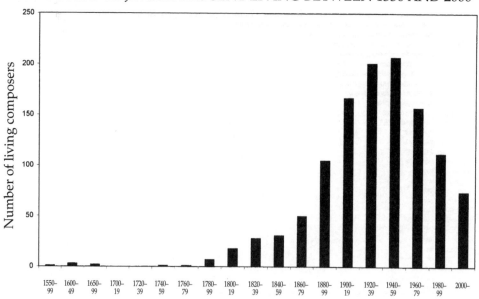

Romania and Italy – to any of the following countries – USA, France, Great Britain, Canada, South America, Australia and Israel. Although not always strictly East to West, the first group of countries are ones that Jews, at various times in the nineteenth and twentieth centuries, were driven from, and those in the second group were those in which they sought a safe haven or better economic prospects. In the East to West category I have also included living composers, where they have taken up citizenship of another country. The third category is more specific. It includes all those who either fled the Nazis or who were imprisoned by the Nazis or were deported to concentration camps and more often than not murdered, and those who were forced to go into hiding. The fourth category includes those who emigrated to Israel (or Palestine before 1948) or making *aliyah la-aretz* (see Glossary). I have only included those who went to Israel with the intention of settling; some settled permanently and others settled for a shorter time, then often moved to America.

Table 2
MIGRATIONS OF COMPOSERS OF JEWISH DESCENT

Category of migration	Numbers/total	Percentage
1. Composers whose country of birth and country of death differs	96/181	53
2. Composers who migrated from East to West	97/257	38
3. Composers who either fled or hid from Nazi persecution or deportation and/or were killed by the Nazis	93/257	36
4. Composers who emigrated to Israel (or Palestine before 1948)	29/257	11

Note: Data taken from the entries in Part II of this book. 'East to West' is defined in the text.

Perhaps the most important conclusion from these analyses is the notion of the 'wandering Jew' being applied to the last 200 years as much as to the earlier centuries. It would seem that being an alien emphasized the need to succeed, often in unfavourable circumstances. This theme is taken up again in sections 3.6 and 3.7.

3.5 THE IMPORTANCE OF CULTURE AND CULTURAL EVOLUTION

When asked the question by an interviewer why there were so many good Jewish musicians, Nathan Milstein responded by saying: 'Well I have known many bad ones!' But on further questioning, Milstein said that he thought it was not genetic but rather was due to upbringing and discipline. He was thinking mainly of performers rather than composers, but the same may hold true for composers.[31]

As mentioned in the previous section, the philsopher Karl Popper stated in his autobiography that musicality runs in families but that the development of European music seems too recent to be genetically based. A complex genetic change is only likely to occur over many generations. Popper also discussed how polyphony arose in European music and went on to draw parallels between the creation of a great work of music and a great scientific discovery, particularly in its initial conception.[32]

Albert Einstein, writing in 1938, believed that the great contribution Jews had made towards progress of knowledge in the widest sense had not been through 'any special wealth of endowment, but to the fact that the esteem in which intellectual accomplishment is held among the Jews creates an atmosphere particularly favourable to the developments of any talents that may exist'. He further pointed out that Jews are 'a mixed race just as are all other groups of our civilization', and that 'even more than its own tradition, the Jewish group has thrived on oppression and on antagonism it has forever met in the world'.[33]

The importance of culture and tradition rather than genetic endowment is well illustrated by historian Steven Beller's discussion of the 'over-representation' of Jews in many areas of intellectual life in *fin-de-siècle* Vienna. Of many factors that he discusses, the differing attitudes of Jews and Catholics in general towards education is relevant. 'The religious Jew had to study as the central tenet of his religion; the Catholic did not have to study unless he was to be a priest.' Although education among practising Jews was primarily focused on the Talmud, with emancipation this broadened into more general education. Attitudes towards authority also differed. Catholic teaching was generally more authoritarian and strongly promoted acceptance of the doctrine handed down by priests. Jewish education promoted discussion. Differing attitudes towards science were particularly significant. Whereas Christian churches came to fear discoveries of science, especially if they conflicted with dogma, Judaism generally welcomed new discoveries as evidence of God's ways. These are simplifications of a number of complex factors, but do nevertheless point to differences in Jewish culture that resulted in better than average education and a greater receptivity towards creative activity.[34]

Michael Chanan has explained the preponderance of important Jewish thinkers and artists such as Marx, Freud, Wittgenstein, Mahler, Schoenberg, Kafka, Chagall and Modigliani, not to some special 'Jewish genius' but rather to the fact of living on the borderlines between cultures, nations and religions, exposed to all their contradictions. Straddling the different cultures and struggling with the internal conflicts that they are forced to negotiate daily, Jewish intellectuals conceive reality as a dynamic process and see society as being in a state of contradiction and flux. This condition was especially acute in *fin-de-siècle* Vienna.[35]

In the preceding paragraphs I have described the views of a musician, philosopher, scientist, historian and music critic. This represents only a small sample of eminent thinkers, but it does all point to the importance of culture in explaining the preponderance of composers of Jewish descent in the last 200 years. How does this fit in with current thinking on cultural evolution? The theory of biological evolution by natural selection proposed by Darwin in the nineteenth century is now widely accepted by scientists and has a very substantial mechanistic framework. Genes have been isolated and fully characterized and their mechanism of action and the nature of mutation is well understood.

By comparison, understanding cultural evolution is in its infancy. In 1976 Richard Dawkins discussed cultural evolution in the final chapter of his book *The Selfish Gene.*[36] Dawkins introduced the term *meme*, a contraction of the Greek *mimeme*, meaning 'imitation'. The meme is proposed as the unit of transmission in cultural evolution, as the counterpart of the gene in biological evolution. 'Culture' in the sense of the total of inherited ideas, beliefs, values and knowledge is transmitted, not only 'vertically' from generation to generation, but also 'horizontally' within populations. The unit of transmission has been described as a meme. A meme might be a mental representation of ideas, behaviours or other imagined concepts. It would be capable of being replicated, and also modified, by analogy with gene replication and mutation. Ideas can be passed from individual to individual; they may also be modified in the process. Memes might be encoded via some form of neuron activation in the brain. Whereas genes are transmitted from cell to cell during cell division, memes would be transmitted from individual to individual. Cultural evolution rests on a foundation of genetic evolution. This applies especially to our brains and the neurons contained within them. Cultural evolution proceeds at a very much faster rate.

Since Dawkins's initial proposal in 1976, there have been many publications on the subject of memetics and cultural evolution, and these have been reviewed.[37] However, the subject is still very controversial and many would say that memetics has not lived up to its potential.[38] Proponents point to the fact that genes were not even a theoretical construct at the time of Darwin's *Origin of Species*. A meme may be a useful concept in trying to explain cultural evolution, but a serious limitation is how to test for its existence. It would not be appropriate here while discussing the preponderance of composers of Jewish descent to consider memes in more detail, but an important conclusion is that cultural rather than genetic evolution is likely to be the basis for understanding this preponderance. Cultural evolution can occur much more rapidly than biological evolution through a community.[39] For example, a piece of information such as a new musical composition can be transmitted to a whole community rapidly, but a new mutant gene for some highly advantageous trait transmits slowly, and therefore having a selective advantage takes many generations. The mechanism of the latter process is well understood, and was explained mathematically in 1908 by Hardy and Weinberg;[40] the former is still poorly understood in scientific terms, although it is assumed to involve some neuronal circuitry. The importance of cultural evolution is highlighted when we consider that the total number of genes in the human genome is relatively small (see section 3.2.2), especially when compared to the number of nerve cells in the brain, which is more than a trillion (US trillion = 10^{12}). Thus the neuronal circuitry in the human brain is far too complex to be completely subject to genetic control.[41] It is very likely that cultural evolution rather than biological evolution is much more important in explaining behavioural phenomena and memory. Thus the expression of Jewish talent, not only in the field of music but also in the arts and sciences more generally, since the beginning of the nineteenth century appears to be largely the result of cultural evolution.

If genes were largely responsible for behavioural traits, and they were subject to natural selection, one might expect the urge to have children to be strongly favoured by selection. This would maximize the transmission of genes present in an individual to subsequent generations. This is the reverse of the cultural trends seen in most of today's societies, where many choose to have small families or no families, thereby making a small or non-existent genetic contribution to the future.[42] Within the Jewish population it is the ultra-Orthodox who come closest to realizing their genetic contribution to future generations; they follow the biblical injunctions 'Be fruitful and multiply; a nation and company of nations shall be of thee, and kings shall come out of thy loins' (Genesis 25:11) and 'My blessing upon you and make your descendents as numerous as the stars in heaven and the sands on the seashore' (Genesis 22:17).

3.6 HOW ARE COMPOSERS OF JEWISH DESCENT PERCEIVED FROM WITHOUT?

Any pronouncements about national characteristics, whilst they may have elements of truth in them when applied to a nation or race collectively, will never be found to apply to all individuals within those groups. This is true of expressions such as 'Teutonic thoroughness', 'canny Scots', and 'American brashness', to name but a few. So whilst it may be possible to make some generalizations about composers of Jewish descent, it is unlikely these will be true in all cases. Among the earliest and certainly the most notorious statements made about Jewish composers since the beginning of the Enlightenment were those made by Wagner (1813–83). He expressed his views on many aspects connected with Jews and Judaism and these have been widely discussed.[43] Here I consider only the points he made about compositions by Jewish composers. A debate on the 'artistic taste of the Hebrews' in the *Neue Zeitschrift für Musik* in 1850 prompted Wagner to write his article *Das Judentum in der Musik*.[44] At the time the article was published anonymously, but Wagner had it reprinted in 1869, together with a preface protesting about Jewish persecution of himself. So much of Wagner's writings and pronouncements about Jews is racist, unreasonable and may be described as immoderate, and this has led, understandably, to many of his opponents dismissing all that is in the article as racist rubbish. Magee[45] points out that within the article there is a proposition that, although couched in emotive language, is worth consideration. Wagner considered that because Jews at that time were not fully assimilated, they were not part of the German culture and therefore, in composing in the style of the time, all they could do was imitate the new culture that surrounded them, but of which they were not yet a part. He considered their compositions to be superficial and imitative. Meyerbeer was the composer most criticized, although not named in the article; Mendelssohn was also criticized. Whilst it may have been true of many German Jews that they were not fully culturally assimilated, it seems hardly true of Meyerbeer and Mendelssohn, both of whom were educated privately and whose families were highly cultured and well educated. To use a similar comparison from the twentieth century, one would not consider someone like Isaiah Berlin, who was born in Riga, as not being part of any British school of philosophy, nor Alexander Goehr, born in Berlin, as not being a British composer.

Both Mendelssohn and Meyerbeer travelled extensively throughout Europe. Although Mendelssohn may not have reached the very highest rank of composers, there can be little doubt that his finest works are inspired and not imitative, and that his best works are outstanding. Meyerbeer's music is much less frequently played nowadays. The conception of his operas has a weak basis, especially when compared to those of Wagner. His operas were often composed in such a way as to make use of the singers whose voices Meyerbeer most admired. Thus a plot would be conceived around particular singers, rather than with the inspiration lying in the story itself. Wagner's approach was, of course, quite the reverse. Wagner describes Meyerbeer's music as being shallow and imitative. Two of Wagner's quotations about Meyerbeer illustrate this. The first concerns the evolution of opera.

> Above all it is noteworthy that he merely *followed* on this march, and never kept *abreast* of, to say nothing of outstripping it. He was like the starling who follows the ploughshare down the field, and merrily picks up the earthworm just uncovered in the furrow.

The second concerns his purported imitation of Rossini.

> Thus he became the weathercock of European opera music, that always veers at first uncertain with the shift of wind, and comes to a standstill only when the wind itself has settled on its quarter.

Nevertheless, Meyerbeer's operas were amongst the most successful Grand Operas of his time, and although his private wealth and having Jewish managers may have helped, these were only some of the factors leading to their success. Paris was the home of Grand Opera. At the time Chopin remarked of Paris: 'I like what I see in this city – the best musicians and the best opera in the world.' Meyerbeer's most successful opera, *Les Huguenots*, was even being compared with *Fidelio*, although Schumann, in his 1837 review, is in no doubt that it is far inferior.[46] Of it he writes scathingly: 'Meyerbeer's ultimate superficiality, want of originality and lack of style are as familiar as his talent for fancy trimmings, the fabrication of brilliant and dramatic episodes, his skill in instrumentation and the great variety of forms.' The reputation of Paris was such that many musicians made it their second home, and besides Meyerbeer these included Rossini, Bellini, Donizetti, Liszt, Chopin and Spontini. So it was no mean feat that Meyerbeer appeared the 'top dog' in a city regarded as the centre of opera.

However, it is important to remember that until after the French Revolution only the aristocracy attended the opera, and that even in the first half of the nineteenth century, although ordinary citizens could attend, the high cost generally prevented this. At the time opera served more a social function and was regarded more for its spectacle than its musical content, whereas by the second half of the nineteenth century, when Wagner and Verdi were regarded as the greatest opera composers, the receptivity of audiences was changing.

Whilst Meyerbeer's operas have their weaknesses, they were also innovative. Meyerbeer challenged the norms of the times. The censors would not allow the performance of *Les Hugenots* in Berlin until six years after its premiere in Paris, because it involved the massacre of Protestants by Catholics. Even before the French premiere the censors forced Meyerbeer to modify the scene involving the blessing of the daggers, because the representation of Catherine de Medici on stage was forbidden. Whilst Meyerbeer was enjoying enormous success with his operas, the only truly French opera composer of note, and contemporary with Meyerbeer, was Berlioz. He had great difficulty in having his operas performed, and arguably his greatest, *Les Troyens*, was not performed during his lifetime. It would be unjust to regard the developments in opera in the latter part of the nineteenth century as simply reaction to the mediocrity of French Grand Opera, since many of its stylistic elements were taken up by later composers, including Wagner, Verdi and Bizet.

Wagner was not only critical of Jewish composers but also of synagogue music, as is evident from the following quotation:

> Who has not had occasion to convince himself of the travesty of a divine service of song, presented in a real folk synagogue? Who has not been seized with a feeling of the greatest revulsion, of horror mingled with the absurd, at hearing that sense-and-sound-confounding gurgle, yodel, and cackle, which no intentional caricature can make more repugnant than as offered here in full, in naïve seriousness?

Liszt was not on the whole favourably disposed towards Jewish musicians, and he considered the achievements of Jewish composers such as Mendelssohn and Meyerbeer to be largely imitative. Nevertheless, he gives a very different picture to that of Wagner, regarding synagogue music:

> In Vienna we knew the famous tenor Sulzer, who served in the capacity of precentor in the Synagogue, and whose reputation was so out-standing ... We went to the Synagogue in order to hear him ... For moments we could penetrate into the real soul and recognize the secret doctrines of the fathers. Seldom were we so deeply stirred by emotion as on that evening, so shaken that our soul was entirely given to meditation and to participation in the service.[47]

It seems to be a case of *chacun à son goût!*

The logic of the argument, that Jews in Europe were not fully assimilated by the mid-nineteenth century because emancipation had only recently occurred, either applies to a much lesser extent, or does not apply at all by the twentieth century. What are the views of twentieth-century writers and composers? The composer and musicologist Vincent d'Indy (1851–1931) argued along similar lines to those of Wagner, although his agenda was some-what different.[48] D'Indy was a staunch French nationalist throughout his life. His became a member of La Ligue de la Patrie Française, was an anti-Dreyfusite and a joint-founder, in 1894, of the Schola Cantorum. At a time of national self-consciousness throughout Europe, towards the end of the nineteenth century and the beginning of the twentieth century, d'Indy was particularly concerned with the maintenance of a pure French culture, free from other national influences. He regarded most of the operas written in nineteenth-century France as 'decadent' and servile meretricious imitations of successful Italian composers. This, he felt, was the inevitable influence of French Jewish composers such as AUBER, ADAM, HALEVY, HEROLD, and Meyerbeer (who although German, lived most of his life in France). In his composition classes d'Indy attempted to explain 'rationally' why a Jew was incapable of writing music of any value. For centuries Jewish culture was totally neglected, just as Jewish religious traditions were ostracized and persecuted. Those traditions were, in any case, of no wide concern and repre-sented no danger, until, with emancipation, the development of a Jewish intelligentsia and the concurrent growth of national self-consciousness throughout Europe. Jewish composers were not only superficial but also incapable of true originality, and were mercenary, in search of gain, as well as derivative in art. 'The Jew possesses a gift of assimilation that allows him to produce amazing, if superficial, imitations, as evidenced by Auber, Hèrold, Felicien David and Offenbach'.[49] For someone who clearly expressed both anti-Semitism and nationalism, d'Indy's views were at times paradoxical. For example, Meyerbeer was the idol of his youth. The idea for d'Indy's opera

Fervaal (1897) was suggested to him by Wagner, and its melodramatic style is very much influenced by Meyerbeer. D'Indy helped in the revival of Salamone Rossi's music, by editing his *Cantiques de S. Rossi*. His anti-Semitism never appeared to upset his good relationship with Dukas. His third opera, *La Legende de Saint Christophe*, is anti-Semitic in tone. After hearing Strauss's opera *Electra*, d'Indy commented to a friend: 'I find it simply hideous – hideous in its subject – hideous in its music – hideous in its orchestra – hideous in its writing … it seems to me the peak of Jewish music, and indeed a monstrous successor to the art of Meyerbeer.' Strauss was not a Jew. His pronouncement on Schoenberg is just as revealing:

> He is a madman, Schoenberg teaches nothing except that you should write everything which comes into your head. This isn't teaching, it's just opinion! His work, interesting at first, is no more than a mass of meaningless notes … Art demands thought, construction, rhythm, form, equilibrium.

These comments reveal ignorance as much as they do prejudice: Schoenberg gave his pupils a thorough grounding in musical theory, a subject about which he was very knowledgeable.[50]

The American 'equivalent' of d'Indy was Daniel Gregory Mason (1873–1953), a composer and writer on music from a musical family going back to his grandfather Lowell Mason. His music is very rarely played today. Mason saw himself as the standard bearer of the white, Anglo-Saxon, upper middle-class New England tradition, particularly against the onrush of black American and other immigrant musicians. He saw, in the works of second generation Russian Jews, such as Gershwin, Copland, Gruenberg, ORNSTEIN, Irving Berlin and Bernstein, the imminent downfall of the cultivated, Europhilic ideals inherited from his father, uncle and grandfather.[51] In 1920 he wrote in an article entitled 'Is American Music Growing Up?':

> The insidiousness of the Jewish menace to our artistic integrity … is due to speciousness, the superficial charm and persuasiveness of Hebrew art, its violently juxtaposed extremes of passion, its poignant eroticism and pessimism.

Eleven years later he was still writing on the same theme:

> Our whole contemporary aesthetic attitude toward instrumental music, especially in New York, is dominated by Jewish tastes and standards, with their Oriental extravagance, their sensuous brilliancy and intellectual facility and superficiality.[52]

Stravinsky (1882–1971) made it clear, in a review of Wagner's prose writings that include *Das Judentum in der Musik*, that he believed Wagner's writing to be both illogical and untrue. Stravinsky also pointed to the eclecticism in his own music as follows:

> But where is the 'truth on the subject'? In the logic which attributes a composer's failure in 'formal productive faculty' to his Jewishness? Then what of the same failure in all the others? And where is the 'truth' in the contention that 'mimicry' is a particularly Jewish characteristic in music? In fact, critics of my own music in the nineteen-twenties might have taken their cue from Wagner's tirade on this subject: 'The Jew musician hurls together the diverse forms and styles of every age and every master.'[53]

Lack of originality is an accusation also made against Mahler. After he visited St Petersburg in 1907 and conducted his fifth symphony, he was strongly criticized by the press and by Rimsky-Korsakov. Typical of the comments was that from the very serious *Russkaya Muzykalnaya Gazeta* (Russian musical gazette): 'his musical ideas with which he works lack originality and fail to reveal a creative personality. At best they are "reminiscences from operas and concerts" whose melodic quality often shows less than good taste.'[54] Few critics would react to his fifth symphony like that nowadays.

Nadia Boulanger (1887–1979) appears to have expressed her views on Jewish musicians, but only verbally.[55] Although at one time she supported liberal causes, Boulanger became sympathetic towards the organization Action Française. This organization was founded at the time of the Dreyfus affair and was a right-wing anti-Semitic organization aimed at protecting French culture. At the same time she still took on Jewish pupils. She thought of Jews as being members of another race and she tried to avoid having too many in her class at one time. She believed that Jews had the abilities to become good performers and teachers, but as a group they had little talent for creative endeavour. She did not reveal these feelings to her Jewish students and their acquaintances, but confided her prejudices to her Catholic friends. Her attitudes at times appear quite inconsistent. Amongst her Jewish pupils were Arthur Berger, BERLINSKI, Copland, Diamond, Irving Fine, Glass, SETER, Shapero, SHLONSKY, Siegmeister, Singer, SPIES, Suzanne Bloch, daughter of Ernest BLOCH, and performers including Daniel Barenboim. Her non-Jewish pupils included Elliot Carter, Roy Harris, Virgil Thomson and Walter Piston in America; Lennox Berkeley and Nicolas Maw in England; Thea Musgrave in Scotland; and Jean Francaix, Igor Markevitch and Marcelle de Manziarly in France. Looking at their present-day standing as composers, it is not obvious that one group has fared better than the other. At times Boulanger praised the music of Schoenberg, Milhaud, Gershwin and Copland. In an interview with Vivian Perlis in 1976 Boulanger describes Copland as a very gifted composer.[56] Unfortunately the topic of Jewish composers does not seem to have been touched on in Monsaingeon's *Conversations with Nadia Boulanger* (1985).

However, she is photographed presenting Leonard Bernstein with the Légion d'Honneur, one of France's greatest honours.[57]

In conclusion, we can say that Wagner, d'Indy, Mason and Boulanger, all of whom at times have shown anti-Semitic leanings, made the point that composers of Jewish origin either lack the imagination, or the cultural background, or both, to be good composers.

The accusation that Jewish composers are imitative was also levelled by the composer and writer Constant Lambert (1905–51), and not at all surprisingly by Theophil Stengel and Herbert Gerigk in their book *Lexikon der Juden in der Musik* (see Appendix I). Lambert, in his iconoclastic book *Music Ho: A Study of Music in Decline*,[58] directed his fire at Jewish jazz composers. Writing in 1933, he pointed out that 'most jazz is written and performed by cosmopolitan Jews'. He continued to elaborate:

> The importance of the Jewish element in jazz cannot be too strongly emphasized, and the fact that at least ninety percent of jazz tunes are written by Jews undoubtedly goes far to account for the curious sagging quality – so typical of Jewish art – the almost masochistic melancholy of the average foxtrot. The masochistic element is becoming more and more a part of general consciousness, but it has its stronghold in the Jewish temperament … There is an obvious link between the exiled and persecuted Jews and the exiled and persecuted Negroes, which Jews, with their admirable capacity for drinking the beer of those who have knocked down the skittles, have not been slow to turn to their advantage. But although the Jews have stolen the Negroes' thunder, although Al Jolson's nauseating blubbering masquerades as savage lamenting, although Tin Pan Alley has become a commercial Wailing Wall, the only jazz music of technical importance is that small section of it that is genuine Negroid. The 'hot' Negro records still have a genuine galvanic energy, while the blues have a certain austerity that places them far above the sweet nothings of George Gershwin.

Norman Lebrecht described Lambert as 'An exotic, toxic growth in the English garden'.[59] One should not be put off by Lambert's forthright style, which in today's parlance is not 'politically correct', when considering whether or not there are some elements of truth in his comments. Lambert's comments are about jazz, which is not the subject of this book. However, I believe the 'masochistic melancholy' having its stronghold in the Jewish temperament, some would consider as a fair description of certain aspects of Mahler's symphonies and songs. When Blitzstein was told that people found Jewish-sounding music in his work, he often agreed, saying that it was the element of self-pity and mysticism they were picking out.[60]

Bryan Magee, in his *Aspects of Wagner: New Light on the Most Controversial Composer of all Time*,[61] examined Wagner's propositions in *Das Judentum in der Musik* over a century after the article was first published. He was particularly concerned to examine the central proposition, whilst fully acknowledging that it was commingled with so much repellent racism that this had led to the central proposition being overlooked. Magee states early on of Jews: 'In no field has their contribution been more outstanding than in music.' And goes on to cite Mahler and Schoenberg as composers, followed by a list of outstanding Jewish performers. A similar point is also made by Goodall, who suggests that 'the Jewish community, beginning in the last half of the nineteenth century, transformed musical culture as profoundly as it did science, law, philosophy, medicine literature art and politics'.[62] The thrust of Magee's argument was that Jews had lived in a closed authoritarian culture where basic assumptions were not challenged. In the area of music and art, the banning of instrumental music and graven images from the synagogue was a major restriction. The Jewish Enlightenment brought about a comparative freedom from authority and allowed creativity to flourish. Magee also pointed out that virtually all the Jews who achieved the highest levels of attainment, for example, Spinoza, Heine, Mendelssohn, Marx, Disraeli, Freud, Mahler, Einstein, Trotsky, Kafka, Wittgenstein and Schoenberg, repudiated Judaism. Only in comparative freedom does individual creativeness flourish, for example in ancient Greece and later in the Renaissance, and that 'Jewish composers of Wagner's day were among the first emancipated Jews, pastless in the society in which they were living and working. They spoke its language with literally a foreign accent.' In effect, because they were not yet fully embedded in their surrounding culture, however gifted, their work would be shallow by the standards of great art. Wagner applied this argument to Mendelssohn as a composer. Magee then pointed out: 'Ones does not need to share Wagner's view of Mendelssohn to see that this argument is substantially correct.' Whilst Wagner's proposition may be substantially correct for the average Jew emerging from the ghetto, when considering the greatest achievers we are not looking at the 'average'. By 1850, when Wagner was writing and certainly by 1869 when he issued the revised version of the article, those Jews whom one might include as the greatest achievers as composers and performers, for example Mendelssohn, Meyerbeer, Hiller, David, Joachim and Moscheles, by the time they were adolescents were well-educated, fluent in languages, widely travelled and, apart from Joachim, came from emancipated backgrounds.

Whilst there is clearly some validity in Wagner's theory, he does not seem to have considered any of its predictive values. As Magee pointed out, any inability of Jews to produce great art that Wagner claimed, should only apply to the transitional period of emancipation, and that it should diminish if full emancipation occurred with subsequent generations.

3.7 ISRAELI COMPOSERS: 'REVERSE ASSIMILATION'

Much of the argument that Wagner, and to some extent Boulanger, used was that Jews were outside the culture of the country in which they lived, and, not being part of it, could only imitate it. Since the founding of the State of Israel in 1948 it has become possible to see what happens when Jews have their own country and form the majority and not the minority of a population. In a sense, as far as musical composition is concerned, a process of 'reverse assimilation' is at work and culture is predominantly Jewish. At the beginning of the Enlightenment many Jews became assimilated and their music was associated with the traditions of the country in which they lived. Schoenberg is an obvious example, where he claimed to be following in the tradition of Beethoven, Brahms and Wagner. In Israel many composers have attempted the reverse this, that is to create a distinctly Israeli music. Half a century has elapsed since the founding of the State of Israel, but this is a relatively short time in which to assess whether a composer will go down to posterity as a great composer. As can be seen from Part II of this book, there is an abundance of Israeli composers; 40 of 258 of those listed are either *sabras* (see Glossary) or have immigrated to Israel either permanently or for a significant period. Gradenwitz[63] gives a full account of music in Israel from earliest times to the end of the twentieth century; the period 1880–1948, prior to the formation of the State of Israel, has been described by Hirschberg,[64] and Fleisher[65] gives a contemporary view by Israeli composers.

There can be no doubt that Israelis have produced outstanding performers during that period, and that Israel has been a receptive environment for music; the Israel Philharmonic has over 30,0000 subscribers, yet Tel Aviv and Jerusalem only have just over a million inhabitants. But has Israel produced outstanding composers? Israeli composers included by Gradenwitz and Fleisher are BEN HAIM, PARTOS, BOSKOVICH, TAL, Seter, STERNBERG, JACOBY, ALEXANDER, BRUN, AVIDOM, DAUS, EHRLICH, GILBOA, ORGAD, AVNI, KOPYTMAN, DORFMAN, RADZYNSKI, SADAI, PAPORISZ, SHERIFF, MA'AYANI, OLIVERO, FLEISCHER, LEEF, RAN, Aharon Harlap, Arik Shapira, Daniel Galay, Gabriel Iranyi, Stephen Horenstein, Noa Permont, Ari Ben-Shabetai and Oded Zehavi. Although their works are widely performed in Israel, they are only occasionally heard outside the country, if at all. They are not in the same 'league' as the outstanding European composers of the mid to late twentieth century, such as Britten in England, Messiaen in France, Henze in Germany, Berio in Italy, Penderecki in Poland and Pärt in Estonia. Apart from Estonia, Israel does, of course, have a much smaller population, roughly the size of Scotland. Half a century at most is also a short period of time to assess whether a work will become an established one in the world's concert repertoire. Nevertheless, there are many contemporary works by other composers from other countries that have now become established. A simple way in which to assess their current popularity throughout the West is assessing a composer's citation in reference books, and how extensively their compositions have been recorded. The latter, of course, partly depends on commercial factors, as well as the intrinsic merit of the work. Using these very rough criteria Israeli composers do not score well. For example, a search of *The Rough Guide to Classical Music,*[66] *The Rough Guide to Opera,*[67] *The Oxford Dictionary of Opera*[68] and *Modern Music and After: Directions Since 1945*[69] produces only a single entry for any of the composers listed above, namely Tal for his operas *Ashmedai* and *Massada 967*. This result may, of course, represent a somewhat western European bias, but it seems unlikely this is the only reason.

Another factor is the focus on a form of national music. As in the case of American music throughout the first half of the twentieth century, composers, for example Copland, felt the need to create a distinctly American style, and now a distinctly American style is widely recognized. However, a 'national style' for Israeli music appears to have a much more limited appeal outside Israel. Arnold Schoenberg's somewhat self-centred reaction was forthright. In 1938 he wrote that Jews 'have never shown any interest in my music ... and now, into the bargain, in Palestine they are out to develop, artificially, an authentically Jewish kind of music, which rejects what I have achieved'.[70] When Schoenberg was asked for his co-operation by the founders of the World Centre for Jewish Music in 1938 he did not bother to reply. Nearly forty years on, in 1977, the musicologist and writer Hans Keller visited Israel. Whilst he was complementary about certain works by Israeli composers, he was quite scathing about the 'national style':[71]

> In order to produce national music, a dangerous undertaking at the most productive of musical times, you have to have an identifiable musical folklore in the second place, and a nationally committed genius like Bedrich Smetana in the first place – in which case your nationally committed music turns international before you can say Arnold Schoenberg, whose *De Profundis* (dedicated to the State of Israel) shows all those Israeli songs where to get off so long as my two conditions are not fulfilled.

This criticism does not apply to other forms of Israeli music, such as *klezmer*, that have been widely recorded and are often heard in concerts throughout the world.

It does seem that on the whole composers of Jewish descent are at their best when feeling outsiders within a culture, when they have something to prove and are able to seize an opportunity, rather than when they are the majority culture, as in Israel, even though many are immigrants from countries as different as America, Russia and the Yemen.

NOTES

1. Steven Beller, *Vienna and the Jews 1867–1938: a Cultural History* (Cambridge: Cambridge University Press, 1989), pp. 33–42 and 47.
2. CE (Christian Era) and BCE (Before the Christian Era) are equivalent to AD and BC.
3. Jonathan Sachs, *Radical Then, Radical Now* (London: Harper, 2000), p. 22.
4. David Goldstein, 'Different Maternal and Paternal Histories in the Founding of Jewish Populations', paper presented to the 21st International Conference on Jewish Genealogy, London, July 2001.
5. Geoffrey Alderman, *Modern British Jewry* (Oxford: Clarendon Press, 1992), pp. 1–2.
6. Darryl Lyman, *Great Jews in Music* (New York: Jonathan David, 1986), p. 15.
7. Raphael Patai and Jennifer P. Wing, *The Myth of the Jewish Race* (New York: Scribner, 1975).
8. Robert C. King and William D. Stansfield, *A Dictionary of Genetics*, 3rd edn (Oxford: Oxford University Press, 1985).
9. Steven Rose, Leon J. Kamin and R. C. Lewontin, *Not in our Genes: Biology, Ideology and Human Nature* (Harmondsworth: Penguin, 1984), pp. 119–27; G. Barbujani, A. Magagni, E. Minch and L. L. Cavalli-Sforza, 'An Apportionment of Human DNA Diversity', *Proceedings of the National Academy of Sciences, USA*, 94 (1997), pp. 4516–19; Paul R. Ehrlich, *Human Natures: Genes, Cultures and the Human Prospect* (Harmondsworth: Penguin, 2000), pp. 290–7; Michael R. Cummings, *Human Heredity: Principles and Issues*, 3rd edn (St Paul, MN: West, 1994), pp. 498–516; Mark Ridley, *Evolution*, 2nd edn (Oxford: Blackwell, 1996), pp. 488–90; Monroe W. Strickberger, *Evolution*, 2nd edn (Sudbury, MA: Jones & Bartlett, 2000), pp. 581–3.
10. K. Owens and M.-C. King 'Genomic Views of Human History', *Science*, 286 (1999), pp. 451–3.
11. Gregory Livshits, Robert R. Sokal and Eugene Kobyliansky, 'Genetic Affinities of Jewish Populations', *American Journal of Human Genetics*, 49 (1991), pp. 131–46.
12. M. F, Hammer, A. J. Redd, E. T. Wood, *et al.*, 'Jewish and Middle Eastern non-Jewish Populations Share a Common Pool of Y-Chromosome Bialleleic Haplotypes'. *Proceedings of the National Academy of Sciences*, 97 (2000), pp. 6769–74.
13. K. Skorecki, S. Selig, S. Blazer, *et al.*, 'Y Chromosomes of Jewish Priests', *Nature*, 385 (1997), p. 32.
14. Jared M. Diamond, 'Jewish Lysosomes', *Nature*, 368 (1994), pp. 291–2; Kelly Owens and Mary-Claire King, 'Genomic Views of Human History', *Science*, 286 (1999), pp. 451–3.
15. R. Durst, R. Colombo, S. Shpitzen, *et al.*, 'Recent Origin and Spread of a Common Lithuanian Mutation, G197delLDLR, Causing Familial Hypocholesterolaemia: positive selection is not always necessary to account for disease incidence among Ashkenazi Jews', *American Journal of Human Genetics*, 68 (2001), pp. 1172–88.
16. Mark Ridley, 'Near the End of the Line? How DNA Can Trace our Ancestry from Fossils to *Homo Sapiens*', *Times Literary Supplement* (19 October 2001), pp. 3–4; Barmak Modrek and Christopher Lee, 'A Genomic View of Alternative Splicing', *Nature Genetics*, 30 (2002), pp. 13–19.
17. Gerald M. Rubin, 'Comparing Species', *Nature*, 409 (2001), pp. 820–1; J. G. Hacia, 'Genome of Apes', *Trends in Genetics*, 17 (2001), pp. 637–45.
18. Mark Ridley, 'How we Got Here and Where we are Going', *Science*, 290 (2000), pp. 1102–3.
19. Peter D. Snustad, Michael J. Simmons and John B. Jenkins, *Principles of Genetics* (New York: Wiley, 1997), pp. 710–12.
20. See Patai and Wing, *Myth of the Jewish Race*, pp. 145–56.
21. See Rose, Kamin and Lewontin, *Not in our Genes*, pp. 95–100.
22. R. Pearson, *Race, Intelligence and Bias in Academe* (Washington, DC: Scott-Townsend, 1991).
23. Stephen J. Gould, *The Mismeasure of Man* (Harmondsworth: Penguin, 1996).
24. See Ehrlich, *Human Natures*, p. 5.
25. Ullica Segerstråle, *Defenders of the Truth: the Sociobiology Debate* (Oxford: Oxford University Press, 2000), pp. 235–40 and 275–94.

26. J. B. Davis, *The Psychology of Music* (London: Hutchinson, 1968), p. 113.
27. Karl Popper, *Unending Quest: an Intellectual Autobiography* (London: Routledge, 1992), p. 53.
28. Reser (1935), quoted in R. Shuter, *The Psychology of Musical Ability* (London: Methuen, 1968).
29. R. Shuter-Dyson, 'Musical Ability', in D. Deutsch (ed.), *The Psychology of Music* (Orlando: Academic Press, 1982), pp. 391–412.
30. D. Drayna, A. Manichaikul, M. de Lange, H. Sneider and T. Spector, 'Genetic Correlates of Musical Pitch Recognition in Humans', *Science*, 291 (2001), pp. 1969–72.
31. Bruno Monsaingeon, *The Art of the Violin: the Devil's Instrument* (Warner Music Group Company, 8573-85801–3, 2000).
32. See Popper, *Unending Quest*, pp. 53–72.
33. Albert Einstein, *Ideas and Opinions* (London: Souvenir Press, 1973), p. 195.
34. See Beller, *Vienna and the Jews*, p. 90.
35. Michael Chanan, *From Handel to Hendrix: the Composer in the Public Sphere* (London: Verso, 1999), pp. 204–5.
36. Richard Dawkins, *The Selfish Gene* (Oxford: Oxford University Press, 1976), pp. 203–15.
37. Susan Blackmore, *The Meme Machine* (Oxford: Oxford University Press, 1999), and 'The Power of Memes', *Scientific American*, 283 (2000), pp. 64–6.
38. Richard Aunger, *Darwinizing Culture* (Oxford: Oxford University Press, 2000).
39. See Ehrlich, *Human Natures*, p. 5.
40. See Snustad, Simmons and Jenkins, *Principles of Genetics*, pp. 722–6.
41. See Ehrlich, *Human Natures*, p. 4.
42. Ibid., p. 8.
43. Barry Millington, *Wagner* (London: Dent, 1984); D. Borchmeyer, *Richard Wagner: Theory and Theatre* (Oxford: Oxford University Press, 1982); Michael Tanner, *Wagner* (London: Panther, 1997); Brian Magee, *Wagner and Philosophy* (Harmondsworth: Penguin, 2000).
44. A. Goldman and E. Springhorn, *Wagner in Music and Drama*, trans. H. A. Ellis (London: Gollancz, 1970), pp. 51–9.
45. See Magee, *Wagner and Philosophy*, pp. 343–80.
46. Henry Pleasants, *Schumann on Music: a Selection from the Writings* (New York: Dover, 1988), pp. 137–40.
47. Arthur Holde, *Jews in Music* (New York: Bloch Publishing, 1974), p. 297; E. Gartenburg, *Vienna: its Musical Heritage* (Pennsylvania State University Press, 1968), p. 111.
48. Pierre Boulez, *Orientations: Collected Writings* (London: Faber, 1986), pp. 223–30; Jane F. Fulcher, 'The Preparation for Vichy: Anti-Semitism in French Musical Culture Between the Two World Wars', *Musical Quarterly*, 73 (1995), pp. 458–75; Jane F. Fulcher, 'A Political Barometer of Twentieth-Century France: Wagner as Jew or Anti-Semite', *Musical Quarterly*, 78 (2000), pp. 41–57.
49. See Fulcher, 'Political Barometer', p. 51, and Vincent d'Indy, 'Une ecole d'art réspondant aux besoins modernes', *La Tribune de Saint-Gervais* (November 1900), pp. 303–14.
50. Andrew Thomson, *Vincent d'Indy and his World* (Oxford: Clarendon Press, 1996), pp. 214–15.
51. John W. Struble, *The History of American Classical Music* (New York: Facts on File, 1995), p. 84.
52. Jonathan Bellman, 'The "Noble Pathways of the National": Romantic and Modern Reactions to National Music', *Pendragon Review*, 1 (2002), p. 52; Richard Crawford, *America's Musical Life: a History* (New York: W. W. Norton, 2001), p. 782.
53. Igor Stravinsky and Robert Craft, *Themes and Episodes* (New York: Alfred A. Knopf, 1967).
54. Henry-Louis La Grange, *Gustav Mahler*, vol. 3, *Vienna: Triumph and Disillusion* (Oxford: Oxford University Press, 1999), pp. 762–4.
55. Léonie Rosenstiel, *Nadia Boulanger: a Life in Music* (New York: W. W. Norton, 1998), p. 98.
56. Aaron Copland and Vivian Perlis, *Copland: 1900 through 1942* (New York: St Martins Press, 1984), pp. 68–70 and 171.
57. Bruno Monsaingeon, *Mademoiselle: Conversations with Nadia Boulanger*, trans. R. Marsack (Manchester: Carcanet, 1985), p. 118.
58. Constant Lambert, *Music Ho: a Study of Music in Decline*, 3rd edn (London: Faber, 1966), pp. 177–88.

59. Norman Lebrecht, *The Companion to Twentieth-Century Music* (London: Simon & Schuster, 1992), p. 194.
60. Eric A. Gordon, *Mark the Music: the Life and Work of Marc Blitzstein* (New York: St Martins Press, 1989), p. 506.
61. See Magee, *Aspects of Wagner*, pp. 29–44.
62. Howard Goodall, *Big Bangs: the Story of Five Discoveries that Changed Musical History* (London: Vintage, 2001), pp. 168–77.
63. Peter Gradenwitz, *The Music of Israel: from the Biblical Era to Modern Times* (Portland, OR: Amadeus Press, 1996).
64. Jehoash Hirshberg, *Music in the Jewish Community of Palestine 1880–1948: a Social History* (Oxford: Clarendon Press, 1995).
65. Robert Fleisher, *Twenty Israeli Composers: Voice of Culture* (Detroit: Wayne State University Press, 1997).
66. Jonathan Buckley (ed.), *Classical Music on CD: the Rough Guide* (London: Rough Guides, 1994).
67. Jonathan Buckley (ed.), *Opera: the Rough Guide* (London: Rough Guides, 1997).
68. John Warrack and Ewan West, *The Oxford Dictionary of Opera* (Oxford: Oxford University Press, 1992).
69. Paul Griffiths, *Modern Music and After: Directions Since 1945* (Oxford: Clarendon Press, 1995).
70. Erwin Stein (ed.), *Arnold Schoenberg Letters* (London: Faber, 1964), p. 205.
71. Hans Keller, *The Jerusalem Diary: Music, Society and Politics, 1977 and 1979*, ed. C. Wintle and F. Williams (London: Plumbago, 2001), p. 20.

Chapter 4

Jewish Consciousness

In the previous chapter I considered how composers of Jewish descent were seen from without. I now want to examine how they saw themselves, in terms of Judaism. Were they conscious of their Jewish roots when composing, and if so did this manifest itself in their composition? Looking generally at individuals of Jewish descent, one sees a complete spectrum of attitudes. At one extreme, there are Chassidic Jews, who by their beliefs, practices, behaviour and dress clearly see themselves as a distinct group and go to great lengths to show this. At the other extreme, there are Jews who regard themselves as wholly assimilated in all aspects of life, but who nevertheless are aware of their origins; their attitude has been neatly summed up by Sidney Morganbesser as *Incognito ergo sum* (parodying Descartes' *Cognito ergo sum* – I know therefore I am).[1] There are also those who are completely unaware of their Jewish descent or perhaps learn about it late in life. Anti-Semitism has often brought about a heightened awareness of Jewish identity, as did the Six-Day War in 1967, but for a different reason.

As far as composers of Jewish descent are concerned, the attitudes of some are evident in the pronouncements they made. Here are some examples from the better-known composers. Mahler's two quotations are perhaps best known: 'An artist who is a Jew has to achieve twice as much as one who is not, just as a swimmer with short arms has to make double efforts'; and 'I am three times homeless: as a native of Bohemia in Austria, as an Austrian among Germans and as a Jew throughout the world. Everywhere an intruder, never welcomed.'[2] Milhaud expressed a quite different sentiment. He was one of a minority of composers of Jewish descent who was a practising Jew. In the opening paragraph of his autobiography *My Happy Life* he wrote: 'I am a Frenchman from Provence and by religion a Jew.'[3] After conducting the revival of Bach's *St Matthew Passion* in 1829, Mendelssohn exclaimed to the actor Eduard Devrient, while still in the middle of the Opern Platz: 'it should be an actor and a Jew that gives back to the people the greatest of Christian works'.[4] Schoenberg, at a time when he was also a Protestant, wrote in a letter to Kandinsky in 1923: 'I have at last learned the lesson that has been forced upon me during this year, and I shall not ever forget it. It is that I am not a German, not a European, indeed perhaps scarcely a human being (at least the

85

Europeans prefer the worst of their race to me) but I am a Jew.'[5] In 1987, Alfred Schnittke made his diverse origins clear as follows: 'Like my German fore-fathers, I live in Russia, I can speak and write Russian far better than German. But I am not Russian … My Jewish half gives me no peace: I know none of the three Jewish languages – but I look Jewish.'[6] What is clear from all five of these examples, only one of which is from a practising Jew, is that all are conscious of their Jewish heritage and in spite of the problems that they may encounter, are probably proud of their heritage.

4.1 ASSIMILATION, CONVERSION AND BAPTISM

From the time of the Jewish Enlightenment up until World War Two, many Jews converted to some form of Christianity; in some cases these were genuine religious conversions, but in many others they were to overcome or to try to overcome legal disabilities or discrimination. There are a number of well-documented cases amongst Jewish composers. Felix Mendelssohn, his older sister Fanny and younger sister Rebecka and brother Paul were all baptized as Protestants in Berlin in March 1816. Felix was 7 years old at the time. However, the decision to bring the children up as Protestants seems to have been taken earlier, because it is clear from a letter written by his mother, Lea, that Felix had not been circumcised. His parents, Abraham and Lea, did not convert until 1822, after the death of Lea's mother, Bella Salomon, partly perhaps so as not to incur her disapproval. On the occasion of Fanny's confirmation, her father wrote to her explaining that he felt the outward form of religion was changeable, and that in effect the core beliefs to which he subscribed were common to both Christianity and Judaism. It is clear from Felix's writings that he had a Protestant faith and was a true believer.

The violinist and composer Joseph Joachim was baptized at the age of 23. At the time he was employed as violinist to the King of Hanover. He described, in a letter to his friend Hermann Grimm, how his baptism was to take place secretly, with the King and Queen acting as godparents.[7] He explains his reactions:

> I feel as if I had shaken off all bitterness for the first time and were armed against all the sordidness of Judaism, against which I became more inimical the more I had to conquer the disadvantages under which I suffered, at first unconsciously, owing to my Jewish upbringing. The basis of Christ's religion seems to me to be a willing surrender to things spiritual and a joyful martyrdom for them – and in the face of this everything else appears unessential to me just now.

This suggests a degree of religious conviction, coupled with convenience.

Schoenberg and Klemperer both converted to Christianity, but several years later, after the rise of Nazism, converted back to Judaism. Schoenberg was baptized as a Protestant in 1898, clearly as the result of religious conviction. Although he had been brought up in the Jewish tradition, his father was a free-thinker, and during his teens Schoenberg became interested in religion and was given a thorough knowledge of the Christian religion by his friend, Walter Pieau. In 1933, as a refugee from Nazi Germany, Schoenberg reconverted to Judaism in the office of a liberal Paris rabbi, in part at least to identify with the plight of the Jews in the hands of the Nazis.[8]

Klemperer also had a traditional, though not particularly observant, Jewish upbringing. In 1915, when Klemperer was 30, he became interested in Roman Catholicism and attended lectures by the Catholic philosopher Max Scheler. In 1919 he was received into the Church of Rome. At the time he accepted most of the doctrine of the Catholic Church, but his temperament was such that at times he had crises of faith and did occasionally visit synagogues. Nearly fifty years later, in 1967, when Klemperer was living in London, he started visiting the Marble Arch synagogue, although this did not prevent him from also visiting the Brompton Oratory. He bought himself a *yarmulke, tallit* and three volumes of writings by the Jewish philosopher Moses Maimonides. His return to Judaism, at the age of 82, appeared less concerned with faith than with a desire to show solidarity with Israel. At the time he said: 'I wanted to demonstrate that I am a Jew and am loyal to Jewish things.' When he died in 1973 he was buried according to the plain Jewish rite in the Jewish cemetery at Friesenberg near Zurich.[9]

Both Schoenberg and Klemperer converted to Christianity from religious conviction rather than to avoid any form of discrimination. Their return to Judaism was principally to identify with the Jewish people at a time of crisis. The circumstances of Mahler's conversion to Catholicism were somewhat different. Mahler was brought up in an observant but fairly liberal Jewish family. There is evidence of his attending synagogue as a child, but he was also allowed to sing in the local Sankt Jakob choir. He would thus have heard synagogue chants and also sung the great Christian choral works. Once he left home there is no evidence to suggest he attended synagogue or associated with the Jewish communities where he was living. His beliefs were pantheistic, believing in the existence of some supreme and mysterious power and in the manifestation of God's will everywhere. His spirituality was the primary inspiration for his major compositions. He was baptized in the Kleine Michaelkirche in Hamburg on 23 February 1897. He did so when it became clear to him that unless he embraced Roman Catholicism he would not be appointed Kapellmeister at the Vienna Court Opera, the position he most coveted. It is clear that becoming a Catholic was something he did not find easy; he explained to Ludwig Karpath, a music critic and nephew of Karl Goldmark, that he converted 'to escape from Pollino's *inferno*' adding that 'I do not hide the truth from you when I say that this action, which I took from an instinct of self-preservation and which I was fully disposed to take, cost me a great deal.'[10] (Pollini was director of the Hamburg municipal theatre.) Another music critic, Ferdinand Pfohl, discussed the matter with Mahler at the time. After congratulating Mahler on his appointment to the Vienna Court Opera, he asked him how it had come about, since 'the strictly Catholic Kaiser appointed only Catholics as a matter of principle to his court. To become conductor at court, Mahler would have needed to submit to the ceremony of baptism. Mahler replied "The cloak has changed" ... Mahler converted for material gain, forced by neither inner conflict nor inner need.'[11] Mahler's conversion is the central theme of a play by Ronald Harwood.[12]

Other examples illustrate the pressures put upon Jews to convert. When OFFENBACH sought to marry Herminie de Alcain, the family imposed two conditions. Offenbach should go on a concert tour to London, and should renounce the Jewish faith and embrace Roman Catholicism. The first condition he found more challenging, but nevertheless arranged it in 1844. On returning from London, Comtesse Bertin de Vaux acted as his sponsor when he was baptized a Catholic, after which he married Herminie on 14 August 1844. Offenbach had a traditional Jewish upbringing, and when he and his brother went to Paris to study, their father arranged for them to sing in a synagogue choir. However Offenbach, although God-fearing, soon dropped the synagogue ritual, and conversion to Catholicism does not appear to have caused him any conflict.[13]

The parents of Anton and Nicolay RUBINSTEIN converted to Christianity, and both children were baptized into the Russian Orthodox church when two years old.[14] These were for the practical purposes of avoiding excessive taxation, other forms of harassment, and to open the children's opportunities to professions such as law, medicine and teaching, which were closed to Jews.

4.2 CHANGE OF SURNAME

There can be many reasons for changing surnames; sometimes this is done by immigrants so that their name is easier for the native population to enunciate, or for the added reason to show identity with a new homeland. For example, Bernard Herrmann's father, on arrival in America from Russia, called himself Abram Finkelpearl. However, on meeting his mother's cousin, Herman Finkelpearl, in Pittsburgh, the latter said, 'Why go by Finkelpearl, a name strange to Americans, why not go by a German name, which is more acceptable in this country', hence Herrmann.[15] Many Jews on emigrating to Israel adopted Hebrew names to identify with their new homeland, for example Ben Haim (Frankenburger), Avidom (Mahler-Kalkstein), Da-Oz (Daus), Seter (Starominsky) and Tal (Gruenthal). Another reason can be to hide a Jewish identity, or at least make it less obvious. When Mendelssohn's parents, Abraham and Lea, converted to Christianity in 1822, they adopted the name Mendelssohn Bartholdy. Bartholdy was the surname originally adopted when Lea's brother, Jakob Salomon, converted to Christianity. Correspondence between Felix and his father Abraham shows that the latter was concerned on seeing that only the name Mendelssohn, and not Mendelssohn Bartholdy, appeared on London concert announcements. Also, Felix refused to use visiting cards that his father had had engraved with the name Felix M. Bartholdy. His father wrote that he wanted him to use the name Felix Bartholdy. He was quite explicit that by using the name Mendelssohn he was *ipso facto* a Jew, and would suffer accordingly.[16]

Koussevitzky (himself a Jew) advised Leonard Bernstein to change his name because of its ordinariness and Jewishness. He suggested a change to Leonard S. Burns (S. for Samuelovitch) would be more suitable for a conductor, but Bernstein adamantly resisted.[17]

Theodor Ludwig Wiesengrund was the son of an assimilated Jewish wine merchant. He taught philosophy at the University of Frankfurt, but when the Nazis came to power in 1933 his right to teach was withdrawn. Initially, he thought the rise of Nazism was just a phase, but nevertheless went into exile in 1934. In 1936 he wrote an article 'On Jazz', using the pseudonym Hektor Rottweiler, which perhaps expressed his faint hope that he might find a position back in Germany. In the article it is clear he had no love for American culture, but nevertheless he accepted an invitation to join Horkheimer's Institute for Social Research in New York, which had been relocated from Frankfurt. In 1938 he took the decision to drop his father's Jewish surname and adopt that of his Catholic mother, Maria Calvelli-Adorno, becoming Theodor ADORNO.[18] He had been baptized as a Catholic, and even briefly toyed with the idea of embracing his mother's Catholicism, although his left-wing political convictions precluded any sectarian, ethnic or religious identification. As the extent of the Holocaust became known, he came to acknowledge the true ramifications of his Jewish heritage. One of his most cited remarks is 'To write poetry after Auschwitz is barbaric.'

4.3 ANTI-SEMITISM AND JEWISH IDENTITY

For many Jews, whether assimilated or not, and those of only partial Jewish heritage, a rise of anti-Semitism such as happened in the Nazi era gave rise to an acute sense of awareness of their heritage. Albert Einstein wrote to a Minister of State in 1929: 'When I came to Germany fifteen years ago I discovered for the first time that I was a Jew, and I owe this discovery more to Gentiles than Jews.'[19]

Primo Levi, who experienced the full horror of Nazism at first hand, eloquently expressed this awareness in his writings. He was brought up in an assimilated middle-class Jewish family. At the age of 13 he became *bar mitzvah* and, while religion was not deeply important to him, *bar mitzvah* and keeping the high holy days was part of the family custom. In 1938, when the racial laws came into force in Italy, he would not have been able to complete his doctorate had it not been for the protection of an anti-fascist teacher. In 1944 Levi was interned in a camp at Fossoli di Carpa in German-occupied Italy. One night, after witnessing a group of Libyan Jewish detainees being sent on their final journey, he felt for the first time a sense of belonging to the Jewish people. Later, when he himself has been transferred to Auschwitz and had the Star of David sewn on his jacket and his flesh marked with a registration number, he wrote: 'My Jewish identity took on a great importance following my deportation to Auschwitz; it is very likely that without Auschwitz I would never have written, and would have given little weight to my Jewish identity.'[20]

Fritz Haber, who won the Nobel prize for Chemistry in 1918 and who was a Protestant since 1893, wrote in 1933 when his career was effectively brought to an end by the Nazi purge of the German universities: 'Never before have I felt more like a Jew than now.'[21]

A number of composers of Jewish descent had similar experiences, particularly those living in Germany and countries that became occupied by Germany. In 1921 Schoenberg and his family were on holiday in Matsee in Austria, which at the time was an ostensibly liberal republic. They were told that Jews were not allowed to stay and that Schoenberg would have to produce his baptismal certificate. They left in disgust and Schoenberg realized that, in spite of his baptism and assimilation, he was still regarded as a Jew.[22] This and other factors eventually led him to return to Judaism.

In 1920 Franz SCHREKER was appointed director of the Berlin Musikhochschule. He had been brought up as a Catholic. His mother was a Catholic and his father converted to Protestantism but was Jewish by birth. Schreker wrote in 1921 about the consequences of this appointment: 'Automatically I became a "Jew" (a new metamorphosis)'. Later, in 1932, because of his Jewish inheritance he was forced to resign his position as director.[23]

Victor Ullman had never been a religious person, even though all three of his marriages were to Jewish women. He was very active in Rudolph Steiner's anthroposophic movement. He seems to have only become aware of his Jewishness when he was deported to the concentration camp at Terezin, after which he composed a number of works on Jewish themes.[24] Likewise, the dramatist Egon Redlich, who collaborated with the composer Gideon KLEIN in the monodrama *The Great Shadow,* and who also composed in Terezin, wrote: 'Four months in Terezin. Sensation: I am becoming a Jew to all intents and purposes here, I am reaching the conviction for which I was heading – to become a real Jew.'[25]

World War Two and the subsequent creation of the State of Israel made otherwise unobservant Jews more aware of their heritage. BLITZSTEIN had no formal Jewish education. According to his biographer, Eric Gordon: 'Blitzstein rarely thought about his Jewishness and took no pains to explore Jewish themes in his work. He knew almost nothing of Jewish history and had never read the Bible.'[26] At a conference on the Jewish Commitment in Creative Arts in Israel in 1962 Blitzstein declared: 'I consider myself addicted to humanism … I know I am a Jew.' And he continued to explain that this was particularly the case when he encountered anti-Semitism; he surmised that when all anti-Semitism had disappeared, he might cease to feel like a Jew.

Composers of Jewish descent living in the Soviet Union, for example Jacob WEINBERG, LOKSHIN and KLYUZNER, suffered particularly during the Stalinist era, because they were identified by the authorities as Jews. This was particularly so during the 1940s and until Stalin's death in 1953. Lokshin lost his post in the Moscow Conservatory, Klyuzner had none of his compositions published during most of this period, and Weinberg was arrested in 1953.

4.4 COMPOSITION AND JEWISH IDENTITY

In the previous sections I have considered how aware composers of Jewish descent were of their identity and the factors that led to an increased awareness of identity. Now I consider whether, and to what extent, awareness of a Jewish heritage influenced their composing. There are a number of ways by which this may manifest itself. The first is by composing Jewish sacred or liturgical music. The second could be by composing on specifically Jewish or Old Testament themes. It is important to distinguish between these two. The Old Testament is common to both Jewish and Christian religions, whereas a specifically Jewish theme might relate to an event occurring since the origin of Christianity. Examples of the latter are: Lipkin's *Clifford's Tower*, which relates to the massacre of Jews in York in 1190; Halévy's opera *La Juif*; LAVRY's opera *Dan the Guard*, the action of which takes place on a kibbutz; or Reich's *Different Trains*, the second movement of which is entitled *Europe – During the War* and includes dialogue from Holocaust survivors. A third way in which a composer's Jewish heritage might be evident would be in the form of the music itself. Unlike the first two categories, the third is more difficult to define and identify. For example, to what extent is Mahler's Jewish heritage reflected in his music (see below).

By examining the first two of these it can be seen how significant these factors are. Of the composers listed in Part II of this book, 15 per cent have composed sacred or liturgical music, while well over 50 per cent have composed music that incorporates Jewish or Old Testament themes.

Some composers are known either principally, or exclusively, as composers of liturgical music, for example, Louis Lewandowski, Salomon Sulzer, Samuel Naumbourg (1815–80), Maier Kohn (1802–75), Hirsch Weintraub (1811–82), Israel Meyer Japhet (1818–92), Samuel Alman, Miriam GIDEON, Maxine Warshauer and Benjie-Ellen Schiller.[27] Others such as Rossi, Bloch, Milhaud, CASTELNUOVO-TEDESCO, Judith Lang ZAIMONT and Hugo WEISGAL have composed complete settings for synagogue services, but this only comprises a part, albeit an important part, of their total outputs. Others have composed minor works for use in synagogues, usually as a result of a commission, for example, Moscheles wrote a cantata for the Vienna synagogue in 1814, Halévy composed a setting of Psalm 130, Korngold composed *A Passover Psalm*, Op. 30 as a commission, and ZEMLINSKY set Psalm 83 to music, in memory of his father who died in 1900. A number of cantors have commissioned music for use in synagogues. For example, David Putterman (1901–79) cantor at the Park Avenue synagogue in New York, commissioned a large number of composers (mainly but not exclusively Jewish) to compose liturgical music. These included Alexander, David AMRAM, Jacob AVSHALOMOV, Berlinski, Ernest Bloch, Suzanne Bloch, Jacob DRUCKMAN, Miriam GIDEON, Tal, Ben-Haim, Lavry, Sholom SECUNDA, Robert STARER, and Stefan Wolpe.[28]

Many composers, both Jewish and non-Jewish, have used Old Testament themes as the basis for compositions.[29] Handel's 14 English oratorios on Old Testament themes are deservedly the best known. There have been several compositions in response to the Holocaust. Those by composers of Jewish descent include Schoenberg's *Survivor from Warsaw*, Josephs's *Requiem*, Frankel's *Violin Concerto in Memory of the Six Million*, Op. 24, Oscar MORAWETZ's *From the Diary of Anne Frank: Oratorio for Voice and Orchestra*, Reich's *Different Trains*, Senator's *Holocaust Requiem*, Waxman's *Song of Terezin* and Zeisl's *Requiem Ebraico*.

The third category, in which the music itself has elements that have been recognized as Jewish, is more difficult to define. This is discussed at length in the article on Jewish music in the *New Grove Dictionary*[30] and is only briefly mentioned here. It may take the form of quoting or adapting some traditional melody. For example, Goldschmidt quotes the traditional hymn *Moôr Tzur* (Rock of Ages) sung during *Chanukah* (the Festival of Lights) in his String Quartet, No. 3. Although this is an abstract work without a programme, it was commissioned by the State of Schleswig-Holstein for the opening of the Jewish Museum in Rendsburg in 1988. In Copland's piano trio *Vitebsk* (Study on a Jewish Theme), a Yiddish folk melody that Copland heard in Ansky's production of the play *The Dybbuk* is used. The title, *Vitebsk*, is the name of the town in Byelorus in which Ansky grew up. Although this is also clearly not programme music, Copland stated that 'it was his intention to reflect the harshness and drama of Jewish life in White Russia'.[31] In Copland's *Piano Variations* (1930) there are echoes of Negro blues and a declamatory style reminiscent of synagogue music. Both Negro and Jew are seen as dispossessed peoples, who become, for Copland, symbolic of urban man's uprootedness. Ernest Bloch wrote a number of 'Jewish works' mostly composed between 1912 and 1919. These contain motifs borrowed directly from biblical cantillation, synagogue prayer modes, or reflect many of the traits in Jewish sacred music without direct quotation. The latter include the use of Near Eastern scales and the microtonal inflection of melody. Many of the traditional

Jewish materials Bloch took from the *Jewish Encyclopaedia* of 1910. Benjamin Frankel at an early stage in his career considered becoming a 'Jewish composer' in the sense that Bloch is regarded. In two early works that he composed, *Elegie Juive* for cello and piano and *Sonate Ebraica* for cello and harp, he identifies with his Jewish roots (but not the Jewish religion itself). He later rejected the idea of becoming a 'Jewish composer' because he felt it too restrictive, believing that in any case his roots would find their voice in his music.

Steve Reich was brought up as a secular assimilated Jew, although he underwent *bar mitzvah*. However, when he married Beryl Korot in 1974 they both began to explore their Jewish roots, including taking lessons in Hebrew. In 1981, after visiting Israel, Reich composed *Tehillim*, a setting of verses from four Psalms. His comment about *Tehillim* is interesting: 'People have listened to *Tehillim* and said, "It's a Jewish-sounding melody." And I say horseshit, it's a Steve Reich-sounding melody, and if I'm Jewish then it is. But it doesn't have anything to do with Hasidic melodies or Jewish folktunes.'[32]

There can be no doubting Leonard Bernstein's awareness of his Jewish identity in both his words and actions. His only work, specifically for use in the synagogue, was *Hashkivienu* for tenor, mixed chorus and organ. A number of his works have Jewish inspiration, for example, *Jeremiah*, Symphony No. 1; *Kaddish*, Symphony No. 3; *Halil*, a nocturne for flute and chamber group; and *Dibbuk*, Suite Nos. 1 and 2. *Chichester Psalms*, which includes Psalms 23 and 100, is sung in Hebrew. It is interesting that arguably his most successful work, *West Side Story*, was originally conceived as a modern version of *Romeo and Juliet*, set in slums during the coincidence of Easter Passover celebrations, with the Capulets as Jews and the Montagues as Catholics. However, Bernstein soon switched these for newly arrived Puerto Ricans and second generation Americans from white immigrant families.[33] Bernstein made many visits to Israel from 1948 onwards. He spent two months in Israel seeing a great deal of suffering in the struggle for independence, and gave his first performance in Israel of Mahler's Resurrection Symphony, insisting on the German text being translated into Hebrew. He was offered the post of director of the Israel Philharmonic Orchestra, which he declined, but he visited Israel many times as guest conductor. At the time of the Six-Day War Bernstein was conducting the Resurrection Symphony in Vienna. He donated his fee to the Israeli Red Cross and flew to Israel as soon as was practical, to conduct three special concerts marking the reunification of the city of Jerusalem; these included an open air concert on the slopes of Mount Scopus.

Bernstein made a large contribution towards bringing Mahler's music to the general public. After Mahler's death in 1911 and up until the end of the 1950s performances of Mahler's symphonies were infrequent, and were not as highly regarded as they are today. Geoffrey Sharp, in a 1949 article about Mahler's symphonies wrote:

Mahler's aim undoubtedly was 'expression' but it is doubtful whether what he wanted to express was always worth the trouble he took over it. ... Two criticisms of Mahler's music which cannot be dismissed lightly: those two corner-stones of contemporary disparagement – pseudo-naïveté and banality ... Mahler's attempts to come to terms with the realms of childlike fantasy were always childishly inadequate and there is no doubt at all that he was often vulgar.[34]

This was a fair reflection of views common at the time, that is, the late 1940s and 1950s, partly as a result of being unable to hear performances of Mahler's symphonies. But things were to change with the 100th anniversary of Mahler's birth in 1960. Bernstein regularly performed the Mahler symphonies during his period as director of the New York Philharmonic Orchestra (1958–69), and he and Rafael Kubelik made the first complete cycles of recordings of Mahler's symphonies. By the 1980s Mahler was one of the most popular symphonists in the concert halls.

Bernstein also brought Mahler to a wider audience in his *Omnibus* programmes for CBS television. In these he analyzed the 'Jewish' elements in Mahler's music. He pointed out that Mahler often resorted to 'heart-rending' semitones of the Phrygian mode that belonged equally to Arabic music, to flamenco, with its Moorish influence, and to *klezmer*, the music of itinerant Jewish musicians in eastern Europe, which combines the ancient modal traces that are found in peasant music from Croatia to Georgia. What Bernstein heard in Mahler's music that he felt made it so unmistakeably Jewish is what he called a 'sob', a sort of lamenting or breast-beating. He pointed out an instance of the Phrygian melodic twists in the song *Das irdische Leben* (Earthly life), one of the *Wunderhorn-Lieder*, which protests the death of a child from poverty and starvation in constant chromatic changes. Bernstein said that it sounded like a child of the ghetto.[35]

Bernstein has been accused of projecting his own identity into that of his hero, Mahler. However, Theodor Adorno also identified Hebraic melodies, both sacred and profane, present in Mahler's music and explained that the 'Jewish feel' is much more than just melodies, but is a spiritual quality, intangible in its detail but pervasive at the highest level. The 'Jewish' element is evident in Mahler's music, both to his detractors and well as his supporters. Rudolf Louis wrote in 1909: 'If Mahler's music spoke Yiddish, it would perhaps be unintelligible to me. But it is repulsive to me because it 'acts' Jewish. This is to say that it speaks musical German, but with an accent, with an inflection, and above all, with the gestures of an eastern, all too eastern Jew.'[36]

There has been much debate as to whether 'Jewishness' can be discerned in Mendelssohn's music. There is no argument about whether or not Mendelssohn was conscious of his Jewish inheritance; the argument centres on his attitude towards Judaism. Detailed arguments can be found in a number of articles in *Musical Quarterly*.[37] Mendelssohn could not have failed to be aware of anti-Semitism from a number of encounters in his youth. Many

German Jews underwent assimilation during the period 1815–48 and their 'cultural identity' was in a state of flux. Mendelssohn was aware of his Jewish inheritance, but at the same time showed growing devotion to Protestantism.[38] This is reflected in his revival of Bach's *St Matthew Passion* in 1829, and in his oratorios *Paulus* (1836) and *Elijah* (1846). *Elijah* was his last major composition, although he was working on an oratorio, *Christus*, at the time of his death in 1847. The aria that begins Part 2 of *Elijah*, 'Hear, Oh Israel, hear the voice of the Lord', must have come from the heart. At a performance of *Elijah* in 1937 organized by Jüdische Kulturbund in the Oranienburger Strasse synagogue in Berlin, Jews believed they were hearing a Jewish work written by a German Jew affirming the greatness of Judaism.[39]

Perhaps one of the most enigmatic composers of Jewish descent was Gerald Finzi. His works are often described as quintessentially English, so much so that Stephen Banfield entitled his biography, *Gerald Finzi: an English Composer*.[40] Although Finzi was surrounded by Jewish relatives in childhood, he later detached himself from his family, and appears to have done his utmost to dissociate himself from Judaism in general. Yet when he heard of the plight of Jews in Germany in the 1930s he was very disturbed. Banfield describes his attitude thus: 'However much he was prepared to fight for the Jews to be saved, he was, underneath it all, fighting for himself *not* to be one of them! ... just as Nazi ideology would have completely discounted all aspects of his identity other than his Jewishness in dealings with him, so did Finzi insist on essentialising himself as entirely English to the complete discountenance of his Jewishness.'[41] Brian Hunt's interpretation is different.[42] He quotes Finzi's son Nigel as saying of his father: 'He was over-sensitive to things. In the Thirties, when the persecution of Jews began in Germany, he couldn't sleep. He couldn't compose. I suppose you would say he was neurotic. It was the injustice and cruelty that hurt Finzi, not racial empathy.'

Finzi's music is considered to be 'very English' and perhaps his desire to expunge his Jewishness provided an additional motivation to develop in the way he did, both musically and culturally. He greatly admired Bloch as a composer, the Jewish composer *par excellence,* although he never used the word *Jewish* when analyzing his works. In spite of this 'Anglicization' on Finzi's part, Banfield[43] detects possible 'Jewish' inflections in the *Grand Fantasia* and in his last complete work, a cello concerto, where the first bar of the slow movement 'might almost be from *Fiddler on the Roof*'. Perhaps Sidney Morganbesser's maxim *Incognito ergo sum* sums up Finzi's dilemma.

NOTES

1. See Jonathan Sacks, 'Love, Hate and Jewish Identity', www.chiefrabbi.org/speeches/identity.html
2. Norman Lebrecht, *Mahler Remembered* (London: Faber & Faber, 1987), p. xx.
3. Darius Milhaud, *My Happy Life,* trans. Donald Evans (London: Marion Boyars, 1995).
4. Wilfrid Blunt, *On Wings of Song* (London: Hamilton, 1974), p. 89.

5. Erwin Stein (ed.), *Arnold Schoenberg: Letters* (London: Faber, 1964), pp. 88–9.
6. Alexander Ivashkin, *Alfred Schnittke* (London: Phaidon, 1996), p. 9.
7. Nora Bickley, *Letters from and to Joseph Joachim* (New York:Vienna House, 1972), p.110.
8. Alexander Ringer, *Arnold Schoenberg: the Composer as Jew* (Oxford: Clarendon Press, 1993), pp. 7–9 and 205.
9. Peter Heyworth, *Otto Klemperer: his Life and Times* (Cambridge: Cambridge University Press, 1983 and 1996), vol. 1, pp. 137–8, and vol. 2, pp. 328–9.
10. Henri-Louis La Grange, *Mahler* (London: Gollancz, 1974), vol. 1, pp. 15 and 411–12.
11. See Lebrecht, *Mahler Remembered,* pp. 92–4.
12. *Mahler's Conversion* by Ronald Harwood was staged at the Aldwych Theatre, London, in 2001.
13. James Harding, *Jacques Offenbach: a Biography* (London: Calder, 1980), pp. 38–40.
14. O. Bennigsen, 'The Brothers Rubinstein', *Musical Quarterly*, 25 (1939), p. 407.
15. Steven C. Smith, *A Heart at Fire's Center: the Life and Music of Bernard Herrmann* (Berkeley, CA: University of California Press, 1991).
16. See Blunt, *On Wings of Song,* pp. 23–30, and Jeffrey S. Sposato, 'Creative Writing: the Self-Identification of Mendelssohn as Jew', *Musical Quarterly*, 82 (1998), pp. 190–209.
17. Humphrey Burton, *Leonard Bernstein* (London: Faber, 1994), p. 85.
18. Martin Jay, *Adorno* (London: Fontana, 1984), pp. 24–34.
19. Albert Einstein, *Ideas and Opinions* (London: Souvenir Press, 1973), pp.171–2.
20. Myriam Anissimov, *Primo Levi: Tragedy of an Optimist* (London: Aurum Press, 1998), pp. 97 and 341.
21. See Ringer, *Schoenberg,* p. 3, and Robert S. Wistrich, *Who's Who in Nazi Germany* (London: Routledge, 1995).
22. H. H. Stuckenschmidt, *Arnold Schoenberg: his Life, World and Work* (London: Calder, 1977), pp. 272–4.
23. Christopher Hailey, *Franz Schreker 1878–1934: a Cultural Biography* (Cambridge: Cambridge University Press, 1993), p. 138.
24. Joža Karas, *Music in Terezin* (New York: Pendragon, 1985), p. 117.
25. Ibid., p. 73.
26. Eric A. Gordon, *Mark the Music: the Life and Work of Marc Blitzstein* (New York: St Martin's Press, 1989), pp. 319 and 506.
27. A. Z. Idelsohn, *Jewish Music in its Historical Development* (New York: Schocken, 1967), pp. 246–95, and *Proceedings of the First International Conference on Jewish Music*, ed. S. Stanton and A. Knapp (London: City University Press, 1994), pp. 1–4 and 19–25.
28. Irene Heskes, *Passport to Jewish Music* (Westport, CN: Greenwood Press, 1994), pp. 305–8.
29. Ibid., pp. 315–22.
30. *New Grove Dictionary.* See Jewish Music, section V, 2, I–iii.
31. Howard Pollack, *Aaron Copland: the Life and Work of an Uncommon Man* (New York: Henry Holt, 1999), pp. 42–6.
32. K. Robert Schwarz, *Minimalists* (London: Phaidon, 1996), pp. 83–90.
33. See Burton, *Bernstein,* pp. 185–7.
34. Geoffrey Sharp, 'Gustav Mahler', in R. Hill (ed.), *The Symphony* (Harmondsworth: Penguin, 1949), p. 302.
35. Michael Chanan, *From Handel to Hendrix* (London: Verso, 1999), pp. 202–5.
36. Henry-Louis La Grange, *Gustav Mahler*, vol. 2, *Vienna. The Years of Challenge* (Oxford: Oxford University Press, 1995), pp. 304–5.
37. Jeffrey S. Sposato, 'Creative Writing: the [Self-]Identification of Mendelssohn as Jew', *Musical Quarterly*, 82 (1998), pp. 190–209; Leon Botstein, 'Mendelssohn and the Jews', *Musical Quarterly*, 82 (1998), pp. 210–19; Peter Ward Jones, 'A Commentary on Jeffrey Sposato's Article "Creative Writing: the [Self-]Identification of Mendelssohn as Jew"', *Musical Quarterly*, 83 (1999), pp. 27–30; Michael P. Steinberg, 'Mendelssohn's Music and German-Jewish Culture: an Intervention', *Musical Quarterly*, 83 (1999), pp. 31–44; Leon Botstein, 'Mendelssohn, Werner, and the Jews: a Final Word', *Musical Quarterly*, 83 (1999),

pp. 45–50; Jeffrey S. Sposato, 'Mendelssohn, Paulus, and the Jews: a Response to Leon Botstein and Michael Steinberg', *Musical Quarterly*, 83 (1999), pp. 280–91.

38. See Steinberg, 'Mendelssohn's Music', p. 32.
39. See Botstein, 'Mendelssohn and the Jews', p. 213.
40. Stephen Banfield, *Gerald Finzi: an English Composer* (London: Faber & Faber, 1997).
41. Ibid., pp. 257–8.
42. Brian Hunt, 'A Cello Concerto Better Than Elgar's', *Daily Telegraph*, 3 July 2001, p. 21.
43. See Banfield, *Gerald Finzi*, pp. 156–9 and 496.

Conclusions

It is widely acknowledged that composers of Jewish descent have made an important contribution to western classical music during the nineteenth and particularly the twentieth centuries.[1] The number of composers of Jewish descent listed in Part II of this book also demonstrates their relative abundance among composers of western classical music. An important question is how great has been their contribution. Since the *Haskalah* Jews have made a major contribution not only to music but also to many other fields of culture and learning. Much has been made of the large number of Nobel laureates of Jewish descent. Nobel prizes are coveted as a mark of the highest distinction in the fields for which they are awarded, and, although no assessments can be completely objective, the Nobel committees make considerable efforts to be thorough and impartial in making their awards. It is remarkable that approximately one-fifth of the recipients since the centenary of the first awards in 1902 has been to individuals believed to be of Jewish descent. Within the six categories the numbers of recipients believed to be of such ancestry are as follows: physics, 37; chemistry, 21; physiology and medicine, 39; literature, 10; peace, 7; and in economics, 13 (only since 1969).[2]

Although Nobel prizes cannot be used as an absolute yardstick, these statistics inevitably lead to the conclusion that individuals of Jewish descent have been and still are major contributors in both the arts and sciences. Certain areas, such as philosophy, are not included in the six categories, but one can also cite many well-known philosophers of Jewish descent, for example, Spinoza, Wittgenstein, Marx, Ayr, Husserl and Popper.

Any assessment of the contribution of individuals of Jewish descent to music is bound to be to some extent subjective. However, it seems clear that while composers of Jewish descent have made a major contribution to western classical music in the nineteenth and twentieth centuries, this contribution, great though it is, is less than that made by individuals of Jewish descent either to musical performance or in other fields, such as science. As evidence to support the first of these contentions, we may compare composers with musical performers over the past 200 years. If asked whom one would list as the 20 greatest violinists, cellists, pianists or conductors during this period, although there would not be complete agreement among music enthusiasts, it is unlikely that the majority in each category would not be of Jewish descent. For example, in the case of violinists one might expect Elman, Heifetz, Joachim, Kreisler, Menuhin, Milstein, Oistrakh, Perlman, Szigeti, Stern, and Wieniawski to feature in most lists. When it comes to composers, the same claim for pre-eminence could not be sustained.

For many, Mahler is perhaps the greatest symphonist of the late Romantic period, and as a lieder composer he would also be listed alongside Schubert, Schumann, Wolf and Beethoven. Mendelssohn, although an outstanding composer of the nineteenth century, would not generally be considered to be on the same high plane as Bach, Beethoven or Mozart. Schoenberg has had an enormous influence on music of the twentieth century, and was a highly original composer, but his fame and contribution rest as much on his legacy as the originator of the Second Viennese School as on his compositions *per se*. Opinions on Schoenberg's own music vary, and this has been clearly described by Malcolm MacDonald.[3]

> There are still composers and writers who honestly detest Schoenberg's music and deeply resent his influence. And his works – with few exceptions – have not gained a place in the general repertoire ... In fact Schoenberg evokes as wide a range of attitudes as he has listeners. There are those for whom he is a godlike creative genius who could do no wrong; and those who regard him as a spiritual and emotional cripple who surrendered his power of inspiration to a straight-jacket of an arbitrary 'mathematical' system. For some he is the arch-bogeyman of tuneless modern music ... And there are some who simply love his music.

Copland ranks as one of the pre-eminent American composers of the twentieth century. Kurt Weill's compositions of the late 1920s and early 1930s rank among the foremost of the period of the Weimar Republic (1919–33). Since the death of Shostakovich, in 1975, Alfred Schnittke (1934–98) has been regularly pronounced as his heir and is regarded as having produced some of the most important music of the late twentieth century.[4] Ligeti composed in a number of different styles, including minimalism, and in some aspects he is regarded as one of the truest heirs of Bartok.[5] Reich and Glass were two of the leaders of the minimalist trend in twentieth-century music, but as regards minimalism itself, it is probably too early to fully assess whether it will have a lasting impact. In this discussion it is pertinent to bear in mind that, in general, performers are judged during their lifetime, whereas for composers a full assessment requires the passage of time.

My second comparison is between composers and scientists of Jewish descent. In contrast to composers, there is no doubt that scientists of Jewish descent have fundamentally transformed their subjects. It would be out of place here to make a detailed comparison; the large number of Nobel laureates in science of Jewish descent speaks for itself. Scientists are not widely known to the public in general, in the way that writers, actors, musicians, sports personalities and politicians are, although the greatest – for example, Einstein, Freud (both Jewish), Darwin, Watson and Crick – are household names.

For Karl Popper, a philosopher of science, music was highly important. He studied the history of music as the second subject for his Ph.D. and in addition was a member of Schoenberg's Society for Private Performances. He came to believe that there are many parallels in the creative processes involved in both science and music.[6] For example, Popper suggested that the creation of polyphonic music that occurred between the ninth and fifteenth centuries in Europe was in part the result of the canonization of Church melodies. The unacceptable restrictions thereby imposed on musicians provided the conditions in which counterpoint evolved. Counterpoint he regarded as a fundamental 'breakthrough' in musical development. This can now be compared, in science, to Gallileo's advocacy of Copernicus's theory (namely, that the sun, and not the earth, is the centre of the solar system) that brought him severe ecclesiastical censure. Popper argues that both breakthroughs arose under circumstances in which the authoritarianism of the Church was too constraining, thereby providing the conditions to stimulate creative minds to make the next leap forward. These two developments were roughly contemporaneous and were unique to western civilization of the period.

In a further comparison between music and science, Popper quotes the astronomer and mathematician Johannes Kepler (1571–1630),[7] who likens astronomy to music:

Thus the heavenly motions are nothing but a kind of perennial concert, rational rather than audible or vocal. They move through the tension of dissonances which are like syncopations or suspensions with their resolutions (by which men imitate the corresponding dissonances of nature) reaching secure and predetermined closures, each containing six terms like a chord consisting of six voices.

There are similarities between the development of music and that of science in that on occasions both may take a leap forward as the result of current theories and practices coming to fit less satisfactorily than heretofore with contemporary attitudes and thought. However, there are important differences between a scientific hypothesis and a musical composition. The success of a scientific theory is judged by its explanatory power after rigorous testing, but what makes for a 'great' piece of music is less easy to define, but is related to how it is perceived by the listener. A common feature, however, is that both require imagination and originality. How these arise is difficult to analyze. Karl Popper admits this in his statement: 'Originality is a gift of the gods – like

100

naïvety, it cannot be had for the asking, or gained by seeking it.'[8] Peter Medawar was more specific when he wrote:

> The analysis of creativity in all its forms is beyond the competence of any one accepted discipline. It requires a consortium of the talents: psychologists, biologists, philosophers, computer scientists, artists and poets will all expect to have their say. That 'creativity' is beyond analysis is a romantic illusion we must outgrow. It cannot be learned perhaps, but it can certainly be encouraged and abetted.[9]

Even now science still has a long way to go in explaining the nature of 'creativity'. However, it is noteworthy that thinkers as diverse as Peter Medawar, a zoologist and Nobel laureate (1915–87), the poet Shelley (1792–1822) and the psychologist Robert Weisberg suggest there is no qualitative difference in creativity in the arts or sciences.[10]

Whilst we cannot explain creativity *per se*, we do understand something of how it can be 'encouraged and abetted'. When Louis Pasteur (1822–95) wrote 'In the field of observation, chance favours only the prepared mind', he was considering the nature of scientific discovery. He meant that an inspired idea is most likely to bear fruit in a mind that is able to recognize the potential of the idea. Thus, when Archimedes observed the overflow of water from his bath, he is said to have jumped out of his bath naked, shouting 'Eureka', 'I have found it.' He had discovered what is now known as Archimedes' Principle; a commonplace observation in a 'prepared mind' had led to a fundamental discovery. Pasteur's aphorism does not only apply in the field of scientific observation, but also in music. In a letter written in May 1826, Schubert wrote to a friend: 'I am not working at all.' When this period of inactivity passed it was followed by a burst of creation. Schubert began and finished what is arguably his greatest string quartet (D877 in G major), a work lasting about 40 minutes, in ten days between 20 and 30 June 1826.[11] This required not only the inspiration but also the technical resources developed over his whole, albeit short, lifetime of musical composition. There are many other musical examples where it is clear that it is not only inspiration or creativity that are required, but also experience, understanding and technical competence.

Creativity is 'abetted' by experience, and since humans are able to hand down experience from generation to generation, the effect is accumulative. This is acknowledged both by scientists and musicians. When Sir Isaac Newton (1642–1727), the physicist and mathematician, stated 'If I have been able to see further, it was only because I stood on the shoulders of giants', he was explaining that his achievements were only possible because of those of his predecessors. Schoenberg made a comparable claim in 1931 when he explained that his teachers were primarily Bach and Mozart, and secondarily

Beethoven, Brahms and Wagner – meaning that all these composers had influenced his musical development.[12]

Although our understanding of the nature of creativity is still far from clear, two basic elements must be considered, namely inherent ability and background and training. In the light of this, is it possible to explain the abundance of composers of Jewish descent? There is some truth in Menuhin's statement that 'Musicans are born not made.' An inherent aptitude is a necessary prerequisite and this undoubtedly has a genetic basis, but nurture, in the broadest sense, is also very important if potential is to be realized. It is impossible to satisfactorily apportion between these factors (nature and nurture) quantitatively. Genetic evidence of a variety of different types indicates that Jews are not a distinct genotype. When comparing Jewish populations with their surrounding populations there are small differences in the average genetic make-up of the populations. These are very much smaller than the wide variations of genotypes within the respective Jewish and surrounding non-Jewish populations. When one considers further that composers represent a minute proportion of a total population, then the chances of picking a more genetically suited potential composer from one of the two populations is almost in balance. It is much more likely that any differences between composers of Jewish descent and those not of Jewish descent arise from differences in upbringing or, as described in Chapter 3, as the result of a process of cultural evolution. The Jewish experience of needing to survive as a minority, of being an outsider, facing restrictions and recognizing the importance of education are some of the factors that have been discussed in Chapter 3, that may have led to the preponderance of composers of Jewish descent. The pianist and conductor Vladimir Ashkenazi was once asked why there were so many outstanding pianists in the former Soviet Union. He replied that when he was a child growing up in the Soviet Union there were fewer distractions for a child than in the West and thus more incentive to practice hard and long. Life was generally harder and success for a musician had many advantages, including opening up possibilities of foreign travel. In this case the disparity between the Soviet Union and the West had largely arisen since the October Revolution of 1917. This would be far too short a time-scale for genetic evolution and thus the disparity is clearly due to environmental differences. Although the emergence of composers of Jewish descent dates back about two centuries to the Jewish Enlightenment, it is also too short a period for significant genetic evolution. Cultural evolution must therefore be the predominant factor.

Finally, the majority of composers listed in Part II, although of Jewish descent, either are not or were not practising Jews. Some were brought up as Christians, either because they or their parents converted to Christianity, and others either were (or are, depending on whether they are still living) atheists or not religious. Nevertheless, the majority listed still show some attachment to or awareness of their Jewish roots. The evidence for this lies in some of their compositions, in commissions to write liturgical music for the synagogue, and in their writings about their attitudes towards Judaism. This emphasizes the difference in being a religious Jew and having a Jewish inheritance; many who are not religious Jews nevertheless acknowledge a Jewish inheritance. The difference is illustrated in the following two quotations.

In 1967 when Soma Morgenstern heard in a letter from Otto Klemperer that he was returning to his Jewish faith at the age of 82, Morgenstern replied: 'You have always belonged to us.'[13]

Stephen Brook eloquently describes the difference in his book *The Club*:

There is in Britain, as in most nations of the Western world, a club known as the Jewish community. Its most curious feature is that new members are not elected but born. Membership, like an ancient title of nobility, is inherited. Some find its inheritance a joy, others a burden, and others are indifferent. The club is difficult for outsiders to join, and new applicants are not sought, despite declining membership. Once you are in the club, it is, as George Steiner once remarked to a colleague who disclosed he was 'no longer Jewish', almost impossible to resign from it. Resignations do occur, and at a rate that alarms the club's directors, but in times of stress the non-Jewish community has been known to fail to distinguish between active and former members. Although club activists scorn those who disregard the club's strict rules, the outside world finds little to choose between observant and non-observant members. Fidelity to the rulebook is an internal matter.[14]

NOTES

1. See for example, Brian Magee, *Aspects of Wagner* (London: Granada, 1969), pp. 31–44; Howard Goodall, *Big Bangs: the Story of Five Discoveries that Changed Musical History* (London: Vintage, 2001), pp. 168–77.
2. Burton Feldman, *The Nobel Prize: a History of Genius, Controversy and Prestige* (New York: Arcade, 2001); Agneta W. Levinovitz and Nils Ringertz, *The Nobel Prize: the First 100 Years* (New York: World Scientific Publishing, 2001).
3. Malcolm MacDonald, *Schoenberg* (London: Dent, 1987), pp. viii–ix.
4. Paul Griffiths, *Modern Music and After* (Oxford: Clarendon Press, 1995), pp. 252–4; Arnold Whittall, *Musical Composition in the Twentieth Century* (Oxford: Oxford University Press, 1999), pp. 353–6.
5. See Whittall, *Musical Composition in the Twentieth Century*, pp. 295–300.
6. Karl Popper, *Unending Quest: an Intellectual Autobiography* (London: Routledge, 1992), pp. 55–60.
7. Popper's translation from Latin of D. Perkin Walker, 'Kepler's Celestial Music', *Journal of the Warburg and Courtauld Institutes*, 30 (1967), pp. 228–50.
8. See Popper, *Unending Quest*, p. 62.
9. Peter B. Medawar, *Induction and Intuition in Scientific Thought* (London: Methuen, 1969), p. 57.
10. Peter B. Medawar, *The Threat and the Glory* (Oxford: Oxford University Press, 1991),

pp. 83–90; Robert W. Weisberg, *Creativity: Beyond the Myth of Genius* (New York: Freeman, 1993), pp. 191–239.

11. Maurice Brown, *The New Grove Schubert* (London: Macmillan, 1982), pp. 51–3.
12. J. Peter Burkholder, 'Schoenberg the Reactionary', in W. Frisch (ed.), *Schoenberg and his World* (Princeton, NJ: Princeton University Press, 1999), p. 163.
13. Peter Heyworth, *Otto Klemperer: his Life and Times* (Cambridge: Cambridge University Press, 1996), vol. 2, p. 320.
14. Stephen Brook, *The Club: the Jews of Modern Britain* (London: Pan, 1989), p. 11.

Part II
BIOGRAPHICAL
SKETCHES OF
COMPOSERS

Composers

Abraham, Paul (b. Apatin, Hungary, 2 November 1892; d. Hamburg, 9 May 1960)   Studied at the Budapest Academic of Music from 1910 to 1916. He composed a cello concerto performed by the Budapest Philharmonic Orchestra and a string quartet, both in 1922. In 1927 he became conductor of the Budapest Operetta Theatre. One of the requirements for the post was that he composed operettas, and this he did from then on. His first complete operetta, *Viktoria und ihr Husar,* was performed in Vienna in 1930 and was a great success. It combines the elements of traditional Viennese operetta with jazz. He continued to write operettas that were successfully performed throughout Germany, but with the rise of Nazism he was forced to leave Germany first for Vienna, then with the outbreak of war for Cuba, eking out a living as a pianist and later moving to New York. He had little success after 1938. He returned to Europe to live in Hamburg in 1956, but suffered mental illness and died in an asylum. He composed the score for the film *Die Privatsekretärin* (1931), and his operettas include *Die Blume von Hawaii* (1931), *Ball im Savoy* (1932), *Märchen im Grand-Hotel* (1934), *Dschainah* (1935) and *Roxy und ihr Wunderteam* (1937).
Bibliography: *G*; Ho*; WW

Abrams, Harriet (b. *c.* 1758; d. Torquay, England, 8 March 1821)   English soprano and composer of Jewish decent. She was baptized at St George's, Hanover Square, in 1791. Not much is known about her parents, John and Esther, except that they were not musicians and were probably servants. Many of her brothers and sisters pursued musical careers. She was better known as a singer than as composer, singing in high society. She could on occasion call upon Joseph Haydn to be her accompanist. She was a pupil of Thomas Arne and made her début age 15 years old at Drury Lane, where she sang a song, *Mayday,* written for her by David Garrick with music by Thomas Arne. William Hopkins's comment in his diary at the time was: 'She is very small, a swarthy complexion, has a very sweet voice and a fine shake, but not quite power enough yet – both the piece and the young lady were received with great applause.' She continued to sing at Drury Lane until 1780. In 1776 she appeared with her sister Theodosia at the Concert of Ancient Music. She gradually moved away from the opera house to concentrate on oratorios and singing at private concerts, which were regarded as more respectable than the theatre. She sang at the Handel Memorial Concerts in 1784. She organized many concerts herself, including a series of 'Ladies Concerts' that took place in Lord Vernon's house. Haydn, when in London, performed at several of her concerts.

She started publishing her own music in the 1780s, and probably sang it at her concerts. She published two sets of Italian and English canzonets for one or two voices with harpsichord and occasionally with violin accompaniment (1785), and also Scottish songs harmonized for two to three voices (1790). All Abrams's surviving music is vocal. A collection of 12 of her songs, dedicated to Queen Charlotte, was published in 1803. It includes *The Gamester, A Ballad of the Eighteenth Century, Female Hardship, Friend of my Heart, Orphan's Prayer, William and Mary* and *The Eolian Harp*. All have imaginative accompaniments. One of her most popular songs was *Crazy Jane*, a setting of verses by Matthew Lewis, first published in about 1800 and was still being printed and arranged after her death in 1821.

Bibliography: *G**; *GW*; *Pan*; J. D. Brown and S. S. Stratton, *British Musical Biographies* (Birmingham: Stratton, 1897); Barry Weinberg, 'Some Thoughts on Jewish Music Contributions to Musical Life in Britain from the Eighteenth to the Twentieth Century', *Proceedings of the First International Conference on Jewish Music* (London: City University, 1994), pp. 193ff.

Achron, Joseph (b. Lazdyai on the Polish-Lithuanian border, 13 May 1886; d. Hollywood, 29 April 1943)   Second of four children. His father was a cantor who also played the violin and his mother was a fine amateur singer. He began to study the violin with his father at the age of 5 and first appeared in public three years later in Warsaw, where his family moved in 1890. He studied in Warsaw with Michalovitch and Isidor Lotto. He was a child prodigy and gave violin concerts in a number of major cities in Poland before the family moved, in 1908, to St Petersburg. There he studied at the St Petersburg Conservatory, where he was one of many pupils (including Heifetz) of the famous violinist Leopold Auer. He studied composition under Lyadov. By the time he graduated, in 1904, he had completed a dozen works, including a violin concerto. He then toured Germany as a solo violinist, performing Beethoven's violin concerto under Nikisch. In 1907 he returned to St Petersburg. He composed a number of salon pieces and developed an interest in Jewish music, becoming a member of the Society for Jewish Folk Music. During this period he also composed a number of works that clearly show his assimilation of Jewish musical language, for example *Hebrew Melody, Hebrew Lullaby, Hebrew Dance, Dance Improvisation* and *Eli Zion*. He served in the army from 1916 to 1918 and was offered a professorship at the St Petersburg Conservatory in 1918, a position he turned down.

For the next four years he was very active, giving over 1,000 concerts, teaching violin and writing articles such as 'Foundations of Violin Playing and Performing the Chromatic Scale'. In need of time to compose, he spent two years in Berlin. In 1924 he spent several months in Palestine, giving recitals and collecting music from various Jewish communities. This served as the basis of some of his later compositions. In 1925 he travelled to the USA, settling in New York at the Westchester Conservatory, and became an American citizen in 1930. One of his major works, his first violin concerto, Op. 60 (1927), was dedicated to Heifetz. He wrote incidental music for plays performed at the Yiddish Theatre in New York, including *The Tenth Commandment*, *Kiddush Hashem*, *Belshazzar*, *Mazltov*, *The Witch* and *Stempenyu*. In 1933 he moved to Los Angeles. He gave the premiere of his second violin concerto, Op. 68 in 1936 and his third violin concerto, Op. 72 in 1938, both with KLEMPERER conducting. In 1934 he went to Hollywood and composed music for films.

Many of his compositions are for violin but he also composed a piano concerto, *The Golem*, a suite for chamber orchestra, *Chazan* (cantor) for cello and orchestra, *Sabbath Eve Service* (1932 commissioned by the Temple Emanu-El in New York) and other choral works. Heifetz played many of his works and popularized his *Hebrew Melody*. He reworked Hassidic melodies in a number of works. High blood pressure led to kidney failure and he died soon after his 57th birthday. At the time of his death, in California in 1943, he had composed more than 100 works, but over half of these were not published before his death. A research student, Philip Moddell, discovered a large number of works at the home of a relative, and many of these have now been published.
Bibliography: *AG*; *G*; *HBD*; Ho*; Biddulph LAW 021 [record sleeve]

Adam, Adolphe (b. Paris 24 July 1803; d. Paris 3 May 1856)   Son of a musician. His father was self-taught and rose to become a composer, pianist and teacher at the Paris Conservatoire from 1797 to 1842. Among his pupils were HÉROLD. Adam's father discouraged him from taking up music, but it was Hérold, twelve years his senior, who encouraged his interest in music. Initially Adam was sent to a boarding school, but when this became too expensive for the family he was sent to a day school, where he became friends with Hérold. Eventually his father agreed to him having lessons provided he intended only to become an amateur musician. Adam wished to compose and theatre music most attracted him. He studied piano with Henry Lemoine and, at the age of 17, he entered the Paris Conservatoire, studying the organ with Benoist, counterpoint with Reicha and composition with Boieldieu. At the time Boieldieu was the leading exponent of Opéra-Comique. By the age of 20 Adam was contributing songs for the Paris vaudeville theatres and was playing in the orchestra at Gymnase. In 1925 he won second prize in the Prix de Rome. He wrote his first full opera at the age of 26 – *Pierre et Catherine* – which was first performed as a double bill with AUBER's *La fiancée* by the Opéra-Comique and was given over 80 performances.

Adam went on to compose over 70 comic operas, 15 ballets and many songs in addition to writings on music. He claimed that his only passion was music and he had few other interests. Nowadays he is only known to the general music public by works such as the ballet *Giselle* (which was written in three weeks), the Christmas carol *Noël* and the high tenor aria from the opera *Le postillon de Lonjumeau*. There is a statue to him in Lonjumeau. His music was very much in the style of the time. In his early days Wagner conducted his operas in Riga and claimed himself an ardent champion of Adam.[1] With the revolution of 1830 Adam moved to London, where his brother-in-law Laporte leased the Theatre Royal, Covent Garden. However, his music was not particularly to the public's liking and he soon returned to Paris.

In 1844 he fell out with Basset, the director of the Opéra-Comique, and in order to continue performing his operas he planned a third opera house in Paris, the Opéra-National. Adam put up half the money for this venture and for a few months the Opéra-National flourished, but when revolution broke out again in Paris in 1848 it closed down. Adam was financially ruined, so much so that he could not pay the funeral expenses for his 89-year-old father, who had just died. Determined to get back on an even keel he took on the post of professor of composition at the Conservatoire and when Basset left the Opéra-Comique he was able to continue having his operas performed there. He continued to compose and write prolifically until his early death at the age of 53. His best-known works, other than those already mentioned, are the operas *Le Chalet* (1834), *Le Roi d'Yvetot* (1842), *Giralda* (1850) and *Si j'etais Roi* (1852). Vincent d'Indy described what he called a 'Jewish or Semitic school' in French music that included MEYERBEER, AUBER, Hérold, Adam, DAVID and OFFENBACH.[2] He also wrote that Wagner helped rid French opera of all that was defiling it – 'musicians whose taste and style was bad', such as Auber, Adam, HALÉVY and Hérold.[3] However, there is no indication that he was of Jewish descent in the standard nineteenth-century French biographies.[4]

Bibliography: *G*; Ha; WW

1. Richard Wagner, *My Life* (New York: Da Capo, 1992), p. 145.
2. Aaron Rothmüller, *The Music of the Jews* (London: Valentine Mitchell, 1953), p. 118.
3. Jane F. Fulcher, *Musical Quarterly*, 73 (1995), pp. 458–75 and 78 (2000), pp. 41–57.
4. Fétis, F. J. *Biographie universelle des musiciens* (Paris: Librairie de Firmin-Didot, 1877), vol. 1, pp. 14–17.

Adler, Samuel Hans (b. Mannheim, Germany, 4 March 1928)   Son of a cantor; his mother was also musical. His father was born in Antwerp in 1894, and was actively associated with the Reform Synagogue movement and composed Jewish liturgical music. The family remained in Mannheim until 1939. His father's oratorio *Akedah* was to be premiered in Stuttgart on 10 November 1938, the day after *Kristallnacht*. Although initially eluding the Nazis, his father was caught and sent to the concentration camp at Dachau. On his release in 1939 the family escaped to America. This traumatic period in Samuel's life

inspired much of his Fifth Symphony, which was written much later in 1975. His father became director of the temple in Worcester, Massachusetts. Samuel learned the viola and was educated at Boston and Harvard Universities. He studied composition with Fromm, COPLAND, Hindemith, Randall Thompson and Piston and conducting with Koussevitsky at the Berkshire Music Center. Whilst in the US army he organized and conducted the Seventh Army Symphony Orchestra in Europe. He was director of music at the Temple Emanu-El in Dallas, Texas, from 1953 to 1956. He is a prolific composer of a wide variety of music styles. His works include six symphonies (for a detailed account see Pollack, *Harvard Composers*), concertos for organ, for piano and for flute, six string quartets and much liturgical music. The latter includes *Shir Chadash* (Sabbath Service, 1960), *The Vision of Isaiah* (1950, revised 1962), *B'Shaaray Tefilah* (Sabbath Service, 1963), *Behold your God* (cantata, 1966), *The Binding* (oratorio, 1967) and *From out of Bondage* (1968). His first symphony uses ancient cantillation as an integral part of the composition.
Bibliography: *G*; *HBD*; Ho*; Ly*; Howard Pollack, *Harvard Composers* (New Jersey, MO: Scarecrow Press, 1992).

Adorno, Theodor Ludwig Wiesengrund (b. Frankfurt-on-Main, 11 September 1903; d. Visp, Switzerland, 6 August 1969)   Only child of a wealthy and assimilated Jewish wine merchant Oscar Wiesengrund, and his Catholic wife Maria Calvelli-Adorno of Corsican and originally Genoese descent. He had a happy and comfortable childhood and although his father appears to have been a somewhat distant figure, his mother showered him with attention. It was through her and her unmarried sister that his early and lasting love for music was encouraged. His other great love was philosophy, which was encouraged by a family friend, Siegfried Kracauer. By the time he entered the University of Frankfurt in 1921 he had already published an article on Expressionism and another on an opera by his piano teacher, Bernard SEKLES. He studied philosophy, sociology, psychology and music at the University of Frankfurt, receiving a doctorate in philosophy only three years later, in 1924. He also studied composition with Alban Berg in Vienna from 1925 to 1927, entering the circle of composers around SCHOENBERG. He returned to Frankfurt in 1927 to study philosophy, but from 1928 to 1931 he gained a reputation as a music critic for *Anbruch* and published articles on music, especially on the works of Schoenberg. He found it difficult to decide between a career in music or in philosophy. From 1931 he taught philosophy at the University of Frankfurt until he was expelled by the Nazis in 1934, when he fled initially to Zurich and then to Oxford. Eventually, in 1938 he emigrated to the USA at the invitation of Max Horkheimer to work at his Institut für Sozialforschung (Institute for Social Research), which had moved from Frankfurt to New York. It was here he adopted his mother's surname, Adorno, rather than his father's Wiesengrund, it is said because Wiesengrund sounded Jewish.[1] In 1937–8 he also wrote briefly under the pseudonym Hektor 'Rottweiler'. Whilst at the institute he worked as musical director of the Princeton Radio Research Project until 1940, when he and the institute moved to Los Angeles.

As a social philosopher he became well known for his left-wing views and as a musicologist he developed Freudian and Marxist ideologies in the service of avant-garde music. He was a great champion of the music of Schoenberg and he disdained mass culture. He believed that 'serious' music had to become abstruse, because simplicity and pleasure were ingredients of the 'accessible music' used for moulding consumer demand. In 1940 he advised Thomas Mann, also in exile in California, on the musical aspects of the latter's novel *Docktor Faustus,* in which the central character is a composer whose musical ideas parallel those of Schoenberg. In 1944 he collaborated with Hans EISLER, also in exile, on a study of film music. The outcome was the book *Composing for the Films.* Adorno seemed uncomfortable with the practical orientation of the book and, at the time of its publication, Eisler's brother was under attack because of his communist affiliations. Adorno was anxious and so left his name off the title of the book; it was only in 1969, when the book was reprinted in West Germany, that Adorno's role in it was acknowledged. In 1949 the Institut für Sozialforschung returned to Frankfurt, where Adorno continued to work, succeeding Horkheimer as director. In 1956 he became a professor at Frankfurt University. He died in Switzerland in 1969 while writing what some believe to be his most important philosophical work, *Aesthetic Theory.*

Adorno is best known for his extensive writings on music and social philosophy, although he did also compose, for example, *Theodor Däubler Songs* (1923–4), *Six Orchestral Pieces* (in a Schoenbergian style) and a number of works for string quartet, including *Six Studies for String Quartet* (1920), *String Quartet 1921* and *Two Pieces for String Quartet*, Op. 2 (1924/5). In recent years Heinz-Klaus Metzger and Rainer Riehn have compiled a two-volume edition of his compositions that will make them more accessible.

Bibliography: *G*; *HBD*; Leb.

1. A. Herbert, *Exiled in Paradise* (London: Viking, 1983); J. Lechte, *Fifty Contemporary Thinkers* (London: Routledge, 1994); Martin Jay, *Adorno* (London: Fontana, 1984).

Alexander, Haim [Heinz] (b. Berlin, 9 August 1915) Studied at the Stern Conservatoire, Berlin, before emigrating to Jerusalem in 1936, where he was a pupil of WOLPE. He finished his studies at what was then the Palestine Conservatoire and became a teacher at the Rubin Academy of Music. In the 1960s he spent a period of study with Wolfgang Fortner at Freiburg-in-Breisgau, Germany. His compositions include *Six Israeli Dances* (1951), the overture *Artza alinu* ('We have come to the Land'), a quintet for clarinet and strings, a suite for two pianos, a quartet for two flutes, cello and piano, *Sonata Brevis* for two pianos (1960), *Sound Figures* for piano, and *Four Quatrains* for voice and chamber ensemble based on poems of Omar Khayyam (1963).

Bibliography: *CC*; Grad; *G*; Ho*

Alkan, Charles Valentin (b. Paris, 30 November 1813; d. Paris, 29 March 1888)   Oldest of five brothers in an Ashkenazi Jewish family living in the Marais Saint-Paul district of Paris. His real surname was Morhange, but he adopted his father's first name Alkan or Elkan (meaning 'The lord has been gracious') as his surname. Marais Saint-Paul was the old Jewish quarter of Paris and Alkan's grandfather also lived there, and probably earlier generations of the family also. His father ran a boarding school in Marais Saint-Paul where young Jewish children were taught music and French grammar. His mother, Julie Abraham, was born in Moselle and married Elkan on 12 April 1810.

Alkan was something of a child prodigy. He went to the Conservatoire, where he was taught piano by Joseph Zimmerman at the age of 6, and won the prize for solfeggio at the age of 7. His first public appearance was as a violinist at the age of 7. By the age of 14 he had published his Op. 1 and a year earlier he was introduced to soirées by his teacher Zimmerman, and at one of these given by the Princess of Moscova, he was surprised to find himself outshone by a pianist two years his senior; the pianist was Liszt. He left home and moved to the most fashionable centre for artists, the Square d'Orleans. Here he met and became friends with Chopin and Georges Sand.

In 1833 he visited London, but this appears to be the only time he went abroad. From 1829 to 1836 he was a part-time teacher of solfeggio. By the 1830s he had become well known as a concert pianist, a composer and teacher. His best pupil was Elie Miriam Delaborde. It is generally thought that Delaborde was his natural son, the mother being a noblewoman, Lina Eraim Miriam. His reputation as a composer rests on works mainly for solo piano, many of them technically very difficult. In 1840–1 he wrote two important chamber works: the *Grand Duo*, Op. 21, for violin and piano, and *Trio*, Op. 30, for piano, violin and bass. He wrote a symphony in B minor in 1844, but the manuscript for this has been lost. In 1847 he published his *Grande Sonate*, Op. 33, which Raymond Lewenthal has described as 'a cosmic event in the composer's development and in the history of the piano'. It was works like this that led the co-editors of his music, Isidore Phillipp (1863–1958) and Ferruccio Busoni (1866–1924), to regard him as one of the five greatest composers of piano music after Beethoven, the other four being Chopin, Liszt, Schumann and Brahms. The year 1847 was an unfortunate time to launch what is one of his greatest works. In 1848 Paris was plunged into revolution and many of the pianists who normally performed in Paris fled to London. The sonata was unplayed and unnoticed at the time.

There were two periods in Alkan's life when he withdrew from public concerts, from 1838 to 1844 and from 1853 to 1873. The reason for the first withdrawal is unclear, but the second is undoubtedly connected with his failure to obtain the post of head of piano teaching at the Consevatoire in succession to Zimmerman. To many, Alkan appeared as Zimmerman's heir apparent. Four candidates were shortlisted; Lacombe, Prudent, Alkan and

Marmontel. Both Prudent and Lacombe were regarded as no mean pianists, although not in Alkan's league. In the event the candidate he least expected, Marmontel, a former pupil of Alkan's and a mere run-of-the-mill product of the Conservatoire and solfeggio teacher, was successful. There was public controversy over the appointment. In the event Marmontel's reign was long (until 1887) and distinguished. His pupils included Bizet and Debussy. This undoubtedly left Alkan a bitter man, and as far as public appearances were concerned he became a virtual recluse. He continued composing and teaching. He had a number of pupils from the aristocracy and this brought him sufficient money to live in the modest way he always had; it also gave him time for composition and his other main interest, the study of the Bible. During this period he became pathologically worried about his health, although there is no evidence that he had any serious illnesses. He had a detailed knowledge of the Bible. His studies included translating two or three verses regularly each day. He is quoted as saying, 'If only I had my life over again, I would set the entire Bible to music.' The Bible provided inspiration for a number of his works as is evident from their dedications, for example, the Cello Sonata, Op. 47, the adagio of which is prefaced 'As dew from the Lord how the Jewish people endure, awaiting the help of God alone' (Micah 5:7), and his piano composition *Super Flumina Babylonis* Op. 52, a kind of wordless operatic scena paraphrasing Psalm 137.

After 1873 Alkan again began a series of *petits concerts*, giving up to six per year until 1880 in both the Salle Erard and Salle Pleyel. He dressed in a severe, old-fashioned and somewhat clerical manner, discouraged visitors and went out rarely. Because of his tendency to be a recluse, mystery surrounds a number of aspects of his life, for example, whether Delaborde was his son and what he did between 1838 and 1844, but perhaps the most controversial event is his death. One story is that he died beneath a collapsed bookcase clutching the Talmud, which he had taken from its position on the highest shelf. This account originated from Isidore Philipp, who gave Robert Collet a full account in 1937 of Alkan's death. It seems a suitable apotheosis for a strictly observant Jew, but its veracity has been questioned.[1] Apart from immediate family there were only four mourners to say Kaddish at Montmartre Cemetery on 1 April 1888 – Blondel, head of Erard's, the violinist Maurin, Isadore Philipp and Alexandre de Bertha. Delaborde was not present.

Since Alkan's death his music has been performed infrequently in public until recently. Many pianists may have been put off by the technical difficulty. Some of his later works were written for the pedal piano, that is, a piano having a pedal board, which had a transient phase of fashion particularly in France for a period in the late nineteenth century but which has long since become obsolete. Nevertheless there are champions of Alkan's music. Ronald Smith has been most responsible for bringing Alkan to the public, both by performing his works and researching his life and works,[2] and by forming the London Alkan Society. Since the 1990s there has been a wider interest in Alkan's music and a number of pianists have risen to the challenge of performing his works.

Bibliography: *G*; *HBD*; Brigitte François-Sappey, *Charles Valentin Alkan* (Paris: Fayard, 1991).

1. Hugh MacDonald, *Musical Times*, 114 (1973), p. 25.
2. Ronald Smith, *Alkan,* volume 1, *The Enigma*, and volume 2, *The Music* (London: Kahn & Averill, 1976).

Alman, Samuel (b. Sobolovska, Podolia, Ukraine, 20 September 1879; d. London, 20 July 1947)   Began to write songs at the age of 13, and at 18 entered the Odessa Conservatory, after which he served as a musician in the Russian Army for four years. After the pogrom in Kishiniev, in the Ukraine, in 1903 he fled to London in 1905 and finished his musical studies at the Royal College of Music. He became choirmaster at the Poets Road synagogue, Highbury, and then at the Great Synagogue in Dukes Place, and from 1916 was choirmaster of the Hampstead synagogue. He was both a composer and an arranger of synagogue music, and was strongly influenced by SULZER.[1] He published two volumes of synagogue music. In addition he arranged folk music and composed secular instrumental music. He composed a Yiddish opera in 1912, *Melech Ahaz* (King Ahaz), a string quartet, *Hebraica*, and set to music many poems on religious texts by Tchernikovsky, Bialik, Heine and Katznelson.

Bibliography: Ho*

1. A. Z. Idelsohn, *Jewish Music in its Historical Development* (New York: Schocken, 1967), pp. 313–14; Aron M. Rothmüller, *The Music of the Jews* (London: Vallentine Mitchell, 1953), pp. 169–70; OCD647 [record sleeve]

Amram, David [Werner] (b. Philadelphia, 17 November 1930)   Learned the horn and piano in his youth and developed a strong interest in jazz. He studied horn at Oberlin College (1948) and history at George Washington University, graduating in 1952. He played the horn in various orchestras until 1955, when he studied with Mitropoulis, Giannini and SCHULLER. He spent more time composing, becoming composer-in-residence with the New York Philharmonic in 1966. He has composed over 100 orchestral and chamber works, many film scores, scores for many Shakespeare productions and two operas, including his Holocaust opera, *The Final Judgment*. His compositions reflect his love of music of different cultures, are generally romantic and are often marked by rhythmic and improvisatory characteristics of jazz. He has been listed as one of the 20 most performed composers of concert music in the USA since 1974. He has been director of the International Jewish Arts Festival since 1982 and has been guest conductor of a number of orchestras. His autobiography, *Vibrations: the Adventures and Musical Times of David Amram* (1968), was reissued in 1980.

Bibliography: *G*; *HBD*; http://www.fmp.com/amram; http://www.cs.bsu.edu/homepages/dlsills*

Antheil, George Johann Carl (b. Trenton, New Jersey, 8 July 1900; d. New York, 12 February 1959)   Of German–Jewish descent. In his youth he Americanized his name from Georg to George. He began piano studies from the age of 6 and by the age of 13 he commuted to Philadelphia to study theory and composition with Constantin von Sternberg, a former pupil of Liszt. Near the end of World War One he joined the aviation branch of the United States Signal Corps, but the war ended before he could be sent into the fighting. Nevertheless his involvement with aeroplanes was to influence some of his later compositions. After the war he continued his music studies, initially with Sternberg, but later with Ernest BLOCH and Clark Smith at the Philadelphia Conservatory. During this period he composed his first major work, Symphony No. 1, *Zingareska*, the last movement of which incorporated jazz elements. He continued piano instruction with George Boyle at the Curtis Settlement School (forerunner of the Curtis Institute of Music, Philadelphia) and in May 1922 he went to Europe as a concert pianist, settling in Berlin, but moving to Paris a year later. Although he performed the traditional repertoire (Bach, Mozart and Chopin) he also performed music by Stravinsky and SCHOENBERG.

He gained a reputation as an *enfant terrible*, largely on account of performances of his own anti-expressive, anti-Romantic and mechanistic works. He loved shocking his audiences by appearing as a 'brutal pianist' with an armoury of tone clusters, splashy glissandos and mechanical rhythms in works such as his second piano sonata, *The Airplane* (1921), *Jazz Sonata* (1922), *Sonata sauvage* (1923) and his third piano sonata, *Death of Machines* (1923). He soon decided that he preferred to concentrate on composing rather than being primarily a concert pianist. He was befriended and championed by artists such as Erik Satie, Picasso, James Joyce, Ezra Pound and W. B. Yeats. In 1923 he collaborated with the American cameraman Dudley Murphy and the French painter Fernand Léger to create a film, *Ballet mécanique*. The music was never synchronized with the film, although the two components gained their reputations separately. It was conceived for 16 electronically controlled player pianos, but this proved unwieldy and the final version (1953) is scored for four pianos, recorded aeroplane sounds, electric bells and various percussion instruments.

He married Boski Markus, a political radical, in 1925, shortly after she had escaped to Berlin from her native Hungary. Antheil's most important work of the late 1920s was the opera *Transatlantic*, which centres on an American presidential election and is a caricature of life in the United States. COPLAND said of him in the mid-1920s that he possessed 'the greatest gifts of any young American now writing'. Copland played one of the pianos in a performance of *Ballet mécanique* in a Carnegie Hall concert of all-Antheil compositions, although he later described the music as '*a reductio ad absurdum'*. The work caused an uproar by shattering the normal conventions both in its structure and percussive instrumentation, including aircraft propellers. In spite of the concert proving to be a disaster, Copland commissioned Antheil to compose a second string quartet (1928) and Antheil later played his *Sonatina* (1932) at Yaddo at Copland's invitation. Unlike many American composers, for example, Copland, DIAMOND and GLASS, who spent a period in Paris studying with Nadia Boulanger, Antheil visited Boulanger and invited her to premieres of his new works but was concerned that she might be too tyrannical as a teacher.

Some of his later works adopt neo-Romantic and neoclassical elements, for example, the *Symphonie en fa* and the piano concerto. Russian influences are strong in a number of his works, which are also rich in other borrowings, a trend that was much more acceptable in the post-SCHNITTKE era. From 1928 to 1929 Antheil was assistant music director of the Berlin State Theatre. After Hitler's rise to power he returned to New York and then moved to Hollywood in 1936, where he composed film scores. He expanded his interests into other areas, acting as war analyst for news media during World War Two. He wrote his autobiography, *Bad Boy of Music,* in 1945, which proved a best-seller and is somewhat reminiscent of Hemingway's writings. His other compositions include six symphonies, a number of songs, several works for piano solo, three string quartets, four operas and incidental music for the stage.
Bibliography: *AG*; *G*; *Ly**; www.schirmer.com/composers/antheil

Auber, Daniel François Esprit (b. Caen, 29 January 1782; d. Paris, 12 or 13 May 1871) Son of a wealthy print seller in Paris, Daniel seemed destined to become a merchant. Although he received piano lessons in his youth from Ignaz Anton Ladurner, these were intended more as a social accomplishment than preparation for a potential career. In 1802 he went to London to study commerce and on returning to Paris in 1803 still intended to become a merchant. At the same time his enthusiasm for music grew. He began composing and wrote several romances, a piano sonata and at least one string quartet between 1793 and 1800. However, there is no indication at this stage that he regarded these as important. At one stage he is said to have composed for a cellist friend, Jacques-Michel de Lamare and allowed the work to appear under the cellist's name. After returning to Paris he wrote two small operas, one of which, *L'erreur d'un moment*, was presented at the house of a friend of Cherubini, Prince Chimay, in 1805. It was praised sufficiently for him to consider the possibility of a musical career, and led to him having lessons with Cherubini.

The next opera he produced in 1813, *Le Sejour militaire*, was a failure and he considered giving up composing. However, after his father's bankruptcy in 1819 and subsequent death, Daniel returned to composing. *La Bergère Chatelaine* (1820) had a measure of success and more so *La Neige* (1823), although this was a work very much in the style of Rossini. The latter was composed with the famous librettist, Eugene Scribe (see also MEYERBEER and HALÉVY). This was to be the first of 36 operas he composed with Scribe between

1823 and the latter's death in 1861. Many of these are included as the greatest successes of Opéra-Comique at the time, and by the time he composed *Le Maçon* in 1825 he had developed a distinctive French Opera-Comique style.

An important landmark was the opera *La Muette de Portico* (1828), which established his name and fame and was to inaugurate the era of French Grand Opera; operas characterized by their length, historically based plots, huge crowd scenes, bold orchestration, dramatic scenic effects and generally the inclusion of a ballet. *La Muette de Portico* influenced Meyerbeer's and Halévy's compositions and also Wagner's *Lohengrin*. At the time Wagner, who was writing in the Dresden Abend-Zeitung, praised Auber as an operatic composer. From then onwards Auber was to average one opera a year until his death in 1871. His most enduring success was the comic opera *Fra Diavolo* (1829), which is one of the few still heard occasionally today. During his lifetime he was renowned as one of France's great composers. Other operas that were particularly successful in his lifetime were: *Gustave III*, *Le Domino noir*, and *Les Diamans de la Couronne*. *Le Domino noir* was performed 1,200 times between its premiere in 1837 and 1910 and travelled as far afield as London and New Orleans.

His operas are generally characterized by the charm and elegance of the vocal writings, but the orchestration is less interesting. The comments of other composers are illuminating. Rossini characterized him as '*piccolo musico, ma grande musicista*' (a small musician, but a great maker of music) – he was small in stature. Wagner, although praising his operas in the 1820s, was later to compare his composing to that of a barber who lathers but does not shave. MOSCHELES said of Auber's *Bal Masqué*: 'The music is often deafening, but often piquant; the ball wonderfully brilliant.' He composed a number of non-operatic works including church music, cello concertos, a violin concerto and chamber music. In 1842 Auber succeeded Cherubini as director of the Paris Conservatoire, a post he held until 1870. He received many honours during his lifetime, including the Legion of Honour (1825) and membership of the Institute Académie (1829), and became musical director of the Imperial Chapel in 1852. He never married.

Vincent D'Indy described what he called a 'Jewish or Semitic school' in French music, which included Meyerbeer, Auber, HÉROLD, ADAM, DAVID and OFFENBACH. He also wrote that Wagner helped rid French opera of all that was defiling it – 'musicians whose taste and style was bad' – such as Auber, Adam, Halévy and Hérold.[1] However, there is no indication that Auber was of Jewish descent in the standard nineteenth-century French biographies.[2]

Bibliography: *G*; *HBD*; WW

1. Jane F. Fulcher, *Musical Quarterly*, 73 (1995), pp. 458ff. and 78 (2000), pp. 41–57.
2. F. J. Fétis, *Biographie Universelle des Musiciens* (Paris: Librairie de Firmin-Didot, 1877), vol. 1, pp. 162-4.

Avidom, Menachem (b. Stanislav, Ukraine, 6 January 1908; d. Tel Aviv, 5 August 1995)   Emigrated to Palestine in 1925. His original name was Mendel Mahler-Kalstein. His mother was a cousin of MAHLER. He studied in the

American University in Beirut (1926–8) and then at the Paris Conservatory (1928–31) before returning to Tel Aviv in 1935, where he taught music. In 1955 he became director-general of Israel's Performing Rights Society. His early compositions show a modern French influence, but many of his later compositions draw on eastern Mediterranean styles and many have biblical or Israeli themes. He composed nine operas, including *From Generation to Generation* (1955), *The Swindler* (1967), *The Farewell* (1971) and *The First Sin* (1980), but perhaps his best-known work is *Alexandra the Hasmonean* (1959), which won the Israel State prize for opera in 1961. It relates the story of the struggle of the Hasmoneans against the tyranny of Herod. He wrote ten symphonies, although some might more accurately be described as symphonic suites. The first he entitled *Folk Symphony* in order to indicate that it could be played by any kind of orchestra for any sort of audience. The second symphony, *David Symphony*, could also be similarly described. His ninth and tenth symphonies are based on twelve-note themes (see SCHOENBERG). Many of his piano works also have descriptive titles, for example, *Pieces for Miriam*, *Little Ballet for Daniella* and *Yemenite Wedding Suite*. His last completed composition was *Peace Cantata* (1994).
Bibliography: Grad; *G*; *HBD*; Ly*

Avni, Tzvi [Jacob] (b. Saarbrücken, 27 September 1927) Emigrated to Palestine and has lived in Tel Aviv since 1933. He studied composition with BEN HAIM, SETER and EHRLICH in Israel and with COPLAND and FOSS at Tanglewood (1962 and 1964), and electronic music with Ussachevsky at Columbia University, New York and with Myron Schaeffer at the University of Toronto. In 1971 he began teaching composition at the Rubin Academy of Music in Jerusalem. He was married to a Polish-born poetess (died 1973) and this heightened his interest in setting poetry to music, for example, *Song Cycle* for wind quintet (1959), *Prayer* for orchestra (after a poem by his wife Pnina Avni, 1973). After 1970 his interest in electronic music became evident in many of his compositions for example, *Collage* for voice, flute percussion and magnetic tape (1968), *Synchromotrask* (1976), *Of Elephants and Mosquitos* (1971) and the ballet *Requiem for Sounds* (1970). His works include six other ballets, *The Heavenly Jerusalem* for choir and orchestra (1968), *By the Waters of Babylon* for orchestra (1971), *Kaddish* for cello and strings (1971), *Two Psalms* for oboe and string quartet (1975), two piano sonatas (1961 and 1979) and *Mashov*, a concertino for xylophone, ten winds and percussion (1988).
Bibliography: Grad; *G*; *HBD*; Ken; Ly*

Avshalomov, Aaron (b. Nikolayevsk, Siberia, 11 November 1894; d. New York, 26 April 1965) Studied in Zurich but was unable to return to Russia at the outbreak of World War One and so went to China in 1914 and emigrated to the US in 1947. He composed music that integrated Chinese melodies and rhythms with western forms and instrumentation, as in the two operas *Kuan*

Yuin (Peking, 1925) and *The Great Wall* (Shanghai, 1945) and the ballet *The Soul of the Ch'in* (1933). He also wrote violin and piano concertos and a symphony. His symphonic fantasy *Peipung Hutung,* which reflects street life in the capital, was performed by Stokowski in 1935.
Bibliography: *AG; G;* Ho*; Ly*

Avshalomov, Jacob, David (b. Tsingtao, China, 28 March 1919)   Spent his youth in China and then emigrated with his father, Aaron, to the USA, where he received his general and musical education. He studied with Bernard Rogers at the Eastman School, graduating in 1942. He also studied with COPLAND, TOCH and his father. He became a naturalized American citizen in 1944. He taught at Columbia University from 1946 to 1954, where he conducted the university chorus and orchestra. He gained publicity as a composer when Stokowski conducted his *Taking of T'ung Kuan* (1943) in 1952. Soon afterwards he won the New York critics award (1953) for *Tom O'Bedlam,* and the Naumburg Award in 1956 for *Sinfonietta* (1946). His music encompasses a broad spectrum from exotic Chinese style to American folk idiom. He conducted the US premiere of Tippett's *Child of our Time.*
Bibliography: *G;* Ho*

Barnes, Milton (b. Toronto, Canada, 16 December 1931; d. Toronto, 27 February 2001)   Studied composition with Weinzweig (1952–5) and Krenek (1955) at the Royal Conservatory, Toronto. He was a drummer playing jazz and popular music (1950–8) and then studied conducting with Boyd Neel and Walter Susskind in Toronto and later at the Berkshire Summer School in 1958 and 1961. He has conducted a number of orchestras in Canada and the USA. After 1973 he took the decision to spend most of his time composing, and received commissions from a number of public and private Canadian organizations. He has composed orchestral music, chamber music, vocal music and music for theatre, mainly in a romantic idiom. A number of his works have Jewish themes: for example, *Chanukah* Suites 1 and 2 (1977); *Shebatim* (Tribes), a tableau for string orchestra (1979); *Poèm Juif* for violin, viola cello and piano (1977); *The Dybbuk,* a masque for dancing (1977); *Shema,* a sacred service (1977); *Three Israeli Chassidic Songs* (1985); and *Shir Hashirim* (Song of Songs), a dramatic cantata (1975).
Bibliography: K. Macmillan, and J. Beckwith, *Contemporary Canadian Composers* (Oxford: Oxford University Press, 1975); http://www.musiccentre.ca/CMC/dac_rca/eng/a_/Barnes_Milton.html; http://www.cs.bsu.edu/homepages/dlsills/*

Ben Haim, Paul [Frankenburger] (b. Munich, 1 October 1897; d. Tel Aviv, 14 January 1984)   Studied piano, composition and conducting with Friedrich Klose and Walter Courvoisier at the Akademie der Tonkunst, Munich, from 1915 to 1920. He was assistant conductor to Bruno Walter and Hans Knappertsbusch in Munich from 1920 to 1924 and conducted at Augsburg until 1931. With the rise of the Nazis he left Germany for Palestine in 1933. His early compositions written in Germany are very much in the western late Romantic tradition, and he was conservative by nature. The most well-known works he composed in Germany were his *String Trio*, Op. 10 (1927); *Concerto Grosso*, Op. 15 (1931); *Pan*, a symphonic poem for soprano and orchestra (1931); and the large-scale oratorio *Joram* (1933), which was completed in Munich. *Joram* was the last work he completed in Germany and is based on a poem by Rudolf Borchardt relating the story in archaic biblical language of a man whose character and fate are reminiscent of that of Job. Although he wrote a number of choral works after emigrating to Palestine, this was the nearest he came to writing an opera.

On arrival in Palestine he changed his German surname from Frankenburger to Ben Haim. It was common for immigrants to take on a new Hebrew name as a sign of throwing off the burden of one culture and adopting a new life. In Ben Haim's case there was a more immediate reason; it was an attempt to prevent the British authorities from noticing that he was performing as a professional pianist during a visit to Palestine when he only held a tourist visa. He settled in Tel Aviv for the rest of his life. He taught at the conservatories in Tel Aviv and Jerusalem. Although conservative by nature, Ben Haim wanted to absorb the culture of Palestine and create music that fused both western and eastern traditions. He was introduced to the singer and folklore collector Braha Zefira and became acquainted with Near Eastern chants and folk music. He worked to notate the melodic and intricate rhythms of oriental folk song. His early compositions were a series of melodic arrangements and songs of his own for concerts with Braha Zefira.

Ben Haim is generally regarded as the oldest of the founding fathers of Israeli music, although he did not obviously fit into any of the groups of immigrant composers. He composed a wide range of music, from orchestral to vocal and chamber music. His large-scale works include two symphonies. Perhaps his best work is the *Symphonia Concertante* for solo instruments and orchestra, *The Sweet Psalmist of Israel*, commissioned by the Koussevitzky Foundation and composed in 1953. The 'sweet psalmist' is King David, and a harpsichord solo is used to represent King David's stringed lyre. A number of Ben Haim's works have resulted from commissions, for example, the *Sonata in G* for solo violin (1951) was commissioned by Yehudi Menuhin; *Music for Solo Cello* (1974) by Uzi Wiesel; and *Music for Piano* (1957 and 1967) by Varda Nishry. Other compositions include *The Chief Musician* (1957–8), *The Eternal Theme* (1965), *Three Songs Without Words* (1952), *Kabbalai Shabbat* (Friday Evening Service), for soprano, tenor, chorus organ and chamber orchestra (1967), *Clarinet Quintet* (1941) and *Serenade* for flute and string trio (1952).
Bibliography: Grad; *G*; *HBD*; Jehoash Hirschberg, *Paul Ben Haim: his Life and Works* (Jerusalem: Israeli Music Publications, 1990).

Benjamin, Arthur (b. Sydney, 18 September 1893; d. London, 10 April 1960) Came to England in 1911 to study composition under Stanford and piano under Cliffe at the Royal College of Music. He then served in the British Army

during World War One, returning to Australia where he taught at the Sydney Conservatory from 1919 to 1921. He resettled in London in 1921, becoming professor at the Royal College of Music in 1926, where Benjamin Britten was one of his pupils. Besides teaching and composing he was also a concert pianist, giving the first performances of Howell's piano concerto (1914) and Lambert's piano concerto (1931) and the first British performance of GERSHWIN's *Rhapsody in Blue*. In 1940 he became conductor of the Vancouver Symphony Orchestra. He composed a wide range of music, including operas, orchestral music and music for television and films. His composing style was unashamedly Romantic and did not acknowledge any influence of either Stravinsky or the Second Viennese School. He composed over 80 works, including five operas, a symphony, concertos and other orchestral works. In Britain he was a pioneer of film music. His best-known operas were *The Devil Take Her* (1931), *The Tale of Two Cities* (1949–50), which won a Festival of Britain prize in 1951, and *Mañana* (1956), a television opera. He wrote a concerto for oboe and strings (1942) and a harmonica concerto for Larry Adler (1953). Some of his music shows the influence of dance band and Latin American music. His best-known orchestral piece is probably *Jamaica Rumba* (1938).
Bibliography: *G*; *HBD*; Ho*; Ken; Leb; Herbert Howells, 'Arthur Benjamin: 1893–1960', *Tempo*, 55 (1960), pp. 2–3.

Benjamin, George (b. London, 31 January 1960)   Started piano lessons at the age of 7 and began composing when he was 9. His teachers were Peter Gellhorn (piano and composition, 1974–6), Oliver Messiaen (composition, 1976–8) and Yvonne Loriod (piano, 1976–8). At King's College, Cambridge he studied with Alexander GOEHR (1978–82). In 1980 he was the youngest composer to have a work performed at the BBC Promenade Concerts – *Ringed by the Flat Horizon*, a work evoking a Mexican desert thunderstorm. This work was followed by *A Mind of Winter* for soprano and chamber orchestra (1981) and *At First Light* for chamber orchestra (1982). He has proved particularly successful at evoking landscape in music through control of timbre and harmony. Many of his titles are suggestive of musical landscape: *Altitude* (1977), *Flight* (1979), *Cascade* (1990), *Helix* (1992) and *Sudden Time* (1993).

He gave the first performance of Britten's *Sonatina Romantica* at the Aldeburgh Festival in 1983. He spent from 1984 to 1987 at the Institut de Recherche et de Coordination Acoustique/Musique (IRCAM), an institute set up by Pierre Boulez where composers, scientists and computer experts could develop new music, and this led in Benjamin's case to composing *Antara* for two electronic keyboards and ensemble (1985–7; revised 1989), which was premiered in 1987. The work shows how electronically generated sound can closely match that of conventional orchestral instruments such as the flute. It also enables a set of electronically recorded panpipes to project into a concert hall and also to stabilize and increase their range.

Benjamin has worked extensively with the London Sinfonietta. He has

performed widely in America and has conducted and taught at the Tanglewood Summer School since 1999. From 2000 he has been composer-in-residence to the Berlin Philharmonic Orchestra. He is professor of composition at the Royal College of Music in London.
Bibliography: *G**; Ken; Leb; Paul Griffiths, *Modern Music and After* (Oxford: Clarendon Press, 1995); www.fabermusic.co.uk

Berger, Arthur Victor (b. New York, 15 May 1912)   Studied at New York University, graduating in 1934; he then studied at the Longy School of Music (1935–7) and at Harvard under Piston in 1936. He was active in COPLAND's Young Composers group. He is as well known as a music critic as he is as a composer. He composed twelve-note pieces in his teens, but later suppressed all of these works except for *Two Episodes* for piano (1933). As such he was the earliest American composer to use twelve-tone technique (see SCHOENBERG). He studied with Nadia Boulanger from 1937 to 1939, and subsequently taught at Mills College, Brooklyn College, the Juilliard School of Music in New York, at Brandeis University and the New England Conservatory. He was music critic of the *New York Herald Tribune* (1946–53) and co-founder of *Perspectives in New Music* (1962). Much earlier, in 1930, he had founded the journal *Musical Mercury*. After studying with Boulanger, whom he found over-dogmatic and didactic, he composed in a neoclassical Stravinskian style, but after 1957 he composed using serial techniques, eventually combining the two. The style of *Chamber Music for Thirteen Players* (1956) is transitional between neoclassicism and serialism. His works include a string quartet (1958), a piano trio (1980), piano pieces, *Serenade Concertante* for violin and chamber orchestra (1951) songs and choral pieces, including a setting of Psalm 92.
Bibliography: *AG*; *G*; *HBD*; Ho*; Ly*; Howard Pollack, *Harvard Composers* (Maryland, NJ: Scarecrow, 1992).

Berger, Jean (b. Hamm, Germany, 27 September 1909)   Was brought up in Alsace-Lorraine in an Orthodox Jewish family. He attended Vienna and Heidelburg Universities. He studied musicology first with Egon WELLESZ and then with Heinrich Bessler, receiving a Ph.D. in Musicology at Heidelberg in 1931. He studied composition in Paris with Aubert. He taught at the Conservatorio Brasileiro de Musica in Rio de Janeiro from 1939 to 1941, then moved to New York, where he worked as vocal coach and arranger for CBS and NBC. He taught in various American colleges. Most of his compositions are choral, including *Brazilian Psalm* (1941), which has entered the standard American choral repertory, *Vision of Peace* (1949), *Fiery Furnace* (1962) and *The Exiles* (1976).
Bibliography: *AG**

Berlinski, Herman (b. Leipzig, 1910)   Born to Polish immigrant parents in Leipzig, where he began studying piano, composition and conducting at the Leipzig Conservatory from 1928 to 1932. Nazi anti-Jewish legislation prevented him from completing his studies there, and he went to Paris in 1933, where he studied piano with Cortot and composition with Nadia Boulanger until 1938. During this period he was also director of the avant-garde Yiddish Theatre. In 1939 he enlisted in the French Army, but with the fall of France he escaped to the USA in 1940. Later he resumed his studies, taking a degree in Sacred Music at the Jewish Theological Seminary, New York. His early compositions are influenced by SCHOENBERG and Hindemith, but after his experiences as a refugee from the Nazis he concentrated on Jewish sacred and secular music. From 1954 to 1963 he served as organist at New York's Temple Emanu-El, and from 1963 to 1977 as minister of music at the Hebrew Congregation of Washington, DC. His compositions include the oratorio *Job*, an instrumental work, *Symphonic Visions: Jeremiah*, and *From the World of my Father* for cello and piano (1948).

Bibliography: *AG*; Ken; Bret Werb, TROY157 [record sleeve]

Berman, Karel (b. Jindrichuv Hradec, Czech Republic, 14 April 1919)   Studied singing at the Prague Conservatory from 1938 until 1940, when his studies were interrupted and he was taken to the concentration camp at Terezin. Although best known as a bass singer, whilst in Terezin he composed *Poupata* (four songs for bass and piano), *Terezin* (suite for piano) and *Three Songs* (for high voice and piano). Towards the end of World War Two he was moved to various concentration camps, but managed to survive; he was liberated in 1945. He then resumed his studies at the Prague Conservatory, graduating as a singer in 1946. He worked in the opera houses at Opava and Pilsen, and then at the National Theatre in Prague and later worked in the field of television and recording.

Bibliography: Joža Karas, *Music in Terezín* (New York: Pendragon, 1985), p. 124.

Bernstein, Leonard (b. Lawrence, Massachusetts, 25 August 1918; d. New York, 14 October 1990)   Son of Jewish immigrants from the Ukraine, Leonard was initially named Louis after his mother Jennie's grandfather in accordance with Jennie's mother's and father's wishes, but from the time he was a child he was called Leonard. His name was officially changed to Leonard when he was 16. Leonard's father Samuel was what might be described as upwardly mobile. He began cleaning fish in New York's Fulton Street Market, but after studying English he obtained a job with a supplier of beauty products to hairdressers, and eventually he ran his own company, the Samuel Bernstein Hair Company, employing about 50 staff. Leonard loved music from an early age. The household was initially without a piano, but had records ranging from Jewish cantors to pop songs. Bernstein had started piano lessons by the age of 10. In 1929 he gained admission to the prestigious Boston Latin School; he also attended the Hebrew school in the evenings. His father discouraged him from becoming a musician, since his idea of a musician was someone playing in a *klezmer* band; he regarded this as not offering good prospects. He preferred to see his son in business, and after Leonard's graduation from Harvard he offered him a job in his business. Although Boston Latin gave Leonard an excellent education, enabling him to proceed to Harvard, his musical abilities were not noticeably encouraged there.

An important turning point for Bernstein was starting piano lessons with Helen Coates in 1932. She was the first teacher to really recognize his talent. He began a friendship that was to span more than 50 years, and Bernstein maintained a regular correspondence with her throughout his life. In 1935 Bernstein entered Harvard, taking a general course in music, and, in his first year, studying English literature, Italian, German and fine arts. He studied harmony under Walter Piston. In 1937 he met Dimitri Mitropoulis, who told Bernstein that he had the makings of a successful composer, but in 1939 he was advised to devote his life to conducting. This was a conflict that Bernstein wrestled with throughout his life. Time and again he expressed the wish to have time to compose, but all too readily took on very heavy conducting schedules. He became close friends with COPLAND, BLITZSTEIN, DIAMOND, SHAPERO and SCHUMAN.

After graduating from Harvard in 1939 he spent two years at the Curtis Institute, Philadelphia, where his teachers were Vengerova (piano), Reiner (conducting) and Thompson (orchestration). It was at Curtis that he had his first experience of conducting. In 1938 Tanglewood opened as a music summer school and in the succeeding years it developed into an international music festival; Koussevitsky was in charge at the outset. Bernstein went there in 1940 and 1941, and so impressed Koussevitsky with his conducting that in 1942 he was invited to become Koussevitsky's assistant. Amongst other advice, Koussevitsky suggested he change his name to one more ordinary and less Jewish, suggesting Leonard S. Burns; S for Samuelovitch, son of Samuel Burns. He adamantly rejected the advice. Bernstein made his first broadcast appearance conducting the Curtis Institute Orchestra in Brahms's *Serenade* in A minor. In 1941 he played the piano part in Copland's trio *Vitebsk*, Study on a Jewish Theme. This music appeared to him to be an example of how to keep faith with one's ancient roots and at the same time use contemporary language, something he was to put into practice in his First Symphony and also in many of his later works. In Boston in 1942 at the premiere of his Clarinet Sonata he played with the clarinetist David Glazer. His first symphony, entitled *Jeremiah*, was entered but did not win a competition organized by the New England Conservatory in 1943.

In 1942 he began working for Harms-Witmark, a music publisher. His job was to note down for eventual publication the improvisations on records of noted jazz musicians and to make piano arrangements of 'novelty pieces for orchestra'. Apart from being useful experience, it enabled him to get both his Clarinet Sonata and the *Jeremiah Symphony* published. The symphony was first performed in January 1944 in Pittsburgh by Reiner.

In August 1943 Artur Rodzinski needed an assistant conductor for the New

York Philharmonic; he is quoted as saying: 'I have gone through all the conductors I know of in mind and finally asked God whom I should take and God said "Take Bernstein".' On 13 November 1943 at 0900 hours Bernstein received a phone call asking him to stand in for Bruno Walter, who was unwell, in a concert to be broadcast live at 1500 hours. '*Oy gevalt*' (Horror!) was his parents' reaction. This was perhaps the most significant turning point in his career. Apart from obviously being able to rise to the occasion, the significance was heightened by two factors: it was towards the end of the war, at a time when the public avidly listened to the radio; and Bernstein was the youngest to conduct the Philharmonic and one of comparatively few American-born conductors at that time. The concert received ecstatic reviews in the press. In 1943 he teamed up with the choreographer Jerome Robbins to compose the ballet *Fancy Free*. Its box office success led him to compose the musical *On the Town*. In 1945 he completed a commission for the Park Avenue synagogue, New York, a setting of the choral prayer *Hashkiveini* for choir, tenor solo and organ. From 1945 to 1948 he was engaged as conductor of the New York City Orchestra. In 1946 he met the Chilean actress Felicia Montealegre Cohn. They were eventually married in the Temple Mishkan Tefila, New York, on 8 September 1951. In 1947 Bernstein made the first of many visits to Israel (Palestine at that time). Following a concert in Jerusalem in which he performed his *Jeremiah Symphony*, Ravel's piano concerto and Schumann's Second Symphony, he was called back more than any conductor since Toscanini in 1936. However, not everyone liked Bernstein's conducting style, which Virgil Thomson described as 'chorybantic choreography' and 'the miming of facial expressions of uncontrollable states'.

Bernstein was proactive when he saw social injustices. He spoke out against the House of Representatives' Un-American Activities Committee, and was one of those who appealed against EISLER's deportation; he was also one of the sponsors of a concert of his music. He had problems himself in 1953, when the State Department refused to renew his passport because he had supported a number of 'communist front' petitions and organizations. He also supported his wife in 1969, when she organized an appeal against what she saw as the prolonged and unfair detention of the members of the Black Panthers group prior to their trial on charges of plotting to kill a policeman. This well-intentioned support by the Bernsteins stunned many American Jews and Israelis, who saw this as an endorsement of the Black Panthers's notorious expressions of anti-Semitism.

In 1947 he conducted the world premiere of the orchestrated version of Blitzstein's *The Cradle Will Rock* – an opera set in the USA describing a bitter fight between bosses and workers struggling to form a union. He had conducted an earlier version whilst a student at Harvard. In 1949 in Israel he completed his second symphony, entitled *The Age of Anxiety*, after a poem by W. H. Auden. It is, in effect, a piano concerto, which he premiered under Koussevitsky in 1949. He first conducted the Israel Philharmonic Orchestra in

1947, served as their musical adviser in 1948–9, and was co-conductor with Koussevitsky when they toured America in 1951.

The idea for *West Side Story*, perhaps his best-known dramatic work, began in 1949, when Jerome Robbins came to Bernstein with the idea for a modern version of Romeo and Juliet set in slums at the coincidence of the Easter and Passover celebrations. Originally it was to be called *East Side Story*, but was changed to *West Side Story* when it was discovered that the notorious tenements on Manhattan's East Side had all been pulled down. Stephen Sondheim was chosen as the lyricist and Jerome Robbins the choreographer. It received its premiere at the New York Winter Gardens in September 1957.

In 1949 Bernstein conducted the premiere of Messiaen's *Turagalîla Symphony*. In 1952 he completed his opera *Trouble in Tahiti*, and its sequel, *In a Quiet Place*, in 1983. In 1955 he completed a comic opera, *Candide*, based on Voltaire's *Candide*. Although the overture and some parts have been quite frequently performed, the opera itself has been revised several times with varying degrees of success to try to turn it into a workable theatre structure. In 1954 Bernstein completed a work he called *Serenade* (after Plato's *Symposium*) for solo violin, strings, harp and percussion. It might more concisely described as a violin concerto. Initially it received a rather mixed reception, but is probably one of his most satisfying works for concert hall.

Many times Bernstein talked of taking a sabbatical from conducting in order to compose, but, as with his heavy smoking, he found it difficult to give up and leaped at the many invitations to conduct that came his way. Between 1957 and 1971, the year of his *Mass*, he completed only two works: the *Kaddish Symphony* in 1963 and *Chichester Psalms* in 1965. The *Kaddish Symphony* had been commissioned by the Koussevitsky Foundation in 1955. A spur to finish it was when the Israel Philharmonic arranged a date for its premiere in Tel Aviv in 1963. The assassination of President Kennedy occurred around the time of its completion, and Bernstein dedicated it to his memory. The assassination gave particular relevance to the part in which the speaker challenges the Almighty with the words: 'You let this happen, Lord of Hosts! You with your manna, your pillar of fire! You ask for faith. Where is your own?' *Chichester Psalms* was composed in the spring of 1965 for performance in Chichester Cathedral. It comprises three movements, each containing a psalm plus one or more verses from a complementary psalm. It was described by critics after its premiere as 'extremely direct and simple and very beautiful' and 'it parades not, neither does it posture'.

His *Mass*, a theatre piece for singers, players and dancers, was commissioned for the opening of the Kennedy Center in Washington, DC, in 1971. It is scored for a rock band, a brass band and an orchestra and Bernstein set the Latin text of the Catholic Mass, interwoven with songs and choruses in English, expressing the difficulty in sustaining faith at a time of recurring wars and human atrocities. Bernstein had something of a block until he found the right collaborator in Stephen Schwartz (the composer of *Godspell*) to work on the lyrics. At the end of the premiere there was complete silence for three minutes, followed by cheering for half an hour. The reception was mixed. Some felt it exalting and moving; others felt it was a cheap and vulgar showbiz mass.

In 1978 Bernstein's wife Felecia died of lung cancer. He missed her a great deal for the last twelve years of his life, but continued a punishing conducting schedule, including the visit to Berlin at the reunification celebrations, where he conducted Beethoven's Ninth Symphony, substituting *Freude* with *Freiheit* ('Joy' with 'Freedom') in the *Ode to Joy* in the final movement. Schiller had used *Freiheit* in his original version of the *Ode to Joy*, but to satisfy the Prussian censor he had replaced it with *Freude*. Bernstein was thus reverting to the original version. He left a number of works unfinished. He wanted to write what he called a Holocaust opera, but never got down to it. In addition to conducting, performing as a pianist, and composing, he spent much time teaching, for example on television programmes, during the summers at Tanglewood, at Brandeis University (1951–6) and at Harvard in 1973, when he gave the Norton Lectures. He wrote a number of books including *The Joy of Music* (1959), *Young People's Concerts for Reading and Listening* (1962), *The Infinite Variety of Music* (1966), *The Unanswered Question* (1976) and *Findings* (1982). Shortly before his death he expressed a thought that had worried him for most of his life, that he would be remembered less as a composer than as a conductor, and that his 'serious' works would be overshadowed by his 'popular' ones.

Bibliography: *AG*; *G*; *HBD*; Leb; Ly*; Humphrey Burton, *Leonard Bernstein* (London: Faber, 1994); P. Myers, *Leonard Bernstein* (London: Phaidon, 1998); Meryle Secrest, *Leonard Bernstein: a Life* (New York: Knopf, 1994); www.leonardbernstein.com

Blacher, Boris (b. Niu-chang, China, 19 January 1903; d. Berlin, 30 January 1975)   Of part-Russian and part-Jewish parentage. His father was a wealthy Baltic German businessman working for a tsarist Russian bank in northern China. He studied violin and piano as a child, and in his teens moved to Irkutsk, Siberia. In 1919 he worked in the opera house in Charbin, China, and in 1922 came with his mother to Berlin, via Paris. At the wish of his parents, he first studied architecture and mathematics, but then went on to study music with Friedrich Ernst Koch at the Berlin Hochschule für Musik from 1924 to 1926. His father disapproved and stopped his monthly allowance. His mother returned to the Baltics in 1925, and he was left very much to his own devices. He read music at Berlin University from 1927 to 1931. Whilst still a student he played the piano and harmonium in movie theatres and started arranging music for dance bands. His first opus was *Jazz-Koloturen* for soprano, alto-saxophone and bassoon (1929). He continued to support himself as a copier, arranger and composer of film music. His early works were tonal, often witty, showing the influence of jazz and the French composers, Satie and

MILHAUD, and also Stravinsky. A number of his works were performed in Berlin in the 1930s, including *Capriccio* and *Konzertante Musik für Orchestra*, but some were not well-received by Nazi critics.

In 1938, with Karl Böhm's help, he was appointed to teach composition at the Dresden Conservatory. However, he was forced to resign after just a few months because he had used works of Milhaud and Hindemith in his classes. He continued composing during World War Two and his music was performed in Germany, for example the ballet *Harlekinade*, staged in Krefeld in 1940, and the opera *Fürstin Tarakinova*, staged in Wuppertal in 1941. His name was not included in the first edition of the Nazi music critic Gerigk's *Lexikon der Juden in der Musik*, which included musicians of Jewish or semi-Jewish origin. However, by the time of the second edition (1943) Gerigk claimed to have evidence that Blacher's father had been an elder in the Jewish community at Riga, and musicians having a quarter Jewish ancestry were included. Blacher's name was now included (see Appendix I), having a Jewish grandmother, Louise Feliciana Boerling, although she was the daughter of baptized Jews; as a result his music was proscribed. As a reaction to this he composed *Drei Psalms* for baritone and piano (1943), the subject being a cry for God's justice and a heartfelt prayer for deliverance. *Partita* for strings and percussion Op. 24 was written in 1945, amongst the devastation in Berlin. It is a sombre work haunted by the memories of war and the copyright of the completed work was sold for a few packets of cigarettes. These two works are in sharp contrast to many of Blacher's earlier works, which are in a much more cheerful vein.

In 1948 he was appointed professor at the Berlin Hochschule für Musik, where in 1953 he was made director. He remained there until he retired in 1970. He also taught at summer schools, for example Bryanston (1949, 1950), the Salzburg Mozarteum (1950, 1951) and Tanglewood (1955). Among his pupils were Erbse, Einem, Klebe, Reimann, SHERIFF and Max Stern. In the 1950s he became interested in serialism, for example, in the ballet *Lysistrata* (1950), and developed a procedure in which not only does the pitch follow certain rules, but also the metrical organization varies according to a predetermined arithmetic formula. *Ornamente* for piano (1950) was his first work in which this was used. He wrote several operas and ballets on a variety of themes, ranging from the Shakespearean to the contemporary, including one satirizing German character traits. Other works include incidental music, film scores, five string quartets, two piano concertos, a work with a strong jazz influence (*Concertante Musik* for orchestra, 1937) and the oratorio *Der Grossinquisitor* (1942, after Dostoyevsky). *Jüdische Chronik* (1960) was a work written in memoriam after World War Two by Jens Gerlach with music by four fellow German composers, Blacher, Wagner-Régeny, Hartmann and DESSAU. Blacher's contribution was to compose the prologue to the words, 'Will the silent call, will the lame walk, will the deaf hear, will the blind see?'

Bibliography: Grad; *G*; *HBD*; Ken; Leb; Michael H. Kater, *The Twisted Muse*

(Oxford: Oxford University Press, 1997), p. 64*; Erik Levi, *Music in the Third Reich* (London: Macmillan, 1994), p. 67*.

Blech, Leo (b. Aachen, 21 April 1871; d. Berlin, 24 August 1958)   Studied piano with Bargiel and composition with Rudorff, and later with Humperdink at the Berlin Hochschule für Musik, starting in 1890. He spent most of his life as a conductor, at the Stadttheater Aachen (1893–9), the German Theatre in Prague (1899–1906), the Berlin Hofoper (1906–23), the Vienna Volkoper (1925) and the Berlin Staatsoper (1926–37). It was in Prague that he established himself as both a conductor and a composer. He worked with Strauss in Berlin and conducted many of his operas. He was particularly successful in conducting Wagner and Verdi, and also Bizet's *Carmen*. He composed five late Romantic operas, which were successful during his lifetime, among them *Das war ich* (1902), *Alpenkönig und Menschenfiend* (1903), *Aschenbrödel* (1905) and *Versiegelt* (1908). In the 1934 edition of Naumann's famous *Illustrierte Musikgeschichte*, Blech's portrait, along with that of other Jewish composers, was removed from the chapter on 'Wagner's followers in Germany'. He was described by the musicologist Hans Moser as having the 'clever consciousness of his tribe' in knowing the limits of his talent.[1] Nevertheless, in spite of such actions he stayed in his post later than many Jewish musicians in Germany, and it was only when he fulfilled a guest engagement in Riga in 1937 that he found he could not return. He remained in Riga until 1941, when Nazi advances forced him to flee to Stockholm, where he obtained a post with the Stockholm Royal Opera. He returned to Berlin in 1949, where he again became conductor of the Berlin Städtische Oper from 1949 to 1953.
Bibliography: *G**, Leb; Erik Levi, *Music in the Third Reich* (London: Macmillan, 1994), p. 47*;
1. Pamela M. Potter, *Most German of the Arts* (New Haven: Yale University Press, 1998), p. 208.

Blitzstein, Marc (b. Philadelphia, 2 March 1905; d. Fort-de-France, Martinique, 22 January 1964)   Born into a middle-class Jewish family. His paternal grandfather and grandmother emigrated from Odessa to the United States via Liverpool, eventually settling in Philadelphia in 1889. His grandfather initially ran a tobacco business, but then moved into banking. His father Samuel was a steam ticket agent in the family bank, although his interests lay more in politics, particularly socialism. Most of the bank employees were Jewish, many being relatives of the Blitzstein family. His mother, Anna Lewyski (later shortened to Levitt), was born in Russia but came to America with her family as an infant. Her father had a clothing business. Marc was the second child. His elder sister, Jo, with whom he was always close, was born three years earlier, in 1902. His parents were not religious and the children were given a secular education.

Marc showed a talent for music at a very early age, playing the piano in public for the first time at the age of 7. In 1912 his parents began divorce proceedings, and his mother had custody of the children. With her financial situation considerably worsened, the mother and both children went to live in California with her relatives, but returned to Philadelphia in 1917. Marc progressed well at school, but the thing that interested him most was playing the piano and composing, and by 1918 he had composed his opus 4, no. 1, a barcarole entitled *Waterfall*. He continued his piano studies with Maurits Leefson from 1917 to 1918, Hendrik Ezerman from 1918 to 1922 and Alexander Siloti in 1924. He studied at the University of Pennsylvania for two years (1921–3) before entering the Curtis Institute, Philadelphia, in 1924, where he studied composition with Rosario Scalero. In 1926 Blitzstein was soloist with the Philadelphia Orchestra in the Liszt Piano Concerto in E flat, but in spite of the ovation he received he had made up his mind that most of all he wanted to be a composer. His composition studies were completed with Nadia Boulanger in Paris and with SCHOENBERG in Berlin. He was the only American to study with both Boulanger and Schoenberg, although he was not impressed by the latter's method or approach. Blitzstein gave the premiere of his own sonata for piano in New York in 1928. The same year he met Eva Golbeck at the MacDowell Colony; they were eventually married in 1933. Eva was aware of Blitzstein's homosexual orientation from the outset.

Blitzstein always had left-wing leanings and joined the Communist Party, probably in 1938, although he supported the activities of the party well before then. In 1934, after attending a communist congress in Belgium, Marc and Eva were deported to Paris, where they previously had been staying. Blitzstein's early compositions are generally complex in structure and are either no longer performed or in some cases have never been performed. However, by the mid-1930s he began composing in a simpler idiom in order to reach a wider proletarian audience, adopting the EISLER model; for example, he composed a cantata, *Workers' Kids of the World Unite!* (1934). His proletarian style culminated in what has become his best-known work, the opera or musical play *The Cradle Will Rock* (1937). Before he could complete it his wife Eva died of anorexia.

In 1935 Blitzstein met Berthold Brecht and played him a song about a street-walker, *The Nickel Under my Foot*. Suitably impressed, Brecht suggested that Blitzstein write a complete opera about all forms of prostitution. Blitzstein wrote the libretto for *The Cradle Will Rock*, as he did with most of his works. It concerns the attempt of steel workers to create a union, and the devious methods of their employers to frustrate the attempt. The capitalist boss uses bribery and coercion to try to smash the union, but fails. The opera was scheduled to open in June 1937 and was directed by Orson Welles. However, just before its opening the politicians became uneasy about the apparent political agenda and pressured the theatre to ban the production. The performers, production team and the awaiting audience responded by moving to another empty theatre, where the first performance took place, the singers in their ordinary clothes located in different parts of the house and Blitzstein playing the piano accompaniment. As the action switched from one performer to another the spotlight was redirected to locate the individuals in the auditorium. This unorthodox performance was a great success, and received much press publicity because of the circumstances of its first performance. It also seemed that the simplified performance, including piano accompaniment rather than a full orchestra, had a spontaneity that increased its popularity; it ran for 124 nights. A notable performance was given in 1939 by the Harvard Student Union, which was reportedly put together in ten days on a budget of just $35. At this performance the roles of clerk and reporter were played from memory by graduating senior Leonard BERNSTEIN, who also played the piano accompaniment. On this occasion it led the Chief of Police to investigate for 'Reds' in the university.

During World War Two Blitzstein volunteered and served in the US Eighth Air Force, where he was stationed in England and assigned musical tasks. He wrote the choral *Airborne Symphony* (1946) dedicated to the Army Air Forces, and *Freedom Morning* (1943), celebrating the unsung role of black soldiers. The latter was performed in the Royal Albert Hall in a concert that featured the first black chorus in the 72-year history of the hall. *Airborne Symphony* has a speaker and chorus and is a description of the history of aviation from Icarus to World War Two, but it also contains a commentary on the futility of war. Blitzstein hoped that it might become for Americans what Shostakovich's *Leningrad Symphony* became for Russians. After the war Blitzstein continued to compose operas. *Regina*, based on Lillian Hellman's play *The Little Foxes*, was premiered in 1949. It is about a predatory family whose members devour each other through hate, deceit, theft and murder, eventually devouring themselves as well. The music is a mixture of styles, including spirituals sung by the black servants, ragtime played by a black band, some Handelian recitatives and some austere *Sprechstimme*. It was from *Regina* that Bernstein 'borrowed' a musical theme for the song *Maria* in *West Side Story*.

Blitzstein's greatest success, along with *The Cradle Will Rock*, was his translation of WEILL's *Dreigroschenoper*. In 1949, when Blitzstein's nephew came back from Prague, he related how he had been spellbound by a performance of *Dreigroschenoper*, which had been banned by the Nazis since the 1930s. This gave Blitzstein the idea that an English version might go down well in America and he began translating some of the numbers. In January 1950 Blitzstein sang his translation of the number *Pirate Jenny* over the phone to Weill and Lotte Lenya, and both felt he had got it 'just right'. Blitzstein was particularly good with lyrics, some would say better than with composing. Weill died later in 1950, but the first performance in English was given in 1952 with Lotte Lenya as Jenny, 24 years after she had first sung the role in German. It proved a great success. After *Threepenny Opera* Blitzstein was never so successful again. His Broadway opera *Reuben Reuben* (1955) was a failure and *Juno* (1959), based on a play by O'Casey, fared only a little better.

The anti-communist witch hunt conducted by Senator McCarthy was at its height between 1950 and 1954, but it was not until 1958 that Blitzstein was ordered to appear before the Un-American Activities Committee. He was kept under surveillance but no further action was taken.

In 1960 Blitzstein received a grant from the Ford Foundation to write an opera on the controversial *Sacco v. Vanzetti* case of the 1920s. Blitzstein had previously alluded to this case in his short opera *The Condemned*, composed in the early 1930s. It concerned two Italian anarchist immigrants who were convicted of killing two men in a payroll robbery in Massachusetts in 1920. Opinion was divided between those who believed they had been convicted because of their political beliefs, and those who felt those beliefs had compounded their guilt; also, some believed that they were victims of mistaken identity. It was a subject with which Blitzstein became obsessed, and he spent much time researching the background, writing the libretto and composing the music. There was concern in conservative quarters that the Ford Foundation should support such a venture. Blitzstein had a contract with the Metropolitan Opera to stage the opera, although Sir Rudolph Bing, the general manager, felt somewhat jittery about the venture. Blitzstein spent the summer of 1960 in a rented cottage at Martha's Vineyard working on it, but by October 1960, when the opera should have been largely drafted, he had not written enough for the Met to make an assessment.

He spent the winter of 1960 and spring 1961 in Rome continuing to research and compose. He was invited to spend the summer of 1962 at an American–Israeli congress on the creative arts, and spent the summer in Israel. This proved very much to his liking, and he was able to make progress with *Sacco and Vanzetti*. For the academic session 1962/3 he was invited to teach playwriting at Bennington College, Vermont, although he had never written a play, only librettos for setting to music. While there he met the writer Bernard Malamud. Impressed with his short stories and freshly back from Israel, Blitzstein was smitten with the idea of setting to music two of these, *The Magic Barrel* and *Idiots First*, both with strong Jewish characters and settings. He temporarily set aside *Sacco and Vanzetti* to work on them. After Bennington he had a number of health problems; he decided to move south for warmer weather and went to Martinique. Sadly, during a visit with a full wallet to a waterfront bar he was robbed and beaten by three sailors and died in hospital in Fort-de-France. *Sacco and Vanzetti*, *The Magic Barrel* and *Idiots First* were left incomplete.

Others works by Blitzstein include the ballet *Cain* (1930), incidental music for *Julius Caesar* (1937), *King Lear* (1956), *A Midsummer Night's Dream* (1958) and *A Winter's Tale* (1958), operas *Triple Sec* (1928) and *No for an Answer* (1940), a piano sonata (1927), two string quartets (1930, 1932), and a piano concerto (1931). Blitzstein composed in so many different styles that he is difficult to characterize. His integration of music with texts in the main written by himself into large-scale theatrical works on socially conscious themes laid down a model for many future American stage composers.

Bibliography: *AG*; *G*; *HBD*; Leb; Eric A. Gordon, *Mark the Music: the Life and Work of Marc Blitzstein* (New York: St Martins Press, 1989)*.

Bloch, Ernest (b. Geneva, 15 July 1880; d. Portland, Oregon, 15 July 1959)   Son of a Swiss-Jewish businessman. His grandfather had been president of a small Jewish community of Lengnau in the Aargau Canton of Switzerland. His father originally planned to study for the rabbinate but later decided on a business career. Ernest was brought up in traditional Jewish surroundings and was familiar with traditional Jewish melodies. His father hoped that he would eventually join his clock business and was not enthusiastic about him becoming a composer. He began violin lessons at the age of 9, although from an early age he was more interested in composition. It is said that he vowed to devote himself to music in a ritual ceremony in which he wrote out his vow, placed it under a pile of stones and set light to it. He continued his music studies from the age of 14 with Emile Jaques-Dalcroze (composition) and Louis Rey (violin) at the Geneva Conservatory. He wrote several juvenile works between 1895 and 1900 that were not published. These include *Symphonie Orientale*, a movement for string quartet, a violin concerto and cello sonata. When he was 17 he went to Brussels and whilst there studied violin under Eugène Ysaÿe and composition under François Rasse. Ysaÿe felt from the outset that he was better as a composer than as a violinist, thus confirming Bloch's own opinion. In 1900 he completed his musical education with Ivan Knorr in Frankfurt-on-Main and Ludwig Thuille in Munich.

From 1902 to 1909, in what might be described as his early mature phase, he composed a symphony in C sharp minor, two short symphonic poems entitled *Hiver–printemps*, a song cycle *Poèmes d'automne* and the opera *Macbeth*. In the symphony the influence of Strauss is evident, and in the expressionist symphonic poems that of Debussy. The last movement of the symphony has the character of a lively Chassidic dance. The opera *Macbeth*, composed in the style of the nineteenth-century Grand Opera, was a four-year undertaking. Roger Sessions, a pupil of Bloch, writing in 1927, suggested that this might be regarded as Bloch's masterpiece, although this view is not now generally held, perhaps because it is rarely heard. In it he moulds the styles of Moussorgsky's *Boris Godunov* and Debussy's *Pelléas et Melisande* but at the same time shows signs of his own emerging originality. It contains elements of irony and profound pessimism. *Macbeth* was performed in 1910 at the Opéra-Comique in Paris, four years after its completion. It received 16 performances in its first season, and was then neglected, not being revived until 1938 and again in 1953.

During this early phase financial difficulties meant that he had to return to his father's business and work as a bookkeeper in the shop. In 1904 he married Marguerite Schneider. It was the music critic Romain Roland who responded favourably to his symphony and the opera *Macbeth* and who persuaded him to abandon shop-keeping and devote his time fully to music.

From 1911 to 1915 Bloch earned his living teaching composition and aesthetics at the Geneva Conservatory. In a letter to his friend, the Swiss poet Edmond Fleg, written in 1906, Bloch expresses the rediscovery of himself as a Jew and indicates his more distant goal: ' I think, I shall write one day songs to be sung in synagogue in part by the cantor, and part by the faithful.' It was another 28 years before this was realized, but it gives an indication of his thinking.

What is often described as his Jewish phase is the period from approximately 1912–19, in which he began writing a projected opera, *Jézebel*, which was never to be completed. His compositions of this period include *Trois poèmes Juif*, dedicated to his father and incorporating themes from the uncompleted opera *Jézebel*, Psalms 137 and 114 for soprano and orchestra, *Schelomo*, Psalm 22 for baritone, the symphony *Israel* and the first string quartet in B minor. In what sense are these works Jewish? Bloch states:

> It is not my desire to attempt a 'reconstruction' of Jewish music … It is the Jewish soul that interests me, the complex, glowing, agitated soul that I feel vibrating throughout the Bible … All this is in us, all this that I endeavour to hear in myself and to transcribe in my music: the venerable emotion of a race that slumbers way down in our soul.

In his 'Jewish' works he does not quote actual Hebrew melodies or synagogual chants, but uses stylistic elements found in Hebrew music, such as quarter tones and rhythmic patterns. *Schelomo* for cello and orchestra is his most frequently performed work. He had been long interested in setting the Book of Ecclesiastes to music. He loved the sonority of Hebrew, but felt insufficiently familiar with the language to proceed with the project. He met the sculptress Catherine Barjansky and her cellist husband Alexandre. At the time Catherine was modeling a figure of King Solomon (the legendary author of Ecclesiastes). This gave him the inspiration to use the cello as the voice of King Solomon in creating this rhapsody. The contrast between the king's great but transient earthly power and the emptiness of all endeavour as portrayed in the first chapter of Ecclesiastes is reflected in the music; on one hand the pomp and splendor of Solomon's court, and on the other an introspective communing with the self. *Schelomo* dedicated to the Barjanskys.

Bloch's *Israel Symphony* of 1912–16 was inspired by the Day of Atonement and is in two movements played without a break. The mood of the first movement is turbulent, disturbed by inner doubts and conflict; the second brings peace to the repentant sinner and concludes with the chorus intoning a Hebrew prayer.

Early in 1916 Bloch visited the United States as touring conductor of the Maude Allen dance troupe. During what was intended to be an extensive tour the company became bankrupt and Bloch was stranded without resources in America. He was engaged primarily in teaching from 1917 to 1920 at Mannes College, New York. During this period his music was performed in a number of concerts and thus became more familiar to American audiences. The Flonzaley Quartet gave the premiere of his first string quartet in 1916, and in 1917 he conducted his *Trios poèmes Juif* with the Boston Symphony Orchestra. The premiere of both *Schelomo* and *Israel* were given that year. In 1919 he received the Elizabeth Sprague Coolidge prize for his Suite for Viola and Piano.

A measure of his growing reputation in America was his appointment as director of the Cleveland Institute of Music in 1920. During this period he took on American citizenship (1924). He was never really happy in this administrative post and many of the reforms he wanted to introduce, such as reducing examinations in favour of more direct practical experience, met with resistance; this led to his resignation in 1925. He then became director of the San Francisco Conservatory. During this period his compositions are more diverse in nature. They include the Suite for Viola and Piano, a sonata for violin and piano no. 1, the suite *Baal Shem* for violin and piano and a piano quintet. These do not belong so overtly to the Jewish cycle and show new strands of interest – in the baroque period, for example *Concerto Grosso* No. 1 (1925), in impressionism, for example *Five Sketches in Sepia* for piano (1923) and in the influence of America, for example the symphonic rhapsody *America*. During this period he became teacher to a whole generation of American composers, including Roger Sessions, Douglas Moore, Quincy Porter, George ANTHEIL and Randall Thompson.

In 1930 he received an endowment that enabled him to give up his post at San Francisco and devote himself entirely to composition. He had become friendly with the cantor of the Temple Emanuel in San Francisco, Reuben Rinder. Rinder was able to persuade the philanthropic Warburg family to give Bloch a 10,000-dollar commission in 1929, in order to write a Sabbath morning service for the cantor. Bloch made thorough preparations by spending one full year studying Hebrew and synagogue music under Rinder's guidance. He wrote nearly 2,000 exercises in sixteenth-century counterpoint and made a careful analysis of the subtleties and sonorities of the Hebrew text. He then returned to Switzerland and lived in isolation at Roverado Capriasco in the Canton of Ticino until he had completed *Sacred Service*, in 1933. On completing this he had fulfilled a wish first expressed in 1906. In contrast to his use of the Book of Ecclesiastes in *Schelomo*, he now felt that his understanding of Hebrew was sufficient to express himself confidently. The work can be regarded as an oratorio in five sections, performed without a break, the text being based on the American Union Prayer Book for Jewish Worship. It is scored for baritone (cantor), mixed choir and a large orchestra. It begins by using a six-note motive, *g-a-c-b-a-g* in the Mixolydian mode, and this theme pervades the whole work. Bloch also uses motives from *Schelomo*, *Trios poèmes Juif* and also from the cantorial chant *Tsur Yisroel* that Rinder sent him. The work received its premiere in Turin on 12 January 1934, and in New York on 11 April 1934. Many consider it Bloch's greatest work.

1 Felix Mendelssohn.

2 Gustav Mahler.

3 Arnold Schoenberg, photographed during his Berlin Years.

4 The Kroll Theatre, Berlin. Klemperer was director of the Kroll Theatre from 1927 to 1931 and Zemlinsky conducted there from 1927 to 1930. During that period it was the leading experimental theatre in Europe staging works by Schoenberg, Weill and Milhaud.

5 The Neues Theatre am Schiffbauerdamm, Berlin, scene of the sensational success of Kurt Weill's Dreigroschenoper in 1928.

6 The American-Soviet Music Society (l-r) Mordeai Bauman, Morton Gould, Betty Bean, Serge Koussevitzky, Elie Siegmeister, Margaret Grant, Aaron Copland, and Marc Blitzstein. Several American musicians had strong socialist leanings.

7 Ferdinand David, violinist and composer, who played the premiere of Mendelssohn's Violin Concerto in 1845.

8 Paul Dukas.

9 Hanns Eisler (right) and Ernst Busch in 1961. With his experience of cabaret singing, Busch was an unrivalled interpreter of many of Eisler's songs.

10 Gerald Finzi in the 1930s.

Other major works that Bloch wrote during the 1930s were the symphonic poem *In the Wilderness* for orchestra with cello obbligato (1936), *Evocations* (1937), a three-movement orchestral suite, and the violin concerto (1938). In *In the Wilderness* the role of the cello is somewhat different from that in *Schelemo*. Bloch described the work, which is in six movements, as 'meditations' describing the 'apparently unhappy destiny of man'. The work is dark and melancholic, suggesting fears and forebodings. The cello plays between each of the six movements rather in the role of a commentator. Although Bloch was not directly involved in the tragedy arising from the rise of Nazism, this work is undoubtedly influenced by those events. The work was given its premiere by the Los Angeles Philharmonic Orchestra under KLEMPERER on 21 January 1937.

A violin concerto was begun in 1930 but did not really take shape until after 1935, when Bloch had returned to America. Bloch uses an American Indian motif right at the start, which repeats itself in each of the three movements. The whole work does not have a single style; at times it has the rhapsodic character of his earlier Hebraic works, and at times the orchestration shows American influence. It was premiered by Szigeti with the Cleveland Orchestra in 1939.

From 1939 Bloch became professor of music at the University of California at Berkeley, where he taught summer courses until he retired in 1952. When not teaching he lived in isolation near Portland, Oregon, in a house on the cliffs overlooking the Pacific, where he was free to compose. He received awards and prizes in his later years: the first gold medal in music of the American Academy of Arts and Sciences (1947) and the New York Music Critics Circle Awards (1952) for Quartet no. 3 and *Concerto Grosso* no. 2. During the 1950s he was very prolific, composing his third, fourth and fifth string quartets, *Rhapsodie hébraique* (1951), *Concerto Grosso* no. 2 (1952), *Sinfonia breve* (1952), a symphony for trombone and orchestra (1954), Symphony in E flat (1955), *Proclammation* for trumpet and orchestra (1955), and *Last Poems* for flute and orchestra (1958).

In 1957 Bloch was diagnosed as having cancer; he underwent surgery but it was not successful and he died in 1959.
Bibliography: *AG*; *G*; *HBD*; Ken; Ly*; Robert Strassburg, *Ernest Bloch: Voice in the Wilderness* (Los Angeles: California State University Press, 1977).

Boskovich, Alexander Uriyah (b. Kolozsvár, Transylvania [Cluj-Napoca, Romania], 16 August 1907; d. Tel Aviv, November, 1964)   Came from a deeply religious family whose ancestors were rabbis. His initial education was in the Jewish Lyceum Tarbut in Cluj; he later took advanced piano lessons with Ebenstein in Vienna, and then with Lazare Levi, followed by composition lessons in Paris with DUKAS. The latter gave him a lifelong predilection for French music. He returned to Cluj in 1930, acting as coach and conductor to a local opera group. He was interested in reviving Jewish national identity in Transylvania, and carried out fieldwork in the Jewish villages in the Carpathian mountains; this inspired one of his first compositions, *Chansons populaire juives* (1936), a suite of arrangements of Yiddish folk songs. In 1938, with the rise of a fascist government in Romania, he lost his position at the Cluj Opera.

He went to Palestine, where his *Chansons populaire juives* was performed. He remained in Palestine and continued composing, but this brought him very little money. He taught for a while at an elementary school and gave private music lessons. It was not until 1946 that he obtained a regular position in the Academy of Music in Tel Aviv. He was inspired by life in Palestine to continue composing music, particularly with Jewish themes. His works include a violin concerto (1942), an oboe concerto (1943), the *Semitic Suite* (1945), which is a series of dances and songs that convey something of the atmosphere of Palestine, a set of piano pieces entitled *Album for the Young*, a setting of Psalm 28 for contralto and orchestra and incidental music for the Habima Theatre. Boscovich had a period of depression during which few new works appeared. He spent much of this period teaching, studying philosophy and analyzing music of contemporary western composers, such as Webern. When he started to compose again the effects of this analytic study were evident. He completed only four new works (*Canto di Ma'alot*, 1960; a cantata, *Bat Israel*; a concerto da camera for violin and chamber orchestra, 1964; and *Ornaments* for flute and orchestra, 1964) before his death in 1964.
Bibliography: Grad; *G*; Ho*; Ly*; Jehoash Hirshberg, *Music in the Jewish Community of Palestine 1880–1948* (Oxford: Clarendon Press, 1995).

Bosmans, Henriëtte [Hilde] (b. Amsterdam, 6 December 1895; d. Amsterdam, 2 July 1952)   Daughter of Henri Bosmans, principal cellist of the Concertgebouw Orchestra, and the Jewish pianist and piano teacher Sarah Benedicts. Henriëtte studied piano with her mother and also at the Amsterdam Conservatory, graduating in 1912. By the 1920s her career as a pianist was firmly established. She gave the first Dutch performance of Berg's chamber concerto for piano, violin and 13 wind instruments. She began composing in her teens and later studied counterpoint with Kersbergen and instrumentation with Cornelius Dopper (1921–2). Many of her compositions are inspired by musicians with whom she performed. Her early works are lyrical, with Romantic influences, but after 1927 her compositions become more expressionistic, reminiscent of Ravel and Debussy. She became engaged to the violinist Francis Koene in 1934, but he died a year later. The *Concertstuk* for violin and orchestra, intended for him, was first performed by Louis Zimmerman in 1935. Being half-Jewish, she was not allowed to perform after 1942, but resumed again in 1945. Her compositions after the war were almost entirely vocal, written for the French singer and close friend Noéme Perugia, whom she accompanied. These included *Lead Kindly Light* (1945) to words by John Henry Newman, *Les Deux enfants du Roi* (1949) to words by Verhaeren,

Aurore (1950) by Verdet, *Das macht den Menschen glücklich* (1951) by Heine and *The Artist's Secret* (1948) with words by Schreiner, composed for Peter Pears and Benjamin Britten. She also wrote a song setting of Heine's *Belsazar* (1936), two cello concertos (1922 and 1924), a piano concerto (1929) and a string quartet (1928).

Bibliography: G; Aaron I. Cohen, *International Encyclopaedia of Women Composers* (New York: Books and Music Inc., 1987), p. 98; www.leosmit.nl/eng/contemporaries/jewish_text.htm]*

Brandmann, Israel (b. Kamenetz-Podolsk, Russia, 1 December 1901)   Began studying the violin at the age of 7, and attended the St Petersburg Conservatory from 1913 to 1917. He was active in his home town as a conductor and violinist. After conducting a choir on a tour of Romania, he emigrated to Palestine in 1921, where he worked as conductor, violinist and teacher until 1924. He then went to Vienna to study composition with Franz Schmidt, and later with Alban Berg at the Hochschule für Musik. After returning to Palestine, he became active as a composer, combining the idiom of modern European music with that of the East. His works include *Variationen über einem Palästinensischen Volktanz* for string quartet, *Variationen über ein Volksthema* for clarinet and piano, a symphonic poem *Hechalutz* (The Pioneer) for large orchestra, *Three Passover Melodies* for clarinet and string quartet, sonata for violin and piano, an arrangement of the *Hatikvah* for solo, chorus and piano, *Mourning Cantata* for baritone and orchestra and two string quartets.

Bibliography: G; Ho*; Aron M. Rothmüller, *The Music of the Jews: an Historical Appreciation* (London: Vallentine Mitchell, 1953).

Brant, Henry Dreyfus (b. Montreal, 15 September 1913)   Interested in music from an early age, building his own instruments at the age of 9. His father was a violinist. Brant studied at the McGill Conservatory from 1926 to 1929, then went to New York (1929–34) to the Institute of Musical Art, and then to the Juilliard School of Music (1932–4) under Rubin GOLDMARK. HE also studied privately with Riegger, ANTHEIL and Fritz Mahler. He earned a living by composing, arranging and conducting. He has a love for burlesque and a sense of humour that perhaps has led to the comment that his compositions are inspired more by gimmick than by human experience. However, this may be unfair: he was interested in instrumental timbre and composed pieces for one family of instruments, for example, *Artists and Devils*, for flute and flute orchestra, 1931, revised 1956 and 1979; *Music for a Five-and-Dime Store* (1931) for kitchenware; and *Orbits* for soprano, organ and 80 trombones (1979). In creating a kind of spatial music he anticipated Stockhausen, although this has been rarely acknowledged. For example, in 1953 he composed *Antiphony 1*, in which he started spatial music experiments with instruments around and outside the hall. He also composed film music, and orchestrated for the bands of Benny Goodman and André Kostelanetz. He orchestrated the score for

BLITZSTEIN's *Valley Town*. He also wrote music for the film *My Father's House*, incidental music for *The Eternal Light* (1945–6) and wrote a symphony entitled *The Promised Land*. He taught at Columbia University (1945–52), the Juilliard School of Music (1947–54) and Bennington College, Vermont (1957–80).
Bibliography: *AG*; *CC*; *G*; Ho*; Leb; Wilfred Mellors, *Music in a New Found Land* (London: Barrie & Rockcliff, 1964).

Braunfels, Walter (b. Frankfurt, 19 December 1882; d. Cologne, 19 March 1954) Came from a literary, musical and half-Jewish background. His father made a well-known translation of Cervantes and his mother was the great-niece of the composer Louis Spohr. He received his first piano lessons from Kwast and later, after a phase of studying law and economics, he reverted to music, studying piano with Leschetizky in Vienna and with Thuille and Mottl in Munich. Affected by his experiences during World War One, he converted to Catholicism and marked this by setting the *Te Deum* in 1921. In 1925 he established and directed the Cologne Hochschule für Musik. In 1933 students reported him to the Reich Education Ministry for allegedly thwarting the promotion of a musicologist and National Socialist supporter, Büchen.[1] With increased Nazi control of educational institutions, he was later forced to resign in 1933. He left for Switzerland until after the war, when he returned to reorganize the Cologne Hochschule für Musik, retiring in 1950. His compositions are mainly in the classical-Romantic tradition. He wrote seven operas, about 15 orchestral works, including a piano concerto, four string quartets and a number of works for voices and orchestra. His operas were banned by the Nazis in the mid-1930s and most never regained the stage. His most successful opera was *Die Vögel*, based on Aristophanes' play *The Birds*. It was first performed in 1920 and was revived and recorded in the 1990s. His string quartets were also revived and performed in the 1990s.
Bibliography: *G*; *HBD*; Martin Anderson, *Tempo*, 210 (1999), pp. 52–6*.
1. Pamela M. Potter, *Most German of the Arts* (New Haven: Yale University Press, 1998), p. 100.

Brod, Max (b. Prague, 27 May 1884; d. Tel Aviv, 20 December 1968) Began studying piano at the age of 6; his teacher was Adolf Schreiber. He studied law at the University of Prague and was employed for a time as a minor government official, but eventually he turned his interest to literature and music. In 1902 he met and became lifelong friends with Franz Kafka. He was instructed by Kafka to destroy all the latter's unpublished works after his death, but he defied his friend's wishes and edited and published many of Kafka's major works. He also wrote a biography of Kafka and edited his diaries and letters. Brod wrote several novels, his most famous being *Tycho Brahes Weg zu Gott* (1916; The Redemption of Tycho Brahe). He was for many years music critic on the *Prager Tagblatt*. He began composing in 1900 and continued until the mid-1950s, completing 38 opuses. Most of the works are vocal and include *Requiem Hebraicum*, Op. 20, which was composed after the death of his wife.

Although less well known as a composer than as a writer on music and advocate of other composers, he was given disproportionately high prominence in *Lexikon der Juden in der Musik* (see Appendix I). One reason for the lengthy article was that he had written an article that purported to prove the intrinsically Jewish nature of MAHLER's music.

Brod had been an active Zionist since 1912, and fled from the Nazi invasion of Czechoslovakia in 1939 on the last train to leave before the arrival of the German Army. He lived in Palestine (Israel) for the rest of his life. He was drama adviser to the Habima Theatre Company in Tel Aviv. He continued both writing, for example, books on Mahler and on the music of Israel, and composing, evolving a style that blended oriental and European traditions. Throughout his life he made important contributions to the work of other composers. After his piano teacher, Schreiber, committed suicide, Brod had some of his songs published and wrote his biography. He translated into German many of Janáček's operas and wrote the first biography of Janáček. He translated WEINBERGER's *Svanda the Bagpiper*, rewriting the first act and persuading Weinberger to modify the music. He also wrote the librettos for DESSAU's oratorio *Hagadah shel Pessach*, composed in the mid-1930s but not performed until much later, and for LAVRY's opera *Dan the Guard*, which premiered in 1941.
Bibliography: *G*; *HBD*; Ho*; Leb; Ly*; www.pitt.edu/~kafka/brod.htm

Brüll, Ignaz (b. Prossnitz, Moravia [Prostejov, Slovakia], 7 November 1846; d. Vienna, 17 September 1907) Eldest son of a prosperous Jewish merchant family living in Prossnitz. In 1850 the family moved to Vienna, where Ignaz was to live for the rest of his life. Although his father initially wanted him to take over the family business, it was apparent at an early age that his great talents lay in music. He studied piano with Julius Epstein and composition with Otto Dessoff and Johann Rufinatscha. He began composing at an early age, writing his first piano concerto at the age of 14, at which time Anton RUBINSTEIN considered he had great potential. His second piano concerto was written when he was 22. This is a more accomplished work than the earlier concerto and shows more imaginative writing. It has been more widely performed. He toured Germany as a concert pianist and when not touring he gave concerts in Vienna. Earlier, in 1864, he wrote his first opera, *Die Bettler von Samarkand*, and although he submitted it to the Court Theatre in Stuttgart nothing became of it. However, his second opera, *Das Goldene Kreuz*, completed in 1875, was a sensational success, boosting his reputation both as a composer and a pianist. In 1878 he toured England as a concert pianist. During this visit his opera received its English premiere. He made a second visit to England as a concert pianist in 1881. In 1882 he married Marie Schosberg, daughter of a Viennese banker, after which he drastically reduced his concert playing to concentrate on composition. He had a large circle of musician friends, including Brahms, Karl GOLDMARK, Gustav MAHLER and the music critic Hanslick. He was a particularly close friend of Brahms, who greatly admired him as a performer. Brahms used to try out his new compositions on a small group of critics and friends before giving public performances. All four of his symphonies and the B flat piano concerto were tried in this way with Brüll playing; in the case of the symphonies as four-handed piano arrangements, with Brahms on the second piano.

There are over 100 opuses in the catalogue of Brüll's works. These include ten operas, a ballet entitled *Ein Märchen aus der Champagne*, a symphony, three orchestral serenades, three overtures, two piano concertos, a violin concerto, chamber music and some Jewish songs. His Third Piano Sonata in E minor, Op. 81 was thought by his contemporaries to be the best after Brahms. In his later years he was somewhat conservative as a composer, refusing to have anything to do with musical developments at the end of the nineteenth century.
Bibliography: Grad; *G*; *HBD*; Ly*; Hartmut-Wecker, CDA67069 [record sleeve]

Brün, Herbert (b. Berlin, 9 July 1918) Emigrated to Palestine and studied composition with Wolpe at the Jerusalem Conservatory from 1936 to 1938 and later at Columbia University from 1948 to 1949. Notable among his early works is the *Concertino for Orchestra* (1947), which uses a twelve-note row (see Schoenberg) in its first movement. In 1949 he was commissioned by Leonard Bernstein to write *Dedication Overture* in honour of Israel's first president, Chaim Weizmann. His early chamber works include *Sonatina for Violin* (1948), *Sonatina for Viola* (1950), *Sonatina for Flute* (1949) and *Poem* for low voice and string quartet (1949) to words by Natan Alterman. He also composed for theatre, radio and television. His first string quartet (1953) was performed at the International Society for Contemporary Music Festival at Baden-Baden in 1955, and his second at Strasburg in 1958. From 1955 to 1961 he carried out research on electronic music in Paris, Cologne and Munich and from 1963 taught electronic and computer music at the University of Illinois. His compositions based on electronic or computer technology include *Gestures for 11* (1964), *Soniferous Loops* for live performers and tape (1964) and *Dust* (1976), *More Dust* (1977) and *Destiny* (1978).
Bibliography: Grad*; *G*; *HBD*

Castelnuovo-Tedesco, Mario (b. Florence, 3 April 1895; d. Los Angeles, 16 March 1968) Came from an Orthodox Jewish family whose ancestors had lived in Florence for 400 years. Neither of his parents was a musician, but his maternal grandfather encouraged him greatly in his musical studies. It was from him that Castelnuovo-Tedesco attributed his musical talent, having found a setting of Hebrew prayers to music by his grandfather. In his early teens the boy studied piano and composition at the Cherubini Royal Institute of Music. His early compositions were songs and pieces for piano, and it was in the area of shorter forms of music that he excelled, so much so that he was able to work as a freelance composer and pianist throughout the interwar years. At around 1920 he turned to larger forms. He wrote *Fioretti* for voice and orchestra (1920) which is a setting of verses by Francis of Assisi, and an opera, *La Mandragola* (1925), with the libretto based on a comedy by Machiavelli. He became more internationally known after the New York Philharmonic under Toscanini gave the first performance of his *Symphonic Variations* for violin and orchestra in 1930. This was followed in 1931 by his first violin concerto (*Concerto Italiano*, Op. 31, composed in 1924), his second violin concerto (1933) and his cello concerto (1935), all three works being performed by the New York Philharmonic under Toscanini. The soloist in the violin concertos was Heifetz, and in the cello concerto Piatigorsky. When Italy was clearly showing solidarity with Nazi Germany, Castelnuovo-Tedesco fled to the USA, initially settling in New York but then establishing a permanent home in California, teaching in the Los Angeles Conservatory. He took on American citizenship in 1946 and lived there for the rest of his life, although making occasional returns to Italy after the war.

He was a very prolific composer, writing over 200 works, including five operas, a number of film scores, two piano, two guitar and one oboe concerto, and a large amount of choral and chamber music. Two major influences inform his music: Shakespeare and the Bible. Two of his operas, *The Merchant of Venice* and *All's Well That Ends Well*, are based on the Shakespeare plays, and 33 song and sonnet settings also use Shakespeare's words. The biblical influence is evident in the *Sacred Service for Sabbath Eve* (1943), in the second violin concerto subtitled *The Prophets*, in a series of biblical oratorios including *The Book of Ruth* (1949), *The Book of Jonah* (1951), *The Song of Songs* (1955), *The Book of Ester* (1962), a biblical opera *Saul* and a piano piece *Le Danze del Re David* (1925). The second violin concerto (*The Prophets*) has movements subtitled *Isaiah*, *Jeremiah* and *Elijah*, although he made it clear that there were no programmatic associations; he was seeking, he said, to represent 'the flaming eloquence of the ancient prophets among the surrounding voices of the people and voices of nature'. A comment that has been made about Castelnuovo-Tedesco (see G) is that he showed exceptional gifts in his youth, but that he failed to bring them to full fruition owing to excessive facility and inadequate self-criticism. His potential is evident in his early compositions, the least successful generally being the large-scale ones. His works are not frequently performed today; the most popular is the guitar concerto (Op. 99).
Bibliography: *AG*; *G*; *HBD*; Ho*; Leb; Ly*

Chasins, Abram (b. New York, 17 August 1903; d. New York, 21 June 1987) Writer, broadcaster, pianist and composer. He studied at the Juilliard with Rubin GOLDMARK, at Columbia University with Ernest Hutcheson, and at the Curtis Institute, Philadelphia, with Josef Hofmann. From 1926 to 1935 he was a teacher at the Curtis Institute. He composed over 100 works; the best known of which are two piano concertos (1928, 1931), *Three Chinese Poems* for piano

(1928) and *Parade* for orchestra (1930). The orchestrated version of *Three Chinese Poems* (1929) was the first work by an American composer to be performed by Toscanini. Chasins broadcast a regular music programme entitled *Arthur Chasin Music Series* from 1932 to 1938.
Bibliography: *AG*; *HBD*; Ho*; Ly*

Copland, Aaron (b. Brooklyn, New York, 14 November 1900; d. Westchester, New York, 2 December 1990)   Fifth child of Russian–Jewish emigrants. His maternal grandfather, Aaron Mittenthal, left a village on the Russian-Polish border in search of freedom and security in America. Aaron's mother, Sarah Mittenthal, came over with his grandmother and four other children and the family settled in Illinois and Texas before settling in New York in 1881. Aaron's father, Harris Kaplan, was born in Shavli, then part of Lithuania. When faced with military conscription, Harris emigrated via Scotland to New York at the age of 17, and it seems probable that whilst in Scotland he changed his name to Copland. The families of both parents had settled in America before the major Jewish migrations. By the time Aaron was born, his father was running a small department store in Brooklyn, selling clothing, shoes, toys and general household items. The family lived above the shop. The business was success-ful and Aaron was brought up in comfortable middle-class surroundings. They employed a maid and by 1914 owned a car. The family celebrated the main Jewish festivals, but the religious practice had to fit round the needs of the business. By the time of Aaron's *bar mitzvah*, Harris had been president of the local synagogue for some years.

His elder brother and sister played the violin and piano and Aaron made his first attempts at composing songs when he was only 8 years old. He had piano lessons from Leopold Wolfsohn and made his first public début in a student concert held, ironically, in the auditorium of a department store in 1917. He went to few concerts in his youth, but a notable one was around 1915, when he heard Paderewski perform; this was a defining moment, when he decided to become a musician. He had further piano lessons with Victor Wittgenstein and Clarence Adler and in 1917 began studies on harmony with Rubin GOLDMARK. Although Goldmark's preference was for German com-posers, Copland became more interested in Russian and French composers, particularly Skriabin, Mussorgsky and Debussy, and this is evident in his apprentice compositions of the period. He graduated from high school in 1918 and decided not to go to college. He had a number of part-time jobs as a pianist in dance bands, and was encouraged by a literary friend, Aaron Schaffer, to study in Paris. In June 1921, with the aid of his savings and a scholarship, Copland set off, intending to stay in Paris for one year. However, after being accepted as a pupil by Nadia Boulanger, who was to have a major influence on him, he stayed until 1924. In Paris he shared rooms with a distant relative, Harold Clurman, who was studying literature and drama at the Sorbonne; both were to have a strong influence on each other in their respective fields.

The period in Paris was a decisive musical experience for him, not only through his study with Boulanger but also from the general musical scene. During this period he met Roussel, Prokofiev, MILHAUD, Koussevitsky, WEILL and EISLER and attended the Diaghilev ballets and the premiere of Ravel's orchestration of Mussorgsky's *Pictures at an Exhibition*. Among his major compositions of the period is *Grogh*, written for an imagined ballet inspired by a film adaptation of Dracula.

On returning to New York in 1924 he obtained a part-time appointment at the New School of Social Research, a position that he held intermittently for the next ten years. This, together with other temporary teaching posts, including standing in for Walter Piston at Harvard, gave him a modest income. Based on this teaching period, he later wrote the book *What to Listen for in Music* (1939). It was not until the late 1930s, by which time he had established a reputation as a composer, that his financial situation could be described as comfortable. By 1960 he was able to afford a second home and drive a Mercedes. The change in circumstances was in part due to his breakthrough in Hollywood and the film music scene. In subsequent years he was to write eight film scores, including *Of Mice and Men* (1939), *Our Town* (1940), *The Red Pony* (1948) and *The Heiress* (1948). Although these are unexceptional in the context of the world film history, he was the most distinguished American-born composer to work so extensively and successfully in Hollywood.

In 1924 Copland wrote the Organ Symphony, commissioned by Boulanger for her first visit to America. It was later transcribed into his First Symphony (without organ) but is not regarded as one of his best works of the period. In 1925 he was commissioned to write a chamber orchestra piece for the Boston Symphony; the outcome was *Music for the Theatre*, which was premiered by Koussevitsky in 1925. One of the movements, 'Burlesque', was partly inspired by Fanny Brice, the daughter of Jewish immigrants and a star attraction of American vaudeville at the time. In 1926 he composed his piano concerto, admitting later that he might have been propelled to do so by the success of Gershwin's *Rhapsody in Blue* (1924). For his piano trio, *Vitebsk* (Study on a Jewish Theme), composed in 1928 he was attracted by a Jewish folk melody he had heard in a production of Ansky's play *The Dybbuk*. *Vitebsk* is the name of the Byelorussian town in which Ansky had grown up and first heard the tune. Copland's intention was to reflect the harshness and drama of Jewish life in the Pale of Settlement. In *Vitebsk* the violin and cello play in quarter-tones and the work is one of his best chamber pieces. From 1928 to 1931 Copland and Roger Sessions organized a series of concerts in New York, focusing mainly on American composers.

From 1930 Copland was involved in the organization of the Yaddo Festival of Contemporary American Arts held in a Gothic-style mansion that had been created as an artists' retreat and was situated in Saratoga Springs, New York. It was there in 1930 that Copland completed his *Piano Variations*, consisting of a theme and twenty variations. It was premiered in New York in 1931 with

Copland at the piano. Although the audience were somewhat baffled by the work, in subsequent performances it became regarded at least by enthusiasts as a landmark composition. It was described at the time as 'the summit of Copland's achievement'. Copland wanted to establish a style in music that could be called 'American', as opposed to that of many earlier American composers, who merely imitated European styles well, although Ives and a few others had blazed the American trail. By the time he had become widely known through his compositions, he was tagged 'Dean of American Music' by the younger American composers. Copland supported many younger American composers in a variety of ways, for example, recommending DIAMOND to Boulanger, reading through manuscripts and advising SCHUMAN. Others whom he helped included BERGER, Irving FINE, FOSS, SHAPERO, LEVANT, AVSHALOMOV, DRUCKMAN, ADLER, WOLPE, Barbara Kolb and Del Tredici. His popularity was not widespread until the US premieres of *El Salón México* and *Billy the Kid* in 1938 – two of his most popular works.

In 1926 Copland met the Mexican composer Chávez in New York, and the two remained friends for over 50 years. They had many interests in common, but one of particular significance was that both showed a strong Pan-American resistance and solidarity in the face of European cultural domination. Chavez invited Copland to Mexico in 1932, offering the prospect of performances in Mexico of Copland's music. Several years earlier when Copland first went to Paris he had overcome a personality crisis and accepted his homosexuality. During his lifetime he had a number of partners for varying periods of time, one of the most long-lasting being with Victor Kraft, whom he met in 1932 shortly before leaving for Mexico. Kraft, a 16-year-old violinist, accompanied him on the trip and the two travelled together over the next decade whenever their schedules permitted. The visit to Mexico was a particularly happy one for Copland, and he returned on many occasions. It was on this first visit that he was inspired to write the orchestral work *El Salón México*, depicting the dance hall in Mexico City of that name. He worked on it intermittently from 1932 to 1936.

The period from the mid-1930s until the late 1940s was Copland's most prolific and successful time as a composer. In addition to the works already mentioned he composed *Quiet City* (1939), *Lincoln Portrait* (1942), *Fanfare for the Common Man* (1942), the ballet *Rodeo* (1942), the Piano Sonata (1941), the Violin Sonata (1944), the ballet *Appalachian Spring* (1944), the Third Symphony (1946), *In the Beginning* (1947), the Clarinet Concerto (1950), and the Piano Quartet (1950). *Quiet City* was composed to accompany the play of that name by Irwin Shaw. The play concerns a half-Jewish businessman, Gabriel Mellon, who rejected his Jewish background, Anglicized his name and married a wealthy socialite. The music evokes a quiet city at night, which is then disturbed by the sound of a trumpet with music reminiscent of a Jewish chant that reminds Gabriel of his spurned Jewish roots, prompting him to examine his life. The theme struck a chord with Copland, who perhaps identified

146

himself with Gabriel. The music has remained popular, but the play did not survive. *Applachian Spring* was written at the behest of Martha Graham for her dance company; it proved to be one of Copland's most popular works, using the Shaker song *Simple Gifts*. (Shakers were a Protestant sect related to the Quakers who settled in America in the late eighteenth century.) The Clarinet Concerto was written for the jazz clarinetist Benny Goodman. The Piano Quartet (1950) is one of very few of Copland's works to employ a form of SCHOENBERG'S twelve-tone method.

Although Copland never belonged to a political party it was clear that he had left-wing liberal sympathies. Between 1935 and 1949 he sponsored more than 20 left-wing causes. At the World Peace Conference held in 1949 a number of public figures attended, including Copland, Leonard BERNSTEIN, Thomas Mann and Arthur Miller, together with visitors from the Soviet Union. Newspaper articles accused the Americans of being communist sympathizers, and this marked the beginnings of Copland's victimization by the anti-communist senator Joseph McCarthy. The FBI examined any conceivable indication of pro-communist activity or sympathy. Copland's *Lincoln Portrait*, which was to be performed at the Eisenhower inaugural concert, was dropped because of 'his suspect political affiliations'. Further action was taken in which, along with certain other composers including Gershwin, Sessions, Thompson, Harris and Bernstein, his works were banned from the 196 official American libraries around the world. Copland was called before the Un-American Activities Committee. The only alleged associations that he admitted were membership of the National Council of American–Soviet Friendship, sponsorship of a concert in support of Hans EISLER (1948) and participation in the World Peace Conference (1949). No action was taken against him other than minor irritants, such as difficulties in securing a passport.

Copland lived until 1990, and although he stopped composing after 1973 he continued to conduct. His last extended work was the Flute Sonata (1971). From the mid-1970s he suffered increasingly from senile dementia. In all, he composed over 100 works that are diverse both in size and range. Many have become part of the standard American repertory. Curiously, although Jewish influences and themes can be detected on many of his works, for example, the piano trio *Vitebsk, Quiet City* and *In the Beginning*, he is one of only two major American composers who did not compose any work specifically for the synagogue (the other is Schuman).[1]

Bibliography: *AG; G; HBD*; Leb; Aaron Copland and Vivian Perlis, *Copland 1900 Through 1942* (New York: St Martins Press, 1984); Howard Pollack, *Aaron Copland: the Life and Work of an Uncommon Man* (New York: Henry Holt, 1999)*

1. Samuel Adler, 'The Aborted Renaissance: Music for the Synagogue since 1945 in America', in S. Stenton and A. Knapp (eds), *Proceedings of the First International Conference on Jewish Music* (London: City University, 1994), p.2.

Daiken, Melanie Ruth (b. London, 27 July 1945)   Daughter of a Russian–Jewish writer from Ireland. In her childhood she visited Israel and Canada before returning to England. She learned the violin at an early age, and at 10 became a junior exhibitioner at Trinity College of Music in London. In 1963 she studied composition with Hugh Wood at the Royal Academy of Music and also went to the University of Ghana for a short period to study rhythms of traditional West African music. After winning a French government scholarship, she spent the period from 1966 to 1969 studying with Messiaen and his wife Yvonne Loriod. Her first important compositions date from this period, for example, *Les Petits justes*, a song cycle to poems by Paul Eluard (1967). Her first opera was *Eusebius*, the first act of which was performed in Paris in 1968; her second opera was *Mayakovsky and the Sun* (1971). The latter is about the life of the Russian poet Mayakovsky and was premiered at the Edinburgh Festival in 1971. Vocal works form a major part of her compositions; she has set texts by Paul Eluard, F. Garciá Lorca, Charles Baudelaire, Rupert Brooke, Georg Trakl and Samuel Beckett to music. She has taught composition at London University, Morley College and the Royal Academy of Music, where she was appointed deputy head of composition and contemporary music in 1986. Bibliography: *GW*: *Pan**

Damrosch, Leopold (b. Posen, 22 October 1832; d. New York, 15 February 1885)   Spent his childhood in Posen, Prussia. His mother died soon after his birth and his father married his mother's sister. His parents were Jewish in origin but not at all religious. His father believed that full emancipation for Prussian Jews would lead to a richer and better life. There is no suggestion that Leopold ever had any instruction in Hebrew or entered a synagogue; his early interest in music was stimulated through non-sectarian schools and individuals. His childhood was not happy, largely because of conflicts with his father, who saw music as a pastime, not as a career. It was his maternal grandmother who arranged for him to have violin lessons as a child. During his teens he was under pressure from his father to spend more time on academic studies and less on music. He went to Berlin University, initially to study law, but later changed to medicine in which he graduated with honours in 1854. He then continued his violin studies, eventually appearing as a violin soloist in the principal German cities. Liszt appointed him leading violinist to the court orchestra in Weimar in 1857. Between 1858 and 1860 he was conductor of the Breslau Philharmonic Society. In 1871 he was invited to New York to conduct. He and his wife, the singer Helene von Heimburg, settled in New York, where he became heavily involved in organizing musical activities. He founded the Oratorio Society in 1873, and in 1878 the Symphonic Society. He was elected conductor of both societies, positions he held until his death. He also became director of the Metropolitan Opera, where he established German opera, introducing Wagner's later works to the United States.

He composed through much of his life, but his more substantial works were

148

composed mainly whilst he was in Breslau. His commitment to organizing music in New York meant that he only had time to devote to composing songs. His compositions include *Concertstuck in Form of a Serenade*, *Festival Overture*, a concerto for violin, *Ruth and Naomi, A Scriptural Idyll* for soloists and chorus (1875) and the oratorio *Sulamith* (1882). In addition, he made a number of song settings to various poets, including von Zesen, Heine, Ruckert, Geibel, Byron and Shelley. His most lasting works are songs for children, included in a collection called *St Nicolas Songs* that appeared in 1885.
Bibliography: *G*; George Martin, *The Damrosch Dynasty* (Boston: Houghton Mifflin, 1983)*

Damrosch, Walter Johannes (b. Breslau, 30 January 1862; d. New York, 22 December 1950)   Son of Leopold DAMROSCH. He was devoted to music from an early age, and studied in Germany with his father (see above) and also with Wilhelm Rischbieter, Anton Urspruch and Hans von Bulow, all before the family emigrated to America in 1871. He was better known as a conductor and musical educationalist than a composer. In many respects he followed in his father's footsteps, becoming assistant conductor at the Metropolitan Opera in 1884 and musical director of the Symphony Society and conductor of the Oratorio Society in New York. In 1894 he organized the Damrosch Opera Company, bringing in first-rate productions of German operas. During World War One, he organized the bandmaster's training school in France for the American Expeditionary Force. He was also involved in the early stages of music broadcasting, giving the first radio broadcast of an orchestral concert in 1925. He composed throughout his life, his most successful compositions being choral and dramatic music. These include the operas *The Scarlet Letter* (1896), *The Dove of Peace* (1912), *Cyrano de Bergerac* (1913) and *The Man without a Country* (1937), and also *Manila Te Deum* for soloists, chorus and orchestra (1898), *Mary Magdalen* for soprano (1899), a violin sonata, a song setting of *Danny Deever* by Kipling and incidental music to *The Canterbury Pilgrims* (1909).
Bibliography: *G*; George Martin, *The Damrosch Dynasty* (Boston: Houghton Mifflin, 1983)*

Da-Oz, Ram [Daus, Avraham] (b. Berlin, 17 October 1929)   Moved to Israel with his parents (see DAUS) in 1934. He studied piano (1945) and oboe (1947) and composition for three years with Hajos in Tel Aviv, graduating in 1953. Before this he was blinded in the (Israeli) War of Independence of 1948. He has composed mainly orchestral and chamber music, including the orchestral work *Alei Yagon Va'Nocham* (Metamorphosis of Grief and Consolation, 1959), *Rhapsody on a Yemenite Jewish Melody* for piano and strings (1971) and three string quartets. His compositions show the influences of Prokofiev, Bartok and SCHOENBERG.
Bibliography: *G*

Daquin, Louis-Claude (b. Paris, 4 July 1694; d. Paris, 15 June 1772)   Son of a Jewish family who emigrated from Italy to Carpentras in southern France and thence to Paris. On his mother's side he was related to Rabelais and on his father's to the Rabbi of Avignon, who converted to Christianity before he died in 1650. His parents, after converting to Christianity, assumed the name D'Aquin. He was one of five children, but the only one to reach adulthood. An uncle of his, the famous physician Dr D'Aquin, was personal physician to Louis XIV. Louis-Claude was a child prodigy, playing the piano before Louis XIV at the age of 6. He studied organ with Louis Marchand and composition with Nicolas Bernier, becoming organist at Petit St Antoine-Cloister, Paris, in 1706. In 1727 he was chosen ahead of Rameau as organist at St Paul, and in 1732 he succeeded Dandrieu as *Organiste du roi*, eventually becoming organist at the cathedral of Notre Dame in 1755. He was regarded as the best organist of his generation. He composed a large number of keyboard works of which the most well known is *Le Coucou*. His extant works are contained in two books, *Premiere Livre de pièces de clavecin* (1735) and *Nouveau Livre de noëls* (*c*. 1740), that contain four suites and 12 carol settings for keyboard and other instruments.
Bibliography: *G*; *HBD*; Ken; Alfred Sendrey, *The Music of the Jews in the Diaspora* (New York: Yoseloff, 1970), pp. 396–7*

Daus, Abraham (b. Berlin, 6 June 1902; d. Tel Aviv 1974)   Began his musical studies under one of Brahms's pupils, Edward Behm, and then continued at the Munich High School of Music, studying composition under Walter Courvoisier. He worked for some years as a theatre *répétiteur* and conductor before emigrating to Palestine, settling in Tel Aviv in 1936. Between 1940 and 1963 he worked and lived in various kibbutzim, composing and conducting. In his early compositions he was often inspired by the countryside. In the 1950s he travelled abroad and absorbed some of the newer musical techniques of the day. Many of his compositions are inspired by poetry, for example, *Songs of Rachel* (1938), *Twelfth Sonnet* for solo cello (1969) and *Five Sonnets* after Shakespeare for soprano, lute, and flute (1963). Other works include an over-ture to the cantata *Gate to the Sea* for large orchestra (1937), *Variations on a Yemenite Song* for flute and piano (1940), *Arabesques after Paintings of Paul Klee* for soprano and chamber ensemble (1961), *Four Dialogues* for violin and cello (1957) and a piano sonata entitled *Confessions of an Angry Man* (1967).
Bibliography: *Grad*; *G*; *Ly**

David Félicien, César (b. Cadenet, Vaucluse, France, 13 April 1810; d. St Germain-en-Laye, 29 August 1876)   Son of a goldsmith, Charles Nicolas David. His ancestors can be traced back to the early seventeenth century in Aix-en-Provence. His father amassed considerable fortune in San Domingos in Guinea, but had to abandon it whilst escaping disruptions in the region. He re-established himself, first in Marseilles and then at Cadenet. However, his young wife, Marie-Anne Françoise Arquier, also from a goldsmith's family, died soon after giving birth to Félicien. Charles also played the violin, and the young Félicien sang to his father's violin accompaniment. Only a few years later his father died, when Félicien was only 5 years old, leaving four orphaned children of whom Félicien was the youngest. A neighbour, who was a former oboe player at the Paris Opéra, recognizing that Félicien had a good singing voice persuaded his relatives in Aix to enter him as a choirboy at the cathedral of Saint-Sauver, where he also received his general education. He progressed well and by the age of 18 had become choirmaster and had also taught himself the violin. In 1830 he studied counterpoint and organ for a year at the Paris Conservatoire, after receiving a small allowance from an uncle.

He supported himself by giving lessons, and in 1832 he joined the Saint-Simonian sect. He composed hymns for the Saint-Simonian apostles. In 1832 David and a small band of Saint-Simonians travelled to the Orient to preach their gospel. He travelled to Constantinople, Smyrna, Jaffa, Jerusalem, Cairo and Beirut. The East fascinated him and formed a powerful musical inspiration. He returned to Paris in 1835, and the following year published a collection of *Mélodies orientales* for piano. This was not particularly well received. His turning point was in 1844, when he conducted a very successful performance of his ode symphony *Le Désert*. He went on to compose the oratorios *Moïse au Sinai* (1846) and *Eden* (1848) and the ode symphony *Christoph Columb* (1947), together with chamber music, choral works and operas. He became an officer of the Legion of Honour (1862), and succeeded Berlioz as member of the Institute of France and librarian of the Conservatoire (1869). He retained his Saint-Simonian faith to the end of his days. It is not clear from the biography by Hagan (1985)[1] or other references that David was of Jewish descent, except that d'Indy[2] included him among a list of Jewish composers 'able to produce amazing, if superficial imitations but not truly creative art'. And in Gradenwitz's article[3] an occasion is referred to when David was taken to a Paris synagogue with a Saint-Simonion friend, d'Eidithal, who was a convert from Judaism, but there is no indication that David was also a convert. There were several Jews amongst Saint-Simonians, amongst them Léon Halévy, brother of the composer Fromenthal HALÉVY.[4]

Bibliography: *G; HBD*

1. D. V. Hagan, *Félicien David 1810–76* (New York: Syracuse University Press, 1985).
2. Jane F. Fulcher, 'A Political Barometer of Twentieth-Century France: Wagner as Jew or Anti-Semite', *Musical Quarterly*, 78 (2000), p. 51.
3. Peter Gradenwitz, 'Félicien David and French Romantic Orientalism', *Musical Quarterly,* 62 (1976), pp. 471–506.
4. Ralph P. Locke, *Music, Musicians and the Saint-Simonians* (Chicago: University of Chicago Press, 1986), pp. 35, 95 and 338.

David, Ferdinand (b. Hamburg, 19 June 1810; d. Kloster, Switzerland, 18 July 1873)   Born a year after MENDELSSOHN, in the Mendelssohn's family home in Hamburg; they became firm friends. He studied violin with Spohr and theory with Hauptmann in Kassel from 1823 to 1825. From 1825 to 1827 he played in Copenhagen, Leipzig, Dresden and Berlin, often performing with his sister Louise, who played piano. Whilst a violinist at Königstadt (1826–9) he often played chamber music with Mendelssohn. In 1836 he moved to Leipzig to lead the Gewandhaus Orchestra under Mendelssohn; he established himself as an important figure in music-making in Leipzig in general. Apart from being leader of the orchestra, he acted as Mendelssohn's deputy conductor. This was an important role for two reasons. At this time conducting was evolving from being merely concerned with the technicalities of orchestral playing to the greater role of interpretation, and also because Mendelssohn spent long periods performing away from Leipzig.

In 1839 David went to England. He gave recitals with MOSCHELES and played his own violin concerto. When the Leipzig Conservatory opened in 1843, David, who had already returned to the city, became head of the violin department. One of his first pupils was JOACHIM, who was sent to him by Mendelssohn. David gave the first performance of Mendelssohn's Violin Concerto in 1845. He was able to give Mendelssohn valuable advice during its composition, and this undoubtedly contributed to its great success. The concerto was dedicated to him. He was one of the pallbearers at Mendelssohn's funeral in 1847.

For the last 15 years of his life, which were marked by poor health, he was mainly a conductor, but he continued to play the violin, giving his last public appearance in 1873. He died of a heart attack whilst holidaying with his children on the Siloretta glacier near Klosters. His most notable achievements were as an orchestral leader, a teacher and a writer. He made the Leipzig Conservatory the place to be for aspiring violinists. Although he was a prolific composer (five concertos and solo pieces for violin and orchestra, concert pieces for woodwind, a string quartet and sextet) only the Suite in G minor (Op. 43) for solo violin, *Introduction and Variations on 'Sehnsucht' Waltzes* (Schubert) for clarinet and orchestra (Op. 8) and *Concertino* for trombone (Op. 4) are played today, and then only rarely. He edited the first practical edition of Bach's unaccompanied violin pieces.
Bibliography: *G*; *HBD*; Ho*; Ly*; Wilfrid Blunt, *On Wings of Song* (London: Hamish Hamilton, 1974)

Davidov, Karl Yul'yevich (b. Goldingen, Kurland [Kuldiga, Latvia], 3 March 1838; d. Moscow, 14 February 1889)   Son of a Jewish doctor who was also an amateur violinist. He began piano lessons at the age of 5 and cello lessons at the age of 12, the latter with Heinrich Schmidt, principal cellist at the Moscow Theatre. He was a child prodigy, appearing as a solo cellist in public concerts from the age of 14. However, his parents insisted on him completing his education before embarking on a career as a cellist. He went to Moscow University to study mathematics, graduating in June 1858. During his time in Moscow he perfected his cello playing and wrote two complete operas. He continued his training as a musician at Leipzig, where he studied under Moritz Hauptmann. Ignaz MOSCHELES and Ferdinand DAVID heard him perform and were sufficiently impressed to invite him to perform his first cello concerto in B minor with the Leipzig Gewandhaus Orchestra. He went on to become a professor of cello at the Leipzig Conservatory and a year later, at the age of 22, the first cellist in the Leipzig Gewandhaus Orchestra. Soon he began to recognize that he was more successful as a cellist than as a composer.

He toured Europe as a cellist, returning to Russia in 1862. In 1876 Tchaikovsky and Davidov were both candidates for the post of director of the St Petersburg Conservatory; Davidov was awarded the position. He was also cellist at the Italian Opera, a post he retained for 20 years. In 1875 he had started to write an opera, *Poltava*, based on a poem by Pushkin. When he had not completed it some years later, he agreed to let Tchaikowsky have the libretto, which the latter composer incorporated into his opera *Mazeppa*. In 1887 Davidov was forced to flee Russia after it was discovered he was having a scandalous love affair with a student at the conservatory, but he returned the following year. He was a member of a famous string quartet that included Henrik WIENIAWSKI and Leopold Auer. He became one of the greatest cellists of his day, setting up a great cello tradition that has continued with three generations of pupils down to Rostropovich. In January 1889, at the age of 50, he was suddenly taken ill whilst performing one of Beethoven's sonatas. He died a few days later.

Davidov's output as a composer was fairly small, as he was primarily a performer, teacher and music director. His works mostly comprise works for cello, including four cello concertos. These are generally not particularly Russian-sounding – in this his works differ from those of his contemporaries, such as Borodin – being more influenced by MENDELSSOHN and Schumann from his days at Leipzig. Among his pupils were Carl Fuchs, Leo Stern and Hanus Wihan, the dedicatee of Dvorak's Cello Concerto.

Davidov possessed a very fine cello, one of about 50 made by Stradivarius that survives today. A particularly fine one was presented to him in 1863 by Count Wilhorsky. After Davidov's death the instrument acquired his name and was taken out of Russia at the time of the revolution. It was later bought by an amateur French cellist, and then later by a wealthy American businessman, Herbert N. Straus. In 1964 the Davidov became famous again when it was bought for the then 19-year-old cellist Jacqueline Dupré.
Bibliography: *G*; *HBD*; Ken; Skans, P., OCD 571 [record sleeve]; http://cello.org/cnc/davidov.htm

Davidovsky, Mario (b. Médanos, Buenos Aires, 4 March 1934)   Came from a musical and religious family. His father Natalio played the violin and clarinet. His mother was a biblical scholar, and one of his grandparents was a rabbi and another a Hebraic scribe. He began violin lessons at the age of 7 and continued his musical education at Collegium Musicum, graduating from the Bartolomé

School in Buenos Aires in 1952. He started to compose when he was only 13. His first composition teacher was Guillermo Graetzer. At Buenos Aires University he initially studied law and music, but at the age of 20 decided to continue entirely with music. His first successful composition was his String Quartet No. 1, which was performed in 1954 and won first prize of the Associación Wagneriana. In 1958, at the invitation of Aaron COPLAND, he went to the USA to participate in the Berkshire Music Festival, where his *Noneto* (1957) was performed. He met Milton Babbitt and learned of the forthcoming electronic music studio at Columbia University.

He returned to the USA in 1960 with the support of Guggenheim and Rockefeller Foundation fellowships to study electronic music at Columbia University. His first commercial recording, *Electronic Study* No. 1, composed in 1961, was released in 1964. This composition was followed by *Contrast* for strings and electronic sounds in 1962. It was the beginning of a number of compositions in which he combined electronic sound with instrumental sound. Between 1962 and 1992 he composed a ten-part work entitled *Synchronisms*, each part of which combines tape or electronic sound with a combination of instruments or chorus. The instrumental performers synchronize their music with the electronic sound. Davidovsky stated that in these works he aimed 'to integrate all levels of sound – both electronic media and conventional instrumental media – into one single coherent musical space, trying to keep as much as possible of what is characteristic of the electronic instrument and what is characteristic of the live performer'. The success of these works resulted in a grant from the Koussevitzky Foundation and in a number of awards, including the Pulitzer prize in 1971. After a 5-year spell devoted to electronic music, he returned in 1965 to a purely instrumental composition, *Inflexions* for fourteen instruments. Other compositions without electronic music include *Chacona* for piano trio (1973), the cantata opera *Scenes from Shir Ha-Shirim* (Song of songs) for soprano, two tenors, bass and chamber ensemble (1975–6), *Pennplay* for 16 instruments (1976) and four string quartets. He became professor of music at the City University, New York, and later professor of music at Harvard and Columbia and chairman of the Electronic Music Center at Columbia. He is director of the Koussevitzky Foundation.
Bibliography: *G*; *HBD*; D. Ewen, *American Composers* (London: Hale, 1982); http:\\gigue.peabody.jhu.edu/~philo/davidovsky.htm; www.americancomposers.org/sa98bios.htm

Dessau, Paul (b. Hamburg, 10 December 1894; d. East Berlin, 28 June 1979) Son of the synagogue cantor Moses Dessau. He had violin lessons from the age of 6, and appeared as a soloist age 11. He went on to the Klindworth-Scharwenka Conservatory (1910–12), initially studying the violin but then going on to study composing and conducting. In 1912 he became a *répétiteur* at the Hamburg Opera House, and thanks to the influence of his cousin, Jean Gilbert, who had built up an operetta empire, he was appointed *Kapellmeister* at the Bremen Tivoli Theatre until his service in the army for three years during World War One. After the war he continued in various conducting posts, including the Cologne Opera, where KLEMPERER appointed him as *répétiteur* and conductor of the Berlin Städtische Oper.

His first compositions were performed as early as 1915. When he won a Schott Prize for his violin concertino in 1925 he decided to give up conducting in favour of composing. His first symphony was performed in Prague in 1927. Other compositions from the 1920s include chamber works, orchestral works, film music and choral music. By 1933, with the rise of Nazism, he went unto exile in Paris, where he continued to write film music. There, in 1936 he met LEIBOWITZ, who introduced him to twelve-note composition; the two were to remain friends until Leibowitz's death in 1972. Later, after emigrating to America during World War Two, he met SCHOENBERG. Of the seven string quartets that Dessau composed between 1932 and 1975, the later ones show a Schoenbergian influence.

During the 1930s Dessau's strong socialist convictions were an important source of inspiration for his compositions. With the onset of the Spanish Civil War he composed the popular marching song *Die Thälmann-Kolonne* (1936) and the Picasso-inspired twelve-note piano piece *Guernica* (1938). Dessau, although assimilated, became aware of his Jewish roots. He had written some psalm settings and synagogue music earlier, but the 1930s and 1940s were his most conspicuous 'Hebraic phase'. In 1933 he recast a fragment of a string trio written in 1927 as a setting for Psalm 3, 'O Lord, how many are my foes! Many are rising against me', and in 1935 he wrote music for the film *Avodah*, which tells of the work of construction by Palestinian immigrants. In 1934 he planned what was to be his largest sacred work, the *Hagadah shel Pessach*. It was written in conjunction with Franz Kafka's biographer and friend Max BROD. Brod wrote the libretto in German, although there is a Hebrew translation by Rabbi Mordechai Langer. There were plans for William Steinberg to perform the work in either Berlin or Palestine. These did not materialize before Dessau left for New York in 1939. The work did not receive its first complete performance until 1994 under Gerd Albrecht with the Hamburg Philharmonisches Staatsorchester, nearly 60 years after its completion.

In 1942 Dessau met Berthold Brecht and went with him to southern California in 1943. Brecht collaborated with Dessau as he had done previously with WEILL and EISLER. Dessau provided the incidental music for Brecht's *Mother Courage* (1946), *The Good Woman of Szechuan* (1947) and *The Caucasian Chalk Circle* (1954). After Brecht's death, Dessau wrote in 1956–7 an orchestral piece, *In Memoriam Bertholt Brecht*.

Dessau had been a staunch Marxist socialist since the 1920s, and after the war, in 1948, he and Brecht were eager to return to the new German Democratic Republic (GDR) in order to contribute to the realization of the anti-fascist socialist state. There Dessau wrote socialist propaganda music, for example *Am meine Partei*, a cantata for solo bass, string orchestra and timpani (1955), and *Appell der Arbeiterklasse* (1960–1), and also operas such as *Die Verteilung des Lukillus* (The Condemnation of Lucillus, 1949), *Puntila* (1957–9), *Einstein* (1971–3) and *Requiem für Lumumba* (1961–3). In 1967, to mark the 50th anniversary of the October 1917 Revolution and the second Russian moon probe landing, he wrote an orchestral suite entitled *Sea of Tempests.*

The GDR authorities had problems with some of his compositions, for example, with *Die Verteilung des Lukillus,* in which he was accused of so-called formalism as opposed to the officially approved socialist realism. The perceived fault was his frequent use of harsh dissonances. However, in spite of this opposition, the work was performed (with some revisions) by Hermann Scherchen in 1951, and it became one of the most successful operas of the GDR. In this context, it is perhaps understandable that Dessau should be so critical of Shostakovich's socialist realism. After hearing Shostakovich's Sixth Symphony in Leipzig, he wrote:

> This weak endless first movement … totally out of context, followed by two fast movements of which the last could serve for a circus-juggling act. Regrettable! New proof that our people do not think at all while listening to music, but merely accept what the weak and ignorant present them.

In 1967 the GDR supported the Arab coalition fighting against Israel. This prompted Otto Klemperer to write to Dessau, who was now regarded as a leading composer of the GDR, saying 'In my view you are a Jew, born of a Jewish father and a Jewish mother' ; as such Klemperer felt it was Dessau's duty to leave the GDR. Dessau replied that he regarded himself as a Jew, not an Israeli (a distinction Klemperer could not accept), and remained in the GDR.

Bibliography: *G*; *HBD**; D. Reinhold, *Paul Dessau:'Let's Hope for the Best'. Briefe und Notizbücher aus den Jahren 1948 bis 1978* (Hofheim: Wolke, 2000); Angermann, K. 10 590/91 [record sleeve]

Diamond, David Leo (b. Rochester, New York, 9 July 1915)   Son of Polish-Jewish immigrants. His father was a carpenter and his mother a dressmaker. The family lived in very modest financial circumstances, such that they could not afford David musical instruction during his childhood. Nevertheless, by the time he was 7 he had learned to play the violin, using an instrument borrowed from a friend of the family. In 1927 the Diamonds moved to Cleveland, where David attracted the interest of a Swiss musician residing there, André de Ribaupierre, who provided funds for Diamond's first musical training. This was at the Cleveland Institute of Music (1927–9), after which the family returned to Rochester, where he studied at the Eastman School of Music (1930–4) and at the Dalcroze Institute in New York (1934–6). The teachers who were to influence his development most were Roger Sessions, at Dalcroze Institute, and Nadia Boulanger, who gave him private lessons in Paris in 1936. There he was to have contacts with Stravinsky, Ravel, MILHAUD and Roussel. In 1935 he was commissioned to write music for the ballet *Tom*, to a scenario by E. E. Cummings, completing it in Paris. His first successful orchestral piece, *Psalm*, was also written in Paris. It was performed by Howard Hanson and the Rochester Symphony Orchestra in December 1936, and won a Juilliard Publication award a year later. It is dedicated to André Gide, whom Diamond met and became friends with in Paris. Diamond conceived the opening of *Psalm* as a voice from the depths; it is scored with a solo tuba part to give 'a deep cantorial sound'. His first violin concerto was given its premiere in New York by Nicolai Berezowsky in 1937.

The main body of his output is his symphonies, the first of which was written in 1940 and the eleventh was premiered in 1992. The second is often regarded as his finest. Diamond's style has been described as one in which the tonality and expressiveness of Romantic music is joined with complex twentieth-century harmony and rhythm. When, in 1949, he discussed with SCHOENBERG the twelve-note technique, and he asked Schoenberg whether he should have taken a course in it with him, Schoenberg replied 'Why do you need to? You are a new Bruckner ... I never meant the technique for everybody.' Most of Diamond's works are diatonic but some of the later ones show a degree of chromaticism.

Diamond was appointed Fulbright professor at the University of Rome in 1951, and in 1953 settled in Florence until 1965, when he returned to the USA for his fiftieth birthday celebrations. In Italy he wrote his eighth symphony, dedicated to his friend and mentor Aaron COPLAND, and also eleven string quartets. His orchestral works have been performed by leading conductors, including Scherchen, Koussevitsky and Mitropoulis, and more recently by Gerard Schwarz and the Seattle Symphony Orchestra. Besides symphonies, he has written three violin concertos, songs and chamber music. He was commissioned to compose *Song of Hope* (for eight solo voices and orchestra, 1978) for Elie Wiesel. The *ad libitum* cello solo was to have been played by Yo-Yo Ma, who was unable to be present. However, Yo-Yo Ma asked Diamond to write him a piece and the result was *Kaddish* for cello and orchestra, which evokes Hebraic mysticism; Yo-Yo Ma played at the premiere in 1990. Besides composing, Diamond has been much in demand as a teacher, teaching at the Juilliard School of Music since 1973 and in Salzburg. He has been very prolific composer. Other works he has composed include: *A Song for Shabat* (children's chorus and piano), *Mizmor L'David* (Sacred Service; tenor chorus and organ 1951), *Ahavah* (symphonic eulogy for male narrator, orchestra, 1954), *Prayer for Peace* (mixed chorus, 1960) and *Hebrew Melodies* (song cycle with texts from Byron, 1967–8).

Bibliography: *AG*; *CC*; *G*; *HBD*; *Ly**; V. J. Kimberling, *David Diamond: a Bio-bibliography* (New Jersey, MD: Scarecrow Press, 1987).

Dorfman, Joseph (b. Odessa, 3 August 1940)   Graduated in music history, composition and piano and completed his studies at the Gnessin Pedagogical Institute in Moscow in 1971, having completed a doctoral thesis on Hindemith's chamber music. He emigrated to Israel and joined the music department of Tel Aviv University in 1973. His compositions include an opera, *The Dragon* (1982–3), concertos for piano (1981), violin (1984) and cello (1985), *Piano Trio in Memoriam Dimitri Shostakovich* (1976), *Kol Nidrei* for violin solo (1975), *Tribes of Israel* for percussion (1974), *Sic et non* for cello and piano (1974) and *Viribus Unitis* for piano, three tapes and ring modulator (1974).
Bibliography: Grad: *G*

Dresden, Sen (b. Amsterdam, 20 April 1881; d. The Hague, 30 July 1957) Came from a family of Jewish diamond brokers. He studied music under Bernard Zweers in Amsterdam, and from 1903 with Pfitzner in Berlin. For most of his working life he was a conductor, chiefly of choral music, and a teacher of composition at the Amsterdam Conservatory. Among his pupils were GOKKES and WERTHEIM. His most important early works are Cello Sonata (1916) and Sonata for Flute and Harp (1918). He was also a music critic for *De Telegraaf*. He was appointed director of the Royal Conservatory in The Hague in 1937, but was dismissed three years later because of his Jewish ancestry and was interned for the rest of the war on an estate in Wassenaar. Most of his important compositions date from the last decade of his life, after his retirement from teaching. His best-known work is his orchestral suite *Dansflitsen* (Dance Flashes, 1951). His compositions include two operas, *ToTo* (1945), *François Villon* (1956–7), choral works, *Chorus Tragicus* (1927), *O Kerstnacht* (1939), *Assumpta est Maria* (1943), *Saint Antoine* (1953), *Rembrandt's Saul en David* (1956), concertos for flute, oboe, organ, piano and for two violins, suites for piano and wind, sonata for solo violin and a suite for solo cello.
Bibliography: *G; HBD;* Ly*

Druckman, Jacob Raphael (b. Philadelphia, 28 June 1928; d. New Haven, Connecticut, 24 May 1996)   Studied violin, composition and theory under Gessensway (1938–40). He also studied piano and was a self-taught trumpeter, playing in jazz ensembles. Later, he studied composition with COPLAND at Tanglewood in 1949, and attended the Juilliard School of Music in New York and the École Normale in Paris (1954). He married the dancer Muriel Topaz in 1954. He taught at Bard College (1961–7), Brooklyn College (1972–6) and Yale University from 1976. At Yale he was chairman of the composition department and director of the electronic music studio. He was composer-in-residence for the New York Philharmonic during the 1980s. His compositions reflect a rich and varied musical tradition. His earliest works, such as *Duo* for violin and piano (1949), are influenced by Stravinsky, early SCHOENBERG and Debussy, and also MAHLER, Ravel and Prokofiev. By 1966 he began composing using recording tape and electronic music. After completing his second string

quartet in 1966 he began working on electronic compositions, the first of which was *Animus I* for trombone and tape. He also began using direct quotations or allusions from music of other composers ranging from the seventeenth to the twentieth centuries, for example, Charpentier, Cherubini, Moussorgsky and Wagner. *Windows*, which won the 1972 Pulitzer prize, manages to combine twentieth-century sonorities with earlier harmonies. *Incentres* (1973) contains jazz elements and chords from the coronation scene in Mussorgsky's *Boris Godunov*. He has composed a wide variety of music including the opera *Medea* (1982), a viola concerto (1978), works for performers and tape such as *Animus I–IV* (1966–77), three string quartets (1948, 1966, 1981) and vocal music such as *Shir Shel Yakov*, a Sabbath Eve Service (1967) and *Counterpoise* for soprano and orchestra (1994).
Bibliography: *AG*; *CC*; *G*

Duarte, Leonora (b. Antwerp, 1610[?]; d. 1678[?])   Flemish amateur musician and composer from a well-known Antwerp family of rich jewellers and diamond merchants of Portuguese–Jewish (*marrano*) origin. She appears to have been baptized on 28 July 1610.[1] Her parents were Gaspar Duarte and Catherina Rodriques. She had three sisters and two brothers, all of whom were active music makers. Together they played lute, viols and keyboard instruments, and their home was a centre for music and the visual arts. Leonora composed a set of seven abstract fantasies for a consort of viols: they are in a late Jacobean style and called 'Symphonies'. Her brother Diego also composed, but none of his works survive.
Bibliography: *G*; http://music.acu.edu/www/iawm/pages/jewishcomp.html
1. See *G*.

Dukas, Paul Abraham (b. Paris, 1 October 1865; d. Paris, 17 May 1935)   Born into a middle-class family. His mother was a very gifted musician who could have had a career as a concert pianist had her parents not intervened to prevent this. She died when Dukas was only 5, and his closest ties were with his father and brother, both of whom worked as bankers but had strong interests in the arts. It is claimed that as a baby he 'gave suck in 9/8 time', although he did not show any particular aptitude for music until he was 13, when he had piano lessons and began to compose. At the age of 16 he began studying piano and harmony at the Paris Conservatoire. He became interested in orchestration, and composed an overture based on King Lear in 1883. He became friends with Debussy and d'Indy, and through the latter became a Wagner enthusiast. In 1888 he came within one vote of winning the Prix de Rome for his work *Vellèda*. In 1891 he composed his first major work, the overture *Polyeucte,* which was first performed at Lamoureux in 1892. It echoed Wagner's orchestration in *Der Fliegende Holländer*. In 1892 he also began as a music critic, writing for *Revue Hebdomadaire* and later *Gazette des Beaux-Arts* and *Chronique des Arts et de la Curiosité*. He was to spend much of his life editing and writing about music. His first attempted opera, *Horn et Rimenhild,* got no further than the first act, although he wrote a libretto for the complete opera himself. He composed his only symphony in 1895 and it was first performed in 1897. The work for which he is widely known, a symphonic scherzo after a ballad by Goethe, *L'Apprenti sorcier,* was premiered in 1897. He made further attempts at operas but only *Ariane et Barbe-bleue,* using the text by Maeterlinck, was completed; it was performed at the Opéra-Comique in Paris in 1907.

Dukas spent two periods teaching at the Paris Conservatoire: from 1910 to 1913 he taught orchestration, and after 1928 he taught composition. Between 1913 and 1928 he worked as an inspector of musical education in the provincial conservatories. Among his pupils at the Paris Conservatoire were Messiaen, Albeniz and MILHAUD. Milhaud thought he was a better composer than a teacher. After 1907 he composed little. Many of his works are incomplete. He destroyed a number of unpublished works before he died, leaving barely a dozen, which, besides those already cited, include a piano sonata (1899–1901), *Variations, interlude et final sur un thème de Rameau* (1899), the ballet *La Péri* (1912) and the *Sonnet de Ronsard* (1924). Dukas set himself high standards and spent much time refining his works, seldom being satisfied with them. He was a retiring and insecure person. Being a Jew living in Paris, and being almost contemporary with Alfred Dreyfus (1859–1935) may possibly have contributed to this. He would not allow his picture to be published.
Bibliography: *G; HBD;* Ken; Leb; Ly*

Eben, Petr (b. Zamberk, Czechoslovakia, 22 January 1929)   Born in Zamberg in north-east Bohemia, near the Polish border with the Czech Republic. He grew up in the medieval town of Cesky Krumlov, near to the Austrian border. His parents were both teachers, and, although the family embraced the Catholic faith, his father was Jewish. Because there was a shortage of organists during the war, Eben played the organ in the main church at Cesky Krumlov from the age of 10, and ever since has had a particular interest in the organ; it features in many of he compositions. He also had considerable experience of chamber music in his youth, playing in a piano trio with his father and brother. In 1943 he was ostracized by friends and expelled from school because of his Jewish descent. During World War Two he worked first for a printer, then on a building site; later he was interned in the concentration camp at Buchenwald.

After the war he resumed his schooling at the Music School in Cesky Budejovice, and in 1948 at the Prague Academy of Music and Drama, studying piano with Frantisek Rauch and later composition with Pavel Borkovec. His interest in Czech folklore was strengthened as a reaction against the Nazi occupation. In 1955 he wrote *Suita Balladica* for cello and piano to express some of his feelings. It reflects no bitterness at his suffering, only faith in human endurance. He was a lecturer in the history of music department at Charles

University, Prague, from 1955 to 1990. Promotion was long denied him because of his refusal to join the Communist Party and his continued attendance at church. During this period he spent a year (1978–9) as professor of composition at the Royal College of Music in Manchester. He has been prominent both as a musical educator and as a composer, publishing a number of folk song arrangements for school use.

Since the Velvet Revolution, in 1989, his musical talent has been recognized; he was appointed President of the Prague Spring Festival. Having lived through the Nazi occupation and communist oppression, Eben describes himself as a humanist.[1] He has written music for use in churches, for example, *Sunday Music* for organ (1957–9), *Laudes* for organ (1964), *Trouvere Mass* for choir, guitar and recorders (1968–9) and *Missa cum Populo* (1981–2). This last work was written to meet the requirements of the Second Vatican Council that the congregation should be able to participate. It uses a four-part choir, organ, brass and percussion and the congregation is given a repetitive unison role in the credo. He has written two organ concertos (1954 and 1982) and a symphonic movement for three trumpets and orchestra entitled *Vox Clamatis* (1969). This work was written in reaction to the Soviet invasion in 1968. The Czechs are likened to a lone voice crying in the wilderness, expressed by the trumpets intoning a synagogue chant; this is followed later by a voice declaiming 'Yasheru Messilah L'Elohenu' (Prepare Ye the way of the Lord) and an early Czech chorale 'Lord Have Mercy on Us'. Other works include *Apologia Sokrates* for soloists, chorus and orchestra (1961–7), *Chad Gadyoh* for male choir (1965), *Song of Ruth* for alto and organ (1970), *Okna* (Windows) for trumpet and organ (1976; inspired by four of Marc Chagall's twelve windows at the Hadassah Hospital Synagogue in Jerusalem, depicting the twelve tribes of Israel), a string quartet (1981) and piano trio (1986), *Faust*, in nine parts for organ (1980), *Curses and Blessings*, a ballet for choir and orchestra (1983), *Job*, an eight-part cycle for organ (1987), *The Labyrinth of the World and Paradise of the Heart* (1991) and *Four Biblical Dances* (1991).

Bibliograpy: CC; Grad*; G; HBD; Leb; G. Melville-Mason (ed.), *A Tribute to Petr Eben* (Dvorak Society, Occasional Publications, no. 2, 2000)*

1. CC.

Ehrlich, Abel (b. Cranz, near Königsberg, East Prussia, 1915)   Left Germany in the 1930s and spent five years in the Zagreb Academy of Music, Yugoslavia, before emigrating to Palestine in 1939. There he taught at the College for Music Teachers at Oranin, near Haifa. Ehrlich has been a prolific composer of short vocal and instrumental works, now numbering over 400. Many of his compositions show the influence of Arabic and Hebrew traditional music, and at the same time an awareness of contemporary developments in western music. In a number of works he uses microtones. Examples of his music are: *Bashrav*, originally composed for unaccompanied violin in 1953 and later developed for violin and choir (1956), and later still for orchestra (1958); a

161

cantata, *The Writing of Hezekiah* for soprano and chamber orchestra (1970); the orchestral suite *A Game of Chess*; and ballet music *Country Girl*.
Bibliography: Gra; G; Ho*

Eisler, Hanns (b. Leipzig, 6 July 1898; d. Berlin, 6 September 1962) Son of the Austrian philosopher Rudolph Eisler. Rudolph edited a philosophical/ sociological periodical and together with the Marxist Max Adler he founded the Vienna Sociological Society in 1907. Although he wrote a number of philosophical works he never had an academic career, probably because he was a Jew. One of Rudolf's recreations was piano playing. Eisler's mother, to whom Hanns was closer, was the daughter of a butcher. Hanns later commented that his parents were from different social classes and from different lands – Austria and Saxony – and he attributes his identification with the cause of the workers as a particularly maternal influence. He was the youngest of three children in the family, Elfriede being three years older and Gerhart one year. The family was never well off, so much so that they had to rent a piano when Hanns began lessons. In 1901 the family moved to Vienna, and Hanns's education was at the 'strictly Catholic' Rasumovsky Gymnasium until he joined a Hungarian regiment of the army from 1916 to 1918.

Musically Eisler was largely self-taught. His first compositions were songs. His brother Gerhart was a member of a progressive youth group from 1912, and Hanns, being close to him, had access through him to socialist writings from an early age. Another interest of his was football, and it was through playing football as a child that he met Jascha Horenstein who was later to become a well-known conductor. His first major composition, written about the time of his call-up in 1916, was an anti-war oratorio (*Gegen den Kreig*); it has not survived. Eisler was injured during the war. In 1918, whilst on two months' convalescence leave, he shared a flat with a girlfriend, Irma Friedmann. She accompanied him in numerous songs he wrote and sang for her. Some forty of these were donated to the Eisler archive by Irma Friedmann in 1965. After the war Eisler appears to have been virtually homeless, having loosened the ties with his parents. His brother and sister moved to Berlin, becoming political revolutionaries, whilst Hanns enrolled as a student at the New Viennese Conservatory in 1919, earning money as a proof-reader for Universal Edition. However, he found the instruction at the Conservatory undemanding and conservative in outlook.

Having heard a performance of SCHOENBERG's Chamber Symphony, and also being informed that Schoenberg was a brilliant (if very strict) teacher, Eisler approached him for lessons. Schoenberg was impressed with the young man's talent and gave him free lessons for the next four years. In spite of a later quarrel, Schoenberg and Eisler had a high regard for one another; Schoenberg was to rate him amongst his best three pupils, the others being Berg and Webern. The period 1919–23 coincided with Schoenberg's transition to serial composition. Eisler's first piano sonata Op. 1 was premiered in Prague in 1923. It received favourable press comment and won the art prize for the City of Vienna in 1925. He also composed *Songs*, Op. 2, Piano Pieces, Op. 3, and the *Divertimento* wind quintet, Op. 4, about this time. But the most interesting of his early works is *Palmström*, Op. 5, a study on twelve-note series, composed to be performed at a concert together with Schoenberg's *Pierrot Lunaire*. *Palmström* is a work for solo voice and chamber orchestra, based on texts by Morgenstern. The work shows a touch of parody, but also admiration for Schoenberg.

Although successful in one sense, Eisler became increasingly disenchanted with the musical life in Vienna, which he saw as unacceptably bourgeois. He moved to Berlin, where his brother and sister were politically active. His sister, using her mother's maiden name Ruth Fischer, was a founder of the Communist Party of Austria. His brother was subsequently to become a celebrated political journalist. Schoenberg had also moved to Berlin in 1926 as the successor to Busoni, leading the master class in composition at the Prussian Academy of Arts.

As the result of a successful performance of his first piano sonata in Berlin, SCHNABEL invited Eisler to write piano music for his pupils. He also obtained a teaching post at the Klindworth-Scharwenka Conservatory in 1926. The environment in Berlin in the 1920s was very different from that of Vienna. In Berlin he was confronted with situations – strikes, demonstrations, mass unemployment, and so forth – that he had previously only read about in political texts. A conflict between his musical and political interests opened up. Symphony concerts and operas were performed to a middle-class minority, whereas his political leanings drew him to consider popular forms of music. At this stage (*c.* 1925) the Communist Party had hardly developed any solutions to the problems of cultural work.

In 1926 Eisler and Schoenberg had a strong disagreement, after which they had no contact for some years. The nub of this was that Eisler had become critical of 'modern music', such as that performed at music festivals. He regarded it as being devoid of social relevance and deaf to the social changes of the time. He said of this music: 'An aimless industriousness celebrates orgies of inbreeding with absolutely no interest or participation from the public.' Schoenberg, who expected complete loyalty from his pupils, took this to be critical of his own music. The resulting break did not result in an immediate change in Eisler's composing technique, but his compositions had an increasingly important social agenda. He became more committed to the Communist Party and began working for the Young Communist agitprop group Das Rote Sprachrohr (The Red Megaphone). It was in about 1927 that Eisler met Bertholt Brecht, probably just after WEILL and Brecht's success with *Threepenny Opera*. Brecht and Eisler began a collaboration that ran for at least as long as that between Brecht and Weill.

In 1927 Eisler married Charlotte Demant and in 1928 their son Georg was born; the year also saw the first performance of *Zeitungausschnitte*, Op. 11

(Newspaper cuttings), a satirical work for voice and piano, in which documentary material is projected and fun made of bourgeois musical conventions. In 1928 Eisler became a teacher at the Marxist School for Workers in Berlin. Works composed in the next five years include militant and marching songs such as *Der Rote Wedding, Stemelleid, Kominternleid* and *Solidaritätsleid; Die Massnahme*, Op. 20, written in collaboration with Brecht; and music for a play, *Die Mütter*, by Brecht. He largely completed his *Kleine Sinfonie*, Op. 29. In addition to compositions he also wrote articles for the journal *Kampfmusik. Die Massnahme* is in the style of a Bach mass with arias, recitatives and choruses representing the Party and making social generalizations. The work was performed in Germany before Hitler came to power and received a mixed reception; it was banned after the *Anschluss*. During a speech on 'The workers' music movement' after one of the early performances of *Die Massnahme*, Eisler said:

> Art no longer has the task of satisfying the listeners' need for beauty, but uses beauty ... to make the present problems of the class struggle tangible and manageable ... not to reflect the troubles and torments of the workers but the right methods for seizing power.

In 1933 Eisler travelled to Vienna at the invitation of Webern to rehearse *Die Massnahme*. Whilst in Vienna the Gestapo searched his apartment in Berlin and a warrant was issued for his arrest. Thus began his 15-year exile from Germany. He, like Brecht, found himself in an increasing dilemma. The rise in support for the Nazis in Germany ran counter to Marxist philosophy. At the same time the Stalinization of the Soviet Union had its affects on the arts. By contrast, artistic life in those countries in the West where exile seemed possible were capitalist. It was through his communist credentials that Eisler sought exile, rather than because of any dangers from anti-Semitism. It seems likely from statements made by him much later (1961), such as 'we exterminate people, gas Jews, and send our young people against Russian tanks', that he did not regard himself as a Jew.

During 1933–4 he travelled to Czechoslovakia, Paris and London and met Brecht, now in Denmark. In 1935 he was invited to join a lecture and concert tour of the USA. The sponsors of this tour included GERSHWIN, COPLAND and Cowell. He toured more than 50 towns. He was struck by the overt capitalism, despite the depression. The Communist Party was numerically small, and although it exerted a marked influence on progressive artists and intellectuals, there were few, apart from Mark BLITZTEIN, who closely identified with communism.

Eisler started work in 1935 on what is now regarded as his greatest work, *Deutsche Sinfonie*, Op. 50. The inspiration for this work came from the need to expose to the world the impact of Nazism upon German cultural and political life. It is a large-scale work in eleven sections, three of which are purely orchestral, but the greater part of the work is vocal and choral, with fiercely anti-fascist texts by Brecht. In 1937 he returned to New York, where he took up a post at the New School for Social Research. In 1940 he received a grant from the Rockefeller Foundation to research the function of film music. In this he collaborated with ADORNO in writing a book, *Composing for Films*. In 1942 he moved to Hollywood and a teaching post at the University of Southern California. There he continued his collaboration with Brecht, working together on *Furcht und Elend des dritten Reiches* and *Galileo*. During his exile in America he started, in 1942, to compile his *Hollywood Song Book: Lieder of the Exile*. On completion, it consisted of nearly 50 songs, including the *Hölderlin Fragments* and a cycle of Hollywood elegies entitled *Fünf Elegien* with words by Brecht.

In 1947, during the McCarthy era, Eisler and others with left-wing leanings were brought before the Un-American Activities Committee. Eisler was questioned about his works and about being the brother of a 'communist spy'. Eventually he was extradited in 1948 and returned to Vienna. In 1949 he and other intellectuals, including Brecht, returned to the German Democratic Republic (East Germany), experiencing the system for which they had strived all their lives, rather than returning to West Germany. They shared in the anti-fascism declared by the GDR to be fundamental to it, and were certain that lessons of more consequence would be learnt from history there, than in West Germany. Although Eisler was highly revered as a person in the GDR, his music was not generally well received. He was never quite free of the tag of being cosmopolitan (i.e. Jewish) and an avant-gardist from the Schoenberg school. He composed rapidly, aiming to use popular material in personal and unconventional ways and to take his audience along with him. However, official acceptance sat uneasily on his shoulders and he managed to be rejected by the musicians of the GDR because he was a communist, and by the communists because he was regarded as a Schoenbergian.

He wanted to compose an opera based on pre-Goethean versions of the Faust legend and also on Thomas Mann's *Doctor Faustus*. He completed the libretto in 1952 and Aufbau Verlag published it in the same year under the title *Johann Faustus – An Opera*. Although the libretto was favourably received by a number of writers and critics, for example, Thomas Mann and Feuchwanger, in the debates that followed the response was more frequently adverse, so much so that in the end Eisler became so disheartened that he did not compose the music for it. Nevertheless, he composed and wrote prolifically for the last twelve years of his life. He composed no chamber music but was more concerned with 'applied music', composing music for 17 films, settings for 36 cabaret chansons and music for theatre. His *Lenin-Requiem* composed in 1937 was given its first performance in Berlin in 1958. Until relatively recently performances of his music have suffered from the post-1945 cultural cold war.

Bibliograpy: *G*; *HBD*; Ken; Leb; Albrecht Betz, *Hans Eisler: Political Musician*

(Cambridge: Cambridge University Press, 1982); David Blake (ed.), *Hans Eisler: a Miscellany* (Luxembourg: Harwood Academic, 1995)*; Alexander Goehr, *Finding the Key* (London: Faber, 1998), pp. 153–4 and 286–8; Julian Silverman, 'Only a Composer: Reflections on the Eisler Centenary', *Tempo*, 206 (1998), pp. 21–8

Elias, Brian David (b. Bombay, 30 August 1948)   Lived in Bombay until the age of 13, when he came to school in England. He began composing at the age of 7. In 1966 he began studying composition with Bernard Stevens and Humphrey Searle at the Royal College of Music in London (1966–7) and later had lessons with Elizabeth Lutyens, whom he met at the Dartington Summer School of Music; he also spent a period at the Juilliard School of Music in New York. Many of his compositions are either chamber works or vocal/choral works. His first composition to gain recognition was *La Chevelure* for soprano and chamber orchestra, written when he was just 19. In 1980 he wrote a large-scale work, *Somnia*, for tenor and orchestra, which was first performed by the BBC Philharmonic Orchestra. His *L'Eylah*, which was commissioned by the BBC, was performed at a 1984 Promenade Concert and was enthusiastically received. This led to another commission by the BBC, for *Five Songs to Poems by Irina Ratushinskaya*, which premiered at the Royal Festival Hall in 1989 and was repeated at a Promenade Concert in 1991. Other works of his include *Proverbs for Hell* for unaccompanied choir (1977), *Tzigane* for violin (1978), the song cycle *At the Edge of Time*, *Pythikos Nomos* for alto saxophone and piano, *Variations* for solo piano, *Song* (a Song of Solomon) for soprano and hurdy-gurdy (1986), *Hymn to Saints Cosmo and Damian* performed by the Hilliard Ensemble in 1991, the ballet *The Judas Tree* (1992) and *Moto Perpetuo* for piano (1996).
Bibliography: *CC*; *G*; Leb; *Newsletter of the Jewish Music Heritage Trust*, 4 (2) (1997); :www.schirmer.com/composers/elias

Engel, Joel Dimitrievich (b. Berdyansk, Ukraine, 4/16 April 1868; d. Tel Aviv, 11 February 1927)   Studied law at Kharkov and Kiev Universities and then music composition under Taniev and Ippolitov-Ivanov at the Moscow Conservatory from 1893 to 1897. He was best known as a music writer, publisher and collector of Jewish folk songs. He was the founder of the Society of Jewish Folk Music in St Petersburg in 1908. He wrote incidental music for Ansky's play *The Dybbuk*, which he later arranged for string quartet, clarinet and bass, and also for piano solo. His other works include *Fünfe Klavierstücke*, *Volksweisenkranz* for piano, *Chabader Nigum* and *Freijlachs* for violin and piano. He left Russia for Berlin in 1922, where he founded Juwal-Verlag for the publication of Jewish music, and then went to Palestine in 1924.
Bibliograpy: *G*; Ly*

Ernst, Heinrich Wilhelm (b. Brno, Moravia, 6 May 1814; d. Nice, France, 8 October 1865)   Ernst was one of the most famous violinists of the nineteenth century. He also composed a number of works for violin, although these are now rather neglected. Ernst first played the violin in public at the age of 9. He entered the Vienna Conservatory in 1825, where he studied violin under Joseph Böhm and composition with Seyfried. When he heard Paganini playing in Vienna in 1828 it made such an impression on him that he followed Paganini on tour, playing his unpublished works by ear so well as to amaze Paganini himself. He made his début in Paris in 1831 and lived there from 1832 to 1838. He performed throughout Europe and Russia, and became one of the outstanding violinists of his day. He was warmly admired by Berlioz, who praised him in the *Journal des Débats*. He performed the viola solo in *Harold in Italy* in Brussels (1842), Vienna (1846), Moscow, St Petersburg and Riga (1847) and in London, where he settled in 1855. Dostoyevsky wrote an early novel, *Netochka Nezvanova* (A 'nameless nobody') in 1849 before he was banished to Siberia. In the novel Netochka's father, a failed musician, believed himself a neglected genius. He blamed his failure on Jewish virtuoso violinists, but one in particular who came to perform in St Petersburg and who stole the father's chances of success. Ernst is believed to be the real-life prototype of this Jewish virtuoso violinist.[1] In 1859 he led the Beethoven Society Quartet with JOACHIM (violin), WIENIAWSKI (viola) and Piatti (cello). His most frequently performed compositions, which are generally in a Romantic style, include *Elègie*, Op. 10 for violin and orchestra (and also piano, 1840), *Othello-Phantasie*, Op. 11 (1839), *Le Carnival de Venise*, Op. 18 (1844), *Airs Hongrois Variés*, Op. 22 (1850), Violin Concerto (also known as *Concerto Pathétique*), Op. 23 (1851). MENDELSSOHN and Ferdinand DAVID were great friends of Ernst. At a concert in the Königstädter Theatre in Berlin, when Ernst was at the height of his performing career, he was pressed in Mendelssohn's presence to put *Elègie* down on the programme twice. He agreed to do so, to Mendelssohn's delight, provided the latter accompanied him, which he did. With David it was not only the violin they had in common: both were keen card players.

Ernst's Violin Concerto was very popular in the late nineteenth and early twentieth centuries, sufficiently so that it was republished in 1896 and revised by H. Mateau in 1913. Szigeti describes it somewhat scathingly as 'a super-annuated work in the virtuoso style of the mid-nineteenth century, bristling with *wunderkind* difficulties'.[2] Ernst's performing career was cut short by illness in 1860s and he sought hydropathic treatment, but the illness proved incurable. In 1862 a concert was given for his benefit at which Joachim, Laub, Molique and Piatti played one of his string quartets, and Joachim played *Elègie*. In a letter to Joachim, Ernst thanked him for his sympathy and support and finished with reference to the gomel blessing (Hebrew *birkat ha gomel*), the thanksgiving benediction recited after surviving a dangerous experience. However, in a letter from Joachim in 1864 it is evident that Ernst was not well enough to play in the concert in London at which his last work, *Six Studies* for unaccompanied violin, was to be performed; Joachim replaced him. Ernst died a year later.

Bibliograpy: *G*; *HBD*; Ho*; Ken; Nora Bickley, *Letters from and to Joseph Joachim* (New York: Macmillan, 1972), p. 256; G. Hart, *The Violin and its Music* (London: Dulan, 1881), pp. 435–9; CDX5102 [record sleeve]

1. David, I. Goldstein, *Dostoyevsky and the Jews* (Austin: University of Texas Press, 1981), pp. 11–12.
2. Joseph Szigeti, *With Strings Attached* (London: Cassell, 1949), p. 87.

Ettinger, Max [Markus Wollff] (b. Lemberg, Galacia [L'viv, Ukraine], 27 December 1874; d. Basle, 19 July 1951)   Left Poland to study piano and harmony in Berlin, and later was a pupil of Thuille and Rheinberger at the Munich Academy. In 1933 he fled from the Nazis to Ascona in Switzerland and remained there for the rest of his life. He was a composer and conductor. Most of his compositions are operas or choral works. Whilst still in Germany he composed a ballet, *Rialon* (1911), the full-length opera *Judith* (1921), and a one-act tragicomic opera entitled *Der Eifersuechtige Trinker* (1925). After fleeing to Switzerland and seeing the fate of his fellow Jews, he wrote works that reflected his early upbringing and his Jewish heritage. These included the oratorios on biblical texts *Das Lied von Moses* (1934–5) and *Königen Ester* (1940–1), and *Yiddish Requiem: Zum Ondenk in di Gefallene vun Warschauer* (In memory of those who fell in the Warsaw Ghetto – a Yiddish Requiem, 1947). Bibliograpy: *G*; Ho*; Ly*

Feinberg, Samuil Yevgenyevich (b. Odessa, 14/26 May 1890; d. Moscow, 22 October 1962)   Better known as a pianist than as a composer. His family moved from Odessa to Moscow when he was 4. His first teacher, A. F. Jensen, encouraged him to study composition as well as piano. He studied piano at the Moscow Conservatory with Alexander Goldenweiser, later becoming his assistant. After his graduation in 1912 he became a concert pianist and toured widely in Europe. He was sent to the Polish front in World War One, contracted typhus, and had to return to Moscow. By the late 1920s his tours abroad were curtailed and remained so throughout the Stalinist era, but this did not diminish his outstanding reputation at home. His repertoire was both classical and contemporary, from Bach to Prokofiev. He was the first Russian to perform in concert the whole cycle of Bach's 48 preludes and fugues. In addition to performing and teaching at the Moscow Conservatory, he composed, mainly for the piano, and his early compositions are much influenced by Skriabin. He refined existing styles rather than developing new ones. His compositions include three piano concertos (1931, 1944 and 1947), twelve piano sonatas, two suites, two fantasies and songs to words of Russian poets. His second piano concerto won the Soviet State Award in 1945, but the third is the most performed. In addition he made a number of Bach transcriptions. He died only a few days after making his last recording of Bach's four-part prelude *Allein Gott in der Höh sei Ehr* (BWV 662). Bibliograpy: *G*; Ho*; Pritsker, M. 81-0002 [record sleeve]

Feldman, Morton (b. New York, 12 January 1926; d. Buffalo, 3 September 1987) Studied the piano at the age of 12 with Madame Maurina-Press, who herself had been a pupil of Busoni. At that time he also started composing short Skriabinesque piano pieces. In 1941 he studied composition with Riegger and in 1944 with WOLPE. However, the person who was to have most influence on him as a composer was Cage, whom he met in 1949. Cage encouraged him to have confidence in his instincts rather than working within any particular system. Also in the 1950s he became friends with the expressionist painters Mark Rothko, Philip Guston, Franz Kline, Jackson Pollock and Robert Rauschenberg, and with the pianist David Tudor.

These associations led him to seek a sound world more direct, more immediate, and more physical than anything that had existed before. He aspired to a kind of contemplative purity, a sustained trance-like concentration that can be aligned with minimalism in its emphasis on repetition and constraints on contrast, but different in its rhythmic passivity and avoidance of tonal-sounding harmony. Of his music, he said: 'To me my score is my canvas, my space. What I do is try to sensitize this area.' Initially, this resulted in him evolving a graphic notation for his compositions, for example, in *Projection I–V* (1950–1). This notation allowed players to select their notes from within a given register (lower, middle or upper pitch) and also the time structure. Feldman wanted players to have a degree of freedom, but found that this relied too heavily on their improvisation skills and so abandoned the practice from 1953 to 1958 in favour of precise notation. By 1960 he had developed a compromise in which pitch was specified but the duration was relatively free, for example, in *Durations I–V*. His last graphically notated score was *In Search of Orchestration* (1967), and in most subsequent works he specified pitch, rhythm, dynamics and duration. From the late 1970s he often expanded the time scale of his works, for example, Second String Quartet lasts up to five and a half hours, and several are between two and six hours, although one of his last works, *Palais de Mari* (1986), lasts only 20 minutes. He intended the music to 'entice the listener to live with the music, the way one would live with a painting on a wall, slowly acclimatizing oneself to its implied universe'. Much of his music is characterized by soft dynamics (between piano and pianissimo), stasis, absence of drama, direction or virtuosity.

From 1973 until his death he was the Edgard Varèse Professor at the University of New York at Buffalo. He collaborated with the playwright Samuel Beckett, whose way of working away at a line with accumulated tiny variations until a deeper meaning had become apparent matched Feldman's own method of composition. These collaborations include *Neither* (1977), a one-act opera for soprano and orchestra, and the play *Words and Music*. Feldman's last orchestral work, *For Samuel Beckett* (1987) has been described as a masterpiece. He was only beginning to receive recognition at the time of his death, although he had been convinced of his own historical importance;

169

in response to an interviewer he admitted that 'I do think about the fact that I want to be the first great composer who is Jewish.'[1]

Bibliography: *AG*; *G*; *HBD*; Leb; Ly*; Thomas Delio, *The Music of Morton Feldman* (Westport, CN: Greenwood Press, 1996)

1. Quoted from http://envill.demon.co.uk/mfkgann.htm

Ficher, Jacobo (b. Odessa, 15 January 1896; d. Buenos Aires, 9 September 1978) Studied violin at the age of 9 with Stolyarsky and later with M. T. Hait. He continued at the St Petersburg Conservatory from 1912 to 1917, where his teachers were Auer, Korguyev, Tcherepnin, and STEINBERG. In 1919 he became the first violinist for the State Opera in St Petersburg. In 1923 he emigrated to Argentina, where he founded a contemporary music group. He was also active conducting and teaching at the University of La Plata and at the Municipal and National Conservatories in Buenos Aires. Ficher composed about 150 works. The influence of his Jewish heritage is evident in the Suite for orchestra (1924) and *Kaddish* (1969), and his interest in Chekhov, in two Chekhov chamber operas, *The Bear* (1952) and *Proposal of Marriage* (1956). Other works include three piano concertos (1945, 1954 and 1960), eight symphonies, a saxophone quartet, a flute concerto, seven piano sonatas, a wind quintet and four string quartets.

Bibliography: Grad*; *G*; *HBD*; Ken

Fine, Irving Gifford (b. Boston, Massachusetts, 3 December 1914; d. Boston, Massachussets, 23 August 1962) Studied piano in his youth, and at Harvard studied composition with Hill and Piston, graduating in 1938. He continued his composition studies with Nadia Boulanger, first at Harvard in 1939, during one of her visits to America, and then in Paris following her return home. The onset of World War Two meant that he had to return to America sooner than he had planned. He studied conducting with Koussevitsky at Tanglewood. He then taught at Harvard from 1939 to 1950, when he was appointed professor of music and chairman of the Brandeis School of Creative Arts. As chairman, he felt it important that students knew the music of their time. He arranged concerts of contemporary music at Brandeis, which in 1952 included BLITZSTEIN's English version of *Threepenny Opera* and BERNSTEIN's *Trouble in Tahiti*.

He was a sensitive and shy person. His membership to the Harvard Musical Association was blocked because he was a Jew, an issue over which Piston resigned his own membership in protest. His earliest compositions were mainly for piano, and he also wrote a number of songs to poems by a friend, Maynard Kaplan, plus a setting of Lewis Carroll's *Alice in Wonderland*. His early style was Stravinskian neoclassical; COPLAND included him, together with Arthur BERGER, Harold SHAPERO and Lucas FOSS, in what he called the American 'Stravinsky School'. One of his most important compositions is his String Quartet (1952), in which he adopted serialism. This is also the case with his Second Symphony (1962) and *Fantasia* string trio (1956). Wilfred Mellors describes his adoption of serial technique in these works as follows: 'The tender, fine-spun lyricism of his slow movements suggests Berg reborn in the clear New England air; if some of the Viennese "morbidity" has gone, so has some of the strength.'[1] He also describes him as elegiac composer. Just a few months after composing his second symphony he died of a massive heart attack.

His other works include five orchestral works, a violin sonata (1946), a wind quintet (1948), *Notturno* for strings and harp (1951) reminiscent of MAHLER'S Fifth Symphony Adagio, choral music and songs. Towards the end of his life he showed an interest, which is clear from his correspondence, in his Jewish heritage. His five-movement *Partita on an Israeli Theme* was well under way when he suffered the heart attack, and there was also a choral work planned based on biblical excerpts from Exodus, Kings, Ezekiel, Isaiah and Daniel. In addition to composing he devoted much time to teaching and writing articles for *Modern Music, Notes, Musical America* and the *New York Times*.

Bibliography: *AG*; *G*; *HBD*; Ho*; Howard Pollack, *Harvard Composers* (New Jersey, MD: Scarecrow Press, 1992).

1. Wilfred Mellors, *Music in a New Found Land* (London: Barrie & Rockcliff, 1964), pp. 143–4.

Fine, Vivian (b. Chicago, 28 September 1913; d. Bennington, Vermont, 22 March 2000) Daughter of Russian-Jewish immigrants. She began piano lessons at the age of 5 with Djane Lavoie-Herz, a pupil of Skriabin. By the age of 11 Herz was sufficiently impressed to recommend that she took lessons in theory and harmony with Ruth Crawford (a former pupil of Herz). She began composing at the age of 13. She left school at 14 in order to spend more time on her music studies with Crawford. In 1929 the first public performance of her *Solo for Oboe* was given at a New York concert of the Pan-American Association of Composers. When Ruth Crawford moved to New York in 1929 Vivian also moved there, where she continued with Crawford's old teacher Adolf Weidig. Her first compositions were dramatically dissonant, possibly the indirect legacy of Skriabin.

In New York she earned her living as a dance accompanist, playing piano scores of works such as Stravinsky's *Petrushka* and Strauss's *Salome*, and began to gain a reputation as a performer of contemporary music. She continued to compose and became the only female member of COPLAND's Young Composers' Group, but she also continued her career as a professional pianist. In 1934 she married the sculptor Benjamin Karp and had two daughters. While receiving composition lessons from Sessions (1934–42), she began composing for ballet companies. Her ballet scores written during this period include *The Race of Life* (1937) for Doris Humphrey, *Opus 51* 1938) for Charles Weidman, and *Tragic Exodus* (1939) for Hanya Holm. After 1937 many of her compositions for dance and ballet were in diatonic mode, but after about 1956 she moved more towards atonality. Her best-known work, *A Guide to the Life Expectancy of a Rose* was written in 1956. It is the comic setting of an article from the gardening column of the *New York Times* for soprano, tenor, flute, violin, clarinet, cello and harp. It was staged by the choreographer Martha Graham, who also commissioned from her the ballet *Alcestis* (1960). In 1972 she composed *Missa Brevis* for four cellos and four-track recording of a mezzo-soprano voice. It sets part of the liturgy in Latin and Hebrew.

She composed her first opera, *The Women in the Garden*, in 1978, after winning a National Endowment for Arts grant to write a feminist opera. It is an opera about women and their attitudes towards their creativity and their lives and experiences, with Emily Dickinson, Isadora Duncan, Gertrude Stein and Virginia Woolf as the central characters. For her 75th birthday she was commissioned by the Bay Area Women's Philharmonic to write *After the Tradition* (1988), a work having its roots in Fine's Jewish background. The first movement is a Kaddish in memory of the cellist George Finkel, and the second movement takes its theme from a poem by the twelfth-century poet Yehuda Ha-Levi. Her last major composition, *The Memoirs of Uliana Rooney* (1994) was a multi-media opera about a female composer in the twentieth century. She was a strong advocate of both American music and of women composers. She held a number of teaching posts, at New York University (1945–8), the Juilliard School of Music (1948), State University of New York at Potsdam (1951), Connecticut College School of Dance (1963–4) and Bennington College, Vermont, from 1964. She was vice-president of the American Composers Alliance, an organization she helped to found, from 1961 to 1965. She died following a car accident in Bennington, Vermont.
Bibliography: *AG*; *CC*; *G*; *HBD*; *Pan**

Finzi, Gerald Raphael (b. London, 14 July 1901; d. Oxford, 27 September 1956) Son of John (Jack) Abraham Finzi (1860–1909), a shipbroker, and his wife Eliza Emma, *née* Leverson. The Finzis were descended from a Sephardic Jewish family that can be traced back to a Jewish money-lending office in Padua as early as 1369. Finzis lived in England from the eighteenth century. Gerald's father, although not a practising Jew, maintained strong cultural ties with the Jewish community; he was educated at University College London, the first great English educational establishment to admit all creeds. Gerald's mother was born in North London and was from the Ashkenazic Jewish community. Gerald lived in North London until 1915, with many of his relatives and other members of the Jewish community living close by. His parents were very comfortably placed financially, and he encountered a number of artists and musicians in his youth. In spite of this, his childhood was far from happy. He was the youngest of five children, but only he and his sister survived beyond World War One. His father died of cancer when Gerald was only 8 years old. He was initially educated by a tutor, then at a small private school, and after his father's death he was sent to a boarding school, where he was not happy. At the age of 12 he performed one of his own piano compositions

172

in a hotel concert and by that age had already decided he wanted to be a composer.

In 1915, after the outbreak of World War One, Gerald's mother and family moved to Harrogate, possibly to be safe from aerial bombardments, and there Gerald began to study with Ernest Farrar, a pupil of Stanford and friend of Vaughan Williams. He struck up a good relationship with Farrar, and was disappointed when in 1916 Farrar enlisted in the Grenadier Guards. He was devastated by Farrar's death in action in 1918. From 1917 to 1922 he studied privately with Sir Edward Bairstow at York Minster. Probably the first work of Finzi's to be performed in public, and given the number Op. 1, was *Ten Children's Songs*, which was performed at York Minster in 1920.

In 1922 Finzi and his mother moved to Painswick in Gloucestershire. It was an area with strong musical associations with Vaughan Williams, Elgar, Parry, Holst, Herbert Howells, Ivor Gurney and the Three Choirs Festival, and there Finzi was to establish himself as part of that English musical tradition. During this period he composed the first of many settings of Hardy's poems, *By Footpath and Style* for baritone and string quartet (1921–2) and the *Severn Rhapsody* for chamber orchestra (1923). Feeling that his composing was limited by his technical understanding, he moved to London in 1925 and studied sixteenth-century counterpoint privately with R. O. Morris. The next few years were important formative years for Finzi, although not productive in terms of the number of completed compositions. He was fortunate in having inherited independent means and not having to depend on composition for his livelihood. He was continually revising works and would then throw away the original. During this period he became friends with Howard Ferguson and Edmund Rubbra, and met Vaughan Williams, Holst and Bliss. Vaughan Williams conducted Finzi's *Violin Concerto* at a Bach Choir concert in 1928, but Finzi later withdrew the work apart from the *Introit*. In 1928 he spent two and a half months in a sanatorium, having been diagnosed as having mild tuberculosis. The *Grand Fantasia*, in which he seems to have achieved a stylistic breakthrough, was perhaps his spontaneous response on being released from the sanatorium. The song cycle *A Young Man's Exhortation*, settings of 15 of Hardy's poems, was completed about 1929 and the first performance given in 1933. From 1930 to 1933 he taught at the Royal Academy of Music in London.

In 1933 Finzi married the artist Joyce Black; this had a liberating effect on his composing. Most of the works that are regarded as the best part of his legacy were composed after his marriage, for example, *Dies Natalis* (1938), many more settings of Hardy's poems, *Earth and Air and Rain, Before and After Summer, I Said to Love* and *Till Earth Outwears, Clarinet Concerto* (1948) and *Intimations of Immortality* (1949). He and Joy went to live in Aldbourne, Wiltshire, from 1935 to 1939. Early in 1937 they found the site of what was to become Finzi's home for the rest of his life. They bought and rebuilt a 16-acre property called Church Farm, in Ashmansworth near Newbury, Berkshire, and lived there from 1939. Not only did Finzi compose his major works here, but he also assembled a library of over 3,000 volumes of English poetry, philosophy and literature and cultivated over 300 varieties of English apples, many of which were in danger of extinction. In 1939 he completed a work begun in 1926, *Dies Natalis* for soprano or tenor and string orchestra to settings by the seventeenth-century cleric Traherne. This is one of the works that has made his reputation. It was scheduled to be performed at the Three Choirs Festival of 1939 but the festival had to be cancelled with the outbreak of war. It was given its premiere in London in 1940.

During the 1930s Finzi was much disturbed by the rise in Nazism in Germany. It was the injustice and cruelty that hurt him, not racial empathy. Finzi had established himself as a thoroughly English composer and saw himself continuing that tradition. This is in sharp contrast to a near contemporary of his, Benjamin FRANKEL. Finzi was completely assimilated and did not have social links with the English Jewish community. Even a Jewish pianist, Myra Hess, did not guess he was Jewish. Nevertheless, he could not help being greatly disturbed by the plight of Jews in Europe, suffering insomnia after *Kristallnacht* and after the German Army overran Czechoslovakia. During the war the Finzis housed many evacuees and Czech and German refugees at Church Farm and Gerald joined the Local Defence Volunteers. From 1941 to 1945 he worked for the Minister of War Transport and was based in London during weekdays, returning to Church Farm at weekends.

In 1940 he founded and conducted the Newbury String Players. His wife Joy organized the players and was herself one of the second violinists. This group, which started in the local parish church, continued in subsequent years to give 379 concerts in local venues throughout Hampshire, Berkshire, Wiltshire and Oxfordshire. Finzi conducted the first 164, and his son Christopher took over in about 1951 and continued until after Finzi's death. As the Newbury String Players developed they invited many well-known soloists. Many promising players and composers found their first opportunities through the group. Apart from supporting young musicians and composers, Finzi devoted much of his time to editing and cataloguing works by Ivor Gurney; he eventually published five volumes of his songs and two of his poems. He was also active in reviving and editing works by Parry, William Boyce, John Stanley and Charles Wesley. Although he had little time to compose whilst at the War Ministry, by the end of the war *Dies Natalis* had transformed his status as a composer and he continued what for him was an important phase of his composing career. During the next five years *Farewell to Arms* (1945), *Lo, the Full, Final Sacrifice* (1946), *For St Cecilia* (1947), *Clarinet Concerto* (1949) and *Intimations of Immortality*, settings of a poem by Wordsworth (1950), were given their premieres.

In 1951 he is diagnosed as having Hodgkin's disease. He felt that by this stage he had overcome many of his earlier technical difficulties and felt in the prime of his creative powers. In a letter concerning his illness he quotes from Tychborne:

My thread is cut, and yet it is not spun;
And now I live, and now my life is done.

In spite of having to have a splenectomy and radiotherapy, he continued to press on with his composing. Before his death he completed a setting of the *Magnificat* for Smith College, Massachusetts (1952) and *White-Flowering Days* for the coronation of Queen Elizabeth II (1953). He was stimulated by John Russell to consider completing a piano concerto begun in 1929. He found he could not do this, but he revised the first movement as the *Grand Fantasia and Toccata* that was premiered in 1953 with Russell playing the piano and Finzi conducting. In 1954 he gave his last premiere and public appearance with *In Terra Pax*, based on a poem by Robert Bridges. His last composition was his Cello Concerto, commissioned by Barbarolli for the Cheltenham Festival of 1956. It was his first work to be taken up by a front-rank conductor during his lifetime, and was first performed the night before he died. The Cheltenham Festival's emphasis at the time was on contemporary British music. Contemporary press comment was to question whether this was indeed 'contemporary music', since the harmonic language and thematic character gave no hint of what had been happening in music during the last 40 years. Nevertheless, it has more than stood the test of time, such that 50 years later it has been described as being on a par with Elgar's Cello Concerto.
Bibliography: *G*; Ken; Stephen Banfield, *Gerald Finzi: an English Composer* (London: Faber & Faber, 1997)*

Fitelberg, Grzegorz (b. Dynaburg, Latvia, 18 October 1879; d. Katovice, Poland, 10 June 1953)   Studied composition with Noskowski and violin with Barcewicz at the Warsaw Conservatory. Originally a violinist, he gained an international reputation as the conductor of the Warsaw Philharmonic Orchestra. With Szymanowski and others he founded the 'Young Poland' group of composers in Berlin in 1905, and he conducted the first performances of almost all the works Szymanowski composed for orchestra. He also conducted the Vienna State Opera (1911–14) and operas in St Petersburg and Moscow, returning to the Warsaw Philharmonic in 1923. He conducted for Diagilev (1921–4), giving the premiere of Stravinsky's *Mavra*. He left Poland in 1939 and returned in 1947. He composed two symphonies (1903 and 1906), a violin concerto (1901) and various violin works and chamber music.
Bibliography: *G*; Ho*; Ly*

Fitelberg, Jerzy (b. Warsaw, 20 May 1903; d. New York, 25 April 1951)   Son of Grzegorz FITELBERG. His first music teacher was his father, but from 1922 to 1926 he studied with Walther Gmeindl and Franz SCHREKER at the Hochschule für Musik in Berlin. He spent six years in Paris (1933–9) and then emigrated to New York in 1940. He composed several orchestral works including three suites, several concertos: a concerto for strings, two for violin, two for piano,

175

and one for cello and one for clarinet. He also composed chamber music, including five string quartets.
Bibliography: *AG*; *G*; *HBD*; Ho*; Ly*

Fleischer, Tsippi (b. Haifa, 20 May 1946)   Studied music at the Rubin Academy of Music in Tel Aviv, graduating in 1969. She also studied Arab language, history and literature at Tel Aviv University, and later continued her music studies at New York University and Bar-Ilan University, where she gained a Ph.D. in musicology. She taught music theory at Tel Aviv and Bar-Ilan Universities and the Hebrew Union College, Jerusalem. In a number of her compositions she attempts to link both Arab and Jewish–Israeli elements as, for example, in *Girl, Butterfly, Girl* for voice and chamber orchestra (1977), which is based on Arab poems, and *A Girl Named Limonad* (1977), which is set to a text by Lebanese Christian poet Shawqi Abi-Shaqra. Other works include: *Lamentations* for soprano, chorus, two harps and percussion (1985); *In Chromatic Mode* for piano and contact microphone (1986); *Ballad of Expected Death in Cairo* for tenor, piano and three violins (1987); *The Gown of the Night* for voices and magnetic tape with text by Muhammad Gana'im (1987); *Like Two Branches*, a chamber cantata for choir, two oboes, psaltery and tar drums (1988); and the trilingual *Oratorio 1492–1992*, which was written in 1991 in commemoration of the expulsion of Jews from Spain.
Bibliography: Grad*; *G*; *GW*

Fleischmann, Benjamin (b. Bezhnetsk, Russia, 7/20 July 1914; d. Krasnoye, near Leningrad, *c.* 14 September 1941)   Studied with Mikhail Yudin at the Mussorgsky Music College, Leningrad, and then was a composition student of Shostakovich for four years at the Leningrad Conservatory. In 1941 he enlisted in the 'People's Brigade' to fight against the Nazis during the siege of Leningrad. Barely trained and poorly armed, like most volunteers, Fleischmann is assumed to have been killed in the district of Luga, Krasnoye Village during the 900-day siege of Leningrad, probably on 14 September 1941.

A single incomplete work of Fleischmann's has been left for posterity. It is also known that he wrote song settings of texts by Lermontov and Goethe and also piano preludes, but these have been lost. As a pupil of Shostakovich, he had begun an opera based on Chekhov's story *Skripka Rotshilda* (Rothschild's violin). After he was killed, Shostakovich found his opera score and decided to complete the orchestration as a tribute to the fallen. Although he completed it by 1943, because of Stalin's anti-Jewish crusade it could not be performed. It was given a first concert performance in Moscow on 20 June 1960 at the Central House of Composers, but the first staged performance was given by Shostakovich's son Maxim in Leningrad by the so-called 'experimental chamber opera studio' on 24 April 1968. The score was published in Moscow in 1965. The first UK performance was in 1997.

The original story on which the short opera is based was written by

Chekhov in 1894; it is set in a *shtetl*. Jacob Ivanov, a Christian coffin maker, from time to time is asked to play the fiddle in a Jewish band at local weddings and celebrations. He shows contempt and hatred for his fellow musicians, particularly the red-bearded Jew nicknamed Rothschild, who is the flautist in the band. However, at the end of the opera, when Jacob is dying he gives his violin to Rothschild as a form of reconciliation. Fleischmann left a somewhat clumsy libretto, possibly because of his inexperience, but a brilliant score was completed, except for a few vocal lines, and the first scene and the closing section unorchestrated. Although the Shostakovich orchestration shows clearly his hallmarks, he is nevertheless sensitive to Fleischmann's own idiom. The opera includes an interlude with a *klezmer*-like dance and a reference to a traditional Chanukah melody.

Bibliography: *G*; Solomon Volkov, *Testimony: the memoirs of Shostakovich* (London: Hamish Hamilton, 1979), pp. 173–4; Ronald Weitzman, 'Fleischmann, Shostakovich, and Chekov's "Rothchild's Fiddle"', *Tempo*, 206 (1998), pp. 7–11; 09026 68434 2 [record sleeve]

Foss, Lucas [Fuchs] (b. Berlin, 15 August 1922)   Showed musical talent at an early age; he began composing at the age of 7 and wrote two operas in his early teens. He studied piano and theory with Julius Goldstein in Berlin, and when he was 11 he went to Paris for four years, studying piano with Lazare Levy also studying composition and orchestration. By 1937, when his family emigrated to America, he had a command of classical European composition techniques. He continued his studies at the Curtis Institute with Vengerova (piano), Scalero and Thompson (composition) and Reiner (conducting). He also studied conducting with Koussevitsky at Tanglewood during 1939–43, and composition with Hindemith as a special student at Yale University from 1939 to 1940. His first big success was the choral setting of Sandburg's poem *The Prairie* (1943). The work received the New York Music Critics Circle Award. The work is quintessentially American, reminiscent of some of COPLAND's work. In his string quartet (1947) Foss was able to combine the more traditional skills he had acquired in Europe with sonorities derived from Copland. In the *Song of Songs* (1946) he combines these influences with that of Jewish cantillation. He was equally at home as a concert pianist and received another New York Critics Circle Award in 1954 for his extrovert second piano concerto, which he premiered in Venice in 1951.

In 1953 he succeeded SCHOENBERG as professor of music at UCLA, where in 1957 he founded the Improvisation Chamber Ensemble. He conducted a number of orchestras, including the Kol Israel Orchestra of Jerusalem in 1972–6. Most of his earlier compositions can be described as neoclassical tinged with Americanism, but after the 1960s he explored serialism in, for example, *Echoi* for four soloists (1961), and minimalism, for example, *String Quartet* No. 3 (1975). The song collection *Time Cycle* for soprano and orchestra (1960) marks the transition between the 'neoclassical phase' and the

177

'experimental phase' of his work, and remains his most performed work. Among his orchestral works are two piano concertos (1943 and 1952) and *Elegy for Anne Frank* (1989). Foss is a prolific and eclectic composer. He has been known as a 'poor man's BERNSTEIN'.[1]

Bibliography: *AG*; *CC*; *G*; *HBD*; Leb; Ly*; Wilfred Mellors, *Music in a New Found Land* (London: Barrie & Rockcliff, 1964)

1. Leb.

Fox, Erika (b. Vienna, 3 October 1936)   Granddaughter of a rabbi; the house in which she originally lived acted as a synagogue. In 1939 she came to England as a refugee and lived in Leeds. She tried composing on the piano at a very early age, and started piano lessons with Millicent Silver at the age of 9. She won a piano scholarship to the Royal College of Music in 1961, where she also studied composition under Bernard Stevens. She married Manfred Fox in 1961. She took further composition lessons with Jeremy Dale Roberts and Harrison Birtwhistle. She became a piano teacher at the Menuhin School and also at the Guildhall School of Music. She has composed for orchestral, chamber, vocal music and opera. Jewish liturgical chant and Chassidic music are the main sources of her inspiration. Her first mature composition was *Eight Songs from Cavafy* (1968) for mezzo-soprano, flute, oboe, bassoon violin and piano. In 1975 she composed a chamber opera, *The Slaughterer*, based on a story by Isaac Bashevis Singer drawing on childhood memories of the *shochet* (ritual slaughterer) when visiting her grandfather's house. In 1983 she visited Jerusalem and produced three works: *Quasi una Cadenza* for horn, clarinet and piano; *Kaleidoscope* for flute, cello harp and vibraphone, which won a Finzi award; and *Shir* for wind quintet, trumpet, trombone, string quartet, double bass, percussion and piano. *Shir* means song, and the work includes part of the Song of Songs and incorporates Chassidic melodies. Other works include: *Nine Lessons from Isaiah* (1970) for bass and string quartet; *The Bet* (1990), a theatre work for narrator, puppets, flute, piano, double bass, percussion and voices to a text by Elaine Feinstein; and *The Dancer Hotoke* (1991), an opera commissioned by the Garden Venture at the Royal Opera House and first performed at the Riverside Studios in London.

Bibliography: *CC*; *G*; Pan*

Franchetti, Alberto (b. Turin, 18 September 1860; d. Viareggio, 4 August 1942) Son of the wealthy Baron Raymondo Franchetti, who was married to Baroness Louise Rothschild. He studied in Turin and Venice, and in Germany with Draesake and Rheinberger. He had no need for regular employment on account of his private wealth, but he directed the Florence Conservatory in 1926–8. His wealth enabled him to stage his nine operas. He also wrote some symphonies and chamber music. His first opera, *Asrael* (1888), was good enough for Verdi to recommend him to compose *Cristoforo Colombo* (1892) to mark the 400th anniversary of the founding of America. His operas were in

the grand style, and were much influenced by Wagner and MEYERBEER. The first two met with some short-term success around the turn of the century, but after that Franchetti's reputation as a composer declined. Caruso sang in *Germania* in 1902 and recorded some of its arias. He was offered Illica's libretto of *Tosca* by Ricordi before Puccini, but was persuaded to decline, acknowledging that Puccini could write a better opera.
Bibliography: G; Ho*; Leb

Franchetti, Arnold (b. Lucca, Italy 1905; d. Middletown, Connecticut, 7 March 1993)   Son of Alberto FRANCHETTI. He studied physics at the University of Florence and enrolled at the Salzburg Mozarteum, where he was awarded a prize for his opera *Bauci*. During World War Two he spent time in Sweden and in the Italian Alps, helping to rescue Allied airmen. He emigrated to the USA in 1947 and taught at the Hart School of Music in Hartford, Connecticut, from 1948 to 1979. Most of his compositions are operas. After exploring late-Romantic and neoclassical styles, he developed a non-serial twelve-note composition language.
Bibliography: G

Frankel, Benjamin (b. London, 31 January 1906; d. London, 12 February 1973) Son of a *shamash* (synagogue beadle). His parents were of Polish–Jewish origin; his father came from Warsaw and had completed military service in the czarist army, and his mother, Golda Adler, came from Tarnopol, a Polish town in the Austro-Hungarian Empire. His father set up as a tobacconist in London's Fulham Road, but later abandoned this to become a *shamash*. To supplement the family income his mother made *kosher* meals for the Jewish boys at St Paul's School. At an early age Benjamin showed a talent for the piano and violin, and whilst he was encouraged by his parents, they did not consider music a reliable profession. Consequently, at the age of 14 he was apprenticed to a watchmaker. During this period and whilst at school he was an avid reader, and taught himself the musical literature, reading everything available at the Hammersmith Public Library. The apprenticeship only lasted for one year. At the age of 14 Frankel so impressed the American pianist Victor Benham that he offered to give him piano lessons free. For two years he studied with Benham, the last six months of which were in Germany. During this period the high inflation in Germany meant that Frankel could manage on a monthly allowance of £1 from his parents.

When civil unrest began Frankel returned to England and earned his living as a jazz pianist and violinist working in cafés, hotels and on ocean liners. With a scholarship from the Worshipful Company of Musicians he was able to continue his music studies under Orlando Morgan at the Guildhall School of Music. To survive financially he played in nightclubs and did some commercial arranging. This led to his composing film scores in the early 1930s. His first film score was in 1934, and over the next 30 years he wrote over 100 film scores, including *The Seventh Veil* (1945), *So Long at the Fair* (1950), *The Man in the White Suit* (1951) and *The Importance of Being Earnest* (1952). *Curse of the Werewolf* (1960) is believed to be the first film score to use twelve-note serial score. In 1946 he became professor of composition at the Guildhall School, where he had earlier studied.

Most of Frankel's output can be divided into film music, chamber music and orchestral music. Whilst he was largely occupied writing film music during the 1930s and 1940s, he also wrote chamber music, but his orchestral music ostensibly began after 1950, and during his later years, when he wrote less film music. His early chamber music included *Three Sketches for String Quartet*, Op. 2, *Sonata for Violin and Piano*, Op. 6, *String Trio*, Op. 3 and *Elegie Juive* for cello and piano, all written in the 1930s. By 1949 he had written four string quartets, the last of which was given its premiere by the then youthful Amadeus Quartet. He wrote a piano quartet, Op. 26 (1953) and a clarinet quintet, Op. 28 (1956), written for Thea King in memory of her husband, and a fifth string quartet (1965).

Besides *Elegie Juive*, two other works have clear Jewish themes, *Sonata Ebraica* for cello and harp, Op. 8, and a violin concerto (1951). The latter was commissioned by Max Rostal for the Festival of Britain in 1951. It is dedicated 'In Memory of the Six Million' and was Frankel's first major orchestral piece. Frankel identified with his Jewish roots, but did not practise the religion. When in 1932 he married out, his father was so upset that he never spoke with him again for the seven years of his life that remained. Frankel joined the Communist Party in 1941, convinced at the time that it was the only way to counter fascism. He resigned in 1952, outraged by the show trials and summary executions of alleged spies in Prague.

In 1957 he moved to Switzerland for seclusion in order to concentrate on composition, particularly of larger-scale work. He completed his first symphony a year later, in 1958. In 1959, whilst visiting London, he suffered a heart attack and was treated in Guy's Hospital. From then until his death in February 1973 he was in poor health. The years of overwork and heavy smoking probably contributed to this, but it was nevertheless a very productive period in his life, in which he composed seven more symphonies between 1962 and 1972. He was commissioned to write his ninth for the 1973 proms, but died before he had committed his ideas to paper. He even requested manuscript paper from his wife when he was admitted to hospital shortly before his death. He said that when composing his symphonies he would work on the ideas in his head over a period of time, and that once these had gelled he would be able to write them down quite quickly. He uses twelve-tone system in many of his symphonies. He studied SCHOENBERG's twelve-note system with his friend the music critic, Hans Keller. Keller explained that both MAHLER and Sibelius had a strong formative influence on his symphonic writings, but that Schoenberg's methods form the basis of his technique. He also likens him to Schoenberg in being a conservative modernist in the tonal

tradition. Although using twelve-tone technique, he rejected the notion of atonality, regarding melody as the stuff out of which music was made.
Bibliography: *G*; Ken; Leb*; E. Dimitri Kennaway, 'Frankel, Benjamin – a Forgotten Legacy', *Musical Times*, 133 (1992), pp. 69–70

Freed, Isadore (b. Brest-Litovsk [Brest], Byelorussia, 26 March 1900; d. New York, 10 November 1960)   Emigrated to Philadelphia at the age of 3. He went to Pennsylvania University, where his teachers were Ernest BLOCH and Josef Hofman. He taught at the Curtis Institute, Philadelphia from 1924 to 1925 and then continued composition studies with d'Indy and Louis Vierne in Paris. He returned to the USA in 1933 and taught at the Temple University (1937–46) and then at the Hart School of Music (1947–60). He wrote two operas and some instrumental music, but is primarily known for his contribution to Jewish sacred music. He wrote a book, *Harmonizing the Jewish Modes* (1958), and composed sacred works in a pan-diatonic and neoclassical style.
Bibliography: *AG*; *G*; *HBD*; Ho*; Ly*

Friedman, Ignaz (b. Podgórze, near Krakow, Poland, 14 February 1882; d. Sydney, Australia, 26 January 1948)   Studied piano with Flora Grzywinska in Krakow from the age of 10. In 1900 he went to the University of Leipzig to study composition with Hugo Rieman, and then later with Guido Adler in Vienna. He also studied piano with Leschetizky in Vienna for four years, making his début as a concert pianist in Vienna in 1904. From 1905 onwards he travelled extensively in Europe, South America and Australia as a concert pianist. He lived in Berlin until 1914 and then in Copenhagen, settling in Australia in 1940. During his career as a concert pianist he gave over 2,800 recitals. He was said to be technically a better pianist than Arthur Rubinstein, and undisputedly a better poker player, winning a substantial sum from Rubinstein on a transatlantic crossing.[1] He appeared with many violinists, including Hubay, Elman, Auer and Huberman and together with Casals in piano trios. In spite of a very active performing career, he also devoted much time to composing. He composed over 100 piano pieces, most romantic character pieces, but also a piano quintet and pieces for cello. He transcribed music by eighteenth-century composers and edited works of Chopin, Liszt and Schumann.
Bibliography: *G*; *HBD*; Ho*; Ken
1. Harvey Sachs, *Arthur Rubinstein* (London: Weidenfeld & Nicolson, 1996), p. 197.

Fuchs, Lillian (b. New York, 18 November 1902; d. Engelwood, New Jersey, 6 October 1995)   Probably best known as a violist and teacher, but she also composed, mainly for viola or violin. She studied violin with Svecenski and Kneisel, and composition with Goetschius at the New York Institute of Musical Art (now the Juilliard School). She performed initially as a violinist but switched to viola in the late 1920s. She was the first to perform and record Bach's six cello suites on viola. She taught at the Manhattan School of Music from 1962, the Aspen Summer Institute in Colorado from 1964 and the Juilliard School of Music from 1971. Her compositions for viola include 12 *Caprices* (1950), *Sonata Pastorale* for viola (1956), 16 *Fantasy Etudes* (1961), and 15 *Characteristic Studies* (1965).

Bibliography: *G*; D. E. Williams, *Lillian Fuchs, First Lady of the Viola* (New York: Edwin Mellon Press, 2001); www.cs.bsu.edu/homepages/dlsills/David_jewish. stml*

Gal, Hans (b. Brunn-on-Gebirge, near Vienna, 5 August 1890; d. Edinburgh, 3 October 1987)   Studied composition with Mandyczewski at Vienna University from 1908 to 1913. From 1919 to 1929 he was a lecturer in musical theory at Vienna University. In 1928 he became director of the Hochschule für Musik and the Conservatory at Mainz. In 1933 he was dismissed and the performance of his music banned by the Nazis. He returned to Austria but was driven out in 1938 by the *Anschluss*, and fled to Edinburgh, where he made his home. He became a lecturer in musical education at Edinburgh University from 1945 to 1965. He helped found the Edinburgh International Music Festival. He published over 100 compositions and also wrote books on Brahms, Wagner and Schubert, including a volume entitled *The Golden Age in Vienna*. He composed five operas (*Der Arzt der Sobeide*, 1919, composed in the Carpathian World War One trenches; *Die Heilige Ente*, 1923; *Das Lied der Nacht*, 1926; *Der Zauberspiel*, 1930; and *Die Bieden Klaus*, 1933), two oratorios (*De Profundis* and *Lebens kreise*) four symphonies, three orchestral suites, a violin and cello concerto, chamber music, piano music and songs. His opera *Die Heilige Ente*, a play about gods and humans, was very successful in its day and was produced in Dusseldorf, Berlin, Prague, Weimar and Karlsruhe. His musical roots were in Brahms and Strauss and were not Schoenbergian, and, although he lived in Vienna at the time of the Second Viennese School, none of his works is atonal. In his later years he composed mainly chamber music. His music was regularly performed until the 1930s and he continued to compose until shortly before his death, at the age of 97. However, after he fled from the Nazis, as a composer he became somewhat marginalized, and unlike Berthold GOLDSCHMIDT, he saw no revival of interest in his music during his lifetime.

Bibliography: *G*; *HBD*; Ho*; Leb; Wilhelm Waldstein, *Hans Gál* (Vienna: Lafite, 1965)

Gardner, Samuel (b. Elisavetgrad [Kirovograd], Russia, 25 August 1891; d. New York, 23 January 1984) Moved with his parents in 1892 to Providence, Rhode Island, USA, where he studied violin with Felix Wendelschaefer from 1897 to 1902. From 1902 to 1908 he continued his violin studies with C. M. Loeffler and Felix Wintermitz in Boston, and studied composition with Percy

Goetschius and violin with Franz Kneisel at the Institute of Musical Art in New York from 1911 to 1913. He taught at the Juilliard School of Music from 1924 to 1941. He was a violinist as well as a composer, playing in the Kneisel Quartet and the Chicago Symphony Orchestra. His compositions include *New Russia* (which won the Loeb prize in 1918), String Quartet No. 1 (which won the Pulitzer prize in 1918), the tone poem *Broadway* (1924), a piano quintet (1925), *Hebrew Fantasy* for clarinet quintet, a violin concerto, String Quartet No. 2 (1946) and *Country Modes* for string orchestra (1946).
Bibliography: *AG*; *HBD*; C. Abravanel,CPO 999 630–2* [record sleeve]

Gernsheim, Friedrich (b. Worms, Germany, 17 July 1839; d. Berlin, 10 September 1916)   Came from a middle-class Jewish family. His father was a doctor and an enthusiastic flute player, and his mother came from an Augsburg merchant family and was a good pianist. Worms had one of the oldest Jewish communities in Germany, dating back over 1,000 years, and Gernsheim's grandfather, Abraham Gernsheim, had been the head of that community. After the French Revolution, as head, Abraham tore down and destroyed the defamatory sign *Judengefängnis* (Jewish prison) at the entrance to the Jewish ghetto. Gernsheim received his first piano lessons from his mother and early musical training from Louis Liebe, a pupil of Spohr. In 1848, because of the upheaval of the revolution that year, the family moved to Mainz, where Friedrich had piano lessons from Ernst Pauer. Later he had piano, violin and musical theory lessons in Frankfurt-on-Main. At the age of 11 he made his first public appearance as violinist and pianist at the Frankfurt Stadttheater. He continued his musical education at the Leipzig Conservatory with Ignaz Moscheles (piano), Moritz Hauptmann (theory), and Ferdinand David (violin). In 1861 he became music director at Saarbrücken, and in 1865 Ferdinand Hiller appointed him to the staff of the Cologne Conservatory. He later held positions at Rotterdam and at the Stern Conservatory in Berlin.

Gernsheim's compositions are strongly influenced by Brahms, his friend and contemporary. His first symphony had its premiere one year before that of Brahms's First Symphony. His best works are considered to be his chamber works, such as the String Quartet in E minor, the Piano Quintet in B minor, and the four symphonies. His Third Symphony in C minor is subtitled *Mirjam*. The inspiration for this came from hearing a performance of Handel's *Israel in Egypt* where the last recitative is Miriam, the prophet's song of triumph at the Red Sea.
Bibliography: *G*; Ho*; Ly*

Gershwin, George (b. Brooklyn, New York, 26 September 1898; d. Hollywood, 11 July 1937)   Second son of émigré Jewish parents. His father, Morris Gershovitz, was born in St Petersburg, which he left sometime in the 1890s to avoid conscription into the army. His mother, Rose Bruskin, was also from St Petersburg and was the daughter of a furrier. Most of the four children's early childhood was spent on the Lower East Side of Manhattan, where George's father worked in a variety of places, including restaurants, Turkish and Russian baths, a pool parlour and a bookmaker's shop at Brighton Beach Race Track. Each time his father sold a business the family moved apartment, living in as many as 25 different apartments during his childhood. There was no musical inheritance in the family. As a child, George was athletic and rather wild, showing little interest in academic activity. The start of his interest in music was in the playground, when he heard the strains of one of his contemporaries, Max Rostal, playing Dvorak's *Humouresque* in the assembly hall. He described it as a flashing revelation to hear him playing. The next important development was when his mother bought a piano. George was 12 at the time and no sooner had it been lifted through the apartment window than George sat down and played a popular tune of the day. He had practised previously on a friend's piano. Although the piano had been purchased with his elder brother Ira in mind, it was decided that George should have the first lessons. Although he was not his first piano teacher, it was Charles Hambitzer who really shaped his future and introduced him to works by Chopin, Liszt and Debussy. He had lessons in theory with Kienyi and later Rubin GOLDMARK.

At the age of 15 Gershwin left school and started working as a song plugger for a Tin Pan Alley publisher, Jerome H. Remick, playing and singing newly published songs to encourage their sales. This proved a useful experience as it enabled him to discern what the public liked. In 1916 his first song was printed and a year later he left Remick. In 1920 he wrote his first real hit song, *Swanee*, in 15 minutes, which Al Jolson adopted and the recording sold over 2,250,000 copies, earning him a royalty of over $10,000 in a year. The composition that launched Gershwin into the concert hall was *Rhapsody in Blue*. Paul Whiteman, the leader of a dance band that played jazz, was sufficiently impressed with Gershwin's *Blue Monday* (1922) to commission him to write and perform at his concert entitled An Experiment in Modern Music. *Rhapsody in Blue* was the successful outcome, bringing American popular music to the concert hall. The *New York Times* music critic wrote that it was 'the finest piece of serious music to come out of America, and the most effective piano concerto written since Tchaikovsky's in B flat minor'. Gershwin wrote the piano part and detailed orchestral sketches, but the complete orchestration was done by Ferdie Grofié. However, for all his subsequent works Gershwin orchestrated for himself. He continued to produce many popular songs, usually in collaboration with his brother Ira, who wrote the lyrics. His next ambitious concert work was the Piano Concerto in F (1925). It combines blues and jazz idioms with elements from the nineteenth-century classical composers. Gershwin continued to have composition lessons from Rubin Goldmark up to 1936, and then from Riegger, Cowell and Schillinber in order to increase his technical mastery.

A visit to Paris gave him the idea of portraying an American visitor's impression of that city. The result was the symphonic poem *An American in*

Paris (1928). The music was used as a ballet in the Ziegfeld production, *Show Girl* (1929). Other orchestral works he wrote were: *Second Rhapsody* for piano and orchestra (1931), *Cuban Overture* (1932), '*I Got Rhythm' Variations* (1934) and *Catfish Row: Suite from Porgy and Bess* (1935–6). His most successful opera was *Porgy and Bess* (1935). In 1926 Gershwin read the novel *Porgy* by DuBose Heyward, about black fishermen in South Carolina. He decided to write an opera but felt he needed first to improve his technical competence. In 1927 a dramatized version of *Porgy* by Heyward's wife Dorothy had proved very successful and so, in 1932, Gershwin began his most ambitious work, the opera *Porgy and Bess* in collaboration with DuBose Heyward and also Ira Gershwin. It is the story of a tragic relationship between Porgy, a crippled beggar, and Bess, a woman of easy virtue. Gershwin described it as a folk opera. In place of the more conventional arias it has show tunes, spirituals and blues composed by Gershwin. It was first performed on Broadway in 1935.

For what were the last eight years of his life Gershwin was also active as a painter. His most successful paintings are portraits, notably those of Arnold Schoenberg and Jerome Kern, and self-portraits. On 11 July he was operated on for a fulminating brain tumour and never recovered from the operation, dying at the age of 38.

Bibliography: *AG*; *G*; *HBD*; R. Greenberg, *George Gershwin* (London: Phaidon, 1998); E. Jablonski, *Gershwin Remembered* (London: Faber, 1992)

Gideon, Miriam (b. Greeley, Colorado, 23 October 1906; d. New York, 18 June 1996)   Came from a German–Jewish family; her father taught philosophy and modern languages and her mother, Henrietta Shoninger, had been a schoolteacher before her marriage. When Miriam was 9, the family moved to Chicago, where she received her first piano lessons from a cousin. A year later they moved to New York, where she took piano lessons from Hans Barth. By the age of 14 she went to live with her uncle, Henry Gideon, who was music director of the Temple Israel, a large reform synagogue in Boston. She went to the College of Liberal Arts, Boston University, graduating in French at the age of 19. She studied composition under Lazare Saminsky, director of the Temple Emanuel from 1931 to 1934, and then on Saminsky's advice she continued with Roger Sessions from 1935 to 1943. During this period she went to study in Europe in 1939, but returned the same year on the outbreak of war. She completed an MA in musicology at Columbia University in 1946.

Her first composition was a one-movement piece for strings entitled *Lyric Piece*, which was first performed by the London Symphony Orchestra in 1944. From 1944 to 1954 she taught harmony, composition and music history at Brooklyn College, then at the City College of New York (1947–55 and 1971–6), the Jewish Theological Seminary (from 1955) and the Manhattan School (from 1967). She received a Doctorate in Sacred Music from the Jewish Theological Seminary in 1970. She composed more than 50 works. Many have a vocal element and most are for small instrumental groups. She set poetry in many different languages to music, in some cases using both the original language and the English translation. She said she was moved by poetry and great prose almost as much as by music, and was fascinated with the challenge of finding an appropriate musical garb for a poetic idea. Her upbringing was such that she was imbued with the Jewish liturgical tradition and is perhaps now regarded as the major female Jewish composer of that genre. Nevertheless, she herself made it quite clear that she preferred to be known as a composer, not as a Jewish composer or as a woman composer. She said: 'I was a *composer* for a long time before I became a *woman* composer.' She appeared to have felt that the rise of feminism in America created a new category and along with it an adversarial feeling between male and female composers, and she refused to join any group of women composers.

She composed a number of works using biblical or sacred texts, and was commissioned to write a Sacred Service for the Temple in Cleveland, Ohio in 1970. This was scored for cantor, soloists, chorus, flute, oboe, trumpet, bassoon, viola, cello and organ and was first performed in 1974. Her second complete service was *Shirat Miriam L'Shabbat* (1974) for cantor, mixed choir and organ, commissioned by the Park Avenue Synagogue in New York. Other works with biblical or Hebrew themes include *How Goodly are Thy Tents*, a setting of Psalm 84 (1946) for women's voices and organ or piano, *Adon Olam* (1954) for soloists, chorus and chamber orchestra, *Three Biblical Masks* (1958) for organ, based on the characters in the Purim story, and *Woman of Valor* (1982) for high voice and piano.

Among the poetical works that inspired her compositions are Shakespeare's sonnets, *The Hound of Heaven* (1945) by Francis Thompson, *Ode to a Nightingale* by Keats, *Woman of Valor* (1982) by her husband Frederick Ewen, poems by Friederich Hölderlein, John Milton, Nancy Cardozo, Felix Pick and Charles Baudelaire, and the Guatemalan poet Miguel Angel.

Bibliography: *AG*; *G*; E. F. Brown, 'Jewish Liturgical Music by American Women since 1945', in S. Stanton and A. Knapp (eds), *Proceedings of the First International Conference on Jewish Music* (London: City University, 1994), pp. 19–25*; http://music.acu.edu/www/iawm/articles/feb97/gray.html

Gilboa, Jacob (b. Košice, Czechoslovakia, 2 May 1920)   Grew up in Vienna and emigrated to Palestine in 1938. Initially, he studied architecture in Haifa and later music at the Music Teachers' Seminary with Josef TAL and Paul BEN HAIM, graduating in 1947. In 1965 he went to Cologne, where he took part in the courses on new music run by Stockhausen; this changed his style from composing in a conservative idiom to using the techniques of avant-garde contemporary composers, including the use of quarter-tones and aleatory techniques. This is evident from the works he composed on returning to Israel, for example, *The Twelve Jerusalem Glass Windows by Chagall* for soprano, voices and chamber orchestra (1966), *Crystals* for five players (1967), *Thistles* for chamber ensemble, and *Pastels* for two pianos (1969). The inspiration for many

of his compositions is pictorial or literary, for example, *Symphonic Paintings to the Bible, Cedars, From the Dead Sea Scrolls, Epigrams for Oscar Wilde, Horizons in Violet and Blue,* and *Red Sea Impressions.* In 1974 he wrote *Lament of Kalonymos,* a lament without words for orchestra. The motto of the piece is taken from a poem by Kalonymos ben Yehuda on witnessing the massacre of the Jews in Mainz by the Crusaders in 1096. In 1977 he was commissioned by Yehudi Menuhin to write *Kathros u-Psantherin: Theme and Variations.* This piece uses oriental motifs and chants contrasted with early church liturgical chant.
Bibliography: *G*; Grad*; *HBD*

Glass, Philip (b. Baltimore, 31 January 1937)   Grandson of Jewish immigrants from Lithuania and Russia. His father ran a radio repair shop that also sold records and he would bring unsold records home to play. In this way Schubert's String Trio became one of Glass's earliest memories, but he also heard Beethoven, Shostakovich and Elliot Carter. He started violin lessons at the age of 6, and later flute lessons at the Peabody Conservatory in Baltimore. By the age of 12 he was working in his father's record department, entering Chicago University at the age of 15 to study mathematics and philosophy. He graduated three years later, in 1956. He then went to the Juilliard School of Music, where one of his contemporaries was Steve REICH. They both studied under Bergsma and Perschetti. Glass says of himself that he was in a sense a 'model student', composing in just the way his teachers wanted, as a kind of homage to them. By the time he graduated he had written something like 70 pieces; some of them are so obviously in the style of his teachers that they are an embarrassment to him.

He then spent a year at Aspen, Colorado, under Darius MILHAUD. This proved to be a useful experience. Discussions of life in Paris in the 1920s may have helped influence Glass to move to Paris to study with Nadia Boulanger from 1963 to 1965. Up until the age of 27 (1964) he composed what could be described as conventional American music. Although he found Boulanger a strict disciplinarian, he liked the model composers she used, for example, Palestrina, Montiverdi and Mozart. Towards the end of his stay in Paris an interesting assignment came his way that was to lead to other things. He was taken on by the film-maker Conrad Rooks as the music director for a film entitled *Chappaqua.* Part of this involved him collaborating with the famous sitar player Ravi Shankar. Glass had to transcribe the music Ravi Shankar was composing into western notation so that it could be played by French musicians. This enabled him to learn the structure of Indian music, in particular the rhythmic pulsatory nature of it and the lack of accents such as are present in western music, with its bar lines. This understanding soon began to influence his own compositions, which began to employ a reductive rhythmically repetitive idiom. This is first evidenced in a piece called *Play.* His string quartet, written in 1966, also foreshadows the minimalism soon to dominate his music. After Paris, Glass and his first wife, Akalaitis, visited

Morocco and then later travelled overland through Turkey, Iran, Afghanistan, Pakistan and to the Punjab. Glass had practised yoga since 1962, and in 1966 began Buddhist meditation; he remains a disciple of Tibetan Buddhism.

His minimalist phase of composition began on his return to New York in 1967. He wrote *Strung Out* for solo amplified violin, *Two Pages* for electric keyboards and winds, and *Music with Changing Parts*. All Reich's and Glass's compositions were performed by their own groups, and initially they worked together, pooling their resources. The collaboration developed into rivalry and they separated into the Philip Glass Ensemble and Steve Reich Players. Reich claimed that Glass's development owed much to his ideas, so much so that he was to repeat what Wittgenstein once said: 'Why didn't Newton acknowledge Leibniz; it would be such a little thing to do?' Glass originally entitled *Two Pages*, *Two Pages for Steve Reich*, but by 1969 the shortened title was used. Glass maintains that there were many composers working simultaneously who developed a minimalist vocabulary.

Glass's earliest minimalist works were performed in universities, museums and galleries and rock clubs. *Music in 12 Parts*, written for three electric keyboards, amplified winds and a soprano, was the first to be played to a conventional concert venue. It plays for five and a half hours, including a one-hour dinner break. The music critic Tim Page called it 'The Art of Repetition', intending to draw the parallel with Bach's 'The Art of Fugue'. In the early 1970s Glass launched his own record company, as he described, 'for the purpose of making my music more widely available since no commercial company would touch it at the time'. Things were to change. From 1974 until 1987 Glass was to concentrate on music theatre. He then began to write orchestral music. The year 1976 saw the start of what was to develop into a trilogy of operas: *Einstein on the beach* (1976), *Satyagraha* (1979) and *Akhnaten* (1984). A feature that these works have in common is that they are what might be described as portrait operas: Einstein, the man of science; Ghandi, the man of politics; and Akhnaton, the man of religion.

For *Einstein* Glass collaborated with Robert Wilson. The opera lasts for five hours. In many ways it broke new operatic ground. It had no formal libretto; its sung texts consisted of numbers and *solfège* notes that reflected respectively the rhythmic and melodic structure of the music. Instead of an orchestra Glass scored it for his own Philip Glass Ensemble (a highly amplified blend of two electric organs, three woodwinds, a female voice and a solo violin) and a group of untrained vocalists, who were to sing, act and dance in equal measure. The opera was a success, and Glass became a celebrity and was commissioned to write a second opera.

The libretto for *Satyagraha* takes extracts from the *Bhagavad-Gita* and is sung in Sanskrit. It is composed for a 51-piece orchestra, rich in strings and woodwind but devoid of brass and percussion. *Satyagraha* has been likened to a modern *Parsifal*, and is more of a religious mystery play or pageant than an opera.

After *Satyagraha*, gaining a commission to write the third opera was not difficult. The subject, *Akhnaton*, was an Egyptian pharaoh whose 17-year reign was cut short by a combined military and religious coup. Akhnaton had deposed Egypt's pantheon of gods by a religion focused on a single god, Aten. Akhnaton has long interested philosophers and historians as to the question of whether his ideas may have inspired the monotheism of the Hebrews. For this opera Glass was assisted by Shalom Goldman, professor of Near Eastern history at New York University. Most of the texts for *Akhnaton* come from the Pharaoh's own time and are sung in Egyptian, Akkadian and Hebrew, but in this opera Glass also has a narration in English.

After this trilogy of operas Glass was to go on to write further operas including *The Juniper Tree* (based on a tale by Grimm), *The Making of the Representative of Planet 8* (from the novel by Doris Lessing), *1,000 Airplanes on the Roof* (a science-fiction opera) and *The Voyage*, which starts in the Ice Age when a spaceship crashes on Earth, proceeds to Columbus's voyage at sea, and comes to its final act in the year 2092. He wrote further operas based on Cocteau's films, reversing the more usual trend of making films out of operas.

In the late 1980s his interest moved more to orchestral music, and since then he has composed a violin concerto and two symphonies, *The Canyon*, *The Light* (a symphonic poem) and *Concerto Grosso*. His Symphony No. 2 (1994) is rather conventional and embraces the European tradition that he once shunned.

Bibliography *AG*; *CC*; *G*; Philip Glass, *Opera on the Beach* (London: Faber, 1988); K. Robert Schwartz, *Minimalists* (London: Phaidon, 1996)*

Glière, Reinhold Moritsovich (b. Kiev, 11 January 1875; d. Moscow, 23 June 1956) Son of a woodwind instrument maker of Belgian extraction. He learned the violin at an early age and also composed music, which was played in his father's house, a meeting place for many musicians. He entered the Kiev Music School to study violin and composition in 1891. Three years later he entered the Moscow Conservatory, continuing to study the violin under Sokolovsky and Hrimaly, harmony under Arensky and Konius, counterpoint under Taneev and composition under Ippolitov-Ivanov. He graduated in 1900 with his diploma work, an oratorio/opera *Earth and Heaven* after Byron. He then taught at the GNESIN School of Music in Moscow. In 1905 as an early revolutionary he went to Berlin after signing an anti-government manifesto, and studied with Oscar Fried until 1907. He made his conducting début in Russia in 1908. He was appointed professor of composition at Kiev Conservatory in 1913 and director in 1914, and later professor of composition at the Moscow Conservatory in 1920, where he remained until his retirement in 1941.

In his compositions Glière followed the Russian late Romantic tradition. Many of his compositions are on a grand scale. He was very much a safe pair of hands as far as the political leadership was concerned. Under Lenin he

visited Azerbaijan to organize its cultural life. A number of his works show the influence of folk culture of the Transcaucasus and central Asia, for example, the opera *Shab-Senem* (1927). His music was held up as a model of social realism. The ballet *The Red Poppy* (1927) is a particularly good example in which a Chinese working girl gives her life to save a rebel leader from vile capitalists. His music won two Stalin prizes (1948 and 1950), the Order of the Red Banner (1937) and the title of People's Artist of the USSR (1938). In 1938 he was appointed chairman of the management committee of the Moscow Union of Composers, a post he held until 1948. The union had considerable control over the publication and performance of compositions. Glière's most popular works are his ballets *The Red Flower* and *The Bronze Horseman* and his third symphony, *Ilya Murometz*, after a Russian folk hero. *The Red Flower* is the 1949 revision of *The Red Poppy*, the change of name being to avoid any opiate connotation. His works include six operas, seven ballets, three symphonies, four string quartets, 123 songs and 175 piano pieces.
Bibliography: *G*; Leb; Ly*; *HBD*

Gnesin, Mikhail Fabianovich (b. Rostov-na-Donu, 2 February 1883; d. Moscow, 5 May 1957)   Came from a family of musicians who established music training institutes. After 1895 these formed the pedagogical basis of teaching throughout Russia and later the Soviet Union. Gnesin studied at the Rostov Technical Institute (1892–9). He then began his musical studies with Georgi Konius in 1899, and later studied composition at the St Petersburg Conservatory under Rimsky-Korsakov, Glazunov and Lyadov from 1901 to 1909. In 1905 he was expelled from the conservatory for taking part in a revolutionary strike, but was allowed to re-enter in 1906; he graduated in 1908. He went to Germany for three years (1911–14), returning to Rostov-na-Donu, where he stayed until 1921, lecturing and composing. He toured Palestine and western Europe, returning to live in Moscow in 1923. Whilst in Palestine he lived in a remote village between Tel Aviv and Jerusalem, where for a year he worked on his opera *Abraham's Youth* (1923), the first Jewish national opera in the Hebrew language. Although parts of it have been performed, the complete opera has not been staged.

From 1925 to 1936 he was professor at the Moscow Conservatory, and from 1935 to 1944 professor at the Lenningrad Conservatory. From 1944 to 1951 he was principal at the Gnesin State Institute for Musical Education, an institute founded some years earlier by his sisters. Among his pupils were Khachaturian and Khrennikov. He composed a number of stage works, including *The Maccabeans*, *Starry Dreams* and incidental music for Sophocles' *Antigone*. His best-known works are the tone poems *After Shelley*, *The Conqueror Worm* (after Poe), *Dithyramb* for voices and orchestra (in memory of the painter Vroubel) and *Requiem* for piano quintet (in memory of Rimsky-Korsakov). He also composed orchestral and chamber works, for example, *Symphonic Monument 1905–1917* (commissioned in 1925 to the words of the

revolutionary poet Yessenin and one of the first works on the subject of the Russian Revolution), *Three Characteristic Melodies* to *The Stone Guest* by Pushkin, Op. 51, *Trio* for piano, violin and cello, Op. 63 (dedicated to the memory of lost children), and *The Jewish Orchestra at the Ball at Nothingtown*, Op. 41.
Bibliography: *G*; Ho*; M. D. Calvocoressi, *A Survey of Russian Music* (Harmondsworth: Penguin, 1944); Nemtsov CD 93.008 [record sleeve]

Goehr, Peter Alexander (b. Berlin, 10 August 1932)   Fled with his family to England in 1933. His father Walter had studied with SCHOENBERG at the Academy of Arts in Berlin and conducted the Berlin Radio Orchestra from 1925 to 1931. He continued his conducting career in England, giving the premiere of Tippett's *A Child of Our Time* and Britten's *Serenade* for tenor horn and strings. After World War Two Alexander became interested in left-wing politics and particularly the Socialist–Zionist Movement. This brought him to Manchester, where he worked as a hospital orderly. At one stage he was undecided between a career in music or politics. Eventually, against family advice, he gave up a scholarship at Oxford, preferring to study music at the Royal College of Music in Manchester from 1952 to 1955. Whilst studying at Manchester he met Harrison Birtwhistle, Maxwell Davis and John Ogdon. Together they formed the Manchester New Music Group, which put on concerts of modern music in the Whitworth and City Art Galleries. They were particularly concerned to promote music by composers such as Schoenberg, Messiaen, Stravinsky and EISLER, whose works were rarely performed in the UK in the early 1950s. Goehr initially became interested in Schoenbergian music not through hearing it, but through the publication of Schoenberg's book of essays, *Style and Ideas* (1950).

His father conducted the first English performance of Messiaen's *Turangalila Symphony* in 1953. After the performance Alexander went along to a private gathering to hear Yvonne Loriod (Messiaen's wife) play Boulez's second piano sonata. He was so overwhelmed that he decided to continue his studies in Paris with Messiaen and Loriod (1955–6). His earliest compositions show a strong Schoenbergian influence, particularly his second piano sonata Op. 2 (1952), but less so in *Fantasias*, Op. 3 (1954).

The work that brought Goehr's music to a wider public and brought him commissions was *The Deluge*, Op. 7, for soprano, alto and chamber ensemble (1957–8), inspired by Leonardo da Vinci. As a result of studying with Messiaen, Goehr developed an interest in medieval music, as seen in, for example, *Paraphrase on the Madrigal 'Il combattimento di Tancredi e Clorinda'*, Op. 28 (1968) and in his opera *Arianna*, a recomposition of Monteverdi's lost opera, which was performed at Covent Garden in 1995. He never abandoned his interest in Schoenbergian music, but in the mid-1960s developed a modal twelve-tone method that can be heard in, for example, *Metamorphosis, Dance and Romanza* for cello and orchestra, Op. 36. His first opera, *Arden Must Die*, Op. 21, written to a German text by the Marxist poet Erich Fried but based on an English play, caused a stir when premiered by the Hamburg State Opera in 1967. This was followed by a triptych of 'dramatic madrigals': *Naboth's Vineyard* (1968), based on the Old Testament; *Shadowplay* (1970), based on Plato's *Republic*; and *Sonata about Jerusalem* (1971), which concerns the false Messiah who deceived the Jews.

From 1960 tp 1968 Goehr worked for the BBC as a producer of orchestral concerts. From 1971 tp 1976 he was professor of music at Leeds University, and from 1976 tp 1999 professor of music at Cambridge University. In the space of some 25 years he had moved from being a left-wing rebel to a pillar of the establishment. In 1987 he was the first musician to be invited to give the BBC's Reith Lectures. Goehr is a prolific composer; his works including four symphonies, concerti for piano, violin, viola and cello, four string quartets, vocal music and four operas, of which *Kantan and Damask Drum*, Op. 67, is the most recent, receiving its premiere in September 1999.

Bibliography: *CC*; *G*; *HBD*; Leb; Alexander Goehr, *Finding the Key* (London: Faber, 1988).

Gokkes, Sim (b. Amsterdam, 1897; d. Auschwitz, 1943)   Student of Sen DRESDEN. He worked as assistant director of the Netherlands Opera, founded the Amsterdam School of Choir Music and directed the choir at the Portuguese Synagogue in Amsterdam. His main compositions are choral and include *Ngolinu Leshabaig* and *Yigdal*, *Cain* (an oratorio for male choir), *Suite* for small orchestra on the Yiddish song *Inter dem Kindem Wiegele*, and *Kinah* for wind quintet. He and his family perished in Auschwitz.

Bibliography: www.leosmit.nl/eng/contemporaries/jewish_text.html*

Goldmark, Karl (b. Keszthely, Hungary, 18 May 1830; d. Vienna, 2 January 1915)   Son of a lower middle-class Jewish family in which there were over 20 children. In 1834 his parents moved to Deutsche-Kreuz, near Ödenburg (Sopron), about 100 km south of Vienna, just inside the present Austrian border. In 1841 he received his first violin lessons from the local choirteacher. After two years at the Ödenburg Music School his father sent him, in 1844, to Vienna, where he began further violin lessons, only to have to give them up for financial reasons after one and a half years. He stayed in Vienna, earning a living in various ways and continuing with the violin by self-teaching. He is said to have started his daily routine by playing Bach for half an hour. He eventually went the Vienna Conservatory for violin lessons and music theory. He played the violin in the theatre, and after teaching himself the piano, gave piano lessons. Among his pupils was Caroline Bettelheim, later well known as a singer in the Vienna Hofoper. She later gave him much support for his vocal works.

Self-teaching formed a large part of Goldmark's musical training, and his compositions reflect an eclectic personal style comprising Hungarian, Jewish, Mendelssohnian and Wagnerian elements. Much of his early composition was vocal music, although it was his string quartet Op. 8 that made him famous overnight. The quartet shows a rich harmonic language and melodiousness that is characteristic of many of his works. Nowadays it is only this quartet, the violin concerto and the *Rustic Wedding Symphony* by which he is known, although some of his overtures and his second symphony are occasionally played. He composed six operas altogether, the most successful of which was his first, *Die Königin von Saba* (The Queen of Sheba, 1875). At the peak of his career he was at the centre of musical life in Vienna, largely as a result of his operatic works. He was an honorary member of the Gesellschaft der Musikfreunde in Vienna and, in 1879, together with Brahms and the music critic Hanslick, he judged the grant awards to artists. His operatic style is between that of Wagner and MEYERBEER. He was a great admirer of Wagner, although they only met once. His operas are now only rarely performed, and he is generally considered at his best in agreeably melodic pieces rather than in large-scale opera. His most performed work, and the one Brahms claimed to be his best, is the *Rustic Wedding Symphony* (*Ländliche Hochzeit*), Op. 26 (1876). It is more of a suite, containing five pictorial movements, in the fourth of which, *Im Garten,* the influence of Wagner is clearly evident.

Goldmark was a great supporter of MAHLER, emphasizing the latter's talent whilst still at the Konservatorium. Mahler is believed to have solicited Goldmark's support in obtaining the appointment at the Vienna Court Opera in 1897.
Bibliography: *G; HBD;* Ho*; Steven Beller, *Vienna and the Jews, 1867–1938* (Cambridge: Cambridge University Press, 1989), p. 24

Goldmark, Rubin (b. New York, 15 August 1872; d. New York, 6 March 1936) Nephew of Karl GOLDMARK. He studied composition with Robert Fuchs and piano with Anton Door at the Vienna Conservatory, and later at the National Conservatory in New York he studied piano with Joseffy and composition with Dvorak, during the latter's stay in New York. He is better known as a teacher than as a composer. He was obliged to move from New York for health reasons and became director of the Colorado Springs Conservatory from 1895 to 1901. After his health improved he returned to New York, establishing himself as a private teacher of composition. Among his students were COPLAND, GERSHWIN, HERRMANN and Giannini. From 1924 he headed the composition department of the Juilliard Graduate School. His compositions are mostly based on the European Romantic tradition and are tinged with Indian or African American themes. These include *Requiem*, inspired by Lincoln's Gettysburg address (1919), *Hiawatha* (1900), a symphonic poem *Samson* (1914), *Negro Rhapsody* (1919) and *The Call of the Plains* for orchestra (1925). His piano quintet won the Paderewski prize in 1909.
Bibliography: *AG; G; HBD;* Ho*; Ly*

Goldschmidt, Berthold (b. Hamburg, 18 January 1903; d. London, 17 October 1996) Second of four children. His father ran a family business, started by his grandfather, importing bedroom furnishings. The family lived above the business premises in Hamburg. Both parents were amateur singers and his father remembered well when MAHLER was in charge of the Hamburg Opera from 1891 to 1897. Berthold went to St George's School in Hamburg and studied harmony with Werner Wolff, a friend of Busoni, from 1918 to 1922. He then studied at the University of Hamburg and at the Friedrich Wilhelm University in Berlin. SCHOENBERG offered him a place in his composition class, but he chose to study composition with Franz SCHREKER and conducting with Rudolf Krasselt at the Hochschule für Musik in Berlin from 1922 to 1925. Among his fellow students in Schreker's class were Alois Hába, Karol RATHAUS and Ernst Krenek. In 1925 he won the Mendelssohn state prize for his composition *Passacaglia*, Op. 4, a composition that was subsequently lost as a result of fleeing the Nazis. Also lost were his *Requiem* and a piano quintet. In compositional style he was more attracted to Busoni than the excessively lush style of Schreker.

Goldschmidt spent a year as assistant conductor to Eric Kleiber at the Staatoper unter den Linden, Berlin, where he was one of the *répétiteurs* for the world premiere of Berg's *Wozzeck*; in 1927 he became conductor of the Darmstadt Opera for two years. During this period his *Passacaglia*, *Concert Overture* and first string quartet received public performances. At Darmstadt he began working on the opera *Der Gewaltige Hahnrei*, which had its successful premiere at the National Theatre in Mannheim in 1932. It was the last opera by a Jewish composer to be premiered in Germany before the National Socialist Party came to power. A further performance was planned to take place in Berlin in 1933, but it was banned and Goldschmidt was dismissed from the post he then held at the Berlin Städtische Oper. He remained in Berlin, training Jewish musicians who were later to become the nucleus of the Palestine Orchestra (later the Israel Philharmonic). In 1935 he was interrogated by the Gestapo, during the course of which the officer whispered in Goldschmidt's ear to get out of Germany as quickly as possible. Goldschmidt left for London the same week.

A year later he composed his second string quartet and the *Ciaccona Sinfonica*, and married the singer Elizabeth Karen Bothe. His only source of income at this time was through teaching. In 1938 he was commissioned to write the music for the anti-fascist ballet *Chronica*, for a dance company of emigrants led by Kurt Loos; this was performed in Cambridge, England, in Scandinavia and in North and South America. It was not until 1944 that he obtained regular employment with the BBC. From 1944 to 1947 he was musical director of the German section, and gained some satisfaction by selecting music banned by the Nazis. In 1947 he was opera coach at the first Edinburgh Festival. In 1951 he was one of the four prize winners in the Festival of Britain composing competition for his opera *Beatrice Cenci*. Although parts of it were performed in 1953, the first complete performance was not until 1988. Between 1952 and 1953 he completed three concerti, for violin, cello and clarinet respectively. He conducted the first complete British performance of MAHLER's Third Symphony in 1960 and advised Deryk Cooke on the 'completion' of Mahler's Tenth Symphony; he conducted its premiere in 1964. He became despondent about getting his own works performed and that, together with his wife's chronic leukaemia from which she died in 1979, led to a cessation in composing from 1964 until 1982, when he composed a clarinet quartet.

His 'rehabilitation' began in 1983, when Bernard Keefe conducted a performance of his *Der Gewaltige Hahnrei* with a student orchestra. A few months later Goldschmidt was invited as guest to the Mürz Valley Workshop – a music workshop sponsored by the Walter Buchebner Society, named after a local poet whose opposition to the Nazis cost him his life. He was invited again in 1985, and on both occasions his works were performed. In 1987 Simon Rattle opened the City of Birmingham Symphony Orchestras concert in Berlin with the German premiere of *Ciaccona Sinfonica*. From then until his death the quality of his previously unplayed works became realized. *Die Gewaltige Hahnrei* was given its Berlin premiere in 1992, 59 years after originally intended. He was also inspired to compose new works, notably *Belshazzar* (1985), a piano trio (1987), a third string quartet (1988–9), which incorporates the traditional *Chanukah* melody *Mo-oz tzur ye shuosi*, a fourth string quartet, *Deux Nocturnes* (1996) and the string trio *Retrospectrum* (1997). From 1935 until his death Goldschmidt lived in the same flat in Hampstead.
Bibliography: G; Ken; Leb; J. Allison, 'Goldschmidt, a Life in Music', *Opera*, 45 (1994), pp. 1020–8*; David Drew, 'Incognito Berthold Goldschmidt (1903–96)', *Tempo*, 200 (1997), pp. 8–13; www.sonyclassical.com/artists/goldschmidt/bio. htm

Golijov, Osvaldo (b. La Plata, Argentina, 5 December 1960)   Lived in Argentina until 1983, then in Jerusalem before moving to the USA in 1986. He studied with George Crumb at the University of Pennsylvania and then with Lukas FOSS and Oliver Knussen at Tanglewood, where he received the Koussevitzky composition prize. He won two Kennedy Center Friedheim awards for chamber music composition for *Yiddishbuk* (1993) and *The Dreams and Prayers of Isaac the Blind* (1995). Other works include *K'vakarat*, a piece for cantor and string quartet, *Last Round*, a homage to Astor Piazzola (1996), *Oceana* (1996) and *Yiddish Ruah* and *La Pasion Segun San Marcos* (Saint Mark Passion, 2000). He teaches composition in Newton, Massachusetts.
Bibliography: Richard Whithouse, *Gramophone,* 79 (2001), p. 71*; www. americancomposers.org/sa98bios.htm; Nonesuch 7559-79444-2 [record sleeve]

Golishev, Yefim (b. Kherson, Ukraine 8/20 September 1887; d. Paris 25 September 1970)   Studied violin with Leopold Auer in Odessa. He left Odessa in 1909 to avoid persecution as a Jew, moving to Berlin, where he became a friend of Busoni and studied at the Stern Conservatory. He composed a string trio

(1914), an opera entitled *Cyrano de Bergerac* (1915–16), and a symphonic poem, *Das Eisige Lied* (1920). He was also a painter and member of the November Group of Berlin Dadaists in 1918–19. At a Dadaist exhibition he presented his *Antisymphonie* and *Keuchmaneuver*, for which he invented new instruments and equipped musicians with kitchen utensils He composed music for the film *Idenbu the Great Hunter* by Eisenstein and Pudovkin. In 1933 he fled again, to Portugal and Spain, this time to avoid Nazi persecution. He lost many of his compositions in the process. After spending part of the war in prison and partly in hiding, he went to Sao Paulo from 1956 to 1956, where he took on Brazilian nationality; he spent the last four years of his life in Paris.
Bibliography: *G*; *HBD**

Gorb, Adam (b. London, 1958)   Showed promise as a teenage composer. In 1973 he wrote *A Pianist's Alphabet*, a selection of which were performed on BBC Radio 3 in 1976. Also in 1976, Benjamin Britten, shortly before his death, examined some of Gorb's early scores and advised and encouraged him (cf. Robert SAXTON). Hans Keller recognized his talent as a composer. At Cambridge University he studied music with Hugh Wood and Robin Holloway, graduating in 1980. He later earned a living as *répétiteur* with Sadler's Wells and the Royal Ballet. He studied composition at the Royal Academy of Music from 1992 to 1993. He taught at the Royal Academy until 1999, when he was appointed head of composition at the Royal Northern College of Music. His works include: *Metropolis* for wind band (1992–3); *Klezmer* for violin (1993); Viola Concerto, first performed in 1992; *Kol Simcha* (1995), a ballet performed over 50 times by the Rambert Dance Company; *Awayday* (1996); a violin sonata (1996); a percussion concerto written for Evelyn Glennie; a synagogue commission, *Ma Towu* (1998); and a clarinet concerto commissioned by the Royal Liverpool Philharmonic Orchestra and premiered by Nicholas Cox in 1999.
Bibliography: Ronald Weitzman, 'Adam Gorb's Clarinet Concerto', *Tempo*, 211 (2000), pp. 35–7*; www.adamgorb.co.uk/bio2.htm

Gottschalk, Louis Moreau (b. New Orleans, 8 May 1829; d. Tijuca, Brazil, 18 December 1869)   First of seven sons of Edward Gottschalk and Marie Aimée (Bruslé) Gottschalk. His father was a London-born Jewish merchant of German descent who was educated at Leipzig University. His mother was of a genteel Creole family, which had fled the slave uprising in Santo Dominga, Haiti, to settle in Lousiana in the 1790s. His father Edward was the only one from his generation of the family not to marry within the faith. Nevertheless, his son Moreau undoubtedly felt the influence of Jewish culture. Many of his Jewish relatives had emigrated to New Orleans, and his father had many Jewish business associates. His father is listed as one of the contributors to the first Jewish Temple in New Orleans. Moreau was baptized in St Louis Cathedral.

He was a child prodigy, showing aptitude as a pianist before his fourth birthday. When he was 5, his parents engaged François Letelier as piano teacher. By the time Moreau was 13 Letelier felt he needed more intensive training and, through his mother's connections, he was sent to Paris. There he was refused entry to the Conservatoire by the head of the piano department, Pierre Zimmermann, on the grounds that 'nothing came out of America except steam engines'. He had lessons with Charles Hallé and later Camille Stamaty. Before he was 16 he gave a highly successful recital in the Salle Pleyel; Chopin was present and predicted that he would become 'the king of pianists'. In fact, he was to become the American equivalent of Liszt as a travelling virtuoso. Three of his compositions of this early Paris period, the so-called 'Louisiana trilogy' of *Bamboula* (1844–5), *La savane* (1845–6), and *Le Bananier* (1845–6), were to make him a household name throughout Europe.

There was a large Negro slave population in New Orleans when Gottschalk was a boy, and he was familiar with their music. Whilst in Paris he was able to recapture the Negro vitality in his music, recreating in pianistic terms extravert dancelike music and introducing a new idiom to European music. *Bambola* is a pianistic arrangement of an authentic New Orleans dance, with the Latin flavour of the music given a Yankee swagger. *Le Bananier* is an elegant version of a French Creole tune with an African drone bass. He made a successful tour as a pianist/composer in Switzerland and France in 1850, and Spain in 1851–2.

He returned to America to begin a concert career in 1853. Up until then he had led a carefree existence, but with the death of his father in 1853, it fell to him to support his mother and six siblings. His father had made it clear to him that as the eldest son, in the event of the father's death, the rest of the family were to regard Moreau as the father figure and provider, as was expected in Orthodox Judaism. Moreau worked tirelessly to this end, but at the same time resented his father not having left the family better provided for. So, although Moreau accepted some of the tenets of the Jewish faith, he also developed a certain coolness towards Judaism. He was forced to give more frequent concerts and to compose pieces very much with their box-office attraction in mind. He was a very colourful character and a womanizer. It was said women fought to touch him, to tear off his clothing and even uproot locks of his hair. A very successful composition, *The Last Hope* (1854), he claimed to have improvised to ease the death-bed melancholy of a Cuban lady. A version of this found its way into sundry hymnals, and in the days of silent cinema was a favoured accompaniment to moments of religious elevation.

Between 1862 and 1866 he toured the Caribbean and parts of Central and South America, performing and organizing massive concerts, giving approximately 1,100 of them. In September 1865 he became involved with a female student at the Oakland Female Seminary, and the widely reported scandal that followed led to him fleeing on the *SS Colorado* bound for South America to escape enraged vigilantes. Eventually his friends managed to clear his name, but he never returned to the USA again. He went to Peru, Chile,

197

Uruguay and Rio de Janeiro, where again he organized large-scale concerts. Weak from yellow fever, he collapsed whilst playing his own lamentation *Morte* (composed in 1868). He was confined to bed and died a month later. Gottschalk was so popular in Brazil, largely through his own compositions, that he received a public funeral in Rio de Janeiro, with thousands lining the route of the cortège. In the press he was described as 'the first Pan-American figure in the arts'. Later his remains were returned to the USA and buried in Greenwood Cemetery, Brooklyn.

His best works were composed during his stay in Paris (1851–2) and in the Antilles (1862–5). The vast majority of his works are for the piano, but also include some instrumental works, songs and operas (most of which are lost). However, he is also one of the first American symphonists; best-known is his second symphony, *A Night in the Tropics*, with its rumba finale, composed 1858–9, whilst he was touring the Caribbean and South America. He is generally regarded as one of the most important nineteenth-century American musicians; pre-echoes of Ives can be discerned in his frequent use of quotation both as a musical and psychological device.
Bibliography: *AG*; *G*; *HBD*; Ho*; S. Frederick Starr, *Bamboula: the Life and Times of Louis Moreau Gottschalk* (Oxford: Oxford University Press, 1995)*

Gould, Morton (b. New York, 10 December 1913; d. Orlando, 21 February 1996)   Started composing at the age of 6. The first concert of his works took place when he was 16. He studied piano, theory and composition at the Institute of Musical Art in New York. He left high school to help support his family by playing in theatre orchestras and jazz bands, and worked as staff pianist at Radio City Music Hall (1931–2). Thus began a long association with radio. He was composer, conductor and arranger for the Mutual Radio Network, New York, from 1935 to 1942. He was a freelance composer and conductor with the New York Philharmonic, with the Philadelphia and Pittsburgh Orchestras, as well as orchestras from Japan (1979), Mexico (1980) and Israel (1981). He composed in a wide range of genres, including orchestral, chamber, vocal, choral and film music, as a remark of his acknowledges: 'I am not a purist and espouse no dogma but am curious and fascinated by the infinite variety of all kinds of musical sounds'.

Gould's lighter works generally draw on American subjects, including jazz and folk music, for example, *American Sinfonietta* (1937), *Lincoln Legend* (1942), *Cowboy Rhapsody* (1942), *Minstrel Show* (1946) and *Homespun Overture*. He wrote *Derivations* (1956) for clarinet and jazz band for Benny Goodman. He employed serial techniques in *Jekyll and Hyde Variations* (1957). He was awarded the Pulitzer prize for *Stringmusic* (1994). He wrote music for the film *Holocaust* (1978) and later arranged it for band (1980). He wrote three symphonies and a viola concerto (1943).
Bibliography: *AG*; *CC*; *HBD*; Ho*; Leb; Ly*; P. W. Goodman, *Morton Gould* (Portland, OR: Amadeus Press, 2000)

Grosz, Wilhelm (b. Vienna, 11 August 1894; d. New York, 10 December 1939) Born into a family of Jewish jewellers. He studied at the Vienna Music Academy from 1910 to 1916 and also musicology at Vienna University, graduating with a doctorate in 1920. His teachers were Heuberger, Fuchs, Adler and Schreker. His *Zwei Phantastische Stucke* was given its first performance by the Vienna Philharmonic Orchestra in 1919. From 1927 he lived in Berlin, where he was involved in broadcasting; he was also artistic director of the Ultraphone Gramophone. In 1933 he was conductor of the Kammerspiele Theater in Vienna, but, as a Jew, was forced to leave Austria. First he went to London, and then to the USA in 1938. In London he failed to gain the interest of music publishers and so turned successfully to Tin Pan Alley composing. Apart from this his main work was a one-act opera buffa written in 1925 and entitled *Sganarell*. He introduced jazz into his works.
Bibliography: *G; Ho**

Gruenberg, Louis (b. Brest-Litovsk, Russia, 3 August 1884; d. Los Angeles, 10 June 1964)   Taken to America at the age of 2 and lived there all his life except from 1903 to 1920. He had music lessons from an early age from Adele Margulies in New York. In 1903 he went to Berlin to study piano and composition under Busoni and Koch, making his début as a pianist under Busoni with the Berlin Philharmonic in 1912. That year he also toured Europe and the USA as a pianist, and was appointed to teach at the Vienna Conservatory. He composed two operas, *The Witch of the Brocken* (1912) and *The Bride of the Gods* (1913), and an orchestral piece, *The Hill of Dreams* (1919). The success of the last work, winning the Flagler prize, led him to abandon a performing career to concentrate on composition and to return to the USA in 1920. He was a co-founder of the League of Composers (1923). He felt that in order to be an American composer, native influences such as jazz and spirituals had to be made use of. His most successful work is probably the opera *The Emperor Jones* (1931), based on a play by Eugene O'Neill. It received 11 performances in its first two seasons and was later revived in Chicago (1946) and Rome (1950). The play centres on a baggage porter who, by brutal force, becomes dictator of an island in the West Indies. His rebellious subjects then force him back into the role of an enslaved Negro. The work uses elements of jazz and spirituals, culminating in an aria based on a Negro spiritual, *Standin' in Need of Prayer*. He was commissioned by Heifetz to write a violin concerto (1944); this also shows the influence of Negro spirituals in the middle movement and in the final movement uses jazz and American folk song. He published four volumes of spirituals in skilful harmonizations. His compositions are wide-ranging, including operas, chamber music, choral and orchestral works and film music.
Bibliography: *AG; G; HBD; Ho*; Ly**

Haas, Pavel (b. Brno, Moravia, 21 July 1899; d. Auschwitz, 17 October 1944) Son of a Czech businessman and his Russian wife. Haas went to school in

Brno, and then to the Music School of the Beseda Philharmonic Society. In 1917 he joined the Austrian Army, although he never saw combat and stayed in Brno during this period. In 1919 he enrolled at the Brno Conservatory and the following year became a pupil of Janáček. He was one of Janáček's most talented pupils, but it was not until the late 1930s that he began to achieve recognition as a composer. He was never successful in obtaining a position in the Brno musical establishment and until 1935 earned his living by working in the family shoe business. In 1935 he married Soňa Jakobsonová, and she was able to support him on her earnings as a doctor. He was able to retire from the business and devote himself to private teaching and composition. His best-known works are the opera *Šarlatán* (Charlatan), two string quartets (Nos. 2 and 3), a wind quintet, an unfinished symphony, four Chinese songs, three film scores and a Hebrew male-voice chorus *Al S'fod*. A weakness of his was that he failed to complete a number of his works.

His works combine a blend of Hebrew, Moravian and French neoclassical sounds. He had both a Czech and a Jewish awareness and had no difficulty in combining both influences in his works. His second string quartet (1925), subtitled *Z opičích hor* (From the Monkey Mountains) is a programmatic piece inspired by a visit to the Czecho-Moravian Highlands. In 1931 he made a setting of Psalm 29 for organ, baritone, female choir and small orchestra.

His first film score, for *Život je pes* (It's a Dog's Life), was written in 1932–3. This was a comedy about a struggling young composer, the main part being taken by Pavel's brother, the actor Hugo Haas. In the 1934 production the company brought out a German version of the film for distribution abroad, but in this production his name was replaced by that of another composer, even though his music was used. It is thought that Moldavia-Film was more likely punishing him for the late delivery of a subsequent film score than it was anticipating the Nuremberg Laws (see Chapter 3, section 3.1), which did not come into effect until September 1935. If it had been the case, such subservience to Hitler's anti-Semitism would have necessitated the removal of both brothers' names.

Much more severe injustices were to come. Haas had not progressed far in the composition of the opera *Šarlatán*, which he began in 1934, when the Nuremberg Laws impinged directly on his work. The idea for the opera came to him after reading the novel *Doctor Eisenbart* by the German writer Josef Winckler. Haas was so inspired by the subject that he quickly drafted a potential libretto, which was completed on 1 July 1934. As the work progressed it was obvious that any collaboration with Winckler would be out of the question because of the Nuremberg Laws, so Haas was forced to conceal the identity of his source material. He did this mainly by giving the characters Czech names. For example, Doctor Eisenbart was given the name Pustrpalk, which is the name of a quack doctor in the old Czech play *Mastičkár* (The Quack). The success of the opera confirmed Haas's status as one of the leading composers of the post-Janáček generation, but the events that followed made his success short-lived.

With the prospect of deportation growing, in April 1940 Haas and his wife divorced, hoping to spare the family as a whole from further persecution. Ironically divorce meant that Soňa Haasová was able to resume work and thus to continue supporting her ex-husband and his father. (As the wife of a Jew, she had been forbidden to practice medicine.) Pavel's brother Hugo and his wife had escaped to France earlier in 1939, leaving behind their infant son. He was taken in by Soňa Haasová, whose Aryan credentials, as defined by the Nazis' racist legislation, enabled one more member of the Haas family to survive the Holocaust.

After completion of *Šarlatán*, Haas composed his third string quartet, a suite for oboe and piano, and a symphony that was to remain unfinished. The third string quartet was written when Czechoslovakia was under threat from Nazi Germany. It includes a quotation from the St Wenceslas chorale *Svaty Václave*. In December 1941 Haas was sent to Terezin, where he still managed to compose. His *Four Songs on Chinese Poems* is full of hope for his return home, for the 'dawning day'. He also composed *Studies for String Orchestra* in the summer of 1943. Ančerl gave its first performance in Terezin, shortly before the composer was taken to Auschwitz and murdered by the Nazis. Only parts of the score survived but Ančerl found it impossible on emotional grounds to reconstruct the work. This was done by Haas's biographer, Lubomir Peduzzi.

From 1945 until the 'velvet revolution' in 1989 virtually nothing was heard of Haas's music. The communist regime encouraged Czechs to think that underground communists were the only heroes of the war years and the reality of Terezin as a staging post for Auschwitz was played down. During the Stalinist era being 'cosmopolitan', that is, a Jew, was tantamount to being a 'bourgeois reactionary and enemy of the working class'. We now know a substantial amount about Haas's life and works; this is largely thanks to Lubomir Peduzzi, who knew him in the 1930s and has spent a lifetime keeping the name of Haas alive.

Bibliography: Grad; *G*; Leb; Joža Karas, *Music in Terezin, 1941–1945* (New York: Pendragon, 1990), pp. 71–84*; Paula Kennedy, *Music and Letters*, 75 (1994), pp. 634–5*; Lubomir Peduzzi, *Život a dilo skladatele* (Pavel Haas: his Life and Work) (Brno, 1993)

Hahn, Reynaldo (b. Caracas, 9 August 1874; d. Paris, 28 January 1947) Born in Venezuela, the youngest in a family of twelve children. His father was a businessman of German-Jewish extraction, and his mother, Elena Maria Echenagucia, came from a Spanish family. At the age of 3, Reynaldo and his family left Caracas to avoid the disturbances there and moved to Paris. Hahn had already shown a talent for music in Caracas, and made his début at the age of 6 at a musical soirée hosted by Princess Matilde, niece of Napoleon I. He continued to give many performances in private houses, dressed in a velvet suit, and quickly took on the manners and style of the Parisian *haut monde*. He entered the Paris Conservatoire in 1885 and began composing songs, one of which, *Si mes vers avaient des ailes* (a setting of poems by Victor Hugo), brought him early fame. It was so popular that four or five rival translations into English were made. His song cycle to poems by Verlaine, *Chansons grises*, was completed at the age of 16, while he was still a student. Hahn had a light baritone voice and, according to many *fin-de-siècle* diarists, would accompany his own singing, often with a cigarette dangling from his lips.

In 1893 he met the novelist Marcel Proust and the two became lovers. Their relationship became an inspiration for them both, as song writer and novelist, respectively. Hahn's piano suite, *Portraits de Peintres*, was inspired by poems of Proust. The first part of Proust's autobiographical novel *À la recherche du temps perdu*, where the character Swann makes a desperate search for his lover Odette in after-hours Paris, is an echo of Proust's own desperate search one night in Paris for his lover Reynaldo Hahn. Later Proust wrote: 'Everything I have ever done has always been thanks to Reynaldo.' Although Hahn was not of French descent, he was, like OFFENBACH, a Francophile, and in 1912 he became a naturalized French citizen.

From 1906 Hahn concentrated on composing for piano, and later for the stage. He composed the ballets *Le Bal de Béatrice d'Este* (1909) and *La Fête chez Thérèse* (1910), before volunteering for the army at the outbreak of war in 1914, even though he was over the official age for conscription. He served as a private, eventually being promoted to corporal. Whilst at the front he composed a song cycle on poems by Robert Louis Stevenson. His most successful operettas were *Ciboulette* (1923), *Brummel* (1931) and *Malvina* (1935). He composed a violin concerto (1927), a piano concerto (1931) and an unfinished and unperformed cello concerto. After its premiere in Paris the violin concerto was not performed again until 1986, by Henryk Szeryng. Altogether he wrote four operas, nine operettas, six ballets, seven sets of songs and works for piano and organ. He was conductor of the Cannes orchestra in 1919 and music critic of *Le Figaro* from 1934; in 1945 he became director of the Paris Opera. From 1940 to 1944, during the Nazi occupation, his music was banned and he was forced into hiding. For many years after his death he was dismissed as a dilettante and composer of salon music, but since the 1970s he has begun to be appreciated, his songs being compared with those of Fauré and Duparc, and his instrumental and orchestral music being performed. He was related to the wife of MOSCHELES, Charlotte née Embden.

Bibliography: *G*; *HBD*; Leb; P. O'Connor, *Gramophone*, 79 (2001), pp. 28–31; www.radio-france.fr/chaines/france-musiques/biographies*

Halévy, Jacques-François Fromental Elie (b. Paris, 27 May 1799; d. Nice, 17 May 1862)   Son of a German Jew, born in Fürth, not far from Nuremberg. After 1795 Jews in France were given full citizenship and were free to practise their religion and take any craft or profession. His father may therefore have come to France to take advantage of these new laws. His Hebrew name was Elyahu Halfon Levy. In France a decree of Napoleon required Jews not to take on a surname taken from the Old Testament, and so he became Elie Halévy. The name Halévy had the merits of conforming with the law and at the same time keeping part reminiscent of his Hebrew name. In Hebrew it means 'The Levite'. In the days of the Temple of Jerusalem Levites were entitled to serve in a musical capacity, so the name Halévy was to become particularly apt. He was a scholar and linguist. He married Julie Meyer, who although born in Lorraine was also of German-Jewish parents. The couple moved to Paris and it was there that their son Jacques-François Fromental Elie Halévy was born. His father eked out a living carrying out small administrative tasks within the Jewish community. His attitude towards emancipation was 'Be loyal to your country and true to the faith of your fathers.'

At school Halévy was taught music by the headmaster's teenage son until he was 9 years old, when he went to the Paris Conservatoire. Among his teachers there, the most influential was Cherubini. In 1816 Halévy made his first attempt to win the Prix de Rome and came second; three years later he came first. The prize carried a five-year grant to enable him to study composition in Italy. In the event, because his mother died in 1819 at the age of 38 he arranged to study for only four years. In 1820 his first notable composition was *Marche funèbre et de profundis* for three voices and orchestra using a text in Hebrew from Psalm 130, composed for the commemorative service for his Royal Highness the late Duc de Berry.

At that time the way to make a success as a composer without large financial support was through the theatre or opera. It was the period when Grand Opera in France flourished. Grand Opera typically consisted of a work with as many as five acts and often included a ballet, elaborate stage settings, with its success depending on a new bourgeois audience with a taste for the grandiose. At the same time the rival form of opera performed at the second opera house in Paris, the Opéra-Comique also flourished. Unlike Grand Opera, Opéra-Comique comprised music and spoken dialogue. During the next 20 years Halévy was to make his reputation composing 32 operas together with small vocal pieces and cantatas. He alternated between the two. His most famous Grand Opera was *La Juive*, completed in 1835. Two years earlier when Ferdinand HÉROLD died leaving his opera *Ludovic* incomplete, Halévy undertook its completion. The success of Halévy's operas depended to no small extent on having a good librettist. Here he was fortunate to have the collaboration of the best librettist of the day, Eugène Scribe, and also his brother Léon Halévy and Vernoy de Saint Georges. His relationship with Saint George was somewhat turbulent; the latter was apt to be late in providing librettos and prone to making hysteric and paranoid accusations. *La Juive* (The Jewess) was Halévy's most successful opera, and the single work by which he is known today. It was shown 550 times during the period 1835–93. In its day its success was equal to that other successful opera, *Les Huguenots* by

MEYERBEER. Scribe's choice of libretto may have been influenced by the knowledge that he was writing for a Jewish composer, and it fired Halévy's imagination as no other story had. It uses leitmotif, as Wagner was to do later. Of his later operas, Halévy only attempted one other with a Jewish theme, *Le Juif errante* (The Errant Jew) in 1852, and its success was much more short-lived.

Besides composing, Halévy was heavily involved in other musical activities. He was *chef du chant* at the Théatre-Italian and then at the Opéra for 16 years in all. It was an arduous task and involved being at the beck and call of directors, artists and fellow composers, but had the benefit of making it easier to stage his own operas and was a source of useful contacts. His composing had to fit in around this. In 1840 he gave up the post in order to spend more time on composition, although he continued as professor of fugue and counterpoint. In 1836 he was elected to the Institute of France, taking the vacancy created by the death of Reicha. In 1854 he became life secretary of the Academy of Fine Arts, one of the five academies of the Institute of France.

He did not marry until the age of 43, when he married 22-year-old Hannah Léonie Rodrigues-Henriques, a member of a wealthy Jewish-Portuguese-Spanish banking family. She had been brought up in luxury and was a compulsive collector of *objets d'art*. Unfortunately, she was prone to mental instability that required occasional retreats to a sanatorium. This instability continued after their marriage and the birth of their two daughters, one of whom was later to marry Bizet. One year before Halévy's death, when he was in failing health, it became clear that his wife was nevertheless unable to cope with looking after him even with a retinue of helpers. She was more accustomed to others looking after her and having stays in sanatoria whenever mental instability threatened her.

Halévy, like his father, was an emancipated Jew but nevertheless showed a loyalty to his faith and heritage. After his marriage he became more involved in Jewish cultural life. He auditioned Samuel Naumbourg for the post of director of music at the synagogue in Rue Notre-Dame-de-Nazareth. Naumbourg was appointed and began compiling an anthology of traditional liturgical songs. In his three-volume compilation there are seven psalm settings, a setting of the *Shema* and *Yigdal*, all of which were composed by Halévy.

Berlioz reviewed many of Halévy's operas. He praised the operas as being innovative and well crafted, but there are also pinpricks in some of his reviews and an element of damning with faint praise. Wagner spent two and a half years in Paris from the autumn of 1839. Whilst trying unsuccessfully to interest the Opéra in his work, he maintained himself during that period by making piano and instrumental arrangements of other composers' works, Halévy's among them. Wagner noted, when making vocal scores of Halévy's operas, 'I have never heard dramatic music which has transported me so completely to a particular historical epoch.' Given Wagner's notorious anti-Semitic views later expressed in *Das Judentum in der Musik*, this praise is surprising.

However, the main weight of his anti-Semitism in music fell on Meyerbeer, whom he contrasted with Halévy as 'frank and honest, no sly deliberate swindler like Meyerbeer'. He went on to say: 'Making arrangements of Halévy's score was far and away more interesting a piece of hack-work than the shameful labour I spent on Donizetti's *La Favorita*' and 'I had taken a great liking to him from the time of *La Juive* and had a very high opinion of his masterly talent'.[1]

Halévy's correspondence reveals his renowned conviviality, generosity and self-deprecation, and also his organizational skills and diplomacy. By the end of his life he was quite a celebrity, and his funeral was like a state funeral, at which 15,000 people were said to be present. Three orchestras and three choirs were stationed at the Jewish section of the cemetery to perform *De Profundis* and the *Marche funèbre* from Act 5 of *La Juive*.
Bibliography: G; *HBD*; Ken; WW; M. Galland, *Fromenthal Halévy: Lettres* (Lucie: Galland Heillbronn, 1999); Ruth Jordan, *Fromental Halévy: his life and Music* (London: Kahn & Averill, 1994)*
1. Richard Wagner, *My Life* (English translation) (New York: Da Capo, 1992), pp. 206–9.

Hársanyi, Tibor (b. Magyarkanisza, Hungary, 27 June 1898; d. Paris, 19 September 1954)   Studied composition with Kodaly and piano with Kovács at the Budapest Academy of Music in 1908. He also received guidance from Bartok. For a time he became a concert pianist in Vienna and the Netherlands before settling in Paris in 1923, where he became one of the group of émigrés known as École de Paris that also included Martinu, TANSMAN and MIHALOVICI. In 1924 he founded a new music group, the Société Triton. His *Nonette* was performed in 1932 at the International Society of Contemporary Music held in Vienna. His music derives from Hungarian folk music with lyrical Romanticism. His most successful works were the opera *Les Invites*, which was performed in Paris in 1937, and his radio opera *Illusion* (1948). Other works include the ballets *Les Pantins* (1938) and *Chota Roustaveli* (1945), *Suite Hongroise* for orchestra (1935), a violin concerto (1941), a symphony (1952), a string quartet (1925), a string trio (1934), a viola sonata (1954) and a number of piano works.
Bibliography: Grad*; G; *HBD*; Ken

Heller, Stephan [István] (b. Pest, Hungary, 15 May 1813; d. Paris, 14 January 1888)   Son of Hungarian-Jewish parents who came from the vicinity of Eger in Bohemia (now Cheb, in the Czech Republic). His grandparents were Austrian. Heller spent the last 50 years of his life in Paris. He was first taught piano by a regimental bandsman stationed near the Hungarian capital, and then by Ferenc Brauer. His first composition lessons were from an organist, Cibalka from Pest. He made his début at the age of 9, when he performed a concerto by Dussek at the Pest Theatre. His father sent him to Vienna to continue his studies from 1824 to 1829 as a pupil of August Halm, who introduced him to Schubert and Beethoven. Infant prodigies were the rage at the time, and by the age of 13 he was playing at concerts in Vienna and Pest. From 1828 to 1830 he toured Hungary, Transylvania, Poland and Germany as a concert pianist, but he reached a state of exhaustion in Augsburg, where he subsequently remained for eight years. There he was encouraged by Count Fugger, a gifted musician and patron, to study composition with Hippolyte Chélard. His earliest compositions were song settings of poems by Goethe, Heine and other poets, but these were not published and are lost. In 1836 Heller sent his *Three Impromptus*, Op. 7 to Robert Schumann, who was the then editor of *Neue Zeitschrift für Musik*. Schumann reviewed the work favourably and as a result it was accepted for publication. Heller himself wrote an article for *Neue Zeitschrift für Musik* under the name of Jeanquirit. In 1838 he moved to Paris but he soon gave up performing, concentrating on composing and teaching and writing musical criticism for *Gazette musicale*. He visited England in 1850 and 1862. Around 1883 his sight began to fail and he was supported by donations organized by his friend Charles Hallé. Although his early compositions were songs, the vast majority of his compositions were works for piano. These amounted to over 160 and include three piano sonatas, three sonatinas, many short piano pieces including dances, many *études*, as well as variations and fantasias on operas by Donizetti, Bellini, HALÉVY, MEYERBEER, AUBER and Weber. He also composed with Heinrich ERNST *Dix pensés fugitives* for violin and piano. During his lifetime it was claimed that his works were of worldwide renown and as important as those of Chopin.[1] However, today only a few of his works are still in print, for example, opuses 16, 45, 46 and 47. *Promenades d'un solitaire*, a set of six piano pieces, Op. 78, is one of his best compositions.[2] Berlioz said of him: 'At once a charming humorist and a learned musician, who has written so many admirable pianoforte works, and whose melancholy spirit and religious zeal for the true divinities of art have always had a powerful attraction for me.'[3]

Bibliography: *G**; *HBD*; Ho*

1. Robert Brown-Borthwick, *Stephen Heller: his Life and Works*, from the French of H. Barbedette (London: Ashdown & Parry, 1877).
2. Styra Avins, *Johannes Brahms: Life and Letters* (Oxford: Oxford University Press, 1997), p. 59.
3. Henry Pleasants, *Schumann on Music: a Selection from the Writings* (New York: Dover, 1988), p. 127.

Henschel, George [Isidor Georg Henschel] (b. Breslau, 18 February 1850; d. Aviemore, Scotland, 10 September 1934)   Both composed and conducted, but was best known as a baritone singer. When he was 9 he sang the solo treble part in MENDELSSOHN's *Hear My Prayer* with the Breslau University Choral Society. He converted to Christianity in his youth. In 1862 he made his début as a pianist in Berlin. He studied at the Leipzig Conservatory from 1867 to 1870 with MOSCHELES (piano), Reinecke and Richter (theory) and Goetze (singing). He sang the part of Hans Sachs in a Leipzig performance of Wagner's *Die Meistersingers von Nürnburg*. He is said to have known everyone worth knowing in musical circles in Leipzig at the time, that is, around the 1870s, and was responsible for introducing Ethel Smyth, then an aspiring composer, to Brahms. In 1870 he entered the Berlin Conservatory to continue composition studies. He sang in Bach's Saint Matthew Passion conducted by Brahms. He made his first appearance as a singer in England in 1877. In 1881 he married the American soprano Lillian Bailey, with whom he later gave joint recitals. He conducted the Boston Symphony Orchestra from 1881 to 1884.

Brahms admired him both as a singer and as a conductor,[1] and recommended him for the post of director of the Breslau Orchestra in 1882, a position that went to Max Bruch. Henschel sang the title roles in Bruch's *Odysseus* and *Achilleus*. Bruch also admired him as a singer for many years, until his anti-Semitism adversely affected his views of Henschel both as a conductor and as a singer.[2]

He settled in England in 1884, taught singing as a professor at the Royal College of Music and founded the London Symphony Orchestra, which he conducted for nine successive years. The family first visited Alvie, near Aviemore in Scotland for summer holidays in 1891 and became very attached to the area, building their own house in 1901. His wife died later the same year and he composed a Requiem Mass in her memory, which was first performed in Boston, USA. In 1907 he retired to Alvie, where he became part of the local community, serving as an elder in the church. Most of his works are choral works and sacred songs, but he also composed a string quartet and 21 piano pieces. He composed three light operas: *Friedrich der Schone*, *The Sea-Change, or Love's Stowaway* (1884) and *Nubia* (1898). He also wrote books: *Personal Recollections of Johannes Brahms* (1907) and *Musings and Memoirs of a Musician* (1918).

Bibliography: G; *HBD*; Ho*; Ken; Ly*; Helen Henschel, *When Soft Voices Die* (London: Westhouse, 1944)

1. Styra Avins, *Johannes Brahms: Life and Letters* (Oxford: Oxford University Press, 1997), pp. 505 and 597–8.
2. Christopher Fifield, *Max Bruch: his Life and Works* (New York: Braziller, 1988), p. 285.

Hérold, Louis Joseph Ferdinand (b. Paris, 28 January 1791; d. Paris, 19 January 1833) Of Alsatian descent. Both his father and grandfather were musicians. He received piano lessons from his father François-Joseph from an early age; his father had received lessons from Ferdinand's grandfather Nicolas Hérold, and also from C. P. E. Bach. He was already composing small pieces by the age of 7. He studied piano with Louis Adam (father of Adolphe ADAM), violin with Kreutzer, harmony with Catel and composition with Méhul at the Paris Conservatory between 1806 and 1812. In 1812 he played his own piano concerto in the Théâtre-Italien and he also won the Prix de Rome for his cantata *La Duchesse de la Vallière*. However, he stayed in Rome for less than a year, since he was suffering from tuberculosis, the disease that killed his father. He was then engaged by the King of Naples to teach his two daughters, eventually returning to Paris in 1815. Whilst in Naples he composed his first opera, *La Gioventù di Enrico Quinto*, two symphonies and three string quartets. Back in Paris in 1815 he became *maestro al cembalo* (accompanist) at the Théâtre-Italien. His first successful operatic composition in Paris was *Les Rosières* in 1817.

His ambition was to compose Grand Opera, although it seems his *métier* was more in the realm of the lighter Opéra-Comique. He composed several operas, but often suffered from lack of a good librettist. He only collaborated with Eugene Scribe in two operas, *La Somnambule* (1827) and *La Belle au Bois Dormant* (1829), unlike his successors in French opera, for example, MEYERBEER, HALÉVY and AUBER, for whom Scribe was their principal librettist. His first real successes in opera were *Les Rosières* and *La Clochette*, both performed at the Opéra-Comique in 1817. He prepared the first Parisian performance of Rossini's *Mosè in Egitto* for the Théâtre-Italien in 1822, but was too ill to attend. It seems that in 1817 he may have intended converting *Mosè* into a French Grand Opera, but this never materialized. His opera *Marie*, composed in 1826, proved to be one of his most successful, with more than 100 performances within the year. For the next three years he concentrated his energies on writing five ballets, including *La Somnambule* and *La Fille Mal Gardé*. The latter has been perhaps the most durable of Hérold's works, particularly when performed in John Lanchbery's 1960 arrangement. His two greatest operas were the last two he completed; *Zampa*, with 682 performances at the Opéra-Comique between 1831 and 1895, and *Les Pré aux clercs*, with 1589 performances between 1832 and 1898.

Adolphe Adam, in his 1857 memoir of Hérold, wrote that 'Of *Les Pré aux clercs* there is no need to speak; everyone knows it by heart.' Today, one only occasionally hears the overture! Hérold died five weeks after the first performance of *Les Pré aux clercs* and before completing his opera *Ludovic*, which was completed by Halévy. Halévy suceeded him as *chef du chant* at the Opéra in 1834. Wagner admired the opera *Zampa* and this is reflected in some of the details of the *Ring*. Judging by the success of Hérold's last operas, had it not been for his early death, he might have become one of the great exponents of French Grand Opera. During his last illness he remarked, 'I was just beginning to understand the stage.'

In his writings Vincent d'Indy went as far as to distinguish a 'Jewish or Semitic school' in French music, including Meyerbeer, Auber, Hérold, Halévy, Adam, David and Offenbach.[1] However, there is no indication that Hérold was of Jewish descent in the standard nineteenth-century French biographies.[2]

Bibliography: *G*; *HBD*; WW

1. Jane F. Fulcher, 'The Preparation for Vichy: Anti-Semitism in French Musical Culture Between the Two World Wars', *Musical Quarterly*, 73 (1995), pp. 458ff. and 'A Political Barometer of Twentieth-Century France: Wagner as Jew or Anti-Semite?', *Musical Quarterly*, 78 (2000), pp. 41–57.*
2. F. J. Fétis, *Biographie universelle des musiciens* (Paris: Libraire de Firmin-Didot, 1878), vol. 4, pp. 303–11.

Herrmann, Bernard (b. New York, 29 June 1911; d. Los Angeles, 24 December 1975)   Best known as a film composer, although he never considered himself as such, but rather as a composer who also scored films.[1] Both of his parents, eastern European Jews, emigrated from Proskurov in the Ukraine in about 1880, during a period of heightened anti-Semitism. However, both arrived in New York independently and met for the first time at the shop where Bernard's mother, Ida Gorenstein, worked as a gloves salesperson. Bernard's father, Abram, was from a well-educated Russian-Jewish family. Abram left Odessa after an argument with his father and became something of an adventurer. He eventually settled in New York and married a Russian-Jewish immigrant, and they had two children. The marriage was short-lived and his first wife together with the surviving child returned to Russia.

Abram then met Ida Gorenstein and, after a prolonged engagement, married her in 1909, by which time he was in his late forties and Ida was 19. It was in many ways a marriage of opposites. Abram was well educated, had a great interest in the arts and music and was from an assimilated family, whereas Ida was from a poor family, poorly educated and orthodox. One thing they had in common was high blood pressure, as did Bernard. His father's adventurous lifestyle fired Bernard's imagination. Bernard's father's name was Abram Moskovitch Dardik, but when he first came to America he changed it initially to August Dardek. His relatives, who had already arrived in America, suggested that a German-sounding name would be more acceptable in America, so he changed it to Abram Herman and later doubled the *r* and *n* to Herrmann, because he thought it looked more unusual.

Bernard was initially named Max Herrmann, but by the time he was brought home from hospital his parents decided to change it to Bernard. He was generally known as Benny. Although his father had no musical training, he had a great interest in music. Benny's mother was Orthodox, but because of his father's overriding views he was given no religious instruction or *bar mitzvah*. He had violin lessons from an early age, but soon found the piano much more to his liking. He showed great interest in music from an early age and composed an opera when he was 7. His father took him to operas and museums from an early age.

In his youth he became a prolific reader, having a passion for English literature, including Dickens, Hardy, the Brontës, Byron and A. E. Housman. He became something of an Anglophile. This is evidenced in some of his later compositions (for example, the opera *Wuthering Heights* and the clarinet quintet inspired by Housman's *A Shropshire Lad*), his promotion of English composers when he was a conductor (for example, Elgar, Vaughan Williams, Delius, Walton, Rubbra, Rawsthorne, Brian and Bax), and in his friendship with Barbirolli and FINZI. He settled in London in 1965. The book that is said to have convinced him to become a composer was Berlioz's *Treatise on Orchestration*.

In 1927 he went to the DeWitt Clinton High School. His school results were patchy. He did well in history, literature, fine arts and music, but poorly in mathematics and science. After graduating from high school he studied first at New York University under Philip James and later under Percy Grainger, and then at the Juilliard School of Music under Wagenaar, Stoessel and Rubin GOLDMARK. The teacher for whom he had the highest regard was Percy Grainger. Grainger was appointed head of music at New York University in 1931 and although he was not generally popular as a teacher, being regarded as rather unconventional, Herrmann saw in him the qualities he was cultivating in himself. Both shared a great love for Delius and Whitman.

At the age of 20 Herrmann founded the New Chamber Orchestra (1931–4), giving concerts in New York and at the Library of Congress. In 1934 he joined CBS radio, initially as director of educational programmes, in 1938 as staff conductor of the CBS symphony orchestra, and from 1942 to 1959 as chief conductor. In the mid-1930s radio was becoming an important form of mass communication and it was the ideal time for innovation. This was an ideal scenario for Herrmann. During the period he composed music for 125 programmes and generally promoted modern music. As chief conductor he gave American premieres of many English works. In 1936, whilst working at CBS radio, he met Orson Welles and when the latter went to Hollywood in 1941 to make the film *Citizen Kane* Herrmann collaborated, composing his first film score. As with many of Herrmann's later film scores, he excelled in using unusual combinations of instruments to heighten the drama. In this case he avoided using strings and instead emphasized brass, woodwind and percussion. The music is not characterized by its melodies, but rather by the use of leitmotif. It was his second film score, for *All That Money Can Buy* (1941), that brought him commercial success and an Oscar. This recognition, together with the financial independence it brought him, meant that he was able to be selective in the films he chose to score. He scored only nine films in his first ten years at Hollywood.

When Herrmann first went to Hollywood in 1941 there was a powerful institutionalized model for setting image to music, and film composers were not expected to orchestrate their own scores, this being done 'in-house'. Herrmann, not only was able to insist on his own orchestration, but was also associated with the films during shooting and in the post-production stages. However, it was his insistence that he had the final say about his music that eventually led to a rift with Hollywood. He was a very successful and original film composer. In all he composed 61 film scores, including several with Hitchcock, for example, *The Trouble With Harry* (1955), *The Man Who Knew Too Much* (1956), *The Wrong Man* (1957), *Vertigo* (1958), *North by Northwest* (1959), *Psycho* (1960) and *The Birds* (1963). In these, perhaps the most striking departure from film music convention is in *Psycho*, where he used exclusively a string orchestra not to produce the typical Hollywood warmth and vibrancy, but to create a cold and piercing sound, and to complement the black and white photography of the film. In 1965 Herrmann demanded 16 horns and 9 trombones for the film *Torn Curtain*, and this led to the final break with Hitchcock. In the event the film was eventually discarded. In 1966 he collaborated with François Truffaut in scoring for the films *Fahrenheit 451* and *The Bride Wore Black*.

In addition to film music Herrmann wrote two television musicals to be performed at Christmas, *Christmas Carol* (1950) and *A Child is Born* (1951), an opera, *Wuthering Heights* (1940–52) and a cantata, *Moby Dick* for two tenors, two basses, choir and orchestra (1937–8). His only musical comedy, *The King of Schnorrers*, adapted from the book by Israel Zangwill, was written in 1968. His two main chamber works, the string quartet *Echoes* (1966) and the Clarinet Quintet (1967), are nostalgic works written after 25 years on mainly film music. Many of his earliest works he later suppressed.

Herrmann had an acerbic, volatile and combative nature that often alienated him from his colleagues and friends, and probably inhibited his conducting career. It has also been proferred as a factor in the breakdown of his first and second marriages.[2] His father and grandfather also had explosive tempers. His father died of a stroke in 1931, as did Bernard in 1975.

Bibliography: *AG*; *G*; Leb; G. Bruce, *Bernard Herrmann: Film Music and Narrative* (Ann Arbor, MI: UMI Research Press, 1985).

1. K. Kalinak, *Settling the Score* (Madison: University of Wisconsin Press, 1992).
2. S. C. Smith, *A Heart at Fire's Center – the Life and Music of Bernard Herrmann* (Berkeley: University of California Press, 1991).

Hiller, Ferdinand von (b. Frankfurt-on-Main, 24 October 1811; d. Cologne, 11 May 1885)   Son of a wealthy Jewish merchant. His talent as a musician was evident at an early age. He received piano lessons from Alois Schmitt and developed so well that he played a Mozart piano concerto in public at the age of 10. In 1825 he went to Weimar to become one of the few pupils of Hummel, returning to Frankfurt in 1827 to continue his studies. His early compositions include incidental music for the Weimar theatres. He went to Paris in 1828 and remained there for seven years, where amongst other achievements he became a successful organ teacher. He became close friends with MENDELSSOHN, Chopin, Liszt and Berlioz. He had first met Mendelssohn earlier in 1822 at Kassel and the two became lifelong friends. He gave first performances of the great keyboard works of Bach and Beethoven, including the Fifth Piano Concerto. He was the dedicatee of Schumann's Piano Concerto. His conducting career began when he deputized for J. N. Scheble in a concert by the Cäcilienverein in Frankfurt in 1837. He composed two oratorios, *Die Zerstörung von Jerusalem* (1840) and *Saul*. In 1840 he replaced Mendelssohn as conductor of the Leipzig Gewandhaus Orchestra, whilst the latter was away. He met Wagner on a number of occasions. Whilst he seems to have taken well to Hiller, he clearly thought less well of his wife. Wagner somewhat gleefully mentions that 'Frau Hiller, an extraordinary Polish Jewess, caused herself to be baptized a Protestant together with her husband, and in Italy to boot.'

Hiller composed six operas, the first of which was *Romilda*, which was performed in Italy but was not a success. The opera *Konradin der Letzte Hohenstaufe* apparently received a favourable reception, which pleased Mendelssohn, but none of the operas has stood the test of time. However, Wagner's account of *Konradin der Letzte Hohenstaufe* puts its reception in a somewhat different light.[1] Hiller felt that after three performances the opera had established itself as a definite success. He persuaded Wagner to attend the fourth performance, although Hiller and his wife were leaving for Dresden that day. Wagner reported that he found almost all the seats empty and then accounts for the apparent success of the earlier performances to hearsay that Frau Hiller had enlisted a crowd of her Polish compatriots, who were living in Dresden at the time and who frequented the Hillers' social gatherings. They had been the 'cheer-leaders' on previous nights.

In 1847 Hiller went to Dusseldorf, in a sense replacing Mendelssohn. There had been little musical activity of note in the town since Mendelssohn left in 1835. Hiller organized concerts and greatly raised the standards and expectations in the town. In 1850 he moved to Cologne, as music director, where he reorganized the Music School along the lines of the Leipzig Conservatoire. In 1852 and 1853 he went to London, where he conducted concerts of the Philharmonic Society, at one of which he included his symphony *In der Freie*. He stayed in Cologne until 1884, when he became gravely ill and was forced to retire. He was a prolific composer (apart from operas and oratorios, he wrote a piano concerto, a violin concerto and a string quartet), but he was more successful as a teacher, conductor and writer, publishing a biography of Mendelssohn in 1874. Schumann, when assessing Hiller as a composer in *Neue Zeitschrift für Musik* in 1835, points to his originality, inventiveness and outstanding poetic talent. However, he finds weaknesses in his tendency to 'distract us from the flatness of his work by the richness of his harmonies' and the 'complexity of rhythms and novel configuration' that are often found in composers who are also virtuoso performers, such as Hiller. His best works are his songs and piano pieces.
Bibliography: *G*; *HBD*; Ho*; Henry Pleasants, *Schumann on Music: a Selection from the Writings* (New York: Dover, 1988), pp. 35–40
1. R. Wagner, *My Life*, English translation (New York: Da Capo, 1992) pp. 294 and 354–5.

Hollaender, Friedrich (b. London, 18 October 1896; d. Munich, 18 January 1976)   Son of the composer and conductor Victor Hollaender (b. Loebschütz, Upper Silesia, 20 April 1866; d. Hollywood, 24 October 1940) and nephew of the violinist and composer Gustav Hollaender (b. Loebschütz, 15 February 1855; d. Berlin, 4 December 1915). He attended the Berlin Hochschule für Musik and studied with Humperdink. After World War One he wrote music for productions by Max Reinhardt at his cabaret *Schall und Rauch*

and became one of the most sought-after cabaret songwriters of the 1920s. In 1929 he began writing for films, for which he is best known, composing songs and scores for over 150 films. His best-known film music was for the Sternberg/Marlene Dietrich film *Der Blaue Engel* (1930). Being a Jew, a jazz musician and a satirist he was forced to emigrate to California with the rise in Nazism. Other films to which he contributed songs include *Destry Rides Again* (1939), *A Foreign Affair* (1948), *Androcles and the Lion* (1952) and *We're No Angels* (1955).
Bibliography: *G*; Ly*; Martin Anderson, 'Degeneration, Regeneration ("Entartete Musik")', *Tempo*, 210 (1999), pp. 52–6*

Jacobi, Frederick (b. San Francisco, 4 May 1891; d. New York, 24 October 1952) Studied composition in New York with Rubin GOLDMARK and Ernest BLOCH and piano with Gallico and Raphael Joseffy, and later at the Berlin Hochschule für Musik with Paul Juon. From 1913 to 1917 he was assistant conductor of the Metropolitan Opera in New York. He studied the music of the Native American Peoples whilst living in New Mexico and Arizona. He returned to New York in 1924 to teach harmony at the Master School of United Arts and later taught composition at the Juilliard School of Music in New York. He included Indian and Hebrew material in some of his compositions, but others were more abstract. His first string quartet (1924) and orchestral suite (1927) are based on Native American themes and were the first works by an American to be published by Vienna's Universal Edition. His other works include: *Hagiographia* for string quartet and piano (1938), based on biblical narratives from Job, Ruth and Joshua; *The Prodigal Son* (1943–4); *Indian Dances* for orchestra; *Sabbath Evening Service*; *Ode to Zion*; and two symphonies, concertos for violin, for cello, and for piano.
Bibliography: *AG*; Grad; *G*; *HBD*; Ho*; Ken; Leb

Jacoby Hanoch [Heinrich] (b. Königsberg [Kalingrad, Russia], March 1909; d. Tel Aviv, 13 December 1990) Studied under Hindemith and Wolfsthal at the Berlin Hochschule für Musik, and, like Hindemith, played the viola. In 1933 with the rise of Nazism he left for Istanbul, where he stayed for a year before settling in Jerusalem, teaching initially at the Conservatoire and then at the Academy of Music. In 1958 he joined the Israel Philharmonic Orchestra. His early works show the influence of Hindemith. He composed in a conservative tonal style and combined oriental Jewish melodic styles with European counterpoint. His compositions include three symphonies (1944, 1951 and 1960), a concertino for viola and orchestra (1939), a violin concerto (1942), two string quartets (1937, 1938), songs and chamber music and music with specific Hebrew or Israeli references, for example *King David's Lyre* for small orchestra (1948), *Capriccio Israélien* (1951) and *Partita Israeliana* for string orchestra (1959).
Bibliography: Grad*; G

213

Joachim, Joseph (b. Kittsee, near Pozsony, Hungary, 28 June 1831; d. Berlin, 15 August 1907)   Seventh of eight children born to Julius and Fanny Joachim. The family lived in the ghetto at Kittsee, but moved to Pest in 1833. He is best known as a virtuoso violinist rather than as a composer, and although he composed a number of works, mainly for violin, they are rather neglected nowadays. He began studying the violin at the age of 5 and made his first public appearance when 7, playing a double concerto by Eik together with his teacher Serwaczynski. When Fanny Figdor, his cousin, heard him play, she was sufficiently impressed to persuade the family that he should go to Vienna to study with the most renowned teachers of the day, Johann Georg Hellmesberger, Joseph Böhm and Miska Hauser. Five years later, in 1843, she convinced the family that Leipzig was where he should go for the next stage of his musical education. In the meantime she had married Hermann Wittgenstein (the grandfather of the philosopher Ludwig Wittgenstein) and was living in Leipzig, and it was here that Joachim came to live. At the age of 12 he made his official début in a programme with the mezzo-soprano Pauline Viardot and MENDELSSOHN accompanying on the piano. At Mendelssohn's suggestion his general musical education was continued under Ferdinand DAVID and Hauptmann. He played Beethoven's Violin Concerto for his London début in 1844, which according to a letter from Mendelssohn to the Wittgensteins was an unparalleled success. He played it again in Berlin in 1852 and was largely responsible for establishing it in the violin repertoire. He was baptized in 1855. His letter to Herman Grimm at the time suggests his conversion was mainly to remove the disadvantages of Judaism.[1]

The physicist Hermann von Helmholtz had demonstrated that Joachim's intonation was more accurate than any other violinist of the time. Joachim was meticulous in keeping exactly to the score, regarding the performer as the 'servant of the composer'. He played under Liszt as leader of the Weimar court orchestra in 1850. After early meetings, both Wagner and Liszt were on sufficiently friendly terms that Joachim used the 'Du' form of address. Two publications were to dramatically cool their relationships.[2] The first was Wagner's 'Das Judentum in der' *Musik*, published in *Neue Zeitschrift für Musik*, and the second, in 1860, was a letter of protest from Brahms and Joachim, published in the same journal, in which they strongly opposed the new German School of Music, that is, music typified by Liszt and Wagner. Joachim's musical affinities were more with Schumann and Brahms. Although MEYERBEER is generally regarded as Wagner's *bête-noir*, Wagner's own words indicate his greater hatred for Joachim.

In 1853 Joachim became leader and soloist to the King of Hanover, but he resigned the post in protest in 1864 because his employer, Count Platen, showed an anti-Semitic attitude towards one of his colleagues, Herman Grimm. In 1868 he went to Berlin (where he was to live for the next 40 years) as director and professor of violin at the Hochschule für ausübende Tonkunst, and the following year formed the Joachim Quartet that became one of the most admired in Europe. He became great friends with Schumann and with Brahms (a friendship of 25 years) and played many of the latter's chamber works with the Joachim Quartet. He was the dedicatee and first to perform Brahms's Violin Concerto, and although the dedicatee of Dvorak's Violin Concerto, he refused to play it.

Schumann wrote his violin concerto intending it for Joachim to play. In October 1853 he sent it to Joachim asking for his comments. The following February Schumann attempted suicide and was taken to an asylum, where he died two years later. Some years later Clara Schumann and Joachim looked at the violin concerto again and decided that it was not worth publishing. It was neglected until 1933, when Joachim's great niece, the violinist Jelly d'Aranyi, announced that during a séance she had heard Schumann asking her to find it. When she tracked it down she was determined to play it, but was beaten to first performance by Georg Kulenkampf, who played it in Berlin in 1937. She performed it in 1938. A further twist was that the anti-Semitic musicologist Karl Blessinger, author of *Judentum im Musik: Ein Beitrag fur Kulture und Rassenpolitik* (1944), claimed that Joachim deliberately withheld Schumann's violin concerto from the public so that it would not supplant that of the Jewish composer, Mendelssohn.

By contrast, Joachim was enthusiastic about Brahms's Violin Concerto, and played an important role in advising Brahms on many of its aspects. Brahms thought very highly of Joachim's creative talent, and felt it a great pity that Joachim virtually gave up composing soon after his marriage to Amalie Schneeweiss in 1863. Instead, Joachim devoted his energies to performing, conducting, teaching and Directing the Royal Conservatory of Music in Berlin. There was a rift in his friendship with Brahms when Joachim sued for divorce in 1881, and Brahms sided with Amalie. From 1881 to 1883 there was virtually no contact between Brahms and Joachim, but by the time Brahms had completed his double concerto, and it had been given its premiere in 1887, with Joachim (violin) and Robert Hausmann (cello), the rift had healed.

Joachim's compositions include three violin concertos, five concert overtures and violin and viola pieces, including, for example, the *Hebraische Melody* for violin and piano. He wrote cadenzas for Beethoven's, Brahms's and Mozart's violin concertos. Although there were complaints to the German Ministry of Propaganda during World War Two, it did not prevent performances of the Joachim cadenzas. Nevertheless, the bust of Joachim was removed from the Hochschule für Musik in Berlin, and from the Beethoven Haus in Bonn, where the Joachim Quartet performed at festivals.[3]

Most of his works have a grave melancholy character. His most important work was his second violin concerto, known as the Hungarian Concerto, Op. 11, that is dedicated to Brahms. It was composed in Hanover in 1857 and was first performed by Joachim in 1860, when he was still only 20. It is a very long violin concerto; the first movement is longer than the whole of the Bruch

G minor concerto, with which it is often compared. When it is occasionally played nowadays, judicious cuts are generally made in the outer movements.

Besides performing and composing, Joachim taught a large number of violinists; however it is clear from a letter he wrote to a friend that he did not regard himself highly as a teacher, 'since of his hundreds of pupils not one has become world famous. They became skilled musicians, excellent chamber-music players, filled the position of orchestral leaders with credit, but none of them really made a career as a solo violinist.'[4] This seems unduly modest, given that Auer, Hubay and Huberman were among his pupils.

Bibliography: G; Ken; Ly*; Styra Avins, *Johannes Brahms: Life and Letters* (Oxford: Oxford University Press, 1997), pp. 91, 270–2, 571 and 750.

1. Nora Bickley, *Letters from and to Joseph Joachim* (New York: Vienna House, 1972).
2. K. Cornish, *The Jew of Linz* (London: Arrow, 1999).
3. Bertha Geissmar, *The Baton and the Jackboot* (London: Hamish Hamilton, 1944).
4. Joseph Szigeti (1949) *With Strings Attached* (London: Cassell, 1949).

Joseph, Jane Marian (b. Notting Hill, London, 31 May 1894; d. London, 9 March 1929)   Came from a Jewish family in which her father was a lawyer. She was a pupil at St Paul's School for Girls from 1909 to 1913, where Gustav Holst was director of music. She read classics at Girton College, Cambridge, from 1913 to 1916. Her family were keen musicians and she played the double bass, which suited her, being very tall, and also the piano. Whilst at Cambridge she studied composition during vacations with Holst. After graduating she began teaching at the Eothen School in Caterham, Surrey, and at the same time was actively involved in welfare work to help the war effort. She died of a kidney disease at the tragically young age of 34, and is better-known today for the assistance she gave Holst than as a composer in her own right. She wrote the libretto for Holst's *The Golden Goose*. She was one of a number of amanuenses whom Holst relied upon after he began to suffer from persistent neuritis. She assisted him in the preliminary translation from Greek of the text used for his *Hymn of Jesus*. She also spent much time in organizing music festivals at which Holst was a major composer. One of her first compositions, *A Festival Venite*, was performed in the Queen's Hall in London in 1923. Most of her compositions were choral works, including a song cycle entitled *Mirage* with string quartet, the songs *Echo, Song in a Cornfield, One Foot in the Sea, and one on Shore*, and settings of carols including *A Little Childe, There is Ibore, Adam Lay Ibounden, Wassail Song* and *Noël*. In addition, she composed *Short String Quartet* in A minor, which was performed in 1922 but was never published and appears to have been lost, as do 33 solo songs mentioned in an article by Holst. Two orchestral pieces, *Morris Dance* and *Bergamask*, survive.

Bibliography: G; Alan Gibbs, 'The Music of Jane Joseph', *Tempo*, 209 (1999), pp. 14–18*

Josephs, Wilfred (b. Newcastle-upon-Tyne, 24 July 1927; d. London, 18 November 1997)   Attended Rutherford Grammar School from 1939 to 1945.

At the age of 16 he had his first lessons in harmony and counterpoint from Arthur Milner. He wrote a large number of works as a schoolboy, but these early works he later destroyed. Parental mistrust of the music profession led him to study dentistry at Newcastle University (then part of the University of Durham), graduating in 1951. He practised dentistry as an army dental officer from 1951 to 1953, whilst doing his national service, but in 1954 won a scholarship to the Guildhall School of Music and studied under Alfred Nieman until 1956, whilst at the same time continuing to practise as a dentist. He spent a year (1958/9) in Paris on a Leverhulme scholarship, studying under Max Deutsch, a former pupil of Arnold SCHOENBERG, and this, together with exposure to the musical scene in Paris at the time (Boulez was coming to prominence), greatly enlarged his musical range. This did not however make him into a wholehearted Schoenbergian. In 1964 he wrote: 'The twelve-note style has come and gone for me, and I have found my own style in works that have appeared abroad – seldom in England.' This is born out by his subsequent works, which stand apart from most of those of his English contemporaries.

In 1961 he was commissioned to write *Viola Concertante*, Op. 30, for a chamber orchestra in Birmingham. He was also in demand as a composer for radio and television. Two of his works written during the period are *Comedy-Overture 'The Ants'*, Op. 7 (1955), that depicts the antlike movement of Londoners in the underground during the rush hour, and *Twelve Letters*, Op. 16 (1957), a setting of Hilaire Belloc's *A Moral Alphabet*. He came to be known by a much wider public after December 1963, when he won first prize in the First International Competition of La Scala and the City of Milan for his *Requiem*, Op. 39. It was conceived at the time of the Eichmann trial, and is in remembrance of the millions of Jews who perished in the Holocaust. The work evolved from his *String Quintet*, Op. 32 (1961), written in memory of Jews who had died, having three slow movements headed *Requiescant pro Defunctis Ludaeis*. It has ten movements in all. The string quintet movements are interspersed with settings of the Kaddish and a purely orchestral movement, *De Profundis*. The music, which is simple and austere rather than dramatic, made a moving impact at the La Scala premiere, and it was particularly adopted in America, where performances were given in New York and Cincinnati in 1967 and by the Chicago Symphony Orchestra under Carlo Mario Guilini in 1972, who at the time stated that it was 'the most important work of a living composer'. After his success with *Requiem* he finally gave up dentistry for full-time composition. His first major work to be performed in the UK was his second symphony, which was performed at the Cheltenham Festival in 1965.

Josephs was a prolific composer, claiming his principal recreation was writing music. He wrote twelve symphonies, two piano concertos, concertos for cello, for two violins, for viola, for percussion, four string quartets, sonatas for violin and piano and for solo violin, many of which deserve to be more

217

widely heard. He wrote a number of operas, including *The Nottingham Captain* (1962), the text of which was by Arnold Wesker, but his greatest was *Rebecca* (1983), commissioned by Opera North and staged in Leeds, which is based on the novel by Daphne du Maurier. His ballet *Cyrano* (1991) was staged at Covent Garden.

In 1981 he composed a setting of the Torah Service to celebrate the Golden Jubilee of the North Western Reform Synagogue at Alyth Gardens. However, he is best known as a film and television composer. Amongst his greatest successes have been the scores for *I Claudius* and *The World at War*. Other well-known scores for television include those for *All Creatures Great and Small*, *Swallows and Amazons* and *Cider with Rosie*. Josephs's strengths lie in his clarity of expression and economy of means, as is particularly evident in his chamber works, for example, *Chaconny*, Op. 38 (1963), Solo Violin Sonata, Op. 15 (1957), Sonatas for Violin and Piano, Op. 46 (1965) and Op. 147 (1986–87), together with his great technical facility.

Bibliography: *G*; *HBD*; Ken; Leb; F. Routh, *Contemporary British Music* (London: MacDonald, 1972)*

Kagel, Mauricio Raúl (b. Buenos Aires, 24 December 1931)   Of Argentinian–Jewish parentage. He failed to gain entrance to Buenos Aires Conservatory of Music and instead went to the Buenos Aires University to study philosophy and literature, where his particular interests were Spinoza and Jorge Luis Borges. As a composer he is largely self-taught, but he studied music theory with Juan Carlos Paz and piano, cello, voice and conducting with Alfredo Schiuma and others. He has wide interests, including literature, philosophy, theatre, film and music. These interests have led him to be particularly concerned with the interaction between the different art forms and this is apparent in many of his compositions. In 1949 he began an association as artistic consultant with Agrupacion Nueva Musica and helped found Ciné-mathèque Argentine in 1950. He worked as chorus master at Teatro Colon from 1949 to 1956.

In 1957 he emigrated to Cologne in Germany, attracted to the electronic studio headed by Karlheinz Stockhausen, and where he became a professor of music. His music is difficult to characterize. Many musical influences can be detected including those of the Second Viennese School, Kurt WEILL, Satie and Cage and more recently minimalism. Although he has written orchestral music and chamber music, vocal music and theatre and film music are perhaps his most important genre. For many of his works the visual aspect is as important as that of the aural. Some examples of his compositions illustrate this point. *Pas de Cinq* for five performers (1965) notates the movement of five actors about the stage, incorporating the tapping of walking sticks but no other sound. *Dessur* (1986) uses a rhythmically banged chair. In *Ludvig van* (1969–70) Kagel uses Beethoven's music showing the distortions that time has made between Beethoven's time and the present. In *Variationen ohne Fuge*

(1972) he takes Brahms's *Handel Variations* and translates them atonally. *Sankt-Bach-Passion* (1985) is a musical biography of Bach with the text drawn from various sources, including historical documents and using some of the conventions of Bach's own Passions.

Bibliography: *CC*; *G*; *HBD*; Leb*; Paul Griffiths, *Modern Music* (London: Thames & Hudson, 1978), pp. 187–90; Arnold Whittall, *Musical Composition in the Twentieth Century* (Oxford: Oxford University Press, 1999), pp. 370–5

Kahn, Erich Itor (b. Rimbach, Germany, 23 July 1905; d. New York, 5 March 1956)   Pianist and composer. He studied at the Frankfurt Conservatory and moved to Paris in 1933, where he worked as a piano accompanist and chamber musician. He toured North Africa with Casals in 1938–9. He was interned in a French concentration camp in 1940–1, where he wrote *Nenia Judaeis Qui Hac Aetate Perierunt* (In memory of the Jews who perished in the Holocaust) for cello and piano, completing it in 1943 when he reached New York. There he formed the Alberni Trio, together with Alexander Schneider and Benar Heifetz in 1944. His other compositions include *Les Symphonies Bretonnes* (1940), *Actus Tragicus* for 10 instruments (1946) and *Ciaccona dei Tempi di Guerra* for piano (1943).

Bibliography: *AG*; Grad; *G*; *HBD*; Ly*

Kahn, Robert (b. Mannheim, 21 July 1865; d. Biddenden, Kent, England, 29 May 1951)   Brought up in a middle-class Jewish family where his music studies were encouraged. He studied at the Berlin Hochschule für Musik in 1882–5 and at the Munich Academy of Music in 1885–6 with Rheinberger. On a number of occasions he met Brahms, who offered to teach him. Kahn declined the offer, it is said out of modesty. Nevertheless, many of his compositions are clearly influenced by Brahms, to the extent that his style remained very much in the nineteenth century and was not generally forward-looking. After living briefly in Vienna and following military service he returned to the Berlin Hochschule, first as piano teacher, then as theory teacher and then as composition teacher from 1894 to 1930. His greatest talent lay in his ability as a teacher. Among his pupils were the pianists Arthur Rubinstein[1] and Wilhelm Kempff. In 1937, when he was 72 he fled to England and lived there for the remaining 14 years of his life. His String Quartet, Op. 8, was performed by the JOACHIM Quartet and his *Orchestral Serenade* was premiered by the Berlin Philharmonic Orchestra under von Bülow. The bulk of his compositions are chamber music and *Lieder*: his best-known chamber music is Violin Sonata, Op. 50, piano quartets Op. 30 and Op. 41 and String Quartet, Op. 60. He composed at least 110 *Lieder* between the 1880s and 1932. These show a directness and simplicity, and are well crafted but conservative in style. His most successful choral work is *Mahomets Gesang*, Op. 24.

Bibliography: *G*; *HBD*; Ho*; Harvey Sachs, *Arthur Rubinstein* (New York: Pheonix, 1995), p. 29.; Johnson, Graham: OP393 [record sleeve]

1. *G*.

Kaminski, Heinrich (b. Tiengen, near Waldshut, Germany, 4 July 1886; d. Ried, near Benediktbeuren, Germany, 21 June 1946)   His father was of Polish descent, originally a priest, and his mother was an opera singer. One of his grandmothers was Jewish. He did not begin to study music until he was an adult. He studied music theory with P. Wolfrum in Heidelberg and later in 1909 briefly studied composition in Berlin with Paul Juon and Hugo Kaun, but otherwise he was largely self-taught. From 1914 to 1930 he lived in Ried, a small village near Lake Kochel, and taught privately. His pupils included ORFF. In 1930 he succeeded Pfitzner, being in charge of the master class in composition at the Prussian Academy of Arts in Berlin until he resigned in 1933. Many of his compositions are vocal, including two operas, a *Magnificat* and a number of psalm settings. He also composed two string quartets, a string quintet, a quartet for clarinet, violin, cello and piano, and a quintet for clarinet, horn, violin, viola and cello. His most successful orchestral work was *Concerto Grosso* (1922). In the mid-1930s his music was discouraged in Germany because he had one Jewish grandmother, although he escaped racial registration. The National Socialist Party condemned him for his opposition to the regime in 1933–5, but noted with satisfaction that by 1940 Kaminski had four children in the Hitler Youth.
Bibliography: *G*; *HBD*; Michael H. Kater *The Twisted Muse* (Oxford: Oxford University Press, 1997), pp. 82–3*

Kaminski, Joseph (b. Odessa, 17 November 1903; d. Tel Aviv, 14 October 1972) Came from an artistic family; his mother was the Jewish actress Esther Rachel Kaminska. He started to learn the violin at the age of 6. His violin teachers were Heller in Warsaw and Barmas and Arnold Rosé, both in Vienna. He also studied composition with Friedrich Koch in Berlin in 1922 and with Hans GAL in Vienna in 1923–4. He became leader of the Warsaw Radio Orchestra and was invited by Bronislav Huberman in 1937 to be one of the leaders of the Palestine Philharmonic Orchestra. He settled in Tel Aviv in 1937. His compositions include incidental music for the Vilna Jewish Theatrical Troupe, *Aggadah ve-Riqqid* for strings (1939), *Concertino* for trumpet and orchestra (1941), *Ha-aliyah* variations for baritone and orchestra (1943), *Comedy Overture* (1944), a suite for violin, cello and piano (1944), a string quartet (1945), *Variations* for cor anglais and strings (1958), a violin concerto (1950), *Israeli Sketches* (1955), *Tryptych* for piano (1958) and *Symphonic Overture* (1960).
Bibliography: *G*; *HBD*; Grad; Aron M. Rothmüller, *The Music of the Jews* (London: Vallentine Mitchell, 1953), p. 202*

Karel, Rudolf (b. Plzeň, Czechoslovakia, 9 November 1880; d. Terezin, 6 March 1945)   Attended the Prague Conservatory, where he was Dvorak's last pupil. He went to Russia, where he taught at the Taganrog Music School and Rostov Conservatory. In 1923 he was appointed professor of composition at the Prague Conservatory, where he remained until forced from his post in 1941,

and in 1943 was arrested by the Gestapo for membership of the Czech resistance movement and sent to Terezin. By then he was suffering from a heart condition and died of dysentery in Terezin in 1945. His early works show the influence of Dvorak and Tchaikovsky. His works include two operas (*Ilsa's heart,* 1909 and *Three Hairs of Old Wise Man*, 1944), the symphonic poem *The Demon*, the oratorio *Resurrection*, and *Nonet* for horn, woodwinds and strings (1944). The two works dated 1944 he composed in prison, in the prison hospital. These had to be written on scraps of paper, which the prison physician then smuggled out for him. They therefore had to be composed in small fragments, and he had to memorize the earlier parts while composing the later parts. After 1945 they were edited and given premieres in Prague after the composer's death.
Bibliography: *HBD*; Ken; Jozǎ Karas, *Music in Terezin: 1941–1945* (New York: Pendragon, 1985), p. 191; Robert Hopkins, 'The Forgotten Generation', in *Czech Music: the Journal of The Dvorak Society*, 21 (1999/2000), pp. 224–48*

Keal, Minna [*née* Minnie Nerenstein] (b. London, 22 March 1909; d. Buckinghamshire, 14 November 1999)   Born in the East End of London. Her parents were Yiddish-speaking Jewish immigrants from Byelorussia. Her father ran a Hebrew publishing and book-selling business near Petticoat Lane. Some of her earliest musical experiences were hearing her mother singing Hebrew folk songs and her uncle playing Paganini on the violin. She had piano lessons as a child and went to Clapton County School in Hackney. When her father died in 1926 plans for her to try for Oxbridge were abandoned, but instead in 1928 she entered the Royal Academy of Music, studying piano with Thomas Knott and composition with William Alwyn. She changed her name from Minnie to the more artistic-sounding Minna on entering the academy. At the same time she helped her mother part-time in the shop. In spite of making excellent progress at the academy, family pressure forced her to abandon her studies in 1929 to work full-time in the shop. Prior to this she had composed some chamber works: *Fantasie in C Minor* for violin and piano, *Ballad in F Minor* for viola and piano, and *Three Summer Sketches* for piano, some of which were played at the Whitechapel Gallery and the People's Palace, but after that she gave up composing.

In 1931 she married Barnett Samuel and had a son, Raphael, who later went on to become a distinguished social historian. During the 1930s and early 1940s she was actively involved in social and political activities. She and her husband set up a committee to help Jewish children escaping from Nazi Germany and she joined the British Communist Party, abandoning Judaism. When her marriage broke down, during the war, she went to Slough to work in an aircraft factory, and it was there that she met her future second husband, Bill Keal. They were married in 1959. After the Soviet invasion of Hungary they left the Communist Party in protest. The Keals moved to Chesham in 1963 and Minna worked in a number of office jobs. She gave piano lessons at the Guildhall School of Music until she retired in 1969.

In about 1980, in her capacity as a piano teacher, she met Justine Connolly, an Associate Board Examiner who was examining one of her pupils. She took the opportunity to show him some of her early compositions, and on seeing them he encouraged her to start writing again. She started having lessons with Justine Connolly, paid for by her son Raphael, now a tutor in social history at Ruskin College, and then later with Oliver Knussen. As a result she composed String Quartet, Op. 1 (1978), Wind Quintet, Op. 2 (1980), dedicated to her first teacher, William Alwyn; Symphony No. 1 (1987), and *Cantillation* (for violin and orchestra). To assist with the composing her husband Bill had their garage converted into a studio. The string quartet was premiered by the Arditti Quartet in 1979 – over 40 years after a composition of hers was first performed in public. In 1991 *Cantillation* was given its premiere with Ann Hooley (violin) and the European Women's Orchestra, conducted by Odaline de la Martinez. Symphony, Op. 3, was performed by the BBC Symphony Orchestra at a Promenade Concert in 1989. One music correspondent wrote: 'A talent frozen like a princess in a fairy tale – a young voice in an old lady.' She was keen to write a cello concerto, but realized that since the symphony took her five years to write, a cello concerto might take a similar length of time; she was 80 years of age at the time. She achieved this by 1994, when Cello Concerto, Op. 5, was given its premiere by Alexander Baillie on 26 August. The work was dedicated to her late husband William Keal. She completed one further short work before her death, *Duetino* for flute and clarinet. In 1992 a BBC 2 documentary was made of her story entitled *A Life in Reverse*.
Bibliography: *GW*; *Pan*; 'Minna Keal', *Musical Times*, 141 (2000), pp. 16–17*; Keal, Minna. LNT110 [record sleeve]

Kernis, Aaron Jay (b. Philadelphia, 15 January 1960)   Took little interest in music until the age of 12, after which he taught himself the piano. In his teens he discovered minimalism. He attended the San Francisco School of Music in 1977–8, where John Adams was his teacher. Subsequently he went to the Manhatten School of Music and Yale School of Music. Amongst his teachers were Charles Wuorinen, Elias Tannenbaum and Jacob DRUCKMAN. In 1984 he won the Rome prize of the American Academy of Rome. By the age of 23 his compositions were sufficiently highly regarded for his *Dream of the Morning Sky* for soprano and orchestra to be performed by the New York Philharmonic Orchestra under Zubin Mehta. His output to date includes orchestral, chamber and vocal music. The descriptive word most frequently used in connection with his music is eclecticism, ranging from baroque to pop. Kernis says that he has been most influenced by nineteenth-century music, minimalism and impressionism. As a pupil of John Adams, he may be regarded in a sense as the third generation of minimalists (Philip GLASS and Steve REICH being amongst the first).

Kernis has been very successful with having works commissioned and in having his works performed by outstanding performers. His first symphony,

Symphony of Waves, was commissioned by the St Paul Chamber Orchestra, Minnesota, who gave the first performance under John Adams in 1989. The vocal work, *Love Scenes* for soprano and cello, was first performed in 1987 by Dawn Upshaw. His first string quartet (*Musica Celestis*) was first performed in 1990 and his second string quartet (*Musica Instrumentalis*) won the 1998 Pulitzer prize.

Kernis has been much troubled by the violence, inhumanity and injustice in the world and this has been the inspiration for some of his works written in the early 1990s. His *Second Symphony* (1992) was written in protest against the Gulf War. He was commissioned by the San Francisco Symphony Orchestra to write a concerto for cor anglais. The resultant work, *Colored Field,* was inspired by a visit to the sites of the concentration camps at Auschwitz and Birkenau. There he noticed a child chewing blades of grass in a field that was once blood-soaked soil. The third movement of this work incorporates Hebrew cantillation and Christian chant, suggesting a Kaddish. The work seems particularly apt for cor anglais, with its plaintive tone colour. In parallel with *Colored Field* he wrote a elegiac piece for piano quartet, *Still Movement with Hymn,* that also shows the influence of medieval church music and Hebrew cantillation. This was followed by *Lament and Prayer* for violin and orchestra, in commemoration of the fiftieth anniversary of the end of World War Two and the Holocaust. In this work the violin and orchestra are personified as the cantor and congregation.
Bibliography: CC; G; www.schirmer.com/composers/kernis/bio.htm

Klebanov, Dmytro Lvovych (b. Khar'kiv, Ukraine, 12/25 July 1907; d. Khar'kiv, Ukraine, 6 June 1987)   Studied violin with Ilya Dobrzynets and composition with Bogatïryov, graduating at the Khar'kiv Institute of Music and Drama in 1926. He worked as a violinist with the State Opera and ballet theatre in Leningrad (1927–9) playing under conductors such as Walter and KLEMPERER. In 1934 he returned to Khar'kiv, where he worked at the conservatory for 50 years, becoming head of composition in 1970. His first successful composition was a ballet for children entitled *Aistienok* (Little stork), which was followed two years later by the ballet *Svetlana* (1939). He composed nine symphonies, two violin concertos, a cello concerto, a number of orchestral suites, six string quartets, song cycles and music for films and television. His music is tonal and shows the influence of Shostakovich. His first symphony (1945) was 'dedicated to the memory of the martyrs of Babi Yar' and is his response as a Jewish Ukrainian to the mass execution of Jews during the German occupation of Kiev in World War Two. It was criticized as being filled with the spirit of nationalism and cosmopolitanism (i.e., Judaism).
Bibliography: G*

Klein, Gideon (b. 6 December 1919, Přerov, Moravia; d. Fürstengrube, 27 January 1945)   The youngest in a Jewish family of four children. His father was a cattle dealer. At the age of 6 Gideon had piano lessons with the local headmaster, Karel Mařik, and soon showed that he had musical talent. By the time he was 11 it was decided that he should have piano lessons with Professor Růžena Kurzová in Prague, initially once a month. In 1931 he moved to Prague, was looked after by his sister, Eliška, and attended the Jirásek Grammar School until 1938. At the same time he continued his piano lessons, initially with Růžena Kurzová and later with her husband, Vilém Kurz, as an extramural student of the Prague Conservatory, graduating in 1938. He then began musicological studies at Charles University, Prague, and studied composition under Alois Hába at the conservatory.

However, by November 1939, within a few weeks of starting university, the Germans closed all Czech universities, and because of the Nuremberg Laws (see Chapter 3, section 3.1) Klein was forced to leave the conservatory in the spring of 1940 and prevented from taking up a scholarship he was offered at the Royal Academy in London. By this time he had begun to perform widely as a pianist, but for public performances, from necessity he had to perform under the assumed name of Karel Vránek. He had contacts in the literary world and performed with theatre groups. He gave his last public performance on 30 January 1940. He continued to be involved in concerts held in private flats, as a pianist, and increasingly with chamber groups. He also taught in a Jewish orphanage in Prague. This all came to an end with the summons on 1 December 1941 to assemble to be sent by the Nazis to Terezin.

Before being sent to Terezin in 1941 Klein gave a suitcase to a friend for safekeeping. The friend also had to leave Prague because of racial persecution. However, it was not until 1990 that the Herzog family found in their possession this locked suitcase, which contained many of Klein's compositions from the 1939–40 period. Until 1990 it was generally assumed that Klein's composing phase was largely from the time of his internment until his murder by the Nazis (1941–5). However, this discovery revealed that a significant number of his 23 completed works date from before his internment. In addition to this there is a large number of uncompleted works. These works reveal a strong interest in the Second Viennese School and also quarter-tone music composed at the time when Hába was his composition teacher. Important works from this period include a duo for violin and viola in the quarter-tone system, a divertimento for eight wind instruments, Three Songs, Op. 1, and a second string quartet dedicated to his sister Eliška.

Although conditions in Terezin were dire – there was gross overcrowding and gross undernourishment – they were not as bad as in some of the other concentration camps. In fact, Terezin was a sort of staging post from which internees were transported to Auschwitz. Within Terezin, Klein, together with others, for example, Victor Ullmann, were in charge of the so-called *Freizeitgestaltung* (leisure activities group). He was responsible for organizing singing and performed in a chamber group, producing some of his finest compositions in this period. In 1941 there were few musical instruments available, and at this stage choral singing was most important. By 1942 there were large influxes of internees with musical instruments from the big cities and so more instrumental music was possible. Most of Klein's compositions are for chamber groups. The combination of instruments for which they are scored depended on the availability of instruments and the availability and skills of the instrumentalists. New internees were frequently arriving and others were being dispatched to Auschwitz, thus the situation was ever-changing.

Klein made a number of arrangements of folk songs for improvised choirs that could be performed in Terezin. Notable amongst these are *Madrigal* for a five-part choir based on a poem by François Villon, *Original Sin,* based on Czech folk poetry, and *Madrigal* for a five-part choir to words by Hölderlin. His most important chamber works composed in Terezin are a piano sonata, *Fantasia and Fugue* for string quartet, and a string trio. The piano sonata is highly chromatic and somewhat reminiscent of Berg's Piano Sonata. The string trio was the last work Klein composed in Terezin, completed nine days before he was transported to Auschwitz. The slow movement is a set of variations on a Moravian folk song. Although Klein was strongly aware of his Jewish roots it appears to have had little impact on most of his compositions. A few works composed in the 1930s have Jewish titles. There is an unfinished sketch, *Shema Israel* for voice and string quartet, and an unfinished Kaddish for tenor and organ.

Before he was transported to Auschwitz on 16 October 1944 he gave his compositions to his girlfriend in Terezin, Irma Semtzka. Both she and Eliška survived, and after the liberation she gave his compositions to Eliška in Prague. Klein was transferred from Auschwitz to a smaller camp at Fürsten-grube, near Katovice, holding about 1,500 prisoners. There he was worked for three months to the point of death in the coalmines. With the advance of the Russians on the eastern front the camp was evacuated, and it is uncertain whether he was shot by the SS or whether he perished on the death march when the camp was evacuated. The date was about 27 January 1945.
Bibliography: Grad; *G*; Leb; Joža Karas, *Music in Terezin* (New York: Pendragon, 1985), pp. 71–6; Milan Slavický, *Gideon Klein: a Fragment of Life and Work* (Prague: Helvetica Tempora, 1995)

Klemperer, Otto Nossan (b. Breslau, 14 May 1885; d. Zurich, July 1973) Born in Breslau, but by the time he was 4 years old his parents had moved to Hamburg, where he grew up. His father was born in the Prague ghetto and was an Orthodox Jew, whereas his mother's family attended the reform synagogue and were much more assimilated. His father was a small and not very successful businessman, and after moving to Hamburg worked as a bookkeeper. He was easy going, whereas his mother was much more austere, a character which Klemperer inherited from her. On moving from a close-knit community in Breslau to Hamburg their religious observance lapsed, although Klemperer underwent *bar mitzvah* when he reached the age of 13.

He showed an interest in music at an early age and initially received piano lessons from his mother. The Klemperers were not at all wealthy, and Helen Rée, his mother's first cousin, paid for his piano lessons with a professional piano teacher, Hans Havekoss. In 1901 he was accepted into the Hoch Conservatory in Frankfurt, but when his teacher, Kwast, moved to the Klindworth-Scharwenka Conservatory in Berlin in 1902, Klemperer transferred with him. Initially it seemed that he was destined to become a concert pianist. In 1905 he suffered his first manic-depressive phase and this was to recur in cycles for the rest of his life. Klemperer studied with Hans Pfitzner for two years and this fired his creative imagination, but it was in 1905, when he was assisting in a performance of MAHLER's Second Symphony by conducting the off-stage band, that he was to meet the composer himself. This was to lead to Klemperer being chorus master in a production of OFFENBACH's *Orpheus in the Underworld* and to his interest in both the theatre and conducting. He had a succession of conducting posts: assistant conductor at the German Theatre in Prague (1907–10), conductor of the Hamburg Opera (1910–12), Cologne (1917–24), Wiesbaden (1924–7) and the Kroll Opera (1927–31).

It was whilst in Cologne that he turned to Catholicism and was baptized in the spring of 1919. The attraction of Catholicism had been growing for some time, and was strengthened by his attendance at lectures by Max Scheler, a Catholic philosopher. In 1919 he received instruction from a Catholic priest. At the time of his conversion he accepted most of the doctrine of the Catholic Church. He told Daniel Barenboim many years later that he had naïvely thought one had to be a Christian in order to conduct the great Christian pieces, such as Bach's *Saint Matthew Passion* or *Saint John Passion*.[1]

In the summer of 1919 he married Johanna Geissler, whom he had met when she was a soprano in the Hamburg Opera. She was a Lutheran and was received into the Church of Rome two days before their civil marriage, when for the first and last time she made confession. At the time Klemperer's sister Marrianne said of Johanna: 'You cannot imagine how vital she is – she must have nerves of steel, she has a lot of humour and is very jolly … she seems most suitable for Otto.' Johanna was destined to give him enormous support throughout his turbulent career until her death in 1956, when his daughter Lotte took over the role until his death.

His four-year directorship of the Kroll Opera in Berlin was to be one of the high points of his long career. The Kroll became the embodiment of a progressive new culture. It was set up as an artistically independent organization in 1927, but at the same time it was to serve as a people's theatre; it is doubtful if both were compatible. Klemperer wanted to reform the staging of opera by introducing new works into a stagnant repertoire, but the nearer he got to bringing in a new operatic age, the less it seemed to please its principal client, the public. The Kroll established a far wider repertoire than any other Berlin opera house at the time, but failed to attract the wider audiences. When the cultural life of Germany began to re-emerge from World War Two, many of the Kroll's innovations were reintroduced.

In 1933 Klemperer and his family were forced to flee the Nazis and emigrated to America, to settle in Los Angeles. His conducting career had vicissitudes and he was never really a success in America. His bouts of manic depression continued to recur and have serious effects on his employability. It was during his manic phases that he did most of his composing. Success, as a conductor, frequently eluded him until his spell with the Budapest Opera (1947–50) and his very successful period during his late seventies and eighties when he was in charge of the New Philharmonia in London. It was during this period that Walter Legge was able to harness his undoubted talents to produce some of the best recordings of the classical repertoire of the twentieth century. From being underrated for a long period, he became an idol of music audiences and continued conducting until the year of his death, at the age of 88.

In 1958 on a visit to Israel he was invited to conduct the Israel Philharmonic. When Klemperer expressed disappointment that on his previous visits to Israel he had not been invited to conduct, the manager replied that as a Jew who had converted to Catholicism, he was a heretic. Klemperer pointed out that the same could be said of Koussevitzky and Walter who had conducted the orchestra. 'Yes' replied the manager 'but without a fee'.

Klemperer attended Mass not infrequently, particularly during his manic phases, but he never overlooked his Jewish roots. Eventually, in 1967 he resolved to leave the Catholic Church. A number of factors contributed to this, but particularly the Church's failure to disassociate itself from anti-Semitism, and the evidence that Pope Pius XII, whom Klemperer met on two occasions, failed to take a stand against the Third Reich. So like SCHOENBERG he returned to the faith of his fathers. He started to attend the Marble Arch Synagogue, but occasionally Brompton Oratory as well. As he put it, 'I wanted to demonstrate that I am a Jew and am loyal to Jewish things.' In 1971, at the age of 86, he began Hebrew lessons with Abraham Kuflik, a stern Orthodox Jew. He even had an Israeli passport, and is said to have been the most famous Israeli conductor never to conduct the Israel Philharmonic. When he died in 1973 he was buried in the Jewish cemetery at Friesenberg in the hills over-looking Zurich.

In conversation with his biographer, Peter Heyworth, in the early 1970s, Klemperer recalled Mahler saying to him in 1907: 'You compose, don't you. I can see you do.' By 1972 Klemperer described himself as follows: 'I am mainly a conductor who also composes. Naturally, I would be glad to be remembered as a conductor *and* as a composer. But, without wanting to be arrogant, I would only like to be remembered as a *good* composer.' He composed a number of works, although few are frequently played. These include six symphonies among 17 works for orchestra, nine string quartets, and about 100 songs. He composed a setting of Psalm 42, *Missa Sacra* for solo and chorus (1919), and *Merry Waltz* (1959). His opera *Das Ziel*, composed in 1915 and revised in 1970,

was never performed. The opera *Juda* (1962) was incomplete, and only the funeral march and libretto of *Thamar* (the daughter of King David) survive. His Second Symphony, Seventh String Quartet and *Merry Waltz* have been recorded. A critic's comment after the performance of his Second Symphony was that it was 'the product of an outstanding conductor musing on the works of composers he has championed throughout his career, notably Mahler, Bruckner and Strauss ... What it does not reflect is their grasp of large-scale structures.' Benjamin Britten's response to the score of the first symphony that Klemperer sent him was: 'I feel that your ideas are often very good ... But, dear Doctor, I am not always so sure that the notes you have chosen are always the exactly right ones to express what is so clearly in your mind.'
Bibliography: *G*; *HBD*; Ken; Peter Heyworth *Otto Klemperer: his Life and Times* (Cambridge: Cambridge University Press, 1983 and 1996), vols. 1 and 2
1. Daniel Barenboim, *A Life in Music* (London: Weidenfeld & Nicolson, 1991).

Klyuzner, Boris Lazaryevich (b. Astrakhan, 19 May/1 June 1909; d. Komarovo, Leningrad Region, 22 May 1975)   Born into the family of an opera singer. He studied under Mikhail GNESIN at the Leningrad Conservatory (as it was then called) from 1936 until graduating in 1941. He also directed amateur choirs. He was a member of the Communist Party of the Soviet Union from 1932. After serving in the army he returned to choral work during the period 1945–8. He moved to Moscow in 1961. His compositions centre on choral, chamber and orchestral music. His work shows the influence of MAHLER. He was not a very prolific composer, but much of his music shows more originality than that of the more prolific party hacks of the time; this is particularly so of the Second Symphony, composed in 1961, which is one of the most original pieces written by a Soviet composer of his generation. His compositions include three overtures, four symphonies (1954–72), concertos for forte piano (1939), violin (1950) and two violins (1960) a clarinet quintet (1935), *Poem About Lenin* for baritone, chorus and orchestra (1954) and *Conversation with Comrade Lenin* for base and orchestra to words by V. V. Mayakovsky (1969). He was a friend of Shostakovich. He held administrative positions in the Composers Union and may have been the camp survivor 'K' mentioned in Solzhenitsyn's *Gulag Archepelago*. There is a conspicuous absence of compositions between 1939 and 1945. His music is at present very little known in the West, and is infrequently played. A combination of reasons may account for this: his personal modesty, his Jewish origin, which automatically ranked him as second-rate in the USSR, and the fact that he remained in St Petersburg rather than moving to Moscow.
Bibliography: *G*; *HBD*; A. Ho and D. Feofanov, *Biographical Dictionary of Russian/Soviet Composers* (New York: Greenwood, 1989); G. V. Keldish (ed.), *The Musical Encyclopaedia* (in Russian) (Moscow, 1990); M. Pritsker,* RD CD 11 162 [record sleeve]

Koffler, Józef (b. Stryj, Poland [Ukraine], 28 November 1896; d. near Krosno, Poland, early 1944?) Studied music in Vienna with Graedener (1914–16) and Adler (1920–4), receiving his doctorate at the University of Vienna in 1925. He taught composition at the Lvov Conservatory (1929–41) and served as music critic on *Ekspres Wierczorny*. He was the first Polish composer to use twelve-note-based serialism. He corresponded with SCHOENBERG in 1929 but the two never met. His serialist folk-tune-based third symphony for wind, harp and percussion was premiered at the last International Society for Contemporary Music meeting before World War Two held in London in 1938. His other works include *15 Variations* for string quartet, a string quartet, a string trio and various choral works. After the Germans attacked Lvov in 1941 he was deported with his family to the ghetto at Wieliczka. He and his wife and child are believed to have gone into hiding in the vicinity of Krosno but were found and murdered by the Nazis in early 1944.
Bibliography: *G*; Grad; *HBD*; Leb*; Ly*

Kohn, Karl [Georg] (b. Vienna, 1 August 1926) Studied piano from an early age; his first teacher was Alice Löwinger-Feldstein. His father was a textile salesman and violinist and his mother was a pianist. His played a Haydn piano concerto with an amateur orchestra of Jewish war veterans (Jüdische Frontkämpfer). He escaped with his immediate family after the *Anschluss* to America, settling in Goshen, New York, in 1939. Many of his relatives were murdered by the Nazis, and his piano teacher committed suicide when she realized escape from the Nazis had become impossible. He attended the New York College of Music, studying piano with Carl Werschinger and conducting with Julius Prüwer. After one semester at Harvard (1944–5) he served two years in the army as a bandmaster, returning to continue his studies with Piston, Ballantine, Irving FINE and Randall Thompson and graduating in 1950. He became professor of music at Pomona College and Claremont Graduate School, California, in 1950.

He gave many concerts with his wife Margaret, performing music for two pianos. His early compositions can be described as American neoclassicism and show the influence of his Harvard teachers, for example, *Fanfare* for brass (1952), *Five Pieces* for piano (1955), and *Castles and Kings* for two pianos (1958). After a visit to Europe, and conscious of his Viennese roots, he became interested in multi-serialism (serialism not only involving pitch, as SCHOENBERG developed, but also involving rhythm and dynamics, as developed by Boulez) in works such as *Two Short Pieces* for clarinet and piano (1959) and *Episodes* (1966). He continued using both styles in a number of works during the 1960s, for example, *Serenade* for piano and wind quintet (1961). In the 1970s he embarked on a Romantic phase in works such as *Reflections* (1970) and *Second Rhapsody* (1971). In *Introductions and Paradies* (1967), *Impromptus* (1969) and *The Prophet Bird* (1976) he quotes from MENDELSSOHN's Violin Concerto, Stravinsky's Octet and Schumann's *Bird of Paradise*, respectively.

Bibliography: *HBD*; Howard Pollack, *Harvard Composers* (New Jersey, MD: Scarecrow, 1992)*

Koppel, Herman David (b. Copenhagen, 1 October 1908; d. Copenhagen, 14 July 1998)   Eldest son of Polish–Jewish immigrants. The synagogue was the source of his earliest musical impressions. He began playing the piano at the age of 5, quickly demonstrating his musical talent, and started to compose while still a child. He studied at the Royal Danish Conservatory from 1925 and graduated in 1929. There he met the director Carl Nielsen, who advised him on composition. He made his début as a pianist in 1930 and travelled to Berlin, Paris and London. He served as *répétiteur* for the Danish Theatre and Danish Radio in the late 1930s. From 1940 to 1949 he taught music at the Royal Institute for the Blind, but he and his family fled the Nazi invaders, and lived in Örebro, Sweden, from 1943 to 1945, where he was a pianist with the Örebro Symphony Orchestra. In 1955 he became a professor at the Copenhagen Conservatory.

His works include an opera, *Macbeth*, which premiered in Copenhagen in 1970, seven symphonies, concertos for piano, violin, cello, oboe and flute, choral work, songs, piano and chamber music and film scores. His early works show the influence of Nielsen, Stravinsky and Bartok as well as jazz.

Since World War Two a number of his works have been on biblical (specifically Old Testament) themes. Early influences of cantorial singing heard in the synagogue can be discerned in his vocal work. After his return from Sweden, the discovery of the extent of the Holocaust inspired him to write a number of works, including *Tre Davidssalmer* for tenor, choir and orchestra, Op. 48 (1949), inspired by the agony of Jewish prisoners under the Nazi regime, *Five Biblical Songs*, Op. 46 (1949), *Four Love Songs* from the canticles of Solomon, Op. 47 (1949) and the oratorio *Moses* Op. 76 (1963–4). In these works he was also encouraged by the Danish tenor Aksel Schiøtz, whom he frequently accompanied at the piano. Other major works composed in the postwar period include a third piano concerto (1948), Piano Sonata, Op. 50 (1950), Cello Concerto, Op. 56 (1952), Fifth Symphony, Op. 60 (1955), Seventh Symphony, Op. 70 (1960–1) and *Memory* for strings composed in 1995 to commemorate the end of World War Two.

Many of his relatives were also musicians. His brother Julius led the Chapel Royal Orchestra from 1939, his daughter Lone Winther became a leading soprano in the Danish Opera and his son Thomas is a pianist and composer and leader of the Danish rock group Savage Rose.

Bibliography: *G*; *HBD*; D. Herman, 'Koppel', *Musical Times* (winter 1998), p. 6.

Kopytman, Mark (b. Kamyanets-Podilsky, USSR [Ukraine], 1929)   Studied both medicine and music at Czernowitz, in the Ukraine, graduating in piano in 1950 and in medicine in 1952. He continued with his dual careers by serving in a hospital near Lviv and concurrently studying composition at the Lviv Academy of Music. In 1958 he continued his music studies in Moscow,

completing a doctorate on the subject of polyphony. He taught in the USSR until 1972, when he emigrated to Israel. He composed a number of works whilst in the USSR, including the opera *Kasa Mare* (1966) that won a prize in Moscow in 1971. Since living in Israel he has composed a number of works for solo instruments, for example, *Lamentations* for solo flute (1973), *For Trombone* (1974), *For Piano I* (1972), *For Percussion* (1975) and *For Harpsichord* (1975). He has also composed a series of works entitled *Cantus*, which incorporates elements of Jewish folklore melody and microtonal Near Eastern music – *Cantus I* for three oboes, *Cantus II* for string trio, *Cantus III* for bass clarinet and orchestra, and *Cantus IV* for violin solo.
Bibliography: Grad; G

Korngold, Wolfgang Erich (b. Brno, Moravia, 29 May 1987; d. Hollywood, 29 November 1957)   Son of the music critic Julius Korngold. Korngold's grandfather, Simon was a wine merchant. Wolfgang's background was that of a typical bourgeois assimilated Jewish family. He was a child prodigy, who has often been compared with Mozart in this respect. The roles played by their respective fathers also have parallels. Korngold's father, being a very respected music critic, was very well placed to nurture the undoubted talent of his prodigy son. This worked both to his son's advantage and disadvantage. A quote Korngold made in joke sums this up: 'I never wanted to compose. I did it only to please my father.' In his childhood his father's contacts undoubtedly meant that Korngold's talents were noticed. In later life his father made clear the course of development he approved for his son. He was strongly opposed to the developments of the Second Viennese School, and he disapproved of his son's move to film music. Julius Korngold lived close to his son for the greater part of his life, escaping to America after the *Anschluss* and living in Hollywood until his death, only 12 years before that of his son Erich.

Korngold showed an interest in and a talent for music at a very early age. At 3 he was beating time with a wooden spoon, at 5 he was picking out melodies on the piano, and at 6 composing his own music. He composed a cantata, *Nixe, Gold*, for soloists, choir and piano. His father thought the piece was inspired by Wagner's *Das Rheingold*, but was disturbed by what he saw as an element of modernism in it. He felt that with further training his son would develop within the 'inner laws of tonal art'. This strongly held belief was to influence his son's development in the years to come. A few weeks after Korngold's tenth birthday he played the cantata from memory to Gustav MAHLER, with whom his father was on good terms. Mahler is said to have declared him a genius and recommended that he should study with ZEMLINSKY. By the time Korngold was 11 he had completed three superb works: *Der Schneeman* (a ballet), a piano sonata and six short pieces for piano based on episodes from *Don Quixote*. His father decided the best way to proceed was to get Universal Edition in Vienna to publish a private printing of these works, which could then be shown to various important musicians. The response was

231

very positive from Strauss, Nikisch and Humperdink. GOLDMARK, although recognizing his undoubted talent, was worried lest it might be beyond the well-established conservative style of the day – a view heartily endorsed by his father. *Der Schneeman* was given its successful premiere, orchestrated by Zemlinsky, at the Vienna Hofoper in 1910. By 1916 Korngold had written two short operas, *Der Ring des Polykrates* and *Violanta*. His most successful opera, *Der Tote Stadt*, which uses Wagnerian leitmotifs, he wrote at the age of 20; it was given its dual premiere at Hamburg and Cologne in 1920. The Cologne premiere was conducted by KLEMPERER, with his wife Johanna singing the role of Marietta.

In 1917 whilst serving in the army he met Luzi von Sonnenthal at a dinner party. She too was very talented, an excellent soprano and a good pianist from a musical and theatrical Jewish family. They married in a civil ceremony in Vienna in 1924. For various reasons both parents had resisted the marriage. Julius may have been over concerned for his son's musical development, no one being good enough for his son. There may also have been an element of jealousy in it.

Korngold's next opera, *Das Wunder der Heliane*, was completed in 1927. This received a mixed reception, partly because it got off to a bad start owing to casting, and partly because of its contrast with another very different opera staged at the same time, *Jonny Spielt Auf* by Krenek. The reception had a depressing affect on Korngold and he did not produce another opera until *Die Kathrin* in 1939. In the meantime he concentrated on the arrangement of operettas, collaborating with Max Reinhardt. He only wrote seven original works between 1927 and 1935.

Like many assimilated Jews living in Austria, Korngold and his family expected the rise of Nazism to be short-lived, and it was only during the succeeding years that they became aware of their Jewish identity. The collaboration with Reinhardt turned out to be very fortuitous. Reinhardt moved to Hollywood in the early 1930s to work on film production, and in 1934 asked Erich to collaborate on a film production of *Midsummer Night's Dream*. What was expected to be an eight-week trip to America lasted six months. It led to further visits to America, to collaborate with Warner Brothers and Paramount. During this period the situation in Austria worsened and eventually Korngold and both his and Luzi's families escaped to America.

Film-making had progressed from silent films (accompanied by music) through 'talkies', in which no music was played, to the next phase in which music provided an important role. Korngold played a leading role in this. He predicted that it would eventually become like writing operas for the screen. He showed a tremendous talent for the medium and was given a much greater degree of independence than other film composers, such as WAXMAN, who was treated as a mere film scorer. Korngold composed for a large number of films and received two Oscars. Amongst his film scores are: *Give Us This Night, Captain Blood, Anthony Adverse, The Prince and the Pauper, The Adventures of Robin*

Hood, The Sea Hawk, The Sea Wolf, Between Two Worlds and *Of Human Bondage.*
One film for which he particularly enjoyed making the film score was *Green Pastures*, a sentimental interpretation of biblical stories seen through the eyes of small Negro children. Untypically, he charged no fee for this score. He was particularly upset when he discovered that the chorus master along with the black cast were discriminated against by not being allowed to eat in the restaurant and in being restricted to the cafeteria. When he realized the situation he left the restaurant to join them in the cafeteria. Korngold was able to command high fees, but he was effectively supporting two households: his own and that of his wife's parents. The only non-film music he composed during the war was *A Passover Psalm*, Op. 30 and *Prayer*, Op. 32, after being approached by the local rabbi. These were the only religious music pieces he ever wrote.

After the death of his father and of Reinhardt he seemed to become tired of film music and began to return to music for concert performance. His health was not good, and perhaps he felt he had not fulfilled his early promise. His late period includes String Quartet, Op. 34 (1945), Violin Concerto, Op. 35 (1945), Cello Concerto, Op. 37 (1946) and Symphony in F sharp major, Op. 40 (1952). In these he uses lush themes from his film music. Unlike in his early days when the public was very receptive, he found that after World War Two tastes had moved on and that his romantic bitonality was out of fashion. His last opera, *Die Kathrin*, fell into this category.

Korngold always had a tendency to being overweight. From his Vienna days the cake shop was important to him, and this trend continued. He suffered a heart attack and was told to go on a strict diet. Eventually he suffered a stroke in the left side of his brain in 1956 and died of a cerebral haemorrhage a year later. Little of his music was heard for nearly forty years, but towards the end of the twentieth century there was a revival of his music and many of his operas have been staged again.

Bibliography: *G*; *HBD*; Leb; Brendon G. Carroll, *The Last Prodigy: a Biography of Erich Wolfgang Korngold* (Portland, OR: Amadeus, 1997); Jessica Duchen, *Eric Wolfgang Korngold* (London: Phaidon, 1996)

Krasa, Hans (b. Prague, 30 November 1899; d. Auschwitz, 17 October 1944)
Born into a prosperous Jewish German-speaking family; his father was a Czech lawyer and his mother was from a German–Bohemian family. The family was musical; two of the five children becoming professional musicians. There was a history of musical talent predominantly from his mother's side. By the age of 6 Krasa was beginning to compose, but he was also an avid reader, particularly of Russian and French literature, and to a lesser extent German and Czech literature. For his tenth birthday his father bought him a genuine Amati violin and arranged for him to have lessons with Frankenbusch, leader of the German Opera House in Prague. By the age of 11 he had pieces of his music performed in Salzburg and St Moritz. He studied at the German Academy of Music in Prague under ZEMLINSKY. Whilst studying he

composed his Op. 1, *Galgenleider* settings of poems by Morgenstern, a fore-runner of the Dadaists. Zemlinsky conducted a very successful performance of Op. 1 with the Czech Philharmonic in May 1921. Because of his comfortable financial circumstances he felt no great pressure to earn his living, but he worked as *répétiteur* in the Prague New German Theatre, where Zemlinsky was chief conductor. He met and became friendly with many writers, poets and journalists during the early 1920s, including Max BROD. In 1921 he composed a string quartet and about 1923 a symphony for small orchestra. The third and fourth movements of the symphony, which was performed in Paris in 1923, are based on the poem by Rimbaud, *Les Chercheuses de Poux*, which Brod translated. The writer and composer ROLAND-MANUEL wrote after this performance: 'His magical world is ruled over by the spirit of ironic poetry, which sometimes mocks its own power to bewitch.'

Krasa spent time working at the Kroll Theatre in Berlin, and received lessons in composition from Roussel in Paris. He was not a prolific composer and composed comparatively little during the 1920s, although he had an ambition to write an opera. It was not until the late 1920s that he found a theme to his liking in a story by Dostoyevsky, *Uncle's Dream*. He began composing what was to be *Verlobung im Traum* (*Betrothal in a Dream*) in the late 1920s. The completed opera was first performed under George Szell at the New German Theatre in Prague on 18 May 1933, and earned Krasa the Czechoslovak state prize for composition that year. The story is a domestic tragedy in which Sina, the principal character, is lured away from her true love, Fedya, by her mother, in order to marry an aging wealthy prince. Eventually Sina tells the confused and ageing prince that he has been tricked into proposing to her. The embarrassed prince departs leaving Sina free to marry Fedya, only to be informed by Fedya's servant that Feyda, who has been ill for some time, has just died. Although the outcome is tragic the opera is given a humorous and at times ironic treatment.

Krasa's best-known work is the children's opera *Brundibar*. Krasa had composed incidental music for a play, *Mládi ve Hře* (Youth at Play) by Adolf Hoffmeister, and it was Hoffmeister who provided the libretto for *Brundibar* to be performed by the Jewish Orphanage in Prague. In 1942 Krasa, along with many other Jews, was imprisoned by the Nazis in the concentration camp at Terezin, north of Prague. A number of other Jewish composers were imprisoned in the camp, including ULLMAN, HAAS and KLEIN. At least fifty works in total were composed in Terezin, of which Krasa composed six.[1] For the performance of *Brundibar* in Terezin, Krasa had to reduce the original score for the available instruments and players. The opera was first performed in Terezin in September 1943 and was performed altogether 55 times, the cast having to be changed a number of times as participants, including child performers, were sent to their deaths. In the opera two children have no money to buy milk for their sick mother. They sing on a street corner and passers-by give them money to buy milk. Brundibar, an organ-grinder, is annoyed by their singing and manages to steal the money from the children. Various animals help the children chase Brundibar until they recover the money and he is defeated. The story probably had a particular resonance with the audience in Terezin, who had been wrongfully deprived of their freedom and belongings; most of whom would be murdered by the Nazis. That was the fate that Krasa, when he, along with the other composers and many others, were transported to Auschwitz and murdered in October 1944.

In addition to the compositions already mentioned, Krasa wrote a number of other works, some of which have not survived. The others include *Fünf Lieder*, Op. 4 (1925), *Die Erde ist des Hern*, a psalm setting for soloist, choir and orchestra (1932), *Theme and Variations* for string quartet (*c.* 1935), *Chamber Music for Harpsichord and Seven Instruments* (1936), *Dance for String Trio* (1944) and a number of songs.

Bibliography: Grad; *G*; Leb; J. Nemtsov and B. Schröder-Nauenburg, *Acta Musicologica*, 70 (1998), pp. 22–44; Kennedy, P.455 587-2 [record sleeve]

1. Joža Karas, *Music in Terezin* (New York: Pendragon, 1985), pp. 103–10.

Krein, Alexander Abramovich (b. Nizhni-Novogorod, Russia, 8/20 October 1883; d. Staraya Ruza, near Moscow, 21 April 1951)   Brought up in a musical family. His father was a fine violinist and collected folk songs, including Jewish melodies and this later led to Krein's interest in Jewish traditional music. His brother Grigori Abramovich KREIN and his nephew Julien Grigorovich KREIN were also musicians and composers. Alexander graduated from the Moscow Conservatory in 1908, where he studied cello with Aleksandr von Glehn and composition with Nikolayev, Taneyev and Yavorsky. He became a member of the Society for Jewish Folk Music, which commissioned a set of *Yevreyskiye Eskizi* (Hebrew sketches) for clarinet and string quartet. His first major composition was the symphonic poem *Solomon*. He taught at the People's Conservatory of Moscow from 1912 to 1917. He composed a number of works that show the influence of Jewish melodies, including: *Songs of the Ghetto*; *Hebraic Caprice* for violin and piano; a cantata Kaddish for tenor, chorus and orchestra; the symphonic poem *Poem of Passion* (1913), based on the story of Salome; the opera *Zagmuth* (1930), concerning the Jewish uprising in Babylon in the eighth century BCE; and the tone poem *Birobidjan*. He composed a number of works during the 1920s to accompany plays staged at the Jewish theatres in the Ukraine, Belarus and Moscow. Other influences on his music were those of Debussy and Skriabin. He succumbed to pressure in the 1930s to compose music with political themes, such as *The Soviet Shock Brigade* for orchestra and chorus, using writings from Marx, Lenin and Stalin, and *Threnody in Memory of Lenin* (1925) for chorus and orchestra. Other works include a symphony (1925), a piano sonata (1922) and the ballet *The Rape of Tatania*.

Bibliography: *G*; *HBD*; Ho*;Ly*; M. D. Calvocoressi, *A Survey of Russian Music* (London: Pelican, 1944)

Krein, Grigory Abramovich (b. Nizhni-Novogorod, 18 March 1879; d. Komarova, near St Petersburg, 6 January 1955)   Brother of Alexander Abramovich KREIN, graduated from the Moscow Conservatory in 1905, where he studied violin with Hímalý and composition with GLIÈRE and Paul Juon. He continued his studies in Leipzig with Max Reger (1907–8). Like his brother his works show the influence of Skriabin and the French impressionists; some are on Jewish themes and some political. His works include *Hebrew Rhapsody* for clarinet and orchestra (1926), a violin concerto (1934), string quartet, 2 piano sonatas, *Three Symphonic Episodes on the Life of Lenin* (1937) and a symphony (1946).
Bibliography: *G*; *HBD*; Aron M. Rothmüller, *The Music of the Jews* (London: Vallentine Mitchell, 1953), p. 163*

Krein, Julian Grigor'yevich (b. Moscow, 5 March 1913)   Son of Grigory Abramovich KREIN, studied with his father, and then in Paris at the École Normale de Musique, where he worked with DUKAS (1928–32). He returned to the Soviet Union and taught at the Moscow Conservatory (1934–7). His music also shows the influence of Skriabin and the French impressionists but less use of Jewish folk song. His works include *Five Preludes* for orchestra (1927), a cello concerto (1931), piano pieces and songs.
Bibliography: *G*; *HBD*

Kreisler, Fritz (b. Vienna, 2 February 1875; d. New York, 29 January 1962) Best known as one of the most outstanding violinists of his generation, but he also composed. He learnt the violin from the age of 4, initially from his father, who was a doctor and amateur violinist. At the age of 7 he entered the Vienna Conservatory as the youngest ever pupil. For three years he studied the violin with Joseph Hellmesberger and musical theory with Anton Bruckner. He first performed in public at the age of 9. He went to the Paris Conservatoire and was taught by WIENIAWSKI until he was 12, after which time he received no further violin instruction. In 1889–90 he toured the USA with Moritz Rosenthal. He then studied as a premedical student, giving it up for military service. After this he returned to the violin and in 1899 began what was to become an international career with the Berlin Philharmonic under Nikisch. Elgar dedicated his Violin Concerto to him and he gave the first performance of it in 1910. However, it was Albert Sammons who really launched the Violin Concerto, with its subsequent performances. In World War One he joined the Austrian Army, but was discharged after being wounded. He left for the USA with his American wife, returning to live in Berlin from 1924 to 1934. He was one of a number of musicians who sent a telegram to Hitler to support colleagues who had been discriminated against, and in 1933 he declined a personal invitation from *Furtwängler* to perform with the Berlin Philharmonic Orchestra.[1] With the rise of the Nazis he fled Austria, first going to France but returning permanently to the USA in 1939. In 1941 he was involved in a traffic accident, which left his hearing impaired, but he continued playing until 1950.

Although primarily an outstanding violinist, he also composed. His best-known compositions are the 'bonbons', but he was also capable of more substantial works, such as his string quartet. His compositions can be divided into three categories: his own original works, acknowledged as such; his own original works, published as being arrangements by other, generally minor composers, the so-called classical transcriptions; and transcriptions of works by other composers.

Within the first category are his operetta *Apple Blossom*, his String Quartet in A minor, numerous short pieces such as *Tambourin Chinois*, *Caprice Viennois*, *Schön Rosmarin*, *Shepherd's Madrigal* and *Gypsy Caprice*, and the cadenzas he wrote for Beethoven's, Brahms's and Mozart's violin concertos. A number of his own works he performed, but he ascribed to seventeenth- and eighteenth-century composers such as Boccherini, Porpora, Couperin, Padre Martini, Vivaldi, Friedmann Bach, Cartier, Pugnani, Dittersdorf, Francoeur, Stamitz and Tartini. He did this because he felt there were fewer short pieces written for the violin than the piano. He decided to make up the shortfall by composing works that he would perform. Modesty is said to be the reason that he attributed these 'classical transcriptions' mainly to minor composers rather than have his own name appear repeatedly on concert programmes. When in 1935 he admitted these pieces were hoaxes, many critics were indignant whilst others accepted it as a joke. His 'acknowledged transcriptions' of works from other composers range from those of Bach, Handel, Beethoven and Mozart to Irvine Berlin, KORNGOLD and Percy Grainger.

During the 'Aryanization' of music in Germany in the period of the Third Reich, works by Jewish composers were banned from performance in Germany. From 1933 radio performance of his works and recordings were banned and his publisher Schott of Mainz was banned from selling them. Implementation of the ban presented a dilemma. In 1938 the Carl Lindström Record Company was reluctant to forgo the profits earned from their extremely popular records made by Kreisler, but anti-Semitic pressure eventually forced the company to remove them from their lists. Nevertheless, as late as 1944 the Kreisler cadenza to Beethoven's violin concerto (and also those by JOACHIM and Fleisch) were still being performed. The ministry justified this on the grounds that it was less creative simply to write a cadenza.

Bibliography: *G*; *HBD*; Ho*; Ken; Leb; Ly*

1. Bertha Geissmar, *The Baton and the Jackboot* (London: Hamish Hamilton, 1944), p. 91.

Laderman, Ezra (b. Brooklyn, New York, 29 June 1924)   Studied composition with Stephan WOLPE from 1946 to 1949, with Miriam GIDEON at Brooklyn College and with Luening and Moore at Columbian University, graduating in 1952. He taught at the the Sarah Lawrence College (1960–1 and 1965–6) and was composer-in-residence at the State University of New York at Binghampton from 1971 to 1982. He was visiting composer at Yale University in 1988, where he became dean of music in 1989–95 and then professor of

music from 1996. He has composed two operas, *Galileo Galelei* (1978) and *Marilyn* (1993), based on the life of Marilyn Monroe, eight symphonies, concertos for piano, flute, violin, viola and cello, nine string quartets and film and television scores, for example, *The Eleanor Roosevelt Story* and *The Black Fox*. A number of his works have Jewish themes, for example: the cantata *And David Wept* (1971); his third symphony, *Jerusalem* (1973); *Meditations on Isaiah* for cello (1973); and *A Mass for Cain* for voices, chorus and orchestra (1983).
Bibliography: *AG*; *CC*; *G*; Grad; *HBD*; Ly*; www.schirmer.com/composers/laderman

Lassen, Eduard (b. Copenhagen, 13 April 1830; d. Weimar, 15 January 1904) Moved to Brussels with his family when he was a child. He studied at the Brussels Conservatory, where he won prizes for piano (1844), composition (1847) and the Prix de Rome in 1851. He composed two operas, incidental music for Goethe's Faust, a ballet, orchestral works and some songs. He met Liszt when he travelled to Weimar. Liszt conducted Lassen's opera *Landgraf Ludwigs Brautfahrt* at Weimar, where Lassen succeeded him as *Kapellmeister* in 1858.
Bibliography: *G*; *HBD*; Ho*; Ken

Lavry, Marc (b. Riga, 22 December 1903; d. Haifa, 24 March 1967) Studied at the Riga and Leipzig Conservatories and privately with Glazunov. He had various appointments as an opera and ballet conductor in Germany. In April 1933, two months after the Nazi rise to power, he returned to Riga, which was the target of a fascist coup a year later. He decided to emigrate, but initially could not decide between Palestine and Russia. He visited Palestine on a tourist visa and was soon employed to write incidental music. His talent was apparent to the authorities and he was allowed to stay. The new pioneering spirit in Palestine at the time strongly influenced his compositions. In 1937 he wrote his successful symphonic poem *Emek*, based on a popular song, expressing the joy of returning to his homeland. It was the first locally composed piece to be played by the Palestine Orchestra. It combines the eastern European traditions that he had left behind with Palestinian folk music, including a hora dance theme.

Further successes were the oratorio *Shir ha'shirum* (Song of Songs, 1944) and the opera *Dan the Guard* (1947). The latter was the first Hebrew opera produced in what was to become Israel. The action takes place on a kibbutz and portrays the conflict between the individual and the collectivism of the kibbutz. Again, its musical style combined the old and new traditions. Lavry conducted the Palestine Folk Opera from 1941 to 1947 and directed the music department of the radio station Kol Zion LaGola, broadcasting to overseas Jewish communities. His second piano concerto was premiered in Paris in 1948, and in 1955 he composed settings for the Sacred Service *Avodat ha'kodesh*, which was commissioned by the Emanu-El congregation of San Francisco. His other works include *From Dan to Beersheva* (1947), *Country Dances from Israel* (1952) and *Israeli Dances*. Although his music was popular in the pioneering days of Palestine and the early days of the State of Israel, it is not performed so often at the present time.

Bibliography: *G*; Grad; *HBD*; Ho*; Jehoash Hirshberg, *Music in the Jewish Community of Palestine, 1880–1948* (Oxford: Clarendon Press, 1995)

Lazarus, Daniel (b. Paris, 13 December 1898; d. Paris, 27 June 1964) Studied at the Paris Conservatoire with Diemer, Leroux and Vidal. After this he became musical director at the Théâtre du Vieux Colombier (1921–5), artistic director at the Opéra-Comique (1936–9), choirmaster of the Paris Opéra (1946–56) and professor at the Schola Cantorum. He was primarily a conductor, but also composed three operas, a piano concerto, a symphony and three ballets. Lazarus was noted for his confrontation with the rising anti-Semitism in France in the 1930s. He became active in the musical programmes of the Popular Front, and composed a large-scale work entitled *Symphonie avec hymne*. This five-movement work traces the history of the Jewish people. Each movement has a title and brief synopsis, for example, *Marche funèbre. En mémoire des combattants Juifs de chaque pays, qui sont morts pendant la grande guerre pour défendre leur patrie* (In memory of the Jewish combatants of each country, who died during the great war to defend their country). His message was to emphasize the patriotism of Jews in their respective nations, despite persecution.

Bibliography: *G*; Jane Fulcher, 'The Preparation for Vichy: Anti-Semitism in the French Musical Culture Between the Two World Wars', *Musical Quarterly*, 73 (1995), pp. 458–75*

Ledec, Egon (b. Ksotele nad Orlici, Bohemia, 16 March 1889; d. Auschwitz, 17 October 1944) Primarily a violinist. He graduated from the Prague Conservatory in 1906 and then joined the Czech Philharmonic as a violinist. After a period in the army he returned to the Czech Philharmonic in 1926 and was made leader in 1927, a position he retained until 1939. He was imprisoned in Terezin and eventually sent to Auschwitz, where he was murdered on 17 October 1944. The only work of his known to have survived is a Gavotte for Strings.

Bibliography: Grad; Joža Karas, *Music in Terezín, 1941–1945* (New York: Pendragon, 1985); http://gray.music.rhodes.edu/musichtmls

Leef, Yinam (b. Jerusalem, 21 December 1953) Studied piano at the Rubin Academy in Jerusalem and composition with KOPYTMAN. He continued his studies at the University of Pennsylvannia with Wernick, ROCHBERG and Crumb, and with Berio at Tanglewood. He returned to Jerusalem to teach composition and music theory at the Rubin Academy. His compositions include *Turns*, for wind trio, *Fireflies*, for soprano, flute and harpsichord, *A Place of Fire*, for mezzo-soprano and chamber orchestra (1985), *Fanfares and*

Whispers, for trumpet and string orchestra (1986), and *Sounds, Shadows*, for chorus (1987).
Bibliography: *G*; Grad

Leibowitz, René (b. Warsaw, 17 February 1913; d. Paris, 29 August 1972) Composer, conductor and musicologist. He is now best known through his writings and teachings concerning the Second Viennese School. He grew up in the household of Arthur SCHNABEL, who was a member of the early Schoenberg circle. From 1930 to 1933 he studied with SCHOENBERG and Webern in Berlin and Vienna and this had a decisive influence on him. In 1933 he had lessons on orchestration from Ravel. In 1937, after studying conducting with Monteux he made his début as conductor, conducting throughout Europe and the United States. During World War Two he went into hiding, first in Vichy and later in Paris. In 1945 he settled in Paris, where he founded the International Festival of Chamber Music. During the 1930s and early 1940s Schoenberg's music was rarely performed; the Nazis made concerted efforts to suppress music composed by Jews and considered twelve-tone music degenerate. Leibowitz, more than anyone else, was responsible for its revival in Europe. This he did through his teachings and writings and by performing his works. It was a revelation to Boulez when in 1945 he heard Leibowitz conduct a performance of Schoenberg's Wind Quintet.[1] Boulez decided to study with Leibowitz and became active in continuing the promotion and development of twelve-tone music. Leibowitz's first two books, *Schönberg et son Ecole* (1946) and *Introduction à la musique de douze sons* (1949) were well received, although his later writings were rather controversial. The techniques and aesthetics of his own compositions, which include five operas, a symphony, three piano concertos and four string quartets, are similar to those of Schoenberg and Berg. He completed Schnabel's last work, *Duodecimet* for strings, which has been described as a minor masterpiece.
Bibliography: *G*; *HBD*; Ho*; Ly*
1. Joan Peyser, *To Boulez and Beyond* (New York: Billboard Books, 1999), pp. 159 and 163*

Levant, Oscar (b. Pittsburgh, 27 December 1906; d. Los Angeles, 14 August 1972)   Composer, pianist, writer and film actor. His initial education was in Pittsburgh, but he later studied piano with Zygmunt Stojowski and composition with SCHOENBERG. He began lessons with Schoenberg in June 1935 and was regarded as one of his most talented pupils. Under Schoenberg's guidance he composed a piano concerto (1936), a string quartet (1937) and a nocturne for orchestra (1937). He discontinued his lessons with Schoenberg when he moved away from Beverly Hills, but maintained friendly relations with him, and in 1939 was able to support him in becoming a member of the American Society of Composers. Levant met GERSHWIN in the mid-1920s and became one of his finest interpreters on piano. He was influenced by Gershwin in his song-writing. He wrote scores for several films, including

Street Girl and *Tanned Legs*, and acted in some, for example, *Dance of Life* and *An American in Paris*. He also composed two sonatinas for piano, two string quartets, orchestral suites and a dirge dedicated to Gershwin. In these the influence of his teacher, Schoenberg, is evident. He also wrote three books of autobiographical reminiscence: *A Smattering of Ignorance* (1940), *The Memoirs of an Amnesiac* (1965) and *The Unimportance of Being Oscar* (1968).
Bibliography: *AG*; *G*; Ho*; Sabine M. Feisst, 'Arnold Schoenberg and Cinematic Art', *Musical Quarterly*, 83 (1999), pp. 93–113; Edward Jablonski, *Gershwin Remembered* (London: Faber, 1992)

Levenson, Boris (b. Ackermann, Bessarabia, 3 October 1884; d. New York, 3 November 1947)   Graduated from St Petersburg Conservatory, where he studied under Glazunov and Rimsky Korsakov. In 1920 he emigrated to America. His compositions include a symphony, *Palestine Suite* (1927), oriental dances for violin and piano, *Hebrew Suite* for eight instruments, and a number of folk-song arrangements.
Bibliography: A. Ho and D. Feofanov, *Biographical Dictionary of Russian/Soviet Composers* (New York: Greenwood Press, 1989); C. Abravanel,* CPO 999 630-2 [record sleeve]

Lévy, Ernst (b. Basel, 18 November 1895; d. Morges, Switzerland, 19 April 1981)   Studied in Basel and Paris and directed a piano master class in Basel University from 1917 to 1921. The rise in Nazism drove him to leave Switzerland for America. He taught in several music schools in the USA from 1941 to 1966 and then retired to Switzerland. His works, written in a tonal style, include 15 symphonies, four string quartets, various psalm settings and songs.
Bibliography: *G*; *HBD*; Ho*

Lewandowski, Louis [Lazarus] **Eleazar** (b. Wreschen, near Posen, Germany [Września near Poznań, Poland], 3 April 1821; d. Berlin, 3 February 1894) Born in what was at the time the province of Posen. When Poland underwent its third partition in 1795 the province of Posen was created as part of Prussia, but nevertheless retained much of its Polish character. His father was the local amateur cantor, and he and his four brothers sang with their father from an early age. The family was poor, and after his mother's death when he was 13 he was sent to Berlin, where he became *singerl* (boy soprano) to the cantor Asher Lion at the Heidereutergasse synagogue. In Berlin he met Alexander MENDELSSOHN, cousin of Felix. Although Alexander had converted to Protestantism, he still felt a strong bond with a poor Jewish boy seeking education, and helped him to obtain a music scholarship to the Sing-Akademie in Berlin, where he was the first Jewish student. A serious nervous disorder meant that he had to give up his studies for a few years.
     Berlin was the centre of the Reform Movement, but Asher Lion was reactionary and not anxious to change the form of the *chazzanuth*. However,

in 1838 Hirsch Weintraub went to Berlin to give a synagogue concert that was so well received the congregation was persuaded to modernize the music at the service. Lion wanted to introduce music like that which SULZER had introduced to Vienna, but was not capable of doing this himself, as he read music only with difficulty. In 1844 the Berlin Jewish community invited Lewandowski to organize the choir and become its director. This was the first post of its kind in a synagogue, since it was normally the cantor who was responsible for the singing. In 1845 cantor Abraham Lichtenstein replaced Asher Lion, and this provided the stimulus for a great leap in Lewandowski's musical development. Lichtenstein had a brilliant tenor voice and also played the violin. It was he who brought the traditional *Kol Nidre* tune to Max Bruch's attention. He inspired Lewandowski to arrange synagogue singing for four-part choral singing. In 1855 the Berlin community sent both Lewandowski and Lichtenstein to Vienna for six months to study with Suzler.

In 1864 Lewandowski was invited to become choir director and Lichstenstein, cantor of the New Oranienburgerstrasse synagogue in Berlin, where he had the opportunity to create complete services with organ accompaniment. His settings for the Sabbath Service and festivals for solo and two-part verse were published as *Kol Rinnah* in 1871, and his four-part settings for choir and congregation and solo pieces with organ accompaniment for the whole year cycle were published in the two-volume *Todah v'Zimrah* (1876 and 1882). He also wrote a number of symphonies, overtures, cantatas and songs. Although his sacred music is extensively used in synagogues throughout world today, his secular music is virtually unknown.
Bibliography: *G*; Ho*; Ly*; A. Z. Idelsohn, *Jewish Music in its Historical Development* (New York: Schocken, 1967), pp. 269–84

Liebermann, Rolf (b. Zurich, 14 September 1910; d. Paris, 2 January 1999) Studied law at the University of Zurich and music at the José Berr Conservatory in Zurich. His composition teacher there was Hermann Scherchen, and after completing his studies he acted as assistant and secretary to Scherchen in Prague, Budapest and Vienna from 1937 to 1938. He returned to Switzerland in 1938, where he undertook lessons in serialism with Vladimir VOGEL. His subsequent contributions to music were split between composition and administration. He was a producer for Swiss Radio in Zurich from 1945 to 1950, manager of the Beromünster Radio Orchestra from 1950 to 1957, music director for North German Radio in Hamburg from 1957 to 1959, general manager of the Staatsoper in Hamburg from 1959 to 1973, general manager of the Paris Opéra from 1973 to 1980, and finally coming out of retirement to return to the Staatsoper in Hamburg from 1985 to 1987. The administrative position in which he achieved most was undoubtedly the Staatsoper in Hamburg. He did much to premiere many modern works by composers such as Krenek, Penderewski, KAGEL and Stockhausen and also presented new stagings of works by Berg, Janáček and Britten.

His most active composing period was during the 1950s. He effectively stopped composing from the early 1960s, but then resumed again after retiring from his managerial duties in the 1980s. Most of his work has a strongly theatrical emphasis. His first opera was *Leonora 40/45*, which premiered in Basle in 1952. It has a multiplicity of styles and at one point in the first act a piano recital takes place in which a piano sonata by Liebermann is followed by the third *Liebestraum* waltz of Liszt. *Concerto for Jazz Band and Orchestra* (1954) uses both serial technique and jazz, and is an attempt to assimilate both high and popular styles of the day. It enjoyed a brief success. *Penelope* (1953–4) was his most successful opera. The *Penelope* of Greek mythology is given a twentieth-century setting in the environs of Paris during the German occupation. The music uses in a rather free twelve-note technique, a Hindemithian form of diatonicism and boogie-woogie. Of his late compositions the most successful are *Liaison* for cello, piano and orchestra (1983) and the opera *Der Wald* (1985–6), which was first performed in Geneva in 1987.
Bibliography: CC; G; Ho*

Ligeti, György Sándor (b. Diciosânmartin, Transylvania [Tîrnǎveni, Romania], 28 May 1923)   Born in Transylvania, then part of Hungary. He came from a middle-class Jewish family of Austrian descent. His father was an economist, who wrote a number of books on economics, and his mother was an ophthalmologist. There was a strong musical tradition in the family; his father played the violin and his great-uncle was the famous violinist Leopold Auer. The name *Ligeti*, which was adopted by his grandfather, derives from the Hungarian *Liget* meaning 'copse' and is a false translation of the German *Aue* meaning 'water meadow'. By the time Ligeti was 6 the family moved to what is now Cluj in Romania.

Although Ligeti wanted to play the violin from an early age, he did not start to learn an instrument until he was 14, and then it was the piano. When he was 18 it was intended that he should go to university to study physics, but at the time, 1941, the anti-Jewish laws made it very difficult to go to university, so instead his father said he could go to the Budapest Conservatory. Soon afterwards he decided he wanted to be a composer. Although 1941 marked the end of his formal science training, Ligeti's scientific/mathematical bent is evident in his subsequent musical career. For example, during his interest in electronic music in the late 1950s he mathematically analyzed Boulez's *Structures 1a*. From 1941 to 1943 Ligeti studied composition with Farkas at the Kolozsvár (Cluj) Conservatory, and in the summers of 1942 and 1943 he took private lessons with Kardosa in Budapest. His first published composition was a song *Kinereti* (Hebrew for the Sea of Galilee), which was published in 1942.

In January 1944 Ligeti was called up for military service. The anti-Jewish laws in force at the time were restrictive for his parents, and Ligeti had to do forced labour, which in his case included the dangerous job of transporting heavy explosives to the front line. By June 1944 the deportation of Jews to concentration camps had begun, and it was around this time that his parents and brother were sent to Auschwitz. His father died in Bergen Belsen and his brother was murdered in Mathausen; his mother survived Auschwitz, largely because she was a camp doctor. There was a brief period when someone in the defence ministry wanted to save Jews in the service of the army. Those called up earlier or later perished. Ligeti was called up during that 'window' and considers he was fortunate to survive. He deserted the labour corps in the front line in October 1944, during a battle, making his way back on foot to Transylvania.

After the war, in May 1945, he went to the Budapest Academy of Music, where he graduated in 1949 and then a year later was appointed professor of harmony, counterpoint and formal analysis. He remained there until 1956. Under the communist regime of the early 1950s, compositions had to be vetted before publication. Ligeti kept most of his important compositions unpublished. In addition to these restrictions it was not possible to gain access to works of the Second Viennese School or musical developments in the West generally, and much of Bartok's music was proscribed. Amongst Ligeti's compositions of this period are his first string quartet (1953–4) and six bagatelles for wind (1953). The influences of Bartok and Stravinsky are evident in works of this period, although elements of a distinctive style are also present. During the period 1953 to 1956, after Stalin's death, some of the restrictions were lifted and so the first five of the six bagatelles were able to be performed, but the sixth, which is chromatic, was not. By 1955 Ligeti was able to receive material from abroad and saw and heard the music of SCHOENBERG and Berg for the first time. In 1956 he began writing a twelve-tone work, *Requiem*.

During the Russian invasion of Hungary in 1956 the jamming of radio broadcasts was stopped and he managed to hear the first broadcast of Stockhausen's *Gesang der Jünglinge*, which impressed him greatly. In December 1956 he and his wife managed, along with ten others, to get to the border in a mail train, hiding under the mailbags. They crossed the border on foot. From February 1957 he settled in Cologne, where Stockhausen organized a scholarship for him. The timing of this move, although dictated by political events, was opportune, for Ligeti was able to interact with the leading musical avant-garde figures who met at Darmstadt each summer between 1957 and 1966 for the International Summer Course for New Music. Initially, when first founded in 1946 these were aimed at awakening young German composers to music forbidden in the Hitler years, but by the mid-1950s they had become the international centre for developments in the musical composition sphere, including electronics and aleatory music.

Ligeti arrived at the same time as Mauricio KAGEL, and visitors included Karlheinz Stockhausen, Pierre Boulez, Bruno Maderna and Luigi Nono. Ligeti was initially silent, whilst he absorbed the new developments and as part of this analyzed Boulez's *Structures 1a* (see above). He concluded that for him, neither Schoenberg's serialism, nor Boulez's form of total serialism, was the way forward. His first composition in the electronic medium was *Glissandi* and his important works of this period include *Apparitions* (1958–9), *Atmosphères* (1961) and *Volumina* for organ (1961–2). For many of Ligeti's works the titles are in French. This he explained is because Hungarian is inaccessible to most audiences, and German too heavy. The successful premiere of *Apparitions* meant that his later works were readily taken up by contemporary music festivals, and his music became more widely known. *Atmosphères* is one of his most performed works. Both works use a technique that he described as micropolyphony. He uses clusters of sounds, the range of pitches of which expand and contract. The clear articulation of melody, harmony and rhythm are abandoned in favour of the timbre and texture of the sound itself. In 1959 he moved to Vienna, where he stayed until 1969. From 1961 to 1971 he was guest professor at the Stockholm Academy of Music. In 1973 he was appointed professor of composition at Hamburg Musikhochschule.

Ligeti was brought to the attention of a wider public in 1968, when Stanley Kubrick used the music from his *Lux aeterna*, a piece for unaccompanied voices, *Atmosphères*, and the Kyrie from *Requiem* (1965) in a very successful film, *2001: A Space Odyssey*. This was without Ligeti's knowledge or permission. His opera *Le Grand macabre*, based on a condensed version of a play by the Belgium writer Michel de Ghelderode, conjures up a Breughel painting. It is a raucous burlesque, composed for the Stockholm Opera, depicting the end of the world as experienced by the characters of 'Breugelland'. Ligeti stated that 'it follows the tradition of the medieval dance of death, the mystery play and punch-and-judy show, the theatre of fairgrounds and suburbs'. Ligeti's humour is evident in many of his works. For example, *Poème symphonique pour 100 metronomes* is a gibe at musicians' rigid adherence to tempo markings.

His works of the 1960s are characterized by dense saturating semitone clusters with an absence of melody, harmony and rhythm, in favour of texture and timbre, what he described as *mikropolyphonie*, and this technique became more refined in works such as *Lux aeterna* (1966) and *Lontano* (1967). By the 1970s and later melody, rhythm and harmony begin to reappear. For example, in *Chamber Concerto* (1969–70) the *mikropolyphonie* is magnified so that individual lines can be audibly discerned and melody evident. During the 1970s to 1980s he showed a greater degree of eclecticism. For example, in *Le Grand macabre* there is a toccata in the manner of Monteverdi, but motor horns are used rather than trombones. The work also makes references to Verdi's *Falstaff* and Rossini's *Barber of Seville*. In other works the influence of Caribbean and rock music is evident. Rhythm is an important element in *Hungarian Rock* (*Chaconne*) for harpsichord (1978). Later works such as *Horn Trio* (1983), *Piano Concerto* (1988) and *Violin Concerto* (1992) show a rich and wide range of harmony. His more recent compositions are generally considered to be in a more accessible style than his music of the 1950s and 1960s.

Bibliography: CC; G*; Leb; Paul Griffiths, *György Ligeti* (London: Robson, 1983)*; R. Toop, *György Ligeti* (London: Phaidon, 1999)

Lilien, Ignace (b. Lemberg [L'viv, Ukraine], 29 May 1897; d. The Hague, 10 May 1964)   Lived in Lemberg until 1914. At the time Lemberg had a high Jewish population and one of his contemporaries was the famous cellist, Feuermen. In 1914 Lilien went on a cycling tour of the museums of Europe and found himself cut off in The Hague at the outbreak of World War One. He decided to stay in the Netherlands and trained as a technical engineer at the Technical University of Delft. He became a chemical engineer and a musician and took Dutch citizenship. After the war he began composing and performing as a pianist. He wrote songs, mostly with his own words, close in style to those of Brecht and WEILL, for example, *Fünf trunkene Lieder* (1920), *Veronica* (1920), *Quatre chansons des mendiant* (1923) and *Mietskaserne* (1932). During the 1930s he lived in the Bohemian town of Reichenberg (Liberec), where he composed *Modern Times*, a sonata for violin and piano (1935), the last movement of which became so popular that it was published separately as *Rondo Brésilien*. He composed two operas, *Beatrys* (1922) and *Great Catherine* (1932). The latter was opposed by the Nazis at its premiere at Wiesbaden. He returned to the Netherlands in 1939 and, as a Jew, spent the war years in hiding. During this time he composed a number of songs on Dutch texts, including *Ballade van Westerbork*, which is a setting of his own poems, depicting the deportation of Jewish children from Westerbork to concentration camps in eastern Europe. After the war he visited South America, and incorporated elements of South American folk music into works such as the symphonic poem *Les Palmes dans le vent* (1955). Among his late works is the school cantata *A Negro Girl Goes to School*, dealing with race problems in the USA.
Bibliography: *G*; http://www.leosmit.nl/eng/contemporaries/jewish_text.htm*

Lipkin, Malcolm (b. Liverpool, 2 May 1932)   Studied piano with Gordon Green (1944–8) and then continued his musical education at the Royal College of Music from 1949 to 1953. He studied privately with Matyas SEIBER from 1954 to 1957, and also with Bernard Stevens and Boris BLACHER (1954–7). He lectured in the department of external studies at Oxford University from 1965 to 1975 and at Kent University. He first gained recognition when his fourth piano sonata was performed at the 1954 Cheltenham Festival, and then his piano concerto at the 1959 Cheltenham Festival. His first symphony, *Sinfonia da Roma* (1965), portrays the dark side of city life, and the second, *The Pursuit* (1977) and third, *Sun* (1986), portray the span of modern life. Other orchestral works include two violin concertos and a flute concerto. The second violin concerto (1960–2) was commissioned by Yfrah Neaman: its slow movement is a lament for the early death in an accident of his teacher Matyas Seiber. He composed a setting of Psalm 96 in 1969, and of Psalms 121 and 92 to celebrate the centenary of the West London Synagogue in 1973. He composed *Clifford's Tower* for instrumental ensemble based on William of Newburg's account of the massacre of Jews in York in 1190, for the Cheltenham Festival of 1980. His chamber works include a string quartet (1951), a wind quintet (1985), a piano

trio (1988), *Naboth's Vineyard* for recorders, cello and harpsichord (1982), *Variations on a Theme of Bartok* for string quartet (1992) and five piano sonatas and songs. *Prelude and Dance* for cello and piano (1988) was written in memory of Jacqueline Du Pré. His orchestral works include three symphonies and *From Across La Manche* for chamber orchestra (1998).
Bibliography: *G*; *HBD*; Leb; A. Burn, *Musical Times*, 124 (1983), pp. 25–7; H. Good, *Musical Times*, 110 (1969), pp. 1237–40; www.malcolmlipkin.co.uk

Lokshin, Alexander Lazarevich (b. Biysk, Russia, 19 September 1920; d. Moscow, 11 June 1987)   Son of Lazar Zaharovich Lokshin, an accountant, and Korotkina Maria Borisovna, an obstetrician. During the extermination of the *kulaks* his family lost their house and property and moved to the large town of Novosibirsk. There he began studying the piano from the age of 6, and from 1930 attended the music school at Novosibirsk. In 1936 he attended the Moscow Conservatory studying composition with Myaskovsky, graduating in 1944. His graduation piece, a symphonic poem, entitled *Wait for Me*, based on verses by Somonov, was performed by Mravinsky and the Leningrad Philharmonic Orchestra. It was later criticized in *Pravda* in an article entitled 'Don't Wait for me'. Although he began teaching musical literature, instrumentation and score reading at the Moscow Conservatory in 1945, he was dismissed in 1948 during a campaign against 'cosmopolitism', that is, against Jews. In spite of Myaskovsky's support he was unable to gain employment in a musical institute. He made a living from paid commissions such as film scores and radio and theatre plays. He led a secluded life during which he composed prolifically. His favoured genre was the vocal symphony. His works have been taken up by international conductors, for example, Mravinsky, Barshai, Rozhdestvensky and Jansons. Shostakovich described his first symphony as a work of genius. Nevertheless, the premieres of many of his works were delayed in the USSR because his choice of texts conflicted with the official ideology. Lokshin had been extremely consistent in his clearly expressed antipathy to Soviet officialdom and any artistic compromise. This meant that until the collapse of the USSR his works were only rarely heard in the West. Rudolf Barsai felt that he had been greatly underrated as a composer.

He composed 11 symphonies, 10 with voices (1st, 1958; 2nd, 1963; 3rd, 1966; 4th, 1968; 5th, 1970; 6th, 1971; 7th, 1972; 8th, 1973; 9th, 1975; 10th, 1976; 11th, 1976). His other works include piano quintet (1940), *Hungarian Fantasia* for violin and orchestra (1952), Clarinet Quintet (1955), a comic oratorio, *The Roach* (1963), *Songs of Margaret* for soprano and chamber orchestra (1973), *Three Scenes from Goethe's 'Faust'* for soprano and orchestra (1980), the cantata *Grieving Mother* (words by Akhmatova, 1981), a string quintet in memory of Shostakovich (1981) and *Symphonietta* for tenor and eight instruments (1983).
Bibliography: *G*; Ken; A. Ho and D. Feofanov, *Dictionary of Soviet/Russian Composers* (New York: Greenwood Press, 1989); G. V. Keldish (ed.), *The Musical*

Encyclopaedia (in Russian) (Moscow, 1990); http://www.df.ru/~loka/lokshin. htm*

Lourié, Arthur Vincent [Lur'ye, Arthur Sergeyevich] (b. Propoisk, Mogilev Province [now Slavogorod, Belarus], 2/14 May 1891; d. Princeton, USA, 12 October 1966)   Studied at the St Petersburg Conservatory. This had become possible because the director, Alexander Glazunov, had succeeded in abolishing the discriminatory quota for Jewish applicants. It coincided with a period of greater Jewish emancipation. Nevertheless, Lourié converted to Catholicism in his teens. He soon abandoned his formal studies at the Conservatory and began experimenting with impressionist and also with atonal and serial techniques, and later used quarter-tones. His early works include three sonatinas, the four *Préludes Fragile* and *Synthesis,* all of which are piano works dating from 1915. He belonged to the artists' circle that included Alexander Blok, Anna Akhmatova and Ossip Mandelstam. He was at first an enthusiastic supporter of the October Revolution, and was appointed commissar for music in the Soviet Republic in 1918, but in 1921 he went on an official visit to Berlin and did not return. There he met Busoni, with whom he had cultural and philosophical interests in common. He moved to Paris in 1924, remaining there until the German occupation in 1941, when he fled to America, becoming a US citizen in 1947. In the 1920s he generally adopted tonal harmony in works such as *Sonata Liturgica* for alto voices and chamber orchestra (1928) and *Concerto Spirituale* for piano solo, voices and orchestra (1929). The former uses melodic ideas akin to plainsong and the whole work is suggestive of Byzantine chant. He composed an opera-ballet entitled *The Feast During the Plague* (1935) and the opera *The Blackamoor of Peter the Great* (1961), both based on Pushkin's writings. His other works include two symphonies, three string quartets, several piano works and other chamber music.
Bibliography: *G; HBD;* Leb; Ly*; J. Nemtsov, J.EDA 012-2 [record sleeve]

Lucký, Štepán (b. Žilina, Slovakia, 20 January 1919)   Studied at the Prague Conservatory under Alois Hába, Otakar Šín and Jaroslav Řídký from 1936 to 1939. After the universities were closed by the Nazis he joined the Resistance and fought in the Slovak National Uprising against the Germans in 1944. He was captured and imprisoned in Auschwitz and Buchenwald concentration camps. He survived, but a serious injury to his right hand made a career as a piano virtuoso impossible after the war. After his release in 1945 he continued his studies with Řídký until 1947, and at the same time studied musicology at Charles University, Prague, from 1945 to 1948. He worked as a music critic, was head of music for Czech television and taught opera production at Prague Academy from 1956 to 1961.

During the 1940s he experimented with his compositions, which include *Three Etudes* for quarter-tone piano, a cello concerto, a piano concerto and *Divertimento,* for three trombones and strings. During the 1950s and 1960s he

concentrated on film music, producing 44 feature films and over 100 short films, later returning to concert music with works such as the Violin Concerto (1965), Sonata for Solo Violin (1969), String Octet (1970), *Tre pezzi per i Due Boeme* for bass clarinet and piano (1970) and *Divertimento* for wind quintet (1974).
Bibliography: *G*; Petar Zapletal, *Czech Music* (1995), pp. 1–2

Lupo family   Family of musicians active in the English Royal Court from 1540 to 1642. It is likely that they were descended from Sephardic Jews expelled from Spain in 1492 and subsequently settled in Milan and Venice. Ambrose Lupo (b. Milan?; d. London, 10 February 1591), a composer and string player, was the founder of the dynasty. His Jewish ancestry is revealed in a probate document of 1542, when he is described as 'Ambrosius deomaleyex', apparently a garbled rendering of 'de Olmaliach' or 'de Almaliach' a version of the Sephardic name 'Elmaleh'. The family included Ambrose's sons, Peter (b. Venice, *c.* 1535; d. London, 1608) and Joseph (b. Venice, *c.* 1537; d. Richmond, *c.* 1616), Joseph's son Thomas (b. London, *c.* 1571; d. London, 1627) and Thomas's son Theophilus. Of these, Ambrose, Joseph, Thomas and Theophilus were composers as well as being string players. They were viol players and played the role of introducing an Italian style of consort playing to England. In addition to playing the viol, Thomas was also a lutenist, singer and composer. He became Court Musician in May 1591, initially to Queen Elizabeth I and then King James I, and from 16 February until his death held the post of Composer to the Violins. His works include vocal music (anthems, motets, songs and madrigals) and instrumental music (fantasias and dances).
Bibliography: *G**; *Grad**; *HBD*; R. Charteris, *Lupo, T. The Six-Part Consort Music* (London: Fretwork, 1993)

Ma'ayani, Ami (b. Ramat Gan, near Tel Aviv, 13 January 1936)   Studied at the New Jerusalem Academy of Music from 1951 to 1953 and also studied composition privately with BEN HAIM and conducting with Eytan Lustig. He studied architecture at the Haifa Technion, graduating in 1960. Between 1961 and 1965 he visited Columbia University, New York to study electronic music with Ussachevsky. He taught at the Jerusalem Academy (1972–3) and was appointed conductor of the Israel National Youth Orchestra in 1971. His compositions include two symphonies, two concertos for harp, two for piano, and one each for violin, viola, cello, and guitar; *Qumran*, a symphonic poem (1971), *Mismorim* for high voice and orchestra (1965), *Hebrew Requiem* for mezzo-soprano, chorus and orchestra (1977) and *Sinfonietta on Popular Hebraic Themes* for chamber orchestra (1982).
Bibliography: *G*; *Grad*; *HBD*; Ken

Maazel, Lorin Varencove (b. Neuilly, France, 6 March 1930)   Best known as a conductor, but also as a violinist and least well as a composer. Although born in France he was brought up in Los Angeles and Pittsburgh. He studied conducting with Vladimir Bakeleinikov, and also took violin and piano lessons. He was a child prodigy. Bakeleinikov, realizing Maazel's talent, put him on the podium to conduct the visiting University of Idaho Orchestra at the age of 5. When Baleinkov moved to Pittsburgh, the Maazel family followed so that he could continue his lessons. After Toscanini watched him at rehearsals, he invited him to conduct the NBC Symphony Orchestra, and by the age of 11 he had conducted his first complete programme. He studied mathematics and philosophy at Pittsburgh University, and then won a Fulbright Scholarship to study baroque music in Italy. In 1948 he joined the Pittsburgh Symphony Orchestra as a violinist. In 1960 he became the first, and the youngest, American to conduct at the Bayreuth Festival. His conducting posts have included the Berlin Radio Symphony Orchestra (1965–75), the Cleveland Orchestra (1972–82) the Orchestre Nationale de France (1977–82), the Pittsburgh Symphony Orchestra (1988–96) and the Bavarian Radio Symphony Orchestra since 1993.

He has conducted the Vienna Philharmonic Orchestra, and was artistic director and general manager of the Vienna State Opera from 1982, but left amid controversy in 1984. There are parallels between his relationship with the Vienna State Opera and that of MAHLER's. A resident diplomat is quoted as saying: 'Maazel is everything the Viennese don't like. He prefers Italian opera to German; he is unemotional; he doesn't care for *schmalz* [excessive sentimentality]; he is American and he is a Jew.' For a spirited account of Maazel as conductor, see Lebrecht.[1]

Maazel has devoted more time to composition since the early1990s. His works include *Music for Violoncello and Orchestra*, Op. 10, *Music for Flute and Orchestra*, Op. 11, *Music for Violin and Orchestra*, Op. 12 and *Symphonic Movement – Farewells*, Op. 14 and *The Empty Pot*, a Chinese fable cantata for treble, narrator, children's chorus and orchestra.

Bibliography: *G*; *HBD*; Ken; M. Anderson, 'Maazel as Composer', *Tempo*, 213 (2000), p. 50; Edward Greenfield, *Gramophone*, 78 (2000), p. 13

1. Norman Lebrecht, *The Maestro Myth* (London: Simon & Schuster, 1991), pp. 205-10.

Mahler, Gustav (b. Kaliste, Bohemia, 7 July 1860; d. Vienna, 18 May 1911) Brought up in a small town near Jihlava (Iglau) on the border of Bohemia and Moravia at a time when the Austro-Hungarian Empire retained a fragile unity, which was to collapse in 1916. Iglau was essentially a German-speaking town surrounded by a Czech-speaking majority in the nearby countryside. The German-speaking majority were Catholics, with a Jewish minority. Tolerance was on the increase with Jews being accorded full civil and political rights in 1867, although anti-Semitism was also much in evidence.

Mahler had an unhappy childhood. His parents were ill-matched and frequently quarrelled, and of the 14 children his mother gave birth to between 1858 and 1879 only 6 survived until adulthood, and one of these committed suicide at the age of 21. Mahler's father, Bernard, was an innkeeper and by temperament exuberant and authoritarian, whereas his mother, Maria, was quiet, affectionate and retiring. By 1872 Bernard was sufficiently well off to be was able to buy the house next door to the inn. This moderate wealth was offset by the needs of a large family. Bernard strove to improve himself both socially and intellectually and had a passion for reading. Once it became clear that Gustav had musical talent his father encouraged him to make the most of it.

A number of events during his childhood and youth made a strong impression on Gustav, and these can be traced in his mature compositions. He witnessed the deaths of a number of his siblings, mostly when they were less than 2 years old. The death that distressed him the most was that of his brother Ernst at the age of 14. He was only a year younger than Gustav and died of pericarditis after a protracted illness. Ernst was Gustav's favourite brother and companion; they played together and shared musical experiences. On one occasion, fleeing into the street because of a quarrel between his parents, he encountered a barrel organ playing *Ach, du Liebe Augustin*. This is often compared with his ability to juxtapose tragedy with banal light amusement in his music. He was very familiar with folk songs from an early age. An infantry regiment was based in Iglau and he often heard soldiers singing as they marched past his home. He was also familiar with synagogue music, although the much-quoted anecdote that as a child he shouted 'Be quiet! It's horrible' in a synagogue service and then began to sing at the top of his voice *Eits a binkel Kasi* suggests he was not enamoured with it on that occasion. His parents realized he had musical talent at an early age. He began piano lessons at the age of 5 and progressed so well that he performed in public at a local concert in 1870. He completed his first composition, *Polka with Introductory Funeral March*, at the age of 6. His reputation locally was such that he was asked to give piano lessons to boys only a little younger than himself. At about the age of 15 Mahler was asked to decipher some manuscripts by Thalberg for the manager of an estate near Iglau. On hearing Mahler sight-read them, the manager, Gustav Schwartz, felt that Mahler should have lessons in a much larger town, such as Vienna.

Schwartz took him to Vienna for Professor Julius Epstein to hear him play, and as a result he became a student at the Conservatory from 1875 to 1877, studying piano with Epstein, harmony with Fuchs and composition with Krenn. He took the Conservatory in his stride, winning prizes for piano in 1876 and for composition with the first movement of a piano quintet, in 1878. Most of his student compositions are now lost. During the period at the Conservatory he gave piano lessons to help support himself. In 1877 he registered as a student of Vienna University to study philosophy and art history and may have attended lectures by Bruckner. Although the two respected each other, their artistic conceptions were very different. Bruckner told Auer that despite his admiration for Mahler his 'Jewishness' worried him.

251

In 1877 he joined the Wagner Society and was a great admirer of the composer's music, embracing his vegetarianism and teetotalism. From 1878 to 1880 he composed text and music for his first large surviving and completed work, the cantata *Das Klagende Lied* (The plaintive song), although it did not receive its first performance until 1901.

After graduation he stayed in Vienna, eking out a living by continuing to give piano lessons. In the summer of 1880 he obtained his first job conducting at the summer holiday resort of Bad Hall, south of Linz. This job as a theatre conductor was a useful formative experience for him. Operettas by OFFENBACH, Johann Strauss and Suppé were performed. However Mahler only stayed for one season. He began composing his first symphony in 1884 and completed it in 1888. His friend and fellow student, Hans Rott, failed to win the Beethoven prize of the Gesellschaft der Musikfreunde, for his first symphony, and is said to have been advised by Brahms to give up music. So depressed was he by this that he became insane and died in an institution in 1884. Recently Rott's first symphony has been revived and in the scherzo and finale there is a close resemblance to themes in Mahler's symphonies. In 1900 Mahler borrowed the score of Rott's first symphony to read and, according to Nathalie Bauer-Lechner, commented: 'His innermost nature was so much akin to mine that he and I are like two fruits from the same tree, produced by the same soil, nourished by the same air. We would have had an infinite amount in common.'

From September 1881 until April 1882 Mahler was principal conductor of the Provincial Theatre at Laibach (now Ljubljana), where he conducted 50 performances of operas, operettas and incidental music before returning to Vienna. His next appointment for three months from January 1883 was at the Royal Municipal Theatre at Olmütz (Olomouc), followed by his longest appointment until then, as assistant conductor at the Royal Theatre in Kassell from August 1883 until April 1885. During this period he not only began his first symphony but also *Lieder eines Fahrenden Gesellen* (Songs of a Wayfarer) written after a love affair with Johanna Richter, to whom the work is dedicated. By the end of his period at Kassell, Mahler had secured the appointment of second assistant conductor to Nikisch at Leipzig at the beginning of 1886. For the interim year he was third assistant conductor at the German Theatre in Prague. These appointments were to set the seal on his fame as an opera conductor. During this period he conducted operas by many major composers, but particularly those of Wagner. He also completed a successful performing version of Weber's posthumous opera *Die Drei Pintos* in 1887. He completed his first symphony under the spell of a love affair with Marion von Weber, the wife of Weber's grandson, who had entrusted him with the sketches for *Die Drei Pintos*. He also wrote the first movement of his second symphony and sketches for *Des Knaben Wunderhorn*.

As in many of his previous positions Mahler had a disagreement with the director and was dismissed. In 1888 he met David POPPER, cellist, composer and professor of the Budapest Academy of Music, who was head-hunting for the vacant post of director of the Royal Hungarian Opera. Mahler made a favourable impression, and unbeknown to him had been strongly recommended by Guido Adler. He was soon to sign a contract for his most prestigious post yet, although at the time the opera was in artistic and administrative decline and subject to nationalistic tensions between the Magyars and other ethnic groups such as the Slovaks, Serbs, Croats and Slovenes. The wide experience and fame he had gained over the past eight years had brought its reward. Mahler sided with the Magyar majority and set about reviving and reconstructing the opera. He put on *Das Rheingold* and *Die Walküre* in Hungarian and insisted that the tickets be sold in pairs, thus ensuring that both operas were seen in sequence. It proved a great success. During this period he conducted the premiere of his first symphony, which met with both hostile reactions and great applause from different sectors of the public.

In 1889, during Mahler's period at Budapest, his father and mother died. His married sister Leopoldine also died, at the age of 26, and he took responsibility for his other sisters and brother, thus having quasi-parental worries in addition to his very busy life. The appointment of a new and anti-Semitic director led to inevitable tensions and disagreements, and Mahler resigned, taking up the post of chief opera conductor at Hamburg in 1891. In Hamburg, although he did not have the same artistic control as at Budapest, he did have a first-rate company of singers to work with, including, after 1895, the soprano Anna von Mildenburg. He shaped her into a leading artist, and also had a love affair with her.

During his six years in Hamburg, apart from conducting duties, Mahler began a routine of composing during the summer vacation, staying at Steinbach-in-Attersee, in upper Austria, where he built a composing hut in a lakeside meadow. He spent the vacations there with his brothers and sisters and a friend of his sisters, Natalie Bauer-Lechner. His sister Justine took on the role of domestic organizer. Natalie began keeping a journal, which has been a valuable source of information about Mahler. Mahler conducted a Ring Cycle at Covent Garden in 1892 and completed his second and third symphonies whilst employed in Hamburg.

For many years he had seen his goal as conductor of the Vienna Opera. After lengthy negotiations, with the support of Brahms and Hanslick, and after conversion to Roman Catholicism in the 'Kleine Michaeliskirche' in Hamburg on 23 February 1897, Mahler became conductor (April 1897) of the Vienna Opera, one of the supreme posts in the German-speaking world, although at the time somewhat in decline. Mahler made a highly successful début by performing Wagner's *Lohengrin* and in September 1897 he was promoted to director. A month later he put on what was regarded as the embodiment of Czech nationalism, Smetana's *Dalibor*. The German-speaking administrative class felt outraged and a police presence was necessary. The conservative and anti-Semitic press was very critical, but Hanslick, the most famous critic of the day, was highly appreciative. Mahler certainly succeeded in raising standards and reversing the decline of the Vienna Opera. Whilst he was much appreciated in some quarters, he was highly criticized by supporters of the old regime at the opera.

He spent the summer of 1898 in the southern Tyrol, convalescing after an operation for haemorrhoids, but in the summer of 1899 he built a second summer home and composing hut by the side of a lake at Maiernigg and began composing his fourth symphony, completing it the following summer. In the summer of 1901 at Maiernigg he began his fifth symphony and composed the *Rückert Lieder* and three of the *Kindertotenlieder*.

On 7 November 1901 Mahler met Alma Schindler, the daughter of a well-known landscape painter and colourist at a dinner party. She was one of the rising stars among Vienna's 'artistic' beauties of the period, and an accomplished musician, having composition lessons from Alexander ZEMLINSKI. They were engaged within a few weeks and married on 9 March 1902; Alma was 22 and Mahler 42. They spent a working honeymoon in St Petersburg, where Mahler conducted three concerts. He finished composing his fifth symphony at Maiernigg in 1902. The adagio of this symphony is said to be a declaration of love for Alma. Their first daughter, Maria, was born in November 1902. In the summer of 1903 they went to Maiernigg, where Mahler started work on his sixth symphony. It was clear that Alma was expected to play the role of selflessly faithful young wife and mother, looking after the children and copying out his manuscripts. She could not play the piano lest the sound reach Mahler's composing hut and disturb him. He also insisted that she herself gave up composing. Their second daughter, Anna, was born in 1904, by which stage their love had cooled. The sixth symphony was completed in 1904 and the seventh in 1905, the last to be composed at Maiernigg. The eighth symphony, a work on a massive scale, was composed in the summer of 1906 and coincided with a reawakening of his love for Alma. She said that at that time Mahler began to have renewed feelings for her, in contrast to his earlier self-absorption.

In raising the standards at the Vienna Opera, Mahler made great demands of his singers and orchestra. He insisted on very strict discipline and assumed that the director had the authority to punish when orders were not carried out. This led to inevitable clashes, sections of the press mounted a campaign against him, and there was tension between him and officials. After a performance of SCHOENBERG's Quartet Op. 7, that Mahler attended, there was a near riot. Mahler became involved, taking Schoenberg's side, to the annoyance of the Vienna Opera officials. Although he claimed to be unable to understand Schoenberg's music, he was very concerned to give him the benefit of the doubt. His position at the Vienna Opera became untenable when he signed a lucrative contract with the Metropolitan Opera in New York for the four-month winter season. Resignation from the Vienna Opera followed. He was to go to New York for four successive seasons, returning home for the rest of the year in order to give himself more time to compose.

Tragedy struck in 1907 when his daughter Maria developed scarlet fever. Mahler and Alma witnessed their daughter's harrowing illness and subsequent death, which came after a tracheotomy. Days after the death the doctor came to examine Alma, who was suffering extreme exhaustion from the stress. In addition, Alma's mother, who was with them at the time, had suffered a heart attack. Mahler suggested that the doctor should also examine him, supposedly the healthy member of the family. The doctor diagnosed a potentially fatal valve defect in his heart and prescribed no mountain climbing, cycling or swimming. Following this traumatic series of events Mahler spent time reading some Chinese poems in German translation that had been given to him, and so *Das Lied von der Erde*, taking these poems as texts, began to take shape. It was completed the following summer.

In December 1907 he left for New York, where he put on successful performances of *Tristan*, *Die Walküre*, *Siegried*, *Figaro*, *Don Giovanni* and *Fidelio*. Whilst in their hotel room in New York, he and Alma witnessed from their window a funeral procession for the Deputy Fire Chief, who had died in the course of his duties. The procession was accompanied by the sound of a muffled drum. This was to provide the inspiration for the finale of his last, uncompleted tenth symphony, although a performing version was completed by Deryck Cooke and given its premiere in London in 1964, conducted by Berthold GOLDSCHMIDT.

After Maria's death Mahler and his wife did not return to Maiernigg, but instead rented a summer home at Toblach, where Mahler had the last of his composing huts at Alt Schluderbach nearby. For his second visit to New York he shared the conducting with Toscanini at the New York Metropolitan Opera, not always to the satisfaction of both conductors, but Mahler was also able this season to conduct the New York Symphony Orchestra at Carnegie Hall, there he was able to include his second symphony for its American premiere.

In the summer of 1909 he returned to Toblach alone and composed his ninth symphony, some of which has been regarded as autobiographical. His marriage was in a poor state, although Alma returned with him to New York. In 1910, when Alma was recovering from stress in a sanatorium near Tobelbad, she met the architect Walter Gropius. They began a love affair and he later became her second husband. Meanwhile Mahler, at Toblach, was working on his tenth symphony. Alma told Mahler of the affair, which greatly wounded him, to the extent that he consulted Sigmund Freud. At the time Alma observed: 'I knew that my marriage was no marriage and that my own life was utterly unfulfilled. I concealed all this from him, and although he knew it as well as I did, we played out the comedy to the end, to spare his feelings.' The eighth symphony, dedicated to Alma, was given its triumphant premiere in Munich in September 1910 – the last that Mahler was to conduct himself.

On the fourth and final visit to New York in 1910 Mahler contracted endo-carditis. It was clear from the diagnosis that it would be fatal. Mahler wanted to die in Vienna. He and Alma travelled by ship across the Atlantic and then travelled by train via Paris to Vienna. He received serum treatment in Paris, although the absence of antibiotics in those days meant that any alleviation was unlikely. Of the last journey from Paris to Vienna Alma said, 'the last journey was like that of a dying king'. Reporters at every station wanted news of his condition. In Vienna he was taken to the Loew Sanatorium, where he died at the age of 50.

During Mahler's lifetime and for nearly 50 years afterwards his sym-phonies were not appreciated by the concert-going majority and there were few performances of his works. During the Nazi era his music was banned in Germany and the occupied countries. The bust of Mahler by Rodin was removed from the Vienna State Opera and Gustav Mahlerstrasse was renamed Meistersingerstrasse. The 1960s saw a revival of his music in London and New York and recordings of his symphonies were made by BERNSTEIN and Kubelik. Since then he has been recognized as one of the greatest composers of the period.

Bibliography: G; HBD; Ken; Leb; Henry-Louis De La Grange, *Gustav Mahler*, 3 vols (Oxford: Oxford University Press, 1995–9); Peter Frankel, *The Life of Mahler* (Cambridge: Cambridge University Press, 1997); Norman Lebrech, *Mahler Remembered* (London: Faber, 1987); Alma Mahler, *Gustav Mahler: Memories and Letters* (London: Cardinal, 1990)

1. Bertha Geissmar, *The Baton and the Jackboot* (London: Hamish Hamilton, 1944), pp. 330–1.

Mamlok, Ursula (b. Berlin, 1 February 1928)   Studied piano and violin as a child. She moved to Ecuador with her family in 1940 and then to the USA in 1941, becoming an American citizen in 1945. She studied at Mannes College (1942–6) with Szell and at the Manhatten School of Music with Giannini, and also privately with WOLPE, Sessions, Steuermann and SHAPEY. Most of her compositions are chamber or piano works; the early works are influenced by Hindemith, the later ones by SCHOENBERG. Her most frequently performed works are *Panta Rhei* (Time in flux) for violin, cello and piano (1981), Violin Sonata (1989), Five Intermezzi for guitar (1991), *Girasol* (Sunflowers) for flute, clarinet, violin, viola, cello and piano (1990) and *Der Andreas Garten* for voice, woodwind and harp (1987).

Bibliography: G; HBD; www.cs.bsu.edu/homepages/dlsills/David_jewish.shtml*

Marx (Friedrich Heinrich) Adolf Bernhard (b. Halle, East Germany, 15 May 1795; d. Berlin, 17 May 1866)   Born a Jew, converted to Christianity as a young man, but, according to his memoirs,[1] embraced his Jewish heritage. At the time of his conversion he changed his forenames from Samuel Moses to Friedrich Heinrich Adolf Bernhard. His father was a doctor in Halle and encouraged his son's interest in music and the arts, although he had no formal instruction.

He trained as a lawyer but also had music lessons from Türk in Halle. He practised law briefly in Narmburg and Berlin, but from 1824 to 1830 became editor of *Berliner Allgemeine Musikalische Zeitung*. He had composition lessons from Zelter, but became dissatisfied with his teaching and fell out with him after criticizing the poor state of Zelter's Singakademie in his periodical. In 1828 he received a doctorate from the University of Marburg and became professor of music at the University of Berlin in 1830, after MENDELSSOHN had declined the post and recommended Marx for it. In 1838 he married Marie Therese Cohn, the daughter of a Jewish merchant from Dessau. In 1850 he founded, with Stern and Kullak, the Berliner Musikschule, later known as the Stern Conservatory.

Marx is now best known as a music writer and critic. He is especially known for his four-volume *Die Lehre von der Musikalischen Komposition* (1837–47), in which he includes detailed discussions on compositional procedures and in which he coined the term *Sonatenform* (sonata form). He became friends with Mendelssohn, 14 years his junior, during the latter's youth. Together with MOSCHELES and Devrient he tried to convince Mendelssohn's father that his son had the ability to become a professional musician. Marx discussed and advised Mendelssohn on the overture *A Midsummer Night's Dream*, and also completed the draft libretto for his oratorio *Paulus*.[2] Mendelssohn's father was somewhat wary of Marx's influence on his son. Zelter helped to prejudice the father by stating of Marx that he 'must have been baptized with soda because his defecations are greenish grey; like flies they stain even the food they enjoy'. However, the friendship lasted until 1841, when Mendelssohn refused to perform Marx's oratorio *Moses* in Leipzig on the grounds that he felt it was not good enough.[3] It had already been performed in Breslau. Marx's compositions include a large number of songs, two oratorios, two cantatas and a few orchestral and piano works. The majority of these received few performances, the exception being *Moses*, which was performed many times, including in Weimar by Liszt in 1853. Like Mendelssohn he contributed to the revival of J. S. Bach's works by publishing the vocal scores of the *Saint Matthew Passion* (1830) and the B minor Mass (1834).

Bibliography: *G*; *HBD*; Ly*

1. Adolph Bernhard Marx, *Erinnerungen aus meinen Leben* (Berlin: Otto Janke, 1865).
2. Jeffrey S. Sposato, 'Mendelssohn, Paulus, and the Jews', *Musical Quarterly*, 83 (1999), pp. 280–91.
3. Wilfred Blunt, *On Wings of Song: a Biography of Felix Mendelssohn* (London: Hamish Hamilton, 1974), pp. 68–70.

Mendelssohn, Fanny Cäcilie (b. Hamburg, 14 November 1805; d. Berlin, 14 May 1847)   Eldest child of Abraham and Leah Mendelssohn and sister of Felix MENDELSSOHN. She was born into a wealthy, cultured, post-Enlightenment Jewish family. Both parents were interested in music and the arts and in their home they entertained important intellectuals and artists of the day. In a letter that Abraham wrote to his mother-in-law announcing the birth of Fanny, he wrote: 'Leah says that the child has Bach-fugue fingers' – a prophecy that proved to be true. In 1809 the family moved to Berlin. Fanny began piano lessons at a very early age with her mother and later with Ludwig Berger until 1816, when she went to Paris for lessons with Marie Bigot. The same year all the children were converted to Lutheranism. However, though baptized, Fanny retained the cultural values of liberal Judaism. A few years later she received theory and composition lessons from C. F. Zelter. When only 13 she was able to play 24 of Bach's Preludes from memory, and this facility for learning music enabled her to have an extensive repertoire of works of classical composers to play in later years.

Fanny and Felix were very close to each other throughout their lives. She acted as Felix's confidante, particularly on musical matters. She played a major role in shaping some of his works, notably the oratorio *Paulus*. Fanny's earliest composition dates from 1819 and is a song she composed for her father's birthday. In 1820 she enrolled at the newly opened Berlin Singakademie. Overall she composed over 500 works, mainly *Lieder* and piano pieces, but also Piano Trio, Op. 11 (1846) and an unpublished string quartet. Although she was encouraged to compose by both her father and Felix, she was discouraged from publishing her works. The general consensus in those days, even in an enlightened family, was that a woman's place was in the home. As a result only 11 compositions were published with opus numbers and 16 songs published without opus numbers. The full extent of her compositions may never be known, some may still be in private hands and others lost.

In 1829 she married the Prussian court painter Wilhelm Hensel. Their only child, Sebastian, was born the following year and was named after J. S. Bach. There is evidence of at least one stillbirth. Because she was discouraged from publishing she allowed some of her compositions to be attributed to Felix, for example his Op. 8 and Op. 9. On one occasion, in 1842, when Felix visited Queen Victoria at Buckingham Palace, the Prince Consort suggested that Queen Victoria be asked to sing one of his songs. She chose a song entitled *Italien*, which she is said to have sung well, so much so that Felix felt he had to admit that it was Fanny's composition, not his own.

During her lifetime, Fanny's musicianship as a performer rather than as a composer was most in evidence. She was the central figure in a flourishing salon at the Mendelssohn's house in Berlin. Here she performed on the piano and trained and conducted a choir. It is thought that she only once performed in public and that was in 1838 at a charity concert, when she played Felix's First Piano Concerto.

Her death at the age of 42 was sudden. She was conducting a rehearsal of her choir on the afternoon of 14 May when she suffered a stroke and died by 11 o'clock in the evening.

Bibliography: G; GW; 'anonymous', 'Fanny by Gaslight', *Musical Times* (1997), pp. 27–31; Françoise Tillard, *Fanny Mendelssohn* (Portland, OR: Amadeus Press, 1996)

Mendelssohn, Jakob Ludwig Felix (b. Hamburg, 3 February 1809; d. Leipzig, 4 November 1847) In order to appreciate the environment in which Mendelssohn grew up and developed it is necessary to go back two generations. His grandfather, Moses Mendelssohn, lived in the period at the beginning of the Jewish Enlightenment (see Chapter 2, section 2.4). Moses (son of Mendel) was the son of a scribe or writer of holy scrolls born in Dessau. From an early age he was an outstanding student of medieval Hebrew philosophy, being taught by Rabbi David Fränkel. Fränkel moved to Berlin, and in order to continue his studies Moses Mendelssohn, then 14 years old, walked the 70 miles from Dessau to Berlin. Some years later, as a result of his studies, he became a philosopher. His most well-known publication was *Phaedo* (1767), a treatise on the immortality of the soul.

Moses was not a Zionist. He believed a Jew is first of all a citizen of the country in which he is born, and he recommended assimilation. Moses had three sons, and they founded a banking empire. It was an opportune time for banking. Industrially, countries were advancing and his sons accumulated considerable wealth during their lifetimes. Abraham (1776–1835) was a representative of the new educated middle class, a man who believed that the privilege of having money carried with it a duty of enriching the mind. He had a great understanding and interest in the arts and music. It was in Hamburg where he founded a banking house and where three of his children, Fanny (1805), Felix (1809) and Rebecka (1811), were born. The youngest child, Paul (1813), was born in Berlin. By 1811, because of the impending French occupation of Hamburg, the family moved to Berlin.

Abraham's banking business was successful enough for him to buy a mansion with a park situated away from the centre of Berlin. This was Felix's childhood home. With his father's interest in music and the arts and his mother being a very capable hostess, they set out to make their home an intellectual centre, entertaining intellectuals and artists of the day. The children were privately educated at home, although Felix did attend Dr Messow's school in Berlin from 1816 to 1818. They were brought up in an environment in which there was no lack of money. However, the work ethic was very strong. They were up at 5 a.m. each day and set work, although they were allowed an extra hour in bed on Sundays. All the children were very gifted and thrived on this regime. Even when Abraham was older and needed to work no longer, he continued at an undiminished pace, believing in the ethical value of work. The same was expected of the children. They became fluent in several languages, were knowledgeable in the arts and sciences, and from an early age met eminent literary figures and musicians of the day. Both Felix and Fanny showed extraordinary talent, both as pianists and composers. They were very close throughout their lives and Fanny was talented enough for Felix to claim some of her compositions as his own. This appears to have been done amicably, and regarded as a way in which her work could become performed.

Abraham's view of religion overlapped with that of his father's, but went further down the path of assimilation. With his wife Lea's approval he decided to bring the children up as Protestants. They were baptized in 1816. However, it seems likely that the decision to bring them up as Protestants was taken earlier, since Felix was never circumcised. Lea's brother, on embracing the Christian faith, changed his surname from Salomon to Bartholdy, the name of a large garden in Berlin that he had recently purchased. By 1822 Abraham had been persuaded to adopt the surname Mendelssohn Bartholdy to distinguish his branch of the family from the Mendelssohn's that had not embraced Christianity. By the time Felix embarked on an international career, his father felt he should drop 'Mendelssohn' altogether and become just Bartholdy. Felix resisted his father's request, saying that he was already known as Mendelssohn, and that the double-barrelled version was too long. Abraham was not baptized until 1822, perhaps significantly not until after his mother-in-law had died.

Felix began his musical studies with violin and piano lessons, and by the age of 10 had studied theory and composition with Zelter, attending classes in his Singakademie in Berlin. He began composing very rapidly, completing 13 string symphonies, concertos, piano pieces and chamber music. Zelter was greatly impressed commenting that 'it would be a truly rare thing, if a person of Jewish blood were to become an artist'. In 1821 he took Felix to Weimar to display his talent to his friend Goethe. Both were impressed with each other – Goethe with Mendelssohn's playing and the latter on meeting the author of *Faust* and *Werther*. They were to meet four times in all. At this stage Abraham was not convinced that Felix should have a musical career, and in 1825 he took Felix to Cherubini in Paris, where the latter declared in the affirmative. In 1826 he wrote his first great masterpiece, the Octet in E flat, the scherzo of which was inspired by Goethe's *Walpurgisnacht*, and in 1827 the *Midsummer Night's Dream Overture*. In April 1827 the Berlin Opera performed his *Die Hochzeit des Camacho*. This first had to be submitted to Spontini, the king's *Kapellmeister*. By string-pulling the Mendelssohn family were able to get it performed, much to the annoyance of Spontini, who wrote to Wagner years later saying: 'Believe me, there was hope for German music as long as I was Sovereign of Berlin's musical life. Now the Prussian King has delivered his music to the confusion created by two wandering Jews, all hope is lost.' The two 'wandering Jews' referred to are Mendelssohn and MEYERBEER (Spontini's successor). The opera house was filled with family and friends, but by the end of the performance even they were questioning whether it was good enough for the Berlin theatre.

Whilst this was a failure, the opposite was true of Mendelssohn's performance of Bach's *Saint Matthew Passion* with the Singakademie on 11 March 1829. Half a century after Bach's death, less of his music was played than has been the case at any time since. Most of his works that were played at this time were organ works, motets and chamber works. The existence of the larger works, such as the Passions and oratorios, was known only to a few scholars.

Ironically, Mendelssohn was given a copy of the *Saint Matthew Passion* by his Jewish grandmother, Bella Salomon. His important contribution and achievement was to realize from the manuscript the greatness of this work, to spend four years studying it with a small group of amateurs in his home, and then with the help of his friend and actor Eduard Devrient, who played the role of Jesus, to persuade Zelter that the *Saint Matthew Passion* should be performed by the Singakademie. He was concerned that he might not be able to hold the attention of the audience for the full length of the Passion and performed a cut version with some adaptations. For the first performance Eduard Rietz and Ferdinand DAVID, then only 19, were the leaders of the double orchestra, and Mendelssohn conducted using a baton for the first time. This revival proved a tremendous success, emotion filled the hall, men and women wept, and it was a measure of Mendelssohn's genius that he was able to achieve this at the age of 20. The performance had a profound influence not only on the appreciation of the *Saint Matthew Passion*, but also on Bach's other great choral works. According to Devrient, Mendelssohn is quoted as saying: 'To think that it was an actor and a Jew who brought back to the German people their greatest Christian work.'

Mendelssohn spent much of his life travelling. This he enjoyed and it formed part of his inspiration. He particularly enjoyed his visits to England and Scotland. On his first visit to London he was met by Ignaz MOSCHELES. They became great friends and Moscheles helped much in the organization of his concerts throughout his many visits, including the final visit in which *Elijah* was performed. His first visit included Scotland and this inspired the *Hebrides Overture* and the *Scotch Symphony*. Although his knowledge of English was rudimentary at the start of his first visit to England, it rapidly improved and he soon spoke fluent English. He always received a warm reception in England. His second tour, lasting two years, was of Germany, Austria and Italy. At Weimar he visited Goethe for the last time. At Munich he began a romance with the pianist Delphine von Schauroth, to whom his first piano concerto is dedicated. In Rome he met Berlioz, whose music he did not understand, although both men respected one another. He visited Paris, meeting Chopin, Liszt and Meyerbeer, but never really felt at home there, and wrote home saying how delighted he was to be back in London (1832). He and Meyerbeer were never great friends (see MEYERBEER).

After Zelter's death in 1833, Mendelssohn applied for the post of director of the Singakademie, but the post was given to Zelter's assistant Rungenhagen, the voting being 148 to 88. Rungenhagen stayed in the post for 18 years and is said to have condemned the academy to mediocrity. Mendelssohn's rejection is often ascribed to anti-Semitism, but any real proof for this in the form of minutes of the Singakademie is lacking, since these were destroyed during World War Two. Anti-Semitism is mentioned in Devrient's reminiscences of the composer, but other documents suggest that there may have been other issues that effected the outcome.

From 1833 to 1835 Mendelssohn held the post of music director at the opera house in Düsseldorf. This was not an altogether comfortable time for him. In a predominantly Catholic town, Mendelssohn began to replace what he regarded as 'frivolous' church music with Masses and motets by Palestrina and Lassus. This upset some of the faithful, and he found that he could not cope with the intrigues associated with the practicalities of running the opera house. His resignation turned out to be for the best, because he felt more at home in his next post, as conductor of the Leipzig Gewandhaus Orchestra. His period in Leipzig was regarded as a great success. Aided by his phenomenal memory, he became one of the first great interpretive conductors. Having Ferdinand David as leader of the orchestra also helped him. He took an interest in all the musical activities of the city, turning it into a 'musical mecca'. He established the Leipzig Conservatory and was one of its teachers, together with Ferdinand David (violin), Moscheles (piano), Hauptmann (music theory) and Robert Schumann (piano and composition). One of the first pupils was the 12-year-old violinist Joseph JOACHIM.

In 1837 Mendelssohn married Cécile Jeanrenaud, the daughter of a French Reformed Church pastor. They had five children, of whom one died in childhood. Less than four months after his marriage Mendelssohn was travelling again, this time to England, where he gave the first performance of *Paulus*. In 1840 he was appointed to the post of royal *Kapellmeister* with the expectation that a new conservatory would be established in Berlin. This was a period of considerable frustration for him, and when it became clear that through bureaucratic and other resistance no conservatory would be established, Mendelssohn asked the king to release him from the post. During this period he still kept up some conducting at Leipzig, except for the 1843–5 seasons, when Ferdinand HILLER took his place.

By the late 1830s the effects of overwork began to tell on his health. He suffered migraines, and would have liked to withdraw from much of his public activities and concentrate on composing. However, he felt a duty to continue a public career, considering it as part of an artist's mission. In 1847 he suffered a series of small strokes, and eventually massive ones, from which he died in November 1847. At the time of his death he was working on the opera *Loreley* and the oratorio *Christus*.

Mendelssohn began his musical career with exceptional promise and was compared with the young Mozart, especially with the early masterpieces *Midsummer Night's Dream Overture* and *Octet*. However, once the freshness of the works of his youth had gone, and for all his unrivalled technical command, nothing quite took its place.[1] Many of his overtures are masterpieces, and some of his late works, such as the Violin Concerto and the oratorio *Elijah*, stand out. The Violin Concerto was completed in 1844 and performed by David. It was a great success at the time and has retained its popularity to this day. *Elijah* achieved a level of popularity similar to that of Handel's *Messiah*, although nowadays it is not as popular. In the context of his musical development, it is interesting that he was able to write the incidental music to the *Midsummer Night's Dream* in 1843, to add to his *Midsummer Night's Dream Overture* of 17 years earlier (1826), without any apparent change in style.

There has been much discussion of the importance that Mendelssohn attached to his Jewish heritage. During the Nazi era his music was proscribed. His memorial outside the Leipzig Gewandhaus was destroyed on 10 November 1936. In one of the most important biographies of Mendelssohn since World War Two, *Mendelssohn: a New Image of the Composer and His Age*, the author Eric Werner suggested that although baptized for pragmatic reasons, Mendelssohn was very conscious and proud of his Jewish heritage. Three pieces of evidence are cited to support this view: (i) Mendelssohn resisted pressure from his father to be known as Bartholdy, preferring to remain 'Mendelssohn'; (ii) in a letter, Mendelssohn comments favourably on the Jewish Civil Disabilities Act passed in the British Parliament, designed to remove the last civil restrictions on Jews, and contrasts it with the 'miserable Posen statutes', which were very restrictive; and (iii) his portrayal of Jews in the oratorio *Paulus*. However, a careful re-evaluation of the evidence by Sposato (1998), including uncovering mistranslation of some of the documentary evidence by Werner, suggests that although Mendelssohn was concerned about the ultimate political fate of the Jews, he tried to distance himself from his heritage in many respects.[2] This issue has stimulated a lively and continuing debate.[3]

Bibliography: *G*; *HBD*; Ken; Wilfred Blunt, *On Wings of Song: a Biography of Felix Mendelssohn* (London: Hamish Hamilton, 1974); Roger Nichols, *Mendelssohn Remembered* (London: Faber, 1997)

1. Stanley Sadie and Alison Latham, *The Cambridge Music Guide* (Cambridge: Cambridge University Press, 1985), pp. 302–7.
2. J. S. Sposato, 'Creative Writing: The [Self-]identification of Mendelssohn as Jew', *Musical Quarterly*, 82 (1998), pp. 190–209.
3. Leon Botstein, 'Mendelssohn and the Jews', *Musical Quarterly*, 82 (1998), pp. 210–19; Leon Botstein, Mendelssohn, Werner, and the Jews: a Final Word', *Musical Quarterly*, 83 (1999), pp. 45–50; J. S. Sposato, 'Mendelssohn, Paulus, and the Jews: a Response to Leon Botstein and Michael Steinberg', *Musical Quarterly*, 83 (1999), pp. 280–91; M. P. Steinberg, 'Mendelssohn's Music and German-Jewish Culture: an Intervention', *Musical Quarterly*, 83 (1999), pp. 31–44.

Meyerbeer [Meyer Beer], **Giacomo** [Jakob Liebmann] (b. Vogelsdorf, near Berlin, 5 September 1791; d. Paris, 2 May 1864)   Changed his surname to Meyerbeer in 1810 in honour of his favourite uncle, Meyer Beer. Then, while staying in Venice around 1815, he Italianized his given name to Giacomo (Italian for Jacob). He was born into an affluent Jewish family. His father, Juda Herz Beer, ran a sugar refinery and his mother, Amalia Liebmann Meyer Wulff, was the daughter of Liebmann Meyer Wulff, who made his fortune delivering supplies to the Prussian troops and as director of the Prussian lottery. One of his brothers became a noted German astronomer and another, who died young, was a poet. In 1815 his father, Beer, was considered to be the wealthiest individual in Berlin. He was interested in culture and in the emancipation of Jews. There are many parallels with the MENDELSSOHN family, but there is one important difference: the Meyerbeers did not convert to Christianity. In 1812 Meyerbeer made a formal vow to his mother to remain true to his father's religion, a vow that he kept for the rest of his life. In 1816 Meyerbeer's mother was awarded the Order of Luisa in recognition of her charitable activities with the wounded in the war of 1813–15. Like Mendelssohn, Meyerbeer was educated by private tutors, in particular the Jewish scholar Aron Wolfssohn, who was responsible for his general education. His music teachers included the court piano teacher Franz Lauska, Carl Zelter, Bernhard Weber and Abbé Vogler. At an early age he acquired a sense of diplomacy, which became particularly important in the career he pursued, both in dealing with artists, impresarios and anti-Semites.

The parental home was a meeting place of Berlin's cultural elite, and members of the court frequented their house, including the future king, whom Meyerbeer met in childhood. His pianistic ability was apparent at an early age when his performance of a Mozart piano concerto in Berlin was enthusiastically applauded. His first large-scale work, composed in 1811, was the oratorio *Gott und die Natur*. After leaving his teacher Vogler in Darmstadt he went to Munich for nine months. His first opera to be performed was *Jephthas Gelübde* in Munich, apparently without success, although in a letter to Gänsbacher asking him to report it in a newspaper he describes its enthusiastic reception and the flattering compliments the queen paid him, including the gift of a diamond ring. The opera is more like an oratorio and is scholastic in style.

He visited Paris in 1814 and London in 1815, and, with the aim of completing his studies, Italy in 1816. He was to stay there for nine years, interspersed with trips to Germany and Austria. His early successes as a concert pianist were in marked contrast to his lack of success as an opera composer at the time. However, after meeting the leading Italian librettists he composed six operas in the style of Rossini, which were performed in Italy; the last of these, *Il Crociato in Egitto*, composed in 1824, was so successful that in Italy at the time he was being compared with Rossini. It was the last opera to be composed for a castrato in the title role, the famous Velluti. This success led to an invitation to perform *Il Crociato in Egitto* in Paris, the place Meyerbeer held in greatest awe. It was received there with great enthusiasm, in contrast to Berlin, where it received a much cooler reception.

In October 1825 his father died while he was still in Paris. According to Jewish tradition the eldest male member of a family should establish his own household after the father's death. Accordingly, Meyerbeer married his cousin Minna Mosson six months later. He set up household in Berlin, but it was to be an incompatible marriage, in spite of having five children, the first two of whom died in infancy. Although the family lived in Berlin, Meyerbeer spent most of the rest of his life in Paris, where he never acquired

11 Louis Moreau Gottschalk, last portrait, December 1869.

12 Joseph Joachim, violinist and composer, photographed in 1867.

13 Gideon Klein, photographed *circa*
1929, the youngest composer to be sent
to the concentration camp at Terezin.

14 A caricature of the child prodigy Erich Korngold, surrounded by aston-
ished musicians of the day: (*l-r*) Siegfried Wagner, Max Reger, Artur
Nikisch, Richard Strauss and Eugene d'Albert. *Neues Wiener Tagblatt*, 1911.

15 Giacomo Meyerbeer photographed circa 1854, from a lost oil painting by Jager.

16 Ignaz Moscheles, pianist and composer.

17 Jacques Offenbach.

18 David Popper, cellist and composer.

19 Anton Rubinstein, pianist and composer.

20 Henryk Wieniawski, violinist and composer.

a permanent residence but instead stayed in rented hotel suites and private lodgings. He never took on French citizenship. His personal life was difficult and this was perhaps why he poured all his energies into musical activities. He travelled extensively, partly because of both his and his wife's ill health. They visited spas for health cures, but also for his opera productions and in order to audition new singers. He was on the move so much of the time that Wagner was to say after one of their early meetings, 'yet he was friendly and well-disposed to me, regretting only that he was about to leave, a condition in which I invariably found him later, whenever I visited him in Berlin'.

Up until about the late 1820s Meyerbeer's operas had mixed receptions, and he came to realize that an essential prerequisite was to have a good librettist. There were no prominent librettists in Germany at the time. Meyerbeer engaged the French librettist Eugène Scribe for his opera *Robert le Diable*, which was premiered in November 1831 in Paris. This was to prove a great success. It was described 'as a masterpiece remarkable in the history of art'. The style was no longer that of the scholarly German or naturalized Italian composer, but of an original, vigorous, passionate and dramatic composer. Within three years it was to be performed in 77 theatres in ten countries. This was the first of five Grand Operas that Meyerbeer was to produce with Scribe as sole or principal librettist; it was followed by *Les Hugenots* (1836), *Le Prophète* (1849), *L'Étoile du nord* (1854) and *L'Africaine* (1865).

The period 1830–60 saw French Grand Opera at its height. Meyerbeer was its principal and most successful exponent. Grand Opera was characterized by grandeur, enormous casts, large orchestras, elaborate stage settings often using the latest technology, and as many as five acts, including ballet. The plots were often elaborate, historical, involving religious conflicts, dynastic clashes and revolution. It was extremely popular at the time, as much for its spectacle as for its music. Critics such as Berlioz claimed that opera was becoming an institution 'madly in love with mediocrity'. Wagner, who himself wrote a grand opera, *Rienzi*, which was modelled on Meyerbeer's style, claimed that Meyerbeer's works were 'effects without causes'.

There is no doubt that Meyerbeer introduced certain innovatory stylistic elements that were taken up by later operatic composers, for example Berlioz, Wagner, Bizet, SCHREKER and KORNGOLD. There were claims that the whole Grand Opera enterprise in Paris was run by Jewish entrepreneurs, especially as Meyerbeer, HALEVY, AUBER, OFFENBACH and HÉROLD were prominent among the composers. Meyerbeer was an astute businessman and had an eye for what the public wanted, and he also had links with the press. Nevertheless, many of the criticisms of Meyerbeer have greatly exaggerated this aspect of his personality. He was certainly very wealthy, but he lent money and helped colleagues in need, and he had the strong conviction that as a Jew he should perform a *mitzvah* (good deed) every day.

In his early aquaintance Wagner was an admirer of Meyerbeer, both as a person and as a musician. Apart from Wagner's later anti-Semitism, one can see the reasons why later he was so critical of Meyerbeer's operas, given the way his own work developed. Wagner's aim was to create a music drama in which music, art and drama were fully integrated. It is clear that in many ways Meyerbeer's aims were different. Meyerbeer was often initially attracted to the timbre of a singing voice as the starting point for an opera. He spent much time travelling to hear new singers and auditioning them, but he was much less interested in seeing the premieres of new operas. He would even consider modifying an opera to include a particular singer, or to achieve what he considered the required balance between male and female singers, such as in *Les Hugenots*, where Act 4 was modified to include female voices. Another example was when, in 1853, he heard the coloratura soprano Marie Cabel sing. He was so impressed with her voice that he wanted to engage her for *L'Étiole du nord*, but the cast had already been completed. In the event, he put aside *L'Africaine*, the opera on which he was working, having to buy the librettist's (Scribe) consent for 10,000 francs, and composed an opera *Le Pardon de Ploërmel* tailored for Cabel in the leading role.

Les Hugenots (1836) is generally regarded as Meyerbeer's most successful work, although it is not often performed today. The plot involved the St Bartholomew's Eve Massacre of Protestants by Catholics in 1572. For this reason the censors would not allow its performance in Berlin during the life of Friedrich Willhelm III. Only six years after its premiere, was it performed in Berlin after the accession of Friedrich Willhelm IV. Even before the French premiere, in 1836, Meyerbeer had to alter the scene of the blessing of the daggers because the censors had forbidden the representation of Catherine de Medici on stage. *Les Hugenots* was an enormous box office success; between 1836 and 1900 it was the first opera to reach over 1,000 performances. Berlioz was to write that the opera had enough musical riches for twenty successful operas.

A year after the premiere of *Les Hugenots* Scribe began writing the libretto for *L'Africaine*, but Meyerbeer did not complete the opera until shortly before his death, and it was given its first performance a year afterwards, in 1865. In between, *Le Prophète* was completed and performed.

In 1832, a year after the success of *Robert le Diable*, Meyerbeer was appointed Knight of the Legion of Honour and granted the title of court conductor by Friedrich Wilhelm III. A year later he became a full member of the Berlin Academy of Arts, at the same time as Mendelssohn. These appointments would not have been possible a few years earlier, since it was only after 1812 that Jews received Prussian nationality as a result of the Emancipation Edict following Napoleon's march into Prussia. In 1842 Friedrich Wilhelm IV, on his accession, made Meyerbeer Music Director-General, the first time a non-Christian had held public office in Prussia. About the same time Mendelssohn was offered the lesser post of director of church music, a post that he did not accept. Meyerbeer, although retaining an official court position for the rest of his life, was granted leave of absence for long periods, during which he took no salary.

There are many examples of Meyerbeer's generosity, but these are often unfairly interpreted as 'buying influence'. The poet Heinrich Heine, as a young newspaper reporter, wrote enthusiastically about Meyerbeer's operas. In 1838 Heine fell out with his wealthy uncle, who had at one stage promised him a lifelong pension, but then refused. Meyerbeer interceded on Heine's behalf and the pension was reinstated. In 1848, when Heine was in very poor health, Meyerbeer made him a further loan of 1,000 francs. According to Meyerbeer, Heine had only one regret, namely that of changing from Judaism to Christianity when believing himself to be mortally ill. He vowed that if he survived he would only eat kosher food! Later it came to light that Heine had written maliciously about Meyerbeer. It has been surmised that this may have been because Meyerbeer failed to set some of Heine's poems to music. When Heine died, in 1856, Meyerbeer learnt that Heine had written abusive poems against him, and eventually he paid 4,500 francs for Heine's widow to agree not to publish the poems. In 1844 Meyerbeer loaned Heinrich Börnstein 3,000 thaler to set up a socialist journal *Vorwärts*, money which was never repaid. He made the loan because he knew Heine was to be one of the contributors to this journal.

In 1851 Meyerbeer helped the instrument maker Adolphe Sax, originator of the saxophone, to avoid bankruptcy. As Prussian Music Director-General he repeatedly spoke out in favour of higher salaries for the orchestra and chorus and he did not draw his own salary when on leave of absence.

The most notorious of his acts of generosity was that of lending money to Wagner, to help him to stage his first two operas. Then later, when Meyerbeer refused further loans after hearing that Wagner had complained that Meyerbeer's patronage was racially motivated, Wagner he made an exceedingly virulent attack on Jews in the world of music. One only has to compare Wagner's descriptions of his early meetings with Meyerbeer in *Mein Leben* and the contents of *Das Judentum in der Musik* to realize the paranoia of the latter. It was perhaps ironic that on the same day Wagner received a note from the young King of Bavaria assuring him of his future patronage, he also learned of Meyerbeer's death.[1]

Somewhat surprising is perhaps the coolness of the relationship between Meyerbeer and Mendelssohn. This is evident when both were made members of the Berlin Academy of Arts in 1834, and Meyerbeer left for Italy to avoid meeting Mendelssohn. There is also evidence of later disagreements over the singer Jenny Lind.

Whilst it is clear that Meyerbeer was an astute businessman well able to look after his investments, it is also clear that he was both just and generous and showed great humanity and capacity for forgiveness. He was abstemious and a 'workaholic'. Because of his wealth and success he brought out the worst in anti-Semites, but he confronted them with a steadfastness and dignity born out of his faith and upbringing. There is now a wealth of detail on his life, the result of 40 years of work by Heinz and Gudrun Becker up until 1991, and since then by Sabine Henze-Döhring. Five volumes of correspondence and diaries (*Briefwechsel und Tagebhcher*, vols 1–5, 1960–98) have been compiled. How the correspondence became available is a story in itself. The papers were stored during World War Two in the attic of Hans Richter in a suburb of Berlin; the house was next door to the residence in which the Nazi leadership planned the final solution of the 'Jewish problem'.[2]

Bibliography: G; Grad; *HBD*; Ly*; WW; Heinz Becker and Gudrun Becker, *Giacomo Meyerbeer: a Life in Letters* (London: Croom Helm, 1983)*

1. Richard Wagner, *My Life*, trans. Andrew Gray (New York: Da Capo, 1992), pp. 738–9.
2. R. I. Letellier, *Cambridge Opera*, 11 (1999), pp. 295–300.

Mihalovici, Marcel (b. Bucharest, 22 October 1898; d. Paris, 12 August 1985) Studied harmony with Cuclin, violin with Bernfeld and counterpoint with Cremer in Bucharest before moving to Paris in 1919, where he remained for the rest of his life, becoming a French citizen in 1955. In Paris he continued his studies from 1919 to 1925 under Lejeune (violin), Gastuoé (Gregorian chant), Saint-Réquier (harmony) and d'Indy (composition). He became part of the loose association of immigrants that also included TANSMAN, HARSÁNYI and Martinu, known as École de Paris. He taught at the Schola Cantorum from 1959 to 1962 and married the pianist Monique Haas (1909–87). His compositions include operas (*Phèdre*, 1948–9; *Die Heimkehr*, 1954–5; *Krapp*, 1959–60; and *Les Jumeaux*, 1962), five ballets (e.g., *Une vie de polilichinelle*, 1922), five symphonies, three string quartets and several sonatas for different instruments.

Bibliography: G; Grad*; *HBD*; Ken; Leb

Milhaud, Darius (b. Aix-en-Provence, 4 September 1892; d. Geneva, 22 June 1974) Belonged to a wealthy Jewish family. His father was an exporter of almonds and his mother was a trained singer from a distinguished Italian family of Sephardic Jews. He began studying the violin at the age of 7 and eventually went to the Paris Conservatoire as a violin student, but gradually became more interested in composing than performing. His first work was a violin sonata composed in 1911. By the time of his death in 1974 he had become one of the most prolific composers in the twentieth century: his final opus number was 441. As early as 1919 he predicted that he would write 18 string quartets. At the conservatoire two of his teachers were DUKAS and Widor, although he thought Dukas a better composer than a teacher. From his days at the *lycée*, Milhaud knew Armand Lunel, who was also from a Jewish family with similar ancestry to Milhaud's. During their schooldays Milhaud set a number of Lunel's poems to music, although they were subsequently burned as he regarded them as not worthy of being preserved. At the same time that Milhaud went to the conservatoire, Lunel studied philosophy at the École Normale. Lunel suggested that Milhaud read a play by Francis Jammes, *La Brebis égarée*. Milhaud was so touched by it that he wanted to set it to music, and sought permission from the author. Meeting Jammes led to him being introduced to Claudel. His early compositions were much influenced by the two writers. He wrote the incidental music to Claudel's *Protée* (1913–19) and the opera *La Brebis égarée* based on the play by Jammes.

Although Claudel was a poet, he was at the time better known as a diplomat, and in 1916 he invited Milhaud to accompany him as his secretary on a visit to Rio de Janeiro. Prior to this Milhaud had been rejected for military service on medical grounds. The two-year trip to Brazil proved to be an early influence on his composing, leading to the ballet *L'Homme et son désir* (1918) and the dance suites *Saudades do Brazil*. On returning to Paris after World War One, Milhaud renewed acquaintance with a number of composers. A group of them would see each other often and go to concerts together. There was a series of concerts in an artist's studio in Montmartre. At one of these Milhaud's fourth string quartet was played, together with the music of five other composers. Henri Collet wrote an article about the concerts entitled 'The Five Russians and Six Frenchmen'. The fact that Honegger was Swiss and Germaine Tailleferre was a Frenchwoman did not seem to be of concern. From that point the name *Les Six* became a label for Auric, Durey, Honegger, Milhaud, Poulenc and Tailleferre. The six were associated by friendship rather than aesthetics and differences in temperaments soon meant that they went on their individual paths. In 1919 Milhaud wrote what is now one of his most popular works *Le Boeuf sur le toit*. It was played for the first time as a piano duet by Auric and Milhaud in Milhaud's flat, where *Les Six* met. *Le Boeuf sur le toit* was the name of a song that Milhaud heard in Rio de Janeiro, and Brazilian influences are evident in the work.

In 1925 Milhaud married his cousin, Madeleine, who was ten years younger than him, and he was to remain happily married for the rest of his life. Madeleine had a highly successful career as an actress and reciter. She was at his side throughout his travels. This was particularly important since, although he enjoyed travelling very much, from the 1940s onwards he was confined to a wheelchair as a result of rheumatoid arthritis.

Many factors influenced Milhaud's compositions. He was naturally eclectic. In 1920 he went to London and heard jazz for the first time, and in 1922 on his first tour of America he went to New York, visiting one of Harlem's night clubs to hear New Orleans-style jazz. Another of his most popular works is *La Création du monde*, a ballet utilizing Negro rhythms. Two of his styles are what Langham Smith describes as neo-Classical and neoclassical. Neo-Classical is the musical language he evolved to parallel Greek tragedy. This includes his short operas (lasting about ten minutes), for example, *Les Malheurs d'Orphée* composed to a libretto by Lunel, *L'Enlèvement d'Europe* (about Jupiters abduction of Europa), *Oresteia* and *Médée*. Neoclassical music includes reworkings of broadly classical music (e.g., Stravinsky's *Dumbarton Oaks* and Bach's *Third Brandenburg Concerto*), as in, for example, *Suite d'après Corrette*.

Milhaud considered himself a thoroughly assimilated Frenchman, but at the same time a Jew from Provence, and thus of Mediterranean culture. Any

Hebraic influence in most of his works is not clearly evident. Fulcher suggests that 'Milhaud preserved the essential elements of Jewish identity, those inimical to French civilization could be jettisoned' and that the interest in Greek tragedy stems from the fact that it is a neutral cultural ground that can be shared by both Jews and Gentiles – a viable path to cultural assimilation. A number of his works have Jewish themes or associations. His earliest, composed in 1916, *Poèmes Juifs* are song settings of eight anonymous poems dedicated either to a living Jewish friend or relative or to the memory of one. The settings are in a style that resembles Debussy. One of his early operas, *Esther de Carpentras* composed in 1925 with a libretto by Lunel, is set in the thirteenth century in Carpentras and is based on the biblical story of Esther.

Other works with Jewish themes are: *Six chants populaires Hébraïque* (1925); *La Reine de Saba* (a Palestinian air for string quartet, 1939); *Sabbath Service* (1948, premiered at the Emanuel Temple in San Francisco in 1949); *L'cho dodi* for cantor, mixed chorus and organ (1948); *David* (an opera, 1952); *Ani Maamin, un chant perdu et retrouvé* (1972); and his last orchestral work, *Ode pour Jerusalem* (1972), which premiered in New York not long before his death. The opera *David*, with libretto by Lunel, was an ambitious undertaking, composed for the 3,000th anniversary of King David's birth, tracing the life of David, from the time when the prophet Samuel visits David's father's house, to the anointment of the boy Solomon as David's successor. It was given its premiere in Jerusalem in June 1954.

Although Milhaud was enormously prolific he did not write his first symphony until he was 47. His intention was not to write one until he was 50, but a commission from the Chicago Symphony Orchestra changed that. He composed rapidly and also eclectically, for example, he set both an encyclical by Pope John XXIII and a seed catalogue (*Catalogue des fleurs*) to music. In his eighth symphony, the *Rhodanienne*, he reworked Smetana's *Vltava* idea, writing a piece about the Rhone. He spent much time travelling, and used this time to compose. He wrote his tenth string quartet whilst on a boat crossing the Atlantic, when the family was forced to flee France at the time of the Nazi occupation, and his opera *Maximilien* from the only book in French in the library of an English cargo ship on which he was returning to America in 1927. He composed orchestral works straight into full scores.

When Milhaud left France in 1940 he was offered a post at Mills College, Oakland, California. He landed in New York City to begin his new life in exile with his wife and son on 15 July 1940, to be met by Kurt WEILL and his wife Lotte Lenya. He spent the war years there, returning to France in 1947, when he combined the post at Mills College with a professorship in composition at the Paris Conservatoire. He continued at Mills College until 1971, when he resigned because of ill health, by which time he was 79 years of age.

In 1940 Milhaud's first symphony was premiered in Chicago. In order to conduct the premiere Milhaud travelled to Chicago from California by train, a journey of two days. He composed *Sonatine* for two violins (Op. 221) on the

270

journey. On the return journey he composed *Sonatine à trois* (Op 221a) for violin, viola and cello. His first violin concerto was written on a train between Portland and Minneapolis. On one occasion the Milhauds were invited to dinner at the Menuhins' in San Francisco, along with the violinist Roman Totenberg. Menuhin asked whether Milhaud had bought anything to play. At the disappointment that he had not, he promptly composed *Duo* for two violins (Op. 258) in forty minutes.

He worked very hard and it has been said that composing distracted him from the pain of rheumatoid arthritis. In spite of this pain and being confined to a wheelchair, he constantly maintained that he led a happy life, as the title of his autobiography proclaims.

Bibliography: *G*; *HBD*; Ken; Paul Collaer, *Darius Milhaud* (New York: Macmillan, 1988); Jane Fulcher, 'The Preparation for Vichy: Anti-Semitism in French Musical Culture between the Two World Wars', *Musical Quarterly*, 73 (1995), p. 469; Richard Langham Smith, 'Mean Milhaud', *Musical Times*, 133 (1992), p. 648; Darius Milhaud, *My Happy Life*, English translation (London: Boyars, 1995); Roger Nichols, *Conversations with Madelaine Milhaud* (London: Faber, 1996)

Monk, Meredith (b. Lima, Peru, 27 November 1942)   Great-grand-daugther on her mother's side of a cantor of a Moscow synagogue. Her grandfather was an operatic bass and her grandparents founded the Zellman Conservatory in New York. She was born in Peru while her mother, Audrey Marsh, a popular singer and well known for her radio commercials, was on tour. Her childhood was spent in New York and Connecticut. She sang before she talked and had started piano lessons with Gershon Konikov and Marcia Poli Kosinsky by the age of 3. As a teenager she became a promising lyric soprano. She went to a Quaker boarding school in Pennsylvania and then to the Sarah Lawrence College in Bronxville, New York, where she studied performing arts, graduating in 1964. She studied piano, composition and singing. After graduation she worked with the Judson Dance Theatre in New York, producing performing pieces such as *Cartoon* (1964) and *Duet for Cat's Scream and Locomotive* (1966).

She is a composer, singer, dancer, film maker and choreographer. Her main interest in composition is theatre music, and central to this is her own voice. Her vocal music involves extended vocal techniques and is influenced by both popular music and minimalism. As a singer she has a three-octave range. She is as interested in medievalism as she is in modernism. The accompanying instruments she has used include piano, harmonium, flute, guitar, dulcimer, accordion, bagpipes and synthesizer. In 1968 she founded the Meredith Monk Vocal Ensemble in order to teach a group of singers her 'extended vocal technique'. They performed in the USA and Europe.

Some representative examples of her works illustrate these interests. In 1969 she was able to use the Guggenheim Museum in New York as performance space for her theatre cantata, *Juice*, for two violins and 85 performers,

who sang and played jew's harps. *Education of the Girlchild* (1972–3) for six solo voices, electric organ and piano has been described as 'a biography of woman-kind'. It follows the span of a woman's life from old age and death back to the earliest years of life. The opera *Quarry* (1976) for 38 voices, two pump organs, two soprano recorders and tape explores images of the Holocaust and uses black and white film that Monk made showing a bleak quarry that is gradually filled with people. Her film *Ellis Island* (1981–2) examines the experience of immigrants, including her own family, at the turn of the century. It opens with a time-lapse sequence of sunrise to dusk on the Hudson River and juxtaposes a tourist commentary on the deserted island where European refugees were 'processed' by American immigration officials with dance sequences showing immigrants arriving in the contemporary empty sheds. *Book of Days* (1985) is a vocal concerto for five voices, chorus and electric organ, which she also made into a film, with a larger group of performers. The film begins with the blasting of a modern wall and behind it a relatively intact medieval village. It centres around a young Jewish girl, Eva Livinf, in fourteenth-century Europe, who has visionary dreams of the twentieth century; comparison is made between the apocalyptic nature of both centuries and the fear of plague, war and religious persecution in the Middle Ages and AIDS, nuclear annihilation and racial strife of the modern age. The theme of being transported through time features in *Education of the Girlhood, Ellis Island* and *Book of Days*.
Bibliography: *AG*; *CC*; *G*; *HBD*; Leb; Pan*; K. Robert Schwartz, *Minimalists* (London: Phaidon, 1996)

Morawetz, Oskar (b. Světlá nad Sázavou, Czechoslovakia, 17 January 1917) Studied in Prague with Karel Hoffmeister (piano) and Kricka (harmony). In 1937 George Szell offered him a conducting post at the Prague Opera, but with the rise of Nazism he fled, first to Vienna and then to Paris, settling with the rest of his family in Toronto in 1940. He resumed his musical education at Toronto University under Leo Smith and Alberto Guerrero. In 1952 he was appointed professor of music at Toronto University, a post he held until 1982. His first compositional success was his first string quartet (1944) and his second, *Sonata Tragica* for piano (1945), both of which won Composers, Authors and Publishers Association of Canada awards. As a composer he is self-taught; whilst absorbing several of the trends of the twentieth century, his music stresses melodic and rhythmic vitality, but does not embrace serial-ism, aleatory or electronic techniques. Among his best-known works are his piano concerto (1962); *Sinfonietta* for winds and percussion (1965); *Memorial to Martin Luther King* (1968) for solo cello, timpani percussion and celesta; and *From the Diary of Anne Frank* (1970) for soprano, timpani, percussion, harp, celesta and strings. This last work has been performed on all four continents and was awarded a special award from the Segal Foundation of Montreal, 'as the most important contribution to Jewish music in Canada'. *Psalm XXII, God Why Have You Forsaken Me?* (1979) for soloist, piano and orchestra was inspired

by the suffering inflicted by the Nazis during World War Two. Morawetz's early works are often optimistic in outlook, featuring lively Slavic rhythms, for example, *Carnival Overture* (1945), *Divertimento for Strings* (1948), and *Overture to a Fairy Tale* (1956), whereas many of his later works are reflective of contemporary tragedies. Works composed in the 1990s reflect composers who have strongly influenced his style, for example, *Tribute to Wolfgang Amadeus* (1990) and *Improvisations on Inventions by J. S. Bach* (1992).
Bibliography: *G*; *HBD*; www.musiccentre.ca/CMC/dac_rca/eng/k_/Morawetz _Dr._Oskar.html

Moscheles, Ignaz (b. Prague, 23 May 1794; d. Leipzig, 10 March 1870)   Son of a cloth merchant, he was born into a happy family of five children. His grandfather was Isaac Schulhof Moscheles, and his great-grandfather Zalman Schulhof, *Dayyan* (a judge who serves on a religious court) in Prague, was burned in 1689.[1] Moscheles's father was very fond of music and wanted to see at least one of the children have a proper training. Ignaz's elder sister was given piano lessons first, but she obviously did not enjoy them, whilst Ignaz looked on, itching to start. At one stage, when Ignaz exclaimed 'Oh how stupid I could do it better myself', the old music tutor, Zahrada, allowed him to try, and must have passed on favourable comments to his father. From then on Ignaz received lessons in place of his sister. He used his pocket money to subscribe to a music lending library to obtain music to practice on his own. By the age of 7 he brazenly tackled Beethoven's *Pathétique* sonata. That same year his father took him to Dionys Weber, director of the Prague Conservatory, to have an assessment of his son's ability. To Ignaz's surprise Weber was very critical of how he performed the *Pathétique*, but nevertheless thought that he had talent and was prepared to teach him, provided he did not play Beethoven until he had mastered Mozart, Clementi and Bach. His father continued to encourage his musical education, taking him to the opera at an early age. Sadly his father developed typhoid fever and died when Ignaz was 14.

Much of what we know of Moscheles's life comes from his diaries and papers. He kept a diary from age of 19 and included in it a retrospective account of his life up to that time. One of his last wishes was to have his diaries and correspondence published, not so much that he should not be forgotten, but rather because he knew personally many leading musicians of the day including MENDELSSOHN, Beethoven, Chopin and Liszt. His diaries are thus a unique account of the musical scene at the time. His devoted wife, Charlotte, had his accounts published in two volumes entitled *Aus Moscheles' Leben*.

After his father's death his mother took advice on his further musical education, and in 1808, at the age of 14, he was sent to Vienna to study counterpoint under Albrechsberger (who had been Beethoven's teacher) and composition under Salieri. One day, when he called on Salieri, he happened to see a note on his teacher's desk with the message, 'Your pupil Beethoven called on you'. This made Moscheles think that if his idol Beethoven still

273

regarded himself a pupil of Salieri, then how much he himself could benefit as his pupil. By 1814 Moscheles was one of Vienna's most popular pianists and had begun his career as a virtuoso. During that year he composed six scherzos, *Variations on a Theme of Handel*, a rondo in A minor for piano duet and minuets and trios for the publisher Artaria's collection of national dances. This led to the publisher commissioning him to prepare a piano reduction of Beethoven's *Fidelio*. Also in 1814 he was asked to write a cantata for the Vienna synagogue, and on the occasion of the victory over Napoleon he conducted the thanksgiving service at which the cantata was performed. Around this time Moscheles converted to Christianity and on becoming baptized assumed the name Ignaz in place of his Hebrew name Isaak.

An interesting and possibly formative association with Beethoven occurred earlier in 1813. At the time Beethoven was going through financial difficulties and was forced to stoop to inferior composition, one result being *The Battle Symphony*. It was performed at charity concerts for war widows and orphans, and the performers at one of the concerts included Spohr, violin; Moscheles, cymbals; Salieri, off-stage guns; Hummel and MEYERBEER[2] on bass drum. In 1815 Moscheles was asked by Countess Hardegg 'to write something quickly and make it sound spectacular' for some charitable event. He responded by writing some variations on a march that was played by the band of Tsar Alexander's own regiment at the time. The piece met with tremendous success and became a favourite with other aspiring pianists, including Schumann. Between 1815 and 1825 Moscheles travelled to give recitals throughout Germany and also in Paris, London and Prague. He was anxious to support his mother and sisters, who had been left with inadequate support after the early death of Moscheles's father.

In 1823 Moscheles visited both Beethoven and his former teacher Salieri. Beethoven greeted Moscheles and his brother warmly, although they had to converse with him in writing on account of Beethoven's deafness. Salieri was mortally ill at the time and his main concern was that Moscheles should tell the world that there was no truth in the absurd rumour that he had poisoned Mozart. Later when Beethoven was terminally ill, Moscheles was involved in arranging for the Royal Philharmonic Society to make him an advanced payment for a concert so that he had enough money to buy medicine and pay the doctor.

A much happier meeting took place in Berlin in 1824 when he first met the 15-year old Mendelssohn. He saw some of Mendelssohn's compositions and also heard his sister Fanny play, and he judged her to be a fine musician. This began a deep friendship, not only between Mendelssohn and Moscheles, but also between Mendelssohn's parents and Moscheles's future wife Charlotte. Mendelssohn's mother asked Moscheles during his stay if he would give their eldest children (Fanny and Felix) lessons. At first Moscheles was reluctant, but on being pressed he agreed.

In January 1825 in Hamburg he met a Jewish girl, Charlotte Embden (1805–89). She had seen him earlier performing at a concert and 'was entranced by his miraculous fingers'. Within two months of meeting they were joined in what was to become a very harmonious marriage. They had five children, all of whom were baptized, and Charlotte was also baptized after the birth of her fourth child. Later that year they settled in London at 3 Chester Place, Regent's Park, where Moscheles taught the piano at the Royal Academy of Music and became conductor to the Philharmonic Society. London was to be their home for the next 21 years. Moscheles continued to lead a very busy life as a virtuoso pianist, teacher, composer and conductor. He also found time to translate Schindler's *The life of Beethoven*.

Most of his compositions are for piano and although there are some works that have stood the test of time and are still played today, for example *Sonata Mélancolique* (Op. 49) and *Grand Sonata* in E flat major (Op. 47), many of the salon pieces are no longer performed. He wrote works for piano and orchestra, including eight piano concertos, and also a symphony, a concert overture, chamber music for piano and several songs. Several publishers persuaded him to write a number of purely fashionable pieces, offering generous payment. These cost him little effort and he did not give them opus numbers. Charlotte's criterion for works of lasting merit was that they were still being performed 30 to 50 years after their composition, and those of Moscheles in that category include: G minor piano concerto, 24 études, *Homage à la Haendel*, *Rondo* in A, *Souvenirs of Ireland*, three *allegri di bravura* and the two sonatas listed above.

In 1829 the family were grieving the loss of their 3-year-old son, who died of whooping cough, but some relief was provided by the visit of the 19-year-old Mendelssohn. During the visit Mendelssohn's *Midsummer Night's Dream* overture was performed twice and also his concerto for two pianos, with Mendelssohn and Moscheles playing together. Both were a great success. Mendelssohn visited again on a number of successive years. Moscheles was responsible for introducing a number of important works to the public. In 1832 he was asked to conduct a performance of Beethoven's *Missa Solemnis* in the large music room of the arts correspondent of the *Times*, Alsager. It was the first time that Moscheles had conducted an orchestra and the first time that the *Missa Solemnis* was performed in England. The first performance in England of Beethoven's Ninth Symphony had been given in 1824, and it had been dismissed by the critics. Moscheles was keen to have it performed again. When he conducted his first performance on 17 April 1837 it was so successful that he gave three further performances in 1838. By 1839, when Moscheles was 45, he decided to retire from performing in public, whilst still at his peak, to make way for younger pianists, for example Thalberg, who was one of his pupils. From 1840 he only performed in public on rare occasions, although he still performed at private functions and conducted for the Philharmonic Society.

In 1846 he left England to become principal professor of piano at the Leipzig Conservatory, which had been recently founded by Mendelssohn.

One of his last assignments in England was to conduct what was to become Mendelssohn's greatest oratorio, *Elijah*, at the Birmingham Music Festival in August 1846. During the rehearsal he became unwell and Mendelssohn replaced him for the evening rehearsal. The oratorio was an outstanding success. Within three weeks of the close of the festival Moscheles's family had left for Liepzig. Moscheles remained at the Leipzig Conservatory for the rest of his life. Mendelssohn's death in 1847 was a profound blow to him, but he resolved to maintain the high standards of teaching that Mendelssohn would have wished. He continued teaching and composing. In 1849 he took his family to Prague so that the children could see his and his ancestors' birthplace and to visit relatives still living in the city. In 1850 his son Felix left for Paris, where he began his art studies. Later that year an anonymous article appeared in *Neuen Zeitschrift für Musik* entitled *Das Judentum in der Musik*, which sought to belittle Mendelssohn and Meyerbeer. Moscheles and his colleagues sought to have the editor, Dr Brendel, a colleague at the conservatory, dismissed. The directorate of the conservatory charged Dr Brendel to name the anonymous author. He refused to disclose, but was not dismissed. Years later, through a listing of his official writings, it became clear that the author was Richard Wagner.

Moscheles remained both physically and mentally fit until shortly before his death at the age of 76. He led a satisfying and happy life and was under no illusions as to the merits of his compositions. He found it difficult to like some of the compositions of the next generation of composers, as is evident in the following quotation: 'May the new composers not reach beyond Beethoven, Haydn and Mozart, nor try to overthrow them – they who till now have been our signposts. We small lights should naturally be buried under this rubble – and I for one would deem this an honour.' Moscheles's son, Felix, became a painter. He lived in London and painted his father's portrait at the age of 72. Moscheles's second daughter, who was an accomplished pianist, emigrated to Jerusalem and married the German consul George Rosen.[3] A number of distant relatives of the family have become noted in the arts, for example, Reynaldo HAHN and Leo Lehmann.[4]

Bibliography: *G*; *HBD*; Ken; Emil F. Smidak, *Isaak-Ignaz Moscheles* (Aldershot, UK: Scolar Press, 1988)

1. A. Z. Idelsohn, *Jewish Music in its Historical Development* (New York: Schocken, 1967), p. 511.
2. E. Gartenberg, *Vienna, its Musical Heritage* (University Park, PA: Pennsylvania State University Press, 1968).
3. Jehoash Hirshberg, *Music in the Jewish Community of Palestine, 1880–1948* (Oxford: Clarendon Press, 1995), p. 6.
4. H. Roche, *Moscheles: Jewish Composer of Prague, Vienna, London and Leipzig,* 21st International Conference on Jewish Genealogy, London, 2001.

Moszkowski, Moritz (b. Breslau, 23 August 1854; d. Paris, 4 March 1925)   Son of a Jewish–Polish businessman who immigrated to Germany. He first studied at Dresden, then Berlin with Wüesrt and Kullak. He settled in Berlin and

taught piano at Kullak's academy for many years, at the same time travelling as a concert pianist. He was a brilliant pianist, a very effective teacher and he also composed, primarily works for piano. His career as a pianist was interrupted during the 1880s by an arm complaint and he retired to Paris in 1897. His piano compositions are generally light and were very popular at the time. They include: *Spanische Tänze*, originally for four hands, Op. 12; *Album Espanol*, Op. 21 (1879); *Aus aller Herren Ländern*, Op. 23; *Concert Studies*, Op. 24; *Barcarolle*, Op. 27; *Miniatures*, Op. 28; *Gondoliera*, Op. 41; and *Suite*, Op. 50. He also wrote violin pieces, a piano concerto, Op. 59 (1898), and an opera, *Boabdil der letzte Maurenkönig*, modelled on the operas of MEYERBEER. The opera was performed in Berlin, Prague and New York but then soon disappeared from the stage.
Bibliography: *G*; *HBD*; Ho*; Ly*

Nathan, Isaac (b.Cantebury, UK, 1790; d. Sydney, Australia, 15 January 1864) Son of Menehem Mona (d. 1823), a Jewish scholar of Polish descent and almost certainly cantor at the synagogue in Cantebury. He was educated at an Anglo-Jewish boarding school established by Solomon Lyon, then at Cambridge after 1805. In 1809 he was apprenticed by his father to Domenico Corri for singing and composition in London. Although Byron was at Cambridge between 1805 and 1807, the two appear not to have met until 1814, when they collaborated in setting 26 of Byron's poems to Hebrew melodies. Nathan adapted the chants to Byron's poetry. In a letter to Byron, Nathan maintains that some of the melodies he used were 'sung by the Hebrews before the destruction of the Temple'. However, according to Idelsohn, with the exception of those for *Chanukah* and *Pesach* they were not traditional, but were created or adopted by various *chazzanim*. They were published in 1815 as *A Selection of Hebrew Melodies, Ancient and Modern, with Appropriate Symphonies and Accompaniments, by J. Braham and I. Nathan; The Poetry Written Expressly for the Work by the Right Honorable Lord Byron*. They were first sung in London by John Braham and were an instant success, remaining in print until 1861. In the summer of 1812 Nathan married Elizabeth Rosetta Worthington, who came from a wealthy and respected Irish family. The marriage took place in St Mary Abbots Church, Kensington, but Nathan did not renounce his Judaism, and the couple were also married three months later in the Western Synagogue in St Alban's Place, London.

Nathan was a composer, teacher and writer. He taught Princess Charlotte, daughter of the future George IV, and he was author of a book entitled *History of Music*. He composed several comic operas. In 1841 he was financially ruined and emigrated to Australia, initially living in Melbourne, where he gave concerts and opened a singing academy. He produced mainly patriotic odes and songs and his last composition was *A Song of Freedom*, which he wrote as a gift for Queen Victoria. He set up his own music publishing business, transcribed Aboriginal music into western notation and composed the first opera written in Australia. Three of his London operas were successfully performed in Australia. He died at the age of 74 in an accident in which he was crushed beneath the wheels of the first horse-drawn tram in Sydney. He has been described as the 'father' of Australian music, not only for his own contribution; one of his descendents, Harry Nathan, is claimed to have written *Waltzing Matilda* and the conductor Sir Charles Mackerras is his great-great-great-grandson.

Bibliography: *G*; Ho*; Ly*; Thomas L. Ashton, *Byron's Hebrew Melodies* (London: Routledge, 1972); A. Z., Idelsohn, *Jewish Music in its Historical Development* (New York: Schocken, 1967), p. 338; Barrie, Weinberg, 'Some Thoughts on Jewish Music Contributions to Musical Life in Britain from the Eighteenth Century to the Twentieth Century', in S. Stanton and A. Knapp (eds), *Proceedings of the First International Conference on Jewish Music* (London: City University, 1994), p. 196; www.us-israel.org/jsource/loc/loc19intro.html

Offenbach, Jacques [Jakob] (b. Cologne, 20 June 1819; d. Paris, 5 October 1880) Grandson of Isaac Juda Eberst, a music teacher in Offenbach-on-Main. His father, also Isaac Juda, earned his living as a bookbinder and music teacher, but in 1799 left Offenbach-on-Main to become a wandering minstrel. In 1802 he settled in Deutz, a suburb of Cologne, where there seemed to be good opportunities for earning a livelihood by playing music for entertainment and as cantor to the large Jewish community there. Instead of being known in Deutz as *der Offenbacher*, he simply changed his name to Offenbach. Shortly afterwards he married the daughter of a money-changer, and from 1807, at two-year intervals until 1825, they had ten children, seven daughters and three sons. Jakob was the seventh child and the second son. His father continued with music, giving violin, flute, guitar and singing lessons, and published a collection of prayers for the use of young Jewish folk. The family was brought up in the Jewish tradition. All the children showed a talent for music, but from an early age Jakob showed most promise. He played the violin at the age of 6, and at 8 began composing. When the family wanted to play a Haydn quartet and lacked a cellist, Jakob, who had been secretly practising, took the cello part. From the age of 9 he was given cello lessons and the instrument became the first instrument on which he was extremely accomplished. Jakob, his sister Isabella (piano) and his brother Julius (violin) played as a trio in Cologne bars.

By the time Julius was 18 and Jakob was 14 their father decided that it would be better for their musical education if they moved to Paris. He also felt that Jews were treated better there than in Germany. He approached Cherubini, the 73-year-old head of the Paris Conservatoire, to ask if Jakob might be enrolled. At first Cherubini was very negative, but after hearing Jakob play the cello he readily agreed to Julius's and Jakob's enrolment. Their father also found positions for them in the synagogue choir before he returned to Cologne. Jakob studied with Vaslin at the conservatoire, but found it dull and frustrating and left after one year. Both boys learned French quickly and changed their names to Jacques and Jules. After leaving the conservatoire Jacques found a position as cellist at the Opéra-Comique. One of the operas for which he played in the orchestra was HALÉVY's *L'Eclair*. Jacques was already very impressed with Halévy's *La Juive*, which at the time was a great success in Paris. He met Halévy, and they saw *La Juive* together.

Halévy became friends with the two brothers, was impressed with their talent and gave them lessons in composition. This sowed the seeds of Offenbach wanting to become a composer. In 1837 a waltz entitled *Rebecca*, composed by Jacques, was performed in the Jardin Turc. It was based on fifteenth-century Hebrew themes he had known as a child. For a time it was a favourite dance in Paris. Offenbach left the Opéra-Comique and met Flotow, a composer well acquainted with the world of the salon, who knew Chopin, Gonoud and MEYERBEER. Through Flotow Jacques gained entry to the Paris salons, where he played the cello and performed some of his own compositions. He received a commission for a score for the vaudeville *Pascal et Chambard*. He gave his first public concert with his brother Jules in January 1839.

Offenbach continued to perform in salons. At one of these he met his future wife, Herminie d'Alcain, the stepdaughter of John Mitchell, a London concert agent. Herminie's family imposed two conditions on their marriage: that he should give up Judaism and embrace Catholicism, and that he should go on a concert tour of London. He agreed to both, apparently without reluctance. In London he played before Queen Victoria and Prince Albert, and also in concerts with JOACHIM and MENDELSSOHN. A musical review stated: '[Offenbach] is on the violoncello what Paganini was on the violin.' He was unsuccessful at getting his works such as *L'Alcôve* staged at the Opéra-Comique. With the revolution of 1848 he returned temporarily to Cologne, where he performed a range of works including a fantasy on Meyerbeer's *Robert le diable* for seven cellos, a Chinese march, a stage work entitled *Marietta* and a variety of salon numbers. He returned to Paris a year later.

In 1850 he was appointed conductor at the Comédie-Française and was responsible for all matters musical with a salary of 6,000 francs. Nevertheless, he still had little success in getting his stage works accepted until the Exhibition year of 1855. He felt that what he described as miniature Grand Operas were being readily performed but that this was not the genre he had in mind. He had watched the success of Hervé's Théâtre des Folies-Nouvelles, which put on burlesques of fashionable operas, satirical revues and vaudeville. Hervé agreed to put on Offenbach's *Oyayaie, ou la reine des iles*, subtitled 'Cannibalism in Music'. Audience reaction to this led Offenbach to decide to set up his own theatre. He bought a dilapidated building owned by a conjurer who had fallen on hard times. The important advantage of this ramshackle building was its proximity to the Palace of Industry, the centrepiece of the Exhibition. He had it renovated and called it Bouffes-Parisiens. It opened in July 1855. It was sufficiently successful for him to give up his position at the

Comédie Française. He eventually moved to the Théâtre Comte. He composed ten staged works during 1855, using various librettists. He had problems with librettists withdrawing at the last minute until he met the librettist Ludovic Halévy, the nephew of the composer Fromenthal Halévy. He collaborated with Ludovic in many of his later stage works, including *La Belle Hélène*.

It was from the opening of Bouffes-Parisiens that he started to achieve success in the performance of his own works. Within the first month of opening the Bouffes-Parisiens showed a clear profit of 11,000 francs. Initially Offenbach's licence did not permit him to have more than three characters on stage at a time. He found various ways of circumventing this. For example, when he wanted a chorus of Greek soldiers in *Agamemnon* he had a troop of Greek soldiers painted on scenery behind and a chorus off-stage. Restrictions were gradually lifted and he was able to compose more ambitious works. The two-act *Orphée aux Enfers* (1858) was highly successful and served as a model for later works. It was a parody of Gluck's opera, *Orpheus*. Initially it caused controversy. Musicians were annoyed by the apparent slight to Gluck. One critical review said that it amounted to sacrilege, but this only had the effect of raising interest, helping it on its way to success. It ran to 228 performances before being taken off, and then only because the cast needed a break. It was revived later. In 1860 Offenbach became a naturalized French subject.

Offenbach was something of a dandy, taking great care with his appearance. He had a wardrobe full of trousers and shoes and had a hairdresser in attendance every day. He suffered from gout. He had little appetite and never weighed more than six and a half stone. He was a workaholic and even had a desk in his brougham so that he could compose whilst on the move.

In a sketch that Offenbach wrote in 1860 entitled *Le Musicien de l'avenir* he makes fun of Wagner's music. At the time Wagner was living in Paris and his opera *Tannhäuser* had been greeted with jeers and catcalls. Wagner never forgave Offenbach; his attitude changed from initially being patronizing to outright hatred, describing his *Orpheus* as an abomination. By the 1860s Offenbach had become established abroad as a composer. His most successful works were written between 1864 and 1868: *La Belle Hélène*, *Barbebleue*, *La Grande-Duchesse de Gérolstein* and *La Périchole*. He was to become one of the most outstanding composers of popular music in the ninetenth century, establishing an international genre that included Johann Strauss, Sullivan, Léhar, and the twentieth-century musical.

The success of many of Offenbach's stage works depended a great deal on having good librettists and good performers. Halévy and Meilhac proved to be his best librettists, and 1855 saw the début of Lady Hortense Schneider, who in *Le Violoneux* was to become his star singer. She was to perform in his most successful works, including *La Belle Hélène*, *La Vie parisienne*, *Barbebleue*, *La Grande-Duchesse de Gérolstein* and *La Périchole*. When Meilhac and Halévy first met they immediately sensed an affinity. Meilhac's strength was in producing the broad outline of the plot, while Halévy provided verse for the musical numbers. The combination of Offenbach, Halévy, Meilhac and Schneider brought Offenbach to the pinnacle of his career and the four became, in effect, the accredited entertainers of the Second Empire. New catchphrases from his operettas were used by people in the streets. They were enjoyed by audiences drawn from all walks of life, including the aristocracy, politicians and financiers. He deflated the morals and manners of the Second Empire. *La Vie parisienne* was one of the early contributors to the perception of 'gay Paris'. Many of Offenbach's operettas have elements of parody and mockery. *La Grande-Duchesse de Gérolstein* mocks the higher echelons of the military. Bismark is said to have choked with laughter and exclaimed: 'That's it That's absolutely how it is.' His suspicion of the French military was confirmed. Halévy, who was very well aware of the political situation, wrote in his journal: 'Bismark is helping to double our takings. This time its war we're laughing at, and war is at our gates.'

Halévy foresaw the dark days ahead, whereas Offenbach did not anticipate them, but rather saw the political manoeuvrings as more satirical material for his operettas. On 19 July 1870 France declared war on Bismark's Germany. In the sombre mood that followed Offenbach fell out of favour, and newspaper articles accused him of being 'a Prussian at heart'. He was wounded by the accusation, as he felt very much a Frenchman at heart and was proud to have been appointed *chevalier* in the Legion of Honour. After the war he attempted to run his own theatre again. He invested a considerable fortune in the Théâtre de la Gaîté, but it was unsuccessful and closed just short of bankruptcy in 1875. In 1876, the year that marked the 100th anniversary of American independence, he received an invitation to go to America to perform 30 concerts. Although at first he was reluctant, the fee of 30,000 dollars came at an opportune time. There was much in America to interest him, including the warmth of the reception, but he missed his family and Paris and returned home in 1878.

During his lifetime Offenbach wrote nearly 100 operettas, but only one serious opera, which was unfinished at the time of his death: *Les Contes d'Hoffmann*. This was his main preoccupation from 1877 until his death. In 1880, while he was working on it at the Pavillon Henri IV in Saint-Germain, his worsening health forced him to return to Paris, where he died in October. The gout from which he had suffered for many years had finally attacked his heart. A Catholic priest administered the last rites. He was given a lavish Catholic funeral, at which the famous tenor Talazac sung extracts from *Les Contes d'Hoffmann* adapted to the words of the *Dies Irae* and *Agnus Dei*. At the request of the family, Guiraud completed the score of *Les Contes d'Hoffmann*. It was given its premiere at the Opéra-Comique in February 1881.

Bibliography: *G*; *HBD*; Ken; Ly*; WW; James Harding, *Jacques Offenbach: a Biography* (London: Calder, 1980)

Olivero, Betty (b. Tel Aviv, 16 May 1954)   Studied piano with Vincze-Kraus and composition with SADAI and SCHIDLOWSKY at the Rubin Academy at Tel Aviv from 1972 to 1978 and then at Yale University School of Music she continued her study of composition with DRUCKMAN and Amy, graduating in 1981. A Leonard Bernstein scholarship enabled her to study at Tanglewood with Luciano Berio, with whom she continued to study in Italy. *Cantes Amargos* for voice and orchestra and *Horizons* were commissioned by the Maggio Musicale Fiorentino. In many of her compositions she is inspired by music from Jewish communities throughout the Diaspora, but uses contemporary composition techniques learned from Berio and Schidlowsky. Her works include: *Tehilim* (Psalm) for 12 cellos and four double basses (1980); *Pan* for five flutes (1984); *Batnun* for double bass and chamber orchestra (1986); *Presenze* for ten players, which was commissioned in 1987 by the Fromm Music Foundation; *Maqamat*, five folk songs for female voice and nine instruments (1988); and *Tenuot* ('Movements' in Hebrew) for solo instruments and orchestra (1990).
Bibliography: *G*; Grad; *GW*

Orff, Carl (b. Munich, 10 July 1895; d. Munich, 29 March 1982)   Came from a military family and was familiar with the sounds of regimental bands from an early age. He learned to play the cello, piano and organ from an early age. By 1905 he had published his first story in a children's magazine. His first serious attempts at composing were songs to his own texts, with his mother helping him to write them down. In 1911, at the age of 16, his first songs were published and he also composed music for puppet plays. He wrote his first opera in 1913, *Gisei: das Opfer*. He studied at the Munich Academy of Music until 1914 and then held positions as *Kapellmeister* in Munich, Mannheim and Darmstadt between 1915 and 1919, with one year of military service in between (1917–18). In 1920 he studied for a year with Heinrich KAMINSKI, after which he became less interested in contemporary music and developed a strong interest in early music and in staging its revival by making arrangements of works such as Monteverdi's *Orfeo* and *The Coronation of Poppea*.

An important event was his meeting with Dorothee Günther, with whom he founded, in 1924, the Günther Schule, which aimed to unify the disciplines of dancing and gymnastics. Orff also became interested in the unification of music, speech and movement. He created a new range of easily played percussion instruments with the help of Curt Sachs and encouraged teachers and pupils to create their own simply constructed music. He published the basis and principles of his method of teaching in five-volume work entitled *Schulwerk* (1950–4). The school continued to function until 1943, when it was disbanded after bombing. In 1937 Orff composed the music for which he is best known, the dramatic cantata *Carmina Burana*. This is based on medieval student songs and stresses the rhythmic aspects of music. It is influenced by the style of Stravinsky's *Oedipus Rex*. It was staged in Frankfurt in 1937 and at

La Scala in 1942. The rhythmic nature, melodic language and inspiration from Bavarian folk material, described in the newpaper *Völkischer Beobachter* as 'the clear, ardent and disciplined music required for our times', made it a suitable showpiece of fascist values. Orff, having one Jewish grandmother, is said to have considered emigrating in 1938, but doubted that he would have had continued success outside Bavaria. He married four times. One of his wives was the anti-Nazi author Luise Rinser, whom he married after World War Two. By this time he had become interested in Greek drama. He composed a trilogy of operas: *Antigone* (1949), *Oedipus the Tyrant* (1959) and *Prometheus* (1969). Most of his mature compositions are for the theatre, and much of his early work he withdrew.
Bibliography: *G*; *HBD*; Ken; Leb; Michael H. Kater, *The Twisted Muse* (Oxford: Oxford University Press, 1997)*; A. Liess, *Carl Orff: his Life and Work* (London: Calder & Boyars, 1966)

Orgad, Ben-Zion [Büschel] (b. Gelsenkirchen, Germany, 21 August 1926) Went to Palestine with his parents in 1933 and showed an interest in music at an early age. He is one of the first generation of Israeli composers with Hebrew as his main language. At the Rubin Academy of Music in Jerusalem he studied violin with Kinari and Bergmann and composition with TAL, and in Tel Aviv he also studied composition with BEN HAIM. He visited the USA and studied with COPLAND at Tanglewood in the summers of 1949, 1952 and 1961, and then with FINE and SHAPERO at Brandeis University from 1960 to 1962. On returning to Israel he became inspector of music studies in the Ministry of Education and Culture. His music is basically tonal and often uses biblical texts, and many of his works are for voice and orchestra. His works include: *Min He'afar* (Out of the desert) for voice, flute, bassoon, viola and cello (1956); *Trio* for strings (1961); *Mismorim* (Psalms) for solo voices and chamber orchestra (1968); *The First Night Watch* for orchestra (1973); *Melodic Dialogues on Three Scrolls* for violin, oboe, percussion, string quartet and string orchestra (1969); *Duo* for violin and cello (1973), *Hymn to the Goddess Hallel* for orchestra (1979); and *She'arim* for brass orchestra (1986). He also published an autobiographical/philosophical book entitled *Colmontage – a Partita for Solo Voice* (1989).
Bibliography: *G*; Grad; *HBD*

Ornstein, Leo (b. Krememchug, Ukraine, 2 December 1892; d. Green Bay, Wisconsin, 24 February 2002) Son of a cantor in Kiev and St Petersburg. He began piano lessons with his father at the age of 3 and had additional lessons from Vladimir Puchalski in Kiev. At the age of10 he played for the famous pianist Josef Hofmann, who was touring Russia at the time. Hofmann recommended that he enter the St Petersburg Conservatory. His father claimed he was older than his real age in order that he could gain admittance to the conservatory. As a child prodigy he played the piano in the salons of St

Petersburg. In 1907 the family emigrated to New York to avoid anti-Semitic disturbances. There he studied at the Institute of Musical Art with Bertha Fiering Tapper. He made his professional début as a pianist in 1911 and toured Europe in 1913 and 1914. Among the works he performed in 1915 were compositions by SCHOENBERG. His first compositions were for piano: *Two Impressions of Notre Dame* (1914), *Dwarf Suite* (1915) and *Wild Men's Dance* (*Danse sauvage*) (*c.* 1915). After performances of these early works he was considered a futuristic composer. His compositions sounded frenzied and were highly dissonant, so much so that one critic wrote 'I never thought I would live to hear Arnold Schoenberg sound so tame.'[1] As a concert pianist he was very popular, provided he was not playing his own music. He ended his concert career abruptly at its height in 1920, afterwards only playing in public occasionally. He concentrated on teaching and composing. His compositional style also changed to that of lush Romanticism. He became head of the piano department at the Philadelphia Musical Academy in 1920, and he founded the Ornstein Music School. He retired from teaching in 1953. He made a reputation as a composer through his dissonant polytonal, polyrhythmic piano compositions, but his music was rarely performed during the period 1950–70. Since then, however, there has been a revival of interest. Although he retired from teaching in 1953 he continued composing until 1990, when he was 98 years of age. He lived in retirement in Wisconsin. He was a prolific composer and published eight volumes of piano works. His first three piano compositions he played in public on a number of occasions, but he never wrote them down at the time. Several years later, when he attempted to do so, he found that he had forgotten them. Most of his compositions are solo piano works, but he has also written three string quartets, *Hebraic Fantasy* for violin and piano (1929), a number of songs and a piano concerto.
Bibliography: *G*; *HBD*; Ho*; Ly*; D. Ewen, *American Composers* (London: Hale, 1982)

1. G. Rumson (1998), www.wiscomposers.org/news/1998_06/feature.html

Paporisz, Yoram (b. Poland, 1944; d. Freiburg, Germany, 1992) Emigrated from Poland to Israel in 1957, where he studied at the Rubin Academy of Music in Tel Aviv under BOSCOVICH. He later studied in Italy and then with Wolfgang Fortner in Freiburg, Germany. Whilst in Freiburg he was diagnosed as having multiple sclerosis and was unable to return to Israel. He was confined to a nursing home, where he continued to write as long as his eyesight permitted. He wrote a five-volume work, *Discoveries at the Piano*, and composed a number of instrumental works, of which *Florianata* for flute solo (1970) written for Aurele Nicolet is the best known.
Bibliography: Grad

Partos, Oedoen [Ödön] (b. Budapest, 1 October 1907; d. Tel Aviv, 6 July 1977) His grandfather was a devout Jew but his parents were completely assimilated and as a young man he was indifferent to Judaism or Zionism. Hubay heard him play at the age of 8 and was sufficiently impressed to take him on as a pupil at the Budapest Academy of Music, where he also studied composition with Kodaly at the Franz Liszt Academy. He graduated at the age of 17 and became leader of the Lucerne Stadtorchestra from 1924 to 1926 and leader of the Budapest Konzertorchestra from 1926 to 1927. In 1929 he moved to Berlin where he performed as a violin soloist with orchestras and also performed in chamber groups. Whilst in Berlin he also composed chamber music and music for theatre and films.

The rise of Nazism prompted him to return to Budapest, and Bronslaw Huberman was interested in auditioning him for the Palestine Symphony Orchestra. However, in 1936 Partos accepted a position teaching violin and composition at the Baku Academy in Azerbaijan. This appealed to his political tendencies and also his interest in Asian music, but when pressurized to join the Communist Party he decided to return to Budapest as leader of the Konzertorchestra. He was about to sign a contract as leader and soloist in Lima, Peru, when Huberman again invited him for audition, this time in Florence. The meeting was so successful that he instantly accepted Huberman's offer to become first violist in the Palestine Symphony Orchestra (later the Israel Philharmonic) and settled in Palestine in 1938. At the time he was steeped in the European musical tradition, being particularly influenced by Bartok and Kodaly, but in the coming years he showed increasing interest in the music of eastern Jewish communities. He stayed with the orchestra until 1956 and also played the viola in the Israel Quartet until 1954. He was appointed director of the Tel Aviv Academy of Music in 1951.

Most of Partos's compositions are for orchestral and chamber music, often with a strong emphasis on strings and many have solo string parts. The best example of his compositions during the European phase is *Concertino for Strings* (1932), which shows the strong influence of Kodaly. After Partos went to live in Palestine he showed great interest in oriental folk song, and Braha Zefira, who sang this music unaccompanied, commissioned him to write instrumental accompaniments. These accompaniments also provided the inspiration for a number of his subsequent works, including *Four Israeli Tunes* for strings and piano (1948), *Hezionot* (Visions) for flute, piano and strings (1957) and *Maqamat* for flute and string quartet (1959). 'Maqamat' is the Arabic Near Eastern equivalent of an Indian *raga*. In 1946 he wrote *Yizkor* (In Memoriam) for viola and string orchestra, which is dedicated to the victims of World War Two. In 1960 he became very interested in serial technique and a number of his compositions after this date reflect this, for example, *Tehilim* (Psalms) for string quartet and chamber orchestra (1960), *Demuyot* (Figures) for orchestra (1960) and *Agadah* (Legend) for piano, viola and percussion (1960). During the 1960s Partos continued to experiment using microtones, clusters and some aleatory writing, but almost invariably maintaining an element of folk music. He wrote three viola concertos: the first entitled *Song of Praise* (1949), the second in 1957 and the third, *Sinfonia Concertante* in 1962. He wrote one violin concerto (1958). One of his last compositions was *Music for Oboe and Chamber Orchestra*, which was first performed by Heinz Holliger in 1976.

Bibliography: *G*; Grad; Ly*; Jehoash Hirshberg, *Music in the Jewish Community of Palestine, 1880–1948* (Oxford: Clarendon, 1995), pp. 161–2

Perle, George (b. Bayonne, New Jersey, 6 May 1915)   Born of immigrant Russian–Jewish parents. He began his first piano lessons when about age 7 from his cousin, who had recently arrived from Russia. However, from an early age Perle was more interested in composing than in playing. He studied with Wesley La Violette at De Paul University (1934–8) and with Ernst Krenek in the early 1940s. In 1937 he was one of the first American composers to recognize and be strongly influenced by the Second Viennese School, a subject about which he was to become an authority. This interest led to a number of writings, for example, *Serial Composition and Atonality: an Introduction to the Music of Schoenberg, Berg, and Webern* (1962; 6th edn 1991) and *The Operas of Alban Berg* (2 volumes, 1980 and 1985). In *Twelve Tonality* (1977, 1996) and *The Listening Composer* (1990) he sets out his own musical language and presents the view that the disparate styles of post-diatonic music share common structural elements that collectively imply a new tonality. He is better known as a musicologist than as composer. He has taught in a number of universities, including the University of Louisville (1949–57), the University of California at Davis (1957–61) and Queens College, City University of New York (1961–84). One of his early compositions is *Hebrew Melodies* for solo cello, composed in 1945 in Okazaki, Japan. As chaplain's assistant he was with the first American troops to occupy Japan after the end of the Second World War. In this role he met the rabbi in charge, a great lover of music, who provided the inspiration and source material for the work. Many of Perle's compositions are for piano and include *Concertino* for piano, wind and timpani (1979), *Serenade* No. 3 for piano and orchestra (1983), piano concertos (No. 1, 1990, and No. 2, 1992). In 1986 he won the Pulitzer prize for his Wind Quintet No. 4. He is a prolific composer but a number of works composed before the 1970s he has subsequently withdrawn.

Bibliography: *G*; *HBD*; Leb; www.sai-national.org/phil/composers/gperle.htm; Werb, B. 1995, Troy 157 [record sleeve]

Pleskow, Raoul (b. Vienna, 12 October 1931)   Emigrated from Austria to the United States in 1939 and became a naturalized American in 1945. He attended the Juilliard School of Music in New York (1950–2) and studied composition with RATHAUS at Queens College and with Luening at Columbia University. He joined the C. W. Post College on Long Island in 1959 and succeeded Stefan WOLPE as chairman of the music department in 1970. He has composed over 170 opuses, mainly songs, piano sonatas and choral and chamber music. His early works are mainly atonal, for example, *Movement for Nine Players* (1966), but his later works combine tonal and atonal styles, such as in his best-known work, *Four Bagatelles* for orchestra (1981).

Bibliography: *HBD*; http://graham.main.nc.us/~bhammel/MUSIC/RP/bio.html; www.cs.bsu.edu/homepages/dlsills/David_jewish.shtml*

Popper, David (b. Prague, 16 June 1843; d. Vienna, 7 August 1913)   Son of Anselmus Popper, cantor at two synagogues in the Josefov district of Prague, namely the Pinkus synagogue and the Zigeiner synagogue. He was the fourth of seven children. The home was musical, as might be expected of a cantor, and there were many family gatherings around the piano. David began improvising at the piano at the age of 5 and started violin lessons at the age of 6. Being a violinist was regarded by the family as a more likely way of earning a living than being a pianist. Violin lessons continued until David was 12. He continued to improvise well on the piano and showed sufficient promise for the family to decide he should apply for admission to the Prague Conservatory. He impressed well at the audition and was offered a place on condition that he studied the cello. There was a shortage of cellists at the National Theatre, the Opera and the Philharmonic Orchestra at the time. He studied under Goltermann (1827–76). At the age of 15 he stood in at the Opera House for Goltermann, who was indisposed, playing the solo cello part in Rossini's *William Tell*. He always spoke highly of Goltermann in later life and dedicated his first cello concerto to him. He graduated in 1861 and toured Germany, where he met Hans von Bülow, who was impressed with his virtuosity and arranged for his engagement as second cellist in the orchestra of the ducal court of Prince Constantine Hohenzollern at Löwenberg in Lower Silesia. It had been mooted that he might succeed DAVIDOV, who was leaving the Leipzig Gewandhaus Orchestra for St Petersburg. Although Löwenberg could have been regarded as provincial, it had a good orchestra nevertheless, as the result of the prince's patronage. Besides playing in the orchestra there were opportunities to develop as a cello soloist and he also began to compose. When the first cellist, Oswald, died in 1862, Popper moved to first cellist. That same year the prince gave him the title of *Kammervirtuoso*, and in appreciation Popper composed *Six Character Pieces*, Op. 3, that contains two pieces, 'Arlequin' and 'Papillon', which were to become two of Popper's most popular works. The bulk of Popper's compositions published between 1865 and 1880 (Op. 3 to Op. 24) were performed from manuscript prior to publication. In 1863 he met Wagner, who conducted the Löwenberg orchestra in a concert at which Popper was solo cellist. He was a great admirer of Wagner as is evident from some of the Wagnerian harmonic progressions that he uses. Many of the cello concertos played in the 1860s are almost unknown today. The concerto by Volkmann was one that Popper played very successfully in public all over Europe. Between 1863 and 1868 he still played at Löwenberg, but spent an increasing amount of time as a travelling virtuoso.

In 1865 he performed his Cello Concerto in D minor (Op. 8) at Löwenburg; it was his first large-scale composition. From 1868 to 1873 he became the cello soloist at the Vienna Court Opera House and the Vienna Philharmonic Orchestra. He married the concert pianist, Sophie Mentor, daughter of the cellist Joseph Mentor, in 1872. The marriage was to last only 14 years. Both Popper and his wife had very busy performing schedules. As cellist at the Vienna Court Opera he was involved in more than 250 concerts a season and travelled extensively. The music critic Hanslick wrote that Popper and Davidov were the outstanding cellists of their day. Sophie also travelled a lot as a concert artist. A combination of the extensive travel that separated Popper and his wife and professional jealousy led to the eventual breakdown of their marriage. Their daughter Celeste was born in 1876, and because of their professional activities she was fostered from a very early age in northern Bohemia. In 1883 Sophie accepted a professorship offered by RUBINSTEIN at the St Petersburg Conservatory and a more permanent separation led to their divorce in 1886.

By 1880 Popper had accumulated 60 published opuses, of which about 30 were played regularly. After one concert in Odessa in the 1880s, when anti-Semitism was especially rife, Popper was approached in his dressing-room by a man who asked him to play *Kol Nidre* there and then in private. Popper obliged, playing it from memory as he remembered it from childhood when his father sang it. In 1886 Popper moved to Budapest to become a professor at the Budapest Music Academy and he married the 20-year-old Olga Löbl, the daughter of a prosperous businessman and founder of a silk firm in Prague. Popper's daughter Celeste remained with her foster parents, but Olga's mother supervised her welfare and she spent holidays with David and Olga. Popper was to remain in Budapest for the rest of his life. A new Hungarian Academy of Music was formed with Liszt as president. As Liszt was anxious to establish an international reputation from the start, the initial appointments were critical. The Hungarian violinist Jenö Hubay was invited to be in charge of violin playing. He accepted on the condition that Popper was appointed in charge of cello teaching. At the time there was resistance from some quarters, who wanted only Hungarian nationals; Popper did not speak Hungarian. Some years later the nationalist elements in the press tried to damage Popper as a 'foreign' professor and criticized him for 'neglecting his daughter by fostering her out'.

Together with Hubay, Popper founded the Hubay Quartet. This group often worked closely with Johannes Brahms, performing his quartets, and Brahms himself played the piano in works for piano and strings. In 1887 Popper's son Leo was born. At an early age it was apparent that he was talented as an artist, but he had health problems and died at the early age of 19. As Popper became older he devoted more time to teaching and less to performing. In 1891 he was shocked at the dismissal by Count Zichy of MAHLER as director of the Budapest Opera; Zichy was the new superintendent of state theatres. Zichy is quoted as saying of the opera house: 'This Jewish Temple must be made into a Temple of Art.'

Popper's compositions show greatest affinities with Schumann and MENDELSSOHN. He achieved greater fame as a performer than as a composer. Most of his works are small-scale and for cello. He was one of Europe's outstanding cellists of the period. In 1891 he gave the first performance of his *Requiem* for three cellos and orchestra, Op. 66, and it remains one of his best-known compositions. Other works include four concertos, a string quartet, a suite for cello and various salon pieces. They are best known by cellists and cello teachers rather than the general listening public. The works are polished and melodious, but are generally not considered to be profound.

Bibliography: *G*; *HBD*; Ken; Steven De'ak, *David Popper* (New Jersey: Paganiniana, 1980)*

Previn, André George [Andreas Ludwig Priwin] (b. Berlin, 6 April 1929) Multitalented musician, conductor, concert pianist, jazz pianist and composer. At the age of 5 his father, a lawyer and also an excellent pianist, gave him piano lessons. At 6 he entered the Berlin Academy of Music, where he studied piano with Rudolf Breithaupt. In 1937 he was expelled from the academy; Breithaupt explained that 'he could no longer have a Jewish pupil, especially such a talented one, who would be noticed by the Nazi authorities'. In 1938 the family left for Paris, where Previn studied at the Paris Conservatoire with the organist Marcel Dupré until, in 1939, they left for America, eventually settling in Los Angeles. His father was unable to practise law in America without undertaking further expensive training, so he resorted to piano teaching. On the advice of a relative, Charles Previn, who already lived in Los Angeles, the family changed their names to remove the trace of their German antecedents. He considered that this would help in André's future professional career. André continued piano lessons with Max Rabinowitsch (whose hands substituted for actors supposedly playing the piano in numerous films), theory with Joseph ACHRON and briefly with Ernest TOCH, and composition with Mario CASTELNUOVO-TEDESCO.

He began working at MGM (Metro-Goldwyn-Mayer) studios at the age of 16 as composer, arranger and conductor and also played as a concert pianist. In 1951 he studied conducting with Pierre Monteux while in San Francisco during military service.He married the jazz singer Betty Bennett in 1952 and during the 1950s made recordings as a jazz pianist. In 1959 he married for a second time, to a lyricist, Dory Langan, and in 1970 for the third time to the actress Mia Farrow. In the early 1960s he moved more towards conducting classical music and performing with the St Louis Symphony Orchestra. This was the beginning of a succession of conducting posts. He was principal conductor of the Houston Symphony Orchestra (1967–70) and while still there was appointed principal conductor of the London Symphony Orchestra (1969–79). He greatly restored the fortunes of the LSO, particularly with his repertoire of English and Russian music. Later he became principal conductor of the Pittsburg Symphony Orchestra (1976–84), the Los Angeles Symphony Orchestra (1985–9) and music director of the Royal Philharmonic Orchestra (1985–91). He has made a large number of recordings. His fourth marriage in 1982 was to Heather Hales.

He has composed in a number of different genres, including orchestral, chamber and vocal, jazz and film music. His orchestral compositions include a symphony for strings (1962), a cello concerto (1968), a guitar concerto (1971) and a piano concerto (1984) commissioned by Vladimir Ashkenazy. His chamber music includes a violin sonata (1964), flute quartet (1964) and a cello sonata written for Yo-Yo Ma. He wrote six settings of *Honey and Rue* by Toni Morrison for Kathleen Battle and other song cycles for Janet Baker and Sylvia McNair. He collaborated with Tom Stoppard in the music drama *Every Good Boy Deserves Favour* (1977) and created an opera based on Tennessee Williams's *A Streetcar Named Desire* (1998). He was knighted in 1996.
Bibliography: *G*; *HBD*; Leb*; Ly*; Norman Lebrecht, *The Maestro Myth* (London: Simon & Schuster, 1991); André Previn, *No Minor Chords – My Early Days in Hollywood* (New York: Doubleday, 1991); www.schirmer.com/composers/previn/bio.html

Radzynski, Jan (b. Warsaw, 18 June 1950)   Went to Israel following a wave of anti-Semitism in Poland in 1969. There he studied composition with SCHIDLOWSKY and cello at the Rubin Academy of Music in Tel Aviv. In 1977 he went to the USA to study with Penderecki and DRUCKMAN, graduating at Yale University, where he subsequently became associate professor of composition. His compositions include: *The Third Face* (1975) for two sopranos, flute, cello, trumpet and percussion, to texts by Tadeusz Rózewicz; *Sonata* for violin solo (1984); *David Symphony* (1987); *Kaddish* for orchestra, dedicated to victims of the Holocaust (1979); *Mizmorim* (Psalms) for solo violin and eight cellos (1983); *Encounters* (1989); *Time's Other Beat* (1990), based on a poem by the Jewish–Welsh poet Dannie Abse; *String Trio* (1995); and *Shirat Ma'ayan* (1997), a setting of Psalms 46 and 137. Many of his compositions reflect the influence of contemporary Israeli music, although he has been resident in the United States since 1977.
Bibliography: *G*: Grad

Ran, Shulamit (b. Tel Aviv, 21 October 1949)   Her German father and Russian mother emigrated to Israel in the 1930s. She started piano lessons at the age of 8, making her début as a pianist at the age of 12. She studied piano with Miriam Boskovich and Emma Gorochov and composition with Alexander BOSKOVICH and Paul BEN HAIM in Tel Aviv before gaining a piano scholarship to study at Mannes College of Music in New York, where she studied from 1962 to 1967. Her composition teacher was Dello Joio and her piano teachers were Nadia Reisenberg and Dorothy Taubman. In 1963 she played her own composition, *Capriccio for Piano and Orchestra*, with the New York Philharmonic conducted by BERNSTEIN, and in 1967 she played the piano solo in the premiere of her *Symphonic Poem* for piano and orchestra with the Kol Israel Radio Orchestra. As a pianist she toured Europe and America and was artist-in-residence at St Mary's University, Halifax, from 1972 to 1973.

She has written many works for piano solo and piano with chamber groups, and a number for harpsichord. In 1969 she composed *Of the Chimneys*, a setting of five poems by Nelly Sachs about the Holocaust. On the strength of hearing this performed Ralph SHAPEY offered her a post in the music faculty at the University of Chicago. There, she was able to make good use of Chicago's Contemporary Chamber Players and also took composition lessons from Shapey. In 1986 she was commissioned to write *Concerto for Orchestra*, her first large-scale piece since her compositions of the early 1970s. In 1990 she completed her first symphony, which was commissioned by the Philadelphia Orchestra; it won the Pulitzer prize for music in 1991. In the same year she became composer-in-residence with the Chicago Symphony Orchestra. Her works include: *Ten Children's Scenes* for piano (1970); *Concert Piece* for piano (1971); *Double Vision* for wind quintet, brass quintet and piano (1976); Piano Concerto (1977); *Apprehensions*, a setting of a poem by Sylvia Plath, for voice, clarinet and piano (1979); *A Prayer* for clarinet, bass clarinet, bassoon, horn and timpani (1981); *Mirage* for flute, clarinet, violin, cello and piano (1990); *Yearnings* for violin and string orchestra (1995); and *Invocation* for horn, chimes and timpani (1995).
Bibliography: *AG*; *G*; Grad; *HBD*; *Pan*

Rathaus, Karol (b. Tarnopol, Galacia [Ternopil, Ukraine], 16 September 1895; d. New York, 21 November 1954)   Moved to Vienna in 1913 to study composition under SCHREKER. He served in the Austrian Army during World War One and made his début as a pianist/composer playing his *Variations on a Theme of Reger*, Op. 1, in Vienna in 1919. In 1920 he moved to the Hochschule für Musik in Berlin, with Schreker and his other students, including Hába and Krenek. He received a Ph.D. at Vienna University in 1922. He remained in Berlin until 1932 and during this period established himself as a promising composer with works such as *Overture*, Op. 22 (1928), *Suite*, Op. 29 (1930), the ballet *Der Letzte Pierrot* (1927), the opera *Fremde Erde* (1929–30) and the score for the film *The Brothers Karamazov* (1931). With the rise of Nazism his music could no longer be readily performed in Germany, although his works were performed by the Kulturbund Deutscher Juden, an organization set up to provide a livelihood for Jewish artists who had lost their jobs after the legislation introduced in 1933. The scores of Rathaus's Symphony No. 2 (1923) and four orchestral dance pieces were included in the 1938 exhibition of *Entartete Musik* (degenerate music) organized by the Nazis in 1938. By that time Rathaus had fled Germany, initially to Paris (1932–4), then to London (1934–8), and finally to the United States in 1938. He became an American citizen in 1946.

After the war contemporary music had changed and Rathaus's compositions of the 1920s and 1930s were hardly performed. In 1939 he became
professor of composition at Queens College, New York, where he remained
until his death. His style is generally neo-Romantic, but some works show his
affinity with Polish tradition, for example, *Polonaise Symphonique* (1943), and
with Jewish tradition, for example, the incidental music to *Uriel Acosta* for the
Habimah Theatre and the documentary film *Histadrut*.
Bibliography: *G*; *HBD*; Ho*; Leb

Reich, Steve (b. New York, 3 October 1936)   Both his parents were Jewish,
but separated when he was 1 year old. His mother, who was a singer and
lyricist, remarried and lived in Los Angeles. Steve lived mainly with his father
Leonard, a lawyer, but spent time shuttling by train between New York and
Los Angeles with his governess, Virginia. Reich's paternal grandparents were
from Kraków and Budapest, and his maternal grandparents from Vienna and
Koblenz. Reich's maternal grandfather had a jewellery business but was also
a vaudeville pianist. Among Reich's early experiences were his grandfather
playing popular songs at the piano, and his mother writing songs and singing.
He started piano lessons, with a certain amount of parental pressure, when
he was about 7 and he gave them up when he was 10. Three important musical
experiences in his early teens were hearing Stravinsky's *Rite of Spring*, Bach
and bebop. He was never particularly enthusiastic about classical and Romantic
music of the late eighteenth to nineteenth centuries (Haydn to Wagner). He
was keen to play the drums and his father arranged lessons with Roland
Kohloff, the principal timpanist of the New York Philharmonic. Much of his
early composition is dominated by percussion instruments and it was only
later that he was to use a wider range of the conventional instruments of the
orchestra.
   At the age of 16 he entered Cornell University, still playing drums at weekends with a band. He wrote a thesis on the later works of Wittgenstein, who
visited the university in the early 1950s, and contemplated entering Harvard
as a graduate student in philosophy. It was the encouragement of Reich's
music history professor, William Austin, that helped ensure that his future
career lay in music, and towards the end of his stay at Cornell he was
increasingly drawn to composition and eventually went to the Juilliard School
of Music in New York. After studying composition at the Juilliard he went
to Mills College in Oakland, San Francisco (1961–3). He was attracted to
Mills College because Luciano Berio was on the staff. Reich had been intrigued
by Berio's music. Although Darius MILHAUD was also on the staff and Reich
studied with him, Milhaud was by then too old and infirm to be of much direct
influence. He found the teaching of Berio exciting and spent his days at
the college and his nights at the jazz workshop. Even before he entered
Mills College, and whilst at the Juilliard, one of his compositions used a
twelve-tone row, albeit repetitively, creating a static effect – in effect, the seeds

of minimalism (see Glossary). After leaving Mills College Reich tried living as a freelance musician; he supplemented his income by cab driving.

In 1964 a group formed by Reich gave an improvised concert at the Mime Troup at which Terry Riley, already known as a minimalist, was present. After the concert they met and Riley showed him the score of his now famous piece *In C*. As a result of their discussion Reich not only offered advice on *In C* but also provided the pulse in its premiere performance, as the drummer in the group. This led to his first mature minimalist composition in 1965, *Its Gonna Rain*. More minimalist pieces followed: *Come Out* (1966), music based on a single vocal segment from an interview of a Harlem youth who had been beaten up by police; *Piano Phase* (1967); *Violin Phase* (1967); *Pendulum Music* (1968); *Four Organs* (1970).

In 1970 Reich's interest in drumming prompted a trip to Ghana, where he had lessons with the Ghanaian master drummer Gideon Alorworye and experienced the polyrhythms of West African music. The visit was curtailed as Reich contracted malaria. Three years later he took courses in Balinese gamelan at the Universities of Washington and California. One of his most important works, which is often regarded as a minimalist masterpiece, is *Drumming* (for bongos, marimbas, voices, glockenspiels, whistle and piccolo), which had its 90-minute premiere in 1971. Other works from this period are *Music for Six Pianos* (1972), *Music for Mallet Instruments and Organ* (1973) and *Music for 18 Musicians* (1976).

After this very successful minimalist period Reich became established as an international composer. He was now to move in a different direction, becoming more aware of his own roots. In 1974 he met a video artist, Beryl Korot, and they eventually married (Reich for the second time) in 1976, but before that they both explored their Jewish roots. Reich had been brought up as an assimilated Jew, and although undergoing *bar mitzvah* he had a very scant Jewish education. Both Reich and Korot took classes at Lincoln Square Synagogue to redress their deficiencies, and Reich went to the Jewish Theological Seminary to be taught scriptural cantillation. They both went to Israel in 1977 and recorded the singing of Yemenite Jews, whose singing had not appreciably changed for over 1,500 years. The first fruits of this interest appear particularly in the flute part of *Octet* (1979), becoming more fully developed in *Tehillim* (1981). *Tehillim* (meaning psalms) is in four movements set to Psalms 19, 34, 18 and 150. It introduced extended melody to Reich's work.

Different Trains has become an important and successful work. It was written for multitracked string quartet mixed in with speech and train sounds, and was completed in 1988. The Kronos Quartet, together with prerecorded sound, gave its first performance. Its inspiration comes from the numerous train journeys that Reich made as a small child across America before the war, and it is an autobiographical meditation on the very different aspects of Jewish experience in the war years. The first movement, 'America Before the War',

293

conveys the innocence, expansiveness and the whole romance of the train in American folklore; the second, 'Europe During the War', the horror of Nazi transports to death camps; and the third, 'After the War', some of the era's lost innocence, tarnished by intervening tragedy. It uses speech fragments by his childhood governess, Virginia, a Pullman porter and Holocaust survivors.

Reich and Korot together composed what is described as a music/theatre piece, entitled *The Cave* (1993), for voices, ensemble and videotape. It refers to the Cave of Machpelah in the city of Hebron, the supposed burial place of the patriarchs and matriarchs, sacred to Jews, Muslims and Christians and presents a series of talking heads whose views on Arab or Israeli history are projected onto five large screens, their speeches punctuated by melodies, performed by strings, percussion and four singers.

Reich is regarded as one of the originators of minimalism, but during the 1970s and 1980s his music evolved and reacted to other influences, including 'mainstream European music', but at the same time retaining elements of his earlier style.

Bibliography: *AG*; *CC*; *G*; *HBD*; Leb; Paul Griffiths, *Modern Music and After* (Oxford: Oxford University Press, 1995), pp. 260–3; K. Robert Schwartz, *Minimalists* (London: Phaidon, 1996)

Reiner, Karel (b. Žatec, Bohemia, 10 June 1910; d. Prague, 17 October 1979) Son of a cantor. He studied law at Charles University in Prague, graduating as a doctor of law in 1933. He then studied music (piano and composition), first with Josef Suk and then microtonal composition with Alois Hába at the Prague Conservatory (1934–5). He had made his piano début earlier in 1926, and pursued a career as a recitalist and accompanist until the Nazi occupation of Czechoslovakia. He worked in the Jewish Community Office in Prague as organizer of musical activities until he was deported to Terezin in 1943. Whilst in Terezin he composed incidental music for the comedy *The Romancers* by Edmund Rostand, and for the play *Esther*, based on a dramatization of the biblical story by E. F. Burian. He also composed a cycle of nursery rhymes, *Kvetovany Kun* (The flower horse). He survived the concentration camp and after the war resumed composing, initially using avant-garde techniques, including the microtonal techniques he had studied with Hába. He had been a communist before the war and after the war composed socialist songs, for example, *The Rocket and the Red Banner*, *The War Atom* and *Yankee No*. He composed a suite for the film *The Butterflies Do Not Live Here*, based on drawings and poetry by the children imprisoned in Terezin. He later reverted to a more conservative style of composition in works such as Concerto for bass clarinet, strings and percussion (1965) and Concertino for bassoon, winds, and percussion (1969).

Bibliography: *G*; *HBD*; Joža Karas, *Music in Terezin* (New York, Pendragon, 1985), pp. 131–2

Reizenstein, Franz Theodor (b. Nuremberg, 7 June 1911; d. London, 15 October 1968)   Son of a doctor who had an interest in the arts, thus providing a good background in which to nurture Franz's talent. It was apparent from his piano playing and his possession of perfect pitch that Franz was a gifted musician from an early age. Throughout his working life he was known equally as a pianist and as a composer. From 1930 to 1934 he studied at the Hochschule für Musik in Berlin under Leonid Kreutzer (piano) and Hindemith (composition). Hindemith was to be a major influence on his compositional style.

With the rise of Nazism, he realized early on that there was no future for a musician of Jewish birth in Germany, and he was one of the first composers to leave Germany because of the Nazis. His move to England was easier than for some, since he had an uncle on his mother's side living in Kingston upon Thames. In England he continued his studies at the Royal College of Music from 1934 to 1936 studying composition under Vaughan Williams, and took piano lessons privately with Solomon.

His first compositions date from 1931, and over three-quarters of his 50 or so opuses are chamber music or music for piano. He wrote relatively few works for large orchestras. His works generally are a development from the classical and Romantic tradition, and his composing was very disciplined – something he learned from Hindemith. He eschewed atonal and serial composition. Reizenstein clearly had a great admiration for Hindemith, but whilst Hindemith recognized Reizenstein as a good pianist he described Reizenstein as 'too pushy for my taste, and I have learnt over the years that it is better to keep him at a slight distance'.[1]

In 1937 Reizenstein went on a concert tour of South America. He wrote *Prologue, Variations and Finale*, Op. 12, in 1938, the first piece to bring him wide acclaim. Some of the ideas came to him whilst travelling between Buenos Aires and Santiago and show the influence of South American rhythms.

In 1939, at the start of the World War Two, Reizenstein was interned on the Isle of Man, along with many others of non-British birth. During this time he was active in arranging and performing music at the camp. Later during the war he volunteered for the army but failed because of his poor eyesight. He was given a job as a railway clerk until the end of the war and continued to perform in wartime concerts. He became professor of piano at the Royal Academy of Music from 1958 to 1968 and also at the Royal Manchester College (1962–8).

He performed regularly in a piano trio (himself on piano, Maria Lidka, violin and Roham de Saram, cello). He spent six months at Boston University as visiting professor of composition in 1966. Apart from these six months he never taught composition at any of the major music colleges, although he did teach it at the Hendon Musical Centre, but this was in evening classes and mainly to amateurs. Reizenstein was not an innovative composer, but used already established techniques, which he found quite adequate to express his musical thoughts.

Apart from the chamber and instrumental works, he composed cello, violin and piano concertos, some film music and vocal music. He wrote a cantata, *Voices of Night*, Op. 27, in 1950–1 and its success led to the commissioning of a radio opera, *Anna Kraus*, Op. 30, and an oratorio, *Genesis*, Op. 35, which was first performed at the Three Choirs Festival in 1958. His most successful period of composing was his 'middle period' from 1947 to 1960. In this period he also composed *Five Sonnets of Elizabeth Barret Browning* for tenor and piano. His most successful chamber works are the Piano Quintet, Op. 23 (1948), the Cello Sonata, Op. 22, the Violin and Piano Sonata, Op. 20 (1945), *Twelve Preludes and Fugues*, Op. 32 (1955) and *The Zodiac*, for piano, Op. 41 (1964). Two light-hearted works that enjoyed popularity for a time were *Concerto Populare* (1958) and *Lets Fake an Opera*, for Gerard Hoffnung's comic concerts. Together with Camhy, Abinum and Papo he edited the *Liturgie Sephardie* (London: World Sephardi Federation, 1959).

Bibliography: *G*; *HBD*; Ken; Leb; F. Routh, *Contemporary British Music* (London: MacDonald, 1972)

1. Geoffrey Skelton, *Selected Letters of Paul Hindemith* (New Haven: Yale University Press, 1995), pp. 81–2.

Reyer, Louis-Étienne Ernest [original name 'Rey'] (b. Marseilles, 1 December 1823; d. Le Lavandou,Var, France 15 January 1909)   Became a composer and music critic. He studied with his aunt, Louise Farrenc, a pianist and composer. He began composing whilst working as a civil servant in Algiers in 1839. There he composed *Messe pour l'arrivée du duc d'Aumale à Alger* in 1847. In 1848 he went to Paris to take up a music career with the help of his uncle Jacques Farrenc, a Paris-based music critic. He composed two opéras-comiques and an opera, *Erostrate* (1862). He was a great admirer of Wagner, although his operas were in a more classical style. His was praised by Berlioz, both as a composer and as a music critic, and eventually succeeded Berlioz as music critic of the *Journal des Débats*. He planned an opera, *Sigurd,* on the Nibelung legends, which he eventually completed in 1884. His compositions include five operas, cantatas, smaller vocal pieces and piano works. Perhaps significantly for a Jewish composer, at the height of the Dreyfus affair, his operas *Salammbô* and *Sigurd* were staged in Paris, in 1899 and 1900 respectively, and he was nominated Grand Officer of the Légion of Honour.

Bibliography: *G*; *HBD*; Ken; WW; Jane Fulcher, *French Cultural Politics and Music* (Oxford: Oxford University Press, 1999), p. 104*; Percy A. Scholes, *Oxford Companion to Music*, 9th edn (Oxford: Oxford University Press, 1955), p. 876

Rochberg, George (b. Paterson, New Jersey, 5 July 1918)   Studied music at Mannes College under George Szell and Leopold Mannes from 1939 to 1942, and, after military service, continued his music studies at the Curtis Institute, Philadelphia, with Rosario Scaleo and Menotti, graduating in 1948. He then taught at the Curtis Institute from 1948 to 1954. He became music editor for the Presser Company in 1951. In 1960 he became chairman of the music department at the University of Pennsylvania.

His compositions written in the 1940s are tonal and show the influence of Bartok and Stravinsky, for example, 'Night Music', which forms the second movement of his first symphony (1948). After meeting Dallapiccola in 1950, whilst in Rome on Fulbright and American Academy fellowships, he became interested in the music of the Second Viennese School and this is reflected in works such as Chamber Symphony (1950), *Twelve Bagatelles* (1952), Symphony No. 2 (1955–6) and String Quartet No. 2 (1959–61). Towards the end of this phase he became interested in the extreme condensation of the musical argument, as Webern had done, resulting in terse compositions such as the *Cheltenham Concerto* (1958). By 1961 he began to have doubts about the merits of serial music. His last piece of entirely serial music is *Piano Trio* (1963), after which he moved back to an earlier traditional idiom. Lebrecht suggests that in so doing he 'broke the dissonant stranglehold on the American musical academia of that period'. It also coincided with the death of his 20-year-old son in 1964. In *Contra Mortem et Tempus* for violin, flute clarinet and piano (1965), written two weeks after his son's death, he quotes from Boulez, Varèse, Ives and Berio. His works after this period become more romantic, for example, his third string quartet (1972) and his violin concerto (1974), an elegiac memorial to his son (see Chapter 2, section 2.6.5). His later string quartets (nos. 3 to 6) sound in style as though they straddle the First and Second Viennese Schools. In his *Quintet for Piano and Strings* the outer movements are atonal and the central movement tonal, creating 'dark to light and back to dark' moods.

He also wrote about music, his most substantial contribution being *The Hexachord and its Relation to the Twelve-Tone Row* (1955). His compositions include an opera, *The Confidence Man* (1982), five symphonies, seven string quartets, an oboe and a clarinet concerto and vocal music, for example, *Four Songs of Solomon* for voice and piano (1946), *David, the Psalmist* for tenor and orchestra (1954), and *Sacred Song of Reconciliation* for bass-baritone and chamber (1970), which was first performed in Jerusalem in 1971.

Bibliography: *AG; CC; G; HBD;* Leb; Ly*; R. R. Reilly, 'The Recovery of Modern Music: George Rochberg in Conversation', *Tempo*, 219 (2002), pp. 8–12

Roland-Manuel, Alexis [Lévy, Roland Alexis Manuel] (b. Paris 22 March 1891; d. Paris, 2 November 1966) Son of Madame Fernand Dreyfus. Roland-Manuel lived for three years in Florida, then for nine years in Liège, before returning to Paris in 1905 following the death of his father. He studied composition with Roussel at the Schola Cantorum and later privately with Ravel. He converted to Roman Catholicism. He was a composer and writer. His compositional style was anti-Romantic, showing the influence of Ravel. His compositions include five operas, ballets, a piano concerto, choral and chamber music. In 1947 he became a professor at the Paris Conservatoire. He became well known as the founder of a radio show entitled *Plasir de la musique*. He wrote books on Ravel, Satie and de Falla.

Bibliography: *G*; *HBD*; Ly*; Jane F. Fulcher, 'The Preparation for Vichy: Anti-Semitism in French Musical Culture between the Two World Wars', *Musical Quarterly*, 73 (1995), pp. 458–75*

Rosenthal, Manuel [Emmanuel] (b. Paris, 18 June 1904)   Learned the violin as a child. His father died when he was 14, leaving Manuel as head of the household. In his teens he played the violin in the cafés of Paris to supplement the family income. He enrolled at the Paris Conservatoire from 1918 to 1923, initially to study violin, but soon became more interested in composition. He composed a sonatina for two violins and piano (1923) that was performed at the Société Musical Independante at its 100th concert. As a result he met Nadia Boulanger and Ravel and the latter became his teacher from 1926 to 1930. The composition that made him well known was his arrangement for ballet of OFFENBACH's *Gaîté Parisienne*, which was premiered in 1938 and has remained popular ever since. He was assistant conductor of the French National Radio Orchestra from 1934 to 1939 and chief conductor from 1944 to 1947.

He spent part of World War Two in the army and was a prisoner-of-war for nine months. When he was freed he was banned from conducting by the Vichy government on racial grounds. However, although he did not conduct during the war he continued to compose. He was most prolific during this period. His works include: two symphonic suites, *Musique de table* and *Noce villagreoise*, two choral works, seven pieces for voice and orchestra, *Les soirées du petit Juas* for voice and string quartet, and seven pieces for voice and piano.

From 1949 to 1951 he was conductor of the Seattle Symphony Orchestra, where he conducted Wagner's *Der Ring des Nibelungen*. He became professor of conducting at the Paris Conservatoire and conducted the Liege Symphony Orchestra from 1964 to 1967. As a composer he belongs to the French neoclassical school; some of his later music is atonal, but not serial. His works also include an oratorio, *Saint François d'Assisi*, the suite *Jeanne d'Arc* and four operettas, *Rayon de soieries*, *Les Bootleggers*, *La Poule noire* and *Les Femmes au tombeau*. He also made orchestral transcriptions of works by Ravel. His last composition was *Juventas* for clarinet, two violins, viola and cello written in 1988, when he was 84 years of age. Although well known as a conductor it has only been since the mid-1990s that his compositions have been recorded.

Bibliography: *G*; *HBD*; Ho*; Ken; Ly*; M. Anderson, *Tempo*, 212 (2000), pp. 31–7; www.hnh.com/composer/rosentha.htm

Rosowsky, Salamon (b. Riga, 27 March 1878, d. New York, 31 July 1962)   Son of the celebrated Riga cantor Baruch Leib Rosowsky (1841–1919). He studied law at Kiev University and music at the St Petersburg Conservatory with

Rimsky-Korsakov, Liadov and Glazunov. In 1905 he studied conducting with Nikisch at Leipzig. He was one of the founder members of the St Petersburg Jewish Folk Music Society (1908). In 1920 he went to Riga, where he founded the first Jewish Conservatory of Music, from there emigrated to Palestine in 1925 for 22 years, and then went to New York, where he lectured at the Jewish Theological Seminary of America. He is best known as a musicologist, but he composed incidental music for the Jewish Art Theatre in St Petersburg and made a number of arrangements of Jewish folk music.
Bibliography: G; Ho*; Ly*

Rossi, Salamone [alternative spellings Salamon de, Shlomo] (b. Mantua, probably 1570; d. Mantua, *c.*1630)   The dates of his birth and death are uncertain. The date of his birth, 19 August 1570, is inferred from the date of a signed copy of his *primum opus* published at around his 19th birthday. After 1628 nothing is recorded about Rossi and he is thought to have died when the ghetto in Mantua was sacked and destroyed in 1630. Little is known about the life of the composer other than that most of the 40 years of his working life (1587–1628) was spent at the court in Mantua, first serving Duke Vincenzo Gonzoga, and, after 1612, his successor Franceso II. He is best known for his First Book of Canzonettes, published in 1589, his five books of madrigals published between 1600 and 1622, his two collections of instrumental work dating from 1607 and 1608 and his *Hashirim asher lish'lomo* (Songs of Solomon – 33 polyphonic settings of Hebrew psalms).

   Rossi was descended from a family whose pedigree can be traced back to the captives of Jerusalem whom Titus brought to Rome. His father, Asarja dei Rossi (died Mantua, 1578), distinguished himself by his religious philosophy, which united elements of Jewish–Hellenistic thought and Talmudic–Rabbinical tradition. Salamone is thought not to be related to the other Mantuan musicians of the same surname (his sister Madama Europa, a virtuoso singer, and his nephew Anselmi Rossi, also a musician at the court, excepted). Madama Europa sang the title role in Monteverdi's now lost opera, *Arianna*. It is clear that Rossi was in a privileged position at court, since in 1606 he was absolved from having to wear the yellow star, a restriction imposed on the Jewish community by the Lateran Council of 1215. Although there is evidence that he was paid by the court of Mantua, his name does not appear on the normal salary roles, but initially under the heading 'extraordinary', which appears to include those not on the regular payroll. His initial salary appears meagre, but this may be because he was also paid by the Jewish community for his musical contributions, possibly from his patron, Moses Sullam. After 1622, when he was listed as one of the string players at the court of Mantua, his salary appears to have increased significantly. It seems clear that he was regarded as a virtuoso violinist. He also seems to have been in commercial partnership with his brother Emanuele.

   Rossi appears to have written and performed in the Jewish theatre troupes that performed not only in the ghetto but also at court. However, all but two examples of this genre (*Intermedia* for Battista Guarini's comedy *L'Idropica* and his *Balletto* for Giovanni Batista Andreini's *La Maddalena*) are lost. Rossi's Italian vocal works that were published in eight collections account for about half of his published musical output. These comprise *canzonetta* for three voices, madrigals for four and five voices and *madrigaletto* for two voices plus continuo. Most of these are settings from poets affiliated to the court of Mantua.

There are four collections of his instrumental works. The first and second books are dated 1607–8, the third 1613, and the fourth 1622 – altogether they comprise 116 instrumental works, most of which are for three instruments. Rossi played an important role in the development of the trio sonata, as seen from books 1 and 2. Up until about 1620 whole consorts (of viols, flutes, double reeds and brasses) requiring no continuo were favoured. Madrigals written in the late sixteenth century generally had four parts without continuo, but they gradually gave way to madrigals having a bass continuo. In these a single melody was dominant, with secondary accompanying parts, in contrast to the previous polyphonic style. Dance music was the basis for instrumental chamber music. In Italy by 1620 the consorts were outmoded and had been replaced by trios. The development and perfection of the violin in northern Italy during this period is closely linked with this type of instrumental grouping. Rossi's early collection of trio sonatas is for two viole de braccia and chitarone, whereas in the later collection, the viole de braccia are replaced by violini (true violins). Rossi mentions the cornetto as an alternative replacement for the violin. Variation sonatas form the majority of the sonatas in books 3 and 4.

Rossi was the first composer to attempt complete reforms in synagogue liturgical music. In *Hashirim asher lish'lomo* (Songs of Solomon), a series of psalms and prayers (not, incidentally from the Songs of Solomon) in Hebrew are set in the musical idiom of contemporary Italy. The title is thought to be a pun on Salomone Rossi's name, since the first line from the book Song of Songs is 'I will sing the song of all songs to Solomon that he may smother me with kisses'. Rossi dedicated these sacred songs to Moses Sullam, a wealthy Jewish citizen of Mantua whose parents had supported Rossi in his youth, presumably after Rossi's father's death. Rossi combined his knowledge and experience of secular music with the demands of sacred music. Whereas his trio sonatas are forward-looking in style, the *Hashirim asher lish'lomo* is more conservative. It is the first known collection of polyphonic works set to Hebrew texts, and not unexpectedly met with resistance from within the Jewish community accustomed to unaccompanied monophonic chant. A further practical obstacle to be overcome was how best to set out Hebrew choral music – the text of which runs from right to left – with musical notation – which runs from left to right. The compromise used was to reverse the Hebrew words but not the syllables on a normal musical line.

Towards the end of the sixteenth century the Jewish communities in Venice, Mantua, Ferrara, Padua and Casale Monferrato, inspired by Renaissance music, wanted to modernize the religious service. In 1605 a Jewish scholar, Leon of Modena, organized the Italian synagogue in Ferrara to have a choir of six to eight voices. This harmonic innovation brought strong opposition from those who argued that joy and song in the Synagogue have been prohibited since the destruction of the Temple. However, the rabbinical assembly in Venice decided in favour. This paved the way for Rossi to compose *Hashirim asher lish'lomo*. The collection is for choir and soloists, for three, four, five, six, seven and eight parts. It was published in 1622, Leon of Modena doing the proofreading. It was subsequently re-edited in modern musical notation by Samuel Naumbourg, cantor of Paris, in 1877. It is written entirely in the Italian Renaissance style, without the slightest sound of Jewish musical tradition, and represents a reconciliation of the two cultures that dominated Rossi's life – the Italian secular and the Hebrew sacred. Technically, the *Hashirim asher lish'lomo* is simpler than his instrumental music, so that it could be performed by Jewish laymen. This music is believed to have been used only for a short period in Italian synagogues, since in 1630 Mantua was swept by war and captured by the Emperor Fredinand II; much later, in 1800, Jews were expelled from the city. Although Rossi's influence on synagogue in Italy was short-lived, it did indirectly influence Jewish communities in central Europe, including Germany, in introducing choral singing with several parts, and even musical instruments into the synagogue. The King of Portugal's library contained the entire works of Rossi, but was unfortunately burned in a fire in 1755. Bibliography: *G*; Grad; Don Harrán, *Salamone Rossi: Jewish Musician in Late Renaissance Mantua* (Oxford: Oxford University Press, 1999); A. Z. Idelsohn, *Jewish Music in its Historical Development* (New York: Schocken, 1967), pp. 196–203 and 265–7

Rothmüller, Aron Marko (b. Trnjani, Croatia, 31 December 1908; d. Bloomington, Indiana, 20 January 1993)   Studied composition and conducting under Dugan, Bersa and Lhotka, and singing under Ourednik at the Zagreb Academy. From 1928 to 1932 he studied under Alban Berg and Franz Steiner at the Vienna Conservatory. He lived in Switzerland from 1935 to 1948. He taught at Indiana University from 1962. He is best known as a baritone opera singer. He sang at the premiere of Hindemith's *Mathis der Maler* (1938) and the first live performance in London of BLOCH's *Sacred Service* in 1949. Most of his compositions are for small groups, for example, piano trio and string quartet, and many have Jewish folk music or dance music as their basis. Bibliography: *G*; *HBD*; Ho*; Ly*

Rubinstein, Anton Grigor'yevich (b. Vikhvatinets, Podolsk, Russia, 28 November 1829; d. Peterhof, near St Petersburg, 20 November 1894)   Of German–Jewish extraction. Both his parents were Jewish, although they converted to

301

Christianity; Anton was baptized in the Orthodox Church. This was largely to enable them to live in St Petersburg. His father, Gregori Romanovich, was a Russian merchant and his mother, Kaleria, was a Silesian Jewess. The family lived in Berdichev, in the Ukraine, but Anton was actually born in a village inn, where they put up when his mother's pangs of childbirth arose whilst they were travelling. Berdichev was one of the many Jewish centres within the Pale of Settlement and at that time had a population of over 40,000 Jews. There were six children in the family, but the first two died young. Anton was the third child and Nicholay the fourth. Anton's mother had the predominant influence over the children; she was a piano teacher and gave him lessons from when he was 5.

In 1834 the family moved to Moscow, travelling in a horse-drawn wagon, which Anton recalls in his autobiography. His mother felt that he showed such promise on the piano that he needed the best of teachers. Alexandre Villoing had that reputation. However, the family were short of money and doubted whether they could afford lessons. There is a story that at a children's party when Anton was 8 he started to explore the rooms of the house and found a piano and started playing. By a stroke of fortune a guest strolled into the room unbeknown to Anton and was so impressed that he offered free lessons to the boy. The guest was Villoing. Rubinstein gave his first public concert in 1839, and between 1840 and 1843 toured Europe with Villoing as a child prodigy. During the tour he met Chopin and Liszt in Paris, the Russian imperial family in the Netherlands and Queen Victoria in London. After a short stay back in Russia the family moved to Berlin in 1844, where MEYERBEER recommended to Rubinstein's mother that Anton should have lessons in counterpoint and harmony from Siegfried Dehn. There, he also met MENDELSSOHN.

The family returned to Russia when Anton's father died in 1846, but Anton spent two years in Vienna eking out a living giving piano lessons. When he returned to Russia, in 1848, the previous meeting with the Russian imperial family proved useful, for he was taken in by the Grand Duchess Elena Pavlovna, given a room in one of her palaces, and played the piano at her soirées, often in the presence of the Tzar and his family. In 1854 he embarked on a concert tour of Europe, and then stayed with the Grand Duchess in Nice.

Although by this time Rubinstein was a very successful concert pianist, his ambition was to be a composer, and he was also very interested in musical education. In his early operas, *Dmitry Donskoy* (1852) and *The Siberian Huntsman* (1852), he was concerned to develop distinctive Russian music, but these operas failed and it led to him attack the whole state of opera and musical composition in Russia. As a result he drew up plans for the improvement of musical education in Russia, to bring it up to the standards he had seen in Europe. He founded the Russian Musical Society in 1859 and the St Petersburg Conservatory in 1862. He conducted concerts with the former and was director of the latter until 1867, when he embarked on yet another concert tour of Europe. In 1865 he married Vièra Tchéknànov; they were to have three children.

Anton was a sought after pianist and in 1872 he toured the United States with WIENIAWSKI. The tour was arranged through William Steinway, who saw it as an opportunity to promote his pianos throughout the United States. The tour was a great success, although Rubinstein and Wieniawski quarrelled and the latter continued the second year of the tour on his own. Up to the age of 50 Rubinstein had a phenomenal memory, but in his later years he claims to have been nervous before concerts, aware that his memory was not what it had previously been. From 1887 until 1891 he resumed the directorship of the St Petersburg Conservatory. At his death, in 1894, his reputation as a pianist was legendary and comparable to that of Liszt. His greatest legacy was improvement in performance standards in Russia. During his career he also composed prolifically, producing over 120 opuses, including stage works, chamber, orchestral and vocal music and works for solo piano, although only a few of these are heard today. He composed quickly; some of his works show evidence of this. Paganini said of him: 'He had not the necessary patience for a composer.' His most successful operas were *The Demon* (1875) and *The Merchant Kalashnikov* (1877–9). The former is in the French lyrical tradition of Gonoud's *Faust* and was admired by Tchaikovsky, one of his pupils. Certain passages in Tchaikovsky's *Eugene Onegin* are derived from similar passages from *The Demon*. Rubinstein's background was cosmopolitan and this may account for him being unable to achieve a 'Russian' style. A famous quote attributed to him is: 'To the Germans I am a Russian, to the Russians a German, to the Christian I am a Jew, to the Jews a Christian, to the Classicist I am a Wagnerite, to the Wagnerites a reactionary; I am neither fish nor fowl – I am unfinished man.'[1] He may have been the model for the composer–pianist, Herr Klesmer, a character in George Eliot's novel *Daniel Deronda* (1878), since she met him when visiting Liszt in Weimar.

Altogether, he wrote 20 operas and oratorios (sometimes called 'sacred operas'), the latter on biblical themes included *Der Thurm zu Babel* (1870), *Die Makkabäer* (1875), *Sulamith* (1882), *Moses* (1892) and *Christus* (1894).

Bibliography: *G*; *HBD*; Ho*; Ken; WW; O. Bennigsen, 'The Brothers Rubinstein', *Musical Quarterly*, 25 (1939), pp. 407ff.; George Eliot, 'From Daniel Deronda', in O. Strunk (ed.), *Source Readings in Music History* (New York: W. W. Norton, 1998), pp. 1076–82; Anton Rubinstein, *Autobiography of Anton Rubinstein, 1829–1889* (St Petersburg, 1889) English translation 1969; http://utopia.knoware.nl/~jsmeets/r/rubinste.htm
1. http://www.emory.edu/MUSIC/ARNOLD/rubinstein_content.html

Rubinstein, Beryl (b. Athens, Georgia, USA, 26 October 1898; d. Cleveland, Ohio, 29 December 1952)   Studied piano with Alexander Lambert before touring the United States as a pianist (1905–11), but his formal début in New York was not until 1916. He studied in Berlin with Busoni and José Vianna da

Motta. He taught piano at the Cleveland Institute from 1921, becoming its director in 1932. His compositions include *Sleeping Beauty* (1938), a piano concerto and many pieces for solo piano.
Bibliography: *HBD*; Ho*

Rubinstein, Nikolay Grigor'yevich (b. Moscow, 14 June 1835; d. Paris, 23 March 1881)   Brother of ANTON RUBINSTEIN, and in many ways followed a similar path to his brother as a pianist and composer. He played the piano from an early age, having lessons from his mother at the age of 4, but did not achieve the same rank as a pianist as did his brother. He also studied in Berlin with Kullak and Dehn from 1844 to 1846, but later studied medicine at Moscow University, graduating in 1855. He also studied with Villoing in Moscow. He founded the Moscow Conservatory in 1866, where he was director until 1881. Among his pupils were Siloti, von Sauer and Taneyev. He died of tuberculosis.
Bibliography: *G*; *HBD*; Ho*; Ken; O. Bennigsen, 'The Brothers Rubinstein', *Musical Quarterly*, 25 (1939), pp. 407ff.

Sadai [Sidi], **Yizhak** (b. Sofia, Bulgaria, 13 May 1935)   Emigrated to Israel with his family in 1949. From 1951 to 1956 he studied with BOSCOVICH at the Tel Aviv Academy of Music, and later with Haubenstock-Ramati. He also studied with TAL (1954). He taught in the Music Academy in Jerusalem from 1960 and in Tel Aviv from 1966. His development as a composer shows three important influences: the Second Viennese School, particularly Alban Berg as seen in *Impressions d'un Chorale* for piano (1960); traditional oriental music, for example, the cantata *Hazvi Israel* (1960); and, after his visit to Pierre Schaeffer in Paris, *musique-concrète* and electronic music, for example *Aria da Capo* for six instrumentalists and two magnetophones (1966), *Anagrama* for chamber orchestra and tape (1973), *Canti Fermi* for orchestra and synclavier (1985) and *Antiphones* for chamber orchestra and synclavier (1985). His other works include: *Piccola Fantasia* for piano (1956); *Impressions of a Chorale* for harpsichord, which is a free fantasy on a chorale melody by J. S. Bach (1956); *Nuances* for chamber orchestra (1966); a string quartet, *Anamorphoses* (1984); and *Reprises* for eight instruments (1986).
Bibliography: *G*; Grad; *HBD*; Ken; Ly*

Salomon [Salmon], **Karel** (b. Heidelburg, 13 November 1897; d. Beit Zayit, near Jerusalem, 15 January 1974)   Studied in Germany with Wulfrum and Richard Strauss. He conducted in Hamburg from 1920 to 1926 but with the rise of Nazism emigrated to Palestine in 1933. By that year he had established himself as a conductor, singer (baritone) and composer. He became musical director of Palestine Radio from its inauguration in 1936, and continued as musical director of Israel Radio from 1948 to 1957. His compositions include two symphonies and concertos for piano, for cello and for glockenspiel, and many works that have specifically biblical or Hebrew inspiration, for example,

the three operas *David and Goliath* (1930), *Nedarim* (Vows, 1955) and *Viermal Methusalem* (1969), and the cantatas *Kibbutz HaGaluyoth* (1952), *Le-Ma'an Yerusalayim* (1958), *Does Not Wisdom Cry* (from Proverbs 8:1–13, 1962) and *Chaye'i Adam* (The life of man, 1967).
Bibliography: Grad; Ken; Ly*

Saminsky, Lazare (b. Vale-Gotzulovo, near Odessa, Ukraine, 27 October 1882; d. Port Chester, New York, 30 June 1959) His paternal ancestors were merchants who had lived near Odessa since the early nineteenth century and his maternal ancestors were landed gentry. There were rabbis among both his paternal and maternal ancestors. He was born into an intellectual family; his mother, *née* Marie Grieber, was musical and his father was interested in literature and politics. Saminsky did not begin piano lessons until he was 15 and it was then that he made his first written compositions. However, at that age he was more interested in philosophy and mathematics. His first proper studies of the theory of music were at the Odessa Music School in 1903–4. He gained a studentship to the Moscow Conservatory in 1905, but was expelled in 1906 for taking part in political demonstrations. Later that year he enrolled for composition and conducting classes at the St Petersburg Conservatory (1906–10), studying under Liadov, Rimsky-Korsakov and Tcherepine, but he also enrolled for mathematics and law at St Petersburg University (1906–9). In 1907 he began conducting the Petrograd University chorus and orchestra. In 1908, together with fellow students, he founded the Hebrew Folk Song Society. From 1909 it became clear that his career would be in music rather than in law or mathematics. His first opus is an overture composed in 1908, written in a classical style and showing the influence of Glazunov.

In 1910 he carried out military service in the Caucasus and while in that region became acquainted with the religious chants of Jewish tribes in Caucasia. This led, three years later, to him receiving a commission from Baron Horace de Guinzbourg to gather traditional Jewish chants from the Transcaucasian region and gave him a lifelong interest in Jewish religious music. From 1913 to 1917 he conducted at Tbilisi, where he was also professor of composition. In 1919 he travelled to Palestine via Constantinople. Whilst in Jerusalem he composed *Conte Hebraïque* (Hebrew fairytale), reflecting the folk song elements that he had collected a few years earlier, and *Danse Rituelle du Sabbuth*, a Hassidic Sabbath celebration; both works are for piano. Later in 1919 he visited and conducted in Paris, also composing another piano piece, *Etude*. He then visited London and eventually emigrated to New York in 1920, where he established himself as a conductor, music organizer and music publisher. In 1924 he became director of the Reform synagogue,Temple Emanuel; a post he held until 1956.

He composed a biblical ballet, *Lamentation de Rachel*, for speaker, dancer, female solo and choir and orchestra in 1913, which he revised in 1920. Many of his early works were songs or song cycles. He composed five symphonies,

each having a title that expresses the prevailing mood of the symphony rather than one which is programmatic. The first, *The Symphony of Great Rivers*, was composed in Tbilisi in 1914 and was inspired by the snow-capped Caucasian mountains. The second, *The Symphony of Great Summits*, was composed in 1918 in the woods of western Georgia and was first performed by Mengelburg in Amsterdam in 1922. The third, *The Symphony of the Seas*, was conceived in 1919, whilst Saminsky was travelling from Constantinople to the coasts of Syria and Palestine, and was completed in 1921 in the United States. The fourth was completed in 1926 and received its premiere in Berlin in 1929; the fifth, *Jerusalem*, was completed in 1930. His other works include two opera-ballets, *Vision of Ariel* (1916) and *The Gagliarda of a Merry Plague* (1924), and many sacred choral works and settings for services. Many of his compositions have Jewish themes or inspiration, for example, his fifth symphony, *Jerusalem*, and his opera *The Daughter of Jephtha* (1928). Amongst his writings on music is the book *Music from the Ghetto and the Bible* (1934).
Bibliography: *AG*; *G*; *HBD*; Domenico de Paoli, *Saminsky: Composer and Civic Worker* (New York: Bloch, 1930); Nemtsov, J. EDA 012-2, and EDA 014-2 [record sleeve]

Sandberg, Mordecai (b. Suceava, Romania, 4 February 1897; d. Toronto, 28 December 1973)   Studied music and medicine in Vienna and then settled in Jerusalem in 1922. In addition to establishing a clinic in Jerusalem, he also began to compose. Whilst in Vienna it is likely that he came in contact with Willi von Moellendorff, a pioneer of quarter-tone music, and this began his interest in microtonal music. He wrote biblical music in microtonal notation, published a music journal and co-founded the Institute for New Music in Jerusalem in 1929. He remained in Jerusalem until 1938, when he travelled to New York, but with the outbreak of war he was compelled to remain there. In 1970 he and his wife moved to Toronto, where he taught at York University. His compositions were principally biblical works and included settings for the 150 psalms and a trilogy of oratorios entitled *Shelomah*, *Ruth* and *Ezkerah*.
Bibliography: *G*; Grad

Saxton, Robert Louis Alfred (b. London, 8 October 1953)   Started composing at the age of 6, and by the age of 9 he was asking his mother how he could be a composer. She told him to write to a composer to ask. He wrote to Benjamin Britten, started up a correspondence with him, and two years later he went to Britten's house for a composition lesson. Among the advice Britten offered was not to try initially to be original, but rather to develop the craft of composition. He continued to correspond with Britten until he was 15. Whilst a pupil at Bryanston School (1967–71) he studied composition privately with Elizabeth Lutyens (1970–4) and composed songs, a musical and an arrangement of *The Art of Fugue* by Bach. His first published composition, when he was 19, was *Ritornelli and Intermezzi* for piano. He studied at Cambridge with

Robin Holloway (1972–5) and at Oxford (1975–6) with Robert Sherlaw Johnson. He also studied privately with Luciano Berio (1976–7). He had a number of teaching posts at English universities before becoming head of the composition department at the Guildhall School of Music from 1986 to 1999, when he became university lecturer and tutorial fellow at Worcester College, Oxford.

One of his earliest compositional successes was *What Does the Song Hope For* for soprano, flute, oboe, piano, string trio and tape, which won first prize at the International Gaudeamus Week in 1975. Saxton comments that many of his works are concerned with religious/philosophical concepts, and especially with the idea of progressing from darkness into light, as can be seen in works such as *In the Beginning* (1987) and *Music to Celebrate the Resurrection of Christ* (1988). Both traditional mainstream and modernist influences are present in his work. From Elizabeth Lutyens he became interested in serial-based techniques. His eastern European Jewish heritage can be gleaned in some of his works. *Concerto for Orchestra* (1984) is inspired by the *Kabbala*, which describes the mystical experience of journeying through the seven heavens and seven palaces in the highest heaven until the Divine presence is reached. The *Viola Concerto* (1986) contains cantillation-like melodic patterns in the slow movement. Other orchestral works include *Elijah's Violin* (1988), a violin concerto (1989), a trumpet concerto (1990) and a cello concerto (1991). Saxton has written chamber music, vocal and choral music and a chamber opera, *Caritas* (1990), based on the play by Arnold Wesker on the subject of a fourteenth-century anchoress. The main character of the story becomes isolated and oppressed by the community, a subject having an obvious Jewish resonance. His more recent works include *Fantasia* for string quartet (1994), *A Yardstick to the Stars* for string quartet and piano (1995) and *Songs, Dances and Ellipses* for string quartet (1997); the latter two are concerned with the mathematical basis of scientific phenomena. Saxton has also written a number of smaller pieces, for example, *Prayer Before Sleep* for soprano, cello and piano (1997), which is dedicated to the memory of Rabbi Hugo Gryn, and a cantata for eight solo voices entitled *The Dialogue of Sion and God* (2000), which is a setting of a poem by Eleazor ben Kallir. BBC Radio 3 commissioned him for the millennium to compose a dramatic radio operatic fantasy, *The Legend of the Wandering Jew*.

Bibliography: *CC*; *G*; *HBD*; Ken; Leb; Humphrey Carpenter, *Benjamin Britten: A Biography* (London: Faber, 1992), p. 442; David Wright, 'Coming of Age', *Musical Times*, 134 (1993), pp. 596–8; David Wright, 'Robert Saxton in the 1990s', *Tempo*, 215 (2001), pp. 1–6; www.schirmer.com/composers/saxton

Schidlowsky, Léon (b. Santiago, Chile, 21 July 1931)   Studied piano at the Chile National Conservatory in his youth and later psychology and philosophy at the University of Chile, pursuing music concurrently with Pedró Allende and Free Focke. He also studied in Europe from 1952 to 1955,

returning to Chile to teach at the Hebrew Institute in Santiago from 1955 to 1961. He taught at the University of Chile and the National Conservatory from 1962 to 1968. He moved to Germany in 1968 and then emigrated to Israel in 1970, where he was appointed professor of music at the Rubin Academy of Music in Tel Aviv. He has composed over 100 works both before and after arriving in Israel. His earlier work is freely atonal, but his later works use serialism to a varying degree and also aleatory techniques. He uses a graphic system of notation. Many of his works are concerned with themes of early and recent Jewish history, for example, *La Noche de Cristal* (1961) and *Invocación* (1964), commemorating the Holocaust; *Kaddish* for cello and orchestra (1967), *Babi Yar* for strings, percussion and piano (1970), *Rabbi Akiba* (1972), *Massada* (1972), *In Eius Memoriam* for orchestra (1974), in memory of the heroes of the Yom Kippur War in 1973, and *Eleven Tombstones* for contralto, brass quintet, percussion and electronic tape (1972), in memory of the eleven-member sports delegation massacred by anti-Israeli Arab terrorists at the 1972 Olympic Games.
Bibliography: *G*; Grad; *HBD*; Ly*

Schnabel, Arthur (b. Lipnik, Austria [Slovakia], 17 April 1882; d. Axenstein, Switzerland, 15 August 1951)   Born into a moderately orthodox Jewish family. However, when they moved to Vienna in 1889 they became outwardly more assimilated in social terms, although still devoted to the faith. When Schnabel was 6 his elder sister started piano lessons, and according to his mother, although at the time he was not having lessons, he succeeded in playing what she had been taught, only with greater facility. He was given a few piano lessons by a local teacher, and received a general education from a tutor, from whom he also started to learn Hebrew. By the time he was 7 he was taken to Vienna to play for Hans Schmidt, in order to have his potential assessed. Schmidt accepted him as a pupil and from then on he was trained with a view to becoming a pianist, although he always maintained he would have preferred to be a composer.

At this stage the family moved to Vienna, except for his father, who remained behind to look after his business. They lived near to Ignaz Kreisler, their family doctor, and thus Arthur came to know his son Fritz KREISLER. Schnabel's parents were not wealthy, and for the next eight years he was able to continue his tuition largely as the result of sponsorship by some wealthy families anxious to promote talent. At the age of 8 Schnabel gave a private concert arranged by Albert Gutmann, who ran the leading music shop in Vienna and sold pianos. Gutmann organized private concerts so that potential benefactors (sponsors) had the chance to see young talent. Schnabel made a good impression playing Mozart's D minor piano concerto, and this ensured continued financial support. His parents were ambitious for their son, but at the same time did not want to exploit him as a prodigy; consequently he did not perform in public until he was 14. By the time he was 9 his mother had been advised that he needed a superior teacher, and he was accepted by Leschetizky, who became his piano teacher for the next few years, although in the first year it was Leschetizky's wife who taught him.

Leschetizky had a high reputation, having pupils from all over the world, particularly America; Paderewski had been one of his former pupils. It was Leschetizky that made the famous comment to Schnabel, 'You will never be a pianist. You are a musician.' At the time Schnabel did not know what to make of the comment, but it is in keeping with his preference for composing rather than for performing. Had he not gone on to be such a famous pianist, he might not have been so overlooked as a composer. At the time Leschetizky also advised his mother that he should have lessons in composition, so she took him to the house of Anton Bruckner, knocked on the door and said she wanted him to give her son lessons in theory. He replied 'I don't teach children' and shut the door. Leschetizky then advised a less-famous teacher, Mandiczewski, who accepted him.

Mandiczewski proved to be a good teacher. Besides teaching he was the archivist of the Society of the Friends of Music in Vienna and amanuensis of Brahms. This gave Schnabel opportunities to meet Brahms and his circle of friends. He was invited to join them on walking parties in the country around Vienna. Through Leschetizky he met Anton RUBINSTEIN and his circle. At the age of 10 Schnabel, who had until then been educated by a tutor, was sent to school. His mother and sisters left Vienna in 1892 to return to his father, but the whole family returned to Vienna three years later and remained there until his father died in 1927. His mother was taken away by the Nazis in 1942, never to be seen again. The brother of a Viennese family whom Schnabel knew, and who was interested in art, invited him to stay with him in Berlin for as long as he liked, so in 1898 Schnabel moved to Berlin. He made his début as a pianist there by playing a Schubert sonata. At that time Schubert sonatas were hardly played.

Schnabel composed a number of works in a late Romantic style, mainly for piano, together with some songs during the 1890s to early 1900s. In 1901 he gave a performance of his piano concerto with the Berlin Philharmonic Orchestra, and at the same concert the first performance in Berlin of Paderewski's piano concerto. In 1906 he married the contralto Therese Behr, who was known for her interpretations of Schubert, Schumann and Brahms. In 1906 he stopped composing, having become dissatisfied with his early compositions, discarding them all except for a rondo theme from his piano concerto, which he used much later in his third symphony of 1948. In 1914 he resumed composing in a new, more progressive style, with the *Notturno* for voice and piano, a setting of a poem by Richard Dehmel. Schnabel first met SCHOENBERG in Vienna around 1900, when both of them used to queue to go to the opera. Both shared an enthusiasm for the new opera director, Gustav MAHLER. Schnabel was particularly impressed by Schoenberg's *Three Pieces for Piano*, Op. 11, and *Five Pieces for Orchestra*, Op. 16. It is thought that Schnabel may have helped Schoenberg financially at this time. Schnabel's next composing phase lasted until 1925 and was influenced by Schoenberg's atonal music, and also by other composers, for example, Busoni, Richard Strauss, Krenek and Hindemith.

During this period he composed four string quartets, a quintet for piano and strings, a sonata for solo violin lasting 50 minutes, a string trio and a dance suite for piano. Schnabel described 1919 to 1924 as the happiest phase in his life. At this time he was most prolific as a composer. His temperament was such that he did not promote his own works, and rarely played them in public. Such works of his that were performed in public were adversely criticized, prompting him to give up composing in 1925. His piano sonata was performed by Eduard Erdmann at the festival of the International Society for Contemporary Music in Venice. The work was not well received; a member of the audience shouted, 'That's enough.' Ten years later Toscanini asked him, 'Are you really the same Schnabel who wrote that horrible music I heard ten years ago?' His fame as a pianist of the classics appeared to be a disadvantage to a composer of complex expressionistic music.

His main repertoire as a concert pianist were the classical works of Beethoven, Mozart, Schubert and Brahms; he also played in trios with Szigeti and Huberman as violinists and Feuermann, Casals or Primrose as cellist. Earlier he had played with JOACHIM and Ysaÿe. It was his interpretations of the 'classics' that have particularly left their mark. He never played modern works in public, in spite of admiring music by twentieth-century composers such as Schoenberg. When Schoenberg completed his piano concerto in 1943 he had in mind either Steuermann or Schnabel to perform its premiere. In a letter to the music publisher Carl Engel, Schoenberg suggests that he read the riot act to Schnabel, saying: 'His [Schnabel's] standpoint to me seems not only foolish but almost criminal. I believe it is the first duty of a real artist to play contemporary music. If all interpreters had behaved as he had done the works of the greatest masters would never have reached the ears of the public.' In the event it was Steuermann, Schoenberg's first choice, who gave the premiere in 1944.

After a break of six years he began composing again, this time with a sonata for solo cello and a sonata for violin and piano. He continued to compose for the rest of his life, mainly during the summers, when he rested from concert performing. In 1938 he composed his first purely orchestral work, his first symphony, and his second in 1941–2. The latter has never been performed in public.

He emigrated to the USA in 1939, to escape persecution by the Nazis, and became an American citizen in 1944. He was never as popular a pianist in America as in Europe. In 1943 he dispensed with the services of an American manager and started organizing his own concerts. He felt that managers had little interest in music and were mainly concerned with sales. He taught at Ann Arbor, Michigan, from 1940 to 1945, and continued to produce a steady stream of compositions for the rest of his life. His last work, *Duodecimet*, for strings, wind and percussion, which he did not complete but which was completed by René LEIBOWITZ, has been claimed as a minor masterpiece. From 1946 Schnabel made several trips to Europe, on the last of which he died, in Axenstein, Switzerland.

Bibliography: *AG*; *G*; *HBD*; Ly*; Arthur Schnabel, *My Life and Music* (Harlow: Longman, 1961); Mark Swed, 'Schnabel the Composer', *Musical Times*, 130 (June 1989), pp. 332–5

Schnittke, Alfred Harrievich (b. Engels, Saratov, Russia, 24 November 1934; d. Hamburg, 3 August 1998)   Engels was once the capital of the German Republic in the Soviet Union. Schnittke's mother was German and his father was German–Jewish; neither had Russian citizenship. His father was born in Frankfurt. Both his paternal grandmother and grandfather were born in Libava, which in 1918 became part of what is now Liepāja in Latvia. In 1987 Schnittke summed up his nationality as follows:

> Although I don't have any Russian blood, I am tied to Russia, having spent all my life here. On the other hand, much of what I have written is somehow related to German music and to the logic which comes out of being German, although I did not especially want this … Like my German forefathers, I live in Russia, I can speak Russian far better than German. But I am not Russian … My Jewish half gives me no peace: I know none of the three Jewish languages – but I look like a typical Jew.

Both his parents spoke Russian with a strong German accent. Schnittke's father worked on a local German newspaper until 1941. Neither his mother nor father was religious, and his paternal grandparents, although Jewish, were anti-religious. His grandparents were enthusiastic supporters of communism, as were many of their generation. Alfred and his brothers and sisters lived not only with their parents, but also with his maternal grandmother. She was a devout Catholic, and was the person with whom he could most easily discuss religious matters in his youth. This may have influenced his eventual decision to become baptized into the Catholic Church in Vienna in 1980.

During World War Two his parents felt uncomfortable due to being both German and Jewish, and Alfred experienced anti-Semitism for the first time. His father became an army interpreter during the war and was posted to Vienna. After the war Alfred's father took up a position in Vienna on the Soviet newspaper *Òsterreichische Zeitung* and the family moved to Vienna for two years. This was to be an important formative experience for Alfred, and he regarded it as one of the happiest periods of his life. Although there was no piano in the house, Alfred was able to learn the accordion. He started to have lessons at the age of 12 in both music theory and piano, which were given by a professional pianist, Charlotte Ruber, who lived in a flat above the Schnittke's home. During the family's period in Vienna (1946–8), he attended a number of concerts and was particularly impressed by KLEMPERER's performance of Bruckner's Seventh Symphony. The Viennese influence is evident in much of Schnittke's later compositions.

When the newspaper for which his father worked closed down in Vienna, the Schnittkes returned to Russia and lived in Moscow. At the time there was a great shortage of housing, and they initially stayed with Alfred's grandparents. They later found accommodation in Valentmovka, some way out of Moscow. Through one of his father's contacts, Alfred was able to gain a place in a music college, the October Revolution College, which had a reputation for folk music and having a strong choir. He had good teachers both for piano and music theory – Shaternikov and Ryzhkin – and by 1953 was able to present his compositions to support his application to the Moscow Conservatory. He enrolled there in the autumn of 1953, the same year that both Stalin and Prokofiev died in Moscow. He studied under Golubev, a pupil of Myaskovsky. His period at the conservatory coincided with the 'Khrushchev thaw', when it became possible for the first time to obtain scores of music by some of the great innovators of the twentieth century – among them, Stravinsky, SCHOENBERG, Berg and Webern. Schnittke met Luigi Nono on a visit to Moscow. He was thus able to become thoroughly conversant with music outside the USSR as well as with that of Russian composers such as Shostakovich. However, unlike Shostakovich, he was not compelled to express himself indirectly and symbolically because the political climate had now improved.

His first marriage to the musicologist Galina Koltsina was short-lived (1956–9), but his second marriage, to his piano pupil, Irina Katayeva, was to be a happy one. She worked as an accompanist and piano tutor and played many of his first compositions. His double piano concerto was written for her and the wife of his friend, the conductor Gernardi Rozhdestvensky. Many of his early compositions were for the piano and for chamber groups.

From 1961 to 1971, after his graduation, he taught composition, instrumentation, polyphony and harmony at the Moscow Conservatory. His eight completed symphonies were composed between 1972 and 1994. In his first and second symphonies (1972 and 1979) he quotes Gregorian chant. In *Requiem* (1975), which is dedicated to the memory of his mother, he moves very close to the Catholic tradition. In his fourth symphony (1984) his search for religious *rapprochement* is found as he links the three main Christian strands, Orthodox, Catholic and Protestant, to their Jewish source, using a three-note motif representing synagogue chant. In the final section of the symphony the choir were to sing the *Ave Maria*. At the time this was not permitted and the choir sang wordlessly, but after *perestroika* the words were used. During the Brezhnev era his symphonies were outlawed and so he concentrated on film music. He wrote about 60 scores in all, at the rate of 3–4 per year, and this brought in a good income.

His music is termed *polystylistic* as he juxtaposed music with styles of different periods and from different cultural origins. Schnittke was a great admirer of MAHLER's music and he once said that 'the seeds for everything I have composed lie in Mahler's work'. Schnittke felt 'homeless' in the country of his birth, as did Mahler. There is also a stylistic similarity in their compositions; the juxtaposing of different styles, the use of irony and quotations. Schnittke composed electronic music and used a prepared piano. At times he used serial technique, which was a reason why some of his music was outlawed in the Brezhnev era. He was fortunate in having good interpreters of his music, particularly the conductor Gernardi Rozhdestvensky, violinists Mark Lubotsky and Gidon Kremer, and violist Yuri Bashmet. He finished his viola concerto just prior to suffering his first stroke in 1985, but nevertheless went on to complete a cello concerto in 1986. He moved to Hamburg in 1990, where he died in 1998.

Bibliography: CC; G; Leb; Anders Beyer, *The Voice of Music* (Aldershot: Ashgate Publishing, 2000), pp. 239–42*; Alexander Ivashkin, *Alfred Schnittke* (London: Phaidon, 1996)*

Schoenberg, Arnold Franz Walter (b. Vienna, 13 September 1874; d. Los Angeles, 13 July 1951)   Although Schoenberg was born in Vienna his father, Samuel Schönberg, was born in Szécsény (Hungary) and his mother, Pauline (*née* Nachod), was born in Prague. Samuel, like many Jews, moved from Pressburg (Bratislava) to Vienna, where prospects for making a living were better. He owned a small shoe shop, having worked his way up from being a boy apprentice. He described himself as a freethinker and was of an iconoclastic frame of mind. His mother came from an old Jewish family in Prague, and had ancestors who had been cantors in the Altneuschul (Old–New Synagogue). She was a practising Jew and was the driving force in seeing that Arnold had a traditional Jewish upbringing; his father, perhaps, gave him a taste for polemics. Samuel was interested in music and was a member of a choral society; among Pauline's relatives were practising musicians. Although brought up as a Jew, by the age of 17 Schoenberg described himself to Malvina Goldschmeid, with whom he was in love at the time, as an 'unbeliever'. In March 1898 he was baptized as a Protestant. A friend of his, Walter Pieau, who became an opera singer and performed some of Schoenberg's songs, is believed to have given him a thorough knowledge of the Christian religion, prior to this conversion.

There was no piano in the Schoenberg's house, but Arnold was given violin lessons from the age of 8 and started composing before his teens. A school friend whom he met when he was 11, Oscar Adler, gave him his early tuition in harmony. He discovered what was meant by 'sonata form' from an encyclopedia. When he was 15 his father died suddenly from influenza and Schoenberg had to work to help support the rest of the family. He worked in a bank, but at the same time kept up with his music in the evenings and soon decided it was a composer that he really wanted to be. In 1893 he met ZEMLINSKY as the result of playing the cello in an amateur orchestra, which Zemlinsky conducted. Zemlinsky, recognizing him as a promising musician, gave him instructions in the principles of composition. By 1895 the bank in which he worked was near collapse and Schoenberg was relieved to be able to give up being a banking clerk. In order to help support the family he conducted a metal workers' orchestra, and found himself very much in sympathy with the socialist views of the muscians.

In 1897 he completed his first string quartet (referred to as No. 0) and it was performed in a concert that year. One of his best-known works, *Verklärte Nacht*, was completed in 1899; this is a programmatic string sextet based on a poem by Richard Dehmel concerning a conversation between a man and a woman about the illegitimate child the woman is carrying. This late Romantic work is unique in that it is composed in the style of a symphonic poem, where the form of the work arises from its programme and not from a classical form, for example, a sonata form. The strongest influence on his works of this period was Brahms, but after becoming steeped in Wagner's music, his next compositions, particularly *Pelleas and Melisande* (1903) and *Gurrelieder* (initial conception, 1900 – see below) show the latter's influence. *Gurrelieder* is a late Romantic Wagnerian-style love tragedy conceived on a massive scale. The first two parts were drafted in 1900, but then Schoenberg had to stop in order to earn some money. The draft of the whole work was completed in 1901, but it was not until 1911 that the orchestration was complete, by which time Schoenberg had composed expressionist works such as *Erwartung* (1909). Many members of the audience were spellbound at the first performance of *Gurrelieder* conducted by SCHREKER in Vienna in 1913.

In his early years Schoenberg was dogged by financial worries and moved first from Vienna to Berlin, and then back to Vienna largely to where the employment prospects as a musician seemed best. This was even more important after his marriage in 1901 to Mathilde Zemlinsky, sister of Alexander Zemlinsky, and after the birth of their first child in 1902. In 1901, in Berlin, he worked as a conductor and arranger in a cabaret theatre. He met Richard Strauss in 1902, who was impressed with his skill in composition and helped him obtain a scholarship and also a teaching post at the Stern Conservatory in Berlin. It was there that Schoenberg was to discover his talents as a teacher. In 1903 he returned to Vienna, where he taught harmony and counterpoint at a private music school, and at the same time did routine work for music publishers. Included among his pupils during this period were Webern, Berg, Jalowetz, WELLESZ and Erwin Stern.

In 1904, together with Zemlinsky, he formed the Vereinigung Schaffende Tonkünstler (Society of Creative Composers). This society aimed to put on performances of only contemporary music and Mahler became its honorary president. Mahler had been greatly impressed with a performance of *Verklärte Nacht*. In 1905 Schoenberg completed his String Quartet in D Minor (No. 1) and in 1906 his first chamber symphony. He had moved away from works requiring a Wagnerian-sized orchestra, such as *Pelleas and Melisande* and *Gurrelieder*, to a much leaner and increasingly atonal style. The premieres of the string quartet no. 1 and the first chamber symphony in Vienna in February 1907 met with uproar. Mahler was present in the audience and a staunch supporter of Schoenberg, although he claimed that he found it difficult to understand the works. He felt that this was probably because he was old and his ear not sensitive enough. Schoenberg was conscious throughout his life of his historical position at the end of a long line of composers, from Bach through to Brahms, Wagner, Mahler and Strauss. He was very much aware of the direction in which Romantic style had developed and felt that it could not remain static but would inevitably develop further. Wagner's *Tristan and Isolde* was regarded as having exhausted the possibilities of tonality. Schoenberg felt that atonality was a consequent progression. In his book *Harmonielehre*, published in 1911, he formulates the view that tonality is an artificial musical device, albeit a powerful one, and in his works composed between 1908 and 1909, for example, String Quartet, Op. 10, the George lieder, Op. 15, *Three Piano Pieces*, Op. 16, and the monodrama *Erwartung*, Op. 17, there is an implied emancipation of dissonance. Significantly the last movement of String Quartet, Op. 10, is a setting of a poem by Stefan George that begins, 'I feel a breath from other planets'.

Another feature of the development of atonality was the avoidance of any repetition that was an important device in previous music. This development reached its extreme in *Erwartung*, which lasts for about 25 minutes without repetition. The music is particularly apposite to accompany what Schoenberg described as an 'anxiety-dream'. A woman wanders through a forest at night and stumbles on what turns out to be the dead body of her lover. Schoenberg composed this not long after a crisis in his own life. In 1907 he began experimenting with painting and eventually a number of his works were exhibited at Kandinsky's *Blaue Reiter* exhibition in 1911. This is sometimes described as his expressionist phase, not only in terms of his paintings but also his music. He took lessons from the young painter Richard Gerstl. Schoenberg's wife Mathilde became attracted to Gerstl and left Schoenberg in the summer of 1908 to live with him. Webern persuaded Mathilde to return to Schoenberg, which she did, and the couple were eventually reunited, but shortly afterwards Gerstl committed suicide at the age of 25.

Ertwartung represented the limit to which Schoenberg was to go in non-repetition. It is not only atonal but athematic and amotivic. One of his next major works was a modern version of a song cycle, *Pierrot Lunaire*, Op. 21. This was warmly received at its first performance in 1912. It is a setting of Albert Giraud's French poems for chamber orchestra and voice. In it Schoenberg introduced *Sprechstimme*, a half-spoken method of singing where the voice only momentarily holds the indicated pitch before rising or falling to the next pitch. The 'atonal period' led on to Schoenberg developing the twelve-note system. The first work in which this was fully developed was *Piano Suite*,

Op. 25, of 1923, although both *Piano Pieces*, Op. 23, and the *Serenade*, Op. 24, have twelve-note movements. In July 1921 Schoenberg declared to a friend, referring to the twelve-tone system, 'Today I have discovered something which will assure the supremacy of German music for the next hundred years.' (For details of the twelve-note system, see Glossary.) In effect, Schoenberg had abandoned the set of restrictions imposed by the tonal system, but had now brought in a new set in developing his twelve-note system. The period leading up to this point, from the start of World War One, had been a lean period as far as Schoenberg's composing was concerned. He had begun the oratorio *Die Jakobsleiter* in 1915, abandoning it incomplete in 1917, and also composed *Four Orchestral Pieces*, Op. 22, a work lasting about ten minutes but which took four years to complete.

In 1915 the family moved back to Vienna. Schoenberg was called up to serve in the Austrian Army. He carried out garrison duties for one year, by which time his health had deteriorated. He suffered from asthma and was given temporary discharge in 1916, and complete discharge in December 1917. After the war he resumed teaching harmony and composition; among his pupils at this time were Rudolph Kolisch, Hans EISLER, Joseph Rufer and Karl Rankl. In 1918 he founded the Society for Private Musical Performances. It existed for four years, during which time about 150 different twentieth-century works were performed. Although still officially a Lutherian, his Christian beliefs had not lasted. With the crisis in his private life (1907–8), and the dreadful events of the war, he found solace in religion, but what he described as the 'Faith of the Disillusioned' – a Judaeo-Christian background modified by his reading of Strindberg and Swedenborg. In 1923 his wife Mathilde died after a short illness, and although their marriage had had its crises, she was a great loss to him. In 1924 he remarried, this time to Gertrud Kolisch, the sister of one of his pupils and about half his age.

In 1926 Schoenberg returned to Berlin for the third time, as director of the masterclass in composition at the Prussian Academy of Arts, succeeding Busoni, who had died in 1924. It was the most prestigious post that he held and was a sign of his international recognition as an outstanding musician. The facilities were good and he was only required to teach for six months a year. Among the staff were Schreker and Rufer, and among his pupils were Walter GOEHR, Skalkottas and Marc BLITZSTEIN. During the seven years that he was there he composed String Quartet No. 3, *Orchestral Variations*, the opera *Von Heute auf Morgen*, *Accompaniment to a Film Scene*, and he began the opera *Moses and Aron*. *Von Heute auf Morgen* is an opera lasting less than an hour and was completed in 1929. Unusually for Schoenberg, this opera is a domestic satire, with a libretto by 'Max Blonda' (alias his wife, Gertrude). In 1931–2 he visited Roberto Gerhard in Spain and during this visit he met Casals, for whom he later wrote the Cello Concerto (1933).

Schoenberg encountered anti-Semitism at many stages of his life, and he came to realize that it made no difference that he had became a Protestant.

When he went to Matsee near Salzburg to spend the summer of 1921 composing, he was visited by a deputation from the town council and told Jews were no longer welcome in Matsee, although if he could give proof of a Christian baptism he could stay. He left in disgust. His appointment to the Prussian Academy of Arts in 1924 was met with anti-Semitic attacks, and a year earlier he fell out with Kandinsky through the latter's anti-Semitism. He saw earlier than many Jews in Germany that the rise in Nazism was not just a transient phase, but that it would lead to dire consequences for Jews. In 1923 he drafted plans for a play, *Der Biblische Weg*, on the subject of creating a new Jewish homeland. He completed it in 1927, although it has never been performed.

In 1933, after Schoenberg returned to Berlin from his visit to Spain, he found that the political situation had worsened. On hearing from the president of the academy, von Schillings, that Hitler resolved 'to break the Jewish stranglehold on western music', Schoenberg took this as a declaration of intent to dismiss him and other Jews from their posts, and by May 1933 the Prussian Ministry of Culture revoked its contract with Schoenberg and Schreker. By this time Schoenberg had made his way to Paris and on 24 July at a simple ceremony witnessed by the painter Marc Chagall he was received back into the Jewish faith. From this time forth he changed the spelling of his name from Schönberg to Schoenberg and stopped using Gothic script. He was fully aware of the impending tragedy for European Jews and spent much of his time while in Paris writing letters, beginning what was to become a ten-year political campaign on behalf of European Jewry. His concerns are also reflected in many of his later compositions, for example, *Kol Nidre*, Op. 39, *Ode to Napoleon*, Op. 41, and psalms. After his illegal dismissal from his post in Berlin and with his bank account in Germany frozen, he needed to seek employment and was offered a teaching post in a small music school in Boston. With his wife and daughter he sailed for America in October 1933. He never returned to Europe.

The climate in Boston and in New York, where the family lived until 1934, did not suit him, given his asthma and a heart condition. Eventually they moved to Los Angeles, where initially he taught private pupils. In 1935 he lectured at the University of Southern California and the following year was appointed professor at the University of California at Los Angeles (UCLA). He was now in close proximity to Hollywood, but although he was interested in composing for films he never completed a film score. As early as 1910 he had thought of using film for his drama *Die Glückliche Hand*, but this never materialized. In 1929 he composed *Begleitungsmusik zu einer Lichtspielszene*, Op. 34, for a small cinema orchestra. It depicts the following scenes: threatening danger; fear; and catastrophe. This was a somewhat theoretical attempt at film music and was not written for a specific film; it is played as a purely orchestral piece. In 1935 he began sketches for a film based on Buck's novel *The Good Earth*, but when he requested $50,000 for a complete score the producer dismissed the idea. His greatest contribution in this area was in giving lessons to many film composers, for example, Rainger, Powell, Rathburn, Raksin, Newman, Friedhofer and WAXMAN. Although he left no completed film music, two films were made of two of his compositions: *Moses and Aaron* (1930) in 1975 and *Von Heute auf Morgen* (1928) in 1996.[1]

Schoenberg continued as professor at UCLA until 1944, when he was 70 years old. He and his family had become American citizens in 1941. In spite of continuing ill health, he needed to continue working because of his poor financial situation, having only a modest pension. He continued to give private lessons. Most of his late compositions reflect his concerns about the scourge of Nazism and the fate of Jews. *Ode to Napoleon* (1942) is based on a poem by Byron, mocking a dictator, but Schoenberg has Hitler in mind in his composition. *Survivor from Warsaw*, Op. 42, for narrator, men's chorus and orchestra (1947), is based on a story reported to him by survivors from the Warsaw ghetto. The group of prisoners is ordered to count their number prior to being forced into the gas chambers, but in the middle of this they break out into a powerful singing of the *Shema* – a last assertion of human dignity against their exterminators. Schoenberg applied unsuccessfully for a Guggenheim fellowship to complete *Die Jakobsleiter* and *Moses and Aron*; neither was completed, although this is probably attributed to his difficulty in determining how to continue with them. He suffered a heart attack in 1946, which nearly killed him. Shortly afterwards, when he had recovered, he wrote what some regard as one of his best works, String Trio, Op. 45. In the last year of his life (1951) he composed the choral works *De Profundis* (Psalm 130), Op. 50b, and *Modern Psalm*, Op. 50c, and he was made the honorary president of the Israeli Academy of Music.

Bibliography: *G*; *HBD*; Ken; Leb; Walter Frisch, *Schoenberg and his World* (Princeton, NJ: Princeton University Press, 1999); Malcolm MacDonald, *Schoenberg* (London: J. M. Dent, 1987); Alexander L. Ringer, *Arnold Schoenberg: the Composer as Jew* (Oxford: Clarendon Press, 1990); Hans H. Stuckenschmidt, *Schoenberg, his Life, World and Work* (London: Calder, 1977)

1. Sabine M. Feisst, 'Arnold Schoenberg and Cinematic Art', *Musical Quarterly*, 83 (1999), pp. 93–113.

Schoenfield, Paul (b. Detroit, 24 January 1947) Has degrees in both music and mathematics from Carnegie Mellon University and the University of Arizona. At the latter he received his doctorate after studying composition with Robert Muczynski. He has lived in Israel on a kibbutz, but now lives in Cleveland, Ohio. His compositions are inspired by a wide range of musical styles, including American folk music and *klezmer*. His interest in folk music stems largely from his desire to explore his Jewish roots. Although he has composed in almost all media, he has a particular affinity for solo piano composition and chamber works that include piano. His works include: *Four Parables* for piano and orchestra, based on four life encounters; *Vaudeville* for piccolo trumpet and orchestra, patterned after Schumann's *Carnival*; *Klezmer Rondos* for flute and orchestra; *Sonatina* for flute, clarinet and piano; and a piano concerto.

Bibliography: *G*; www.dranoff2piano.org/paul.htm

Schreker, Franz (b. Monaco, 23 March 1878; d. Berlin, 21 March 1934). His father, Isak, was a German-speaking Jew born in Bohemia. He became a photographic artist in the early days of photography, and his clients included those of the imperial court. He worked in Vienna and resorts such as Spa in Belgium and Monaco. Three weeks before he married his second wife, Eleonore von Klossmann, in 1876, Isak was baptized Ignaz and became a Roman Catholic. Their first child died and Franz, their second, was born in Monaco, where his father was working at the time. Franz's early childhood was spent in Monaco, where he encountered a grand clientele who were keen to have their portraits made using the latest technology. Glimpsing European high society made an early impression on Franz. The peripatetic nature of Ignaz's work, and the enthusiasm of both he and his wife for travel, meant that the family settled only briefly during the 1880s in Spa (Belgium), Brussels, Paris, Pola on the Adriatic, Trieste, and Linz in upper Austria. The family was relatively prosperous until Ignaz's death in 1888. By this time Eleonore had four children, and her savings were quickly depleted. She settled in the Döbling district of Vienna, where she had various occupations to try to make ends meet, including seamstress, and running a small general store. Franz's younger sister died of meningitis in 1890.

Franz began formal musical studies at the age of 11 with piano, organ and theory. His first violin and harmony teacher was Karl Pfleger. He showed Pfleger his first composition, 'Ode on the Death of Napoleon the First'. Unlike Schoenberg's mocking *Ode to Napoleon,* Schreker's expressed admiration for Napoleon. By the age of 14 his self-confidence was such that he moved from the family home to a small room in a hotel, where he begun to be the family wage-earner by tutoring reading, writing and mathematics and by freelancing as a violinist. Through a priest, Schreker, who was raised as a Catholic, obtained a part-time post as organist at Döbling parish church. In 1892 he obtained a place in the Vienna Conservatory as a violin student, where a benefactor, Princess von Windischgrätz, paid his fees. His teachers were Ernst Bachrich and Arnold Rosé.

The first public performance of his work was a piece for string orchestra and harp, *Love Song*, that the Budapest Opera orchestra performed in London in July 1896. The one-act opera *Flammen* (1901) was his first completed opera; it premiered in 1902 with Schreker playing the piano accompaniment. His early works are generally regarded as being well constructed technically, but lacking individuality. In 1903 he began what was to become the best known of his six major operas, *Die Ferne Klang*. For five of his operas he wrote his own librettos. He had completed the first two acts of *Die Ferne Klang* in outline by

1906, but seems to have stopped working on it for a while; perhaps lacking confidence in what he was producing. However, in 1907 he went to a performance of Strauss's *Salome*, and this convinced him that he was not on the wrong path with *Die Ferne Klang*. In August 1912 it received its premiere in Frankfurt. Although at the time Schreker was hardly known outside Vienna, after he arrived in Frankfurt and in the weeks before the premiere there was a buzz in the air that an important event was in the offing. The premiere was an enormous success and Schreker took 25 curtain calls. It was 30 years since the death of Wagner, and at the time there appeared to be no one, except possibly Richard Strauss, to carry Wagner's mantle. One critic hailed *Die Ferne Klang* as the most important opera in central Europe since *The Ring* and *Parsifal*. The event put Schreker right at the forefront of the new generation of composers. He also conducted the premiere of Schoenberg's *Gurrelieder* in 1912 to great acclaim.

Both Schreker and Schoenberg were invited to teaching posts at the Vienna Academy of Music in 1912. Both invitations were on the initiative of the director of the academy, Wilhelm Bopp. Only Schreker accepted, and his appointment was not without stiff opposition from the conservative elements within the academy. Earlier, in 1908, he met a young singer, Maria Binder, who was the daughter of a well-established hotel owner. She sang in the Philharmonia Chorus, of which Schreker was conductor. Their marriage in 1909 helped Schreker gain entry into Vienna's social circles.

Schreker wrote most of his own librettos, and in 1911 ZEMLINSKY asked him to write him a libretto about the tragedy of an ugly man. The outcome was *Die Gezeichneten* (The branded one), but Schreker was so pleased with it that he decided to keep it for himself. The opera *Die Gezeichneten* was given its first very successful performance in Frankfurt in 1918, confirming in many critics' minds that Schreker was the greatest opera composer since Wagner. During World War One Schreker was not called up because he had varicose veins. He continued to teach at the Vienna Academy and had to undertake additional teaching to help offset staff shortages caused by colleagues being called up. His third major opera, *Der Schatzgräber*, which like *Die Gezeichneten* was composed during the war years, was premiered in Frankfurt in 1920 and was also a great success. Between 1917 and 1921 his three major operas received 32 productions and over 250 performances. For many he was Germany's foremost opera composer; at the time he was more successful than Richard Strauss.

After the war the relative importance of the two capitals, Berlin and Vienna, shifted, with Berlin in the ascendancy. Schreker, now at the pinnacle of his career, was appointed to the directorship of the prestigious Berlin Akademische Hochschule für Musik, founded by Joseph JOACHIM in 1869. He remained there for the rest of his life. He was given considerable freedom both in the running of the school and in being given the time to compose and conduct. This drew the comment that he was a *Schatzgräber* (a treasure seeker) at the beginning of the month, on payday, and a *ferner Klang* (distant sound) at the end of the month. Whilst his operas had been well received in many major centres, *Die Gezeichneten* received a mixed reception in Berlin. In the meantime his reputation as a composition teacher attracted many students from outside Germany.

A combination of circumstances led to Schreker's ultimate decline into obscurity. Before the First World War he had been considered avant-gardist, his harmonic structures and bold shifting between tonality and atonality seemingly pointing the way to the future. But after the war his opulent style rapidly went out of favour, being regarded by the younger generation as an outpouring of sentimentality and bathos. SLOMINSKY has described it as 'impressionistic nebulosity', and KLEMPERER referred to it as 'inflation music', a reminder of Weimar culture and the hyper-inflation of its currency. A more acerbic style suited a Germany recovering from defeat, with its associated economic problems. Anti-Semitism and conservative nationalism were also factors in the hostility towards Schreker. The inspiration for his next opera, *Irrelohe*, came to him while travelling between Dresden and Nürnberg on a train of the same name: *Irrelohe* means 'flames of madness'. He completed the opera in two and a half years and it was given its premiere by Klemperer in 1924, but its reception was far from enthusiastic and it only received eight productions. Schreker's operas were becoming less popular and his relations with his publisher, Universal Edition, who was now losing all the money it had made on his earlier successes, deteriorated. In 1927 he wrote to Universal Edition describing Kurt WEILL's music as 'garbage that stinks to high heaven' and that 'he [Weill] should give up writing and composing. His text is completely idiotic.'

By 1927 Schreker's operas had all but disappeared from the repertoire. However, he wrote another opera, *Der Singende Teufel*, that was performed in 1928 but which sustained only a brief staging. Reviewers found the libretto obscure and lacking in contemporary relevance, trapped in bourgeois-historical tradition. He wrote one comic opera, *Der Schmeid von Ghent* – the only one for which he did not write the libretto. It was performed in Berlin on 29 October 1932. The performance went well and the singer in the title role was applauded with genuine enthusiasm, but when Schreker appeared there were boos and catcalls, which appear to have had political and anti-Semitic overtones. Another opera, *Christophorus*, was completed and was scheduled to be performed in Freiburg in 1933, but the appointment of Hitler as chancellor, and sweeping gains by the National Socialist Workers Party on 5 March, caused it to be cancelled.

The political situation and anti-Semitism made Schreker's last years particularly tragic. By 1929 he was experiencing considerable opposition to some of his policies at the Hochschule, opposition that was led by the violinist Gustav Havemann, an active supporter of National Socialist policies. In 1932 Havemann and his allies denounced the presence of Jews on the faculty and in the student body. Havemann tried to force a vote of no confidence in

321

Schreker, and when unsuccessful went to the Ministry. Eventually Schreker resigned in exchange for a master-class at the Prussian Academy. He realized that things would become increasingly difficult and looked for posts in America but without success.

The stress of the situation left him physically and mentally exhausted. In April 1933 he went into a sanatorium near Dresden for treatment for nervous exhaustion. When he returned to Berlin he and Schoenberg received letters indicating they had been suspended from duties but would receive their salary pending further notice. By June Schreker received the questionnaire concerning his racial ancestry that would determine his fate, and by this time he also received documents from Hungary proving that his father had converted from Judaism. On 26 September he and Schoenberg received notice that they had been dismissed. Schreker also learned that his pension was to be much less than he expected. All the stress he encountered may have contributed to his stroke in late December. After a second stroke he died, on 21 March 1934. In 1938 at the exhibition of *Entartete Musik* held in Düsseldorf, Schreker's music was included and the theatre manager Hans Severus Ziegler referred to his work as 'that of a Jewish scribbler', adding, 'there is no sexual-pathological aberration that he did not set to music'.

Schreker's operas form the major part of his output, but he also wrote a number of songs, and orchestral music.

Bibliography: *G*; *HBD*; Leb; Christopher Haley, *Franz Schreker: A Cultural Biography* (Cambridge: Cambridge University Press, 1993)

Schul, Zikmund (b. Kassell, Germany, 11 November 1916; d. Terezin, 20 June 1943)   Studied composition with Hindemith in Berlin. He fled from the Nazis to Prague and continued his studies with Alois Hába from 1937 to 1938. Hába also helped to support him financially. Schul became friendly with Rabbi Lieben and, with Hába's encouragement, carried out research on and transcription of Hebrew manuscripts found in the Altneuschul (Old–New Synagogue) in Prague. Hába, who had used quarter-tones in a number of his own compositions, was intrigued by the use of quarter-tones and sixth-tones in some Hebrew chants. After the Nazi invasion of Prague, Schul was imprisoned in the Terezin concentration camp on 11 November 1941. He continued composing whilst in Terezin and most of his works show the influence of Hebrew chants, for example, *Two Hassidic Dances* for viola and cello; *Cantata Judaica* for men's chorus and tenor solo; *Ki tavoa al-harerez* (When you go to the land) for boys chorus; *Uv'tzeil K'nofecho* (In the shadow of your wings) for string quartet. He also wrote *Duo* for violin and viola (parts of which were lost) and *Schicksal* (Fate) for alto, flute, viola and cello. His health deteriorated in the harsh conditions of Terezin and he did not compose in the last year of his life, eventually succumbing to tuberculosis.

Bibliography: Grad; Joža Karas, *Music in Terezin, 1941–1945* (New York: Pendragon, 1985), pp. 121–4

Schulhof, Erwin (b. Prague, 8 June 1894; d. Wülzburg, Bavaria, 18 August 1942)   Born into a prosperous German–Jewish family in Prague, He received a German education. His father, Gustav (1860–1942), was a wholesale wool and cotton merchant, and his mother, Louisa (1861–1938, *neé* Wolff), came from Frankfurt, where her father was leader of the local theatre orchestra. His first teacher was Eduard Schütz, to whom Schulhof dedicated his first work, *Melody*, for violin and piano, which he wrote at the age of 9. The work was subsequently published by H. Weiner, a Prague music publisher, probably impelled by Schulhof's mother, who was ambitious for her gifted son. On Dvorak's advice he studied with Kaan at the Prague Conservatory from 1904 to 1906 and was then a pupil of Thern in Vienna; he continued at the Leipzig Conservatory (1908–10), completing his musical education at the Cologne Conservatory (1911–14), where his composition and conducting teacher was Fritz Steinbach. He also took lessons from Reger and Debussy. His *Suite* for violin and piano, listed as Op. 1, was written about 1911–12, whilst Steinbach was his teacher. In 1913 he won the Mendelssohn prize for piano, and in 1918 the prize for composition.

During the interwar years he was to become equally well known as a concert pianist and as a composer. His first piano concerto was completed whilst at Cologne in 1913, although the work probably did not get a public performance at the time. He began an opera in 1914, based on a play by Goethe, *Die Mitschuldigen* (The accomplices), but was also conscripted into the Austrian Army the same year. After returning from the First World War he had no interest in performing the concerto or completing the opera. The war experience affected him profoundly; he became a pacifist and showed strong leanings towards communism. In 1916 he wrote in his diary, 'I can only place the years of 1914, 1915 and 1916 on humanities lowest rank.'

After the war he settled in Dresden from 1919 to 1923, and during this period the strongest influences evident in his music are those of the Second Viennese School and the Dadaist movement. He was particularly fond of Berg's Piano Sonata Op. 1, which Glen Gould has described as having been written in the twilight of tonality. He performed this in piano recitals, and its influence is evident in his String Sextet. The latter was begun in this period but was dropped in favour of his interest in the Dadaist movement, and was not to be completed until 1924. The Dadaist movement was a bitter and pessimistic denunciation of a supposedly civilized world capable of war and slaughter on an unprecedented scale. It originated with a group of exiles in Zurich in 1917. If this made sense, they implied, it was better to be nonsensical. The title, *Dada* (meaning hobby-horse), was a word picked at random from a French–German dictionary.

Schulhoff joined artists Otto Dix and Georg Grosz in their Dadaist attacks on bourgeois society. Three works of his written during this period show the Dadaist influence: *Bassnachtigall*, a double bassoon solo; *Symphonica Germanica*; and *Sonata Erotica*. The first two have what appear to be nonsensical subtitles.

The third, *Sonata Erotica*, is the musical equivalent of Georg Grosz's obscene drawings that offended the petty bourgeois pretence of morality. It is subtitled *Nur für Herren!* (Only for men) and requires the female solo singer to emit loud expressions of delight as in the act of love. Its first performance was not until 1994, when the production's reported success was colossal.

During the 1920s Schulhoff was active as a jazz pianist and the jazz influence is evident in a number of his works. His music shows influences of many styles, including neoclassicism and Czech folk music. His best music was written during the 1920s and includes two string quartets, a double concerto for flute and piano, the ballet *Ogelala* and his only opera, *Die Flammen*. The last of these is a reworking of the Don Juan story. The story is that by Karel Beneš and was translated from Czech by Max BROD, who was also Kafka's biographer. The opera illustrates Schulhof's eclecticism in mixing jazz, tango and sumptuous late Romanticism; flute parts reminiscent of Debussy, and 'echos of Mozart'.

Schulhof returned to Prague, teaching at the university from 1929 to 1931. From 1935 to 1938 he worked for Czech radio, first in Ostrava and then in Brno. At the same time he performed jazz and new music on the piano. He was one of the first to play the quarter-tone music of Alois Hába. He joined the Communist Party in the early 1930s and wanted his music to be accessible to the working masses – as expected of a communist (*cf.* EISLER). One of his compositions from this phase was a setting of *Communist Manifesto* by Marx and Engels, entitled *Manifesto Cantata*. He lost his job as a radio pianist in 1939 when the Nazis invaded Czechoslovakia. After the Munich agreement he took on Soviet citizenship. He was placed under house arrest in June 1941 and transported to the concentration camp at Wülzburg, where he died of tuberculosis eight months later.

Bibliography: *G*; *HBD*; Leb; J. Bek, *Erwin Schulhoff. Leben and Werk* (Hamburg: Von Bockel Verlag, 1994)

Schuller, Gunther (b. New York, 22 November 1925)   Son of a German–Jewish immigrant family. His paternal grandfather was a conductor, band-master and music teacher in Germany. His father was a violist and violinist in the New York Philharmonic Orchestra. At the age of 12 Gunther entered the St Thomas Choir School in New York City. He continued his music education at the Manhatten School of Music. He left high school in 1942 and never completed his formal education. Earlier he began learning the flute, but switched to the French horn, at which he became very accomplished, even-tually becoming the principal horn in the Cincinnati Symphony Orchestra (1943–5) and then principal horn at the Metropolitan Opera Orchestra New York (1945–9). He also became interested in jazz and played with Miles Davis in the 1950s. He taught at the Manhattan School of Music and has had a distinguished teaching career in various posts, including professor of compo-sition at the Yale School of Music, president of the New England Conservatory at Boston, and Artistic Director at Tanglewood Berkshire Music Center (1965–84).

He began composing as a teenager and was influenced both by jazz and the Second Viennese School. His most prolific period of composing was in the late 1950s and 1960s. He has composed over 160 works. A number of these show the dual influences of jazz and twelve-tone music, such as: *Twelve by Eleven* (1955), written for the Modern Jazz Quartet; *Transformation* (1956) for small ensemble; Woodwind Quintet (1958); *Concertino* for jazz quartet and orchestra (1959); and Piano Trio (1984). In a 1957 lecture at Tanglewood he proposed the term *Third Stream* to encompass such music that amalgamated jazz and 'classical music', although it has not been generally adopted. Other works in which the influence of jazz is evident are String Quartet No. 1 (1958), *Seven Studies on Themes of Paul Klee* for orchestra (1957), *Spectra for Orchestra* (1958), *Conversations* for jazz quartet and string quartet (1959) and *Journey into Jazz* for narrator, jazz quintet and orchestra (1962). He wrote an opera, *The Visitation* (1966), which was commissioned by Hamburg Opera and was based on Kafka's *The Trial*. He won the 1994 Pulitzer prize for the orchestral work *Of Reminiscences and Reflections*. His other works include two symphonies, concertos for horn, double bassoon, saxophone, violin and trumpet, two concertos for orchestra, two string quartets and two wind quintets. He is a prolific writer; his most recent book is *The Compleat Conductor* (1997).
Bibliography: G: HBD; Leb; Ly*; Eaken, J. 8.559062 [record sleeve]; www.schirmer.com/composers/schuller_bio.html

Schuman, William (b. New York, 4 August 1910; d. New York, 16 February 1992) His parents, Samuel and Rachel, were middle-class Jews with a strong respect for education. They expected their son to take some practical profession, and music played a relatively minor role in his childhood. He was much more interested in sport, and also had an early interest in poetry, especially Walt Whitman. In his early teens he had violin lessons, but showed no great enthusiasm. Whilst still at school he did, however, organize a jazz band and wrote popular songs. His band played at weddings, *bar mitzvahs* and fraternity parties. He gave up Latin in order to take up the double bass.

In 1928 he went to New York University's School of Commerce, having decided on a business career. On 4 April 1930 he reluctantly accompanied his sister to Carnegie Hall to hear Toscanini conducting the New York Philharmonic Orchestra in a programme of Wagner, Kodaly and Schumann. It was the first symphony concert that he had attended and he was captivated by it, so much so that the following day he gave up university and on walking home passed the Malkin Conservatory of Music. There he began harmony lessons with Max Persin, who proved to be an admirable teacher able to greatly expand Schuman's musical horizons. At the same time he lost interest in composing popular music. He later had private lessons with Charles Haubiel. He also attended the Columbia University Teachers' College, receiving a

Bachelor of Science in 1935. Whilst he wanted to be a composer he needed to earn a living, and so he took up teaching music at the Sarah Lawrence College (1935–45) – a music school for girls in Bronxville, New York.

In 1935 he approached the composer Roy Harris, who recognized his talent. He was admitted to Harris's summer courses at the Juilliard School of Music in New York. Later, he also took lessons from him privately. During 1936–7 he composed a symphony, a string quartet and a choral setting of Whitman's poem *Pioneers*. He was to become dissatisfied with all of these and they were later withdrawn. His second symphony was performed by Koussevitsky with the Boston Symphony Orchestra. It received a mixed reception; Leonard BERNSTEIN, then a student, reported on it favourably. In 1938 Schuman entered his second symphony for a competition run by the Musician's Committee in aid of Spanish Democracy and won. His next significant piece was the *American Festival Overture*, which received a more favourable reception. His works around this time (1939) began to show a style that was becoming quite distinct from that of his teacher, Roy Harris. His first and second symphonies he later withdrew. His third symphony, completed in 1941, received a favourable reception and is regarded as one of his best works, along with his fifth symphony (Symphony for Strings). Symphonies form the backbone of his compositions. They neither echo nineteenth-century Romanticism nor are obviously American in style. Many are characterized by sustained melodies. April 1945 saw the premiere of his ballet *Undertow*. It received a mixed reception, probably due to a large extent because of its subject matter, which includes a graphic depiction of rape and murder.

At a time when Schuman was beginning to find teaching at Sarah Lawrence College rather restrictive in not allowing him enough time for composition, he was offered a post as director of publications for the music publishers Schirmer. This greatly increased his earnings, but more importantly gave him more time to compose. However, within a short time of assuming the post of director he was head-hunted for the presidency of the Juilliard School of Music. At first he was reluctant because he perceived that many changes in the organization of the school were required, and it was only when it became clear that he would be allowed great latitude in reorganizing the school that he accepted. One feature that particularly concerned him was that while students obtained excellent instrumental tuition from some of the best teachers of the day, he felt they were often not receiving a broad musical education. He introduced a programme of academic studies leading to a bachelor's degree. He also increased the emphasis on contemporary music.

In 1950 he composed what was to become a successful ballet, *Judith*. The same year, at the age of 41, he injured his leg in an improvised baseball game. During the weeks of confinement that followed he fulfilled a commission from the Elizabeth Spray Coolidge Foundation, composing his fourth string quartet. In the mid-1950s plans were afoot to build a new arts complex, the Lincoln Center, that would be the home of the New York Philharmonic and the Metropolitan Opera. Schuman worked hard and eventually succeeded in persuading the authorities that the Juilliard School of Music must be included as part of the complex. The authorities felt that an able administrator was needed to head the Lincoln Center, and so a former chief-of-staff of the US Armed Forces was appointed as the first president. However, he was only there for four months before being called away to advise President Kennedy during the Cuban crisis. Schuman was elected as the second president and served from 1962 until shortly after he suffered a mild heart attack in 1968, when he resigned. He continued to compose whilst president of the Lincoln Center, completing his ninth symphony in 1968. It is subtitled *Le Fosse Ardeatine* (The Ardeatine Caves) and is inspired by the Nazi atrocity of 1944 in which 335 Italian men, women and children were murdered. It is an evocation of the feelings aroused by a visit to the victims' graves within the caves. In 1969 he composed *In Praise of Shahn*, a canticle for orchestra, in honour of the artist Ben Shahn. He is said to be one of two major American composers of Jewish decent between 1900 and 1990 who did not compose any works for the synagogue (COPLAND being the other).[1]

Bibliography: *AG*; *G*; *HBD*; Leb; Ly*; C. Rouse, *William Schuman, Documentary* (New York: Schirmer Inc., 1980)

1. Samuel Adler, 'The Aborted Renaissance: Music for the Synagogue Since 1945 in America', in S. Stanton and A. Knapp (eds), *Proceedings of the First International Conference on Jewish Music* (London: City University, 1994), p. 2.

Secunda, Sholom (b. Alexandria, Russia, 4 September 1894; d. New York, June 1974)   Emigrated with his family to New York in 1907. He studied there at the Cooper Union (1912–13), Columbia University (1913–14) and the Institute of Musical Art (1914–19). As a boy he had a remarkable voice and sang in the synagogues of New York, but after completing his studies he went on to make a name as composer of Yiddish-language operettas as well as Jewish films. He composed *Three Symphonic Sketches* for orchestra, two oratorios *If Not Higher* (1964) and *Yizkor – In Memory of the Six Million* (1967), the song *A Gemore Nigun* (song for Guemara) which has been arranged for clarinet quintet by Simeon Belison, a string quartet and much Jewish liturgical music.

Bibliography: *HBD*; Ly*

Seiber, Mátyás (b. Budapest, 4 May 1905; d. Kruger National Park, South Africa, 24 September 1960)   Born into a musical family. He started to learn the cello at the age of 10. He went to the Budapest Academy of Music, where he continued with the cello under Adolf Shiffer and studied composition with Zoltan Kodály. After completing his studies he took up a teaching post at the Hoch Conservatory in Frankfurt in 1926. During 1927 he joined a ship's orchestra as a cellist and visited South and North America. His early compositions show the influence of Hungarian folk music and of Bartok, but his interest in music was wide and included jazz, early music, light music, film music and serialism. His interest in jazz led him on his return to Frankfurt in 1928 to become one of the first teachers of jazz theory and practice at the Hoch Conservatory, where he stayed until 1933. In that post he attracted students from all over the world. Whilst in Frankfurt he also played as cellist in the Lenzewski Quartet. When, in April 1933, the Nazi law was passed preventing Jews from holding professional posts, he and Bernard SEKLES were sacked from their positions at the Conservatory. Hans Brückner and Christa Maria Rock's book indexing Jewish musicians failed to list either of them. It proved so inaccurate that in 1940 the Nazis commissioned another, this time authored by Stengel and Gerigk (see Appendix I).

Seiber came to England in 1935 and from 1948 until his death he lived in Caterham, Surrey. During his early days in England he had to make a living from music taking whatever opportunities came along, including writing an accordion tutor. In 1942 Michael Tippett offered him a teaching post at Morley College, where he taught for 15 years. He quickly established a reputation as a good teacher, and over the years taught many students who were to become established musicians, including Hugh Wood, Peter Racine Fricker, Malcolm LIPKIN and Francis Chagrin. In 1945 he founded the Dorian Singers, who performed both sixteenth-century and modern choral music. Two important qualities of Seiber were his catholic taste in music and his method of teaching. It is perhaps because his interests were so wide that he is not now widely known. He cannot be easily 'labelled'. Although he was perhaps best known as a teacher, he composed a number of works. He had a particular liking for James Joyce. He composed a large-scale cantata for tenor, chorus and orchestra, entitled *Ulysses* (1946–7), and a chamber cantata for speaker, wordless small choir and chamber ensemble, entitled *Three Fragments*, from *A Portrait of an Artist as a Young Man*. His other works include three string quartets, *Elegy for Viola and Small Orchestra*, a sonata for violin and piano (1960), *Two Jazolettes* for chamber orchestra (1929, 1932) and *Four French Folk Songs* for soprano and strings (1948). He also wrote the film score for George Orwell's *Animal Farm* that includes a mock-Russian folk song and a Bach-like chorale.

He died in a car accident when the steering wheel came off in his hands while driving in the Kruger National Park, South Africa.

Bibliography: *G*; *HBD*; Ho*; Ken; Leb; Michael Graubert, 'Matyas Seiber: 1905–1960', *Composer*, 86 (1985), pp. 1–4; J. Silverman, 'Some Thoughts on Matyas Seiber', *Tempo*, 143 (1982), pp. 12–14

Sekles, Bernhard (b. Frankfurt, 20 March 1872; d. Frankfurt, 8 December 1934) Studied at the Hoch Conservatory in Frankfurt and later with Humperdink. From 1893 to 1894 he was *Kapellmeister* at the Heidelberg Opera and from 1895 to 1896 *Kapellmeister* at the Mainz Opera. He taught theory and composition at the Hoch Conservatory in Frankfurt from 1923, where Hindemith was one of his pupils. He was dismissed in 1933 as the result of the Nazi law preventing those not of Aryan origin being employed in the civil service. He was

interested in introducing music outside the European mainstream and collaborated with SEIBER in introducing jazz (regarded as degenerate by the Nazis) theory into music teaching. His works include the opera *Scheherazade* (1917), which was successfully staged in a number of German theatres, and *Die Zehn Küsse* (1926), a string quartet (1923), the orchestral prelude *Der Dybbuk* (1928) and Symphony No. 1 (1930).
Bibliography: *G*; *HBD*; Ho*

Senator, Ronald (b. London, 17 April 1926) Studied at Oxford University under WELLESZ (1944–7) and with Arnold Cooke at London University (1957–60). He taught at London University, was professor of composition at the Guildhall School of Music in London, and has been visiting professor at the Massachusetts Institute of Technology, the University of Southern California, the City University, New York, and at a number of Canadian and Australian universities. His compositional style shows the influence of both Wellesz (Schoenbergian) and Cooke (Hindemithian). He has composed musicals and operas (*Joseph and Pharaoh* – a children's opera, 1968; *He Has Come Back* – a liturgical drama, 1971; *The Wolf of Gubbio*, 1980; *Insect Play*, 1986; *Echoes*, 1986; and *Trotsky in New York* – a musical, 1997), chamber music (*Mobiles for Piano*, 1983; *Spring Changes* for clarinet and piano, 1983; *Polish Suite* for viola, 1990 and *Lament for Senesh* for piano strings and percussion, 1993) and the song cycles (*Cabaret*, 1989; *Suns in the East*, 1975; and *A Poet to His Beloved*, 1984). His best-known work is the oratorio *Holocaust Requiem* for narrator, soprano, baritone, children's and adult choirs (1986). It is based on poems and diaries of children who died in the concentration camp at Terezin, poems by Nelly Sachs and Paul Celan, and texts common to both Jewish and Christian liturgies. It was first performed in Canterbury Cathedral in 1986, and received its New York premiere in 1990. When it was performed at the Moscow Conservatory in 1992, it was the first time in the history of post-World War Two Russia that public recognition of the Holocaust had been made. The work is dedicated to Senator's first wife, a concentration camp survivor, who died of cancer in 1980. It was also performed at the Terezin 50th anniversary commemoration in 1995.
Bibliography: *G*.

Seroussi, Ruben (b. Montevideo, Uruguay, 1 January 1959) Immigrated to Israel in 1974. He studied composition with Jan Radzynski at the Rubin Academy of Music in Tel Aviv, where his teachers were also SCHIDLOWSKY and SETER. Besides being a composer he is an accomplished guitarist and a number of his compositions are for that instrument. His works include: *Ludi* for two trombones; *Partita* for two guitars; *Jacob and Esau* for voice, oboe, violin and percussion (1985); *Two Poems by Antonio Machado* for voice, flute and guitar (1985); *Echo* for children's choir (1987); *Differencias* for guitar and chamber orchestra (1990); *Canto Al Antigo Sol* for two oboes, xylomarimba, timpani,

harp and double bass (1982); *Victim from Terezin* for narrator and ensemble (1995); and *Lux: In Memoriam Mordecai Seter* for chamber orchestra (1995).
Bibliography: G; Grad

Seter [Starominsky], **Mordecai** (b. Novorossiisk, Russia, 26 February 1916; d. Tel Aviv, 8 August 1994)   Studied piano in Novorossiisk and Tbilisi before his family emigrated to Palestine in 1926. In Paris in 1932–7 he studied piano with Lazar Levy and composition with Nadia Boulanger, DUKAS, and Stravinsky. His first composition was a set of piano preludes (1933) that show the influence of Debussy. His first major work was *Cantata for Shabbat* for solo, chorus and string orchestra, which was premiered in 1941. The text is from the Psalms and the Song of Songs; it uses a style that he was to develop further in later works, which combines ancient liturgical and modal elements. He also used serial techniques in some of his compositions. His works include: the Yemenite rhapsody *Midnight Vigil* (Tiqqun hatsot, 1961), which has been claimed as the finest oratorio in Israeli music; a symphony, *Jerusalem,* for choir, brass instruments and strings; five ballets; *Monodrama* for clarinet and piano; *Epigrams* for flute and cello; a quartet from flute, clarinet, cello and piano; *Janus* for piano; and *Expressivo* for thirteen stringed instruments.
Bibliography: G; Grad; *HBD*; Ho*; Ly*

Shapero, Harold Samuel (b. Lynn, Massachusetts, 29 April 1920)   Studied composition in his teens with SLOMINSKY and Krenek, and piano with Eleanor Kerr. He also played in dance bands and worked as an arranger for Benny Goodman. At Harvard University (1937–41) he studied composition under Piston, then at Tanglewood (1940) with Hindemith, and then at the Longy School with Nadia Boulanger (1942–3). Shapero thus had some excellent teachers and he composed prolifically during the 1940s. His *Nine-Minute Overture* (1940) won the American Prix de Rome and was typical of the kind of piece other American composers were producing at that time (*cf.* SCHUMAN's *American Festival Overture* (1939) and DIAMOND's *Psalm* (1938), often as a prelude to writing a great American symphony. Shapero, however, then followed another path. He composed a number of works in a neoclassical style, some modelled on that of earlier composers, for example Haydn, Scarlatti and C. P. E. Bach. Examples are Trumpet Sonata (1940), three sonatas for piano (1944) and Symphony for Classical Orchestra (1947). This last work was commissioned by the Koussevitsky Foundation and was inspired by Beethoven's Fifth Symphony; it has the structure of a classical symphony in four movements.

In 1952 Shapero was appointed as one of the founding professors at the music department at Brandeis University, Massachusetts, a post he held until 1985. He composed less during the whole of this period than in the 1940s. He experimented with twelve-tone techniques in *Partita* in C for piano and small orchestra (1960), with electronic instruments in *Three Studies in C sharp* for

synthesizer and piano (1969), and with jazz-derived idioms in *On Green Mountain* for jazz ensemble (1957). He was commissioned to write *Hebrew Cantata* for soloists, chorus and flute, trumpet, violin, harp and organ (1954) for the American Jewish Tercentenary. He also wrote *Hebrew Cantata* for chorus (1943), *Two Psalms* (1952, adapted from Psalms 100, 117 and 146) and *Three Hebrew Songs* ('They who sow at night' by Shalom, 'Eagle! Eagle over your mountains' by Tchernikovsky and 'Will there yet come days of forgiveness' by Goldberg, 1988).
Bibliography: *AG*; *CC*; *G*; *HBD*; Ly*

Shapey, Ralph (b. Philadelphia, 12 March 1921; d. Chicago 13 June 2002) Son of Russian–Jewish immigrant parents. He studied violin with Emmanuel Zeitlin and composition with Stepan WOLPE. By the age of 17 he was assistant conductor of the National Youth Symphony Orchestra (1938–47). He continued conducting throughout his career in Buffalo, Chicago, New York and in Europe. He taught music at the University of Pennsylvania (1963–4) and then composition and conducting at the University of Chicago (1964–85). Whilst at Chicago he founded the Contemporary Chamber Players and was very active in promoting a wide range of new works.

He began composing chamber music whilst serving in the army in World War Two. His earliest works to be heard in public were his second string quartet, which was performed by the Juilliard Quartet in 1949, and a concerto for clarinet and chamber ensemble, which was performed by the New York Philharmonic Chamber Society in 1954. The three orchestral works that established his wider reputation were *Ontogeny* (1958), *Invocation* for violin and orchestra (1959) and *Rituals* (1959). Shapey's music, although not serial in technique shows the influence of SCHOENBERG and WOLPE (who studied with Webern in 1933). It also shows the influences of Varèse, whose music Shapey admired and was active in promoting. When Shapey was honoured by the National Institute of Arts and Letters his music was described as exciting and dynamic, full of rugged power and high originality developed over a number of years in response to an intensely personal vision, influenced by changing fashion.

Shapey had a temperament for controversy, but also showed warmth and passion. In 1969 he withdrew his music from public performance in protest against conditions in the musical world and the difficulties facing new composers. However he continued to compose and in 1976 he was persuaded by friends to end the moratorium. This he did with a performance of *Praise*, an oratorio on biblical texts, dedicated to the State of Israel. He composed another explicitly religious work in 1977, *The Covenant* for soprano and sixteen players with texts from the Bible and from Walt Whitman. He has composed over 100 works, including: seven string quartets; *Song of Eros* for soprano orchestra and tape (1975); *Song of Songs I, II* and *III* for soprano, bass, tape and chamber ensemble (1979–80); *Concerto Grosso* for string quintet (1981); *Double Concerto*

for violin and cello (1983); *Symphonie Concertante* (1985); *Variations* for organ (1985); and *Concerto Fantastique* (1991).
Bibliography: *AG*; *CC*; *G*; Grad; *HBD*; Leb

Sheriff, Noam (b. Tel Aviv, 7 January 1935) Studied horn and piano in his youth. Between 1949 and 1957, as a private student, he took lessons in composition with BEN HAIM and conducting with Zeev Priel. He studied philosophy at the Hebrew University of Jerusalem and founded and conducted the Hebrew University Symphony Orchestra from 1955 to 1959. He also conducted the Israeli Army band. From 1960 to 1962 a scholarship enabled him to study with BLACHER at the Berlin Hochschule für Musik. He returned to Israel in 1963 and from 1966 became teacher of orchestration at the Jerusalem Academy of Music. In 1989 he founded an orchestra for Russian immigrants at Rishon-le-zion. His compositions generally show a combination of western European musical influences, Middle Eastern music and Jewish liturgical music. He has also composed using electronic media. His works include: *Festival Prelude*, which was premiered by BERNSTEIN in 1957; *Song of Degrees* (1960); *Ashrei* (Psalms, 1961); 2 *Epigrams* (1968); *A Stone in the Tower of David* (1970); and String Quartet (1973). In 1987 he composed a Resurrection symphony, *Mechaye Hametin* (Revival of the dead). The title is taken from the 18 blessings of the Hebrew liturgy and the work traces Jewish life from the Diaspora through the Holocaust to redemption. It uses material from the Kaddish and is Mahlerian in style. Sheriff was commissioned to compose *Passion Sefardi* (Spanish passion) in eight movements for soloists, choir and orchestra to commemorate the 500th anniversary of the expulsion of Jews from Spain. It was first performed in May 1992 in the courtyard of the military academy in Toledo.
Bibliography: *G*; Grad; *HBD*; Ken; Leb

Shlonsky, Verdina (b. Kremenchug, Ukraine, 22 January 1905; d. Tel Aviv, 20 February 1990) Studied piano with Egon Petri and Arthur SCHNABEL at the Berlin Hochschule für Musik and went to live in Tel Aviv in 1929. In 1930–2 she studied with Nadia Boulanger, Edgar Varèse and Max Deutsch. She composed her first symphony in 1937, whilst studying with Enescu. After the German invasion she fled to London, where she wrote *Piano Concerto in Two Movements* (1942–4). She settled in Tel Aviv in 1945. Her works include a song cycle, *Images Palestiniennes* (1930), the symphonic poem *Jeremiah* (1936), a string quartet (1948), *Eleven Musical Postcards* for piano (1956), *Euphony* for chamber orchestra (1967), *Space and Esprit* for vocalise, bassoon and piano (1969), a piano concerto and a symphonic composition entitled *Meditations* (1971).
Bibliography: *G*; Grad

Shulman, Alan (b. Baltimore, USA, 4 June 1915) Began cello lessons at the age of 8 and later studied cello, harmony and theory at the Peabody Conservatory in Baltimore. He studied with Felix Salmond (cello), Bernard Wagenaar

(composition) and Albert Stoessel (orchestra) at the Juilliard School of Music in New York (1932–7) and also with Feuermann in 1939 and Hindemith in 1942. He is best known as a cellist, having played in the NBC Symphony Orchestra under Toscanini, and as co-founder of the Stuyvesant Quartet (1938–54), which became noted for its performances of contemporary music, including BLOCH's first string quartet and quartets by Paganini and by KREISLER. His first composition was at the age of 10. Most of his compositions are for cello or strings, and include a cello concerto (1948) dedicated to Leonard Rose, *Theme and Variations* for viola and piano (1940), and the incidental music for the play *The Chinese Lantern*.
Bibliography: G; www.capital.net/ggjj/shulman/ and www.cs.bsu.edu/homepages /dlsills/David_jewish.shtml*

Siegmeister, Elie (b. New York, 15 January 1909; d. Manhasset, New York, 10 March 1991)   Studied piano at the age of 9, with Emil Friedberger, a pupil of Leschetizky. At Columbia College he studied composition with Bingham and counterpoint privately with Riegger. After graduation he spent five years (1927–31) in Paris with Nadia Boulanger, then returned to the Juilliard School of Music in New York to study conducting from 1935 to 1938. He travelled extensively throughout the United States gathering folk tunes, which he then used in combination with his own modern idiom as a base for his compositions. He wanted his music to have an American identity. This interest led him to edit, with Olin Downes, *A Treasury of American Song*. He was also concerned about the inequalities in American society and suffered for his left-wing political views in the McCarthy era. His career never really recovered. Much of his music has a distinct American flavour, which can be discerned from his titles, for example: *Ozark Set* for orchestra (1943 – the Ozark Mountains are mainly in Missouri and Arkansas); *American Piano Sonata* (1944); *Western Suite* (1945); *Wilderness Road* for orchestra (1945); *Sunday in Brooklyn* (1946); *I Have a Dream* (1967), a cantata for baritone, narrator, chorus and orchestra from the famous Martin Luther King speech. His late operatic works, *Angel Levine* (1984–5) and *The Lady of the Lake* (1984–5) explore Siegmeister's Jewish identity. *Angel Levine* employs Hebrew chants and intonations.
Bibliography: G; Ho*; Leb

Singer, Malcolm (b. London, 13 July 1953)   Studied at the Royal Academy of Music in London and at Magdalene College, Cambridge, and later with Nadia Boulanger (1974–7) and LIGETI (1975–6). He taught composition at the Menuhin School of Music at Stoke d'Abernon, Surrey (1977–96), and at the Guildhall School of Music in London. He was director of the Zemel Choir (1983–93) and has been the director of the Menuhin School of Music since 1998. His main compositions are chamber music and choral music and include *Kaddish* (1990), for the BBC Singers, and *A Hopeful Place* (1996), for children's choir, string octet and symphony orchestra.
Bibliography: G

Slominsky, Nicolas Leonodovich (b. St Petersburg, 27 April 1894; d. Los Angeles, 25 December 1995)   Best known as a musicologist, although he was also a conductor and composer. He studied piano with his aunt, Isabella Vengerova, from the age of 6, and composition with Kalafati and STEINBERG at the St Petersburg Conservatory. He left St Petersburg in 1918, travelling via Kiev, where he worked as a rehearsal pianist to the Kiev Opera, then went to teach at the Yalta Conservatory. He later moved to Paris, where he worked as secretary and accompanist to Koussevitsky in 1920. In 1923 he went to the United States where he lived for the rest of his life, becoming an American citizen in 1931. He conducted first performances of works by Ives, Varèse, Cowell, Riegger and Chávez. He composed orchestral works and works for solo piano, for example, *Russian Prelude* (1914), *Five Advertising Songs* (1925), *Studies in Black and White* (1928) in which the left hand plays on black keys and the right hand on white, and *Minitudes* (1977). It was as a writer of music that he found he métier, editing four editions of Thompson's *International Cyclopedia of Music and Musicians* (1946–58), the fifth to eighth editions of *Baker's Biography of Musicians* and writing a number of books on music and its history.
Bibliography: *AG*; *G*; *HBD*; Leb; Ly*

Slominsky, Sergei Mikhailovich (b. Leningrad, 12 August 1932)   Nephew of Nicolas SLOMINSKY. He studied music at the Leningrad Conservatory (1945–50). In 1959 he was appointed to teach counterpoint and analysis at the Leningrad Conservatory. He composed in a number of different genres and was interested in folk music, and this is reflected in a number of his compositions. He also experimented with serial and aleatory techniques. His compositions include the operas *Virineia* (1967), *Master and Margarita* (1973) and *Mary Stuart* (1980), the ballet *Icarus* (1971), ten symphonies, a violin concerto (1983), several cantatas and chamber music.
Bibliography: *G*; *HBD*; Ken

Spies, Claudio (b. Santiago, Chile, 26 March 1925)   Born to German–Jewish parents. He lived in Santiago until 1942, when he left for Boston to study at the New England Conservatory. Then he studied with Nadia Boulanger, and from 1947 to 1954 at Harvard with SHAPERO, Piston, Irvine FINE and Hindemith. He taught at Swarthmore College, Philadelphia, from 1958 to 1970 and then at Princeton University from 1970. He became an American citizen in 1966. Spies has a very cosmopolitan background, one which includes Jewish, German, Spanish and American connections, and he speaks fluent English, Spanish, German and Italian. This has enabled him to set texts in all these languages as well as in Hebrew and Latin. His early compositions, for example, *Three Intermezzi* for piano (1950–4), were shaped by American neoclassicism. He was a friend of Stravinsky, whose influence can be seen in *Movements* and in the way in which he uses serialism, for example, *Five Psalms* for chorus (1959), *Impromptu* for piano (1963), *Anima, Vagula, Bandula* for vocal quartet and piano (1964) and *Five Sonnet Settings* for vocal quartet and piano (1977). His later works are mainly for voice, for example, *Three Songs on Poems by May Swenson* for voice and piano (1969), *Seven Enzensberger Lieder* for baritone, clarinet horn, cello and percussion (1972) and *Shirim Le Hathunatham* (texts by Yehuda Halevi) for soprano, flute, clarinet, violin, cello and piano (1975).

Bibliography: *G*; *HBD*; Ken; Howard Pollack, *Harvard Composers* (New Jersey, MD: Scarecrow Press, 1992)*

Starer, Robert (b. Vienna, 8 January 1924)   Began piano lessons at an early age and was requested to join the Vienna Boys Choir on account of his voice, but his mother would not allow him to join because she wanted him to have a 'normal' childhood. He entered the Vienna State Academy at the age of 13 and briefly studied with Victor Ebenstein, but with the *Anschluss* in 1938 he was expelled and his parents sent him to Palestine. His parents were Zionists but not Orthodox Jews. He studied at the Jerusalem Conservatory with TAL, PARTOS and ROSOWSKY from 1938 to 1943. His first compositions date from this period. He also took lessons with the Arabic musician Ezra Aharoni and composed a work for oud and orchestra. He volunteered for the British armed forces in World War Two (1943–6). In 1947 he left for New York to continue his studies at the Juilliard School of Music with Frederick Jacobi, supporting himself as a vocal accompanist. He was a pupil of COPLAND's at the Berkshire Music Center in the summer of 1946. He became an American citizen in 1957. He taught at the Juilliard School of Music from 1949 to 1974 and also at Brooklyn College, City University of New York, from 1963.

He has composed in a wide variety of genres. Most of his music is based on tonal principles, but he has experimented with serial technique, for example, *Trio* for clarinet, cello and piano (1964), and also with jazz. One of his first works to be performed was his first piano concerto (1947), followed by *Prelude and Dance* for orchestra (1949) and *Koholet* (Ecclesiastes) for soloists, chorus and orchestra (1952). He has written several ballets, for example, *The Story of Esther* (1960) and *The Dybbuk* (1960), including works for Martha Graham's ballet group, for example, *Samson Agonistes* (1961), *The Lady of the House of Sleep* (1968) and *The Holy Jungle* (1974). His other works include: operas for which his second wife the novelist Gail Godwin wrote the librettos, for example, *The Last Lover* (1974), *Apollonia* (1978); three symphonies (1950, 1951, and 1969); a violin concerto (1981); a Sabbath Eve Service (1967); and a number of vocal works with biblical texts, for example, *Visions of Isaiah* (1959), *Joseph and his Brothers* (1966) and *Psalms of Woe and Joy* (1975).

Bibliography: *AG*; *G*; *HBD*; Leb; Ly*; Robert Starer, *Continuo: a Life in Music* (New York: Random House, 1987)

Steinberg, Maximilian Osseivich (b. Vilnius, 4 July 1883; d. Leningrad, 6 December 1946)   Learned the violin as a child and studied at St Petersburg

University, where he graduated in 1907, and at the St Petersburg Conservatory, where he graduated in 1908. At the latter institution his teachers were Lyadov (harmony), Glazunov (instrumentation) and Rimsky-Korsakov (composition), whose daughter he later married. His compositions in the decade preceding the October Revolution of 1917 reflect the influence of his teachers and also those of Skriabin and the French Impressionists: for example, *Metamorphoses* (1914), a ballet on a theme of Ovid; a setting of Byron's *Heaven and Earth* (1918) for voice and orchestra; an overture to Maeterlinck's drama *Princess Malen*; and his second symphony. After the revolution he composed a number of works based on folk songs from the Soviet Union, for example, his third symphony is a comprehensive arrangement of national songs of many of the peoples of the USSR. He wrote works that would be acceptable in the Stalinist regime (e.g., his fourth symphony, *Turksib* (1933), dedicated to the builders of the Turkestan Siberian railway), but he also composed using outside sources, for example, his ballet *Till Eulenspiegel* (1936), which uses Spanish and Flemish folk music sources. He edited several of Rimsky-Korsakov's posthumous works for publication.

Steinberg spent almost the whole of his working career as a teacher at the St Petersburg Conservatory, and amongst his pupils were Popov, Shostakovich and Shaporin. Shostakovich initially found his approach to teaching too dogmatic, inhibiting and dull, but later he acknowledged the benefits he had received from Steinberg's thorough analytical methods. Steinberg, for his part, whilst enthusiastic on hearing Shostakovich's first symphony, was guarded on hearing the second, commenting 'can this really be New Art?'.[1] Steinberg was on the executive committee of the Soviet Composers' Union from its inception in 1932 and received a number of awards, including the Order of Red Workers' Banner (1938) and People's Artist of the Uzbek SSR (1944).
Bibliography: G; Ly*
1. Elizabeth Wilson, *Shostakovich: a Life Remembered* (London: Faber & Faber, 1994).

Sternberg, Erich Walter (b. Berlin, 31 May 1891; d. Tel Aviv, 15 December 1974) Studied law at Kiel University. In 1918 he decided to make his career in music, studying composition under Hugo Leichtentritt and piano with H. Praetorius. His musical style was influenced by Hindemith and SCHOENBERG, but at the same time it is rich in quotes from Jewish folk song and cantillation. For example, his first string quartet (1924) quotes *Shema Yisrael*, a theme he was to use again in his symphonic poem *Harken, O Israel* (1947). His piano cycle *Visions from the East* has a movement entitled 'At the Synagogue'. *David and Goliath* for baritone and orchestra was first performed by the Berlin Philharmonic Orchestra in 1927. In his second string quartet (1926) he quoted from a popular Yiddish song 'Trag Dein Peckele, Yudele'; this was first performed in 1928 by the Amar Quartet, with Hindemith playing the viola. Herman Scherchen conducted the first performance of *Halochem ha'amitz* (The gallant soldier) at the 1928 Scherin Festival. From 1925 to 1931 he visited Palestine annually, so that by the time he decided to emigrate he had a number of friends in the *Yishuv* and was invited to give two concerts dedicated to his works. He continued to compose mainly vocal music, for example, *Yistabach* (Praise ye, 1946), *Ha'orev* (The raven, 1949, but also some orchestral music, such as *The Story of Joseph*, a suite for string orchestra (1937) and *The Twelve Tribes of Israel* (1942). This last work is a set of variations on an original theme; each of the biblical tribes is characterized by one variation. Unlike most of the Israeli composers of his generation, although many of his compositions use texts from the Bible his style is very much that of late German Romanticism. He collaborated with Huberman in forming the Palestine Symphony Orchestra and he taught at the Tel Aviv Conservatory.

Bibliography: *G*; Grad; Ho*; Ly*; Jehoash Hirshberg, *Music in the Jewish Community of Palestine, 1880–1948* (Oxford: Clarendon Press, 1995).

Strauss, Johann (b. Vienna, 14 March 1804; d. Vienna, 25 September 1849) Generally known as Johann Strauss Senior to distinguish him from his eldest son Johann Strauss Junior (1825–99). He was the founder of the Strauss family dynasty of composers of Viennese waltzes. Strauss Senior's father was a Viennese innkeeper, who drowned in the Danube when his son was 12. His mother died when he was 7. According to the marriage register in St Stephan's Cathedral, Vienna, Strauss Senior's grandfather was baptized, but of Jewish parentage when he married in 1762. Because the music of both Johann Strauss Senior and Junior was so popular in Germany and Austria, after the *Anschluss* in 1938 the marriage records were removed by the Nazis to hide their Jewish ancestry.

Strauss Senior was largely self-taught as a musician, initially playing the violin in his father's inn, and later at the age of 15 he played the viola in a dance orchestra. The violinist Josef Lanner invited him to join his ensemble, which in time grew into a full orchestra. Both Lanner and Strauss composed dance music for the orchestra. In 1825 Strauss formed his own orchestra, and in 1829 he became musical director at the Sperl, the largest dance hall in Vienna. After 1827 he published many of the waltzes and gallops that he had composed. His music became very popular and from 1833 to 1838 he toured Hungary, Austria, Germany, Holland, Belgium, France and England. He died of scarlet fever at the age of 45.

He composed over 250 works, of which 152 were waltzes; his most famous composition is the *Radetzky March*. His fame became eclipsed by that of his son, Johann Junior who was more inventive as a composer. The music of the latter is played both in the ballroom and concert hall; he also composed operettas, the best known of which is *Die Fledermaus* (1874). Although Strauss Junior was only one-eighth Jewish by descent, his third wife was Jewish, and he is quoted as saying, 'In my heart I am more Jewish than Protestant.'[1]

Bibliography: *G*; *HBD*; Ken

1. Robert Dachs, *Johann Strauss: Was geh ich mich an? Glanz und Dunkelheit in Lebens des Walzerk Önigs* (Germany: Styria, 1999).

Stutschewsky, Yehoyachin [Joachim] (b. Romny, Ukraine, 7 February 1891; d. Tel Aviv, 14 November 1982)   Born into a family of musicians. His father was a *klezmer* musician. Joachim became proficient at the cello at an early age. He studied with Julius Klengel, Paul and Sitt at the Leipzig Conservatory from 1909 to 1912. In 1912 he joined the Jena Quartet and later the Kolisch Quartet. He met Joel ENGEL in Vienna in 1914 and became active in performing Jewish music. He remained in Vienna until the *Anschluss*, when he emigrated to Palestine. He wrote a treatise on the cello completed in 1938, *Die Kunst des Cellospiels*. He was primarily a performer, teacher and collector of Jewish music. On arrival in Palestine he invested much time in the organization of concerts. Most of his composing was in the 1950s and 1960s and includes: *Israeli Melodies*; *Israeli Suite*; *Hasidic Suite* for cello and piano; *Kol Korèh* (A voice is calling) for French horn; *Concertino* for clarinet and strings (1958); *Fantasia* for oboe, harp and strings (1959); *Tsfat*, a symphonic poem (1960); the symphonic suite *Israel* (1964); and compilations of eastern European Jewish songs. Bibliography: *G*; Grad; Ly*; Jehoash Hirshberg, *Music in the Jewish Community of Palestine, 1880–1948* (Oxford: Clarendon Press, 1995), pp. 164–5

Sulzer, Salamon (b. Hohenems, Austria, 1804; d. Vienna, 17 January 1890) The name Sulzer is derived from the small Austrian village Sulz in which his ancestors, originally named Loewy (Levy), settled temporarily when they were exiled from Hohenems. Surnames derived from the town of origin were not uncommon (*cf.* OFFENBACH). Sulzer was to become famous both as a cantor of the Viennese Seitenstettengasse synagogue and for his work in revising the music for the synagogue, *Schir Zion* (Harp of Zion). It was through accidental circumstances that he was to follow this path. He was the son of a rich family of manufacturers. In early boyhood he fell into a river and was nearly drowned. His mother, frantically summoning aid, vowed that if he survived he should devote himself to a sacred career. He was tutored in his early youth by the cantor of Hohenems, Salamon Eichberg (1786–1880). He later went to Switzerland to study with Cantor Lippmann, but his general musical education was acquired in Karlsruhe, Germany, and in Vienna, where he studied with Ignaz von Seyfried (a pupil of Haydn and a friend of Mozart and Beethoven), Josef Fischof and Josef Weigl. In 1820, at the age of 16; he returned to Hohenems, where he served as cantor until 1825.

Towards the end of the eighteenth century, under the Emperor Josef II, liberalism began to enlighten Vienna and many of the restrictions on Jews were lifted. The Jews were officially allowed to re-establish their community in 1790, and eventually in 1826 to build a new synagogue, the Seitenstettengasse, replacing the older Latzenhof. Some members of the community sought to introduce Reform services akin to those already introduced in the Hamburg Temple. This included 'modernizing' the music used in the synagogue; Ignaz MOSCHELES also composed for the synagogue in 1814.

As part of this modernization Rabbi Mannheimer initially wanted to abolish the role of cantor altogether, but imbued with the spirit of Judaic reform, eventually decided to appoint a new cantor, Salomon Sulzer. Because Sulzer had been brought up in a small community away from the centre of Jewish life, and because of his musical training in Vienna, he was more influenced by European culture than Orthodox Judaism. He believed that the Jewish liturgy must satisfy musical demands whilst remaining Jewish, and that it should not be necessary to sacrifice Jewish characteristics to artistic forms. This fitted well with both the wishes of the community and with Rabbi Mannheimer's intentions, and Sulzer remained in that post from 1825 to 1881. During this time he was to become famous, both within the wider Jewish community and also with musicians and music lovers further afield. Apart from having an excellent baritone-tenor voice and being a genuine artist, he had a profound influence on European synagogue music. Two quotations illustrate this. Francis Trollope, a British author and traveller who heard Sulzer's service in 1837 states:

> There is so wild and strange a harmony in the songs of the children of Israel as performed in the synagogue [of Vienna] that it would be difficult to render full justice to the splendid excellence of the performance without falling into the language of enthusiasm ... The volume of sounds exceeds anything of the kind I have ever heard; and being accompanied by no instrument ... while a dozen voices make up a glorious chorus, it produces an effect equally singular and delightful ... Some passages of these majestic chants are so full of pathos that the whole history of the nation's captivity rushes upon the memory as we listen.[1]

Franz Liszt was also moved and wrote the following:

> We went to the synagogue in order to hear him [Sulzer] ... For moments we could penetrate into the real soul and recognize the secret doctrines of the fathers. Seldom were we deeply stirred by emotion, as on that evening, so shaken that our soul was entirely given to meditation and to participation in the service.[2]

Other musicians including Schubert, Schumann and MEYERBEER admired his skills. In July 1828 Schubert set Psalm 92 (in Hebrew) for baritone solo (Sulzer) and mixed chorus (D.953) for the synagogue. Sulzer created a kind of vogue amongst cantors, which was summed up by Idelsohn:

> There was a striking power in him; and this was his great, almost unique talent as singer. It was not so much the music which convinced the people, as the manner and marvelous beauty of rendition which fascinated and bewitched them. A mania spread among the *chazzanim* to sing *à la Sulzer*, to dress *à la Sulzer*, to wear their hair *à la Sulzer*, to cough *à la Sulzer*.[3]

Sulzer produced a monumental opus that was published in two volumes, the first in 1840 and the second in 1865. This work constitutes the earliest complete and thoroughly organized repertory in Hebrew for synagogue services throughout the year set for cantor and four-part male choir and has become the standard liturgical collection used throughout synagogues in Europe and the USA. Sulzer was able to create a style that sounded oriental to the gentile, while carrying distinctly modern overtones to the Jew.

Sulzer received many honours, including a medal from the Grand Duke of Baden for his *Schir Zion* (1843), a professorship at the Vienna Music Society (1845–8), the Ottomanic Mejidiye medal (1864), honorary membership of the Academy of Arts in Rome, and, on his 70th birthday, he was made Knight of the Order of Franz Josef and an honorary citizen of Vienna. After retiring as cantor, he founded the Österreich-Ungarischer Kantorenverein. His son, Professor Joseph, director of the combined Vienna synagogue choirs, helped him revise his *Schir Zion* in the last years of his life. His second son, Julius, was a violinist and became director of the Hofburgtheater in Vienna.

Bibliography: *G*; Grad; Ly*; E. Gartenberg, *Vienna – its Musical Heritage* (University Park: Pennsylvania State University Press, 1968); A. M. Hanson, *Musical Life in Biedermeier Vienna* (Cambridge: Cambridge University Press, 1985); A. Z. Idelsohn, *Jewish Music in its Historical Development* (New York: Schocken, 1967), pp. 246–60

1. Egon Gartenburg, *Vienna: Its Musical Heritage* (Pennsylvania: Pennsylvania State University Press, 1968), p. 111.
2. Ibid.
3. A. Z. Idelsohn, *Jewish Music in its Historical Development* (New York: Schocken, 1967), p. 256.

Tal [Gruenthal], Joseph (b. Pinne, near Posen, Germany [Poznan, Poland], 18 September 1910) Studied composition and piano with Tiessen, Trapp and Hindemith at the Berlin Hochschule für Musik from 1928 to 1930. In 1927 he established an electronic studio. He also worked as a pianist, accompanying dancers and silent films. In 1934 with the rise of Nazism he wanted to emigrate to Palestine, but he knew that the British immigration authorities were unlikely to grant a visa to a pianist, so he trained as a photographer for a year and a half and then applied successfully for a visa as a photographer. He first worked in a photographer's shop in Haifa before going to live at the kibbutz Gesher for over a year. On a young and struggling kibbutz, being a musician was not regarded as an essential occupation, and he eventually moved to Jerusalem, where he became a piano and composition teacher at the conservatory, which, after 1948, became the Israel Academy of Music. From 1948 to 1952 he was its director. From 1965 to 1971 he was head of the musicology department at the Hebrew University.

In his compositions Tal has largely drawn on European avant-garde trends, although many of his compositions have Jewish inspiration. He has been Israel's foremost composer of electronic music. The best known of his early

works are the symphonic cantata *A Mother Rejoices* (1948–9) and the choreographic poem *Exodus* (1945–6). *A Mother Rejoices* recreates the Maccabean legend of Hannah and her seven sons. In 1958 Tal composed an electronic version of Exodus entitled *Exodus II*. He has composed several operas: *Saul at En Dor*, *Amnon and Tamar*, *Ashmedai*, *Die Versüchung* (The temptation), *Der Garten* (The garden), *Massada 967*, *Der Turm* (The tower), *Elsie* and *Josef*. *Massada 967* recreates the tragic events of 73 BCE when the Romans captured the last stronghold defended by the Jews, who then took their own lives rather than going into captivity. *Josef*, with a Kafkaesque libretto by Eliraz, was premiered in 1995. *Der Turm* was composed in 1983, with a libretto by Hans Keller. *Der Garten*, which is a contemporary reinterpretation of the biblical story in which Adam and Eve attempt to reclaim their 'paradise lost', was first performed in Hamburg in 1988, and given a first English performance in London in 1998. Other compositions of Tal's include six symphonies, six piano concertos (three with tape), a viola concerto, a harpsichord concerto with tape, a woodwind quintet and an oboe sonata.
Bibliography: *G*; Grad; *HBD*; Ho*; Ken; Ly*; Jehoash Hirschberg, *Music in the Jewish Community of Palestine, 1880–1948* (Oxford: Clarendon Press, 1995), pp. 167–8

Tansman, Alexandre (b. Lódz, Poland, 12 June 1897; d. Paris, 15 November 1986)   Born of Polish–Jewish parents. He began his musical studies at the age of 5 at the Lódz Conservatory from 1902 to 1914, having lessons in piano, harmony and counterpoint. He then studied law and philosophy at Warsaw University and at the same time took lessons in composition with Piotr Rytel. In 1919 he entered two of his compositions, *Fantasie* for violin and piano, and a piano sonata, under different pseudonyms, to the Polish National Music Composition. They won first and second prizes, respectively. This success enabled him to move to Paris in October 1919. He met Ravel, ROLAND-MANUEL, MILHAUD, Honegger and Golschmann, who conducted his *Intermezzo Sinfonica* in 1920. Other successful works of this period are *Danse de la sorcière* (1924) and his first piano concerto (1926). The latter was performed under Koussevitzky with Tansman as soloist. In 1927 he went on tour with Koussevitzky and the Boston Symphony Orchestra, where his second piano concerto and his first symphony were introduced. He toured extensively in Europe, Canada, Palestine and the Far East. He settled in Paris in the interwar years, finding it an ideal location for a composer, because of the large number of composers including *Les Six*, the Surrealist painters and the café life. In 1937 he took on French citizenship. When Paris fell to the Germans in World War Two, he fled to America. He wrote film scores during the war but returned to Paris in 1946. The city was to remain his home for the rest of his life. In 1955 he introduced the 12-year-old Daniel Barenboim to the pianist Arthur Rubinstein and later to Stokowski. Tansman became close friends with Stravinsky and wrote his biography, completing it in 1948. After Stravinsky's death in 1972 he was inspired to write one of his most moving works, *Stèle* (for low voice and chamber ensemble).

His music shows many influences and styles, for example, Ravel and Stravinsky, but in some ways resembles that of Milhaud, with its lively rhythms, for example, in his Piano Trio No. 2 and wind septet (1930). After 1946 he adopted a neoclassical style in much of his music. His other works include: operas *Les Serment* (1955) and *Sabbatat Lévi, le faux messe* (1961); an oratorio, *Isaïe le prophète* (1951); seven symphonies; a violin concerto; viola concerto (1936); concerto for orchestra (1954); eight string quartets; five piano sonatas; and *Sonatine transatlantique* for piano (1930). Nathaniel Shilkret (1889–1982) commissioned a biblical suite, *Genesis*, in which Tansman (along with other Jewish composers) composed a section entitled 'Adam and Eve'. His *Rhapsodie polonaise* is dedicated to the defenders of the Warsaw ghetto.
Bibliography: *G*; *HBD*; Ly*

Tausig, Carl [Karol] (b. Warsaw, 4 November 1841; d. Leipzig, 17 July 1871) Studied piano, initially with his father, Aloys Tausig, a professional pianist. When Tausig was 14 his father took him to see Liszt at Weimar, and he soon became one of Liszt's favourites, accompanying him on tours as well as studying composition, counterpoint and piano with him. However Brahms, who was a friend of Tausig, claims that he was not a Liszt devotee.[1] Tausig made his début as a concert pianist in 1858. His technical feats were extraordinary, but some audiences disliked his showmanship, which he later moderated and became a quite exceptional pianist. In 1865 he opened a piano school in Berlin, but he abandoned it after a few years, as he did not like teaching. He died of typhoid at the age of 29. His compositions are for the piano and include *Das Geisterschiff* and *Études de concert*, Op. 1; *Tarantelle* and *Réminiscences de Halka de Moniuzko*, Op. 2; *L'Espérance*, Op. 3; *Rêverie*, Op. 5; and an etude, *Le Ruisseau*, Op. 6. He also transcribed a number of works.
Bibliography: *G*, *HBD*, Ly*

1. Styra Avins, *Johannes Brahms, Life and Letters* (Oxford: Oxford University Press, 1997), pp. 257, 293 and 556.

Tausinger, Jan (b. Piatra Neamt, Romania, 1 November 1921; d. Prague, 29 July 1980)   Studied at the Bucharest Conservatory with Dimitrie Cuclin, and later settled in Czechoslovakia, continuing his studies with Alois Hába and Pavel Bořkovec at the Prague Academy from 1948 to 1952. He conducted the radio orchestras of Bucharest, Ostrava and Plzen from 1954 to 1958. He became head of the Prague Conservatory (1971–5). His compositions are mostly chamber or choral works, for example, the song cycle *Cmaranice* (Scrawls across the sky, 1967) and the cantata *Ave Maria* (1972), and date from the 1960s and 1970s. He also composed a ballet, *Noc* (Night, 1967), and an opera, *Oskliva prihoda* (Nasty event, 1969).
Bibliography: *G*; *Czech Music '95*, pp. 1–2*

Toch, Ernst (b. Vienna, 7 December 1887; d. Los Angeles, 1 October 1964) Second child of Moritz Toch, a Jewish leather merchant, and his wife Gisela. There were nine children. The family was not particularly devout, although Toch could read Hebrew and underwent *bar mitzvah*. His family was not particularly musical, but Toch showed an interest in music at an early age. He was largely self-taught until his early twenties. He first encountered a piano as a child in his grandmother's pawnshop. He also watched friends play the piano, and correlated the sounds with the musical notations. He began composing when he was 6, ruling his own manuscript paper. He later acquired technical knowledge by copying the music of Bach, Beethoven and Mozart – particularly Mozart's quartets. The string quartet was his favorite form of composition at this stage, and he completed six by the age of 17. A schoolfriend of his, Joseph Fuchs, noticed him writing the finishing touches to a string quartet and asked to borrow the music. As a result of this music being shown to Arnold Rosé, the Rosé Quartet premiered his first string quartet in 1905. At about this time he had become sufficiently competent to give piano lessons to other school pupils, including the young prodigy George Szell.

His father was opposed to a musical career and wanted him to train for a profession. He entered Vienna University in 1906 to study medicine. An important turning point from a career in medicine to one in music was the award of the Mozart prize for composition on the recommendation of Max Reger in 1909. The prize included a four-year stipend, enabling Toch to enter the conservatory in Frankfurt-on-Main. He studied piano with Willy Rehberg and composition with Iwan Knorr. In 1910 he received the Mendelssohn prize, and four years in succession won the Austrian prize for composition.

In 1913 he was appointed teacher of theory in the Hochschule für Musik in Mannheim. His teaching was interrupted by World War One, during which time he served in the Austrian Army, resuming his teaching at Mannheim in 1918. He married Alice Babette Zwack on 23 July 1916. He completed his doctorate at the University of Heidelberg in 1921 with a thesis on *Melodielehre*. This was to become a useful asset as a teaching qualification when he later fled Vienna for America.

His early compositions were mainly chamber music. They include nine string quartets written by 1919 and sonatas for violin, piano and clarinet, and are in traditional form and tonal idiom; later compositions are more dissonant and some nearly atonal. Works that brought him public recognition were his cello concerto, which was performed by Feuermann in 1925, his first piano concerto, which was performed by Walter Gieseking in 1926, and his comic opera *Der Prinzessin auf der Erbste*, which was performed at the Baden-Baden festival in 1927. He became one of the foremost protagonists of the *Neue Musik* that dominated Berlin in the 1920s and early 1930s and was regarded by many as being on a par with Hindemith. Between 1919 and 1935, his most prolific period, he composed more than 35 works out of his life's total of over 145, of which 49 remain unpublished.

In 1928 he moved to Berlin and four years later he was sufficiently well known to become the first German composer to be invited to tour the United States under the auspices of the Pro Musica Society, giving performances of his chamber works and piano music. On returning to Berlin he completed his second piano concerto (1932), but its premiere was disrupted by the Nazis and its publication cancelled. With Hitler's rise to power in 1933, Toch resolved to flee Germany. He was a member of the Allgemeiner Deutscher Musikverein (ADMV), the prestigious organization founded by Liszt in 1861 devoted to enhancing the cause of German music, mainly by promoting festivals at which the latest German music was featured. In 1935 the music critic Herbert Gerigk accused the ADMV of being infiltrated and controlled by Jews, citing Ernst Toch specifically. However, by this time Toch had left Germany. He had been selected to represent Germany at a musical convention in Florence in April 1933. From there he travelled to Paris, where he arranged for his wife to join him with their 5-year-old daughter Franzi. From there the family went to London and in the autumn of 1934 to America.

In August 1934 he was able to play the premiere of his second piano concerto at a Promenade Concert in London, with Sir Henry Wood conducting. The reception was mixed. The *Musical Times* (September 1934) commented: 'the busy Bach-like movements were pleasant enough and reflect the fashion of yesterday and today, but the dissonance is chronic and the music becomes immobile and drab'. Whilst on the boat to America he composed *Big Ben Variations*, Op. 62, a tone poem evoking the Westminster Chimes as they sounded one foggy midnight to a departing wanderer. In America he was invited to teach composition at the New School for Social Research in New York. He eventually settled in California, which he and the family much preferred, and he became an American citizen in 1940.

In 1937 he received news of the death of his mother. This event moved him to write *Cantata of the Bitter Herbs*, Op. 65, commemorating the Exodus of the Jews from Egypt. One of his finest chamber works, Piano Quintet, Op. 64, commissioned by Mrs Elizabeth Sprague Coolidge, was premiered in Pittsburg in 1938 by the Roth Quartet with Toch at the piano. Whereas in Germany he had been considered one of the foremost composers of his day, in America he was not so enthusiastically received. This, together with being greatly upset at the thought of the many friends and more than 60 cousins he had left in Germany, many of whom perished, left him very depressed.

Like other émigré composers, for example, Korngold and Waxman, he turned to composing film music, although with less distinction. Nevertheless he composed effective scores for *Catherine the Great*, *Peter Ibbetson*, *The Outcast*, *The Ghostbreakers*, *Address Unknown* and *The Unseen*. Copland was particularly complimentary about *Peter Ibbetson*, commenting that there were not enough people in Hollywood 'who could appreciate a good score when they hear one'.[1] Whereas Korngold saw the immediate potential of music to accompany films, Toch was to write an article 'The Cinema Wields the Baton' in the *New York Times* on 11 April 1937 in which he states:

> The focus of film music to come is the original film opera. This cannot be done by adapting old operas for the screen, for the conception of stage-opera music is bound to be different from what film-opera must be ... Music of film-opera has to create and develop its own forms, combining its different laws of space, time and motion. The first film-opera, once written will evoke a host of others.

However, this has not proved to be the case, and relatively few operas have been created specifically for either film or television screen.

The period 1938–45 was his leanest composing period. In 1948 he wrote a book, *The Shaping Forces of Music*, which was reissued as a paperback on his 75th birthday. The last fifteen years of his life were as prolific as he early days and in some ways more remarkable. He suffered a heart attack in 1948. From 1950 to 1958 he lived mainly in Switzerland, and it was there that he started, at the age of 62, to begin composing symphonies. During that period he wrote seven symphonies. His third, completed in 1955, was commissioned by the American Jewish Tercentenary of Chicago, and received its premiere with William Sternberg and the Pittsburgh Symphony Orchestra. It was awarded the Pulitzer prize and is his most performed symphony. Its mood is suggested by the quotation in the score from Goethe: 'Indeed am I but a wanderer, a pilgrim on earth – what are you?' The fifth, sixth and seventh symphonies were composed in the last 18 months of his life, when he was suffering from cancer. His fifth symphony began as a project based on a novel by an émigré friend, Lion Feuchtwanger, *Jefta und seine Tochter*. The novel itself is based on the account of Jephtha, which is to be found in Judges chapters 11 and 12. However, Toch could not wait for a suitable libretto, perhaps sensing that his days were numbered, and so wrote a single movement rhapsodic poem – his fifth symphony. Within a few months of completing his seventh symphony he died in Los Angeles. He worked frantically until the very end, leaving the sketches of a new string quartet by his bedside. In addition to being a composer and writer he was also a teacher; among his students were André PREVIN and Larry Adler.

Bibliography: *AG*; *G*; *HBD*; Ho*; Diane P. Jezic, *The Musical Migration and Ernst Toch* (Ames, IA: Iowa State University Press, 1989)

1. Howard Pollack, *Aaron Copland* (New York: Henry Holt, 1999), p. 350.

Ullmann, Victor (b. Teschen, Austria [Cieszyn, Poland], 1 January 1898; d. Auschwitz, 14 October 1944)   Son of an Austrian army officer. From 1909 he lived in Vienna, where he received a good school education, which included history, literature, philosophy and music. He studied music theory with Josef Polnauer from 1914 until 1916, when he left to serve in the Austrian

Army, becoming a second lieutenant in 1918. He enrolled as a law student at the University of Vienna in 1918, and joined SCHOENBERG's circle of pupils. His teachers were Joseph Polnauer, Heinrich Jalowetz and the pianist Eduard Steuermann. He impressed Schoenberg sufficiently to be recommended to his brother-in-law, Alexander ZEMLINSKY, as his assistant at the New German Theatre in Prague, where he worked from 1920 to 1927. During this period, in addition to being involved in putting on performances of Schoenberg's *Gurrelieder* and Berg's *Wozzeck*, he began composing. When Zemlinsky left Prague in 1927, Ullmann became *Kapellmeister* at Aussig, but probably because the avant-garde operas he chose to stage did not suit the audience he only stayed for one season. He then became *Kapellmeister* from 1929 to 1931 at the Zurich Schauspielhaus.

Ullmann was attracted by the teachings of Rudolph Steiner's Anthroposophical Movement, and when he had difficulty in continuing his conducting career he moved to Stuttgart in 1931 to work in the bookshop of the Anthroposophical Society. With Hitler's rise to power the bookshop was closed. Ullmann returned to Prague in 1933. There he managed to earn a bare living as a teacher and music critic. Because of the stressful conditions during this period, he found composing difficult, but nevertheless completed the opera *Der Sturz des Antichrist* (The fall of the Antichrist) with a libretto by Albert Steffen, the successor of Rudolf Steiner as chairman of the Anthroposophical Society. In 1935–7 he studied with the quarter-tone composer Alois Hába, who was also a member of the Anthroposophical Society. The influence of both Schoenberg and Hába is evident in many of Ullmann's compositions. By 1941 he had 38 works that had been given opus numbers, including four piano sonatas, song cycles, a piano concerto, *Variations on a Theme by Arnold Schoenberg*, and *Der Sturz des Antichrist*, but many of these have been lost.

By 1939, when the Nazis had appropriated Sudetenland, Ullmann, a Jew with a Jewish wife, must have seen the dangers ahead and considered emigration. The details of this period of his life are not clear. When compared with other composers who became imprisoned in Terezin, Ullmann was more assimilated and identified more with Christianity, and this perhaps made him less alert to the dangers. In September 1942 he was deported to Terezin, a concentration camp about 60 km north of Prague, together with his third wife, Elizabeth; for a time his first and second wives were also there, along with their sons. Terezin was in effect a transit camp for Auschwitz. The Nazis allowed music-making in the 'recreational periods' and used the camp for propaganda purposes, making a film entitled *Der Führer schenkt den Juden eine Stadt* (The Führer donates a town to the Jews) showing the musical activities. Ullmann became 'director' of the 'Studio for New Music' and as such organized concerts of works by his fellow prisoners. He was also the main music critic and wrote reviews of many of the performances held in Terezin. In these terrible conditions he composed more prolifically than ever before, stating:

it must be emphasized that Terezin has served to enhance, not to impede my musical activities, that by no means did we sit weeping on the banks of the waters of Babylon, and that our endeavour with respect to Arts was commensurate with our will to live.

By 1935 he had composed only seven works; within two years in Terezin he had composed sixteen works, including three piano sonatas, at least one of which appears to be the sketch for a symphony, a string quartet, a song cycle, a number of Hebrew and Yiddish songs, song settings of Persian and Chinese poems, and an opera. These represent his most profound compositions. In all he wrote seven piano sonatas; Op. Nos. 10 (1936), 19 (undated), 26 (1940) and 38 (1941) were written in Prague and the last three in Terezin. The third, together with his Piano Concerto, Op. 25, was dedicated to the pianist Juliette Arányi, who was later murdered in Auschwitz in 1944. The fifth and seventh appear to be the sketches for symphonies, which Ullmann may have felt he could no longer orchestrate as they could not be performed by a full complement of players under the circumstances. The seventh piano sonata is dedicated to his three children, the eldest of whom perished in Auschwitz along with their mother, while the younger two were sent to England. It was reconstructed as a symphony by Bernhard Wulff and was given its premiere in 1989. The sonata has evocations of MAHLER and the Second Viennese School. In its last movement there are quotations from the Czech Hussite hymn 'Ye, who are God's warriors'; it also contains variations and a fugue on a Hebrew folk song. The sonata was completed shortly before Ullmann was sent to Auschwitz. He wrote three string quartets, but the first (1923) and second (1936) have been lost. The third was composed in Terezin in 1943.

His opera *Der Kaiser von Atlantis* uses a libretto by Peter Kien, a painter and poet, and also a prisoner in Terezin. It is an allegory on the nature of fascism and the low value it places on human life. The main character, Death, goes on strike. When the Emperor sends his troops to battle this causes chaos, with nobody dying. Eventually the Emperor, conducting the battle over the telephone, sees Death in the mirror. Death offers to resume his work provided the Emperor will be the first victim. The Emperor allows himself to be led away. The opera, which quotes a distortion of *Deutschland über alles* in the first scene, was ready to be performed in 1944, but at the final rehearsals an SS delegation were present. They recognized the likeness between the Emperor and Hitler, and the opera was never performed in Terezin. It was first performed in Amsterdam in 1975.

All the prisoners in Terezin saw the regular disappearance of many of their number in the regular transports to Auschwitz. Before Ullmann was sent there to be murdered by the Nazis, along with other composers including HAAS, KRASA and KLEIN, he gave his manuscripts to a fellow prisoner, who survived and passed them to H. G. Adler after the war. Through Adler the manuscripts came to the Goetheanum in Dornach, Germany, where they are now kept.

347

Only 18 of about 50 of Ullmann's compositions written before 1942 have survived.
Bibliography: G; Grad; Leb; Ken; Joža Karas, *Music in Terezin, 1941–1945* (New York: Pendragon, 1985), pp. 111–20; EDA 005-2 [record sleeve]; Kennedy, P., 440 854-2 [record sleeve]; Schröder-Nauenburg, B., BR 100228 [record sleeve].

Vainberg, Moisei Samuilovich   *see* **Weinberg, Moisei Samuilovich**

Veprik, Alexander   *see* **Weprik**

Vogel, Vladimir Rudolfovich (b. Moscow, 29 February 1896; d. Zurich, 19 June 1984)   Son of a German–Jewish father and a Russian mother. Skriabin, whom he saw perform in Moscow, influenced his composing. As a German national he was interned during World War One at Birsk in the Urals. He left Moscow for Berlin in 1918, where he studied with Heinz Tiessen (1919–21) and Busoni (1922–4); taught composition and radiogenetic interpretation at the Klindworth-Scharwenka Conservatory from 1929 to 1933; and became involved in the workers' movement, writing for *Die Welt am Abend* and *Kampfmusik* and setting Weinert's *Der Heimliche Aufmarsch gegen die Sowjetunion* and other political songs to music. With the rise of Nazism he fled Germany in 1933, initially going to Belgium before finally settling in Switzerland. His compositions show the influence of both Busoni and SCHOENBERG. In his first important work, *Sprechlieder* for bass and piano (1922), he uses Schoenbergian *Sprechgesang*, which he also uses in *Wagadu's Untergang durch die Eitelkeit* for soloists, chorus, speaking chorus and five saxophones (1930). In his violin concerto (1937) he wrote two movements in classical style and two in serial. Whilst in Belgium he composed the oratorio *Thyl Claes* for soprano, two speakers and speaking chorus. He also wrote *Epitaffio per Alban Berg* for piano (1936).
Bibliography: *G*; *HBD*; Ho*, Ken; Leb; Ly*

Waxman [Wachsmann], **Franz** (b. Königshütte, Upper Silesia [Chorzów, Poland], 24 December 1906; d. Los Angeles, 24 February 1967)   Pursued a career in banking for two years, then studied at the Dresden Music Academy and the Berlin Conservatory and intended to become a composer. However, in order to earn a living he became a café musician in Berlin. While playing with a jazz orchestra, the Weintraub Syncopaters, he met Friedrich HOLLAENDER. This led to him being commissioned to arrange and conduct Hollaender's film score for *Der Blaue Engel* in 1930. This and his original composition for Ferenc Molnar's *Lilion* in 1933 established his name. However, after being physically attacked by Nazis in 1933 he fled Germany, initially to Paris and then to Hollywood, where in 1934 his first film assignments were *Music in the Air* and *Bride of Frankenstein*. He went on to become a very successful film composer of over 140 films, including *Sunset Boulevard* (1950) and *A Place in the Sun* (1951), both of which won Oscars.

In 1947 he founded the Los Angeles Music Festival and remained its chief conductor until his death. In this capacity he introduced many new twentieth-century works by composers including Stravinsky, Shostakovich, MAHLER, Egk, MILHAUD, Piston, Prokofiev, Honneger, BERNSTEIN, LIEBERMANN, Von Einem, ORFF and Britten.

From the 1950s onwards he devoted more time to composition and only accepted selected film score commissions. One of his best-known compositions is the *Carmen Fastasie*, which was commissioned by Jascha Heifetz in 1947. He also composed *Sinfonietta* for string orchestra and timpani (1965), the oratorio *Joshua* (1959) and the song cycle *The Song of Terezin* (1965). He began an opera based on Stevenson's *Dr Jekyll and Mr Hyde*, but it was never completed, although he did write music for a film of the same name in 1941. He composed *The Song of Terezin* after reading the collection of poems entitled *I Never Saw a Butterfly* written by children in the concentration camp at Terezin, very few of whom survived. He was very moved by the poems, conscious of his own escape from Germany and his Jewish heritage. He wrote the work in three months and it was first performed by the Cincinnati Symphony Orchestra with Waxman conducting in 1965.

Bibliography: *AG*; *G*; *HBD*; Leb; Ly*

Weigl, Karl (b. Vienna, 6 February 1881; d. New York, 11 August 1949)   Born into a prosperous Jewish family. His father was a banker and came from Temesvar, part of the Austro-Hungarian Empire. His first composition lessons were arranged by his mother with Alexander ZEMLINSKY. After leaving school in 1899 he studied musicology at Vienna University with Guido Adler, eventually graduating with a Ph.D. in 1904. He also studied piano with Anton Door and composition with Robert Fuchs. During his studies he met Webern and SCHOENBERG, and kept contact with the latter for the rest of his life. Schoenberg and Zemlinsky, together with Weigl and others, founded the Vereinigung Schaffender Tonkünstler (Society of Creative Composers) and MAHLER became its patron. From 1904 to 1906 Weigl was engaged by Mahler as the opera coach at the Vienna Court Opera. He regarded the period he spent under Gustav Mahler as the most instructive of his entire life. It was through Mahler that he was introduced to Arnold Rosé (Mahler's brother-in-law), whose quartet premiered Weigl's String Quartet No. 3 in A major (1909), which won the Beethoven prize. His String Quartet No. 1 in C minor was not premiered until 1925, and then by the Kolbe Quartet. His String Quartet No. 5 in G major (1933) was premiered by the Busch Quartet in 1934. Weigl was a Hungarian citizen until 1912, when he became an Austrian citizen; he was drafted into the army in 1914. After the war he obtained a post at the New Vienna Conservatory from 1918 to 1928, where he taught theory and composition. He was professor of music theory at Vienna University from 1931 to 1938, where his pupils included EISLER, KORNGOLD and ZEISL. In 1922 his choral work *Hymne* was awarded a prize by the Philadelphia Mendelssohn Club, and in 1924 the City of Vienna awarded him a prize for the symphonic cantata *Weltfeier*. His piano concerto for the left hand (1925) was commissioned by Paul Wittgenstein. In 1929 he succeeded Hans GÁL as lecturer in harmony and counterpoint at Vienna University.

After the *Anschluss* in 1938 Weigl was struck off the music publishers' lists. His mother died in October 1938, after which he fled to America. Initially he found it difficult to get work, in spite of recommendations from Schoenberg, Richard Strauss and Bruno Walter, but later managed to get teaching posts at the Hartt School of Music (1941–2), Brooklyn College (1943–5) and the Boston Conservatory (1946–8). He became an American citizen in 1944. In the last five years of his life he led a rather withdrawn existence, but managed to compose two symphonies and three string quartets. He was a prolific composer, writing in all six symphonies, two piano concertos, eight string quartets, two violin sonatas, a viola sonata and several songs. He composed in a late Romantic style, with musical roots in Brahms, and was hardly influenced by the Second Viennese School.

Bibliography: *AG*; *G*; *HBD*; Ho*; Leb; Ken

Weil, Ernst   Almost nothing is known about this Czech composer, except that a package of music containing the manuscript of a violin sonata written by him was found in the warehouse of the Majdanek concentration camp near Lublin in 1944. He had undoubtedly been killed in the camp.

Bibliography: J. Szigeti, *With Strings Attached* (London: Cassell, 1949), p. 34

Weill, Kurt (b. Dessau, 2 March 1900; d. New York, 3 April 1950)   Son of Albert Weill, cantor and schoolteacher to the Jewish community in Dessau. The Weills were able to trace their ancestors back as far as one born Judah in 1360 in the village of Weil der Stadt, near Stuttgart. When Judah's son Jacob left his birthplace he added the name that became regarded as the family name (*cf.* OFFENBACH and SULZER). Kurt was the third of four children, having two older brothers and a younger sister. The family lived adjacent to the synagogue. The Jewish community in Dessau was what might be regarded as liberal, being one of the first synagogues to have sermons in the vernacular. Kurt received his first piano lessons from his father at the age of 6. From an early age he imbibed the ambience of the synagogue.

Dessau was a small town, but it had historic and cultural associations. The dukes of Anhalt had made it their capital since the beginning of the seventeenth century, and Moses MENDELSSOHN, philosopher and grandfather of Felix, was born there. The town had a theatre where operas were performed. Both synagogue and theatre were to have an influence on Kurt's musical development. After piano lessons with his father, he had lessons from Evelyn Shapiro until he was 15. By this time his interest in and talent for music were very apparent and he was given lessons by Albert Bing, *Kapellmeister* at the court theatre. Kurt was of an age that meant he just missed serving in

World War One. When he reached school leaving age he enrolled both at the University of Berlin and the Hochschule für Musik, but his interest in music was clearly his first love and he soon dropped his academic studies at the university. He studied composition under Humperdink and then returned to Dessau to work as assistant conductor under his former teacher, Albert Bing. In 1920 his parents and their daughter moved to Leipzig, where his father had been appointed as director of an orphanage run by B'nai B'rith, the Jewish fraternal society. At this point Kurt also left, for what was to be a short stay as musical director of the opera in the small Westphalian town of Lündenscheid.

In 1920, in spite of the economic and political consequences of the war, Berlin was very much a centre of artistic developments. Busoni, a virtuoso pianist, composer and teacher was invited to return from exile in Zurich to Berlin to conduct a small and exclusive master-class in composition at the Prussian Akademie der Künste. Busoni had a class of six students, whom he would select from those who approached him. As a result of seeing some of Weill's compositions, Busoni admitted Weill to his class; he became Busoni's favourite pupil until the latter's death in 1924. From 1921 to 1924 Weill's musical development owed much to Busoni's guidance. His works during this period include his first symphony, a string quartet, Op. 8, and his concerto for violin and wind band, Op.12.

Weill's meetings with Georg Kaiser in 1924 and later with Berthold Brecht in 1927, and their subsequent collaborations, were to influence the next stages of his development. The playwright Georg Kaiser lived at Grünheide and approached Weill with the suggestion that they might work together on a musical drama project. The two of them worked on the composition of *Der Protagonist* while Weill stayed with him at Grünheide. It was there that Lotte Lenya was staying as an au pair whilst looking for employment. She first met the composer when she was sent to row across the lake to fetch him from the railway station. Her real name was Karoline Wilhelmine Charlotte Blauer, and she was brought up in a working-class district of Vienna, where her father was a coachman and her mother took in laundry. *Der Protagonist* was finished in 1925 and dedicated to Lotte Lenya, whom Weill married in 1926. The first performance in Dresden was a great success and it was predicted that Weill would become the musical dramatist of the future. At the time young musicians regarded opera as a dying and outdated art form. The correspondent of *Dresdner Neueste Nachrichten* commented: 'This one-actor restores our faith in the future of opera ... with its grand dramatic sweep it is pure theatre, theatre at its most vivid.' (See Taylor 1991, p. 90.) In the following years it was to be performed at Frankfurt, Hanover, Leipzig and Berlin. In 1925 Kaiser introduced Weill to the poet Ivan Goll (pseudonym of Isaac Lang), a Jewish expressionist-surrealist, born in Alsace, who settled in Paris and also spent time in Berlin. Weill set his poem *Der neue Orpheus*, a modern tale set in a large city with adapted mythological characters, as a cantata for soprano, violin and orchestra. Orpheus sees Eurydice as a painted prostitute, loses her and shoots

351

himself in the waiting room of a railway station. Goll subsequently wrote the libretto for Weill's ballet-opera *Royal Palace*. Weill collaborated with Kaiser in 1927 in a second opera, the comedy *Der Zar Lässt sich Photographieren* (The Tzar has his picture taken), and that same year met Bertolt Brecht.

In 1927 Brecht had published a volume of poems with the ironic title *Bert Brechts Hauspostille*, a 'domestic breviary' arranged as a mock-liturgical anthology of prayers. Weill set five of these poems to music to form the *Mahagony Songspiel*. When first performed in Baden-Baden in June 1927 it created a sensation. It used very stark staging, with workers in overalls carrying posters inscribed with provocative socialist slogans, and Lotte Lenya standing in the middle of a boxing ring singing Weill's music. Weill and Brecht developed this work further into a full opera, *Aufsteig und Fall der Stadt Mahagonny* (Rise and fall of the city of Mahagonny), which was first performed in 1930, but this was only after what was to be their greatest collaborative effort, namely *Dreigroschenoper* (Threepenny opera).

For *Dreigroschenoper* Brecht took as his model the 1728 opera by John Gay and John Pepusch, *The Beggar's Opera*. This collaboration was in large measure due to Elisabeth Hauptmann. She collected material for Brecht, particularly from English literature that she thought he might use. *The Beggar's Opera* had been revived in London at the Lyric Theatre, Hammersmith, by Nigel Playfair in 1920. Elisabeth Hauptmann translated it into German and presented it to Brecht. The potential of this play for the German market had already been seen by Schott the publishers, but Hindemith, to whom they suggested it, was not interested. The tale involving thieves, pimps and prostitutes appealed to Brecht. It was first performed in 1928, with Lotte Lenya among the cast. It was a sensational success at the time. People could be heard in the streets whistling the well-known numbers. Theodor ADORNO, the musicologist and composer, said it was 'the most important event in musical theatre since Wozzeck'. Brecht himself said: 'Only the consistent use of pleasing and easily assimilated melody made it possible to achieve what the *Dreigroschenoper* succeeded in doing: the creation of a new type of musical theatre' (see Stuckenschmidt 1970, p. 142).

Weill's music theatre entailed the use of a good actor or actress, but often with more limited singing ability. Lotte Lenya fitted this category. In the space of five years Weill's compositions had taken a dramatic change of direction from the time of his string quartet, when a pupil of Busoni.

He continued to produce works in a similar genre, including *Happy End*, *Lindberghflug* (Lindbergh's flight), *Jasager* (Yes-man), *Die Bürgschaft* (The surety) and *Die Sieben Todsünden* (Seven deadly sins). Although Brecht and Weill collaborated in Weill's most successful and original works, they did not have an easy relationship, and after 1930 they all but ceased to collaborate. *Mahagony* had its film premiere in Berlin in 1931.

By 1933, with the rise in Nazism, Weill made his escape to Paris. By this time Lotte Lenya was having an affair with Otto von Pasetti. Eventually this was to lead to Lenya and Weill's divorce. Nevertheless, when Weill escaped to Paris, Lenya made all the arrangements possible regarding his possessions left in Berlin. Strangely, it was Lenya who wanted the divorce, but once it had been brought about she gradually became more and more in need of his stabilizing influence. In 1935 Weill was invited by Max Reinhardt to write the music for a biblical super-*revue* describing the wanderings of the Jewish people, *The Eternal Road*, which was to be performed in New York. Weill and Lenya sailed to America, where they eventually were to become American citizens and were remarried in 1937. *The Eternal Road* was a failure, but it led to other commissions. For many composers escaping from the Nazis, such as SCHOENBERG, MILHAUD and EISLER, living in America meant living in exile, but not so for Weill; for him it meant future and promise. By 1938 all of his immediate family had emigrated either to America or Palestine (Israel).

In New York he made new friends, including George GERSHWIN, Marc BLITZSTEIN and Maxwell Anderson. Anderson was a dramatist like Kaiser and Brecht and was looking for a composer to write music for a play for Broadway, *Knickerbocker Holiday* (1938), about New York in the 1880s. Weill's contribution to this proved sensational; *September Song* was the greatest hit in the score. This proved to be another turning point in Weill's career. His songs lost their satirical bite, something that had characterized many of his greatest successes in Berlin, and took a more sentimental note. He composed for *Lady in the Dark* (1940), *One Touch of Venus* (1943), *Down in the Valley* (1948) and *Street Scene* (1946). After the success of *Lady in the Dark*, Kurt and Lotte were able to buy a country house in New City, New York State, on the banks of the Hudson River, where Weill found the surroundings congenial for work. He was a workaholic, anxious for success but not money, and he was the most generous of friends.

Elliot Carter (see Taylor 1991, p. 282) admired his adaptability and comments on the dichotomy of his musical style as follows:

> Where in pre-Hitler days his music underlined the bold and disillusioned bitterness of economic justice, now, reflecting his new environment and the New York audiences to which he appeals, his social scene has shrunk to the bedroom … In the atmosphere of Broadway, where so much music is unconvincing and dead, Weill's workmanlike care and his refined sense of style make up for whatever spontaneity and freshness his music lacks.

In the mid-1940s Weill composed three works strongly reflecting his Jewish heritage. *Kiddush* for tenor, mixed choir and organ was composed in 1946 for the 75th anniversary of the Park Avenue Synagogue, New York, and is dedicated to his father. He arranged *Hatikvah* for full orchestra to celebrate Chaim Weizmann's birthday. He wrote the music for *The Flag is Born*. The story of the latter, written by Ben Hecht, is of a young Holocaust survivor who fashions his *tallit* into a battle flag and joins the Irgun (Irgun Zvai Leumi – National

Military Organization, a dissident underground organization led by Menachim Begin), who are fighting for the liberation of the land of their fathers.

In the late 1940s a medical check-up revealed that Weill had high blood pressure and an uneven heart beat. Hypertension ran in the Weill family; his mother and father suffered from it, and his brother Hans had died of it in 1947. He changed his diet, but continued to work hard. He died in 1950 whilst working on songs for *Huckleberry Finn* with Maxwell Anderson.

After Weill's death, Lotte Lenya continued to work tirelessly on behalf of his music, supervising the German and American performances of his main works.

Bibliography: *AG*; *G*; *HBD*; Leb; Jürgen Schebera, *Kurt Weill: an Illustrated Life* (New Haven: Yale University Press, 1995); Hans Stuckenschmidt, *Germany and Central Europe: Twentieth-Century Composers* (New York: Holt, 1970) p. 142; Ronald Taylor, *Kurt Weill: Composer in a Divided World* (London: Simon & Schuster, 1991)

Weinberg, Jacob [Yacov Vainberg] (b. Odessa, 7 July 1879; d. New York, 11 February 1956)   Brought up in a family with a musical background. One of his uncles was married to the sister of Anton RUBINSTEIN. His formal musical training did not begin until he was 17 years old, when he entered Moscow University to study law. He studied music under K. N. Igumnov (piano) and Sergei Taneyev (composition) at the Moscow Conservatory, graduating in 1906. He then studied with Leschetitsky in Vienna from 1910 to 1911. On returning to Moscow he joined the Society for Jewish Folk Music. This was a society based in St Petersburg and which had been founded by Joel ENGEL in 1908 after receiving permission from the government. From 1916 to 1921 Weinberg was director of the Odessa Conservatory, and in 1923 he and his family emigrated to Palestine. There he helped to organize the Jewish National Conservatory at Jerusalem. In 1928 he went to America, where he lived for the rest of his life, working as a pianist, composer and teacher. He published settings of the Sabbath Eve Service (1935), the Sabbath Morning Service (1938–9) and sacred music for other occasions. Whilst in Palestine he wrote the national opera *Hechalutz* (The pioneer), which was performed in New York in 1934. The opera depicts the rejection of the Diaspora and the victory of the Zionist dream with the action taking place in a small town in Poland followed by a kibbutz in Palestine. Different styles of music are used to contrast the two locations. He also wrote two oratorios, *Isaiah* (1948) and *Life of Moses* (1952), a cantata entitled *The Seagull, Purim Suite*, a piano concerto, a violin sonata, a piano trio on Hebrew themes, a clarinet quintet and a number of vocal works.

Bibliography: *AG*; Ho*; Jehoash Hirshberg, *Music in the Jewish Community of Palestine, 1880–1948* (Oxford: Clarendon Press, 1995), pp. 256–8; Aron M. Rothmüller, *The Music of the Jews* (London: Vallentine Mitchell, 1953), p. 165

Weinberg, Moisei Samuilovich [Miesczylaw Weinberg] (b. Warsaw 8 December 1919; d. Moscow, 26 February 1996)   Prolific composer, but the importance of his music is only gradually being recognized, particularly in the West, where it was only since the 1990s that a range of his recordings became available. Shostakovich described Weinberg as 'one of the most outstanding composers of the present day'. He composed seven operas, three ballets, a Requiem, four cantatas, 27 symphonies, 17 string quartets, 19 sonatas (piano solo or with other instruments), two sinfoniettas, Moldavian and Slavonic rhapsodies, concertos for violin, flute, trumpet, clarinet and cello, and over 150 songs. He was also a fine pianist who performed with, among others, Oistrakh and Rostropovich and Vishnevskaya. He often played four-handed piano, together with Shostakovich, and they recorded the piano version of Shostakovich's Tenth Symphony.

Weinberg came from a musical family; his father was a composer and violinist at the Yiddish theatre in Warsaw. At the age of 10 Moisei played the piano in the theatre where his father worked and two years later he went to the Warsaw Conservatory, where he studied with Jozef Turczinski. His talent was noticed by Joseph Hoffman, who arranged for him to study in America, but the plan was forestalled by the outbreak of World War Two. In 1939 his family was murdered (burned alive) by the Nazis, and he fled to Minsk. There he studied composition under Vasili Zolotaryov, graduating in 1941. After the Germans attacked Russia, he fled further and worked at the opera in Tashkent, where he married the daughter of the actor and director of the Yiddish Theatre, Solomon Mikhoels. He suffered further tragedy in 1948, when Solomon Mikhoels was murdered by the secret police during the Stalinist period. The secret police fabricated a story about the existence of a 'pro-American Jewish conspiracy', which was followed by the arrest of leading officials and public figures of Jewish origin. According to Krushchev, Mikhoels was murdered in the plot and his killer was rewarded by Stalin, although Mikhoels was then buried with honours.[1]

Earlier in 1943 Weinberg sent the score of his recently completed first symphony to Shostakovich, asking the latter's opinion of it. Shostakovich made sure that Weinberg received an official invitation to Moscow – this was particularly important for a composer hoping for recognition. Shostakovich and he became friends, and Weinberg described himself as a pupil of Shostakovich, although he never had lessons from him. The regard they had for each other is evident from Shostakovich's dedication of his tenth string quartet to Weinberg, and Weinberg's twelfth symphony dedicated 'In memory of Dimitri Shostakovich, 1976'. The influence of Shostakovich is evident in some of Weinberg's works, for example, Piano Quintet, Op. 18, particularly the biting satirical humour.

By 1948 Weinberg had produced 40 opuses, and he had the dubious privilege of being praised by the newly elected head of the Composers Union, Tikhon Khrenikov, as this quotation shows:

A shining proof of the fruitfulness of the realistic path is the *Sinfonietta* by Weinberg. As a composer Weinberg was strongly influenced by the modernist music which badly mangled his undoubted talent. Turning to the sources of Jewish folk music, Weinberg created a bright, optimistic work dedicated to the theme of shining, free working life of the Jewish people in the land of Socialism. In this work Weinberg has shown uncommon mastery of creative imagination.[2]

In January 1953 Weinberg was arrested, apparently because his wife's uncle, the Kremlin physician Vovsi, had been labelled an enemy of the people, and also because Weinberg appeared to be emphasizing the Jewish elements in his music. The Jewish elements were said to appear in the *Sinfoniettas, Moldavian Rhapsody, Trio,* Op. 24, and some 40 songs based on poems by Izhak Peretz. Weinberg was released in March 1953, after Stalin's death.

During the last two decades of his life Weinberg continued to compose prolifically, including symphonies, chamber music (for example, *Twenty-Four Preludes* for solo cello, Op. 100) and operas.

Bibliography: *G*; Leb; Martin Anderson, 'Moisei Vainberg', *Tempo,* 197 (1996), p. 22

1. Jerrold Schecter and Vyacheslav Luchkov, *Khrushchev Remembers: the Glasnost Tapes* (Boston: Little, Brown, 1990), p. 101.
2. Marma A. Ledin (1993) RD CD 11006 [record sleeve].

Weinberger, Jaromir (b. Prague, 8 January 1896; d. St Petersburg, Florida, USA, 8 August 1967)   Studied under Jaroslav Křička, Václav Karel, and Vitězslav Novak at the Prague Conservatory from 1910–15 and then with Max Reger in Leipzig in 1916. He taught in the Ithaca Conservatory, New York, in 1922 and then returned to Prague. It was whilst at Ithaca that he wrote the folk opera *Schwanda, der Dudelsackpfeifer* (Schwanda the bagpiper, 1926), which contains his best-known piece, the Fugue and Polka. In the opera the bagpiper wanders the world, but with a nostalgia for his homeland. It was a popular success at the time, but more so abroad than in Prague where it has rarely been heard since 1933. He wrote several operas, but the only real success was *Wallenstein,* which was first performed at the Vienna State Opera in 1937. He conducted a performance of *Schwanda, der Dudelsackpfeifer* with the Jüdische Frontkämpfer Orchestra (Jewish War Veterans' Orchestra), also in Vienna. He composed the orchestral work *Neima Ivrit* (Hebrew song, 1936), but with the *Anschluss* he fled to America in 1939. There he wrote *A Lincoln Symphony* (1941), orchestral variations on the song *Under the Spreading Chestnut Tree* (1940), *The Song of the High Sea,* and the cantata *Ecclesiastes.* He committed suicide in 1967, during a period of depression.

Bibliography: *AG*; *G*; Ho*; Leb; Ly*; John Tyrrell, *Czech Opera* (Cambridge: Cambridge University Press, 1988), pp. 251–2

Weiner, Lazar (b. Cherkassy, Kiev, Ukraine, 24 October 1897; d. New York, 10 January 1982) Began his interest in music on hearing his mother sing as a child. He joined the Brodsky Synagogue choir at the age of 7. He was in the children's chorus that sang in Mussorgsky's *Boris Godunov* with the Kiev Opera, and studied piano, theory and composition at the Kiev Conservatory from 1910 to 1914. In 1917 the family emigrated to New York, where Lazar worked initially as a vocal coach. He also began composing by setting Yiddish poems to music. However, when he sent some of his compositions to ENGEL, the founder of the Society of Jewish Folk Music at St Petersburg, Engel criticized them as having a too western style. Weiner then made a detailed study of Yiddish folk songs and biblical cantillation and took formal tuition in composition from Frederick Jacobi and Joseph Schillinger. He directed a number of choirs and became director of music at the Central Synagogue in New York (1930–75). Prior to this he had become an American citizen (1926). Most of his compositions are of vocal music, which was undoubtedly his strength, and many are of a Jewish/Yiddish character. His compositions include an opera, *Golem* (1957), the cantata *The Last Judgement* (1966), a setting of the Friday Evening Service, *Shir l'Shabat* (1963), a string quartet (1937), suite for violin, cello and piano (1929) and a number of solo songs and pieces for piano.
Bibliography: *G*; *HBD*; Ho*; Ly*

Weisgall, Hugo David (b. Ivančice, Moravia [Czech Republic], 13 October 1912) Son of an opera singer, cantor and composer of synagogue music who emigrated with his family to Baltimore, USA, in 1921. Hugo became an American citizen in 1926. He studied at the Peabody Conservatory, Johns Hopkins University, the Curtis Institute of Music under Rosario Scalero and Fritz Reiner and privately with Roger Sessions. In the 1930s he conducted the Baltimore String Orchestra and a synagogue choir and he also composed songs, liturgical works and ballet. The orchestral suite from his ballet *Quest* was performed by the New York Philharmonic Orchestra in 1942. He served in the American armed forces during World War Two, and after the war he was an assistant military attaché and then cultural attaché with the United States Embassy in Prague, where his ballet *Outpost* was performed at the National Theatre in 1947. Whilst in Prague his own *American Comedy* and BLITZSTEIN's *Freedom Morning* were recorded under his baton. He returned to America in 1948. He taught at the Jewish Theological Seminary in New York from 1952, then at the Juilliard School in New York (1957–8). He was professor at Queens College, New York (1961–83). His wrote nine operas, including *Six Characters in Search of an Author* (1956), *Purgatory* (1958) and *Nine Rivers from Jordan* (1968), ballet music and songs.
Bibliography: *AG*; *G*; *HBD*; Bruce Saylor, 'Music of Weisgall', *Musical Quarterly*, 59 (1973), pp. 239–62

357

Wellesz, Egon Joseph (b. Vienna, 21 October 1885; d. Oxford, 9 November 1974)   Only child of Samú Wellesz and Ilona Lovenyi. Both parents came to Vienna independently, from different parts of the Hungarian empire. His mother was a piano pupil of Carl Frühling, and at the age of 7 Egon was sent to study with him. At school he specialized in ancient history and literature, Latin and Greek. His decision to become a composer was taken after he had seen MAHLER conduct Weber's *Der Freischütz*. He was able to see many other performances of music under Mahler's baton. He studied musicology at Vienna University from 1904 to 1906 with Guido Adler, who was a great inspiration to him as a music scholar. In the years to come Wellesz was to make his name perhaps more as a music scholar than as a composer, in spite of being a prolific composer of over 100 works. His earliest composition was *Drei Capriccios*, a trio for violin, cello and piano (1902).

At the age of 19 he studied privately with SCHOENBERG, before Webern and Berg became Schoenberg's pupils. In 1908 he married Emmy Stross, whom he had known since he was a child of 8. She studied eastern art history and this was to reinforce his interest in Byzantine music. In 1909 he completed a doctorate on the subject of the eighteenth-century Italian composer Guiseppe Bonno. *Der Abend*, a cycle of four impressions for piano (1909), was his first composition to be published as the result of being introduced by Bartok to the latter's music publisher. He composed two atonal pieces in 1911 and 1913, *Drei Skizzen*, Op. 6, for piano and *Lieder aus der Fremde*, Op. 15. The former was modelled on Schoenberg's *Drei Klavierstücke*, Op. 11. His early compositions are mainly songs with piano accompaniment. After World War One he wrote five operas and four ballets, the style generally late Romantic reflecting the influence of Mahler and the Second Viennese School. He met and became friends with Hugo von Hofmanstal, who helped and advised him with his opera librettos.

As a music scholar he became interested in Byzantine music. The hymns of the Byzantine church were a distinctive contribution to the music of early Christendom, but there was a fundamental problem in deciphering the notation of this eastern chant. Wellesz played a major role in deciphering the notation and published, with others, facsimile editions and systematic transcriptions of source material (*Monumenta Musicae Byzantinae*, 1935). A decade later he produced the definitive work, *A History of Byzantine Music and Hymnography*. Earlier in 1921 he produced the first biography of SCHOENBERG, in so doing incurring the latter's wrath.

Wellesz was of part Jewish descent, but in the early 1930s he converted to Catholicism. Significantly, in 1934 he wrote a mass (Op. 51). By 1932 he had become professor of music history at the University of Vienna, and in recognition of his contributions to music he received an honorary doctorate at the University of Oxford in the same year. He composed a large cantata, *Mitte des Lebens*, Op. 45, which he dedicated to Oxford University in gratitude. At the same time honorary doctorates were conferred on two friends of his, Edward

J. Dent and H. C. Coles. Wellesz was a pioneer member of the International Society for Contemporary Music. During the 1920s and 1930s many of his operas and ballets were performed throughout Germany and Austria, for example, *Die Prinzessin Girnara* premiered with great success at Frankfurt in 1921, *Alkeltis* (with a libretto by Hofmanthal) in Mannhein in 1924, *Persisches Ballett* in Donaueschingen in 1924 and *Die Bakchantinnen* in Vienna in 1931.[1] His success lasted throughout the period of the Weimar Republic, but once Hitler became chancellor in 1933 performances of his works became more difficult to stage.

In 1938 Bruno Walter conducted the first performance of Wellesz's *Prosperos Beschwörungen*, five symphonic pieces after characters in Shakespeare's *The Tempest*, in Vienna. A further performance that year was given, again by Walter, in Amsterdam. While Wellesz was attending the performance he heard of the *Anschluss* and was warned by telegram that it would be unsafe to return home. Through his friendship with H. C. Coles and the publisher Edward Dent he was able to settle in England, where he was elected fellow of Lincoln College, Oxford. From 1938 until his death in 1974 he made Oxford his home. Back in Germany, in 1939 all his music was banned from performance by the Reichsmusikprüfstelle.

In spite being able to settle in Britain this was a traumatic period for him. He was interned as an alien on the Isle of Man for a time. He found it difficult to compose, although he continued his musical scholarship. In 1947 a readership in Byzantine music was created especially for him at Oxford University. He began composing again near the end of the war, producing two masterpieces: String Quartet No. 5, Op. 60; and a setting of *The Leaden Echo and the Golden Echo* by Gerald Manley Hopkins, for soprano with instrumental accompaniment. Encouraged by their successes, and whilst holidaying in the Lake District in 1945, he was inspired to write his first symphony at the age of 60. He continued over the next 26 years writing a further eight symphonies (1948, 1951, 1952, 1956, 1965, 1968, 1970 and 1971), following the Romantic tradition of Bruckner and Mahler with elements of serialism. Other important compositions written whilst in Oxford were the *Octet* for wind and strings (1949), his only English-language opera, *Incognito*, which premiered in Oxford in 1951, and the violin concerto (1961), written for Eduard Melkus.

Bibliography: *G*; *HBD*; Ho*; C. C. Benser, *Egon Wellesz (1885–1974); Chronicle of a Twentieth-Century Musician* (New York: Peter Lang, 1985)*; http://www.musicweb.force9.co.uk/music/wellesz.htm

1. Philip Ward, 'Egon Wellesz: an Opera Composer in 1920s Vienna', *Tempo*, 219 (2002), pp. 22–8.

Weprik, Aleksander Moiseyevich (b. Balta, near Odessa, 11/23 June 1899; d. Moscow, 13 October 1958)   Born in the Ukraine and brought up in Poland, where he studied piano at the Warsaw Conservatory until he was 10. To escape the pogroms he fled with his mother and siblings to Leipzig, where she had relatives. There he studied composition with Janáček and Reger, and piano with Karl Wendling at the Leipzig Conservatory from 1909 to 1914. His studies continued at the St Petersburg Conservatory with Dubasov (piano) from 1914 to 1917 and with Alexander Zhitomirsky (composition) who was a founding member of the Society for Jewish Folk Music (see ENGEL) from 1917 to 1920. He completed his studies under Myaskovsky at the Moscow Conservatory, where he became a teacher in 1923. He was very active in the organization of musical education and in 1927 and 1928 was sent with Lunacharsky, the Soviet minister for culture, on an official extended tour of Europe to visit many musical institutions. Among those whom they met were SCHOENBERG, Ravel, Hindemith and Honegger. After the 1930s Weprik was an activist in building up of music in the small Soviet National Republics, particularly Kirgiz (a republic to the east of the Caspian Sea), the intention being to show the world how national cultures thrived under socialism.

His most creative period was from 1922 to 1928, during which time he composed a number of works on specifically Hebrew themes, including *Songs and Dances of the Ghetto* for orchestra, *Hebrew Songs* for orchestra, and *Kaddish* (1928). Other works include: *1905*, a set of five episodes for orchestra and chorus; *Song of Joy* and *Song of Mourning* for orchestra; a tone picture, *Stalinstan*; and two piano sonatas. Much of his later work was conventional and imbued with socialist ideology. Nevertheless Weprik was among the few leaders of the Composers Union who were courageous enough to support Shostakovich in the *Lady Macbeth* controversy. After the 1930s Stalinist repression effectively silenced Jewish culture until after Stalin's death in 1953, and in 1950 Weprik was sent to the Gulag. Although he was relieved of the hardest labour in order to organize the prison orchestra, his health deteriorated and by the time he was released, in 1954, he was seriously ill. He died in 1958. Bibliography: G; Ho*; M. D. Calvocoressi, *A Survey of Russian Music* (London: Pelican, 1944); Nemtsov, J. EDA 012-2, EDA 014-2 and 93.008 [record sleeve]

Wertheim, Rosy [Rosalie Marie] (b. Amsterdam, 19 February 1888; d. Laren, the Netherlands, 27 May 1949)   Born into a well-known family of Jewish bankers in Amsterdam. She studied composition with Sem DRESDEN and Bernard Zweers. She was very concerned about social issues, particularly poor working-class children. She gave piano lessons to poor children, conducted the children's choir in a working-class neighbourhood and financially supported a number of families. She also conducted the Jewish women's chorus of Religieus Socialistisch Verbond in Amsterdam. She began to be interested in the music of Debussy, Ravel and Stravinsky and went to Paris from 1929 to 1935 where she studied with Louis Aubert, leaving for Vienna in 1935 to study counterpoint with Karl WEIGL, then for New York in 1936 and returning home to Amsterdam in 1937. She was forced to go into hiding for much of the Second World War. Most of her music is cheerful and in a neoclassical in style. It includes mainly songs, with some orchestral and chamber music. Bibliography: G; http://www.leosmit.nl/eng/contemporaries/jewish_text.htm*

Wiéner, Jean (b. Paris, 19 March 1896; d. Paris, 8 June 1982)   Studied at the Paris Conservatoire with André Gédalge and was a classmate of MILHAUD, Ibert and Honegger. He first encountered jazz in 1912, an interest he continued for the rest of his life. He was active in promoting it in France in the 1920s and formed a piano duo for jazz improvisation with Clément Doucet, giving more than 2,000 concerts between 1925 and 1939. He lost track of Milhaud after leaving the Conservatoire, but the two met again after World War One, by which time Wiéner was earning a living playing American syncopated music in the Bar Gaya. The group of composers sharing a taste for the music of Satie, known as *Les Six*, joined Wiéner at the Bar Gaya for Saturday evening musical get-togethers. The accommodation became too small and so the owner rented a larger space, and it was Wiéner who asked Milhaud's authorization to name it after one of Milhaud most popular works, *Le Boeuf sur le toit*, by which name the cabaret became known.

Wiéner was best known as a concert promoter and pianist. He was active in promoting concerts of new music by the Second Viennese School and also by de Falla and Stravinsky. As a concert organizer he was attacked in the *Courier Musical* in 1923 for organizing 'Concerts métèques' (concerts by aliens or half-breeds), a veiled reference to his Jewishness. He organized the concert in 1923 at which Milhaud conducted the French premiere of SCHOENBERG's *Pierrot lunaire*. Wiéner's own compositions are generally composed in a jazzy, Gershwin-like manner and include *Concerto francoaméricain* for clarinet and strings (1922–3), *Sonatine syncopée* for solo piano (1923) and the songs *Chantefables pour les enfant sages*, *Les Chantefleurs*, and a piano concerto (1970). During World War Two he worked anonymously and underground, mainly producing film scores, which he continued to do after the war. His political affiliations were left-wing. He also wrote music for radio, television and theatre.
Bibliography: G; Leb; Jane F. Fulcher, 'The Preparation for Vichy: Anti-Semitism in the French Musical Culture between the Two World Wars', *Musical Quarterly*, 79 (1995), pp. 458–75; Roger Nichols, *Conversations with Madeleine Milhaud* (London: Faber, 1996), pp.23–5

Wieniawski, Adam Tadeusz (b. Warsaw, 27 November 1879; d. Bydgoscz, Poland, 27 April 1950)   Nephew of Henryk and Józef WIENIAWSKI. He studied piano and composition at the Warsaw Conservatory and then continued his studies in Berlin with Woldemar Bargiel. In 1906 he moved to Paris and studied with Vincent d'Indy and Gabriel Fauré. He was an officer in the French Army during World War One and then returned to Warsaw. In 1928 he became director of the Chopin Music School. He mainly composed music for the theatre in the late French Impressionist style.
Bibliography: G

Wieniawski, Henryk (b. Lublin, Poland, 10 July 1835; d. Moscow, 31 March 1880)   Brought up in a musical family. His mother, Regina Wieniawski, was a pianist as was her brother, Edouard Wolff. His father, Tadeusz Wieniawski, joined the November Uprising in Poland in 1830, as a staff doctor for the fourth regiment of rifles. After the uprising was crushed he spent some time abroad before returning from exile to take up medical practice in Lublin. Henryk's mother was the daughter of a well-known Warsaw doctor, Jozef Wolff, and she is alleged to have been disinherited as a result of her marriage. Henryk's talent for the violin was recognized by the age of 6 by his teacher, Jan Hornziel. When Hornziel left to become a soloist in the Warsaw Orchestra, Stanislaw Serwacyński, one-time leader of the Budapest Opera House, continued Henryk's musical tuition. The Czech violinist Panofka on hearing him play in Warsaw at the age of 8 exclaimed, 'He will make a name for himself!' At this age he was admitted to the Paris Conservatoire, although the minimum age required was 12. His mother hoped that her brother Edward, who was a conservatoire professor, would use his influence to get Henryk admitted, but on hearing how good his playing was, that proved unnecessary.

He studied violin under Lambert Massart and won the first prize for violin in 1846. He continued to study as a private pupil under Massart until 1848, and the two became lifelong friends. After a concert in Paris in which he was accompanied by with his brother Józef on piano, he gave further concerts in St Petersburg, Moscow and Warsaw, returning to the Paris Conservatoire in 1849 to study harmony with Colet. In addition to performing he then began composing, almost exclusively for solo violin or violin with accompaniment. By 1853 he had fourteen of his opuses published. His first violin concerto was completed and first performed in Leipzig in 1853. A few works were written jointly with his brother, for example, *Allegro de Sonate*, Op. 2, and *Grand Duo Polonais*, Op. 8. Between 1851 and 1853 he toured extensively as a virtuoso violinist, giving over 200 concerts in Russia that included many of his own compositions. Until 1855 he and his brother Józef performed together, but afterwards they usually performed separately

In 1858 Henryk played with Anton RUBINSTEIN in Paris, and in London in 1859 as a member of the Beethoven Quartet Society, an association whose members included Josef JOACHIM and Heinrich Wilhelm ERNST. In 1858 he also gave concerts in London. Although he was very popular in England he avoided high society because he often felt offended by the elite's attitude towards the profession of the artist. However, he was persuaded by Rubinstein to visit the Hampton family, where he met Mrs Hampton's brother, the pianist and composer George Osborne (1806–93), and also her daughter Isabella, whom he married in 1860. According to Wieniawski's grandson, Isabella's father, Thomas Hampton, disinherited Isabella because of the marriage. Wieniawski's *Legend*, Op. 17, a romance for violin and orchestra, was composed about the time of their meeting.

Wieniawski was persuaded by Rubinstein, who was working to improve musical conditions in Russia, to go to St Petersburg, and it was there that Wieniawski settled from 1860 to 1872. During this period he was very active as a performer and teacher. He was solo violinist to the Tzar, led the orchestra and string quartet of the Russian Musical Society and became professor of violin at the St Petersburg Conservatory, a post he gave up after two years because it conflicted with his performing career. During this period he composed some of his best works, including *Etude-caprice* (1863), *Polonaise brillante* No. 2 (1870) and a second violin concerto (1872). He toured North America in 1872–4, the first year of which he was accompanied by Rubinstein.

In 1875 he succeeded Henri Vieuxtemps at the Brussels Conservatory, but continued his extensive concert tours. Eugène Ysaÿe was one of his private pupils whilst he was in Brussels. His punishing schedule, together with a heart condition, took its toll and in November 1878 in Berlin he broke down whilst giving a performance of his second violin concerto. JOACHIM, who was in the audience, stepped on to the stage and played Bach's *Chaconne*, by which time Wieniawski had recovered sufficiently to embrace Joachim on stage. He continued to perform for about another year, although he was unwell and at one stage was admitted to the Mariinsky hospital. Although he was at one time wealthy, he died impoverished owing to his inveterate gambling. He was considered one of the great violinists of his day and in addition composed about 30 works, of which the two violin concertos and his polonaises are best known.
Bibliography: *G*; *HBD*; Ho*; Ly*; Wladyslav Duleba, *Wieniawski: his Life and Times* (New Jersey, MD: Paganiniana, 1984)

Wieniawski, Józef (b. Lublin, Poland, 23 May 1837; d. Brussels, 11 November 1912)   Brother of Henryk WIENIAWSKI. His career has many parallels with that of his brother, with the important difference that the piano was his instrument. After early piano tuition from Synek in Lublin, he went to the Paris Conservatoire from 1847 to 1850 where he continued piano studies with Pierre Zimmermann, Antoine Marmontel and ALKAN. From 1851 to 1853 he went to Russia on concert tours with his brother. In 1855–6 he studied with Liszt in Weimar and then studied music theory in Berlin with Adolf Bernhard MARX. In 1866 he became a member of the piano faculty at the newly founded Moscow Conservatory under the directorship of Nikolay RUBINSTEIN, but only stayed there for one term. He was appointed professor of piano at the Brussels Conservatory, a post he held until his death. He was a distinguished pianist, although never as famous as his violinist brother. He was a sought-after piano teacher, and was a more versatile composer than his brother, although his compositions are hardly played today. He composed over 50 opuses, including orchestral, chamber and vocal works and music for solo piano.
Bibliography: *G*; *HBD*; Ho*; Ly*

Wolpe, Michael (b. Tel Aviv, 4 March 1960)   Studied composition at the Rubin Academy, Jerusalem and Cambridge University (1994). He is strongly attached to socialist ideology, and settled in the kibbutz Sdeh Boker, where he founded a regional school of music. His compositions include vocal, orchestral and

363

chamber music, for example, *Hatanim hazru* (The jackels have returned) for orchestra and tape (1996); *Capella Kolot* (Capella of voices) for mezzo-soprano, oboe, cello and piano (1988); *Stabat Mater* (1994), String Quartet (1995) and Trio for violin, cello and piano (1996).
Bibliography: G

Wolpe, Stefan (b. Berlin, 25 August 1902; d. New York, 4 April 1972) His father was of Russian origin and his mother of Viennese origin. He began piano and musical theory studies at the age of 15, and from 1919 to 1924 attended the Berlin Hochschule für Musik, where Franz SCHREKER and Paul Juon were among his teachers. He met Ferruccio Busoni in 1920, from whom he received encouragement and valuable counsel. At about this time he was associated with the Berlin Dadaists and became a member of the November-gruppe, a band of artists dedicated to furthering the socialist aims of the Russian Revolution of 1917; he appeared in their concerts as a composer and pianist. An important work that he composed in 1924 and revised in 1935 was the piano setting of five songs to poems by Hölderlin. In 1925 he joined the German Communist Party. Wolpe was very much a rebel leading the Bohemian life of a leftist avant-garde composer. From 1925 until 1933 much of his music was political cabaret and songs with piano accompaniment. It included marching songs and union anthems, and piano works ranging in style from tonal to exuberant atonal expressionism and stylized jazz idioms.

In 1927 he married the painter Ole Okuniewski; their daughter is the pianist Katherina Wolpe. In 1931 he wrote incidental music for the cabaret *Die Mausefalle* by Gustav von Wangenheim that received over 300 performances in Germany and Switzerland. With the Nazi rise to power in the early 1930s, Wolpe was in great danger, being a Jew and a communist and also producing what the Nazis regarded as degenerate art. He managed to escape from Germany to Zurich via Czechoslovakia with the help of his friend and future second wife, the Romanian pianist Irma Schoenberg (no relation of Arnold Schoenberg). She also managed to retrieve his manuscripts. In May 1933 he went to Moscow to visit the International Workers' Theatre Olympiad. He considered settling in the city, but 'some instinct prompted him to attend to the inner needs that he had so long neglected'.[1] The result was that from September to December 1933 he studied in Vienna with Anton Webern, who taught him free of charge. Although the lessons lasted for only a short period of time, Webern was to have a marked influence on Wolpe's future develop-ment. This can be seen in a number of his later works. For example, in his *Chamber Piece* No. 1 (1965) Wolpe uses the same set of pitches as in the tone row that Webern invented for his concerto for nine solo instruments, Op. 24, which was completed during Wolpe's visit.

From Vienna Wolpe and Irma went to Romania, where after five months she convinced him they should go to Palestine. She had favourable memories of a well-received recital that she gave in Jerusalem in 1931. He went there, not as a Zionist but as a stateless Jewish refugee who would be able to obtain a passport there. His upbringing had been secular and he had given little thought to his Jewishness until he reached Palestine.

Wolpe lived in Palestine from 1934 to 1938. His musical activities during this time can be divided into two aspects. Firstly, he spent time instructing folk composers in kibbutzim. He described his travels with his harmonium strapped to his back in order to organize and conduct choruses in various kibbutzim as being his happiest hours of activity in Palestine. Secondly and much less happily, he spent time in Jerusalem, where he was appointed as composition teacher at the conservatory, and was involved in the inauguration of the Palestine Orchestra. Although he had a number of devoted and enthusiastic private composition pupils and although there was vibrant musical life at their home, Wolpe's role at the conservatory was not wholeheartedly approved of by the management and some staff. There was resistance to his avant-garde style. His high expectations for the Palestine Orchestra ignored the need for a new and heterogeneous ensemble to build up its performance expertise. He was upset that they failed to invite Irma as piano soloist and when they rejected one of his most recent works. Added to this, he feared for his life after he was injured in a car accident in which an Arab driver forced his car into a ditch. He believed this was intentional. His departure for America in 1938 deprived the nascent avant-garde and the musical scene of the kibbutz movement of their most committed spokesman. During his period in Palestine he studied Hebrew and composed settings of Hebrew texts from the Bible and also of contemporary Hebrew and Yiddish poets. He composed folk songs for solo voice and choir. At the same time he developed his own less-restrictive form of serialism. Eric Salzman has described his later work as 'a kind of flashing fantasy serialism'.[2]

In 1938 he settled in New York and held a number of different teaching posts in the Settlement Music School, Philadelphia (1939–42), the Brooklyn Free Music Society (1945–8), the Contemporary Music School (1948–52) and the Philadelphia Academy of Music (1949–52). During this time much of his music could be described as abstract expressionism and the influence of jazz is more evident. He was commissioned to write the cantata *Yigdal* for the Fifth Avenue Synagogue in New York, which he completed in 1945. This was his only music composed for the synagogue. Another biblical work he began in 1942 was a ballet entitled *The Man from Midian* to a scenario by Winthrop Palmer. Midian is the region where Moses fled from a cruel Egyptian overseer and where he received divine instructions to save the Israelites. The ballet is set as seven scenes and an overture; which span the time of suffering of the Israelites to the death of Moses. The first performance was given in 1951 by Dimitri Mitropoulis and the New York Philharmonic Orchestra.

During the 1950s Wolpe continued both to teach and compose. In the summer of 1952 he taught at Black Mountain College in North Carolina, an outpost of aesthetic experimentalism in literature and the arts where Cage and Lou Harrison were among the staff. Wolpe was invited to stay on as music director. Also in 1952 he married the poet Hilda Morley. During his four years at Black Mountain College he composed three substantial works: *Enactments* for three pianos (1950–3), *Piece* for oboe, cello percussion and piano (1955), and his only symphony (1955–6). *Enactments* is a vast, exuberant, five-movement work, and the symphony is complex but does not use the hierarchical structure of the traditional symphony orchestra. The latter was revised in 1964. It was planned that Boulez would give the premiere, but he fell sick at the time and BERNSTEIN stepped in at short notice, although he only had time to rehearse and perform the first two movements. Wolpe was still a political left-winger; in his *Quartet* for trumpet, tenor saxophone, percussion and piano (1950–4) he let be known privately that it was written in celebration of the founding of the People's Republic of China.

When Black Mountain College closed in 1956 Wolpe spent a year in Germany on a Fulbright fellowship and lectured at the Darmstadt Summer Course for new Music on several successive summers. He returned to New York in 1957 to become head of the fledgling music department of C. W. Post College, Long Island University. He was teacher to a number of American composers, including FELDMAN, Tudor, SHAPEY, Sollberger and Wuorinen. In 1963 he was diagnosed as having Parkinson's disease and although he continued to compose, the physical effort of writing scores became progressively more arduous. In the last twelve years of his life he refined and concentrated his musical language and wrote mainly for smaller groups and solo instruments. Amongst the works of this later period are *Piece in Two Parts* for violin alone (1964), *Solo Piece* for trumpet (1966), *Second Piece* for violin (1966), a string quartet (1968–9), *Chamber Piece* No. 1 (1965) and *Chamber Piece* No. 2 (1968).

Bibliography: *AG; G; HBD;* Ly*

1. Jehoash Hirshberg, *Music in the Jewish Community of Palestine, 1880–1948* (Oxford: Clarendon Press, 1995), pp. 159–60 and 176–83.
2. Austin E. Clarkson, 'Stepan Wolpe in Conversation with Eric Salzman', *Musical Quarterly,* 83 (1999), pp. 378–412.

Zaimont, Judith Lang (b. Memphis, 8 November 1945)   Studied piano as a teenager with LeLand Thompson at the Juilliard School of Music, New York, and then with Khachodourian at Long Island Institute of Music until 1966. She studied composition with Hugo WEISGALL at Queens College and with Jack Beeson and Otto Luening at Columbia University, New York, graduating in 1968. She took private lessons with André Jolivet in France in 1971–2. She has taught at Hunter College, New York (1980–8), Adelphi University, New York (1989–91) and the Peabody Conservatory (1980–7) and became a professor of composition at the University of Minnesota in Minneapolis. Her compositions are tonal and romantic in style, with choral and vocal compositions forming a major part of her output. She has received a number of com-

missions. From 1972 for several years she was resident composer for the Great Neck Choral Society. During this period she wrote *Sacred Service for the Sabbath Evening* for baritone, mixed chorus and orchestra (1976), based on a service from the old Reform Prayer Book, which has 16 movements. Her best-known works are song cycles and piano pieces, for example, *Songs of Innocence* for soprano, tenor, flute, cello and harp (1974); *The Magic World* for baritone, piano and percussion (1979); *A Calendar Set* for piano (1978); *Nocturne: la fin de siècle* for piano (1979); and *From the Great Land* for mezzo-soprano, clarinet, piano and drums (1982). She is author of a textbook on composition, *Twentieth-Century Music: an Analysis and Appreciation* (1980) and edited *Contemporary Concert Music by Women* (1981) and the on-going series *The Musical Woman: an International Perspective*. She has composed over 100 works.
Bibliography: *G*; *GW*; *HBD*; Emily Freeman Brown, 'Jewish Liturgical Music by American Women Since 1945', in S. Stanton and A. Knapp (eds), *Proceedings of the First International Conference on Jewish Music* (London: City University, 1994), p. 22*; www.music.umn.edu/fac_rsch/bios/zaimont.htm

Zeisl, Eric (b. Vienna, 18 May 1905; d. Los Angeles, 18 February 1959)   His parents owned a coffeehouse in Vienna. From an early age he had an ambition to compose, but his parents tried to dissuade him from a musical career because they felt it would be difficult to earn a living. Nevertheless, at the age of 14 he entered the Akademie für Musik und Darstellende Kunst in Vienna, where he studied under Richard Stöhr for four years until 1923. By 1921 he had three songs published by Edition Strache. In spite of being a promising composer he was obliged to augment his living by teaching. He was primarily a lyric vocal composer of songs and choral music. During his early period he set to music works by leading German writers, for example, *Mondbilder* (Morgenstern, 1928), *Kinderlieder* (From *Das Knaben Wunderhorn*, Dehmel, 1931), and *Sechs Lieder* (one of each by Eichendorf, Lingg, Mörike, Eidlitz, Lessing and Busch, 1935). In 1934 he won the Austrian state prize for his work *Requiem Concertante* (1933–4). By the late 1930s he was beginning to receive wider recognition; he had an offer of a position at the Vienna Conservatory and was negotiating a publishing contract with Schott. His greatest ambition was to compose an opera. He wrote a *Singspiel* entitled *Leonce und Lena* (an adaptation of Büchners' play) that was due to be premiered at the Schönbrunn Schlosstheater, but with the *Anschluss* of 1938 this was cancelled. It did not receive its premiere until 1952, and then in Los Angeles.
    The Zeisl family escaped from Vienna on 10 November 1938, the day after *Kristallnacht*. They initially sought refuge in Paris, where they met MILHAUD and also Alma Mahler-Werfel, with whom they became lifelong friends. They sailed to New York in September 1939 where their daughter was born soon after. They rented a house in Mamaroneck, New York, where Zeisl began composing an opera entitled *Job*. The inspiration for this was twofold. A few

years earlier Zeisl had read the Joseph Roth novel *Hiob, Roman eines einfachen Mannes* (Job, the story of a simple man), which relates the story of a Polish Jew who emigrates to America. The parallel with his own plight now struck him. Although he began what he hoped would be a four-act opera, circumstances prevented him from continuing with the work at the time, although he was to resume it again later.

Various negotiations for work in New York failed to materialize, and in 1941, like many other immigrant composers, he moved to Hollywood, where he worked as a film composer in 1941, composing the music for *Lassie Come Home* and *The Postman Always Rings Twice*. Disillusioned with the film industry he turned to teaching. Initially he taught at Southern California School of Music and then at Los Angeles City College from 1949, until he died of a heart attack after an evening class in 1959 at the age of 53. In 1945 he had become an American citizen.

Over half of his compositions date from his time in America. His forced move to America brought on a sense of artistic exile, which he seemed to counter by changing his style. Most of the works dating from his American period reflect his Jewish roots, either in subject matter or in style. When asked about his style he described it as 'Classical music in a romantic religious vein'. A chantlike melody appears as a leitmotif in many of his later works, giving them a liturgical flavour. This is particularly evident in the opera *Job*. At the end of 1944, when Zeisl had been commissioned to write music for the synagogue service, he received news that his father, Siegmund Zeisl, had been interned in the concentration camp at Terezin, then transported to Treblinka, where he had been killed. Zeisl decided to write a requiem dedicated to the memory of his father. *Requiem Ebraico* is based on Psalm 92 and is one of his most frequently played works. During the 1950s he was composer-in-residence at the Brandeis Arts Institute for Jewish Culture in California, and in 1957 and 1958 he received grants from the Huntington Hartford Foundation and this enabled him to resume work on the opera *Job* (begun in 1939), but he had only completed the second act at the time of his death. Other works with Old Testament themes include *Four Songs for Wordless Chorus* (1948), inspired by the story of Jephtha's daughter, a cantata entitled *From the Book of Psalms* (1952) using texts from Psalms 55 and 57, and the ballets *Naboth's Vineyard* (1953) and *Jacob and Rachel* (1954). In addition he wrote a piano concerto, a cello concerto, three violin sonatas, a cello sonata, a string quartet, a concerto grosso and a symphony.

Bibliography: *AG*; *G*; *HBD*; Malcolm S. Cole, 'Eric Zeisl: the Rediscovery of an Emigre Composer', *Musical Quarterly*, 64 (1978), pp. 237–44; Moskovitz, M., 1998, CD QS 6225 [record sleeve]; Schwartz, M., 1998, 460 211-2 [record sleeve]

Zemlinsky, Alexander von (b. Vienna, 14 October 1871; d. Larchmont, New York, 15 March 1942) Had an unusual ethnic background. His maternal grandfather, Shem Tov Shemo, was a Sephardic Jew and his maternal grandmother was a Muslim. Both his paternal grandparents were Catholics, but his father, Adolph von Zemlinsky, converted to Judaism out of conviction. When eight days old Alexander was circumcised and he was brought up in a family who were members of the local Sephardic synagogue and imbued with the Jewish traditions. Both his first wife, Ida, and his second wife, Louise, were Jewish. Following the appointment of Karl Lueger as mayor of Vienna in 1897, there was a marked increase in anti-Semitism. Many Jews, including SCHOENBERG, converted to Protestantism in 1898 and Alexander Zemlinsky did so around 1906. About this time he also became a Freemason. These measures were primarily aimed at easing 'career progression' and were taken along with other measures, including eliminating the pseudo-Hungarian z and suppressing the spurious *von* from his surname, so that 'von Zemlinszky' became 'Zemlinsky'. Nevertheless, after the *Anschluss* in 1938, when he realized the family must leave Vienna, he sought the necessary documents from the Catholic Registry in Vienna. Each certificate was stamped 'Valid only in conjunction with application for a certificate of Aryan Origin'. This certificate was held in the achives of the Isräelitisches Kultusgemeinde, which by then was in the hands of the Gestapo. His name was omitted from the 1940 edition of Stengel and Gerigk's *Lexikon der Juden in der Musik*, but in the revised 1943 edition his name was included (see Appendix I).

Zemlinsky showed an interest in the piano from the age of 4 and was a member of the synagogue choir from his early teens. At the age of 13, although his parents could ill afford it, he was sent to the preparatory school of the Vienna Conservatory, progressing to the senior school three years later, where his piano teacher was Anton Door and his theory teachers, Robert Fuchs and Franz Krenn and later J. N. Fuchs (1890). Although he won a number of prizes for his piano performances, he was more interested in composition. He was a sensitive person and generally shunned publicity. The earliest of his compositions that are preserved date from 1887 and include piano music, *Lieder* and chamber music. His first major work was the Symphony in D minor, completed in 1893, which was praised by the critic Hanslick at its first performance. In 1893 he enrolled with the Weiner Tonkünstlerverein (musicians association) that organized performances of *Lieder* and chamber music. He made his début as composer and performer with a piano quartet in D major, and in 1896 won third prize with his Clarinet Trio, Op. 3. As a consequence of joining the Weiner Tonkünstlerverein he met Brahms, the honorary president, who suggested improvements to his String Quintet in D minor, often regarded as his finest work of his early period. He also met Schoenberg, to whom he later gave lessons in counterpoint. Schoenberg's best-known early work, *Verklärte Nacht* for string sextet (1899), is a musical declaration of love to Zemlinsky's sister, Mathilde. Zemlinsky won third prize in a competition for his first opera *Sarema* (1895), which although well received at the time was only performed once more in the succeeding century. The only surviving liturgical text that he set to music was that of Psalm 118, which he composed for the wedding of Isidor Kahan and Helen Bauer in 1896, the same year in which he completed his first string quartet in A major, Op. 4. In 1897 MAHLER, who was musical director of the Vienna Hofoper, encouraged Zemlinsky to write his new proposed opera, *Es was Einmal*. After its completion Mahler and Zemlinsky both revised it before it was given its successful world premiere at the Hofoper in 1900. A new production was staged in Mannheim in 1912, but despite this initial success it was then not performed for another half-century.

Zemlinsky first met Alma Schindler (later Alma Mahler) at a dinner party and shortly after she asked him to look through some of her songs. They met regularly and his early romantic songs, Op. 7, are dedicated to her. Their love affair was broken off after Alma married Mahler in 1902, but they remained friends and corresponded intermittently for the rest of Zemlinsky's life. Zemlinsky's father died in 1900 and he composed a setting of Psalm 83 in his memory, which Schoenberg tried to persuade a Berlin choral society to perform in 1902. However it did not receive its first performance until 1987. From 1899 Zemlinsky was *Kapellmeister* at the Carltheatre in Vienna, and from 1904 (apart from one season at the Hofoper) he conducted opera performances at the repertory opera house, the Volkoper, until 1911. In 1901 Schoenberg married Zemlinsky's sister. That same year Zemlinsky collaborated with Hugo von Hofmannsthal in composing the ballet *Der Triumph von Zeit*. However, neither Mahler nor Strauss would perform it and so Zemlinsky adapted parts of it for *Ein Tanzpoem* (which was not staged until the 1990s). Around 1903 Zemlinsky composed an orchestral fantasy based on a tale by Hans Christian Anderson entitled *Die Seejungfrau* (*The Little Mermaid*). This work reflects his emotions towards Alma during this period. It was premiered in 1905 at a concert at which Schoenberg's *Pelleas et Melisande* was also performed, after which Alma Mahler unfairly concluded 'At first Schoenberg's teacher, he later became his pupil.' A year earlier Schoenberg and Zemlinsky founded the Vereinigung Schaffender Tonkünstler to promote the performance of new music. His third opera, *Der Traumgörge*, was to have been premiered by Mahler, but by 1905 Mahler had resigned from the Hofoper, before the opera was complete. Like a number of Zemlinsky's works, it lay dormant and was not performed until 1980. In 1907 Zemlinsky married Ida Guttmann. In the same year, on the recommendation of Mahler, the 12-year-old Erich KORNGOLD was sent to Zemlinsky for lessons in composition. A number of Korngold's early works were composed under Zemlinsky's supervision. Zemlinsky's fourth opera was the comic opera *Kleider Machen Leute*, which had its premiere at the Volkoper in Vienna in 1910. It received a mixed reception, one of the most positive comments coming from Erich Korngold's father, Julius.

The most important position that Zemlinsky held was at the Deutsches Landestheater in Prague from 1911 to 1927 where he was an outstanding opera conductor. He conducted the Czech premiere of Schoenberg's *Gurreleider* in

1921 and the world premiere of Schoenberg's *Erwartung* in 1924. In 1910, in response to a request, he set Psalm 23 to music that in some ways is reminiscent of the music he would have heard in the synagogue as a child.[1] His second string quartet (1913–14) is dedicated to Schoenberg and quotes from *Verklärte Nacht* in the opening moderato. It coincides with a time of reconciliation with Schoenberg after the distressing period when Zemlinsky's sister, Mathilde, left Schoenberg to live with Richard Gerstl, the latter eventually committing suicide (see SCHOENBERG). Musically it represents a departure from the influence of Brahms seen in the first quartet (1896) but not crossing the threshold of tonality. It was premiered by the Rosé Quartet in 1918. Zemlinsky wrote two operas based on texts by Oscar Wilde, *A Florentine Tragedy* (1917) and *Der Zwerg* (The dwarf, 1922).

Although he had written two symphonies in the 1890s, the best-known work of his that is described as a symphony is the *Lyric Symphony* of 1923. This is best described as a song symphony and is modelled on Mahler's *Das Lied von der Erde*, which sets to music the poems by Rabindranath Tagore, translated into German. The moods are of yearning, love, ecstasy and peace. The work was completed in 1923 and first performed in the Deutsches Landestheater in Prague with Zemlinsky conducting. His third string quartet was conceived partly as a reaction to events following his sister's death in 1923; its style is more modern than that of the second string quartet, although it remains tonal. In 1927 Zemlinsky left Prague and spent four seasons at the Kroll Oper in Berlin under KLEMPERER. He also taught at the Musikhochschule until 1933. From a compositional viewpoint the next few years were barren, and by the early 1930s he had grown wise as a composer through disappointment and was concerned to find a voice that others would listen to. In 1929 his first wife, Ida, died of leukaemia. Had it not been for her failing health, Zemlinsky, who was then having an affair with Louise Sachsel, would have sought a divorce. In 1930 he married Louise. As a wedding present he composed an opera based on Klabund's *Der Kreidkreis* (The chalk circle). In 1931, with the collapse of the stockmarket, the Kroll Oper closed. By 1933, with the rise of Nazism, Zemlinsky moved to Vienna, thinking he would be out of danger. There he continued composing and found work conducting the Vienna Concert Orchestra. During this period he composed String Quartet No. 4, *Six Songs* (originally *Abendlieder*), Op. 22, *Sinfonietta*, Op. 23, a setting of Psalm 13 and an opera, *Der König Kandaules*, based on Gide's *Le Roi Candaule*.

In December 1938 Zemlinsky, his wife and his daughter Hansi left for America. There he resumed work on a clarinet quartet, but only 127 bars of the first movement were completed. Louise's mother and aunt were sent to Terezin and were presumed murdered by the Nazis. In 1939 Zemlinsky suffered a cerebral haemorrhage that left him paralyzed. He made a partial recovery but died in 1942.

Zemlinsky was not a good self-publicist and many of his works were not performed during his lifetime. For about a quarter of a century after his death very little of his work was performed. However, increasingly since the late 1960s his work has been performed and its true worth is becoming appreciated.

Bibliography: *G*; *HBD*; Ken; Leb; Anthony Beaumont, *Zemlinsky* (London: Faber, 2000)

1. Erik Levi, *Music in the Third Reich* (London: Macmillan, 1994), pp. 64–7.

Appendix

Lexikon der Juden in der Musik by Theophil Stengel and Herbert Gerigk

The first edition of *Lexikon der Juden in der Musik*, published in Berlin in 1940, was compiled on the orders of the Reich leadership of the National Socialist German Workers' Party (NSDAP) on the basis of official documents checked by the party. A second edition was published in 1943.[1] The purpose of the book is explained in the Foreword, an abridged extract of which is given below.

> The purification of our cultural and therefore also of our musical life from all Jewish elements has been successfully completed. Clear legal regulations ensure that in Greater Germany the Jew cannot be publicly active in any artistic sphere, either as an exponent or creator of works, or as a writer, publisher or impresario. The 'great' names, from the time since the end of the World War until the new order of the Reich, have sunk without trace. They have indeed been so completely forgotten, that when by chance one of these names surfaces again, some people can hardly remember that this was a notorious Jew whose name was often in people's mouths. This will be particularly true of the present younger generation who did not consciously experience that decadent time, and who therefore from the very beginning of their working life were involved in the building up of our new state. Because of the large number of these names however, it is natural that occasionally some doubt still arises in people's minds about the origins of a particular composer or of someone active in the musical sphere in some other capacity.
>
> This situation made it a necessary task to create a reference work that, despite the difficult nature of the material, would reflect perfectly the state of our knowledge. The most reliable sources had to be sought out in order to give the musician, the music teacher, the politician and also the music lover that absolute certainty which must be achieved with respect to the Jewish question. A lexicon like this will retain its

importance for the future also, when the Jewish question in German art
will be merely a distant historical episode

…

We measure by the standards of *our* race, and in doing so we come to
the conclusion that the Jew is uncreative, and that in the sphere of music
it is merely by imitation that he can achieve a certain degree of crafts-
manship. His parasitical capacity for understanding enables him to
achieve amazing virtuoso results, which however on closer inspection
prove to be devoid of content, because his oriental sensibility must always
falsify the essence of a western musical creation.

It is in our time that the relationship between music and race is for
the first time being scientifically researched in a systematic way. It took
a long time for Richard Wagner's article *Das Judentum in der Musik*,
which clearly focussed attention on the Jewish question in music as
early as the middle of the nineteenth century, to find a positive response.

…

The present lexicon lays claim to the greatest possible reliability. This
is the main reason for our omission of all those names that cannot with
sufficient certainty be identified as Jewish.

…

So that the book would not become unnecessarily voluminous, it
was decided to sacrifice lists of works and exhaustive bibliographical
information. Clarity would have suffered otherwise, and after all it is
not our intention to facilitate a perpetuation of Jewish products, but
rather to provide a tool for the swiftest possible eradication from our
intellectual and cultural life of all the remnants of these which may
by accident still linger there. Being masters of disguise, one or two
individual Jews are even now managing to slip through the net here
and there, unrecognized.

Thus the lexicon will be a reliable guide for cultural policy-makers, for
theatre managers and conductors, radio producers, leading personalities
in the offices of party branches and in the associations connected to
them, and not last for the directors of light entertainment bands. The
music teacher and scholar too will have to use it as an indispensable tool.

…

Since the lexicon is above all intended to provide political educational
material for the NSDAP itself, it seems necessary within this foreword
to draw attention to some cases that have been found by experience to
be unclear in many respects. Among the living quarter-Jews who by
mistake have often been performed, even at events of party organisa-
tions, the most important are Boris Blacher and Heinrich Kaminski …
Mistakenly suspected of being Jewish (and sometimes claimed by Jews

as racial comrades) were (and are) above all Georges Bizet (who was married to a Jewess), and Max Bruch (whose bad luck it was that his version of 'Kol Nidre' became one of his best known compositions), Bernhard Klein, Sigfreid Karg-Elert and the Frenchman Camille Saint-Saëns, who, despite being most vehemently anti-German, was nevertheless an Aryan. The once fiercely controversial composer Alban Berg is also free of Jewish blood.

COMPOSERS INCLUDED IN THE *LEXIKON DER JUDEN IN DER MUSIK* WHO ARE ALSO INCLUDED IN PART II ABOVE

The German spellings and names given below are as they appear in the Lexicon

Abraham, Paul
Achron, Joseph
Adorno *see* Weisengrund
Alexander, Heinz-Gunther
Alkan, Charles*
Antheil, George*
Ben Haim, *see* Frankenburger
Benjamin, Arthur*
Blacher, Boris
Blitzstein, Marc*
Bloch, Ernest
Brandmann, Israel
Brod, Max
Brüll, Ignaz
Castelnuovo-Tedesco, Mario
Copland, Aaron*
Damrosch, Leopold
Damrosch, Walter
Daus, Adolf
David Ferdinand
Davidov, Karl
Dessau, Paul
Dresden, Sen
Dukas, Paul
Eisler, Hans
Ernst, Heinrich*
Ettinger, Max
Feinberg, Samuil*
Fitelberg, Grzegorz
Fitelberg, Jerzy
Franchetti, Alberto

Frankenburger, Paul
Gál, Hans
Gernsheim, Friedrich
Gershwin, George
Gnesin, Mikhail
Goldmark, Karl
Goldschmidt, Berthold
Golyscheff, J.
Gottschalk, Louis*
Grosz, Wilhelm
Gruenberg, Louis*
Halevy, Jacques
Henschel, George
Hensel, Fanny
Holländer, Friedrich
Joachim, Joseph
Kahn, Erich
Kahn, Robert
Kaminski, Heinrich
Klemperer, Otto
Korngold, Wolfgang
Krein, Alexander
Krein, Gregory
Kreisler, Fritz
Lassen, Eduard
Lewandowski, Louis
Mahler, Gustav
Mannuel Roland, Alexis
Marx, Adolf Bernhard
Mendelssohn, Fanny, *see* Hensel
Mendelssohn, Felix

Meyerbeer, Giacomo
Milhaud, Darius
Moscheles, Ignaz
Moscowski, Moritz
Nathan, Isaac
Offenbach, Jacques
Popper, David
Rathaus, Karol
Reizenstein, Franz
Rosowsky, Salamon
Rossi, Salomone
Rubinstein, Anton
Rubinstein, Nikolai
Saminsky, Lazare
Sandburg, Mordecai
Schnabel, Arthur

Schönberg, Arnold
Schreker, Franz
Schulhof, Erwin
Steinberg, Maximil ian*
Sternberg, Erich
Stutschewsky, Joachim
Sulzer, Salamon
Toch, Ernest
Weigl, Karl
Weill, Kurt
Weinberger, Jaromir
Weisengrund-Adorno, Theodor
Wieniawski, Heinrich
Wieniawski, Joseph
Zemlinsky, Alexander

NOTES

1. For an excellent discussion of *Lexikon der Juden in der Musik* see Erik Levi's *Music in the Third Reich* (London, Macmillan, 1994), pp. 64–8.

* Those musicians (according to Stengel and Gerigk) whose Jewish ancestry can be regarded as reliably established, but for whom the available documentary evidence is not conclusive.

Index

Major entries are shown in bold, and these include all the composer entries in Part II